BRIEF EDITION

GOVERNMENT
BY THE
PEOPLE

Second Edition

James MacGregor Burns
*University of Maryland, College Park
and Williams College*

J.W. Peltason
University of California

Thomas E. Cronin
Whitman College

David B. Magleby
Brigham Young University

Prentice Hall, Upper Saddle River, New Jersey 07458

Library of Congress Cataloging-in-Publication Data

Government by the people / James MacGregor Burns [et al.].
    Brief ed., 2nd ed.
        p.   cm.
    Includes bibliographical references and index.
    ISBN 0-13-533639-2
    1. United States—Politics and government.   I. Burns, James
MacGregor.
JK274.B8525   1997
320.473—dc20
                                    96-41010
                                        CIP

Editorial Director: Charlyce Jones Owen
Editor in Chief: Nancy Roberts
Acquisitions Editor: Michael Bickerstaff
Marketing Manager: Chaunfayta Hightower
Project Manager: Serena Hoffman
Director of Production and Manufacturing: Barbara Kittle
Manufacturing Manager: Nick Sklitsis
Prepress and Manufacturing Buyer: Bob Anderson
Creative Design Director: Leslie Osher
Interior Design: Jerry Votta
Illustrations: Gary Moore
Photo Research: Beura K. Ringrose
Supervisor of Production Services: Lori Clinton
Electronic Page Layout: Joh Lisa
Cover Design: Maria Lange
Cover Art: Comstock, Inc

This book was set in 11/12 Garamond by HSS Formatting
and was printed and bound by Courier Companies, Inc.
The cover was printed by Courier Companies, Inc.

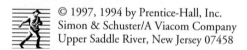
© 1997, 1994 by Prentice-Hall, Inc.
Simon & Schuster/A Viacom Company
Upper Saddle River, New Jersey 07458

Printed in the United States of America

10 9 8 7 6 5 4

ISBN 0-13-533639-2

Prentice-Hall International (UK) Limited, *London*
Prentice-Hall of Australia Pty. Limited, *Sydney*
Prentice-Hall Canada Inc., *Toronto*
Prentice-Hall Hispanoamericana, S.A., *Mexico*
Prentice-Hall of India Private Limited, *New Delhi*
Prentice-Hall of Japan, Inc., *Tokyo*
Simon & Schuster Asia Pte. Ltd., *Singapore*
Editora Prentice-Hall do Brasil, Ltda., *Rio de Janeiro*

BRIEF CONTENTS

CONTENTS

FEATURES

A Closer Look

We the People

From Coast to Coast

You Decide!

A MESSAGE FROM THE AUTHORS

With the collapse of communism, the agenda of American politics has shifted to domestic affairs. Issues like the economy, jobs, and the federal budget were central to the 1992, 1994, and 1996 elections. As the protracted budget battle between Bill Clinton and the Republican 104th Congress demonstrated, consensus about how to proceed on these issues is lacking. The public agrees that the budget deficit should be reduced, but not at the expense of popular programs like Medicare. Yet if popular programs cannot be cut, reducing the deficit will be difficult without raising taxes—something few politicians want to do. Social policy, in areas like health care, welfare, crime, and education, is important to many people, yet Congress was unable to pass any significant legislation. The complexity of these issues, the powerful interests involved, and the difficulty of building bipartisan coalitions make action in these policy areas difficult.

State and local governments have in some respects become more important as the policy agenda has shifted to domestic issues. State concerns about unfunded mandates, excessive red tape, Washington bureaucracy, and the lack of flexibility in policy implementation have all been expressed by a visible and activist set of governors. But whether states have the ability or willingness to play a much expanded role is debatable.

Not surprisingly, our elections reflect this same uncertainty about the future direction of American politics. In 1992, voters rejected the Republicans and denied George Bush a second term as president. Then two years later voters turned on the Democrats and put Republicans in charge of the House of Representatives for the first time in forty years. House Speaker Newt Gingrich and a large class of freshmen Republicans set out on an ambitious legislative agenda built on their Contract with America. Early successes turned to deadlock in a protracted budget battle with President Clinton and a cautious approach to policy taken by the Senate. By the 1996 election, Democrats had turned public opinion against Gingrich in much the same way that Republicans had attacked Bill Clinton during the 1994 election. The 1996 election did not resolve many of these issues, as voters appeared to favor gridlock rather than give one party control of both the executive and legislative branches.

American politics has entered a volatile period, with voters willing to switch back and forth and with the parties trying to find a basis for a new and lasting majority coalition. Although our defense policy changed with the collapse of communism, the world has not suddenly become a safe place in which to live. Regional strife and terrorism continue, and the United States had entered a period of reassessment of its role in the world, in the United Nations, in regional defense organizations like NATO, and in its economic relations with other countries.

These domestic and foreign policy debates all demonstrate how dynamic American politics and government is as we enter the final years of the twentieth century. This text is geared to analyzing these changes in terms of how the institutions and processes of American government deal with such far-reaching and contentious issues.

Even in the twentieth century, constitutional democracy has been the exception rather than the rule. In the past, most people lived under autocratic or tyrannical regimes in which a small group imposed their will on everyone else. And today, less than one-third of the nation-states around the globe exist as viable, healthy democracies. This is a testing time for new democracies as well as old ones. Contempt for government and politics is being expressed here in the United States and abroad. Yet politics and partisan competition are the lifeblood by which free people can achieve the ideals of a government by and for the people.

Constitutional democracy—the kind we have in the United States—is exceedingly hard to win, equally hard to sustain, and often hard to understand without rigorous study. The form of constitutional democracy that has emerged in the United States requires continual participation by caring, tolerant, and informed citizens. The framers of our Constitution warned that we must be vigilant in safeguarding our rights, liberties, and political institutions. But to do this, we first have to understand these institutions and the forces that have shaped the United States' political and constitutional systems.

We hope you will come away from reading this book with a richer understanding of American politics and government, and we hope that in the years to come, many of you will participate actively in making our constitutional democracy more vital and responsive to the urgent problems of the twenty-first century.

AMERICAN POLITICS ON THE INTERNET

The advent of the Internet, particularly the World Wide Web (WWW), has brought with it a flood of information on government and politics. Information that was once available only by searching through stacks in a library is now accessible on any computer in the world that is connected to the Internet. Opinions of the Supreme Court, presidential speeches, and congressional legislation are now available almost instantaneously.

Some WWW sites of interest are on this book's home page (http://www.prenhall.com/burns). A bit of surfing will yield many more sites. A good source of links to government information is often found on home pages of political science departments at different universities. Other excellent sources are:

> The National Election Study of the University of Michigan (www.umich.edu/~nes)
>
> PoliticsNow, the Web page sponsored by *National Journal*, ABC News, and *The Los Angeles Times* (http://www.politicsnow.com)
>
> The United States Census Bureau (www.census.gov)

> The American Political Science Association (gopher://apsa.trenton.edu:70/1)
>
> The White House (http://www.whitehouse.gov)
>
> The Library of Congress (http://www.loc.gov)
>
> The Federal Election Commission (www.fec.gov)

Although there is a great deal of information available, there are also some precautions that should be taken when accessing this information. It is important to consider the source of the information. A report from *The New York Times* (www. nytimes.com) on a potential scandal involving a Republican Congress member is less biased than a report from a Democratic party Web site. That is not to say that biased reports are not useful. Indeed, examining both sides of an issue allows you to draw your own conclusions about what the facts are.

Remember, using text from another source without citing it is plagiarism. It is easy to copy text with computers, and it is also easy to cite it, so make sure you do.

REVIEWERS

The writing of this book has profited from the informed professional, and often sharp, critical suggestions of our colleagues around the country. This and previous editions have been considerably improved as a result of reviews by the following individuals, for which we thank them all:

David Gray Adler, Idaho State University
James Anderson, Tulane University
David Barnum, De Paul University
Robert Bartlett, Purdue University
Robert C. Benedict, University of Utah
Thad Beyle, University of North Carolina
Gary Bryner, Brigham Young University
Jeanne Clarke, University of Arizona
Leif Carter, University of Georgia
Morgan Chawawa, De Kalb College
Richard Chesteen, University of Tennessee
Peggy J. Connally, North Central Texas College
Gary Cornia, Brigham Young University
Gary Covington, University of Iowa
Douglas Crane, De Kalb College
Richard Davis, Brigham Young University
James D. Decker, Macon College
Lois Lovelace Duke, Clemson University
Pat Dunham, Duquesne University
Robert Elias, University of San Francisco
Steven Finkel, University of Virginia

Mark Gibney, Purdue University
L. Tucker Gibson, Trinity University
Jim Graves, Kentucky State University
Paul Herrnson, University of Maryland
Marjorie Hershey, Indiana University
Michael J. Horan, University of Wyoming
Ronald J. Hrebenar, University of Utah
Diane P. Jennings, De Kalb College
J. Landrum Kelly, Georgia Southern University
Donald F. Kettl, University of Wisconsin
Dwight Kiel, Central Florida University
Ron King, Tulane University
Michael E. Kraft, University of Wisconsin
Fred A. Kramer, University of Massachusetts
Paul Light, University of Minnesota
William Louthan, Ohio Weslyan University
Richard Matthews, Lehigh University
Robert McCalla, University of Wisconsin
Max Neiman, University of California
David Nice, Washington State University

Richard Pacelle, University of Missouri
Glen Parker, Florida State University
Kelly D. Patterson, Brigham Young University
George Pippin, Jones County College
John Portz, Northeastern University
Pamela Rodgers, University of Wisconsin
David Rosenbloom, American University
Alan Rosenthal, Rutgers University
H.E. Scruggs, Brigham Young University
Henry Shockely, Boston University
Steven Shull, University of New Orleans
Christine Marie Sierra, University of New Mexico
Robert W. Small, Massasoit Community College
Gregory W. Smith, Gettysburg College
Richard Smolka, American University
Neil Snortland, University of Arkansas at Little Rock
Roy Thoman, West Texas A&M University
John Tierney, Boston College
Richard Valelly, Massachusetts Institute of Technology
R. Lawson Veasey, University of Arkansas

ACKNOWLEDGMENTS

We wish to acknowledge the help we have received from our colleagues, research assistants, and support staff, who have helped each of us in the preparation of this Brief Edition. Thus we thank Chris L. Gianos at the University of California, Irvine, for his research assistance, especially his help in providing the Internet information. At Whitman College, special thanks to JoAnn Collins, Ryan McFarland, Donna Jones, and Ken Singer for their assistance. At Brigham Young University, we give particular thanks to research assistants Quin Monson and Derall Riley.

Our very special thanks go to our production editor, Serena Hoffman, who once again brilliantly guided us in the rewriting of this book. We also thank our Prentice Hall friends: Phil Miller, Charlyce Jones Owen, Nancy Roberts, Mike Bickerstaff, and Chaun Hightower. We must also thank the many other skilled professionals at Prentice Hall who assisted in the publication of this edition: Joh Lisa for superb layouts; Beura Ringrose for photo research; and Gary Moore for illustrations.

Finally, we thank the dozens of students and professors who have sent us letters with suggestions for improving *Government By The People.* We welcome your notes or calls concerning any errors or ways we can further improve the book. Please write us care of the Political Science Editor at Prentice Hall, 1 Lake Street, Upper Saddle River, New Jersey 07458, or to us directly.

James MacGregor Burns
Center for Political
Leadership
University of Maryland
College Park, MD 20742

J.W. Peltason
University of California
School of Social Sciences
Irvine, CA 92717-5700

Thomas E. Cronin
Whitman College
Walla Walla, WA 99362

David B. Magleby
Brigham Young University
Provo, UT 84602

A MESSAGE FROM THE PUBLISHER

The gratifying success *Government By The People* has enjoyed over the years results from a distinguished authorship team who always write a superb book with a distinctive combination of features. Treating each new edition as a fresh challenge—and, in many ways, a virtually new book—the authors capture American government and politics as the dynamic ventures they are.

Comprehensive and Balanced Presentation

Known for its balanced coverage of constitutional principles, political processes, and central political institutions, this Brief Edition offers exciting changes in content that include:

- A thematic examination of constitutional democracy— its ideals, its conditions, and the American struggle to realize its possibilities and potential. The American political experiment is frequently assessed in a comparative light.
- Full integration of the results of the 1996 elections, with analysis of party control of the House and Senate.
- A new chapter, "Domestic Policy" (Chapter 14), covers current policy priorities in health care, welfare, crime, and education. Past policy initiatives, such as the New Deal and the Great Society, as well as current debates on health and welfare reform, crime control, and education policies, are examined.
- A unique chapter, "The American Political Landscape," examines social and economic diversity in American society and some of the political consequences of living in an increasingly multicultural nation. This chapter provides the framework of the social fabric of our nation, which needs to be put in context before students can fully appreciate the role that public opinion, interest group politics, and voting behavior play in America.
- Discussion of the "new" Supreme Court, including the nominations of Justices Ginsburg and Breyer and the politics of their selection and confirmation, with full updates and integrated analysis of recent Supreme Court cases.
- A much-revised treatment of the changing character of United States foreign and defense politics, including our greater involvement in the United Nations and other multinational peacekeeping organizations. Chapter 15 reflects the changing focus of our government in the post-cold war era and the increasing interdependence of foreign and defense policies.
- Innovative treatment of political participation and voting turnout, voting behavior, and campaign financing.
- The examples in *Government By The People* are drawn from a wide range of current and historical sources. Complete lists of suggested readings at the end of each chapter and detailed footnotes at the back of the book highlight sources of lasting and recent importance.

This Brief Edition includes redesigned charts, graphs, figures, and graphics to enhance the content and clarity and visual appeal of the text.

Accessible and Engaging Features for the Student

Written with the student in mind by experienced scholars and teachers, *Government By The People* has always been admired for its elegant, yet engaging narrative style. To assist accessibility, key terms appear on first use in the text in boldfaced type, followed by a precise definition. These terms are also listed in the full Glossary at the end of the book.

Of particular appeal to students will be the wealth of boxed features. Boxes in the margins provide amusing anecdotes and historical, biographical, and additional facts of interest about American politics that will enhance student learning. Several special features reinforce this goal as well:

You Decide! This participatory question-and-answer feature is designed to strengthen students' critical thinking skills as well as introduce interesting and challenging issues. A question is presented on the left page, and on the facing page a Thinking It Through discussion examines possible answers (although, as in real life, not all questions have definitive answers).

A Closer Look Journalistic-style boxes combine text, tables, photographs, or art on relevant issues of high student appeal. Like a good lecture, they provide a pause in the narrative to allow the pursuit of a particular topic beyond the scope of the material at hand.

We the People These unique boxes are designed to reflect the concerns and experiences of ethnic and minority groups in American politics. The many instances in the text where ethnic and minority concerns, histories, and stories are told have made *Government By The People* the strongest and most complete text available that integrates *all* Americans into the story of American politics.

From Coast to Coast Four-color maps provide visual state-by-state comparisons on a broad range of topics.

Supplements Available for the Instructor

- **Instructor's Manual** (0-13-541954-9). For each chapter, a summary, review of concepts, lecture suggestions and topic outlines, and additional resource materials—including a guide to media resources—are provided.
- **Strategies for Teaching American Government:** *A Guide for the New Instructor* (0-13-339003-9). This unique guide offers a wealth

of practical advice and information to help new instructors face the challenges of teaching American government. From setting course goals, conducting the class, constructing and evaluating tests or written assignments, to advising students, many of the issues and questions related to teaching are covered.

- **Test Item File** (0-13-542235-3). Thoroughly reviewed and revised to ensure the highest level of quality and accuracy, this file offers over 1800 questions in multiple choice, true/false, and essay format with page references to the text.
- **Prentice Hall Custom Test** DOS (0-13-542268-X), MAC (0-13-542276-0). A computerized test bank containing the items from our Test Item File. The program allows full editing of questions and the addition of instructor-generated items. Other special features include random generation, scrambling question order, and test preview before printing.
- **Telephone Test Preparation Service.** With one call to our toll-free 800 number, Prentice Hall will prepare tests with up to 200 questions chosen from the Test Item File, on bond paper or ditto master. Within 48 hours of your request, you will receive a personalized exam with answer key.
- **American Government Transparencies, Series III and Series IV.** These sets of 75 to 100 four-color transparency acetates reproduce illustrations, charts, and maps from the text as well as from additional sources.
- **Instructor's Guide to American Government Transparencies, Series III and IV.** This brief guide provides descriptions, teaching suggestions, and discussion questions for each transparency. There is a separate guide for each set of transparencies.

ABC News/Prentice Hall Video Library: Images in American Government (0-13-364498-7); Issues in American Government (0-13-304023-2); Election 96 (0-13-258393-3). Prentice Hall and ABC News bring this innovative video collection to your American government classroom. This video library brings chapter concepts to life by illustrating them with newsworthy topics and pressing issues. The library consists of feature segments from such award-winning programs as *Nightline, 20/20, World News Tonight/The American Agenda,* and *This Week with David Brinkley.*

- **Instructor's Guide to ABC News/Prentice Hall Video Library** (0-13-364696-3). Available for use with the ABC News/Prentice Hall Video Library, this guide provides a brief synopsis and discussion questions for each segment in the library.
- **Prentice Hall Laserdisk:** Images in American Government (0-13-075565-6). The story of American government is vividly illustrated with this exciting technology. This disk contains approximately 200 still images and over one hour of moving images to support the concepts in the text. Accompanying manuals are provided.

Supplements Available for the Student

- **Study Guide** (0-13-542227-2). Includes chapter outlines, study notes, a glossary, and practice tests designed to reinforce information in the text and help students develop a greater understanding of American government and politics.

- **The Write Stuff: Writing as a Performing and Political Art, 2nd Edition** (0-13-364746-3). Written by Thomas E. Cronin, this booklet provides a brief, pithy, and sometimes humorous guide to good writing skills and style.
- **A Guide to Civic Literacy** (0-13-304015-1). Written by James Chesney and Otto Feinstein, both at Wayne State University, this brief booklet provides ideas and suggestions for students to get involved in politics. It includes nine political activities on topics such as agenda building, coalition building, registering, educating and mobilizing voters, and increasing accountability.
- **Prentice Hall Critical Thinking Audio Cassette** (0-13-678335-X). A 60-minute cassette teaches students how to develop their critical thinking and study skills. The first 50 minutes concentrate on critical thinking skills, specifically on how to ask the right questions. The final 10 minutes offer helpful tips on how to study, take notes, and be a more active, effective learner.

The New York Times/Prentice Hall *Themes of the Times.* Prentice Hall joins forces with the premier news publication, *The New York Times,* to provide a student newspaper supplement containing recent articles pertinent to American government. These articles augment the text material and provide real-world examples. Updated twice a year.

- **American Government Simulation Games, Series III:** 3.5" DOS (0-13-566282-6), Windows (0-13-566308-3), Macintosh (0-13-566332-6). Seven simulations that engage students in various role-playing situations: Bill of Rights; House of Representatives; Presidential Budget; Secretary of State; Supreme Court; Washington Ethics; and Crime and Social Policy. Developed by G. David Garson, North Carolina State University.
- **Multimedia Guide to American Government:** Windows (0-13-340456-0). This unique student resource provides text, video, simulations, quizzes, timelines, and study guide tools in CD-ROM format to engage students in the study of government and politics. Developed by G. David Garson, North Carolina State University.
- **Web Site.** Students and professors can now take full advantage of the World Wide Web to enrich the study of American Government through the *Government By The People* Web site. This resource correlates the text with material available on the Internet. Featured on the Web site are chapter objectives, study questions, and news updates, as well as links to information from other sites on the Web that reinforce the content of each chapter. Address: http://www.prenhall.com/burns
- **Political Science on the Internet** (0-13-266594-8). This brief guide introduces students to the origin and innovations behind the Internet and provides clear strategies for navigating the complexity of the Internet and World Wide Web. Exercises within and at the end of the chapters allow students to practice searching for the myriad resources available to the student of political science. This 48-page supplementary book is free to students when purchased as a package with *Government By The People, Brief Second Edition.*

ABOUT THE AUTHORS

James MacGregor Burns is a Senior Scholar, Center for Political Leadership and Participation, University of Maryland, College Park, and Woodrow Wilson Professor Emeritus of Government at Williams College. He has written numerous books, including *The Power to Lead* (1984), *The Vineyard of Liberty* (1982), *Leadership* (1979), *Roosevelt: The Soldier of Freedom* (1970), *The Deadlock of Democracy: Four-Party Politics in America* (1963), and *Roosevelt: The Lion and the Fox* (1956). His most recent book is *A People's Charter: The Pursuit of Rights in America* (1991), which he wrote with his son, Stewart Burns. Burns is a past president of the American Political Science Association and winner of numerous prizes, including the Pulitzer Prize in Writing.

J.W. Peltason is a leading scholar on the judicial process and public law. He is Professor Emeritus of Political Science at the University of California, Irvine. As past president of the American Council on Education, Peltason has represented higher education before Congress and state legislatures. His writings include *Federal Courts in the Political Process* (1955), *Fifty-Eight Lonely Men: Southern Federal Judges and School Desegregation* (1961), and *Understanding the Constitution* (1993). Among his awards are the James Madison Medal from Princeton University and the American Political Science Association's Charles E. Merriam Award.

Thomas E. Cronin is a leading student of the American presidency, leadership, and policy-making processes. He served recently as president of the Western Political Science Association. He teaches at and serves as President of Whitman College. He served as a White House Fellow and a White House aide. His writings include *The State of the Presidency* (1980), *U.S. v. Crime in the Streets* (1981), *Direct Democracy: The Politics of Initiative, Referendum, and Recall* (1989), *Colorado Politics and Government* (1993), and *The Paradoxes of the American Presidency* (1997). Cronin is a past recipient of the American Political Science Association's Charles E. Merriam Award.

David B. Magleby is nationally recognized for his expertise on direct democracy, voting behavior, and campaign finance. He is Professor of Political Science and department chair at Brigham Young University. He has taught at the University of California, Santa Cruz, and the University of Virginia. His writings include *Direct Legislation* (1984), *The Money Chase: Congressional Campaign Finance Reform* (1990), and *The Myth of the Independent Voter* (1992). He has been president of Pi Sigma Alpha, the national political science honor society, has received numerous teaching awards, and during 1996 was a Fulbright Scholar at Nuffield College, Oxford University.

CONSTITUTIONAL DEMOCRACY

The word "democracy" is nowhere to be found in the Declaration of Independence or in the U.S. Constitution, nor was it a term used by the founders of the Republic. Democracy is hard to define. It is both a very old term and a new one. It was used in a loose sense to refer to various undesirable things: "the masses," mobs, lack of standards, and a system that encourages **demagogues*** (leaders who gain power by appealing to the emotions and prejudices of the rabble). It is also used in a very positive sense to refer to everything good and desirable.

Because we are using the term **democracy** in its political sense, we will be more precise. The distinguishing feature of democracy is that government derives its authority from its citizens. In fact, the word comes from two Greek words: *demos* (the people) and *kratos* (authority or power). Thus democracy means government by the people, not government by one person (a monarch, a dictator, a priest) or government by the few (an oligarchy or aristocracy).

Ancient Athens and a few other Greek cities had a **direct democracy**, in which citizens came together to discuss and pass laws and select their rulers by lot. These Greek city-states did not last, and most turned to mob rule and then resorted to dictators. When the word "democracy" came into English usage in the seventeenth century, it denoted this kind of direct democracy and was a term of derision, a negative word usually used to refer to mob rule.

James Madison, writing in *The Federalist*, No. 10, reflected the view of many of the framers of the U.S. Constitution when he wrote "such democracies [as the Greek and Roman] . . . have ever been found incompatible with personal security, or the rights of property; and have in general been as short in their lives, as they have been violent in their deaths" (*The Federalist*, No. 10 appears in the Appendix). Democracy has taken on a positive meaning only in the last one hundred years.

These days it is no longer possible to assemble the citizens of any but the smallest towns to make their laws or to select their officials directly from among the citizenry. Rather, we have invented a system of representation. Democracy today means **representative democracy**, or, to use Plato's term, a **republic** in which those who have governmental authority *get and retain* authority directly or indirectly as the result of winning free elections in which all adult citizens are allowed to participate.

The framers preferred to use the term "republic" to avoid any confusion between direct democracy, which they disliked, and representative democracy, which they liked and thought secured all the advantages of a direct democracy while curing its weaknesses. Today, and in this book, *democracy* and *republic* are often used interchangeably.

Like most political concepts, democracy encompasses many ideas and has many meanings. Democracy is a way of life, a form of government, a way of governing, a type of nation, a state of mind, and a variety of processes. We can

*Words in bold type throughout the text are defined in the Glossary at the end of this book.

divide these many meanings into three broad categories: democracy as a system of interacting values, a system of interrelated political processes, and a system of interdependent political structures (see box).

DEFINING DEMOCRACY

Democracy as a System of Interacting Values

As we enter the twenty-first century, the democratic faith may be as near a universal faith as the world has. A belief in human dignity, freedom, liberty, individual rights, and other democratic values is widely shared in most corners of the world. The essence of democratic values is contained in the ideas of popular consent, respect for the individual, equality of opportunity, and personal liberty.

POPULAR CONSENT   The animating principle of the American Revolution, the Declaration of Independence, and the resulting new nation was **popular consent**, the idea that a just government must derive its powers from the consent of the people it governs. A commitment to democracy thus entails a community's willingness to participate and make decisions in government. Intellectually these principles sound unobjectionable, but in practice they mean that certain individuals or groups may not get their way. A commitment to popular consent must involve a willingness to lose if most people vote the other way.

RESPECT FOR THE INDIVIDUAL   Popular rule in a democracy flows from a belief that every individual has the potential for common sense, rationality, and a notion of fairness. Individuals, democrats insist, have important rights; collectively, those rights are the source of all legitimate governmental authority and power. These notions pervade all democratic thought. They are woven into the writings of Thomas Jefferson, especially in the Declaration of Independence: "All men . . . are endowed by their Creator with certain unalienable rights" (the Declaration of Independence appears in the Appendix). Constitutional democracies make the person—rich or poor, black or white, male or female—the *central* measure of value. The state, the union, and the corporation are measured in terms of their usefulness to individuals. Not all political systems, of course, put the individual first. Some promote **statism**, considering the state supreme. Democrats, however, believe that the state, or even the community, is less important than are the individuals who compose it.

EQUALITY OF OPPORTUNITY   The importance of the individual is enhanced by the democratic value of equality: "All men are created equal and from that equal creation they derive rights inherent and unalienable, among which are the preservation of liberty and the pursuit of happiness." So reads Jefferson's first draft of the Declaration of Independence, and the words indicate the primacy of the concept. Alexis de Tocqueville, James Bryce, and other international visitors who investigated American democracy have all been struck by the strength of egalitarian thought and practice in both our political and our social lives.

But what does equality mean? What kind of equality? *Equality of opportunity* (almost all Americans say they want that), but also *equality of condition*? Does equality of opportunity simply mean that everyone should have the *same place at the starting line*? Or does it mean an effort should be made to equalize most

"The Athenians are here, Sire, with an offer to back us with ships, money, arms, and men—and, of course, their usual lectures about democracy."

Drawing by Ed Fisher. ©1983 The New Yorker Magazine, Inc.

or all the factors that during the course of a person's life might determine how well he or she fares economically or socially?

PERSONAL LIBERTY Liberty has been the single most powerful value in American history. It was for "life, liberty, and the pursuit of happiness" that independence was declared; it was to "secure the Blessings of Liberty" that the Constitution was drawn up and adopted. Even our patriotic songs extol the "sweet land of liberty." *Liberty* or *freedom* (used interchangeably here) means that all individuals must have the opportunity to realize their own goals.

DEMOCRATIC VALUES IN CONFLICT The basic values of democracy do not always coexist happily. Individualism may conflict with collective welfare or the public good. Freedom as liberation may become freedom as alienation. Self-determination may conflict with equal opportunity. The right of General Motors to run its automobile factories to maximize profit, as compared to the right of automobile workers in those factories to join unions or to share in the running of the plants, illustrates this type of conflict in everyday life.

Liberty and equality engage each other at some points and oppose each other at others. Sometimes they do not relate at all. At the extreme, the pursuit of liberty might become license for unbridled selfishness or anarchy, while the pursuit of equality might mean a leveling to dull mediocrity and even the erosion of liberty. Much of our political combat revolves around how to strike a balance between these values.

More people dream about democracy than ever experience it, and many new democracies fail. To be successful, democratic government requires a political process as well as a governmental structure. In both areas, the American experiment is instructive.

Democracy as a System of Interrelated Political Processes

To become reality, democratic values must be incorporated into a political process, a set of arrangements for making decisions and managing the public's business. The essence of the democratic process is respect for the rules of fair play, which can be realized in free and fair elections, majority rule, freedom of expression, and the right to assemble and protest.

FREE AND FAIR ELECTIONS Democratic government is based on free and fair elections held at intervals frequent enough to allow citizens some voice in major public policy choices. Elections are one of the most important devices for keeping officials and representatives accountable.

We previously defined *representative democracy* to mean a system of government in which those who have the authority to make decisions with the force of law acquire and retain this authority either directly or indirectly as the result of winning free elections in which the great majority of adult citizens are allowed to participate. Crucial to modern-day definitions of democracy is the idea that *opposition political parties* can exist, can run candidates in elections, and can at least have a chance to replace those who are currently holding public office. Thus political competition and choice are crucial to the existence of democracy.

While all citizens should have equal voting power, free and fair elections do not imply that everyone must or will have equal political influence. Some people, because of wealth, talent, or position, have more influence than others. How much extra influence key figures should be allowed to exercise in a democracy is an ongoing question for democrats. But at the polls a president or a pick-and-shovel laborer, a newspaper publisher or a lettuce picker, casts only one vote.

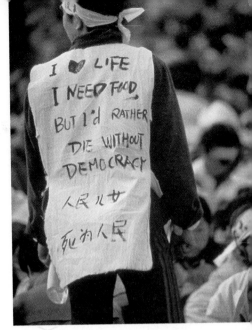

The ideal of liberty still inspires people today, as it did in the Tiananmen Square demonstrations in China that were repressed so brutally.

MAJORITY (PLURALITY) RULE The basic rule of a democracy is that those with the most votes take charge of the government, at least until the next election, when a new majority may be voted in to take charge. In practice, *majority rule* is often *plurality rule*, in which the largest bloc takes charge, even though it may not constitute a true majority, with more than half the votes. While in charge, those elected have no right to curtail the attempts of political minorities to use all peaceful means to become a majority. So even as the winners take power, the losers can go to work to try to get it back at the next election.

The American system of constitutional democracy allows people a say in who will decide important issues. Through the system of representation, people can participate indirectly in the great debates and decisions about laws and public policies.[1]

Should the will of the majority prevail in all cases? Americans answer this question in a variety of ways. Some insist that majority views should be enacted into laws and regulations. But perhaps the more widely held view is that an effective representative democracy involves far more than simply ascertaining and applying the statistical will of the people. It is a more complicated and often untidy process by which the people and their agents inform themselves, debate, compromise, and arrive at a decision, and do so only after thoughtful deliberation.

The Constitution reflects the framers' fear of tyranny by majorities, especially momentary majorities that spring from temporary passion. The framers wanted to guard society against any one part acting unjustly toward any other part. To accomplish this end, they insulated certain rights and institutions from popular choice. The effective representation of the people, the framers insisted, could not and should not be an unthinking mouthpiece for parochial interests or for each shifting breeze of opinion. Note the care with which the framers, most especially James Madison, explained in *The Federalist*, Nos. 10 and 51 (see Appendix) how and why the Constitution was constructed to prevent majority tyranny.

FREEDOM OF EXPRESSION Free and fair elections depend on access to information relevant to voting choices. Voters must have access to facts, competing ideas, and the views of candidates. Free and fair elections require a climate in which competing, nongovernment-owned newspapers, radio stations, and television stations can flourish. Expression by such media should be protected from government censorship.

Here, again, the extent to which different ideas actually receive equal attention is determined by access to the mass media, especially television, where the costs are beyond the reach of most people. Still, the principle and practice of free and fair competition of ideas, especially during election, is essential.

THE RIGHT TO ASSEMBLE AND PROTEST Citizens must be free to organize for political purposes. Obviously, individuals can be more effective if they join with others in a party, a pressure group, a protest movement, or a demonstration. The right to oppose the government, to form opposition parties, and to have a chance of defeating incumbents is not only vital; it is a defining characteristic of a democracy.

Democracy as a System of Interdependent Political Structures

Democracy is, of course, more than values and processes. It also entails a system of political structures that safeguard these values and processes. In this country, the Constitution and the Bill of Rights create an ingenious structure—one that both grants and checks government power. This constitutional structure is reinforced by a political system of parties, interest groups, media, and other institu-

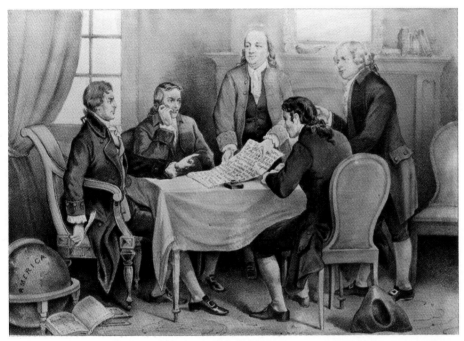

The Declaration of Independence committee set down on paper the ideas and goals that would later be incorporated in the Constitution. Shown here are (*left to right*) Thomas Jefferson, Roger Sherman, Benjamin Franklin, Robert Livingston, and John Adams.

tions that mediate between the electorate and those who govern and thus help to maintain democratic stability.

This structure is remarkable for four elements: One is *federalism*, the division of powers between the national and state governments. Another is the *separation of powers* among the legislative, executive, and judicial branches. Liberty is further safeguarded by a system of *checks and balances*, which gives each branch its own powers as well as the "necessary constitutional means and personal motives to resist the encroachments of the others."[2] This combination of separation of powers and checks and balances was one of the most important creations of the framers in 1787. The fourth element, the *Bill of Rights*, is also important, for it is a *written, explicit* guarantee of individual liberties and due process before the law. The chapters that follow will explain both the principles and the architectural features of American-style democracy in more detail.

CONDITIONS CONDUCIVE TO CONSTITUTIONAL DEMOCRACY

How do we explain the relatively low number of long-lived, strong democracies (see Figure 1-1)? Although it is hard to specify the precise conditions that are essential for the establishment and maintenance of a democracy, here are a few things we have learned.

Educational Conditions

Clearly, the exercise of voting privileges takes some level of education on the part of the citizenry. But a word of caution: A high level of education does not "cause" or "guarantee" democratic government, as the example of Nazi Germany readily illustrates; and there are some democracies, such as India, where large

Thinking it Through

Goals

Not everyone agrees with the goals we list here, and you may weigh them differently, according to your own values. How would you rank these goals? Are some more essential than others?

- Government by popular consent
- Liberty—personal, religious, economic
- Protection for property rights
- Justice—fairness and equality before the law
- Equality of economic opportunities
- Peace and stability

Means and Protections

- Constitutional democracy backed by a written constitution enumerating government powers and their limits
- Federalism
- Separation of powers
- Checks and balances
- Free and frequent elections
- Freedom of speech and press
- Competitive political parties
- Majority rule
- Government protection of minority rights, tolerance for diversity and dissent
- Right to petition government and courts for redress of grievances
- Rule of law, granting citizens due process and making government officials subject to impeachment and criminal prosecution
- Civilian control over the military

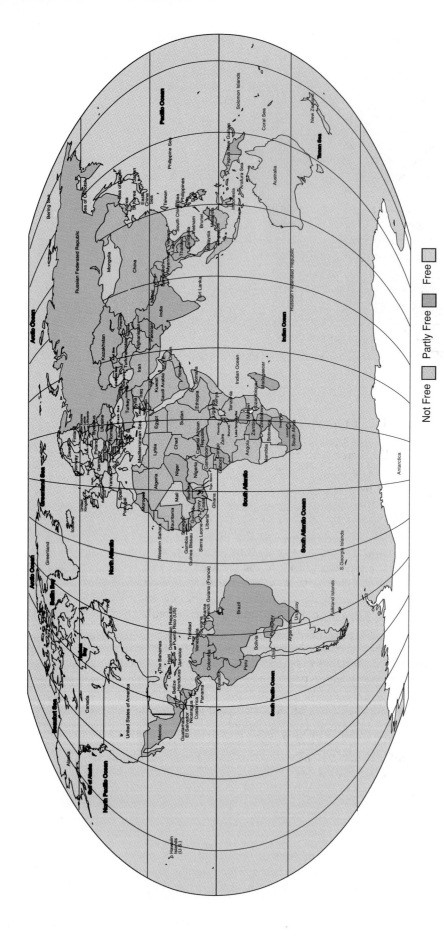

FIGURE 1-1   The Map of Freedom

SOURCE: *Freedom Review*, January–February 1994, pp. 41–42. © 1994 by Freedom House.

numbers of people are illiterate. Still, voting makes little sense unless a considerable number of the voters can read and write and express their interests and opinions. The poorly educated and illiterate get left out in a democracy.

Economic Conditions

A relatively prosperous nation, with an equitable distribution of wealth, provides the best context for democracy. Starving people, by contrast, are more interested in food than in voting. Where economic power is concentrated, political power is likely to be concentrated. Thus well-to-do nations have a greater chance of sustaining democratic governments than do those with widespread poverty. The reality is that extremes of wealth and poverty undermine the possibilities for a healthy constitutional democracy.

Some measure of private ownership of property and a relatively favorable role for the market economy are also related to the creation and maintenance of democratic institutions. Democracies can range from heavily regulated economies with public ownership of many enterprises, such as Sweden, to those in which there is little government regulation of the marketplace. But there are no examples of a democracy with a command (government controlled) economy and little private ownership of property, although there are many examples of nations with a market economy and no democracy. There are no truly democratic communist states, nor have there ever been any.

Social Conditions

Economic development generally makes democracy possible, yet political leadership and proper social conditions are necessary to make it real. In a society fragmented into warring groups that differ fiercely on fundamental issues, government by discussion and compromise is difficult. When ideologically separated groups consider the issues at stake to be vital, they may prefer to fight rather than accept the verdict of the ballot box. But in a society that consists of many overlapping associations and groupings, individuals are not as likely to identify completely with a single group and give their allegiance to it. For example, Joe Brown is a Baptist, an African American, a southerner, a Democrat, an electrician, and a member of the National Rifle Association, and he makes $50,000 a year. On some issues Joe thinks as a Baptist, on others as a southerner, and on still others as an African American. Sue Jones is a Catholic, a Republican, an auto dealer, a member of the National Organization for Women, from a Polish background, and she makes $100,000 a year. Sometimes she acts as a Republican, sometimes as an American of Polish descent, and sometimes as a member of NOW. Jones and Brown differ on some issues, yet agree on others. In general, the differences between them are not likely to be greater than their common interest in maintaining a democracy.[3]

Democracy is also more likely to survive where other social institutions reinforce democratic habits. The family, the church, and the school are all institutions regulating important areas of life affected by and affecting government. If these institutions support and reinforce the idea of government by democratic procedures, then the habits of discussion, compromise, and respect for differences are strengthened by constant use.

Ideological Conditions

Ideology refers to our basic beliefs about power and government and political practices—beliefs that arise out of the educational, economic, and social conditions we experience. Out of these educational, economic, and social conditions must also develop a general acceptance of the ideals of democracy, the willing-

Weaknesses of the Articles of Confederation

1. Congress could not levy taxes to support the army and navy or to carry out its other activities. It could only request funds from the states.
2. Congress could not regulate trade between the states or with other nations. States taxed each others' goods and even negotiated their own trade agreements with other nations.
3. Congress could not forbid the states from issuing their own currencies, further complicating interstate trade and travel.
4. Because there was no executive branch, Congress had to handle all administrative duties.
5. The lack of a judiciary system meant that the national government had to rely on state courts to enforce national laws and settle disputes between the states. In practice state courts could overturn national laws.

ness of a substantial portion of the people to agree to proceed democratically. This quality is sometimes called the *democratic consensus*. A well-known student of democratic ideas writes:

> Prior to politics, beneath it, enveloping it, restricting it, conditioning it, is the underlying consensus on policy that usually exists in a society among a predominant portion of the politically active members. Without such a consensus, no democratic system would long survive the endless irritations and frustrations of elections and party competition.[4]

THE CONSTITUTIONAL CONVENTION OF 1787

During and after the Revolution, Americans experimented with a **confederation**—a weak central government. The resulting **Articles of Confederation** provided some national unity but not enough to deal with rival powers like Britain and Spain or with internal disunity (see box, Weaknesses of the Articles of Confederation). The individual states also appeared powerless to deal with their problems. The bloody **Shays's Rebellion** by farmers in western Massachusetts in 1786 confirmed the leaders' worst fears. They resolved to frame a new national constitution that would ensure both liberty and order. Soon they elected delegates to a convention that would transform the system.

The delegates who assembled in Philadelphia in May 1787 were presented with a condition, not a theory. They had to establish a national government powerful enough to prevent the young nation from dissolving. What these men did continues to have a major impact on how we are governed. It also provides an outstanding lesson in political science for the world.

The Delegates

Seventy-four men were selected as delegates to the **Constitutional Convention** by the various states, but only 55 arrived in Philadelphia. Of these, approximately 40 took a real part in the work of the convention. It was a distinguished gathering. Many of the most important men of the nation were there: successful merchants, planters, bankers, lawyers, and former and present governors and congressional representatives (39 of the delegates had served in Congress). Most had read the classics of political thought. Most had participated vigorously in the practical task of constructing local and state governments. Many had helped to create the Articles of Confederation.

The convention was as representative as most political gatherings at the time: The participants were all white male landowners. These well-read, well-fed, well-bred, and often well-wed delegates were mainly state or national leaders, for in the 1780s ordinary people were not likely to participate in politics. Even today farm laborers, factory workers, and truck drivers are seldom found in Congress, although a haberdasher (Harry Truman), a self-styled peanut farmer (Jimmy Carter), and a movie actor (Ronald Reagan) have made their way to the White House. Most of those in attendance eventually supported the Constitution in the ratification debates.

Several of the participants at the convention stand out as the prime movers. As early as 1778, Alexander Hamilton had been urging that the national government be made stronger. Hamilton had come to the United States from the West Indies and while still a college student had won national attention for his brilliant pamphlets in defense of the Revolutionary cause. During the war he served as General Washington's aide, and his experiences confirmed his distaste for a Congress so weak it could not even supply the Revolution's troops with enough food or arms.

From Virginia came two of the leading delegates: George Washington and James Madison. Although active in the movement to revise the Articles of Confederation, Washington had been reluctant to attend the convention. He accepted only when persuaded that his prestige was needed for its success. He was selected unanimously to preside over the meetings. According to the records, he spoke only twice during the deliberations, yet his influence was felt in the informal gatherings as well as during the sessions. The assumption that Washington would become the first president under the new constitution inspired confidence in it. James Madison was only 36 years old at the time of the convention, yet he was one of its most learned members. He had helped frame Virginia's first constitution and had served both in the Virginia Assembly and in the Confederation's Congress. Madison was also a leader of those who favored the establishment of a stronger national government.

The proceedings of the convention were kept secret. To encourage everyone to speak freely, delegates were forbidden to discuss the debates with outsiders. It was feared that if a delegate publicly took a firm stand on an issue, it would be harder for him to change his mind after debate and discussion. The delegates also knew that if word of the inevitable disagreements got out, it would provide ammunition for the many enemies of the convention. There were critics of this secrecy rule, but without it, agreement might not have been possible.

Consensus

The Constitutional Convention is usually discussed in terms of its three famous compromises: the compromise between large and small states over representation in Congress, the compromise between North and South over the regulation and taxation of foreign commerce, and the compromise between North and South over the counting of slaves for taxation and representation. There were many other important compromises. On many significant issues, however, most of the delegates were in agreement.

Although a few delegates might have personally favored a limited monarchy, all supported a republican form of government. This was the only form seriously considered and the only form acceptable to the vast majority of the people. Equally important, all the delegates were constitutionalists who opposed arbitrary and unrestrained government.

The common philosophy accepted by most of the delegates was that of *balanced government*. They wanted to construct a national government in which no single interest would dominate. Because most of the delegates represented citizens who were alarmed by the tendencies of desperate farmers to interfere with or abuse the property rights of others, they were primarily concerned with balancing the government in the direction of protection for property and business. Most of them respected the remark of Elbridge Gerry, delegate from Massachusetts: "The evils we experience flow from the excess of democracy. The people do not want virtue, but are dupes of pretended patriots." Likewise, there was substantial agreement with Gouverneur Morris's statement that property was the "principal object of government."

Benjamin Franklin, the 81-year-old delegate from Pennsylvania, favored extending the right to vote to all white males, but most of the delegates believed that owners of land were the best guardians of liberty. James Madison voiced the fear that those without property, if given the right to vote, would either combine to deprive property owners of their rights or would become the "tools of demagogues." The delegates agreed in principle on restricted franchise, or voting rights, but differed over the kind and amount of property one must own in order to vote. Because the states were in the process of relaxing qualifications for the

James Madison

Alexander Hamilton

"Remember, gentlemen, we aren't here just to draft a constitution. We're here to draft the best damn constitution in the world."

Drawing by Steiner. ©1982 The New Yorker Magazine, Inc.

vote, the framers recognized they would jeopardize approval of the constitution if they made the right to vote in federal elections more restricted than the franchises within the states. As a result, each state was left to determine the qualifications for electing members of the House of Representatives, the only branch of the national government in which the electorate was given a direct voice.

Within five days of its opening, the convention—with only Connecticut dissenting—voted that "a national government ought to be established consisting of a supreme legislative, executive, and judiciary." This decision to establish a national government that rested on and exercised power over individuals profoundly altered the nature of the central government and changed it from a loose league of states to a national government.

Few dissented from proposals to give the new Congress all the powers of the old Congress plus all other powers necessary to ensure that the harmony of the United States would not be disrupted by the exercise of state legislation. The framers agreed that a strong executive, which had been lacking under the Articles of Confederation, was necessary to provide energy and direction. An independent judiciary was also accepted without much debate. Other issues, though, sparked considerable conflict.

Conflict and Compromise

There were serious differences among the various groups, especially between the delegates of the large and small states. One of the most contentious issues was the distribution of the land extending to the Mississippi, land that had been secured through the Revolution. Several large states asserted claims to these western lands, but the small states generally refused to go along. The large states also favored a strong national government (which they expected they could dominate), while the delegates from the small states were anxious to avoid being dominated.

This tension surfaced in the first discussions of representation in Congress. Franklin favored a single-house national legislature, but most states had had two-chamber legislatures since colonial times, and the delegates were used to the system. **Bicameralism**—the principle of the two-house legislature—also implemented the delegates' belief in the need for balanced government. The smaller chamber would represent the aristocracy and offset the larger, more democratic House of Representatives.

THE VIRGINIA PLAN The Virginia delegation took the initiative. It had met during the delay before the convention, and as soon as the convention was organized, presented 15 resolutions. These resolutions, the **Virginia Plan**, called for a strong central government. The legislature was to be composed of two chambers. The members of the more representative chamber were to be elected by the voters; those of the smaller and more aristocratic chamber were to be chosen by the larger chamber from nominees submitted by the state legislatures. Representation in both houses was to be on the basis of either wealth or numbers, which gave the more populous and wealthier states—Massachusetts, Pennsylvania, and Virginia—a majority in the national legislature.

The Congress thus created was to be given all the legislative power of its predecessor under the Articles of Confederation, as well as the right "to legislate in all cases in which the separate States are incompetent." Further, it was to have the authority to veto state legislation in conflict with the proposed constitution. The Virginia Plan also called for a national executive to be chosen by the legislature and a national judiciary with rather extensive jurisdiction. The national Supreme Court, along with the executive, was to have a qualified veto over acts of Congress.

THE NEW JERSEY PLAN   For the first few weeks the Virginia Plan dominated the discussion. But by June 15 additional delegates from the small states had arrived, and they began a counterattack. They rallied around William Paterson of New Jersey, who presented a series of resolutions known as the New Jersey Plan. Paterson did not question the need for a strengthened central government, yet he was concerned about how this strength might be used. The **New Jersey Plan** would give Congress the right to tax and regulate commerce and to coerce states, yet it would retain the single-house legislature (as under the Articles of Confederation) in which each state, regardless of size, would have the same vote. The plan contained the germ of what eventually came to be a key provision of our Constitution: the *supremacy clause*. The national Supreme Court was to hear appeals from state judges, and the supremacy clause would require all judges—state and national—to treat laws of the national government and the treaties of the United States as superior to the constitutions and laws of each of the states.

Paterson maneuvered to force concessions from the larger states. He favored a strong central government, but not one the big states could control. Further, he raised the issue of practical politics. To adopt the Virginia Plan, which would create a powerful national government dominated by Massachusetts, Pennsylvania, and Virginia and eliminate the states as important units of government, would all but guarantee that the states would reject the new constitution. Still, the large states resisted, and for a time the convention was deadlocked. The small states believed all states should be represented equally in Congress, at least in the upper house. The large states insisted representation in both houses be based on population or wealth and that national legislators be elected by the voters rather than by state legislatures. Finally, a Committee of Eleven was elected to devise a compromise. On July 5 it presented its proposals.

THE CONNECTICUT COMPROMISE   Because of the prominent role of the Connecticut delegation, this plan has since been known as the **Connecticut Compromise**, or as it is sometimes called, the Great Compromise. It called for one house in which each state would have an equal vote and a second house in which representation would be based on population and in which all bills for raising or appropriating money would originate. This proposal was a setback for the large states, which agreed to it only when the smaller states made it clear that this was their price for union. After equality of state representation in the Senate was accepted, most objections to establishing a strong national government dissolved.

NORTH–SOUTH COMPROMISES   Other issues at the convention split the delegates North and South. Southerners were afraid that a northern majority in Congress might discriminate against southern trade. They had some basis for this concern. John Jay, secretary of foreign affairs for the Confederation, had proposed a treaty with Great Britain that would have given advantages to northern merchants at the expense of southern exporters. To protect themselves, the southern delegates insisted a two-thirds majority be required in the Senate before presidents could ratify treaties.

Differences between the North and South were also evident on the issue of representation in the House of Representatives. The question was whether to count slaves for purposes of apportioning seats in the House. The South wanted to count slaves and thereby enlarge its number of representatives; the North resisted. After heated debate, the delegates agreed on the **three-fifths compromise**. Each slave would be counted as three-fifths of a free person for the purposes of apportionment in the House and of direct taxation. The explanation for "three-fifths," as opposed to some other fraction, was that it maintained a

Creating the Republic

April 1775 American Revolution begins at Lexington and Concord

June 1775 George Washington assumes command of Continental forces

July 1776 Declaration of Independence approved

November 1777 Articles of Confederation adopted by Continental Congress

March 1781 Articles of Confederation ratified by the states

October 1781 British defeated at York-town

April 1784 Congress ratifies peace treaty with British

Late 1786 Shays's Rebellion in western Massachusetts

May 1787 Constitutional Convention opens in Philadelphia

September 1787 Constitution for the United States adopted by Convention

June 1788 Constitution ratified by nine states

Early 1789 First national elections

March 1789 United States Congress meets for the first time in New York

April 1789 George Washington inaugurated as first president

September 1789 John Jay becomes first chief justice of the United States

September 1789 Congress proposes Bill of Rights

December 1791 Bill of Rights (first 10 amendments) ratified as part of the U.S. Constitution

Note: It took about 15 years to win independence, form an interim government that tried to govern, fashion a "more perfect union," and actually get a national government, with functioning legislative, executive, and judicial branches.

balance of power between North and South. The issue of "balance" would recur in the early history of our nation as territorial governments were established and territories applied for statehood.

OTHER ISSUES The delegates found other issues about which to argue. Should the national government have lower courts, or would one federal Supreme Court be enough? This issue was resolved by postponing the decision; the Constitution states that there shall be one Supreme Court and that Congress *may* establish inferior courts. How should the president be selected? For a long time the convention accepted the idea that the president should be elected by Congress. Yet the delegates feared Congress would dominate the president, or vice versa. Election by the state legislatures was rejected because these bodies were distrusted. Finally, the electoral college system was devised. This was perhaps the most novel and contrived contribution of the delegates, and today it is one of the most criticized provisions in the Constitution.[5] (Consult Article II, Section 1, of the Constitution.)

After three months the delegates stopped debating. On September 17, 1787, they assembled for the impressive ceremony of signing the document they were recommending to the nation. All but three of those still present signed; others who opposed the general drift of the convention had already left. Their work well done, delegates adjourned to the nearby City Tavern to relax and celebrate.

TO ADOPT OR NOT TO ADOPT?

The delegates had gone far. They had neither hesitated to disregard Congress's instruction to do no more than revise the Articles nor did they hesitate to ignore Article XIII of the Articles of Confederation. This article declared the Union to be perpetual and prohibited any alteration of the Articles unless agreed to by Congress and *by every one of the state legislatures*, a provision that had made it impossible to amend the Articles. The convention delegates, however, boldly declared that their newly proposed Constitution should go into effect when ratified by *popularly elected conventions in nine states*. They turned to this method of ratification for practical considerations as well as for reasons of principle. Not only were the delegates aware that there was little chance of securing approval of the new Constitution in all state legislatures; many also believed the Constitution should be ratified by an authority higher than a legislature. A constitution based on popular approval would have higher legal and moral status. The Articles of Confederation had been a compact of state governments, but the Constitution was to be based on "we the people." Nevertheless, even this method of ratification would not be easy. The nation was not ready to adopt the Constitution without a thorough debate.

Federalists versus Antifederalists

Supporters of the new government, by cleverly appropriating the name **Federalists**, took some of the sting out of charges that they were trying to destroy the states and establish an all-powerful central government. By calling their opponents **Antifederalists**, they pointed up the negative character of the arguments of those who opposed ratification.

The great debate was conducted with pamphlets, papers, letters to the editor, and speeches. The issues were important, but in the main the argument was carried on in a quiet and calm manner. Out of the debate came a series of essays known as ***The Federalist***, written by Alexander Hamilton, James Madison, and John Jay to persuade the voters of New York to ratify the Constitution. *The Fed-*

eralist is still, said Charles and Mary Beard, "widely regarded as the most profound single treatise on the Constitution ever written and as among the few masterly works in political science produced in all the centuries of history."[6] (Three of the most important *Federalist* essays, Nos. 10, 51, and 78, are found in the Appendix of this book. We urge you to read them.) The great debate stands even today as an outstanding example of free people using public discussion to determine the nature of their fundamental laws.

The Antifederalists' most telling criticism of the proposed Constitution was its failure to include a bill of rights.[7] The Federalists believed a bill of rights unnecessary. They contended that the proposed national government had only the specific powers delegated to it by the states and people, so there was no need to specify that Congress could not, for example, abridge freedom of the press because it had no power to regulate the press. Moreover, the Federalists argued, to guarantee *some* rights might be dangerous, because it would then be thought that rights *not* listed could be denied. The Constitution already protected some important rights—trial by jury in federal criminal cases, for example. Hamilton and others also insisted that paper guarantees were weak supports on which to depend for protection against governmental tyranny.

The Antifederalists were unconvinced. If some rights were protected, what could be the objection to providing constitutional protection for others? Without a bill of rights, what was to prevent Congress from using one of its delegated powers to abridge free speech? If bills of rights were needed in state constitutions to limit state governments, why was a bill of rights not needed in the national constitution to limit the national government? This was a government farther from the people, they contended, with a greater tendency to subvert natural rights.

The Politics of Ratification

The absence of a bill of rights in the proposed Constitution dominated the struggle over its adoption. "There is no Declaration of Rights" was the first sentence of an attack on the document by Virginia delegate George Mason. In taverns and church gatherings and newspaper offices up and down the eastern seaboard, people were muttering, "No bill of rights—no constitution!" This feeling was so strong that some Antifederalists who were far more concerned with *states'* rights than *individual* rights joined forces with bill of rights advocates in an effort to defeat the proposed Constitution.

The Federalists were first off the mark in the struggle over the Constitution that opened as soon as the delegates left Philadelphia in mid-September 1787. The Federalists' immediate tactic was to secure ratification in as many states as possible before the opposition had time to organize. The Antifederalists were handicapped. Most newspapers were owned by supporters of ratification. Moreover, Antifederalist strength was concentrated in rural areas, which were underrepresented in some state legislatures and difficult to arouse to political action. They needed time to perfect their organization and collect their strength. The Federalists, composed of a more closely knit group of leaders throughout the colonies, moved in a hurry.

In most of the small states, now satisfied by equal Senate representation, ratification was gained without difficulty. Delaware was the first state to ratify. By early 1788, Pennsylvania, New Jersey, Georgia, and Connecticut had also ratified. In the view of the grass-roots political observer Mercy Warren of Massachusetts, there seemed to be few Americans who did not "unite in the general wish for the restoration of public faith, the revival of commerce, arts, agriculture, and industry, under a lenient, peaceable and energetic government."[8]

Reports were coming in from Massachusetts, however, that opposition was broadening, especially in the hinterland of the state. The position of such key

TABLE 1-1

Ratification of the U.S. Constitution

State	Date
Delaware	Dec. 7, 1787
Pennsylvania	Dec. 12, 1787
New Jersey	Dec. 19, 1787
Georgia	Jan. 2, 1788
Connecticut	Jan. 9, 1788
Massachusetts	Feb. 6, 1788
Maryland	April 28, 1788
South Carolina	May 23, 1788
New Hampshire	June 21, 1788
Virginia	June 25, 1788
New York	July 26, 1788
North Carolina	Nov. 21, 1789
Rhode Island	May 29, 1790

leaders as John Hancock and Samuel Adams was in doubt. The debate in the ratifying convention in Boston pitched some of the most polished Federalist leaders against an array of eloquent but plainspoken Antifederalists. The debate raged for most of January 1788 and into February. At times it looked as though the Constitution would lose, as Antifederalists raised the cry of "Why no Bill of Rights?" and other objections. But in the end the Constitution was narrowly ratified in Massachusetts, 187 to 168 (see Table 1-1).

The Federalists were elated; yet, in fact, both sides had won. To gain votes for the Constitution, the Federalists had to make a deal, one of the most important compromises in U.S. history. The Federalists adopted the strategy of accepting their opponents' most convincing argument—the lack of a bill of rights—and offered to add a bill of rights to the Constitution, but only *after* the new government under the Constitution was set up. Thus the Federalists sidetracked proposals for a *second* convention, which might have turned into a "runaway" gathering. In turn, the Antifederalists, led by such notables as Samuel Adams, won a promise for bill of rights amendments—a promise later honored by Madison and his fellow Federalist leaders.

The struggle over the Constitution continued throughout the spring of 1788. By June 21, Maryland, South Carolina, and New Hampshire had ratified, putting the Constitution over the top in the number (nine) required for ratification. But two big hurdles remained: Virginia and New York. Virginia was crucial, as the most populous state, the home of Washington and other heroes, a link between North and South. The Virginia ratifying convention rivaled the Constitutional Convention in the caliber of its delegates. Madison, who had only recently switched to favoring the bill of rights position after saying earlier it was unnecessary, captained the Federalist forces. The fiery Patrick Henry led the opposition. In an epic debate, Henry cried that liberty was the issue—"Liberty, the greatest of earthly possessions . . . that precious jewel!" But Madison quietly rebutted him and then played his trump card, a promise that a bill of rights embracing the freedoms of religion and speech and assembly would be added to the Constitution. At a critical moment, Washington himself tipped the balance with a letter urging ratification. News of the Virginia vote, 89 for the Constitution and 79 opposed, was rushed to New York.[9]

When the convention assembled, the Federalists were outnumbered, but they were aided by the strategy and skill of Hamilton and by word of Virginia's ratification. New York approved by a margin of three votes. Although North Carolina and Rhode Island still remained outside the Union (the former ratified in November 1789, and the latter six months later), the new nation was created. In New York, a few members of the old Congress assembled to issue the call for elections under the new Constitution. Then Congress adjourned without setting a date for reconvening.

THE LIVING CONSTITUTION

Although only a few people liked all parts of the recently drafted constitution, most figured it was better than the weak Articles of Confederation. The original, unamended Constitution was a skinny document of only 4,543 words (you can carry it around in your coat pocket), yet it packed a powerful punch. It was intended to be only a framework for governing; it was a document into which citizens could, if optimistic, read their hopes, or, if pessimistic, their fears. Most of the founders would be surprised to learn that more than two hundred years later we still have not written another constitution—let alone two or three!

Soon after the adoption of the Constitution, economic prosperity returned. Markets for American goods were opening in Europe, and business was pulling out of its postwar slump. Such events seemed to justify Federalist claims that adoption of the Constitution would correct the nation's problems. Within a surprisingly short time, the Constitution lost its partisan character; both Antifederalists and Federalists honored it. Politicians differed less and less over whether the Constitution was good; they began to argue over what it meant.

The 1791 adoption of the Bill of Rights made the Constitution more popular than ever.[10] As the Constitution won the support of Americans, it began to take on the aura of **natural law**, law that defines right from wrong, law that is higher than human law. "The Fathers grew ever larger in stature," wrote Max Lerner, "as they receded from view; the era in which they lived and fought became a Golden Age; in that age there had been a fresh dawn for the world, and its men were giants against the sky."[11] This early Constitution worship helped bring unity to the diverse new nation. Like the Crown in Britain, the Constitution became a symbol of national loyalty, evoking both emotional and intellectual support from all Americans, regardless of their differences. The framers' work became part of the American creed.[12] It stood for liberty, equality before the law, limited government—indeed, for just about whatever anyone wanted to read into it.

The Constitution, however, is more than a symbol. It is also a *supreme and binding law that both grants and limits powers.* "In framing a government which is to be administered by men over men," wrote James Madison in *The Federalist*, No. 51, "the great difficulty lies in this: you must first enable the government to control the governed; and in the next place oblige it to control itself." (Take a look at *The Federalist*, No. 51, in the Appendix at the back of this book.) The Constitution is both a *positive* instrument of government, which enables the governors to control the governed, and a *restraint* on government, which enables the ruled to check the rulers.

In what ways does the Constitution limit the power of the government? In what ways does it create governmental power? How has it managed to serve as a great symbol of national unity and at the same time a somewhat adaptable and changing instrument of government? The secret is an ingenious separation of powers and a system of checks and balances that combine to check power with power.

CHECKING POWER WITH POWER

It may seem strange to begin by stressing the ways in which the Constitution limits governmental power, but we must keep in mind the dilemma the framers faced. They wanted a *stronger and more effective* national government than they had under the Articles of Confederation. At the same time, they were keenly aware that the people would not accept too much central control. Efficiency and order were important concerns, yet they were not as important as *liberty*. The framers wanted to ensure domestic tranquillity and prevent future rebellions, but they also wanted to forestall the emergence of a home-grown King George III. Accordingly, they allotted certain powers to the national government and reserved the rest for the states, thus establishing a system of *federalism* (whose nature and problems we take up in Chapter 2). Even this was not enough. They believed they needed additional means to limit the national government.

The most important way to make public officials observe the constitutional limits on their powers is through *regular and fair elections*; voters have the ability

"And there are three branches of government, so that each branch has the other two to blame everything on."

Dunagin's People by Ralph Dunagin. © 1978 Field Newspaper Syndicate. By permission of the News America Syndicate.

to throw out of office those who abuse power. Yet the framers were not willing to depend solely on such political controls, because they did not fully trust the people's judgment. "Free government is founded on jealousy, and not in confidence," said Thomas Jefferson. "In questions of power, then, let no more be heard of confidence in man, but bind him down from mischief by the chains of the Constitution."[13]

Even more important, the framers feared that a majority faction might use the new central government to deprive minorities of their rights. "A dependence on the people is, no doubt, the primary control on the government," Madison admitted in *The Federalist*, No. 51, "but experience has taught mankind the necessity of auxiliary precautions." What were these "auxiliary precautions" against popular tyranny?

Separation of Powers

The first step was the **separation of powers**—that is, the allocation of constitutional authority to each of the three branches of the national government. In *The Federalist*, No. 47, Madison wrote, "No political truth is certainly of greater intrinsic value, or is stamped with the authority of more enlightened patrons of liberty, than that . . . the accumulation of all powers, legislative, executive, and judiciary, in the same hands . . . may justly be pronounced the very definition of tyranny." (Chief among the "enlightened patrons of liberty" to whose authority Madison was appealing were John Locke and Montesquieu, whose works were subscribed to by most educated Americans.)

The intrinsic value of the principle of dispersion of power does not by itself account for its incorporation into our Constitution. Such dispersion of power had been the general practice in the colonies for more than one hundred years. Only during the Revolutionary period did some of the states and the Articles of Confederation concentrate authority in the hands of the legislature, and that unhappy experience confirmed the framers' belief in the merits of separation of powers. Many attributed the evils of state government and the lack of energy in the central government to the fact that there was no strong executive both to check legislative abuses and to give energy and direction to administration.

Still, separating power was not enough. There was always the danger—from the framers' point of view—that different officials with different powers might pool their authority and act together. Separation of powers by itself might not prevent governmental branches and officials from responding to the same pressures—from the demand of an overwhelming majority of the voters to suppress an offensive book, for example, or to impose confiscatory taxes on rich people. If separating power was not enough, what else could be done?

Checks and Balances: Ambition to Counteract Ambition

The framers' answer was a system of **checks and balances**. "The great security against a gradual concentration of the several powers in the same department," wrote Madison in *The Federalist*, No. 51, "consists in giving to those who administer each department the necessary constitutional means and personal motives to resist encroachments of the others. . . . Ambition must be made to counteract ambition."

Each branch, therefore, has a role in the actions of the others (see Figure 1-2). We have a "government of separated institutions sharing powers."[14] Congress enacts laws, yet the president can veto them. The Supreme Court can declare laws passed by Congress and signed by the president unconstitutional,

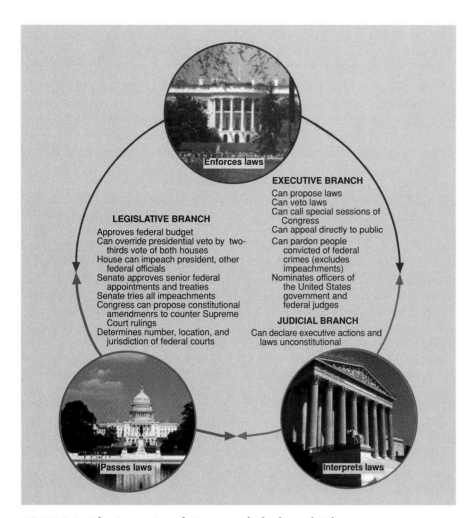

Enforces laws

EXECUTIVE BRANCH
Can propose laws
Can veto laws
Can call special sessions of
   Congress
Can appeal directly to public
Can pardon people
   convicted of federal
   crimes (excludes
   impeachments)
Nominates officers of
   the United States
   government and
   federal judges

LEGISLATIVE BRANCH
Approves federal budget
Can override presidential veto by two-
   thirds vote of both houses
House can impeach president, other
   federal officials
Senate approves senior federal
   appointments and treaties
Senate tries all impeachments
Congress can propose constitutional
   amendmenrs to counter Supreme
   Court rulings
Determines number, location, and
   jurisdiction of federal courts

JUDICIAL BRANCH
Can declare executive actions and
   laws unconstitutional

Passes laws

Interprets laws

FIGURE 1-2   The Separation of Powers and Checks and Balances

but the president appoints with the Senate's approval the justices and all the other federal judges. The president administers the laws, yet Congress provides the money. Moreover, the Senate and the House of Representatives have an absolute veto over each other in the enactment of a law, because bills must be approved by both houses.

Not only does each branch have some authority over the others, but each is *politically independent of the others.* The president is selected by electors (now popularly elected). Senators are now chosen by the voters in each state, and members of the House are chosen by voters in their districts. And although federal judges are appointed by the president with the consent of the Senate, once in office they hold terms virtually for life.

The framers also ensured that a majority of the voters could win control over only part of the government at one time. Although a popular majority might take control of the House of Representatives in an off-year (that is, a nonpresidential) election, the president, representing a previous popular majority, would still have two years to go. Further, senators are chosen for six years. Finally, independent national courts, which have developed their own powerful checks, were also provided. In fact, judges have become so important in our system of checks and balances that they deserve special attention.

JUDICIAL REVIEW AND THE "GUARDIANS OF THE CONSTITUTION"

Judges did not claim the power of **judicial review**—the power of a court to *refuse* to enforce a law or a government regulation that in the opinion of the judges conflicts with the Constitution—until some years after the Constitution was in operation. From the beginning, however, judges were expected to restrain legislative majorities. "The independence of judges," wrote Alexander Hamilton in *The Federalist*, No. 78 (which appears in the Appendix), "may be an essential safeguard against the effects of occasional ill humors in the society."

The Constitution says nothing about who should have the final word in disputes that might arise over its meaning. Whether the delegates to the Constitutional Convention of 1787 intended to give the courts the power of judicial review is a question long debated. The framers clearly intended for the Supreme Court to have the power to declare *state* legislation unconstitutional, but whether they intended to give it the same power over *national* legislation is not clear. The late Edward S. Corwin, the outstanding authority on the American Constitution, concluded that unquestionably "the framers anticipated some sort of judicial review. . . . But it is equally without question that the ideas generally current in 1787 were far from presaging the present vast role of the court."[15] Why, then, did the framers not specifically provide for judicial review? Probably because they believed the power could readily be inferred from certain general provisions.

The Federalists generally supported a strong role for federal courts and favored judicial review. Their opponents, the Jeffersonian Republicans (called Democrats after 1832), were less enthusiastic. In 1798 and 1799 Jefferson and Madison (who by this time had left the Federalist camp) were behind the Virginia and Kentucky Resolutions that came close to the position that state legislatures—and not the Supreme Court—had the ultimate power to interpret the Constitution. These resolutions seemed to question whether the Supreme Court even had the final authority to review state legislation, something about which there had been little doubt.

When the Jeffersonians defeated the Federalists in the elections of 1800, it was still undecided whether the Supreme Court would actually exercise the power of judicial review. The idea was in the air, logical reasons to support a doctrine of judicial review were at hand, and some precedents could even be cited; nevertheless judicial review was not an established power. Then, in 1803, came *Marbury v Madison*, one of the most famous Supreme Court decisions of all time.[16]

Marbury versus Madison (1803)

The elections of 1800 marked the rise to power of the Jeffersonian Republicans. President John Adams and fellow Federalists did not take their defeat easily. Before he left office, Adams and the lame-duck Federalist-controlled Congress created dozens of new federal judicial posts. (**Lame duck** is the term applied to elected officials who have recently been defeated for office but are serving out the rest of their term before being replaced by their successors.) Jefferson, now inaugurated as president, was angered by this "packing" of the judiciary. When he discovered that some of the commissions were still lying on a table in the Department of State, he instructed a clerk not to deliver them.[17]

Among the commissions not delivered was one for William Marbury. After waiting in vain, Marbury decided to seek action from the courts. Searching through the statute books, he came across Section 13 of the Judiciary Act of 1789, which authorized the Supreme Court "to issue writs of mandamus, in cases warranted by the principles and usages of law, to . . . persons holding office under the authority of the United States." A **writ of mandamus** is a court order directing an official, such as the secretary of state, to perform a ministerial duty, a duty about which the official has no discretion, such as delivering a commission.

On February 24, 1803, the Supreme Court delivered its decision. Section 13 of the Judiciary Act, announced Chief Justice John Marshall, conflicts with Article III of the Constitution. Article III gives the Supreme Court original jurisdiction only when an ambassador or other foreign minister is affected or when a state is a party. Even though this is a case of original jurisdiction, Marbury is neither a state nor a foreign minister. If we follow Section 13, wrote Marshall, we have jurisdiction; if we follow the Constitution, we have no jurisdiction.

Marshall then asked: Should the Supreme Court enforce an unconstitutional law? Of course not, he concluded. The Constitution is supreme and binding law, and the courts cannot enforce any action of Congress that conflicts with it.

The tough question remained unanswered. Congress and the president had also read the Constitution, and according to their interpretation, which was also reasonable, Section 13 was compatible with Article III. Where did the Supreme Court get the right to say they were wrong? Why should the Supreme Court's interpretation of the Constitution be preferred to that of Congress and the president?

Paralleling Hamilton's argument in *The Federalist*, No. 78, Marshall reasoned: The Constitution is law; judges—not legislators or executives—interpret law. Therefore, judges should interpret the Constitution. "If two laws conflict with each other, the courts must decide on the operation of each," he said. Case dismissed.

Jefferson fumed. For one thing, Marshall had said that a court with the proper jurisdiction could issue a writ of mandamus, even against the secretary of state, one of the president's closest advisers. Yet there was little Jefferson could do about what he thought was Marshall's arrogance. There was not even a court order he could refuse to obey. In a single stroke, Marshall had lectured the Jeffersonian Republicans for failing to perform their duties, and he had gone a long way toward acquiring the power for the Supreme Court to review acts of Congress. And he had done it in a manner that made it difficult for the Republicans to challenge.

Marbury v Madison is a masterpiece of judicial strategy. Marshall went out of his way to declare Section 13 unconstitutional. He could have interpreted the section to mean that the Supreme Court could issue writs of mandamus in those cases in which it did have jurisdiction. He could have interpreted Article III to mean that Congress could add to, though not subtract from, the original jurisdiction the Constitution gives to the Supreme Court. He could have dismissed the case for want of jurisdiction without discussing Marbury's right to his commission. But none of these would have suited his purpose. Marshall was fearful for the Supreme Court's future; unless the Court spoke out, he reasoned, it would become subordinate to the president and Congress.

Marshall's decision, important as it was, did not by itself establish the Supreme Court's power to review and declare acts of Congress unconstitutional. Not until the *Dred Scott* case in 1857 did the Supreme Court declare another act of Congress unconstitutional,[18] and not until after the Civil War did the modern use of judicial review become established.

Marbury v Madison might have been interpreted by subsequent generations in a very limited way, so that the Supreme Court had the right to determine the scope of its *own* powers under Article III, but that Congress and the president had the authority to interpret *their* own powers under Articles I and II, respectively. One scholar insists that is what Marshall intended and that the more expansive interpretation of *Marbury v Madison* is part of a myth designed to perpetuate judicial dominance.[19] However, Marshall's decision has not been

Chief Justice John Marshall (1755–1835), our most influential Supreme Court justice. Appointed in 1801, Marshall served until 1835. Earlier he had been a staunch defender of the U.S. Constitution at the Virginia ratifying convention, a member of Congress, and a secretary of state. He is one of those rare people who served in all three branches of government.

The Exercise of Checks and Balances, 1789–1996

Vetoes

The president has vetoed about 2,500 acts of Congress.

Congress has overridden presidential vetoes about 100 times.

Judicial Review

The Supreme Court has ruled 150 congressional acts or parts thereof unconstitutional. Its 1983 decision on legislative vetoes (*INS v Chahda*) affects another 200 provisions.

Impeachment

The House of Representatives has impeached 16 federal officials, including 13 federal judges; of these, the Senate has convicted 7.

Confirmation

The Senate has refused to confirm 9 cabinet nominations, and many other cabinet and subcabinet appointments were withdrawn because of likely Senate rejection.

interpreted in this way. On the contrary, building on Marshall's precedent over the decades, the Court has taken the commanding position as the authoritative interpreter of the Constitution.

Several important consequences follow from the acceptance of Marshall's argument that judges are the official interpreters of the Constitution. The most important is that even a law enacted by the Congress and approved by the president may, under many circumstances, be challenged by a single person. Simply by bringing a lawsuit, those who lack the clout to get a bill through Congress or influence a federal agency may often secure a judicial hearing. And organized interest groups often find that policy goals unattainable by legislation can be achieved by litigation. Litigation thus supplements, and at times takes precedence over, legislation as a way to make public policy.[20]

CHECKS AND BALANCES: DOES IT WORK?

What if a majority of the people gain control of all branches of government and force through radical measures? If a great majority of the voters want to take a certain step, the framers knew that nothing could stop them—nothing, that is, except despotic government, and that the framers did not want. They reasoned that all they could do—and this is quite a lot—is to prevent, temporarily, full control by the popular majority.

Distrustful of both the elites and the masses, the framers deliberately *built inefficiency into our political system.* They designed the decision-making process so that the national government can act decisively only when there is a general agreement—a consensus—among most of the interest groups and after all sides have had a chance to have their say.

Two centuries after the ratification of the Constitution, Americans continue to debate the desirability of these limits under the vastly different conditions of our times. Crucial questions remain: Are these checks necessary or sufficient to prevent abuses of political power? Is the greater danger that governments will not do the right things, or that they will do the wrong things? Do these limitations work to prevent abuses, or do they result in a "deadlock of democracy," making coherent governmental action for the general welfare difficult, if not impossible?

Modifications of Checks and Balances

Even though fragmentation of political power remains, several developments have modified the way the system of checks and balances works.

1. *The rise of national political parties.* Political parties can serve as unifying factors—at times drawing together the president, senators, representatives, and sometimes even judges behind common programs. Yet the parties, in turn, can be splintered and weakened by having to work through a system of fragmented governmental power, so they find it difficult to become strong or cohesive. Moreover, when one party controls the Congress and the other the White House, as has generally been the case since the end of World War II, parties may intensify checks and balances, rather than moderate them, to the point that definitive action on some major issues may be difficult, even impossible, as was the case when it took months to reconcile the differences between President Clinton and the Republicans in charge of Congress over the 1997 federal budget.[21]

Divided government may lead to such competition between the two branches that we find "each institution protecting and promoting itself through a broad interpretation of its constitutional and political status, even usurping the other's power when the opportunity presents itself."[22] Thus, we have had battles over presidential impoundments, budgeting deadlocks, and unseemly and angry confirmation hearings for the appointment of federal judges, especially for the justices of the Supreme Court. Divided government also makes it difficult for the voters to hold anybody or any party accountable. "Presidents blame Congress . . . while members of Congress attack the president. . . . Citizens genuinely cannot tell who is to blame."[23]

Yet when all the shouting dies down, concluded David R. Mayhew after a careful review of the evidence, "control by one party has not made all that much difference." There have been just as many congressional investigations and just as much important legislation passed when one party controls Congress and another controls the presidency as when the same party controls both branches.[24] Another major scholar, Charles Jones, after another review of recent legislative history, comes to the same conclusion: that divided government not only is not that important in determining how our government responds to crises, but it is precisely what the voters have wanted throughout much of our history.[25]

2. *Expansion of the electorate and changes in electoral methods.* The framers wanted the president to be chosen by wise, independent citizens free from popular passions and hero worship. Almost from the beginning, however, presidential electors have pledged prior to elections to cast their votes for their parties' presidential candidates. Further, senators, originally elected by state legislatures, are today chosen directly by the people.

The "people" entitled to vote has expanded from white property-owning males to all citizens over 18 years of age. During the past century, American states have expanded the role of the electorate within the states by adopting **direct primaries**, in which voters select party nominees, and by permitting voters in about half the states to vote directly on laws (**initiative** and **referendum**) and even to remove elected state and local officials from office (**recall**). At the national level the electorate has been given a major voice in choosing party nominees not merely for the House and the Senate but even for president.

3. *Establishment of agencies deliberately designed to exercise legislative, executive, and judicial functions.* When the national government began seriously to regulate the economy, it issued detailed rules on such complex matters as railroad safety, bank and stock exchange practices, employment conditions, union negotiations, and oil and gasoline emissions. It has been difficult to assign regulatory responsibilities without blending the powers to make and apply rules and to decide disputes. Beginning in 1887, Congress created independent regulatory commissions such as the Interstate Commerce Commission (which went out of business in 1995) and the Federal Communications Commission, and in this century it established independent executive agencies such as the Environmental Protection Agency.

4. *Changes in technology.* The system of checks and balances operates differently today from the way it did in 1787. Back then there were no televised congressional committee hearings, no electronic listening devices, no *Larry King Live* or *Rush Limbough* or other radio talk shows, no *New York Times*, *Wall Street Journal*, *USA Today*, CNN, C-Span, no nightly news programs with national audiences, no presidential press conferences, and no live coverage of wars and of Americans being held hostage in foreign lands. Nuclear bombs, television, computers, cellular telephones, fax machines, public opinion polls,

Thinking it Through

Although most of us do not think we should change our Constitution very often, in recent years some members of Congress have suggested amendments that would:

Require a two-thirds majority in both chambers of Congress to raise taxes

Give Congress and the states the power to make flag desecration illegal

Require a balanced federal budget

Permit state-sponsored prayers in public schools

Provide for equal rights under the law for women

Abolish the electoral college and provide for the direct election of the president

Permit citizens to participate directly in national law making by initiative petitions, to be approved or rejected by a direct vote of the people

Provide for a single, nonrenewable six-year term for the president

Confirm what Congress passed in 1996 and give the president an item veto over appropriations (a veto over part of a bill while accepting the rest)

Impose a twelve-year limit on the terms of members of the House of Representatives and the Senate.

the World Wide Web—these and other innovations create conditions very different from those of two centuries ago. In some ways these new technologies have added to the powers of presidents by, among other things, permitting them to appeal directly to millions of people and giving them immediate access to public opinion. These new technologies have also added leverage to organized interests by making it easy for them to target thousands of letters and calls at Congress, to organize letters to the editor, and to stage media events. New technologies have also given greater independence and influence to nongovernmental agencies such as the press. They have made it possible for rich people like Ross Perot and Steve Forbes and religious leaders like Pat Robertson, who have access to large resources, to bypass political parties and carry their message directly to the electorate.

5. *The emergence of the United States as a world power and the existence of recurrent crises.* Today, problems anywhere in the world—China, Bosnia, the Persian Gulf, Somalia—often become crises for the United States. The need to deal with perpetual emergencies has concentrated power in the hands of the chief executive and the presidential staff. The president's role as the most significant player on the world stage, and the immediate coverage of summit conferences with foreign leaders, enhance his status as domestic leader. Headline-producing ceremonial and substantive events give the president a visibility no congressional leader can achieve. The office of the president has sometimes served to impose some measure of national unity. Drawing on constitutional, political, and emergency powers, the president has sometimes been able to overcome restraints imposed by the Constitution on the exercise of cohesive governmental power—to the applause of some and the alarm of others.

The British and American Systems: A Study in Contrasts

Although many Americans question the usefulness and functions of some government institutions, we still tend to take the system of checks and balances for granted, considering it necessary for constitutional government. Like Madison, we view the amassing of power by any one branch of government as leading to tyranny, especially since such scandals as Watergate, in which President Richard Nixon tried to use federal agencies to suppress evidence of his administration's involvement in a break-in at Democratic party headquarters, and the Iran-Contra affair, in which the Reagan administration worked covertly to sell arms to Iran in order to get around congressional limitations on giving aid to the Nicaraguan government.

Yet it is quite possible for a government to be constitutional without these checks and balances. The British system is a good example (see Figure 1-3). Under the British system, voters elect members of Parliament from districts throughout the nation, much as we elect members of the House of Representatives. Members of the House of Commons have almost complete constitutional power. Leaders of the majority party serve as executive ministers, who collectively form the cabinet, with the prime minister as its head. The prime minister, like the other cabinet members, represents a constituency (a district) and is in effect chosen by the majority party. When the executive officers lose the support of the majority in the Commons on a major issue, they must resign or call for new elections. Formerly, the House of Lords could check the Commons, but it is now almost powerless. There is no high court with the power to declare acts of Parliament unconstitutional. The prime minister cannot veto them, although he or she may ask the Crown to dissolve Parliament and call new elections for members of the House of Commons.

FIGURE 1-3 A Comparison of the British and American Systems

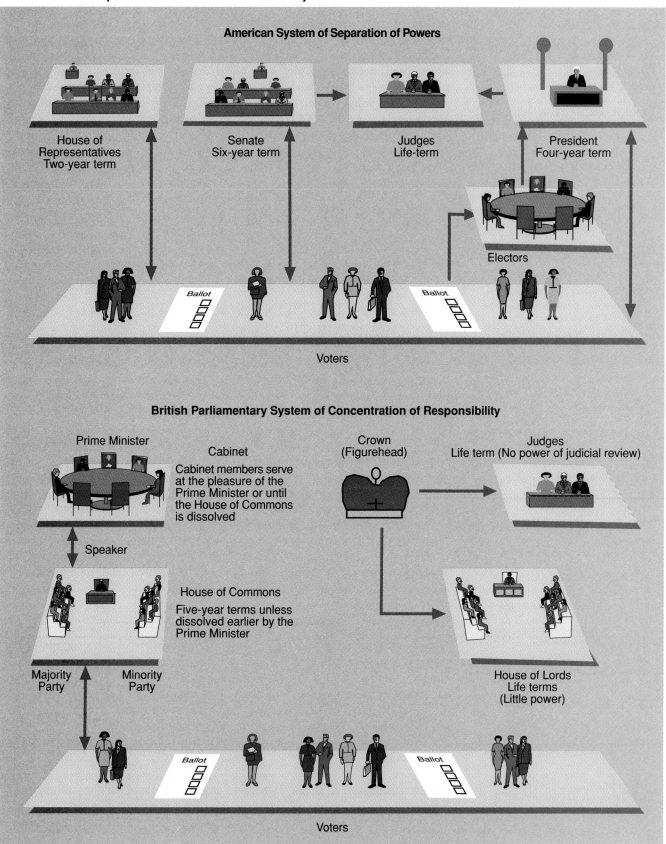

American System of Separation of Powers

House of Representatives
Two-year term

Senate
Six-year term

Judges
Life-term

President
Four-year term

Electors

Ballot

Ballot

Voters

British Parliamentary System of Concentration of Responsibility

Prime Minister

Cabinet
Cabinet members serve at the pleasure of the Prime Minister or until the House of Commons is dissolved

Crown
(Figurehead)

Judges
Life term (No power of judicial review)

Speaker

House of Commons
Five-year terms unless dissolved earlier by the Prime Minister

Majority Party   Minority Party

House of Lords
Life terms
(Little power)

Ballot

Ballot

Voters

How the Amending Power Has Been Used

To Add or Subtract National Government Power

The Eleventh took some jurisdiction away from the national courts.

The Thirteenth abolished slavery and authorized Congress to legislate against it.

The Sixteenth enabled Congress to levy an income tax.

The Eighteenth authorized Congress to prohibit the manufacture, sale, or transportation of liquor.

The Twenty-first repealed the Eighteenth and gave states the authority to regulate liquor sales.

The Twenty-seventh limited the power of Congress to set members' salaries.

To Limit State Government Power

The Thirteenth abolished slavery.

The Fourteenth granted national citizenship and prohibited states from abridging privileges of national citizenship; from denying persons life, liberty, and property without due process; and from denying persons equal protection of the laws. This amendment has come to be interpreted as imposing restraints on state powers in every area of public life.

To Expand the Electorate and Its Power

The Fifteenth extended the suffrage to all male African Americans.

The Seventeenth took the right to elect their United States senators from state legislatures and gave it to the voters in each state.

The Nineteenth extended suffrage to women.

The Twenty-third gave voters of the District of Columbia the right to vote for president and vice-president.

The Twenty-fourth prohibited any state from taxing the right to vote (the poll tax).

The Twenty-sixth extended the suffrage to otherwise qualified persons 18 years of age or older.

The British system is based on *majority* (51 percent) or *plurality rule* (largest number); that is, a plurality of the voters elects a parliamentary majority. Like us, the British elect legislators from districts, and the party with the most votes in that district wins the seat, so that even with three or more parties, a plurality of the popular vote usually results in a majority of the parliamentary seats. So long as the parliamentary majority stays together, it can enact into law the majority party's program. British parties are cohesive and disciplined; party members vote together and support their parliamentary leaders. In Britain the party that wins an election has a very good chance of seeing its *platform*, or policy goals, enacted. Our system usually depends on the agreement of many elements of society. The party that wins a presidential or congressional election or even one that controls both these branches will still have a tough time carrying out its platform promises. The British system *concentrates* control and responsibility in the legislature; ours *diffuses* control and responsibility among several organs of government.

We have a written document called the Constitution; Britain has no such single document. Yet both systems are constitutional in the sense that the rulers are subject to regular restraints. The limits our written Constitution and the conventions the unwritten British constitution impose rest on underlying values and attitudes.

THE CONSTITUTION AS AN INSTRUMENT OF GOVERNMENT

As careful as the Constitution's framers were to limit the powers they gave the national government, the main reason they had assembled in Philadelphia was *to create a stronger national government*. Having learned that a weak central government, incapable of governing, is a danger to liberty, they wished to establish a national government within the framework of a federal system with enough authority to meet the needs of all times. They made general grants of power, leaving it to succeeding generations to fill in the details and organize the structure of government in accordance with experience.

Hence our formal, written Constitution is only the skeleton of our system. It is filled out by numerous rules that must be considered part of our constitutional system in its larger sense. In fact, it is primarily through changes in our informal, *unwritten* Constitution that our system is kept up to date. These changes are to be found in certain basic statutes and historical practices of Congress, presidential practices, customs and usages of the nation, and decisions of the Supreme Court.

Congressional Elaboration

Because the framers gave Congress authority over many of the structural details of the national government, it is not necessary to amend the Constitution every time a change is needed. Rather, Congress can act from year to year. Examples of congressional elaboration appear in such legislation as the Judiciary Act of 1789, which laid the foundations of our national judicial system; in the laws establishing the organization and functions of all federal executive officials subordinate to the president; and in the rules of procedure, internal organization, and practices of Congress.

IMPEACHMENT AND REMOVAL POWER A dramatic example of congressional elaboration of our constitutional system is the use of the impeachment and removal power. An **impeachment** is a formal accusation against a public official and the first step in removal from office. Constitutional language is sparse. Take a look at your copy of the Constitution, and note that according to Article I—the Legislative Article—it is up to Congress to give meaning to that language. Article I gives the House of Representatives the sole power of impeachment, and the Senate the sole power to try all impeachments. When sitting for that purpose, senators "shall be on Oath or Affirmation." In the event the president is being tried, the chief justice of the United States presides. Article I also requires conviction on impeachment charges to have the agreement of two-thirds of the senators present. Judgments shall extend no further than removal from office and disqualification from holding any office under the United States, but a person convicted shall also be liable to indictment, trial, judgment, and punishment according to the law. In Article II—the Executive Article—the Constitution provides that the "President, Vice President and all civil Officers of the United States, shall be removed from Office on Impeachment for, and Conviction of, Treason, Bribery, or other High Crimes and Misdemeanors." This article also exempts cases of impeachment from the president's pardoning power. Article III—the Judicial Article—exempts cases of impeachment from the jury trial requirement. That is all the relevant constitutional language. We must look to history to answer most questions about the proper exercise of these powers.[26]

Fortunately, our experiences have triggered few acute constitutional disputes about the interpretation of impeachment procedures, and there is little history to go on. The House of Representatives has investigated 66 individuals for possible impeachment and has impeached 16 (one resigned after the impeachment resolutions were adopted, so the House voted on articles of impeachment for only 15); the Senate has convicted 7 (all federal judges). The recent spate of impeachment proceedings—three since 1986—caused the Senate to decide, not without controversy, that the responsibility to hear evidence can be delegated to a committee. The Supreme Court has ruled that the Senate may so delegate and, in fact, that the House and Senate possess the constitutional authority to decide what the impeachment process shall be, subject to little, if any, judicial review.[27]

Only one president—Andrew Johnson—was impeached, in 1868, but the Senate failed by one vote to muster the two-thirds necessary to support the charges. Another president—Richard Nixon—resigned on August 9, 1974, to avoid impeachment after the House Judiciary Committee recommended three articles of impeachment against him. The House did not press the matter further, but the articles of impeachment were submitted by the committee and were "accepted" by the House.

Even though congressional precedents have rejected the broadest view—that the Constitution authorizes removal of officers by impeachment because of *political* objections to them or because of their unpopularity (a view that might have moved us more in the direction of a parliamentary type of government)—Congress has also rejected the *narrowest* construction—that impeachable offenses are *only* those that involve violations of the criminal laws. Rather, the firmly established position is that impeachment and conviction are only justified if there have been serious violations of constitutional responsibilities and a clear dereliction of duty.[28]

Presidential Practices

Although the president's formal constitutional powers have not changed, the office is dramatically more important and more central today than it was in 1789. Vigorous presidents—George Washington, Thomas Jefferson, Andrew Jackson, Abraham Lincoln, Theodore Roosevelt, Woodrow Wilson, Franklin Roosevelt, Harry Truman, Lyndon Johnson, Bill Clinton—have boldly exercised their political and constitutional powers, especially during times of national

How the Amending Power Has Been Used (continued)

To Reduce the Electorate's Power

The Twenty-second took from the electorate the right to elect any person to the office of president for more than two full terms.

To Make Structural Changes in Government

The Twelfth corrected deficiencies in the operation of the electoral college that were revealed by the development of a two-party national system.

The Twentieth altered the calendar for congressional sessions and shortened the time between the election of presidents and their assumption of office.

The Twenty-fifth provided procedures for filling vacancies in the vice-presidency and for determining whether presidents are unable to perform their duties.

crises. Such presidential practices have become important precedents, building the power and influence of the office. Even John Tyler made his contribution to constitutional elaboration. Upon becoming president through vice-presidential succession, Tyler established the precedent that the vice-president becomes the president, not merely the acting president.

Presidential practices include **executive privilege** (the right of the president to withhold information), **impoundment** of funds previously appropriated by Congress, the right to send armed forces into hostilities, and, most important, the right to propose legislation and work actively to secure its passage by Congress.

Foreign and economic crises as well as nuclear-age realities add force to the president's role as the nation's "final arbiter." Political scientist Richard Neustadt says, "When it comes to action risking nuclear war, technology has modified the Constitution: the President, perforce, becomes the only such man in the system capable of exercising judgment under the extraordinary limits now imposed by secrecy, complexity, and time."[29] Following the Great Depression of the 1930s and World War II, the president become the chief legislator as well as the nation's chief executive. By the end of the twentieth century, however, there was a reemergence of the Congress as an instigator of legislation, and, as one scholar put it: it became clear once again that "Ours is not a presidential system . . . . It has been from the start a separated system with three coequal branches sharing, and sometimes competing for power.[30]

Custom and Usage

Custom and usage round out our governmental system. Although not specifically mentioned in the Constitution, certain practices are now fundamental. It has been primarily the development of structures outside the formal Constitution—such as national political parties or the extension of the suffrage within the states—that democratized our Constitution. Through these developments, the president has become responsive to the people and has a political base different from that of Congress, so the constitutional relationship among the branches today is considerably different from that envisaged by the framers.

What is the difference between a custom and a usage? Not much. One could distinguish between them by reserving **custom** to refer to practices of non-

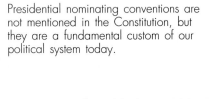

Presidential nominating conventions are not mentioned in the Constitution, but they are a fundamental custom of our political system today.

governmental institutions such as political parties or of the electorate—not nominating or voting for persons who are not residents of the district they wish to represent—and reserving **usage** to refer to long-standing practices of Congress, the president, and the courts. The two terms are used together to refer both to customs of nongovernmental agencies and usages of governmental institutions, a practice we adopt here.

Judicial Interpretation

Judicial interpretation of the Constitution, especially by the Supreme Court, has played an important part in keeping the constitutional system up to date. As social and economic conditions have changed and new national demands have developed, the Supreme Court has changed its interpretation of the Constitution accordingly. In the words of Woodrow Wilson, "The Supreme Court is a constitutional convention in continuous session." Because the Constitution adapts to changing times, it does not require frequent formal amendment.

The advantages of this flexibility may be appreciated by comparing the national Constitution with the rigid and often overly specific state constitutions. Many state constitutions, more like legal codes than basic charters, are so detailed that they excessively tie the hands of the public officials. Such constitutions must be amended frequently or replaced every generation or so.

A Rigid or a Flexible Constitution?

The idea of a constantly changing system disturbs many people. How, they contend, can you have a constitutional government when the Constitution is constantly being twisted by interpretation and changed by informal methods? This view fails to distinguish between two aspects of the Constitution. As an expression of *basic and timeless personal liberties*, the Constitution does not and should not change. For example, a government cannot destroy free speech and still remain a constitutional government. In this sense the Constitution is unchanging. But when we consider the Constitution as an *instrument of government* and a positive grant of power, we realize that if it does not grow with the nation it serves, it will soon be pushed aside. The framers could not have conceived of the problems faced by a government of a large, powerful, and wealthy nation of about 275 million people in the last decade of the twentieth century. Although the general purposes of government remain the same—to establish liberty, promote justice, ensure domestic tranquillity, and provide for the common defense—the powers of government adequate to accomplish these purposes in 1787 are simply insufficient two hundred years later.

"We the people"—the people of today and tomorrow, not just the people of 1787—ordain and establish the Constitution. "The Constitution," wrote Jefferson, "belongs to the living and not to the dead." So firmly did he believe this that he suggested there might be a new constitution for every generation. New constitutions have not been necessary, however, because in a less formal way, each generation has taken part in the process of developing and changing the original Constitution. Because of its remarkable adaptability, the Constitution has survived democratic and industrial revolutions, the turmoil of civil war, the tensions of major depressions, and the dislocations of world wars.[31]

CHANGING THE LETTER OF THE CONSTITUTION

The framers knew that future experiences would call for changes in the text of the Constitution and that some means for formal amendment were necessary. In Article V they gave responsibility for amending the Constitution to Congress and

The Twenty-seventh Amendment: Is Two Hundred and Three Years a Reasonable Time?

In March 1982, Gregory Watson, a student at the University of Texas writing a paper on the Equal Rights Amendment, came across an amendment proposed in 1789 as part of the Bill of Rights that would prohibit a pay raise for members of Congress until the intervention of an election for members of the House. He found that only 6 of the original 13 states had ratified it, and that during the intervening years only 3 more states had done so.

Watson decided to start a ratification movement. He got some publicity for his efforts and, with the help of Texas Republican State Representative Don Mielke, persuaded 6 more state legislatures to ratify this long-forgotten proposed amendment. (By the way, Watson only got a C on his paper, although he "is credited with influencing 26 state legislatures to ratify the congressional amendment."*)

After Congress tried unsuccessfully in 1989 to avoid public heat by delegating the decision to increase congressional salaries to an independent commission, anti-Congress sentiment began to grow, and the ratification movement began to pick up steam. On May 7, 1992, the Michigan legislature became the thirty-eighth state to ratify it, and on May 18, 1992, the United States archivist certified that the amendment was part of the Constitution and had it printed in the *Federal Register*.

The first reaction of some congressional leaders was to question this action because the Supreme Court had made it clear that amendments must be ratified within a "reasonable time." However, when members of Congress realized that the issue could be used against them in the next election, they declared the Twenty-seventh Amendment to be "valid as part of the Constitution of the United States." The vote was not even close: 99 to 0 in the Senate, 414 to 3 in the House. Only the representative from Iowa spoke against ratification. He told his colleagues, "The principle of contemporary consensus . . . is just too important to ever waive just because it appears popular at the moment."

*Ruth Ann Strickland, "The Twenty-seventh Amendment and Constitutional Change by Stealth," *P.S. Political Science and Politics* (December 1993), p. 720.

to the states; the president has no formal authority over constitutional amendments. Presidential veto power does not extend to them, although presidential political influence is often crucial in getting amendments proposed by Congress and ratified by the states. Nor may governors veto ratification of amendments.[32]

Proposing Amendments

The first method for proposing amendments—and the only one used so far—is by a two-thirds vote of both houses of Congress. Dozens of resolutions proposing amendments are introduced in every session. Thousands have been introduced since 1789, most of them during the last two decades. Few make any headway. Throughout our history Congress has proposed only 33 amendments (21 plus the Bill of Rights, including the Twenty-seventh, which was originally part of the Bill of Rights but took more than two hundred years for ratification).

In recent years there has been a flurry of congressional consideration of constitutional amendments. None has been formally proposed by both chambers; many are currently under consideration. One being given serious consideration is the so-called Balanced Budget Amendment. It has the support of a majority in both the House and the Senate, but so far not the required two-thirds necessary for passage. It has several times secured the two-thirds vote it needs in the House but failed to do so in the Senate. In 1986, 1994, and again in 1995, it fell short of the 67 needed. The 1995 version called for a balanced budget starting in 2002 unless three-fifths of both houses voted to suspend the requirement. The 1995 version also contained a clause specifying "the judicial power of the United States shall not extend to any case or controversy arising under this article," unless Congress were specifically to authorize such judicial intervention. It seems likely that the issue again will be before the Congress.

Why has proposing amendments to the Constitution become such a popular pastime? In part because interest groups unhappy with Supreme Court decisions seek to overturn them. In part because groups frustrated by their inability to get things done in Congress—balancing the budget, for example—hope to bypass the Congress. And in part because scholars or interest-group representatives (not necessarily mutually exclusive categories) seek to change the procedures and process of government to make the system more responsive.[33]

The second method for proposing amendments—by a convention called by Congress at the request of the legislatures in two-thirds of the states—has never been used. This method presents some difficult questions.[34] First, can state legislatures apply for a convention to propose specific amendments on one topic, or must they request a convention with full powers to revise the entire Constitution?[35] How long do state petitions remain alive? How should delegates be chosen? How should a convention be run? Congress has considered bills to answer some of these questions but has not passed any, in part because most members do not wish to encourage a constitutional convention for fear that once in session it might propose amendments on any and all topics. Scholars are divided, however, on whether Congress has the authority to so limit what a constitutional convention might propose.[36]

Despite several organized efforts to force Congress to call a constitutional convention (or to propose the amendment itself), Congress has never done so.[37] We came close to a convention in 1967, when the thirty-third state legislature—only one short of the required number—petitioned Congress to call a convention to propose an amendment to set aside a Supreme Court ruling that both chambers of a state legislature must be apportioned on the basis of population. A thirty-fourth state never petitioned for a convention, and as state legislatures completed the process of reapportionment, pressures for an amendment abated.

Ratifying Amendments

After an amendment has been proposed, it must be ratified by the states. Again, two methods are provided: approval by the legislatures in three-fourths of the states, or approval by specially called ratifying conventions in three-fourths of the states. Congress determines which method is used. All amendments except one—the Twenty-first (to repeal the Eighteenth, the Prohibition Amendment)—have been submitted to the state legislatures for ratification.

Seven state constitutions specify that their state legislatures must ratify a proposed amendment to the U.S. Constitution by majorities of three-fifths or two-thirds of each chamber. Although a state legislature may change its mind and ratify an amendment after it has voted against ratification, the weight of opinion is that once a state has ratified an amendment, it cannot "unratify" it.[38]

Submitting amendments to legislatures rather than ratifying conventions allows changes to be made in the Constitution without any direct expressions by the voters. Legislators may have been elected before the proposed amendments were submitted to the states. In any event, state legislators are chosen because of their views on schools, taxation, or other matters, or because of their personal popularity. They are almost never elected because of their stand on proposed constitutional amendments, although the candidates' position on the Equal Rights Amendment (ERA) did surface as a key issue in several state legislative elections.

Procedures can make a difference. The decision to submit the Twenty-first Amendment repealing Prohibition to ratifying conventions came about because the "wets" rightly believed that repeal had a better chance of success with conventions than with the rural-dominated state legislatures. For similar tactical reasons, southern Democrats joined with eastern Republican conservatives in an unsuccessful effort to submit the Nineteenth Amendment to give women the vote, also called the Susan B. Anthony Amendment, to ratifying conventions. Let the voters decide—the male voters, that is—they argued.[39] For the Twenty-first Amendment, Congress left it up to each state legislature to determine how the ratifying conventions would be organized and delegates elected. State delegates ran at large on tickets that pledged they would vote for or against ratification. As a result, when state conventions were called to order, they quickly ratified the decision the voters had already made. In effect, ratification had been submitted to the voters.

The Supreme Court has said ratification must take place within a "reasonable time." It suggested that it is up to Congress to police this requirement. Congress, at the time it proclaims the amendment to be part of the Constitution, must decide whether an amendment has been ratified within a reasonable time so that it is "sufficiently contemporaneous to reflect the will of the people."[40] However, since Congress has approved ratification of the Twenty-seventh Amendment, which had been before the nation for almost 203 years, there seems to be no limit to what it will consider to be a reasonable time for ratification to take place. It is conceivable, but not likely, the Supreme Court could some day rule that the Twenty-seventh Amendment had not been properly ratified.[41]

The question of reasonableness of time for ratification is not likely to become an issue with respect to other amendments. At the time it "certified" the ratification of the Twenty-seventh Amendment, the Senate declared the other three outstanding amendments to be "dead." For future amendments, Congress will probably continue the current practice of stipulating that an amendment will not become part of the Constitution unless ratified by the necessary number of states within seven years from the date of its submission. In fact, ratification ordinarily takes place rather quickly.[42]

Thinking it Through

A constitutional convention to consider the Balanced Budget Amendment is necessary and desirable because:

1. The fiscal excesses of the federal government threaten irreparable damage to the nation.

2. We must correct this situation through constitutional reform with a tax limitation or balanced budget amendment. But Congress has refused to propose a constitutional amendment to control its fiscal practices.

3. The framers provided the people with a direct method of proposing amendments to the Constitution.

4. Thirty-two states have passed resolutions calling for a constitutional convention. Completion of this process is essential to the future of our nation.

No constitutional convention should be called because:

1. The Constitution does not define or limit the scope of such a convention.

2. Our only precedent, the 1787 Constitutional Convention, broke every legal restraint the Confederation Congress had designed to limit its power.

3. Assurances that limits can now be imposed are without substance; if a convention meets, it will do whatever the majority wants it to do. A number of secondary agendas have already been suggested.

4. Assurances that the threat of a convention, when backed by 33 states, will force Congress to pass an amendment limiting its spending are historically unsound and legally suspect.

SOURCE: Lewis K. Uhler, president of the National Tax-Limitation Committee, Roseville, Calif., and Linda Rogers-Kingsbury, president of Citizens to Protect the Constitution, Washington, D.C. Quoted in *Liberty* (March/April 1991), pp. 2, 3.

AMENDING THE CONSTITUTION

The framers set up two ways to propose amendments and two ways to ratify them, and they saw to it that amendments could not be adopted by simple majorities. Each amendment must be both proposed and ratified.

The Thirteenth, Fourteenth, and Fifteenth Amendments put an end to slave auctions like this and granted basic rights to all races.

The Nineteenth Amendment extended the right to vote to women.

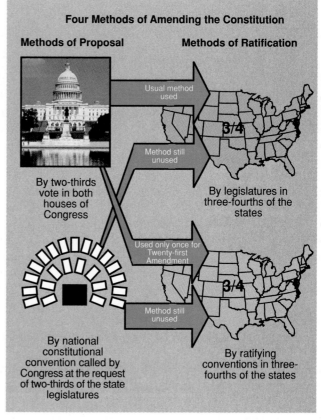

Four Methods of Amending the Constitution

Methods of Proposal　　　　**Methods of Ratification**

Usual method used

Method still unused

By two-thirds vote in both houses of Congress

By legislatures in three-fourths of the states

Used only once for Twenty-first Amendment

Method still unused

By national constitutional convention called by Congress at the request of two-thirds of the state legislatures

By ratifying conventions in three-fourths of the states

The 27 Constitutional Amendments and Their Times for Ratification

Amendment	Time to Ratify	Ratified	Amendment	Time to Ratify	Ratified
1-10. Bill of Rights	2 years, 2½ months	1791	19. Women's suffrage	1 year, 2½ months	1920
11. Lawsuits against states	3 years, 10 months	1795	20. Terms of office	11 months	1933
12. Presidential elections	8½ months	1804	21. Repeal of prohibition	9½ months	1933
13. Abolition of slavery	10½ months	1865	22. Limit on presidential terms	3 years, 11½ months	1951
14. Civil rights laws	2 years, 11½ months	1868	23. Washington, D.C., vote	9 months	1961
15. Suffrage for all races	1 year, 1 month	1870	24. Abolition of poll taxes	1 year, 5½ months	1964
16. Income tax	3 years, 7½ months	1913	25. Presidential succession	1 year, 6½ months	1967
17. Senatorial elections	1 year, ½ month	1913	26. 18-year-old suffrage	4 months	1971
18. Prohibition	1 year, 1½ months	1919	27. Congressional salaries	202 years, 7½ months	1992

SUMMARY

1. *Democracy* is an often misused term, and it is used by many people to mean many different things. Here we use it to refer to a system of interacting values, interrelated political processes, and interdependent political structures. The vital principle of democracy is that a *just* government must derive its powers from the *consent* of the people, and that this consent must be regularly renewed at free and fair elections.

2. Stable constitutional democracy is encouraged by various conditions, such as an educated citizenry, a healthy economy, and overlapping associations and groupings within a society in which major institutions interact to create a certain degree of consensus about the importance of democratic procedures. Civilian control over the military and a general acceptance of the ideals of democracy are also essential.

3. *Constitutionalism* is a general label we apply to those arrangements such as checks and balances, federalism, separation of powers, due process, and the Bill of Rights that force our leaders and representatives to listen, think, deliberate, bargain, and explain before they act and make laws. And a constitutional government enforces recognized and regularly applied limits on the powers of those who govern.

4. A *constitutional democracy* is a governing process in which the voice of the people is regularly heard through free and fair elections. It is also a government in which recognized limits are regularly applied to those who govern. Constitutional democracy remains in many ways a goal rather than an achievement, and, as we enter the twenty-first century, a number of questions remain about its vitality and its capacity to mature.

5. Our Constitution both grants and limits powers. The framers established a government to be operated by ordinary people. They did not anticipate that Americans would be so virtuous and civic minded that they could be trusted to operate a government without checks and balances. The framers were suspicious of people, especially of those having political power, so they separated and distributed the powers of the newly created national government in a variety of ways.

6. The framers were also concerned that the national government be strong enough to solve national problems. They wanted it to be responsive to the wishes of the people and to carry out those wishes; that is, the matured and refined wishes of the people. Thus they gave the national government substantial grants of power. But these grants were made with such broad strokes that it has been possible for the national government and the constitutional system to remain flexible and adapt to changing conditions.

7. Although the American governmental system has its roots in British traditions, our separation of powers and checks and balances systems differ sharply from the British system of concentrated responsibility. It is also different because our courts have the power of judicial review.

8. The system of checks and balances has been modified over time. The Constitution has been adapted to new conditions through congressional elaboration, modern presidential practices, custom and usage, and judicial interpretation.

9. Although adaptable, the Constitution itself needs to be altered from time to time, and the document provides a procedure for its own amendment. An amendment must be both proposed and ratified: proposed by either a two-thirds vote in each chamber of Congress or by a national convention called by Congress on petition of the legislatures in two-thirds of the states; ratified either by the legislatures in three-fourths of the states or by specially called ratifying conventions in three-fourths of the states. The Constitution has been formally amended 27 times. The usual method has been proposal by two-thirds vote in both houses of Congress and ratification by the legislatures in three-fourths of the states.

FURTHER READING

BRUCE A. ACKERMAN, *We the People* (Harvard University Press, Belknap Press, 1991).

THORTON ANDERSON, *Creating the Constitution: The Convention of 1787 and the First Congress* (Pennsylvania State University Press, 1994).

BERNARD BAILYN, ED., *The Debate on the Constitution: Federalist and Antifederalist Speeches, Articles, and Letters During the Struggle over Ratification*, 2 vols. (Library of America, 1993).

RICHARD B. BERNSTEIN, *Amending America: If We Love the Constitution So Much Why Do We Keep Trying to Change It?* (Time, 1993).

JAMES BRYCE, *The American Commonwealth*, vols. 1 and 2 (Macmillan, 1889).

JAMES MACGREGOR BURNS, *The Vineyard of Liberty* (Knopf, 1982).

JAMES MACGREGOR BURNS AND STEWART BURNS, *The People's Charter* (Knopf, 1991).

RUSSELL L. CAPLAN, *Constitutional Brinkmanship: Amending the Constitution by National Convention* (Oxford University Press, 1988).

ROBERT LOWRY CLINTON, *Marbury v. Madison and Judicial Review* (University Press of Kansas, 1989).

THOMAS E. CRONIN, *Direct Democracy: The Politics of the Initiative, Referendum, and Recall* (Harvard University Press, 1989).

ROBERT A. DAHL, *Democracy and Its Critics* (Yale University Press, 1989).

SCOTT DOUGLAS GERBER, *To Secure These Rights: The Declaration of Independence and Constitutional Interpretation* (New York University Press, 1995).

ALEXANDER HAMILTON, JAMES MADISON, AND JOHN JAY, *The Federalist Papers*, ed. Clinton Rossiter (New American Library, 1961). Also in several other editions.

CHARLES O. JONES, *Separate But Equal Branches: Congress and the Presidency* (Chatham House, 1995).

BARBARA B. KNIGHT, *Separation of Powers in the American Political System* (George Mason University Press, 1989).

SANFORD LEVINSON, ED., *Responding to Imperfection: The Theory and Practice of Constitutional Amendment* (Princeton University Press, 1995).

LIBRARY OF CONGRESS, CONGRESSIONAL RESEARCH SERVICE, *The Constitution of the United States of America: Analysis and Interpretation*, Senate Document 100-9 (U.S. Government Printing Office, 1991).

DONALD G. MATHEWS AND JANE SHERRON DE HART, *Sex, Gender, and the Politics of ERA: North Carolina and the Nation* (Oxford University Press, 1990).

DREW R. MCCOY, *The Last of the Fathers: James Madison and the Republican Legacy* (Columbia University Press, 1989).

FORREST MCDONALD, *Novus Ordo Seclorum: The Intellectual Origins of the Constitution* (University Press of Kansas, 1985).

RICHARD B. MORRIS, *Witnesses at the Creation: Hamilton, Madison and Jay, and the Constitution* (Holt, Rinehart & Winston, 1985).

J. W. PELTASON, *Understanding the Constitution*, 13th ed. (Harcourt Brace, 1994).

BARBARA A. PERRY, *Unfounded Fears: Myths and Realities of a Constitutional Convention* (Greenwood Press, 1989).

ALEXIS DE TOCQUEVILLE, *Democracy in America*, 2 vols., 1835 (Vintage, 1955).

JOHN R. VILE, *Rewriting the United States Constitution: An Examination of Proposals from Reconstruction to the Present* (Praeger, 1991).

JOHN R. VILE, *The Constitutional Amending Process in American Political Thought* (Praeger, 1992).

On Reading The Constitution

More than two hundred years after its ratification, our Constitution remains the operating charter of our republic. It is neither self-explanatory nor a comprehensive description of our constitutional rules. Still, it remains the starting point. Yet many Americans who swear by the Constitution have never read it seriously. Copies can be found in the back of most American government and American history textbooks.

Justice Hugo Black, who served on the Supreme Court for 34 years, kept a copy of the Constitution with him at all times. He read it often. Reading the Constitution as amended would be a good way for you to begin (and then reread again to end) your study of the government of the United States. Thus, we have included a copy of it at this point in the book. Please read it carefully.

The Constitution
of the
United States

The Preamble

We the People of the United States, in Order to form a more perfect Union, establish Justice, insure domestic Tranquility, provide for the common defense, promote the general Welfare, and secure the Blessings of Liberty to ourselves and our Posterity, do ordain and establish this Constitution for the United States of America.

Article I—The Legislative Article

Legislative Power

Section 1 All legislative Powers herein granted shall be vested in a Congress of the United States, which shall consist of a Senate and House of Representatives.

House of Representatives: Composition; Qualifications; Apportionment; Impeachment Power

Section 2 The House of Representatives shall be composed of Members chosen every second Year by the People of the several States, and the Electors in each State shall have the Qualifications requisite for Electors of the most numerous Branch of the State Legislature.

No Person shall be a Representative who shall not have attained to the Age of twenty five Years, and been seven Years a Citizen of the United States, and who shall not, when elected, be an Inhabitant of that State in which he shall be chosen.

Representatives and direct Taxes[1] shall be apportioned among the several States which may be included within this Union, according to their respective Numbers, *which shall be determined by adding to the whole Number of free Persons, including those bound to Service for a Term of Years, and excluding Indians not taxed, three fifths of all other Persons.*[2] The actual Enumeration shall be made within three Years after the first Meeting of the Congress of the United States, and within every subsequent Term of ten Years, in such Manner as they shall by Law direct. The Number of Representatives shall not exceed one for every thirty Thousand, but each State shall have at least one Representative; and until each enumeration shall be made, the State of New Hampshire shall be entitled to chuse three, Massachusetts eight, Rhode-Island and Providence Plantations one, Connecticut five, New-York six, New Jersey four, Pennsylvania eight, Delaware one, Maryland six, Virginia ten, North Carolina five, South Carolina five, and Georgia three.

When vacancies happen in the Representation from any State, the Executive Authority thereof shall issue Writs of Election to fill such Vacancies.

The House of Representatives shall chuse their Speaker and other Officers; and shall have the sole Power of Impeachment.

Senate Composition: Qualifications, Impeachment Trials

Section 3 The Senate of the United States shall be composed of two Senators from each State, *chosen by the Legislature thereof,*[3] for six Years; and each Senator shall have one Vote.

Immediately after they shall be assembled in Consequence of the first Election, they shall be divided as equally as may be into three Classes. The Seats of the Senators of the first Class shall be vacated at the Expiration of the second Year, of the second Class at the Expiration of the fourth Year, and of the third Class at the Expiration of the sixth Year, so that one third may be chosen every second Year; *and if Vacancies happen by Resignation, or otherwise, during the Recess of the Legislature of any State, the Executive thereof may make temporary Appointments until the next Meeting of the Legislature, which shall then fill such Vacancies.*[4]

No person shall be a Senator who shall not have attained to the Age of thirty Years, and been nine Years a Citizen of the United States, and who shall not, when elected, be an inhabitant of that State for which he shall be chosen.

The Vice President of the United States shall be President of the Senate, but shall have no Vote, unless they be equally divided.

The Senate shall chuse their other Officers, and also a President pro tempore, in the Absence of the Vice President, or when he shall exercise the Office of President of the United States.

The Senate shall have the sole Power to try all Impeachments. When sitting for that Purpose, they shall be on Oath or Affirmation. When the President of the United States is tried, the Chief Justice shall preside: And no Person shall be convicted without the Concurrence of two thirds of the Members present.

Judgment in Cases of Impeachment shall not extend further than to removal from Office, and disqualification to hold and enjoy any Office of honor, Trust or Profit under the United States; but the Party convicted shall nevertheless be liable and subject to Indictment, Trial, Judgment and Punishment, according to law.

Congressional Elections: Times, Places, Manner

Section 4 The Times, Places and Manner of holding Elections for Senators and Representatives, shall be prescribed in each State by the Legislature thereof; but the Congress may at any time by Law make or alter such Regulations, except as to the Places of chusing Senators.

The Congress shall assemble at least once in every Year, *and such Meeting shall be on the first Monday in December, unless they shall by Law appoint a different Day.*[5]

---

[1]Modified by the 16th Amendment
[2]Replaced by Section 2, 14th Amendment

[3]Repealed by the 17th Amendment
[4]Modified by the 17th Amendment
[5]Changed by the 20th Amendment

Powers and Duties of the Houses

Section 5   Each House shall be the Judge of the Elections, Returns and Qualifications of its own Members, and a Majority of each shall constitute a Quorum to do Business; but a smaller Number may adjourn from day to day, and may be authorized to compel the Attendance of absent Members, in such Manner, and under the Penalties as each House may provide.

Each House may determine the Rules of its Proceedings, punish its Members for disorderly Behaviour, and, with the Concurrence of two thirds, expel a Member.

Each House shall keep a Journal of its Proceedings, and from time to time publish the same, excepting such Parts as may in their Judgment require Secrecy; and the Yeas and Nays of the Members of either House on any question shall, at the Desire of one fifth of those Present, be entered on the Journal.

Neither House, during the Session of Congress, shall, without the Consent of the other, adjourn for more than three days, nor to any other place than that in which the two Houses shall be sitting.

Rights of Members

Section 6   The Senators and Representatives shall receive a Compensation for their Services, to be ascertained by Law, and paid out of the Treasury of the United States. They shall in all Cases, except Treason, Felony and Breach of the Peace, be privileged from Arrest during their Attendance at the Session of their respective Houses, and in going to and returning from the same; and for any Speech or Debate in either House, they shall not be questioned in any other Place.

No Senator or Representative, shall, during the time for which he was elected, be appointed to any civil Office under the Authority of the United States, which shall have been created, or the Emoluments whereof shall have been encreased during such time; and no Person holding any Office under the United States, shall be a Member of either House during his Continuance in Office.

Legislative Powers: Bills and Resolutions

Section 7   All Bills for raising Revenue shall originate in the House of Representatives; but the Senate may propose or concur with Amendments as on other Bills.

Every Bill which shall have passed the House of Representatives and the Senate, shall, before it becomes a Law, be presented to the President of the United States; if he approve he shall sign it, but if not he shall return it, with his Objections to that House in which it shall have originated, who shall enter the Objections at large on their Journal, and proceed to reconsider it. If after such Reconsideration two thirds of that House shall agree to pass the Bill, it shall be sent, together with the Objections, to the other House, by which it shall likewise be reconsidered, and if approved by two thirds of that House, it shall become a Law. But in all such Cases the Votes of both Houses shall be determined by yeas and Nays, and the Names of the Persons voting for and against the Bill shall be entered on the Journal of each House respectively. If any Bill shall not be returned by the President within ten Days (Sundays excepted) after it shall have been presented to him, the Same shall be a Law, in like Manner as if he had signed it, unless the Congress by their Adjournment prevent its Return, in which Case it shall not be a Law.

Every Order, Resolution, or Vote to which the Concurrence of the Senate and House of Representatives may be necessary (except on a question of Adjournment) shall be presented to the President of the United States; and before the Same shall take Effect, shall be approved by him, or being disapproved by him, shall be repassed by two thirds of the Senate and House of Representatives, according to the Rules and Limitations prescribed in the Case of a Bill.

Powers of Congress

Section 8   The Congress shall have Power To lay and collect Taxes, Duties, Imposts and Excises, to pay the Debts and provide for the common Defence and general Welfare of the United States; but all Duties, Imposts and Excises shall be uniform throughout the United States.

To borrow Money on the Credit of the United States;

To regulate Commerce with foreign Nations, and among the several States, and with the Indian Tribes;

To establish an uniform Rule of Naturalization, and uniform Laws on the subject of Bankruptcies throughout the United States;

To coin Money, regulate the Value thereof, and of foreign Coin, and fix the Standard of Weights and Measures;

To provide for the Punishment of counterfeiting the Securities and current Coin of the United States;

To establish Post Offices and post Roads;

To promote the Progress of Science and useful Arts, by securing for limited Times to Authors and Inventors the exclusive Right to their respective Writings and Discoveries;

To constitute Tribunals inferior to the supreme Court,

To define and punish Piracies and Felonies committed on the high Seas, and Offences against the Law of Nations;

To declare War, grant Letters of Marque and Reprisal, and make Rules concerning Captures on Land and Water;

To raise and support Armies, but no Appropriation of Money to that Use shall be for a longer Term than two Years;

To provide and maintain a Navy;

To make Rules for the Government and Regulation of the land and naval Forces;

To provide for calling for the Militia to execute the Laws of the Union, suppress Insurrections and repel Invasions;

To provide for organizing, arming, and disciplining, the Militia, and for governing such Part of them as may be employed in the Service of the United States, reserving to the States respectively, the Appointment of the Officers, and the Authority of training the Militia according to the discipline prescribed by Congress;

To exercise exclusive Legislation in all Cases whatsoever, over such District (not exceeding ten Miles square) as may, by Cession of particular States, and the Acceptance of Congress, become the Seat of the Government of the United States, and to exercise like Authority over all Places purchased by the Consent of the Legislature of the State in which the Same shall be, for the Erection of Forts, Magazines, Arsenals, dock-Yards, and other needful Buildings;—And

To make all Laws which shall be necessary and proper for carrying into Execution the foregoing Powers, and all other Powers vested by this Constitution in the Government of the United States, or in any Department or Officer thereof.

Powers Denied to Congress

Section 9   The Migration of Importation of such Persons as any of the States now existing shall think proper to admit, shall not be prohibited by the Congress prior to the Year one thousand eight hundred and eight, but a Tax or Duty may be imposed on such Importation, not exceeding ten dollars for each Person.

The privilege of the Writ of Habeas Corpus shall not be suspended, unless when in Cases of Rebellion or Invasion the public Safety may require it.

No Bill of Attainder or ex post facto Laws shall be passed.

No Capitation, or other direct, Tax shall be laid, unless in Proportion to the Census or Enumeration herein before directed to be taken.[6]

No Tax or Duty shall be laid on Articles exported from any State.

No Preference shall be given by any Regulation of Commerce or Revenue to the Ports of one State over those of another; nor shall Vessels bound to, or from, one State, be obliged to enter, clear, or pay Duties in another.

---

[6]Modified by the 16th Amendment

No Money shall be drawn from the Treasury, but in Consequence of Appropriations made by Law; and a regular Statement and Account of the Receipts and Expenditures of all public Money shall be published from time to time.

No Title of Nobility shall be granted by the United States; And no Person holding any Office of Profit or Trust under them, shall, without the Consent of Congress, accept of any present, Emolument, Office, or Title, of any kind whatever, from any King, Prince, or foreign State.

Powers Denied to the States

Section 10 No State shall enter into any Treaty, Alliance, or Confederation; grant Letters of Marque and Reprisal; coin Money; emit Bills of Credit; make any Thing but gold and silver Coin a Tender in Payment of Debts; pass any Bill of Attainder, ex post facto Law, or Law impairing the Obligation of Contracts, or grant any Title of Nobility.

No State shall, without the Consent of the Congress, lay any Imposts or Duties on Imports or Exports, except what may be absolutely necessary for executing its inspection Laws: and the net Produce of all Duties and Imposts, laid by any State on Imports or Exports, shall be for the Use of the Treasury of the United States; and all such Laws shall be subject to the Revision and Controul of the Congress.

No State shall, without the Consent of Congress, lay any Duty of Tonnage, keep Troops, or Ships of War in time of Peace, enter into any Agreement or Compact with another State, or with a foreign Power, or engage in War, unless actually invaded, or in such imminent Danger as will not admit of Delay.

ARTICLE II—THE EXECUTIVE ARTICLE

Nature and Scope of Presidential Power

Section 1 The executive Power shall be vested in a President of the United States of America. He shall hold his Office during the Term of four Years and, together with the Vice President, chosen for the same Term, be elected as follows:

Each State shall appoint, in such Manner as the Legislature thereof may direct, a Number of Electors, equal to the whole Number of Senators and Representatives to which the State may be entitled in the Congress: but no Senator or Representative, or Person holding an Office of Trust or Profit under the United States, shall be appointed an Elector.

The Electors shall meet in their respective States, and vote by Ballot for two Persons, of whom one at least shall not be an Inhabitant of the same State with themselves. And they shall make a List of all the Persons voted for, and of the Number of Votes for each; which List they shall sign and certify, and transmit sealed to the Seat of the Government of the United States, directed to the President of the Senate. The President of the Senate shall, in the Presence of the Senate and House of Representatives, open all the Certificates, and the Votes shall then be counted. The Person having the greatest Number of Votes shall be the President, if such Number be a Majority of the whole Number of Electors appointed; and if there be more than one who have such Majority and have an equal Number of Votes, then the House of Representatives shall immediately chuse by Ballot one of them for President; and if no person have a Majority, then from the five highest on the List the said House shall in like Manner chuse the President. But in chusing the President, the Votes shall be taken by States, the Representation from each State having one Vote; A quorum for this Purpose shall consist of a Member or Members from two thirds of the States, and a Majority of all the States shall be necessary to a Choice. In every Case, after the Choice of the President, the person having the greatest Number of Votes of the Electors shall be the Vice President. But if there should remain two or more who have equal Vote, the Senate shall chuse from them by Ballot the Vice President.[7]

The Congress may determine the Time of chusing the Electors, and the Day on which they shall give their Votes; which Day shall be the same throughout the United States.

No Person except a natural born Citizen, or a Citizen of the United States, at the time of the Adoption of this Constitution, shall be eligible to the Office of President; neither shall any Person be eligible to that Office who shall not have attained to the Age of thirty five Years, and been fourteen Years a Resident within the United States.

In Case of the Removal of the President from Office, or of his Death, Resignation, or Inability to discharge the Powers and Duties of the said Office, the same shall devolve on the Vice President, and the Congress may by Law provide for the Case of Removal, Death, Resignation, or Inability, both of the President and Vice President, declaring what Officer shall then act as President, and such Officer shall act accordingly, until the Disability be removed, or a President shall be elected.[8]

The President shall, at stated Times, receive for his Services, a Compensation, which shall neither be encreased nor diminished during the Period of which he shall have been elected, and he shall not receive within that Period any other Emolument from the United States, or any of them.

Before he enter on the Execution of his Office, he shall take the following Oath or Affirmation:—"I do solemnly swear (or affirm) that I will faithfully execute the Office of President of the United States, and will to the best of my Ability, preserve, protect and defend the Constitution of the United States."

Powers and Duties of the President

Section 2 The President shall be the Commander in Chief of the Army and Navy of the United States, and of the Militia of the several States, when called into the actual Service of the United States, he may require the Opinion, in writing, of the principal Officer in each of the executive Departments, upon any Subject relating to the Duties of their respective Offices, and he shall have the Power to grant Reprieves and Pardons for Offences against the United States, except in Cases of Impeachment.

He shall have Power, by and with the Advice and Consent of the Senate to make Treaties, provided two thirds of the Senators present concur; and he shall nominate, and by and with the Advice and Consent of the Senate, shall appoint Ambassadors, other public Ministers and Consuls, Judges of the supreme Court, and all other Officers of the United States, whose Appointments are not herein otherwise provided for, and which shall be established by Law: but the Congress may by Law vest the Appointment of such inferior Officers, as they think proper, in the President alone, in the Courts of Law, or in the Heads of Departments.

The President shall have Power to fill up all Vacancies that may happen during the Recess of the Senate, by granting Commissions which shall expire at the End of their next Session.

Section 3 He shall from time to time give to the Congress Information of the State of the Union, and recommend to their Consideration such Measures as he shall judge necessary and expedient; he may, on extraordinary Occasions, convene both Houses, or either of them, and in Case of Disagreement between them, with Respect to the Time of Adjournment, he may adjourn them to such Time as he shall think proper; he shall receive Ambassadors and other public Ministers; he shall take Care that the Laws be faithfully executed, and shall Commission all the Officers of the United States.

Section 4 The President, Vice President and all civil Officers of the United States, shall be removed from Office on Impeachment for, and Conviction of, Treason, Bribery, or other High Crimes and Misdemeanors.

ARTICLE III—THE JUDICIAL ARTICLE

Judicial Power, Courts, Judges

Section 1 The judicial Power of the United States, shall be vested in one supreme Court, and in such inferior Courts as the Congress may from time to time ordain and establish. The Judges, both the supreme and inferior

---

[7]Changed by the 12th and 20th Amendments

[8]Modified by the 25th Amendment

Courts, shall hold their Offices during good Behaviour, and shall, at stated Times, receive for their Services, a Compensation, which shall not be diminished during their Continuance in Office.

Jurisdiction

Section 2 The judicial Power shall extend to all Cases, in Law and Equity, arising under this Constitution, the Laws of the United States, and Treaties made, or which shall be made, under their Authority;—to all Cases affecting Ambassadors, other public Ministers and Consuls;—to all Cases of admiralty and maritime Jurisdiction;—to Controversies to which the United States shall be a Party;—to Controversies between two or more States; *between a State and Citizens of another State*;[9]—between Citizens of different States;—between Citizens of the same State claiming Lands under Grants of different States, and between a State, or the Citizens thereof, and foreign States, Citizens, or Subjects.

In all Cases affecting Ambassadors, other public Ministers and Consuls, and those in which a State shall be Party, the supreme Court shall have original Jurisdiction. In all the other Cases before mentioned, the supreme Court shall have appellate Jurisdiction, both as to Law and Fact, with such Exceptions, and under such Regulations as Congress shall make.

The Trial of all Crimes, except in Cases of Impeachment, shall be by Jury; and such Trial shall be held in the State where the said Crimes shall have been committed; but when not committed within any State, the Trial shall be at such Place or Places as the Congress may by Law have directed.

Treason

Section 3 Treason against the United States, shall consist only in levying War against them, or in adhering to their Enemies, giving them Aid and Comfort. No Persons shall be convicted of Treason unless on the Testimony of two Witnesses to the same overt Act, or on Confession in open Court.

The Congress shall have Power to declare the Punishment of Treason, but no Attainder of Treason shall work Corruption of Blood, or Forfeiture except during the Life of the Person attainted.

ARTICLE IV—INTERSTATE RELATIONS

Full Faith and Credit Clause

Section 1 Full Faith and Credit shall be given in each State to the public Acts, Records, and judicial Proceedings of every other State. And the Congress may by general Laws prescribe the Manner in which such Acts, Records and Proceedings shall be proved, and the Effect thereof.

Privileges and Immunities; Interstate Extradition

Section 2 The Citizens of each State shall be entitled to all Privileges and Immunities of Citizens in the several States.

A person charged in any State with Treason, Felony or other Crime, who shall flee from Justice, and be found in another State, shall on Demand of the executive Authority of the State from which he fled, be delivered up, to be removed to the State having jurisdiction of the Crime.

No person held to Service or Labour in one State, under the Laws thereof, escaping into another, shall, in Consequence of any Law or Regulation therein, be discharged from such Service or Labour, but shall be delivered up on Claim of the Party to whom such Service or Labour may be due.[10]

Admission of States

Section 3 New States may be admitted by the Congress into this Union; but no new State shall be formed or erected within the Jurisdiction of any other State; nor any State to be formed by the Junction of two or more States, or Parts of States, without the Consent of the Legislatures of the States concerned as well as of the Congress.

The Congress shall have Power to dispose of and make all needful Rules and Regulations respecting the Territory or other Property belonging to the United States; and nothing in this Constitution shall be so construed as to Prejudice any Claims of the United States, or of any particular State.

Republican Form of Government

Section 4 The United States shall guarantee to every State in this Union a Republican Form of Government, and shall protect each of them against Invasion; and on Application of the Legislature, or of the Executive (when the Legislature cannot be convened) against domestic Violence.

ARTICLE V—THE AMENDING POWER

The Congress, whenever two thirds of both Houses shall deem it necessary, shall propose Amendments to this Constitution, or, on the Application of the Legislatures of two thirds of several States, shall call a Convention for proposing Amendments, which, in either Case, shall be valid to all Intents and Purposes, as Part of this Constitution, when ratified by the Legislatures of three fourths of the several States, or by Conventions in three fourths thereof, as the one or the other Mode of Ratification may be proposed by the Congress; Provided that no Amendment which may be made prior to the Year One thousand eight hundred and eight shall in any Manner affect the first and fourth Clauses in the Ninth Section of the first Article; and that no State, without its Consent, shall be deprived of its equal Suffrage in the Senate.

ARTICLE VI—THE SUPREMACY ACT

All Debts contracted and Engagements entered into, before the Adoption of this Constitution, shall be as valid against the United States under the Constitution, as under the Confederation.

This Constitution, and the Laws of the United States which shall be made in Pursuance thereof; and all Treaties made, or which shall be made, under the Authority of the United States, shall be the supreme Law of the Land; and the Judges in every State shall be bound thereby, any Thing in the Constitution or Laws of any State to the Contrary notwithstanding.

The Senators and Representative before mentioned, and the Members of the several State Legislatures, and all executive and judicial Officers, both of the United States and of the several States, shall be bound by Oath or Affirmation, to support this Constitution; but no religious Test shall ever be required as a Qualification to any Office or public Trust under the United States.

ARTICLE VII—RATIFICATION

The Ratification of the Conventions of nine States, shall be sufficient for the Establishment of this Constitution between the States so ratifying the Same.

Done in Convention by the Unanimous Consent of the States present the Seventeenth Day of September in the Year of our Lord one thousand seven hundred and Eighty seven and of the Independence of the United States of America the Twelfth *In Witness whereof We have hereunto subscribed our Names.*

AMENDMENTS

The Bill of Rights

[The first ten amendments were ratified on December 15, 1791, and form what is known as the "Bill of Rights."]

AMENDMENT 1—RELIGION, SPEECH, ASSEMBLY, AND POLITICS

Congress shall make no law respecting an establishment of religion, or prohibiting the free exercise thereof; or abridging the freedom of speech, or of the press; or the right of the people peaceably to assemble, and to petition the government for a redress of grievances.

---

[9]Modified by the 11th Amendment
[10]Repealed by the 13th Amendment

AMENDMENT 2—MILITIA AND THE RIGHT TO BEAR ARMS

A well regulated Militia, being necessary to the security of a free State, the right of the people to keep and bear Arms, shall not be infringed.

AMENDMENT 3—QUARTERING OF SOLDIERS

No Soldier shall, in time of peace be quartered in any house, without the consent of the Owner, nor in time of war, but in manner to be prescribed by law.

AMENDMENT 4—SEARCHES AND SEIZURES

The right of the people to be secure in their persons, houses, papers, and effects, against unreasonable searches and seizures, shall not be violated, and no Warrants shall issue, but upon probable cause, supported by Oath or affirmation, and particularly describing the place to be searched, and the persons or things to be seized.

AMENDMENT 5—GRAND JURIES, SELF-INCRIMINATION, DOUBLE JEOPARDY, DUE PROCESS, AND EMINENT DOMAIN

No person shall be held to answer for a capital, or otherwise infamous crime, unless on a presentment or indictment of a Grand jury, except in cases arising in the land or naval forces, or in the Militia, when in actual service in time of War or public danger; nor shall any person be subject for the same offence to be twice put in jeopardy of life or limb; nor shall be compelled in any criminal case to be a witness against himself, nor be deprived of life, liberty, or property, without due process of law; nor shall private property be taken for public use, without just compensation.

AMENDMENT 6—CRIMINAL COURT PROCEDURES

In all criminal prosecutions, the accused shall enjoy the right to a speedy and public trial, by an impartial jury of the State and district wherein the crime shall have been committed, which district shall have been previously ascertained by law, and to be informed of the nature and cause of the accusation; to be confronted with the witnesses against him; to have compulsory process for obtaining Witnesses in his favor, and to have the Assistance of Counsel for his defense.

AMENDMENT 7—TRIAL BY JURY IN COMMON LAW CASES

In Suits at common law, where the value in controversy shall exceed twenty dollars, the right of trial by jury shall be preserved, and no fact tried by a jury shall be otherwise re-examined in any Court of the United States, than according to the rules of the common law.

AMENDMENT 8—BAIL, CRUEL AND UNUSUAL PUNISHMENT

Excessive bail shall not be required, nor excessive fines imposed, nor cruel and unusual punishments inflicted.

AMENDMENT 9—RIGHTS RETAINED BY THE PEOPLE

The enumeration in the Constitution, of certain rights, shall not be construed to deny or disparage others retained by the people.

AMENDMENT 10—RESERVED POWERS OF THE STATES

The powers not delegated to the United States by the Constitution, nor prohibited by it to the States, are reserved to the States respectively, or to the people.

AMENDMENT 11—SUITS AGAINST THE STATES
[Ratified February 7, 1795]

The Judicial power of the United States shall not be construed to extend to any suit in law or equity, commenced or prosecuted against one of the United States by Citizens of another State, or by Citizens or Subjects of any Foreign State.

AMENDMENT 12—ELECTION OF THE PRESIDENT
[Ratified June 15, 1804]

The Electors shall meet in their respective states, and vote by ballot for President and Vice-President, one of whom, at least, shall not be an inhabitant of the same state with themselves; they shall name in their ballots the person voted for as President, and in distinct ballots the person voted for as Vice-President, and they shall make distinct lists of all persons voted for as President, and of all persons voted for as Vice-President, and of the number of votes for each, which lists they shall sign and certify, and transmit sealed to the seat of the government of the United States, directed to the President of the Senate;—The President of the Senate shall, in presence of the Senate and House of Representatives, open all the certificates and the votes shall then be counted;—The person having the greatest number of votes for President, shall be the President, if such number be a majority of the whole number of Electors appointed; and if no person have such majority, then from the persons having the highest numbers not exceeding three on the list of those voted for as President, the House of Representatives shall choose immediately, by ballot, the President. But in choosing the President, the votes shall be taken by states, the representation from each state having one vote; a quorum for this purpose shall consist of a member or members from two-thirds of the states, and a majority of all states shall be necessary to a choice. And if the House of Representatives shall not choose a President whenever the right of choice shall devolve upon them, *before the fourth day of March next following*, then the Vice-President shall act as President, as in the case of the death or other constitutional disability of the President.[11] The person having the greatest number of votes as Vice-President, shall be the Vice-President, if such a number be a majority of the whole numbers of Electors appointed, and if no person have a majority, then from the two highest numbers on the list, the Senate shall choose the Vice-President; a quorum for the purpose shall consist of two-thirds of the whole number of Senators, and a majority of the whole number shall be necessary to a choice. But no person constitutionally ineligible to the office of President shall be eligible to that of Vice-President of the United States.

AMENDMENT 13—PROHIBITION OF SLAVERY
[Ratified December 6, 1865]

Section 1 Neither slavery nor involuntary servitude, except as a punishment for crime whereof the party shall have been duly convicted, shall exist within the United States, or any place subject to their jurisdiction.

Section 2 Congress shall have power to enforce this article by appropriate legislation.

AMENDMENT 14—CITIZENSHIP, DUE PROCESS, AND EQUAL PROTECTION OF THE LAWS
[Ratified July 9, 1868]

Section 1 All persons born or naturalized in the United States, and subject to the jurisdiction thereof, are citizens of the United States and of the State wherein they reside. No State shall make or enforce any law which shall abridge the privileges or immunities of citizens of the United States; nor shall

---

[11]Changed by the 20th Amendment

any State deprive any person of life, liberty, or property, without due process of law; nor deny to any person within its jurisdiction the equal protection of the laws.

Section 2 Representatives shall be apportioned among the several States according to their respective numbers, counting the whole number of persons in each State, excluding Indians not taxed. But when the right to vote at any election for the choice of electors for President and Vice President of the United States, Representatives in Congress, the Executive and Judicial officers of a State, or the members of the Legislature thereof, is denied to any of the male inhabitants of such State, being twenty-one[12] years of age, and citizens of the United States, or in any way abridged, except for participation in rebellion, or other crime, the basis of representation therein shall be reduced in the proportion which the number of such male citizens shall bear to the whole number of male citizens twenty-one years of age in such State.

Section 3 No person shall be a Senator or Representative in Congress, or elector of President and Vice President, or hold any office, civil or military, under the United States, or under any State, who, having previously taken an oath, as a member of Congress, or as an officer of the United States, or as a member of any State legislature, or as an executive or judicial officer of any State, to support the Constitution of the United States, shall have engaged in insurrection or rebellion against the same, or given aid or comfort to the enemies thereof. But Congress may by a vote of two-thirds of each House, remove such disability.

Section 4 The validity of the public debt of the United States, authorized by law, including debts incurred for payment of pensions and bounties for services in suppressing insurrection or rebellion, shall not be questioned. But neither the United States nor any State shall assume or pay any debt or obligation incurred in aid of insurrection or rebellion against the United States, or any claim for the loss or emancipation of any slave; but all such debts, obligations and claims shall be held illegal and void.

Section 5 The Congress shall have power to enforce, by appropriate legislation, the provisions of this article.

AMENDMENT 15—THE RIGHT TO VOTE
[Ratified February 3, 1870]

Section 1 The right of citizens of the United States to vote shall not be denied or abridged by the United States or by any State on account of race, color, or previous condition of servitude.

Section 2 The Congress shall have power to enforce this article by appropriate legislation.

AMENDMENT 16—INCOME TAXES
[Ratified February 3, 1913]

The Congress shall have power to lay and collect taxes on incomes, from whatever source derived, without apportionment among the several States, and without regard to any census or enumeration.

AMENDMENT 17—DIRECT ELECTION OF SENATORS
[Ratified April 8, 1913]

The Senate of the United States shall be composed of two Senators from each State, elected by the people thereof, for six years; and each Senator shall have one vote. The electors in each State shall have the qualifications requisite for electors of the most numerous branch of the State legislatures.

When vacancies happen in the representation of any State in the Senate, the executive authority of such State shall issue writs of election to fill such vacancies: *Provided*, That the Legislature of any State may empower the executive thereof to make temporary appointment until the people fill the vacancies by election as the legislature may direct.

This amendment shall not be so construed as to affect the election or term of any Senator chosen before it becomes valid as part of the Constitution.

AMENDMENT 18—PROHIBITION
[Ratified January 16, 1919 Repealed December 5, 1933 by Amendment 21]

Section 1 After one year from the ratification of this article the manufacture, sale, or transportation of intoxicating liquors within, the importation thereof into, or the exportation thereof from the United States and all territory subject to the jurisdiction thereof for beverage purposes is hereby prohibited.

Section 2 The Congress and the several states shall have concurrent power to enforce this article by appropriate legislation.

Section 3 This article shall be inoperative unless it shall have been ratified as an amendment to the Constitution by the legislatures of the several states, as provided in the Constitution, within seven years from the date of the submission hereof to the States by the Congress.[13]

AMENDMENT 19—FOR WOMEN'S SUFFRAGE
[Ratified August 18, 1920]

The right of the citizens of the United States to vote shall not be denied or abridged by the United States or by any State on account of sex.

Congress shall have power, by appropriate legislation, to enforce the provision of this article.

AMENDMENT 20—THE LAME DUCK AMENDMENT
[Ratified January 23, 1933]

Section 1 The terms of the President and Vice President shall end at noon on the 20th day of January, and the terms of the Senators and Representatives at noon on the 3rd day of January, of the years in which such terms would have ended if this article had not been ratified; and the terms of their successors shall then begin.

Section 2 The Congress shall assemble at least once in every year, and such meeting shall begin at noon on the 3rd day of January, unless they shall by law appoint a different day.

Section 3 If, at the time fixed for the beginning of the term of the President, the President elect shall have died, the Vice President elect shall become President. If a President shall not have been chosen before the time fixed for the beginning of his term, or if the President elect shall have failed to qualify, then the Vice President elect shall act as President until a President shall have qualified; and the Congress may by law provide for the case wherein neither a President elect nor a Vice President elect shall have qualified, declaring who shall then act as President, or the manner in which one who is to act shall be selected, and such person shall act accordingly until a President or Vice President shall have qualified.

Section 4 The Congress may by law provide for the case of the death of any of the persons from whom the House of Representatives may choose a President whenever the right of choice shall have developed upon them, and for the case of the death of any of the persons from whom the Senate may choose a Vice President whenever the right of choice shall have devolved upon them.

---

[12]Changed by the 26th Amendment

[13]Repealed by the 21st Amendment

Section 5 Sections 1 and 2 shall take effect on the 15th day of October following the ratification of this article.

Section 6 This article shall be inoperative unless it shall have been ratified as an amendment to the Constitution by the legislatures of three-fourths of the several States within seven years from the date of its submission.

AMENDMENT 21—REPEAL OF PROHIBITION
[Ratified December 5, 1933]

Section 1 The eighteenth article of amendment to the Constitution of the United States is hereby repealed.

Section 2 The transportation or importation into any State, Territory, or Possession of the United States for delivery or use therein of intoxicating liquors, in violation of the laws thereof, is hereby prohibited.

Section 3 This article shall be inoperative unless it shall have been ratified as an amendment to the Constitution by conventions in the several States, as provided in the Constitution, within seven years from the date of the submission hereof to the States by the Congress.

AMENDMENT 22—NUMBER OF PRESIDENTIAL TERMS
[Ratified February 27, 1951]

Section 1 No person shall be elected to the office of the President more than twice, and no person who has held the office of President, or acted as President, for more than two years of a term to which some other person was elected President shall be elected to the Office of the President more than once. But this Article shall not apply to any person holding the office of President when this article was proposed by the Congress, and shall not prevent any person who may be holding the office of President, or acting as President, during the term within which this Article becomes operative from holding the office of President or acting as President during the remainder of such term.

Section 2 This Article shall be inoperative unless it shall have been ratified as an amendment to the Constitution by the legislatures of three-fourths of the several states within seven years from the date of its submission to the States by the Congress.

AMENDMENT 23—PRESIDENTIAL ELECTORS FOR THE DISTRICT OF COLUMBIA
[Ratified March 29, 1961]

Section 1 The District constituting the seat of Government of the United States shall appoint in such manner as the Congress may direct:

A number of electors of President and Vice President equal to the whole number of Senators and Representatives in Congress to which the District would be entitled if it were a State, but in no event more than the least populous State; they shall be in addition to those appointed by the States, but they shall be considered, for the purposes of the election of President and Vice President, to be electors appointed by a State; and they shall meet in the District and perform such duties as provided by the twelfth article of amendment.

Section 2 The Congress shall have power to enforce this article by appropriate legislation.

AMENDMENT 24—THE ANTI-POLL TAX AMENDMENT
[Ratified January 23, 1964]

Section 1 The right of citizens of the United States to vote in any primary or other election for President or Vice President, for electors for President or Vice President, or for Senator or Representative in Congress, shall not be denied or abridged by the United States or any State by reason of failure to pay any poll tax or other tax.

Section 2 The Congress shall have power to enforce this article by appropriate legislation.

AMENDMENT 25—PRESIDENTIAL DISABILITY, VICE PRESIDENTIAL VACANCIES
[Ratified February 10, 1967]

Section 1 In case of the removal of the President from office or his death or resignation, the Vice President shall become President.

Section 2 Whenever there is a vacancy in the office of the Vice President, the President shall nominate a Vice President who shall take the office upon confirmation by a majority vote of both houses of Congress.

Section 3 Whenever the President transmits to the President pro tempore of the Senate and the Speaker of the House of Representatives his written declaration that he is unable to discharge the powers and duties of his office, and until he transmits to them a written declaration to the contrary, such powers and duties shall be discharged by the Vice President as Acting President.

Section 4 Whenever the Vice-President and a majority of either the principal officers of the executive departments, or of such other body as Congress may by law provide, transmit to the President pro tempore of the Senate and the Speaker of the House of Representatives their written declaration that the President is unable to discharge the powers and duties of his office, the Vice President shall immediately assume the powers and duties of the office as Acting President.

Thereafter, when the President transmits to the President pro tempore of the Senate and the Speaker of the House of Representatives his written declaration that no inability exists, he shall resume the powers and duties of his office unless the Vice President and a majority of either the principal officers of the executive departments, or of such other body as Congress may by law provide, transmit within four days to the President pro tempore of the Senate and the Speaker of the House of Representatives their written declaration that the President is unable to discharge the powers and duties of his office. Thereupon Congress shall decide the issue, assembling within forty-eight hours for that purpose if not in session. If the Congress, within twenty-one days after receipt of the latter written declaration, or, if Congress is not in session, within twenty-one days after Congress is required to assemble, determines by two-thirds vote of both houses that the President is unable to discharge the powers and duties of his office, the Vice President shall continue to discharge the same as Acting President; otherwise, the President shall resume the powers and duties of his office.

AMENDMENT 26—EIGHTEEN-YEAR-OLD VOTE
[Ratified July 1, 1971]

Section 1 The right of citizens of the United States, who are eighteen years of age, or older, to vote shall not be denied or abridged by the United States or by any State on account of age.

Section 2 The Congress shall have power to enforce this article by appropriate legislation.

AMENDMENT 27—CONGRESSIONAL SALARIES
[Ratified May 7, 1992]

No law, varying the compensation for the services of the Senators and Representatives, shall take effect, until an election of Representative shall be intervened.

AMERICAN FEDERALISM

2

A s is true of Americans today, most early Americans put at the top of their worry list a fear that governments might threaten their liberties. Questions about how powers were to be divided between the new national government and the states were much on their minds. *Federalism*—the constitutional division of powers between the national government and the states—has from our beginnings been hailed as a potent barrier against tyranny.[1]

Questions about the relations between the national government and the states did not end with the founding period. In 1861, men and women fought and died for Virginia or Texas or for the Union (although it would be a mistake to think of the Civil War as merely a particularly heated debate over the principles of federalism). Today questions about the relations between the national government and the states have again become a major issue for Americans. This debate was one of the central themes of the 1994 congressional and the 1996 presidential elections, with Republicans leading the charge against the national government and urging a massive return of powers and responsibilities to the states. Antigovernment themes, most particularly those directed against entitlements, were part of the campaign rhetoric of candidates from both political parties.

But it is not just in the United States that federalism issues have come to the top of the political agenda. In Canada the very nature of their federal system is at stake as the French-speaking province of Quebec demands special status and a considerable measure of autonomy.[2] The former Soviet Union—a highly centralized government that was federal only in form but not in fact—broke apart into 15 independent nations. Russia itself is going through a struggle to define its federal relationship, with Chechnya being the most extreme case. Throughout Central Europe tensions erupt into violence as nations divide and subdivide. And even in the United Kingdom there are calls for rethinking the relationship between Scotland, Wales, and England. "In the last few years sentiment for independence for Scotland has grown by leaps and bounds."[3] There are similar calls in Wales for a local parliament.

From the days of the New Deal in the 1930s to today, there has been a steady drift of power and responsibility from the states to the national government. Presidents Nixon, Reagan, and Bush tried to slow down the growth of the national government under the banner of *New Federalism*. President Nixon declared, "For a third of a century, power and responsibility have flowed toward Washington. We intend to reverse this tide." "It is my intention to curb the size and influence of the federal establishment," President Reagan vowed in 1981."[4] But although Presidents Carter and Clinton put some brakes on the growth of the national government, it was not until 1995, when the Republicans took control of both houses of Congress, that a major, almost revolutionary, attempt to return many functions back to the states—the "Devolution Revolution"—occurred.

Although in 1995, to the surprise of most observers, some Supreme Court justices reopened *constitutional* questions about the powers of the national government,[5] debates today are not likely to be about the constitutional division of authority between the national government and the states. Despite the Supreme Court declaring that congressional attempts to regulate firearms around schools was unconstitutional,[6] the national government's constitutional authority over an enormous range of subjects is clearly established, whether it concerns civil rights, highway speed limits, or the sale of holiday lights. Nonetheless, we can still argue about the proper division of responsibilities between the national and state governments: whether Congress should regulate welfare, Medicare, Medicaid, the environment, or leave regulation to state discretion.

Such arguments, although couched in terms of national-state relations, almost always reflect differences among various interests about public policy. National and state governments are the arenas in which and through which battles take place between consumers and producers, workers and employers, airlines and railroads, pro-choice and right-to-life advocates, pro-growth and anti-growth forces, and all the other contending groups that make up our political system. People who think they can get more of what they want from the national government are likely to advocate national action; those who see state governments as more sympathetic are likely to argue for decentralization. Advocates of environmental protection, for instance, have generally found a more receptive audience in Washington than in their state capitals, especially in the West. They are likely to complain about "special interests" at the state house. Opponents of such regulation are likely to denounce the Washington bureaucrats.

In this chapter we begin by defining federalism and discussing its advantages. Next we look at the constitutional basis of our federal system. Then we see how the Supreme Court and political developments have shaped, and continue to shape, our modern system of federalism.

DEFINING FEDERALISM

Scholars have argued and wars have been fought about what federalism really means. One scholar counted 267 definitions.[7] **Federalism**, as we define it, is a form of government in which a constitution distributes powers between a central government and subdivisional governments—usually called states or provinces or republics—giving to both the national government and the regional governments substantial responsibilities and powers, including the power to collect taxes and to pass and enforce laws regulating the conduct of individuals.

The mere existence of both national and state governments does not make a system federal. What is important is that a *constitution divides governmental powers between the national government and the constituent governments* (called *states* in the United States), giving substantial functions to each. Neither the central nor the constituent government receives its powers from the other; both derive them from a common source—a constitution. This constitutional distribution of powers cannot be changed by the ordinary processes of legislation—by, for example, an act of either a national or a state legislature. Both levels of government operate through their own agents and exercise power directly over individuals. Other countries with federal systems include Canada, Switzerland, Mexico, and Australia. "Nearly 40 percent of the people of the world now live in nations with a federal form of government. Another third live in countries that use some elements of federalism."[8]

Constitutionally, the federal system of the United States consists of only the national government and the 50 states. "Cities are not," the Supreme Court has reminded us, "sovereign entities." But in a practical sense, we are a nation of almost 87,000 governmental units—from the national government to the school board district (see Table 2-1). This does not make for a tidy, efficient, easy-to-understand system; yet, as we shall see, it does have its virtues.

Interpretations of Federalism

Federalism is a powerful but elusive concept, leading both scholars and politicians to add adjectives that reflect their ideas:

Dual Federalism interprets the Constitution as giving a limited list of powers—primarily foreign policy and national defense—to the national government, leaving most power to sovereign states. Each level of government is dominant within its own sphere. The Supreme Court serves as the umpire between the national government and the states in case of a dispute over which government is in charge of a particular activity. During our first hundred years, dual federalism was the favored interpretation most of the time by the Supreme Court.

Cooperative Federalism stresses federalism as a system to deliver governmental goods and services to the people and calls for cooperation among various levels of governments in "getting the job done."

Marble Cake Federalism, coined by political scientist Morton Grodzins in 1960, conceives federalism as a marble cake in which all levels of government are involved in a variety of issues and programs, rather than a layer cake with uniform divisions between layers or levels of government.[a]

Competitive Federalism, a term created by political scientist Thomas R. Dye, brings to the fore the fact that federalism provides us with a national government, 50 states, and thousands of other units, each competing with the others in the way in which they put together packages of services and taxes and vying for the support of citizens. Applying the analogy of the marketplace, Dye emphasizes that at the state and local levels we have some choice which state and city we want "to use," just as we have choices about which automobile we wish to drive.[b]

Permissive Federalism implies that although federalism provides "a sharing of power and authority between the national and state government, the states' share rests upon the permission and permissiveness of the national government."[c]

New Federalism, favored by Richard Nixon, Ronald Reagan, George Bush, and Bob Dole, emphasized their view that we should return fiscal resources and management responsibilities to the states in the form of large block grants and revenue sharing, and that we should sort out functions between national and state governments.

[a] Morton Grodzins, "The Federal System," in *Goals for Americans: The Report of the President's Commission on National Goals* (Columbia University Press, 1960).

[b] Thomas R. Dye, *American Federalism: Competition Among Governments* (Lexington Books, 1990), pp. 13–17.

[c] Michael D. Reagan and John G. Sanzone, *The New Federalism* (Oxford University Press, 1981), p. 175.

TABLE 2-1

Number of Governments

States	50
Counties	3,043
Municipalities	19,296
Towns	16,666
School Districts	14,556
Special Districts	33,131
Total	86,742

SOURCE: U.S. Department of Commerce, Bureau of the Census, *1992 Census of Governments.*

Alternatives to Federalism

Among the alternatives to federalism are **unitary systems** of government in which a constitution vests all governmental power in the central government. The central government, if it so chooses, may delegate authority to constituent units, but what it delegates it may take away. Britain, France, Israel, and the Philippines have unitary governments. In the United States, state constitutions usually create this kind of relationship between the state and its local governments.

At the other extreme are **confederations** in which sovereign nations by a constitutional compact create a central government but carefully *limit* the power of the central government and do not give it the power to regulate the conduct of individuals directly. The central government makes regulations for the constituent governments, but it exists and operates only at their direction. The 13 states under the Articles of Confederation operated in this manner, as did the southern Confederacy during the Civil War (see Figure 2-1).

To complicate this matter, the framers of our Constitution used the term "federal" to describe what we would now call a *confederate* form of government. Moreover, today the term "federal" is frequently used as a synonym for national; people often refer to the government in Washington as "the federal government." But it is the states and the national government *together* that make up our federal system.

Why Federalism?

In 1787, federalism was an obvious choice. Confederation had been tried and found wanting, but a unitary system was out of the question. Most of the people were too deeply attached to their state governments to permit subordination to central rule. Federalism was, and still is, thought to be ideally suited to the needs of a heterogeneous people spread over a large continent, suspicious of concentrated power, and desiring unity but not uniformity. Federalism offered, and still offers, many advantages for such a people.[9]

FEDERALISM CHECKS THE GROWTH OF TYRANNY Although in the rest of the world federal forms have not been notably successful in preventing tyranny and many unitary governments are democratic, Americans tend to associate freedom with federalism.[10] As James Madison pointed out in *The Federalist*, No. 10: If "factious leaders . . . kindle a flame within their particular states," national leaders can check the spread of the "conflagration through the other states." Moreover, when one political party loses control of the national government, it is still likely to hold office in a number of states. It can then regroup, develop new policies and new leaders, and continue to challenge the party in power at the national level.

Such diffusion of power creates its own problems. It makes it difficult for a national majority to carry out a program of action, and it permits those who control a state government to frustrate the consensus expressed through Congress and national agencies. To some of our Constitution's framers, these obstacles were an advantage. They were more fearful that a single-interest national majority might capture the national government and attempt to suppress the interests of others than that minority interests might frustrate the national will. Of course the size of the nation and the many interests within it are the greatest obstacles to the formation of a single-interest majority, a point often overlooked today but emphasized by Madison in *The Federalist*, No. 10. If such a majority were to occur, having to work through a federal system would act to check its power.

FIGURE 2-1 A Comparison of Federalism and Confederation

Government under the Articles of Confederation: 1781-1788

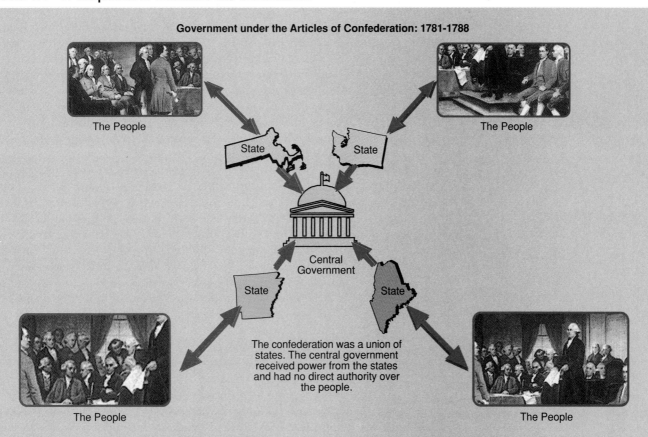

The People

The People

State

State

Central
Government

State

State

The People

The People

The confederation was a union of
states. The central government
received power from the states
and had no direct authority over
the people.

Government under U.S. Constitution (Federation): 1789-

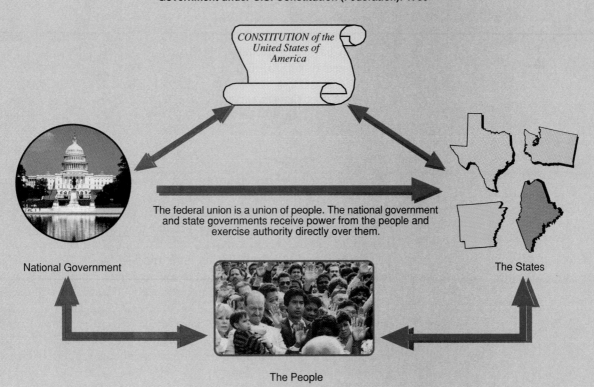

CONSTITUTION of the
United States of
America

The federal union is a union of people. The national government
and state governments receive power from the people and
exercise authority directly over them.

National Government

The States

The People

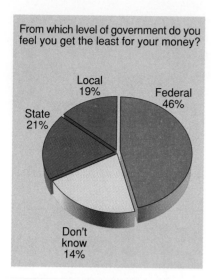

From which level of government do you feel you get the least for your money?

Local 19%

Federal 46%

State 21%

Don't know 14%

FIGURE 2-2 The Least Popular Level of Government

SOURCE: Advisory Commission on Intergovernmental Relations, *Public Attitudes on Governments and Taxes, 1994* (Government Printing Office, 1994), p. 29.

FEDERALISM ALLOWS UNITY WITHOUT UNIFORMITY National politicians and parties do not have to iron out every difference on every issue that divides us, whether it be abortion, divorce, gun control, gambling, capital punishment, education financing, or comparable worth. (**Comparable worth**, which mandates comparable pay for jobs requiring comparable skills, has been advanced as one way to correct pay inequities between higher-paying, male-dominated fields, such as plumbing, and lower-paying, female-dominated fields, such as teaching.) Instead, these issues are debated in state legislatures, county courthouses, and city halls. This advantage of federalism is becoming less significant as more local issues become national and as events and outcomes in one state immediately affect policy debates at the national level.

FEDERALISM ENCOURAGES EXPERIMENTATION Supreme Court Justice Louis Brandeis pointed out that state governments provide great "laboratories" for public policy experimentation, with states serving as proving grounds. If they adopt programs that fail, the negative effects are limited; if programs succeed, they can be adopted by other states and by the national government. Georgia, for example, was the first state to permit 18-year-olds to vote; Oregon is holding elections by mail; New York has been vigorous in its assault on water pollution; California has pioneered air pollution control programs, especially automobile emission standards. After federal leadership on environmental matters waned in the 1970s, New Jersey initiated programs to handle toxic wastes, radon gas testing, and mandatory recycling. Many states legalized abortion under certain conditions before the Supreme Court acted. (Whether these laws and regulations are good or bad depends, of course, on one's values, as do so many questions of politics.) "Sunset laws" (requiring periodic reauthorization for programs), equal housing, no-fault insurance, and "lemon laws" (providing consumer protection for faulty automobiles) are other examples of programs that originated in the states. Oregon and Hawaii are pioneers in creating new systems for the delivery of health care. Nevada is the only state, so far, to legalize statewide gambling, but some aspects of legalized casino gambling are now found in more than half the states. Not all innovations, even those considered successful, are widely adopted. Nebraska is the only state to have a unicameral legislature, although in 1996 it was momentarily discussed in California.

FEDERALISM KEEPS GOVERNMENT CLOSER TO THE PEOPLE By providing numerous arenas for decision making, federalism involves many people and helps keep government closer to the people. Every day thousands of Americans are busy serving on city councils, school boards, neighborhood associations, and planning commissions. And since they are close to the issues and have firsthand knowledge of what needs to be done, they may be more responsive to the problem than the experts in Washington.

We should be cautious, however, about generalizing that state and local governments are necessarily "closer to the people" than is the national government. True, more people are involved in local and state politics than in national affairs, and in recent years confidence in the ability of state governments has gone up while respect for national agencies has diminished (see Figure 2-2). Yet national and international affairs are often more on people's minds than are state or even local politics. Fewer voters participate in state and local elections than in congressional and presidential elections. Some caution against "the romantic notion of power to the people" by pointing out "The only thing worse than the U.S. Postal Service is the local motor vehicle department. . . . There is no efficiency magic in devolution."[11]

THE CONSTITUTIONAL STRUCTURE
OF AMERICAN FEDERALISM

Dividing powers and responsibilities between the national and state governments requires thousands of court decisions, hundreds of books, and endless speeches to explain—and even then the division lacks precise definition. Nonetheless it is helpful to get a basic understanding of how the Constitution divides these powers and responsibilities among the national and state governments and what obligations it imposes on each level of government in its relations to the other.

Powers of the National Government

The Constitution, chiefly in the first three articles, delegates legislative, executive, and judicial powers to the national government. In addition to these **express powers**, such as the power to appropriate funds, the Constitution delegates to Congress **implied powers**, such as the power to create banks, which may be inferred from express powers. (We will see an example when we discuss the landmark case of *McCulloch v Maryland.*) The constitutional basis for the implied powers of Congress is the **necessary and proper clause** (Article I, Section 8, Clause 18). This clause gives Congress the right "to make all Laws which shall be necessary and proper for carrying into Execution the foregoing Powers, and all other Powers vested . . . in the Government of the United States."

In the field of foreign affairs the Constitution gives the national government **inherent powers**, so that the national government has the same authority to deal with other nations as if it were the central government in a unitary system. These inherent powers do not depend on specific constitutional grants. For example, the government of the United States may acquire territory by discovery and occupation, though no specific clause in the Constitution allows such acquisition. Even if the Constitution were silent about foreign affairs—which it is not—the national government would have the right to declare war, make treaties, and appoint and receive ambassadors.

Together, these express, implied, and inherent powers create a flexible system that has allowed the Supreme Court, Congress, the president, and the people to expand the central government's powers to meet the needs of a modern industrial nation operating in a global economy. This expansion of central government functions has rested on four constitutional pillars.

NATIONAL SUPREMACY ARTICLE   One of the most important pillars is found in Article VI of the Constitution: "This Constitution, and the Laws of the United States which shall be made in Pursuance thereof; and all Treaties made . . . under the Authority of the United States, shall be the supreme Law of the Land; and the Judges in every State shall be bound thereby; any Thing in the Constitution or Laws of any State to the Contrary notwithstanding." All officials, state as well as national, are bound by constitutional oath to support the Constitution of the United States. States may not use their reserved powers to override national policies; this restriction also applies to local units of government since they are agents of the states. National laws and regulations of federal agencies *preempt* the field, so that conflicting state and local rules and regulations are unenforceable.

THE WAR POWER   The national government is responsible for protecting the nation from external aggression and, when necessary, for waging war. In today's world military strength depends not only on troops in the field but also on the ability to mobilize the nation's industrial might and to apply scientific knowledge to the tasks of defense. The national government has the power to wage war and

Constitutional Division of Power

The formal constitutional framework of our federal system may be stated relatively simply:

1. The national government has only those powers *delegated* to it by the Constitution (with the important exception of the inherent power over foreign affairs).
2. Within the scope of its operations, the national government is supreme.
3. The state governments have the powers not delegated to the central government, except those *denied* to them by the Constitution and their state constitutions.
4. Some powers are specifically denied to *both* the national and state governments; others are specifically denied *only* to the states; still others are denied *only* to the national government.

An Expanding Nation

A great advantage of federalism—and part of the genius and flexibility of our constitutional system—has been the way in which we acquired territory and extended rights and guarantees by means of statehood, commonwealth, or territorial status, and thus grew from 13 to 50 states.

Louisiana Purchase	1803
Florida	1819
Texas	1845
Oregon	1846
Mexican Cession	1848
Gadsden Purchase	1853
Alaska	1867
Hawaii	1898
Philippines	1898–1946
Puerto Rico	1899
Guam	1899
American Samoa	1900
Canal Zone	1904
U.S. Virgin Islands	1917
Pacific Islands Trust Territory	1947

to do what is necessary and proper to do so successfully. Thus the national government has the power to do almost anything not in direct conflict with constitutional guarantees.

The Power to Regulate Interstate and Foreign Commerce Congressional authority extends to all commerce that affects more than one state and to all those activities, wherever they exist or whatever their nature, whose control Congress decides is necessary and proper to regulate interstate and foreign commerce. *Commerce* includes the production, buying, selling, renting, and transporting of goods, services, and properties.[12] The **commerce clause**—Article 1, Section 8, Clause 3—packs a tremendous constitutional punch; it gives Congress the power "to regulate Commerce with foreign Nations, and among the several States, and with the Indian Tribes." In these few words the national government has been able to find constitutional justification for regulating a wide range of human activity, including agriculture, transportation, finance, product safety, labor-relations, and the workplace. Few, if any, aspects of our economy today affect commerce in only one state and are thus outside the scope of the national government's constitutional authority.

The commerce clause can also be used to sustain legislation that goes beyond commercial matters. When the Supreme Court upheld the 1964 Civil Rights Act forbidding discrimination because of race, religion, or national origin in places of public accommodation, it said: "Congress's action in removing the disruptive effect which it found racial discrimination has on interstate travel is not invalidated because Congress was also legislating against what it considers to be moral wrongs." Discrimination restricts the flow of interstate commerce; therefore, Congress could legislate against the discrimination. Moreover, the law could be applied even to local places of public accommodation because local incidents of discrimination have a substantial and harmful impact on interstate commerce. "If it is interstate commerce that feels the pinch, it does not matter how local the operation that applies the squeeze."[13]

After sixty years of almost unquestioned authority to regulate interstate commerce, in the Gun-Free School Zones Act of 1990 banning the possession of a firearm inside school zones, Congress did not even bother to specify how the presence of guns in schools affects interstate commerce. In 1995 the Supreme Court, in the case of *United States v Lopez*, declared that law unconstitutional by a vote of 5 to 4.[14] Chief Justice Rehnquist stated for the majority that not only must Congress show that the possession of guns in schools affects interstate commerce, but it must show that it *substantially* affects interstate commerce. Some commentators called the *Lopez* case "the opening cannonades of a constitutional revolution"; others were doubtful.[15] Most likely it was just a judicial reminder to Congress that it has no general police power to regulate whatever it thinks is in the public interest. As the dissenting justices pointed out, if Congress wants to make it a federal crime to possess a gun in a school, it must make the case, which should not be difficult, that "gun-related violence near the classroom poses a serious economic threat" to interstate commerce.

The Power to Tax and Spend Congress lacks constitutional authority to pass laws solely on the ground that they will promote the general welfare, but it may raise taxes and spend money for this purpose. This distinction between *legislating* and *appropriating* makes little difference most of the time. Congress, for example, lacks constitutional power to regulate education or agriculture directly, yet it does have the power to appropriate money to support education or to pay farm subsidies. By attaching conditions to its grants of money, Congress may thus regulate what it cannot directly control by law.

When Congress puts up the money, it determines how the money will be spent. By withholding or threatening to withhold funds, the national government can influence or control state operations and regulate individual conduct. For example, Congress has stipulated that federal funds should be withdrawn from any program in which any person is denied benefits because of race, color, or national origin; subsequently the categories of sex and physical handicap were added. Congress has also used its power of the purse to force states to raise the drinking age to 21 by tying such a condition to federal dollars for highways. (Louisiana is the only state to refuse to do so.)

Congress frequently requires states to do certain things—for example, provide services to indigent mothers and take action to clean up the air and water—or else Congress will impose even more stringent federal regulations. These requirements are called **federal mandates**. Often, Congress does not supply the funds required to carry out these mandates, and its failure to do so has become an important issue in states facing growing expenditures with limited resources.

These four constitutional pillars—the national supremacy clause, the war power, the power over interstate commerce, and, most especially, the power to tax and spend for the general welfare—have permitted a tremendous expansion of the functions of the national government, so much so that the national government has in effect almost full power to enact any legislation that Congress thinks will promote the general welfare, so long as it does not conflict with those provisions of the Constitution designed to protect individual rights.

The power to regulate interstate commerce allowed Congress to forbid discrimination in places of public accommodation in the 1964 Civil Rights Act.

Powers of the States

The Constitution *reserves for the states* all powers not granted to the national government, subject only to the limitations of the Constitution. Powers not given *exclusively* to the national government, by provision of the Constitution or by judicial interpretation, may be concurrently exercised by the states, as long as there is no conflict with national law. Each state has **concurrent powers** with the national government, such as the power to levy taxes and regulate commerce internal to each state (see Table 2-2).

Precisely how federalism limits the states' taxing powers is not simple to explain or understand. In general, a state may levy a tax on the same item as the national government, but a state cannot, by a tax, "unduly burden" commerce among the states, interfere with a function of the national government, complicate the operation of a national law, or abridge the terms of a treaty of the United States.

TABLE 2-2

The Federal Division of Powers

Types of Powers Delegated to the National Government	Types of Powers Reserved for the States	Some Concurrent Powers Shared by the National and State Governments
• Express powers stated in Constitution • Implied powers that may be inferred from express powers • Inherent powers that allow nation to present a united front to foreign powers	• To create a republican form of government • To charter local governments • To conduct elections • To exercise all powers not delegated to the national government or denied to the states by the Constitution	• To tax citizens and businesses • To borrow and spend money • To establish courts • To pass and enforce laws • To protect civil rights

Federalism issues are even more complicated with states using their so-called police powers to protect the public well-being. Where Congress has not preempted the field, states may even regulate interstate businesses, provided these regulations do not cover matters requiring uniform national treatment or unduly burden interstate commerce. Who decides what matters require uniform national treatment or what actions might place an undue burden on interstate commerce? Congress does, subject to final review by the Supreme Court. When Congress is silent or does not clearly state its intentions, courts—ultimately the Supreme Court—decide if there is a conflict with the national Constitution or if there has been federal preemption by law or regulation.

Constitutional Limits and Obligations

To make federalism work, the Constitution imposes certain restraints on both the national and the state governments. States are prohibited from:

1. Making treaties with foreign governments
2. Authorizing private persons to prey on the shipping and commerce of other nations—what the Constitution refers to as "granting letters of marque and reprisal," a practice common during times of war in the eighteenth century
3. Coining money, issuing bills of credit, or making anything but gold and silver coin a tender in payment of debts

Nor may states without the consent of Congress:

1. Tax imports or exports
2. Tax foreign ships
3. Keep troops or ships in time of peace (except the state militia, now called the National Guard)
4. Enter into compacts with other states or foreign nations that "tend to increase the political power in the States, which may encroach upon or interfere"[16] with the supremacy of the national government
5. Engage in war, unless invaded (an invasion of one state would be an invasion of the United States itself) or in such imminent danger as will not admit of delay.

The national government, in turn, is required by the Constitution to refrain from exercising its powers, especially its powers to tax and to regulate interstate commerce, in such a way as to interfere substantially with the states' abilities to perform their responsibilities. Today, whatever protection states have comes primarily from the political process—in restraints that our system provides because individuals elected from the states participate in the decisions of Congress—rather than from judicially enforced limitations.

The Constitution also requires the national government to guarantee to each state a *republican form of government*. The framers used this term to distinguish a republic from a monarchy, on the one side, and from a pure, direct democracy, on the other. Congress, not the courts, enforces this guarantee and determines what is or is not a republican form of government. By permitting the congressional delegation of a state to take its seat in Congress, Congress in effect acknowledges that the state has the republican form of government guaranteed by the Constitution.

In addition, the national government is obliged by the Constitution to protect states against *domestic insurrection*. Congress has delegated to the president the authority to dispatch troops to put down such insurrections when so requested by the proper state authorities. If there are contesting state authorities, the president decides which are the proper ones.[17] The president does not have to wait, however, for a request from state authorities to send federal troops into a state to enforce federal laws. Today it is hard to imagine a situation of domestic insurrection against a state that would not also involve federal laws.

Horizontal Federalism: Interstate Relations

Three clauses in the Constitution, taken from the Articles of Confederation, require states to give full faith and credit to each other's public acts, records, and judicial proceedings; to extend to each other's citizens the privileges and immunities of their own citizens; and to return persons who are fleeing from justice.

FULL FAITH AND CREDIT The **full faith and credit clause** (Article IV, Section 1), one of the more technical provisions of the Constitution, requires that state courts enforce the civil judgments of the courts of other states and accept their public records and acts as valid. (It does not require states to enforce the criminal laws of other states; in most cases, for one state to enforce the criminal laws of another would raise constitutional issues.) The clause applies especially to noncriminal judicial proceedings, such as enforcement of judicial settlements and court awards.

INTERSTATE PRIVILEGES AND IMMUNITIES Under Article IV, Section 2, states must extend to citizens of other states the privileges and immunities granted to their own citizens, including the protection of the laws, the right to engage in peaceful occupations, access to the courts, and freedom from discriminatory taxes. Further, because of this clause, states may not impose unreasonable *durational residency* requirements, that is, withhold rights to American citizens who have recently moved to the state and thereby have become citizens of that state. For example, a state may not set unreasonable time limits to withhold state-funded medical benefits from new citizens or to keep them from voting. How long a residency requirement may a state impose? A day seems about as long as the Court will tolerate to withhold welfare payments or medical care, 50 days or so for voting privileges, and one year for eligibility for in-state tuition for state-supported colleges and universities.

EXTRADITION In Article IV, Section 2, the Constitution asserts that when individuals charged with crimes have fled from one state to another, the state to which they have fled is to deliver them to the proper officials upon the demand of the executive authority of the state from which they fled. This process is called **extradition**. "The obvious objective of the Extradition Clause," the courts have claimed, "is that no State should become a safe haven for the fugitives from a sister State's criminal justice system."[18] Congress has supplemented this constitutional provision by making the governor of the state to which fugitives have fled the agent responsible for returning them.

Despite their constitutional obligation, governors of asylum states have on occasion refused to honor a request for extradition. So far in modern times no federal judge has had to try to enforce an extradition request. When the governor of Indiana refused to extradite Bobby Knight, the celebrated Indiana University basketball coach who had been convicted in absentia by a Puerto Rican court of assaulting a police officer during the Pan-American Games in Puerto Rico, the governor of Puerto Rico decided to drop the matter.

INTERSTATE COMPACTS The Constitution also requires states to settle disputes with one another without the use of force. States may carry their legal disputes to

Same-Sex Marriages and the Full Faith and Credit Clause

The full faith and credit clause is likely to become an issue of public concern if and when any state (Hawaii seems to be the most likely one) recognizes same-sex marriages. The question then will arise, "Must other states give full faith and credit to such marriages?" The Supreme Court has yet to address this issue squarely, and past precedents provide no clear answer. It is the view of one authority that in light of recent Court rulings showing the present Court's tilt toward states rights and "the fact that marriage has traditionally been an almost exclusive sphere of state authority, the Court would likely maintain the noncentralized and dual nature of American domestic relations that exist today, and allow the states to decide whether to recognize Hawaiian same-sex marriages."*

*John P. Feldmeier, "Federalism and Full Faith and Credit: Must States Recognize Out-of-State Same-Sex Marriages?" *Publius, The Journal of Federalism* 25, no. 4 (Fall 1995), p. 126.

Thinking it Through

It is easier to answer questions about unfunded mandates in the abstract; it is hard when faced with specific problems. We need to get behind the abstraction. When we ask "Should the federal government" or when we talk about "the state," remember, we are talking about our own pocketbook, not somebody else's. The "national government" is just a shorthanded way to ask, "Should we as federal citizens and taxpayers set standards for drinking water, or could we do it better and cheaper at the state level?" The answers to such questions are political in the best sense of the word; that is, they are policy choices, preferences among competing but legitimate values. Nonetheless, when called on to make these policy choices as citizens, we need to be informed so as to increase the probability that we will choose people and policies that will be responsive to our concerns.

Qualifying for In-State Tuition

Financially independent adults who move into a state just before enrolling in a state-supported university or college may be required to prove that they have become citizens of that state and intend to remain after finishing their schooling by supplying such evidence of citizenship as tax payments, a driver's license, car registration, voter registration, and a continuous, year-round off-campus residence. Students who are financially dependent on their parents remain citizens of the state of their parents.

One of the Great Society programs that has survived and is seen as successful is Head Start. Here a Head Start teacher reads to a class.

the Supreme Court, or they may negotiate **interstate compacts**. More often interstate compacts are used to establish interstate agencies to handle interstate problems. Before most interstate compacts become effective, congressional approval is required. After a compact has been signed and approved by Congress, it becomes binding on all signatory states, and its terms are enforceable by the Supreme Court. A typical state belongs to 20 compacts dealing with such subjects as environmental protection, crime control, water rights, and higher education exchanges.[19]

THE POLITICS OF FEDERALISM

This outline of the constitutional structure of federalism is oversimplified and even misleading—especially in terms of the division of powers between the national government and the states. The formal structures of our federal system have not changed much since 1787, but the political realities, especially during the last half-century, have greatly altered how federalism works. To understand these changes, we need to look at some of the trends that continue to fuel the debate about the meaning of federalism.

The Growth of Big Government

Over the past two hundred years there has been a drift of power from other institutions—families, churches and synagogues, the marketplace—to governments, and especially to the national government. "No one planned the growth," explains the Advisory Commission on Intergovernmental Relations, "but everyone played a part in it."[20] How did this come about? For a variety of reasons. One is that many of our problems have become national in scope. Much that was local in 1789, in 1860, or in 1930 is now national—even global. State governments could supervise the relations between small merchants and their few employees, but only the national government can supervise relations between a multinational corporation and its thousands of employees, many organized in national unions.

As industrialization proceeded, powerful interests made demands on the national government. Business groups called on the government for aid in the form of tariffs, a national banking system, and subsidies to railroads and the merchant marine. Farmers learned that the national government could give more aid than the states, and they, too, began to demand help. By the beginning of this century, urban groups in general, and organized labor in particular, pressed their claims. Big business, big agriculture, and big labor all added up to big government.

The growth of the national economy and the creation of a national transportation and communications network altered people's attitudes toward the national government (see Figure 2-3). Before the Civil War, the national government was viewed as a distant, even foreign, government. Today, in part because of television, most people identify as closely with Washington as with their state capitals. We are apt to know more about our president than about our governor, more about our national senators and representatives than about our state legislators or even the local officials who run our cities and schools.

The Great Depression of the 1930s stimulated extensive national action on such issues as welfare, unemployment, and agriculture surpluses. World War II brought federal regulation of wages, prices, and employment, as well as national efforts to allocate resources, train personnel, and support engineering and inventions. After the war the national government helped veterans obtain college degrees and inaugurated a vast system of support for university research. The United States became the most powerful leader of the free world, maintaining substantial military forces even in times of peace. The Great Society programs of the 1960s poured out grants-in-aid to states and localities. City dwellers who had migrated from the rural South to northern cities began to seek federal funds for—at the very least—housing, education, and mass transportation.

Although economic and social conditions created many of the pressures for expansion of the national government, so did political claims. Members of Congress, presidents, federal judges, and federal administrators actively promoted federal initiatives. And until the recent years of overwhelming budget deficits, Congress in particular encouraged this trend. True, when there is widespread conflict about what to do—how to reduce the federal deficit, adopt a national energy policy, reform Social Security, provide health care for the indigent—Congress waits for a national consensus. But when an organized constituency wants something and there is no counterpressure, Congress "responds often to everyone, and with great vigor."[21] Once established, federal programs generate groups with vested interests in promoting, defending, and expanding them. Associations are formed, alliances are made. "In a word, the growth of government has created a constituency of, by, and for government."[22]

The politics of federalism are changing, however, and Congress is pressured to reduce the size and scope of national programs. Tax laws no longer permit automatic increases to compensate for inflation, so Congress faces reduced federal revenues. Second, the cost of entitlements programs such as Social Security and Medicare are going up because there are more older people and they live longer. These programs have widespread public support, and to cut them is politically risky. "With all other options disappearing, it is politically tempting to finance tax cuts by turning over to the states many of the social programs. . .that have become the responsibility of the national government."[23] Thus, it is increasingly tempting for Congress to turn over the problems to the states by using block grants (see Figure 2-4).

The Devolution Revolution[24]

Throughout our history there has been an ebb and flow of power from the states to the national government, with more and more responsibilities vested in Washington. But as we approach the end of this century, there appears to be a trend toward substantial *devolution* of federal functions back to the states and local governments.

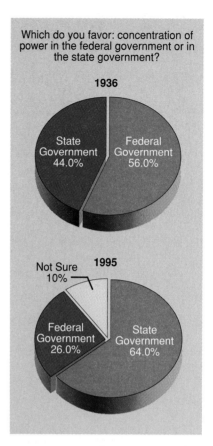

FIGURE 2-3   A Changing View of the Federal Government

SOURCE: Richard P. Nathan, "The Devolution Revolution: An Overview," *The Devolution Revolution* (Rockefeller Institute of Government, 1996).

FIGURE 2-4   Public Trust in Government
SOURCE: Surveys by ABC News/*Washington Post*, March 16–19, 1995.

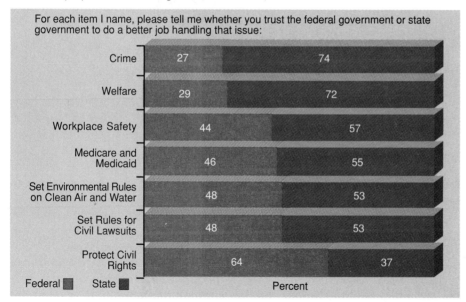

Should the national government be made stronger or weaker?

Should we take major functions from the national government such as welfare and Medicare and give these responsibilities back to the states? If the national government sets the standards, should it provide the funds but leave the details to the states? Do the facts, as you know and perceive them, support the need for federal standards, or can state and local governments be trusted to handle most domestic problems in their own way?

The federal debt now stands at $5 trillion. We have annual budgets of over $1.5 trillion, with annual budgets deficits of $150 billion. The annual budgets are 22 percent of our gross domestic product. Deficits have become a major constraint on the expansion of federal programs. Through adjustments for inflation and the growth in the number of people who qualify, annual outlays for **entitlements** increase each year. (Entitlements are programs such as Social Security and Medicare in which Congress has promised to provide all the funds necessary to all individuals who qualify. Moreover, for most entitlement programs, Congress has also promised to provide an annual cost-of-living adjustment, a COLA.) As a consequence, there is not much room for the federal government to undertake additional programs, even with the reduction of defense expenditures following the end of the cold war.

As the twentieth century comes to a close, despite pressures for the national government to "do something" about urban poverty and crime on the streets, fear of an increase in federal taxes or expansion of the national debt moderates— at least for the moment—the expansion of national government spending. Even so, total federal outlays for fiscal 1997 are $1,519 trillion.[25] That is big government by any measure.

The Republican sweep of the Congress in the 1994 elections carried with it a pledge to return many functions, most especially welfare, back to the states. "Nothing on this scale has ever been attempted before," commented Georgetown University political scientist A. James Richley. Richard Nathan, a longtime student of American federalism, stated, "This is bigger than Lyndon Johnson's Great Society, because it is going to profoundly affect American federalism and social policy."[26]

President Clinton, in his State of the Union Address to the Congress in 1996, agreed with his Republican opponents that "the era of big government is over." However, he tempered his comments by saying, "But we cannot go back to the time when our citizens were left to fend for themselves." He vetoed many congressional proposals for returning major programs to the states, insisting that the federal government continue to guarantee funds for Medicare and student loans and grants. Then, in the summer of 1996, as the elections approached, Congress and the president finally came together on a major overhaul of welfare with the adoption of the Personal Responsibility and Work Opportunity Reconciliation Act of 1996. This act, while retaining Medicaid as a federally funded entitlement program, gives states the option to deny Medicaid to immigrants, even those legally here. But the act ended the 61-year-old federally backed guarantee of welfare checks to all eligible mothers and children and substituted for it a block grant to each state, with caps on the amount of federal dollars that the state will receive.

The Great Debate—Centralists versus Decentralists

The growth of big government was not without constitutional controversy. During the Great Depression of the 1930s, the nation debated whether Congress had the constitutional authority to enact legislation on agriculture, labor, education, housing, and welfare. Only 40 years ago some questioned the constitutional authority of Congress to legislate against racial discrimination. The debate continues, although no longer couched primarily in constitutional terms, between **centralists**, those who favor national action (or as we used to call them, *nationalists*) and **decentralists**, those who favor action at the state and local levels (or by the old-fashioned name, *states' righters*). The victory for the nationalists is relatively recent and not likely to be the last word. Throughout our history and into the present, powerful groups have favored states' rights, and they still do today.

The constitutional arguments revolving around federalism grew out of specific political issues: Did the national government have the authority to outlaw slavery in the territories? Did states have the authority to operate racially segregated schools? Could Congress regulate labor relations? The debates were frequently phrased in constitutional language, with appeals to the great principles of federalism. But they were also arguments over who gets what, where, and how.

Among those favoring the decentralist or states' rights interpretation, with varying emphasis, were Thomas Jefferson, John C. Calhoun, the Supreme Court from the 1920s to 1937, and more recently, Ronald Reagan, George Bush, Bob Dole, the Republican leaders of Congress, most especially the House of Representatives, Chief Justice William H. Rehnquist, Justices Antonin Scalia, Clarence Thomas, and Sandra Day O'Connor. Most decentralists contend that the Constitution is a treaty among sovereign states that created the central government and gave it carefully limited authority. As Justice Thomas, a modern-day ardent decentralist, wrote in his recent dissenting opinion supporting the argument that a state has the power to impose limits on terms of members of Congress, "The ultimate source of the Constitution's authority is the consent of the people of each individual State, not the consent of the undifferentiated people of the Nation as a whole."[27] Thus, the national government is nothing more than an agent of the states, and every one of its powers should be narrowly defined. Any question about whether the states have given a particular function to the central government or have reserved it for themselves should be resolved in favor of the states.

Decentralists hold that the national government should not be permitted to exercise its delegated powers in a way that interferes with activities reserved for the states. The Tenth Amendment, they claim, makes this clear: "The powers not delegated to the United States by the Constitution, nor prohibited by it to the States, are reserved to the States respectively, or to the people." Decentralists insist state governments are closer to the people and reflect the people's wishes more accurately than does the national government. The national government, they add, is inherently heavy-handed and bureaucratic; to preserve our federal system and our liberties, central authority must be kept under control.

The centralist position has been supported by Chief Justice John Marshall, Abraham Lincoln, Theodore Roosevelt, Franklin Roosevelt, and throughout most of our history by the Supreme Court. Centralists reject the whole idea of the Constitution as an interstate compact. Rather, they view the Constitution as a supreme law established by the people. The national government is an agent of the people, not of the states, because it was the people who drew up the Constitution and created the national government. The sovereign people gave the national government sufficient power to accomplish the great objectives listed in the Preamble to the Constitution. They intended that the central government's powers should be liberally defined and that the central government should be denied authority only when the Constitution clearly prohibits it from acting.

Centralists argue that the national government is a government of all the people and that each state speaks for only some of the people. Although the Tenth Amendment clearly reserves powers for the states, as Chief Justice Harlan Stone said, "The Tenth Amendment states but a truism that all is retained which has not been surrendered."[28] The amendment does not deny the national government the right to exercise to the fullest extent all the powers given to it by the Constitution. On the other hand, the supremacy of the national government, it is argued, restricts the states, because governments representing part of the people cannot be allowed to interfere with a government representing all of them.

Chief Justice Rehnquist, joined by Justices Antonin Scalia, Clarence Thomas, Sandra Day O'Connor and frequently Justice Anthony Kennedy, have veered the Court back to a more decentralist position. President Clinton's two appointees, Justices Ruth Bader Ginsburg and Stephen Breyer, joined by Justices David Souter and John Paul Stevens are resisting this movement back to a states' rights

Thinking it Through

The great debate about which level of government can best perform functions continues to rage. The Republican party started its history as the party of the National Union, while the Democrats were then the champion of states rights. For the past several decades there has been a switch. After winning majority status in Congress in 1994, Republicans led the charge on Washington, demanding the return of functions back to the states. Although Democrats are not strong champions of the national government, they tend to be reluctant about removing all federal standards, especially with respect to regulation of the environment and of the workplace, and they tend to be in favor of providing minimum standards for programs, especially welfare and health care.

Centralists' Arguments

1. State and local officials tend to be less competent than national officials.
2. State and local officials tend to be concerned only with the interests of their own areas.
3. State and local governments are unable or unwilling to raise taxes needed to carry out vital government functions.
4. State and local governments are more apt to reflect local racial and ethnic biases as well as the biases of dominant local industries.
5. State and local governments are afraid to regulate industries for fear the industries will move elsewhere.

Decentralists' Arguments

1. Increased urbanization has made states more responsive to the needs of city people.
2. In recent years state and local governments have shown greater willingness to raise taxes than the national government.
3. State and local governments have become as sensitive to the needs of the poor and minorities as is the national government.
4. State and local governments have reformed and modernized and thus become more effective governments.

interpretation of our federal system. However, the Court is so narrowly divided on federalism issues that the outcome of the debate may well turn on the views of the next appointees.

THE ROLE OF THE FEDERAL COURTS

The political process ultimately decides how power will be divided between the national and the state governments. Still, the federal courts—and especially the Supreme Court—have often been called on to umpire the ongoing debate about which level of government should do what, for whom, and to whom. This role for the Courts was claimed in the celebrated case of *McCulloch v Maryland*.

McCulloch versus Maryland

In *McCulloch v Maryland* (1819), the Supreme Court had the first of many chances to choose between a centralist and a decentralist interpretation of our federal system.[29] Maryland had levied a tax against the Baltimore branch of the Bank of the United States, a semipublic agency established by Congress. James William McCulloch, the cashier of the bank, refused to pay on the grounds that a state could not tax an instrument of the national government. Maryland's attorneys responded that, in the first place, the national government did not have the power to incorporate a bank, but even if it did, the state had the power to tax it.

Maryland was represented before the Court by some of the country's most distinguished lawyers, including Luther Martin, a delegate to the Constitutional Convention. Martin left the convention early when it became apparent that a strong national government was in the making. Basing his argument on the states' rights view of federalism, Martin said the power to incorporate a bank is not expressly delegated to the national government. He maintained that the necessary and proper clause gives Congress only the power to choose those means and to pass those laws absolutely essential to the execution of its expressly granted powers. Because a bank is not absolutely necessary to the exercise of any of its delegated powers, Congress has no authority to establish it. As for Maryland's right to tax the bank, Martin's position was clear: The power to tax is one of the powers reserved to the states; they may use it as they see fit.

The national government was represented by equally distinguished counsel, chief among whom was Daniel Webster. Webster conceded the power to create a bank is not one of the express powers of the national government. However, the power to pass laws *necessary and proper* to carry out Congress's express powers is specifically delegated to Congress. This delegation of implied powers should be interpreted to mean Congress has authority to enact any legislation convenient and useful for carrying out its delegated national powers. Therefore, Congress may incorporate a bank as an appropriate, convenient, and useful means of exercising the granted powers of collecting taxes, borrowing money, and caring for the property of the United States.

Although the power to tax is reserved to the states, Webster argued that states cannot use their reserved powers to interfere with the operations of the national government. The Constitution leaves no room for doubt; in cases of conflict between the national and state governments, the national government is supreme.

Speaking for a unanimous Court, Chief Justice John Marshall rejected every one of Maryland's contentions. He wrote:

> We must never forget that it is a constitution we are expounding . . . a constitution intended to endure for ages to come, and consequently, to be adapted to the various crises of human affairs. . . . The government of the Union, then, . . . is,

emphatically, and truly, a government of the people. In form and substance it emanates from them. Its powers are granted by them, and are to be exercised directly on them, and for their benefit. . . . It can never be to their interest and cannot be presumed to have been their intention, to clog and embarrass its execution, by withholding the most appropriate means.

Marshall summarized his views on the powers of the national government in these now-famous words: "Let the end be legitimate, let it be within the scope of the Constitution, and all means which are appropriate, which are plainly adapted to that end, which are not prohibited, but consist with the letter and spirit of the constitution, are constitutional."

Having thus established the doctrine of *implied national powers,* Marshall set forth the doctrine of **national supremacy**. No state, he said, can use its reserved taxing powers to tax a national instrument. "The power to tax involves the power to destroy. . . . If the right of the states to tax the means employed by the general government be conceded, the declaration that the Constitution, and the laws made in pursuance thereof, shall be the supreme law of the land, is empty and unmeaning declamation."

The long-range significance of *McCulloch v Maryland* in providing support for the developing forces of nationalism cannot be overstated. The arguments of the states' righters, if accepted, would have strapped the national government in a constitutional straitjacket and denied it powers needed to handle the problems of an expanding nation.

An Expanding Role for the Federal Courts

The authority of federal judges to review the activities of state and local governments has expanded dramatically in recent decades because of modern judicial interpretations of the Thirteenth, Fourteenth, and Fifteenth Amendments (especially the Fourteenth) and the congressional legislation enacted to implement these amendments. Today almost every action by state and local officials is subject to challenge before a federal judge as a violation of the Constitution or of federal law.

In carrying out their judgments, federal judges sometimes have, in effect, taken over the supervision of state prison systems, public hospitals, public schools, and other public facilities. Although a more recent decision called the validity of this holding in doubt, the Supreme Court has gone so far as to sustain a federal judge's right to order a local school board in Missouri to ignore the state's constitutional constraints and to raise taxes and sell bonds to fund the operation of a racially integrated magnet school.[30]

One of the major instruments for opening these issues for federal court review is the Supreme Court's revitalization—some would say rewriting—during recent decades of an 1871 civil rights act originally written to combat the Ku Klux Klan. This act (now called Section 1983 after its designation in Title 42 of the United States Code) permits individuals to go into federal court to sue cities and counties for damages or seek injunctions against any person acting under the color of law—that is in an official capacity—who they believe has deprived them of any right secured by the Constitution or by any one of the several thousands of federal laws.[31] Although federal judges can order states to stop acting in a manner that violates the federal Constitution or laws or treaties, the Eleventh Amendment constrains federal courts from hearing damage suits against the states, but not against local government officials.

Federal judges have also become agencies to enforce federal mandates. Any citizen can now sue a state to make it carry out these duties. For example, doctors and hospitals may sue a state to force it to provide "reasonable" reimbursement

From 1937 until 1995 the Supreme Court took most of the constitutional issues arising from federalism out of play. The Court gave an expansive interpretation of the commerce clause, allowing Congress to exercise whatever powers it thought necessary to promote the common good. In 1985, by a 5 to 4 vote, in *Garcia v. San Antonio Metro*, the Supreme Court in essence told federal courts to get out of the business of protecting the states from congressional interference. Congress, not the courts, said the court majority, decides which actions of the states should be regulated by the national government.* And in interpreting the restraints on the states' right to regulate any aspect of interstate commerce, the Supreme Court deferred to congressional judgment about what the states were allowed to do without being called to task for infringing on congressional territory.

In 1995 the Supreme Court dealt with two major federalism issues in a way that called into question whether future federal courts will remain passive in resolving state's rights issues. In the first of these two important cases the Supreme Court, for the first time in sixty years, declared an act of Congress unconstitutional because Congress lacked authority under the commerce clause. In this case, the Gun-Free School Zones Act of 1990, Congress had made it a federal offense "for any individual knowingly to possess a firearm at a place that the individual knows, or has reasonable cause to believe, is a school zone."

Speaking for four other justices, Chief Justice Rehnquist declared the law unconstitutional. He conceded that Congress has wide powers to regulate state or private activities that affect interstate commerce, but there are, he argued, some limits, and "the proper test requires an analysis of whether the regulated activity 'substantially affects' interstate commerce."** The dissenters pointed out how inconsistent this ruling was with those of the Supreme Court from John Marshall's time to today, except for the decades just prior to the Civil War and from about 1896 to 1937, when a state's rights interpretation of the Constitution had prevailed.

It is likely that if Congress had been more careful in documenting why it had the constitutional authority to regulate guns around schools, this legislation would have been sustained. Congress, after sixty years of no serious questioning of its right to act under the commerce clause, made almost no findings in the Gun-Control Act of why it felt compelled to act.

as required by federal Medicare law.[32] Parents may sue a state for allegedly failing to provide their disabled children with a "free appropriate public education" or otherwise reimburse such parents for tuition in a private school.

Federal judges spend a considerable portion of their time deciding cases in which the central issue is whether some provisions of federal laws have preempted state and local action. **Preemption** occurs when a federal law or regulation takes over and precludes enforcement of a state or local law or regulation. State and local laws are preempted not only when they conflict directly with federal laws and regulations, but also if they touch a field in which the "federal interest is so dominant that the federal system will be assumed to preclude enforcement of state laws on the same subject."[33] Examples of federal preemption include the Coast Guard Authorization Act directing the secretary of transportation to develop standards for determining when people are considered intoxicated while operating a marine recreational vessel; dozens of laws regulating hazardous substances, water quality, and clean air standards; and many civil rights acts, most especially the Civil Rights Act of 1964 and the Voting Rights Act of 1965.

Over the years federal judges, under the leadership of the Supreme Court, have favored national powers (including their own). However, recently the Supreme Court has returned to the states several explosive political issues. Perhaps most notably in 1989 in *Webster v Reproductive Health Services*, and in 1992 in *Planned Parenthood v Casey*, the Court gave states considerable latitude to regulate abortion, setting off intense clashes between pro-choice and right-to-life groups in the state legislatures.[34]

Despite the Supreme Court's bias in favor of national over state authority, few would deny the Supreme Court the power to review and set aside state actions. As Justice Oliver Wendell Holmes once remarked: "I do not think the United States would come to an end if we lost our power to declare an Act of Congress void. I do think the Union would be imperiled if we could not make that declaration as to the laws of the several States."[35]

FEDERALISM AND THE USE OF FEDERAL GRANTS

Congress authorizes programs, establishes general rules for how the programs will operate, and decides whether and how much room should be left for state or local discretion. Most important, Congress appropriates the funds for these programs and, until recently, has had deeper pockets than even the richest states. One of Congress's most potent tools for influencing policy at the state and local levels has been the federal grant.

Types of Federal Grants

There are three types of federal grants presently being administered: categorical-formula grants, project grants, and block grants (or as the Clinton administration calls them, flexible grants). From 1972 to 1982 we had revenue sharing—federal grants to state and local governments to be used at their discretion and subject only to very general conditions. But when, in the second Reagan administration (1985-89), federal budget deficits soared and there was no revenue to share, revenue sharing was terminated—to the states in 1986 and to local governments in 1987.

CATEGORICAL-FORMULA GRANTS Congress appropriates funds for specific purposes, such as school lunches and the building of airports and highways. These funds are allocated by formula and are subject to detailed federal conditions, often on a matching basis; that is, the government receiving the federal funds must put up some of its own dollars. Categorical grants, in addition, provide federal supervision to ensure that the federal dollars are spent as Congress wants. There are hundreds of grant programs, but two dozen, including Medicaid and Aid to Families with Dependent Children, account for almost 85 percent of total spending for categoricals.

PROJECT GRANTS Congress appropriates a certain sum, which is allocated to state and local units and sometimes to nongovernmental agencies based on applications from those who wish to participate. Examples are grants by the National Science Foundation to universities and research institutes to support the work of scientists or grants to states and localities to support training and employment programs.

BLOCK GRANTS While categorical grants provide whatever federal funds are needed to support persons who qualify for the funds, block grants, on the other hand, are usually capped. Block grants are broad grants to states for prescribed activities—welfare, child care, education, social services, preventive health, and health services—with only a few specific strings attached. States have great flexibility in deciding how to spend block-grant dollars, but when the federal funds for any fiscal year are gone, there are no more matching federal dollars.

Block grants are favored by Republicans and governors but opposed by many Democratic members of Congress and big-city mayors. Big-city mayors oppose block grants because such grants threaten to take both dollars and discretion from them. They also deprive members of Congress of the opportunity to take credit for grants to their particular districts. As a result, until the Republican takeover of Congress in 1994, most proposals for block grants did not get far. Now, with not enough federal dollars to go around, Congress is much more willing to turn over to state governors and legislatures the task of deciding how to allocate scarce dollars.

This move to block grants marks a fundamental realignment of the relationship between the national and state governments. It is also likely to lead to greater disparities in welfare and other programs among the states.[36] The new welfare block grants give states considerable flexibility in how they provide for welfare, but there are some federal strings attached. Most important, no federal funds can be used to cover recipients who do not go to work within two years, and no persons can receive federally supported benefits for more than five years. And in order to slow down "the race to the bottom" in which states may try to make themselves "the least attractive state in which to be poor,"[37] Congress also stipulated that in order for states to receive their full share of federal dollars, they must continue to spend at least 75 percent of what they have been spending on welfare.[38]

The Politics of Federal Grants

Arguments about the form of federal aid involve more than questions of efficiency. They reflect differences about what constitutes desirable public policy, where power should be located, and who will gain or lose by the various types of grants. And the debate is not just a dispute over whether state and local governments can be trusted to spend federal dollars wisely. It is also a debate about which state and local officials should be given control over the spending.

Specialists who work for state and local governments often have more in common with their fellow specialists working for the national government

The Rehnquist Revolution (continued)

The second case, dealing with term limits, questioned a state's right to add qualifications for serving in the Congress. The Court again returned to first principles of federalism. Justice Stevens, writing for the five-person majority, built his argument on the concept of the federal union as a compact among the people and the national government serving as their agent.[†] Justice Clarence Thomas, writing for the minority of four, espoused a view of federalism not heard from a justice of the Supreme Court since prior to the New Deal. He would interpret the Tenth Amendment as requiring the national government to justify its actions in terms of an enumerated power and granting to the states all other powers not granted to the national government.

In the very next term, in a third case, *Seminole Tribe of Florida v. Florida,*[††] the court majority—Chief Justice Rehnquist and Justices O'Connor, Scalia, Kennedy, and Thomas—again declared that Congress had exceeded its powers. This time the Court declared that the Indian commerce clause did not empower Congress, in the face of the Eleventh Amendment, to authorize federal courts to hear suits brought against states by Indian tribes. The effect of this decision goes beyond Indian tribes. Except to enforce rights stemming from the Fourteenth Amendment, which the Court explicitly acknowledges is within Congress's power, Congress may no longer authorize individuals to bring suits in federal courts against states.

Garcia v San Antonio Metro, 469 US 528 (1985).

**United States v Lopez*, 131 L Ed 2d 626 (1995).

†*U.S. Term Limits, Inc. v Thornton*, 131 L Ed 2d 881 (1995).

††*Seminole Tribe of Florida v Florida*, 134 L Ed 2d 2542 (1996).

than they do with their own governors, mayors, or state legislators. These specialists (highway engineers, welfare administrators, educators) confer at meetings, read common journals, and jointly defend the independence of their programs from attempts by elected national or state officials to regulate them.[39] When interest groups, congressional committee staffers, and federal bureaucrats (who in turn are connected to state and local bureaucrats) join forces, they create **issue networks or iron triangles**, and they can be very effective in protecting programs.[40]

Republicans "have consistently favored fewer strings, less federal supervision, and the delegation of spending discretion to the state and local governments."[41] The Republican-controlled 104th Congress, although giving high priority to the creation of block grants, ran into trouble in trying to lump together welfare, school lunch and breakfast programs, prenatal nutrition programs, and child protection programs in one block grant. They did, however, succeed in making the main cash welfare program, Assistance to Families with Dependent Children (AFDC), into a block grant, and the major federal child care program into another such grant. But despite their avowed support for local discretion, Republican conservatives insisted upon some restrictions—for example, to prevent states from using federal funds to give welfare assistance to additional children born to welfare mothers and to make immigrants ineligible for many welfare programs or not to receive food stamps until they became citizens or worked in the United States for ten years.

The battle over the appropriate level of government to control the funds tends to be cyclical. A scholar of federalism explains, "Complaints about excessive federal control tend to be followed by proposals to shift more power to state and local governments. Then, when problems arise in state and local administration—and problems inevitably arise when any organization tries to administer anything—demands for closer federal supervision and tighter federal controls follow."[42]

REGULATORY FEDERALISM
AND FEDERAL MANDATES

Fewer federal dollars did not mean fewer federal controls. On the contrary, the federal government imposed mandates on states and local governments, often without any offsetting federal funds. State and local officials complained that new federal regulatory devices were far more intrusive than the old-fashioned conditions they used to complain about.[43] One observer concluded, "The role of Congress has changed since 1965 from a generous supplier of funds to a preemptor imposing costs that have the potential for bankrupting many small rural local governments and fiscally strained cities by the year 2000."[44] Nobody knows for sure how much unfunded federal mandates cost, but one study concludes that they may impose a cost on states and cities of $90 billion over the next five years[45] (see Figure 2-5).

Protests from state and local officials against unfunded federal mandates were effective. President Clinton issued an executive order prohibiting federal agencies from issuing regulations that impose unfunded mandates on states and localities, and in 1995 Congress, with President Clinton's support, passed the Unfunded Mandates Reform Act of 1995.[46] The act calls on the Advisory Commission on Intergovernmental Relations, the Congressional Budget Office, and federal agencies to issue reports about the impact of unfunded mandates and to provide judicially enforceable cost-benefit analyses of mandates and regulations, as well to consult state and local officials prior to the issuance of regulations. In addition, the act imposes constraints on Congress itself. A congressional committee that approves any legislation containing a federal mandate must draw attention to the mandate in its report and describe its cost on state and local governments as well as on private companies. If the committee intends any mandate to be partially unfunded, it must explain why it is appropriate for the cost to be borne by the state and local government. With many significant exceptions—such as laws or regulations enforcing constitutional rights, prohibiting discrimination, requiring compliance with accounting and auditing procedures—any member of Congress may raise a point of order against proposals for unfunded mandates.

Whether the Unfunded Mandate Reform Act significantly slows downs federal mandates remains to be seen. The Americans with Disabilities Act, for example, calls on state and local governments to build ramps and alter curbs—renovations that will cost millions. The Environmental Protection Agency regulations require states to build automobile pollution-testing stations and take other actions to reduce pollution, but without corresponding federal dollars. Will the states put up a battle against such expenses? Will the courts sustain their objections?

New Techniques of Federal Control

DIRECT ORDERS In a few instances, federal regulation takes the form of direct orders that must be complied with under threat of criminal or civil sanction. Examples are the Equal Opportunity Act of 1982, barring job discrimination by state and local governments because of race, color, religion, sex, and national origin, and the Marine Protection Amendments of 1977, prohibiting cities from dumping sewage into the ocean. Because such direct orders raise mild constitutional concerns and more serious political ones, Congress favors other techniques for imposing the federal will on the states.

Goals of Federal Grants

Federal grants serve four purposes, of which the most important is the fourth:

1. To supply state and local governments with revenue

2. To establish minimum national standards for such things as highways and clean air

3. To equalize resources among the states by taking, through federal taxes, money from people with high incomes and spending it, through grants, in states where the poor live

4. To attack national problems yet minimize the growth of federal agencies.

FIGURE 2-5 The Curtailment of Federal Aid

SOURCE: Advisory Commission on Intergovernmental Relations, *Significant Features of Fiscal Federalism*, Vol. 2 (Government Printing Office, 1992), p. 60.

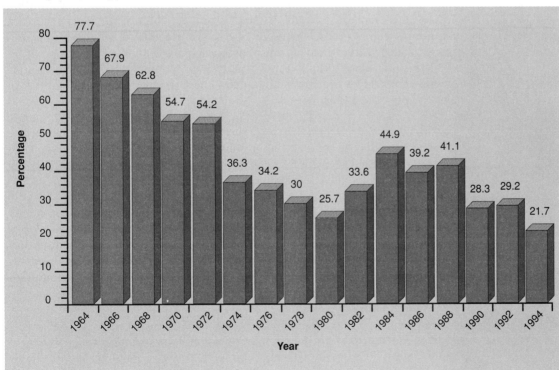

From Coast to Coast

Fiscal Capacity to Raise Revenue Through Taxes

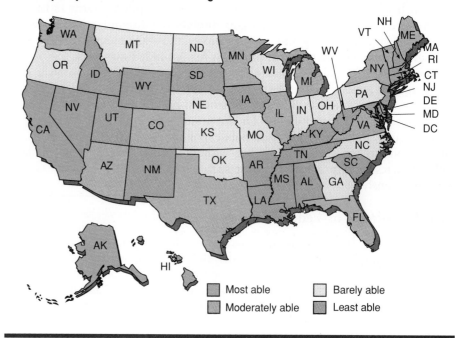

■ Most able	□ Barely able
■ Moderately able	■ Least able

SOURCE: Advisory Commission on Intergovernmental Relations, *Significant Features of Fiscal Federalism*, Vol. 2, (Government Printing Office, 1992), p. 268.

CROSS-CUTTING REQUIREMENTS   The first and most famous of these requirements (so-called because a condition on one federal grant is extended to all activities supported by federal funds regardless of their source) is Title VI of the 1964 Civil Rights Act, which holds that no person may be discriminated against in the use of federal funds because of race, color, national origin, sex, or handicapped status. More than 60 cross-cutting requirements concern the environment, historic preservation, contract wage rates, access to governmental information, the care of experimental animals, the treatment of human subjects in research projects, and so on.

CROSS-OVER SANCTIONS   These sanctions permit the use of federal dollars in one program to influence state and local policy in another. One example is a 1984 act that threatened to reduce federal highway aid by up to 15 percent for any state that failed to adopt a minimum drinking age of 21 by 1987.

TOTAL PREEMPTION   This kind of control rests not on the national government's power to spend but on its powers under the supremacy and commerce clauses to preempt conflicting state and local activities. Building on this constitutional authority, federal law in certain areas just preempts state and local governments from the field. "There are fourteen types of total preemption laws, ranging from ones removing all regulatory powers from the states to ones authorizing states to cooperate in enforcing a statute."[47]

PARTIAL PREEMPTION   In these instances federal law establishes basic policies but requires states to administer them. Some programs give states an option to participate, but if a state chooses not to do so the national government then steps in and directly runs the programs. Even worse from the state's point of view is *mandatory partial preemption*, in which the national government requires the state to act on peril of losing other funds but provides no funds to support the state action. The Clean Air Act of 1990 is an example of mandatory partial preemption; the federal government sets national air quality standards and requires states to devise plans and pay for their implementation and enforcement.[48] If a state fails to adopt air pollution plans that are deemed to be adequate, so-called hammer provisions require federal implementation plans to be imposed on the state.[49] State violations of the clean air requirements can be "punished" by a variety of sanctions, including withholding of federal funds for a variety of purposes. Medicaid is another example of the national government providing some dollars but mandating states to provide services that cost more than the federal funds cover.

These new forms of federal regulation accelerated during the 1970s and abated only slightly during the 1980s. More than half the federal statutes preempting state and local authority have been enacted in the last two decades.[50] Despite the Reagan-Bush emphasis on retrenchment of federal regulations, their administrations sought national controls to force states to adopt drunk-driving legislation, to cut off federal funds to cities enacting rent controls, and to force on states and localities certain busing, abortion, and school prayer policies.

Liberals and conservatives alike tend to favor fewer federal controls over state and local officials in the abstract, yet are willing to make exceptions in policy areas when they feel strongly something must be done to correct or prevent an injustice. Because there are plenty of injustices, federal regulation of state and local governments remains a continuing feature of our political system.

POLITICS AND FEDERALISM: A LOOK TO THE FUTURE

The ongoing debate about federalism can be understood on several levels. On one level, it is an argument about which government can most effectively deal with a particular problem—the national government or the states. On another

Steve Benson, Arizona Republic.

level, it is an attempt by interest groups to find the forum—Washington or their state capitals—where they have the greatest chance of a sympathetic hearing. And on yet another level, it is a debate about the best way to protect liberty and promote equality.[51]

Until the civil rights revolution of the 1960s, for example, segregationists feared that national officials—responding to different political majorities—would work for racial integration. Thus they praised local government, emphasized the dangers of overcentralization, and argued that the protection of civil rights was not a proper function of the national government. As one political scientist observes, "Federalism has a dark history to overcome. For nearly two hundred years, states' rights have been asserted to protect slavery, segregation, and discrimination."[52]

Today the politics of federalism, even with respect to civil rights, is more complicated than in the past.[53] With changing political power distributions, the national government is not necessarily more favorable to the claims of minorities than most state or city governments. With the Supreme Court's abandonment of rigorous constitutional protection for women's right to abortions and its refusal to extend marital privacy rights to gays and lesbians, some state constitutions and state courts now provide more protection for these rights than does the U.S. Constitution. State and local governments also "have become the principal agents for advancing the cause of comparable worth. This role challenges the conventional wisdom that only centrist alternatives can advance equal opportunity and civil rights for all citizens."[54]

As states more actively regulate the economy, some business interests have been arguing that conflicting state regulations are unduly burdening interstate commerce and are asking for preemptive federal regulation to save them, not only from stringent state regulations but from having to adjust to 50 different state laws.[55] "One national dumb rule is better than 50 inconsistent rules of any kind," says a lawyer who represents trade groups in the food industries and medical devices.[56]

The Reemergence of the States

When the national government slowed the rate of growth of its domestic spending, the states took over some of its responsibilities.[57] "Instead of getting government off the backs of the American people," Ronald Reagan "presided over a huge growth of big government at the state level."[58] Not only were programs shifted to the states, so were the costs of running them. For example, in 1970 Medicaid cost the states about 4 percent of their budgets; now it is in excess of 20 percent.[59] If given more responsibilitiy for Medicare and Medicaid, "states will have to go through an unbelievable transformation. The states will have to write laws to define disability and benefits. . .design new application forms. . .redo computer programs, cope with new political pressures."[60]

Abandoned by the national government, cities and counties turned again to their own state capitals. States responded to this plea with mixed results. Some states—Florida, Massachusetts, New Jersey, New York, and Oklahoma—tried with some success to replace the withdrawn federal funds for their cities and schools until they, too, fell upon hard times in the early 1990s. Other states— California, for example—made little effort to replace the federal dollars.[61] Higher education was hard hit in most states, while spending on corrections was up. "Medicaid was at the heart of state fiscal policy during these years."[62] States shifted funding to the Medicaid program in order to get the matching federal dollars they needed to avoid reductions in other programs or having to raise taxes.

By the 1990s, states were staggering under these additional burdens and were forced to raise taxes, lower the level of services, or use mandates to make local governments provide additional services without state aid.[63] These fiscal realities and the economic recession of the early 1990s stalled the states' resurgence.[64] Their costs for education, for welfare, for prisons, for health care were going up much faster than their revenues. The rate of growth of state governments had slowed; the rate of growth of the problems they faced had not. Nonetheless, the states reestablished their balanced budgets and had a combined surplus of $18 billion in 1994, while the federal government had a deficit in excess of 160 billion.[65]

Block grants give large sums to the states, and also major obligations. Some are concerned that this shift of responsibility back to the states may in fact create 50 budget crises. The coming years will be a severe test for the states, especially for their legislatures, many of which consist of citizen lawmakers. "State legislatures are much more competent than they were 25 years ago. They do have much more ability to make the important decisions, but that doesn't mean they are magicians."[66]

The Future of Federalism

In 1933, seeing state governments helpless during the Great Depression, one writer stated, "I do not predict that the states will go, but affirm that they have gone."[67] Those prophets of doom were wrong. States are stronger than ever. During recent decades state governments have undergone "a major transformation." Most have improved their governmental structures, taken on greater roles in funding education, launched programs to help distressed cities, and—despite new constitutional limitations—expanded their tax bases. Able men and women have been attracted to many governorships. "Today, states, in formal representational, policymaking, and implementation terms at least, are more representative, more responsive, more activist, and more professional in their operations than they ever have been. They face their expanded roles better equipped to assume and fulfill them."[68]

The national government, however, is not likely to retreat to a pre-1930 posture or even a pre-1960 one. The underlying economic and social conditions that generated the demand for federal action have not substantially altered. On the contrary, in addition to such traditional issues as helping people find jobs and preventing inflation and depressions that still require national action, countless new issues have been added to the national agenda by the growth of a global economy based on high technology, service, and information. It is worth remembering that in terms of gross domestic product, many American states are larger than many nations—California, for example, has an economy larger than that of Great Britain—yet most states still lack the jurisdiction by themselves to clean up the air, modernize the air traffic control system, regulate the economy, prevent pollution of rivers, deal with drug abuse, or prevent the spread of AIDS and find its cure. And there are issues such as the lack of decent housing and access to health care for inner-city African Americans and Hispanics and the skyrocketing costs of health care for all Americans that are beyond the capacity of the states to solve alone.

One prominent student of federalism has written: "On the whole, the problems of American federalism have been greatly exaggerated. The state and local fiscal crises caused by the 1991 recession now seem to be temporary phenomena, not a harbinger of a torturous future. The national government is at least for the moment concentrating more on what it does best: caring for the sick, the poor, and the needy. State and local governments continue to foster the country's economic development."[69] Whether this division of labor continues depends in large part on the outcome of our elections.

Most Americans have strong attachments to our federal system—in the abstract. They remain loyal to their states and show a growing and healthy skepticism about the national government. In the thirty years since 1964, distrust in the federal government has grown from 22 percent of the people to 78 percent of the people. Yet most of the time for most of the people, the concerns are about more immediate problems—clean air, safety in the streets, relations between men and women, jobs, the cost of medical care, heating fuel for their homes, and gasoline for their cars. They are not much concerned about the nature of federal grants or arguments about the virtues of national versus state action. "Some evidence suggests that the anti-government, anti-Washington consensus is 3,000 miles wide but only a few miles deep."[70] Most Americans are willing to use whatever governmental agencies or combinations of agencies they feel can best serve their needs and represent their interests.

American federalism has modified, and been modified by, the political and social issues facing us during the last two hundred years. It will continue to shape our society. Our federal system remains firmly rooted in our political system as well as our constitutional democracy. We are not about to abolish it or modify it drastically. But just as the federalism of today is as different from that of 1787 as a jet airplane is from a stagecoach, so federalism will continue to evolve as we move into the twenty-first century.

SUMMARY

1. Our federal constitutional system has evolved into something only slightly different in form, yet significantly different in operation, from the 1789 version.

2. It is not possible to divide functions between the national and state governments neatly and noncontroversially.

3. The national government has the constitutional authority to do whatever Congress thinks is necessary and proper to promote the general welfare and to provide for the common defense.

4. Although the Supreme Court has put forward some cautionary warnings, there are few if any judicially enforced limits to restrain Congress from interfering with the actions of the states.

5. Today we no longer spend much time debating the constitutional structure of federalism; we have moved on to the politics of federalism. As now interpreted, the Constitution gives voters the option to decide through the political process what to do, who is going to pay, and who is going to get it done.

6. The centralization of constitutional power at the national level over the last two centuries does not mean that federalism is dead. Political power remains dispersed, and states remain active and significant political realities.

7. An individual's ideological bias in favor of either national or state action is likely to reflect concrete political objectives. However, conservative support for states'

rights and liberal preference for national action are no longer predictable as shifting political issues lead to shifting allegiances among the various levels of government.

8. The drive toward a greater role for the national government has been fueled more by underlying economic and social changes than by concerns about federalism, but we detect a vigorous trend toward the view that federalism as a political principle is worthy of being preserved.

9. The major instruments of federal intervention have been various kinds of financial grants-in-aid, of which the most prominent are categorical-formula grants, project grants, and block grants.

10. The national government controls the activities of state and local governments and creates national programs by direct orders, cross-over sanctions in the use of federal funds, total preemption, and partial preemption.

11. In the 1990s the underlying political struggles between Republicans and Democrats, combined with a very tight federal budget, have kept Congress from inaugurating new federal programs and put pressure on it to shift some existing programs back to the states.

12. These political realities have accelerated trends that started in the 1970s. We may be in the midst of a Devolution Revolution, but how many functions will be turned over to the states and for how long waits further political and economic developments.

FURTHER READING

ADVISORY COMMISSION ON INTERGOVERNMENTAL RELATIONS, *Intergovernmental Perspective* (U.S. Government Printing Office, published four times a year).

SAMUEL H. BEER, *To Make a Nation: The Rediscovery of American Federalism* (Harvard University Press, Belknap Press, 1993).

CENTER FOR THE STUDY OF FEDERALISM, *Publius: The Journal of Federalism* (Temple University, published quarterly; one issue is an "Annual Review of the State of American Federalism").

THOMAS R. DYE, *American Federalism: Competition Among Governments* (Lexington Books, 1990).

DANIEL J. ELAZAR, *The American Mosaic: The Impact of Space, Time, and Culture on American Politics* (Westview Press, 1994).

DANIEL J. ELAZAR, *Exploring Federalism* (University of Alabama Press, 1987).

MICHAEL FIX AND DAPHNE A. KENYON, *Coping with Mandates* (Urban Institute Press, 1990).

AL GORE, *From Red Tape to Results—Creating a Government That Works Better and Costs Less: Report of the National Performance Review* (U.S. Government Printing Office, 1993).

CHRISTOPHER HAMILTON AND DONALD T. WELLS, *Federalism, Power and Political Economy* (Prentice Hall, 1990).

JOHN KINCAID, ED., "American Federalism: The Third Century," *Annals of the American Academy of Political and Social Science* 509 (May 1990).

SUE O'BRIEN AND MARSHALL KAPLAN, *The Governors and the New Federalism* (Westview Press, 1991).

VINCENT OSTROM, *The Meaning of American Federalism* (ICS Press, 1991).

PAUL E. PETERSON, *The Price of Federalism* (Brookings Institution, 1995).

WILLIAM H. RIKER, *The Development of American Federalism* (Academic Publishers, 1987).

HARRY N. SCHEIBER, *Federalism and the Judicial Mind: Essays on American Constitutional Law and Politics* (Institute of Governmental Studies, University of California at Berkeley, 1992).

THOMAS R. SCHWARTZ AND JOHN E. PECK, *The Changing Face of Fiscal Federalism* (M. E. Sharpe, 1990).

DAVID B. WALKER, *The Rebirth of Federalism: Slouching Toward Washington* (M. E. Sharpe, 1990).

JOSEPH F. ZIMMERMAN, *Contemporary American Federalism: The Growth of National Power* (Praeger, 1992).

FIRST AMENDMENT RIGHTS

"Congress shall make no law," declares the First Amendment, "respecting an establishment of religion, or prohibiting the free exercise thereof; or abridging the freedom of speech, or of the press, or the right of the people peaceably to assemble, and to petition the Government for a redress of grievances." In this one sentence our Constitution lays down the fundamental principles of a free society: freedom of conscience and freedom of expression.

Although it was the framers who wrote the Constitution, in a sense it was the people who drafted our basic charter of liberties. As we have seen, the Constitution drawn up in Philadelphia included guarantees of a few basic rights, but it lacked a specific bill of rights similar to that found in most state constitutions. This omission aroused widespread suspicion among the people. In order to persuade delegates to the state ratification conventions to vote for the Constitution, the Federalists had to promise to correct this deficiency. In its first session, the new Congress proposed twelve amendments, ten of which were ratified by the end of 1791 and became part of the Constitution. These ten amendments are known as the Bill of Rights.[1] (As we saw in Chapter 1, another of those proposed amendments was ratified 202 years later to become the Twenty-seventh Amendment.)

Note that the Bill of Rights literally applies *only to the national government*. As John Marshall held in *Barron v Baltimore* (1833), the Bill of Rights limits the national government, not the state governments.[2] Why not the states? The people were confident they could control their own state officials, and most of the state constitutions already had bills of rights. It was the new and distant central government they feared. As it turned out, those fears were largely misplaced. The national government, responsive to tens of millions of voters from a variety of races, creeds, religions, and economic interests, has shown less tendency to curtail civil liberties than have state and local governments. Until recently, for the most part, state judges have not used the bills of rights in their respective state constitutions to protect civil liberties.

When the Fourteenth Amendment, which *does* apply to the states, was adopted in 1868, some contended that its **due process clause**—which states that no person shall be deprived of life, liberty, or property without due process of law—limits states in precisely the same way the Bill of Rights limits the national government. At least, they argued, freedom of speech should be protected by the Fourteenth Amendment. For decades the Supreme Court refused to interpret the Fourteenth Amendment in this way. Then in 1925, in *Gitlow v New York*, the Court announced: "For present purposes we may and do assume that freedom of speech and of the press—which are protected by the First Amendment from abridgment by Congress—are among the fundamental personal rights and 'liberties' protected by the due process clause of the Fourteenth Amendment from impairment by the States."[3]

THE NATIONALIZATION OF THE BILL OF RIGHTS

Gitlow v New York was a revolutionary decision. For the first time, the U.S. Constitution protected freedom of speech and of the press from abridgment by state and local governments. By the 1940s the other provisions of the First Amendment—religion, assembly, petition—had been brought within the scope of the Fourteenth Amendment. Today the First Amendment's restraints are applied to all who exercise governmental authority, at national, state, or local levels.

If the First Amendment applies to the states, why not the other parts of the Bill of Rights, most of which have to do with the rights of persons accused of crimes and with restraints on police procedures? Beginning in the 1930s, and continuing at an accelerated pace during the 1960s, the Supreme Court **selectively incorporated** provision after provision of the Bill of Rights into the due process clause.[4] Today the Fourteenth Amendment imposes on the states all the provisions of the Bill of Rights except those of the Second, Third, Seventh, and Tenth Amendments and the grand jury requirements of the Fifth Amendment. When we talk about the Bill of Rights today, we are really talking about limits on the power of all who govern, whether they do so on behalf of the national government, the states, or local units of government.

How are we to distinguish between those provisions of the Bill of Rights that are incorporated into the Fourteenth Amendment—that is, made to limit state and local governments—from those that are not? The rights *not* incorporated are those the Supreme Court has concluded could be replaced by other procedures without necessarily resulting in a denial of justice or liberty. Whereas no nation could be considered free without freedom of speech, for example—which is why it is incorporated as part of the due process clause of the Fourteenth Amendment—justice could be done without necessarily requiring a grand jury indictment before bringing people to trial. That is why this provision in the Fifth Amendment has not been incorporated.

In addition to the rights specifically protected by the Constitution, the Supreme Court has found constitutional protection for other fundamental rights. For example, the rights of association and of privacy, as well as the right to travel, are not mentioned anywhere in the Constitution. Yet these important but unexpressed rights have nonetheless been found to share constitutional protection in common with explicit guarantees.[5]

After the Supreme Court incorporated most of the national Bill of Rights into the Fourteenth Amendment, little attention was paid by state judges—or anybody else—to the bills of rights in their respective state constitutions. "The Supreme Court took such complete control of the field that state judges could sit back in the conviction that their part was simply to await the next landmark decision."[6] Recently, however, stimulated in part by the U.S. Supreme Court's more limited interpretation of some provisions of the national Bill of Rights, there has been a renewal of interest in state constitutions as independent sources of additional protection for civil liberties and civil rights.[7]

Advocates of what has come to be called **new judicial federalism** contend that the U.S. Constitution should set minimum but not maximum standards to protect our rights. There is nothing, they argue, to keep state courts from using similar provisions of the bill of rights in their own state constitutions to provide more protection for rights than is to be found in the U.S. Constitution. Moreover, state bills of rights sometimes have language that encourages a more expansive protection of rights than does the national Bill of Rights. For example, a dozen states have an equal rights amendment in their constitutions, and eleven explicitly protect the right of privacy.[8] The Louisiana state constitution prohibits age discrimination; 35 state constitutions affirm the right of free speech; 36 state

The Nationalization of the Bill of Rights

1890 No taking of property without just compensation (*Chicago, Milwaukee and St. Paul Ry v Minnesota*, 134 US 418, 1890)

1925 Freedom of speech (*Gitlow v New York*)

1931 Freedom of press (*Near v Minnesota*)

1932 Fair trial (*Powell v Alabama*)

1934 Free exercise of religion (*Hamilton v Regents of California*, confirmed in 1940 by *Cantwell v Connecticut*)

1937 Freedom of assembly (*De Jonge v Oregon*)

1942 Right to counsel in capital cases (*Betts v Brady*)

1947 Separation of church and state; establishment of religion (*Everson v Board of Education*)

1948 Right to a public trial (*In re Oliver*)

1949 Right against unreasonable searches and seizure (*Wolf v Colorado*)

1958 Freedom of association (*NAACP v Alabama*)

1961 Exclusionary rule (*Mapp v Ohio*)

1962 Right against cruel and unusual punishments (*Robinson v California*)

1963 Right to counsel in felony cases (*Gideon v Wainwright*)

1964 Right against self-incrimination (*Mallory v Hogan*)

1965 Right to confront witnesses (*Pointer v Texas*)

1965 Right of privacy (*Griswold v Connecticut*)

1966 Right to an impartial jury (*Parker v Gladden*)

1967 Right to a speedy trial (*Klopfer v North Carolina*)

1967 Right to compulsory process for obtaining witnesses (*Washington v Texas*)

1968 Right to a jury trial for all serious crimes (*Duncan v Louisiana*)

1969 Right against double jeopardy (*Benton v Maryland*)

1972 Right to counsel for all crimes involving a jail term (*Argersinger v Hamlin*)

In this and the next several chapters, we discuss constitutional rules at length, and to talk about the Constitution is to talk about Supreme Court decisions. Many of these decisions are cited in the notes at the back of the book so that you can look them up if you wish. Two forms of citation are used:

1. Official Supreme Court reports are cited as: *Gitlow v New York*, 268 US 652 (1925). This means that this case can be found in the 268th volume of the *United States Supreme Court Reports* on page 652, and it was decided in 1925. These reports are published by the U.S. Government Printing Office.
2. For more recent cases, see the advance sheets of *United States Supreme Court Reports*, published by the Lawyers' Cooperative Publishing Company. An example is a case relating to Indian tribes, gambling, powers of Congress, and the Eleventh Amendment. The case is *Seminole Tribe of Florida v Florida*, which we noted in Chapter 2. It is cited as 134 L Ed 252 (1996). This means that it can be found in volume 134 of the Lawyers' Edition, second series, starting on page 252, and it was decided in 1996.

constitutions have clauses that could easily be construed as going beyond the Second Amendment in protecting the right to bear arms.[9]

Thirty-two state supreme courts have found some rights protected to a greater extent than the Supreme Court of the United States has found to be secured by the national Bill of Rights.[10] Nevertheless, state court decisions extending rights beyond the limits secured by the U.S. Constitution are exceptions and are to be found in a substantial manner in relatively few states, such as California, Alaska, Florida, and Massachusetts.[11]

If a state supreme court goes too far beyond public sentiment in its own state, its decisions run the risk of being overturned by an amendment to the state constitution. In 1990, for example, in California and Alaska, after their respective state courts extended to criminal defendants some rights beyond those provided by the U.S. Constitution, "victims' rights" amendments were added to these state constitutions to reverse the effect of those decisions and to forbid state judges from so extending the rights of criminal defendants beyond those provided by the U.S. Constitution. And since most state judges lack lifetime tenure and are subject to electoral contests, state judges "who stray too far from most of the people of their state's understanding of their state constitutions are likely to get chucked out of office,"[12] as happened in California in 1988 with the defeat of Chief Justice Rose Bird and two other liberal justices. Thus, despite the revival of interest in state bills of rights, the U.S. Supreme Court and the national Bill of Rights remain the dominant protectors of civil liberties and civil rights.

CONGRESS SHALL MAKE NO LAW RESPECTING AN ESTABLISHMENT OF RELIGION

The first words of the First Amendment are emphatic and brief: "Congress shall make no law respecting an establishment of religion." The framers were reacting to the English system, wherein the Crown was the head not only of the government but also of the established church—the Church of England—and public officials were required to take an oath of support for the established church as a condition of holding office.

The **establishment clause** goes beyond merely forbidding the establishment of a religion. "A given law might not establish a state religion but nevertheless be one 'respecting' that end in the sense of being a step that could lead to such establishment and hence offend the First Amendment."[13] On the other hand, the clause does not prevent governments from accommodating to religious needs. To what extent and under which conditions governments may accommodate to these needs is at the heart of much of the debate among the justices in interpreting the clause.

Establishment clause cases are not easy. They stir deep feelings, and the justices, reflecting differences in the nation, are often divided among themselves. As Justice Clarence Thomas put it bluntly, "Our Establishment Clause jurisprudence is in hopeless disarray."[14] The prevailing doctrine, though under attack inside the Supreme Court and within the country, stems from a 1947 decision of the Supreme Court, *Everson v Board of Education*, that the establishment clause created a wall of separation between church and state, and that it prohibits any law or governmental action designed to confer any benefit on religion, even if all sects are treated the same.[15] This strict separation of church and state doctrine was further elaborated in *Lemon v Kurtzman* (1971), and despite considerable criticism of the so-called *Lemon test*, it has never been specifically overruled. Under this three-part test, (1) a law must have a secular legislative pur-

The constitutional separation between church and state becomes blurred during the Christmas season, when religious displays appear in front of government buildings.

pose; (2) its primary effect must neither advance nor inhibit religion; and (3) it must avoid "excessive government entanglement with religion." The establishment clause is designed to prevent three evils: "sponsorship, financial support, and active involvement of the sovereign in religious activity." [16] The *Lemon* test of what violates the establishment clause apparently still retains the support of Justices John Paul Stevens, Ruth Bader Ginsburg, and Stephen Breyer.[17]

A rival test championed by Justice Saundra Day O'Connor is the *endorsement test*: O'Connor believes that the clause forbids governmental practices that a reasonable observer would view as endorsing religion, even if there is no coercion.[18] The endorsement test has been honed in a series of decisions as the Court has struggled with the question of what governments may or may not allow religious symbols to be displayed on, in, or near public properties and in public places. For example, the Court concluded that when a city displayed a crèche (Nativity scene) in a shopping district along with Santa's house and other secular and religious symbols of the Christmas season, there was little danger that a reasonable person could conclude that the city was endorsing religion.[19] On the other hand, the Constitution does not permit a county to display the Nativity scene in a courthouse because, in this context, the county gives the impression that it is endorsing the display's religious message.[20]

Justice Anthony Kennedy has put forward a *coercion test*, under which he interprets the establishment clause not to prevent governmental actions that may accommodate to religious activities but to forbid governments from imposing any pressure on persons to participate in religious activities, even if such pressure falls short of legal compulsion, such as prayer at high school graduations.[21]

There is also a *neutrality test* emerging. As Justice David Souter recently restated for the Court, "The heart of the Establishment Clause [is] that government should not prefer one religion to another, or religion to irreligion."[22] The clause does not require or even allow a government to provide a religious exemption "from neutral laws of general applicability, even if religion is incidentally benefited.[23] Justice Antonin Scalia, speaking for a plurality of the Court, after going out of his way to repudiate an endorsement test, applied the neutrality test and announced: "Religious expression cannot violate the Establishment Clause where (1) it is purely private and (2) occurs in a traditional or designated public forum, publicly announced and open to all on equal terms, even if a reasonable observer would see the expression as indicating state endorsement."[24]

Chief Justice William Rehnquist and Justices Scalia and Thomas are edging toward a *nonpreferentialist test.*[25] They appear to believe that the Constitution simply prohibits favoritism toward a particular religion, but does not prohibit governmental accommodation of religious activities or even some nonpreferential support for religious organizations, so long as individuals are not legally coerced into participating in religious activities, and religious activities are not singled out for favorable treatment.

Applying these generalities, we find that the establishment clause forbids states, including state universities, colleges, and school districts, to introduce any kind of devotional exercises into the public school curriculum. However, the Supreme Court has not, as it is sometimes said, prohibited prayer in public schools. It is not unconstitutional for people to pray in a school building. What is unconstitutional is sponsorship or encouragement of prayer by public school authorities.[26] In 1992 the Court extended the ban against school-endorsed prayer in public schools to forbid the use of a nondenominational prayer at primary and secondary school graduations. The Court concluded that such a practice coerces students into participating in religious ceremonies.[27]

Devotional reading of the Bible, recitation of the Lord's Prayer, and posting of the Ten Commandments on the walls of classrooms in public schools are also prohibited by the Constitution. A state may not forbid the teaching of evolution or require the simultaneous teaching of "creation science"—that is, the belief that human life did not evolve but rather was created by a single act of God.[28]

Tax exemptions for church property, along with that of other nonprofit institutions, are constitutional. State legislatures and Congress may hire chaplains to open each day's legislative session—a practice that has continued without interruption since the first session of Congress. But if done in a public school, this practice would be unconstitutional. Apparently, the difference is that legislators, as adults, are not "susceptible to religious indoctrination or peer pressure."[29] Also, as the joke goes, legislators need the prayer more.

Parochial School Aid

A troublesome area involves attempts by many states to provide financial assistance to parochial schools. The Supreme Court has tried to draw a line between permissible public aid to students, including those in sectarian schools, and impermissible public aid to religion.

At the college level the problems are relatively simple. Tax funds may be used to construct buildings and operate educational programs at church-related schools, as long as the money is not spent directly on buildings used for religious purposes or on teaching religious subjects. Even if students choose to attend religious schools and become ministers, governmental aid to these students is permissible. Such aid has a secular purpose; its effect on religion is the result of individual choice, "and it does not confer any message of state endorsement of religion."[30]

At the elementary and secondary levels, however, the constitutional problems become more complicated, and "the current law on government aid to religious schools is a quagmire."[31] Here the secular and religious parts of institutions and instruction are much more closely interwoven. Students are younger and more susceptible to indoctrination, and the chances are greater that aid given to church-operated schools might seep into aid for religion.

Despite the constitutional obstacles, some states have attempted to provide tax credits or deductions for those who send their children to private, largely church-affiliated schools. Deductions or credits available only to parents of children

The courts have allowed the use of public funds to provide books and remedial services to parochial schools.

attending nonpublic schools are unconstitutional, but allowing taxpaying parents to deduct or take a credit from their state income taxes for what they paid for tuition and other costs to send their children to school—public or private—is constitutionally permissible, even if most of the benefit goes to those who send their children to private religious schools.[32]

The Supreme Court has also approved using tax funds to provide students who attend primary and secondary church-operated schools (except those that deny admission because of race or religion) with textbooks, standardized tests, lunches, transportation to and from school, diagnostic services for speech and hearing problems, and other kinds of remedial help—provided such services take place outside of the school building and away from the "pervasively sectarian atmosphere of the church-related schools."[33]

Tax funds may not be used in religious schools to pay teachers' salaries, purchase equipment, provide counseling for students, produce teacher-prepared tests, repair facilities, or transport students on field trips. School authorities may not permit religious instructors to come into public school buildings during the school day to provide religious instruction on a voluntary basis.

However, in 1993, the Court upheld the assignment of a sign-language interpreter, paid for by public funds, to accompany a deaf child to a parochial school. The Court held that this was aid to a student, not to a religion. In the context of a state program that made such services generally available, there could be no danger that such a practice could be construed as an endorsement of religion. The minority contended that since the interpreter would be obliged to follow the deaf student throughout his day, including attendance at Mass, "the interpreter's every gesture would be infused with religious significance."[34]

Why is it constitutional for state governments to pay for books but not for maps? For bus trips but not for field trips? For standardized tests but not for tests prepared by teachers? For a sign-language interpreter, but not for teachers? Those on the "approved" side meet the three-part Lemon test, but those on the "forbidden" side fail one of the requirements. Thus, transportation to and from school, which is permitted, involves a routine trip that every student makes every day; it is unrelated to any aspect of the curriculum. Field trips, which cannot be paid for by tax funds, are controlled by teachers and are aids to instruction. Books and standardized tests, which can be bought by tax funds, can be easily evaluated to ensure that they are not designed to promote religion, whereas maps or teacher-prepared tests cannot be so readily checked. And in cases involving teaching by public teachers in parochial schools, the supervision to ensure avoidance of religious influences creates excessive entanglement of church and state, whereas a sign-language interpreter does no more than accurately interpret whatever material is presented to the class as a whole.

Right to Worship as One Chooses

The Constitution not only forbids the establishment of religion, but it also contains a **free exercise clause** that forbids Congress and the states from passing any law "prohibiting the free exercise thereof." "The Court has struggled to find a neutral course between the two religion clauses, both of which are cast in absolute terms, and either of which, if expanded to a logical extreme, would tend to clash with the other."[35] In addition, religious speech is protected by the Constitution. As the Court has pointed out: "There is a crucial difference between *government* speech endorsing religion which the Establishment Clause forbids, and *private* speech endorsing religious which the Free Speech and Free Exercise Clauses protect."[36]

Thinking it Through

The board decided not to allow the Klan to put up the cross because to do so might be construed as state support for a religion contrary to the establishment clause. But the courts, ultimately the U.S. Supreme Court, concluded that under these circumstances the board had violated the Klan's free speech rights. Justice Antonin Scalia, speaking for three other justices, wrote: "Religious expression cannot violate The Establishment Clause where (1) it is purely private and (2) occurs in a traditional or designated public forum, publicly announced and open to all on equal terms." Justice Sandra Day O'Connor concurred to create a majority because she concluded that in these circumstances there was no endorsement of religion.*

*Capitol Square Review Board v Pinette, 132 L Ed 650 (1995).

The tension between the two religion clauses became evident when the University of Virginia denied a student group student fee funds to pay a printer for their religious newspaper. The university felt that because of the establishment clause it could not give public moneys to support a newspaper that "primarily promotes a belief in or about a deity." The students alleged that this action deprived them of their right to freedom of speech, including religious speech. The Supreme Court agreed with the students that the establishment clause did not justify a state agency making this kind of "viewpoint discrimination." As long as the state's action was neutral there was no violation of the establishment clause. On the contrary, "the neutrality commanded of the State by the separate Clauses of the First Amendment was comprised by the University's course of action."[37]

Unconventional religions are entitled to the same constitutional protection as are the more traditional ones. The Constitution provides no definition or a church or religion, and the Supreme Court has been reluctant, understandably, to get into these questions. The free exercise clause extends to those who act on sincerely held religious beliefs, not just to those who respond to a specific command of a particular church. But, although the Court does not "underestimate the difficulty of distinguishing between religious and secular convictions and determining whether a professed belief is sincerely held,"[38] only beliefs rooted in a religion are protected by the free exercise clause.

The right to hold any or no religious *belief* is one of our few absolute rights. No government has authority to compel the acceptance of any creed or to censor it. A state may not compel a religious belief or deny persons any right because of their beliefs or lack of them. Requiring religious oaths as a condition of public employment or as a prerequisite to running for public office is unconstitutional. In fact, the only time the Constitution mentions the word religion is to state: "No religious Test shall ever be required as a Qualification to any Office or public Trust under the United States" (Article VI).

Although carefully protected, the right to *practice* a religion has had less protection than the right to hold particular beliefs. Religious convictions do not ordinarily exempt one from obeying an otherwise valid and nondiscriminatory law or government regulation. Prior to 1990 the Supreme Court applied what is known as the *compelling interest test* and carefully scrutinized laws alleged to infringe on religious practices. The Court insisted that the government provide some compelling public purpose to justify the infringement: "Only those interests of the highest order and those not otherwise served can overbalance legitimate claims to the free exercise of religion."[39] In other words, the Constitution was thought to throw "a mantle of protection" around religious practices, and the burden was on the government to justify interfering with them.

Then, in 1990, the Rehnquist Court significantly altered the interpretation of the free exercise cause. In *Employment Division v Smith*, the Court discarded the compelling interest test, except as it applied to laws denying people unemployment compensation. Outside of this narrow field, so far as the Constitution is concerned, a government no longer has to show a compelling interest in order to apply its general laws to religious practices. As long as a law does not single out and ban religious practices because "they are engaged in for religious reasons, or only because of the religious belief they display," a general law may be applied to conduct even if it is religiously inspired. In this particular instance, Oregon was allowed to deny unemployment benefits to two Native Americans who were fired because they used peyote as part of their religious rituals.[40]

Three years later, however, the city of Hialeah, Florida was told that it could not apply its ordinances forbidding the slaughtering of animals as part of religious rituals to the Santeria religious services since other forms of ani-

Brookins, *Richmond Times Dispatch.* © 1982 Field Enterprises, Inc.

Compulsory education laws cannot force Amish children to attend public schools beyond eighth grade.

mal slaughtering are allowed, and it was clear that these ordinances had been designed specifically to forbid the slaughter of animals as part of religious rituals in the Santeria religion.[41] Similarly, in 1993, the Court declared unconstitutional a public school practice that made its facilities available after school hours to any organization except religious ones. The Court struck down this practice more as a content-based restriction on speech than as an interference with religious freedom, but it also held that to allow religious groups the same right to use school facilities outside of school hours as any other group did not violate the establishment clause.[42]

Even prior to *Employment Division v Smith*, when the Supreme Court was using the compelling interest test, it nonetheless upheld laws and regulations outlawing business activities on Sunday, as applied to Orthodox Jews, and forbidding military officers to wear headgear while indoors, as applied to an Orthodox Jew's wearing of a yarmulke (skullcap). Congress subsequently intervened to make such practices permissible. The Court has also sustained an Internal Revenue Service regulation denying tax exemption to religious schools that admit members of only one race.[43] The Forest Service was allowed to construct a road through a portion of national forest held sacred by Native Americans and used by them for religious ceremonies.[44]

On the other hand, a state may not require Jehovah's Witnesses (or anyone else, for that matter) to participate in public school flag-salute ceremonies. Although a state may compel parents to send their children to some kind of accredited school, parents have a constitutional right to send their children to a church-sponsored rather than to a public school. Similarly, a state's compulsory school laws cannot compel the Amish to send their children to school beyond the eighth grade. Through the eighth grade the interests of the state in ensuring that all children learn basic skills overbalance religious convictions; after the eighth grade, religious convictions are given priority.

The Religious Freedom Restoration Act of 1993

The Supreme Court's decision in *Employment Division v Smith* promoted "an unprecedented coalition of political forces and an extraordinary congressional reaction."[45] In 1993 Congress passed and President Bill Clinton signed the Religious Freedom Restoration Act, which was explicitly designed to reverse that decision and restore the use of the compelling interest test. The Religious Freedom Restoration Act exempts people from laws and governmental actions that burden their religious freedom, even if the burden results from "a rule of general

Thinking it Through

Not necessarily, said the Supreme Court by a 5 to 4 vote. In *Bowen v Kendrick*, 487 US 589 (1988), Chief Justice William H. Rehnquist delivered the opinion of the majority of the Court. He applied the three-pronged *Lemon* test but with a strong accommodationist twist. The act was, he held, clearly motivated by a legitimate *secular purpose:* the elimination or reduction of the problems caused by teenage sexuality and pregnancy. Its effect has not been to promote religion, to advance substantial federal funds to churches, or to create a crucial symbolic link between government and religion; and finally, there has been no *excessive governmental entanglement* with religion.

Justice Sandra Day O'Connor, in a concurring opinion, joined with the Chief Justice and Justices Antonin Scalia, Anthony M. Kennedy, and Byron R. White in upholding the law on its face, but gave her vote only on the condition that the case be returned to the trial court to be sure that the law as applied had not in fact been used to permit "public funds to promote religious doctrine."

The Best Test of Truth

Justice Oliver Wendell Holmes, Jr., dissenting in *Abrams v United States*, wrote:

Persecution for the expression of opinions seems to me perfectly logical. If you have no doubt of your premises or your power and want a certain result with all your heart, you naturally express your wishes in law and sweep away all opposition. . . . But when men have realized that time has upset many fighting faiths, they may come to believe even more than they believe the very foundations of their own conduct that the ultimate good desired is better reached by free trade in ideas—that the best test of truth is the power of the thought to get itself accepted in the competition of the market, and that truth is the only ground upon which their wishes safely can be carried out. That at any rate is the theory of our Constitution. It is an experiment, as all life is an experiment.

SOURCE: *Abrams v United States*, 250 US 616 (1919).

applicability," except where the government can demonstrate that the burden is "the least restrictive means of furthering a compelling interest." By the terms of this law, "A person whose religious exercise" has been violated by a law or regulation may "assert that violation as a claim or defense in a judicial proceeding and obtain appropriate relief against [the] government."[46] It is not clear precisely how in practice one asserts this right.

In signing the bill, President Clinton said that reversing a decision of the Supreme Court "is a power that is rightly hesitantly and infrequently exercised by the United States Congress. But this is an issue in which that extraordinary measure was clearly called for."[47] That Congress can confer such a defense for persons who refuse to comply with federal laws and regulations is one thing; but that it can confer such a right on persons who do not comply with their own state and local laws and regulations raises interesting questions of federalism. It is not clear by what authority Congress can so diminish the power of state governments and restrict their power to legislate. If a religion permits individuals, under some circumstances, to avoid laws applied to others, it is predictable that people will claim this status, even though they may not be acting because of religious convictions or because of the commands of a church.

FREE SPEECH AND FREE PEOPLE

Government by the people is based on every person's right to speak freely, to organize in groups, to question the decisions of the government, and to campaign openly against it. Only through free and uncensored expression of opinion can government be kept responsive to the electorate and political power be transferred peacefully. Elections, separation of powers, and constitutional guarantees are meaningless unless all persons have the right to speak frankly and to hear and judge for themselves the worth of what others have to say.

Despite the fundamental importance of free speech to a democracy, some people seem to believe speech should be free only for those who agree with them. Americans overwhelmingly support principles of tolerance when such principles are presented in general, abstract fashion—for example, "Do you believe in freedom of speech?" They are less tolerant, however, when the speech is directed at them or is critical of their race, religion, or ethnic origin.

Free speech is not simply the personal right of individuals to have their say; it is also the right of the rest of us to hear them. John Stuart Mill, whose *Essay on Liberty* (1859) is the classic defense of free speech, put it this way: The peculiar evil of silencing the expression of opinion, is that it is robbing the human race. . . . If the opinion is right, they are deprived of the opportunity of exchanging error for truth; if wrong, they lose what is almost as great a benefit, the clearer perception and livelier impression of truth, produced by its collision with error.[48]

Freedom of speech is, as Justice Robert H. Jackson said, "freedom to differ as to things that touch the heart of the existing order."[49] Yet some who say they believe in free speech draw the line at ideas they consider dangerous. What is a dangerous idea? Who decides? In the realm of political ideas, who can find an objective, eternally valid standard of right? Or as Chief Justice William H. Rehnquist put it for the Supreme Court, "The First Amendment recognizes no such thing as a 'false' idea."[50] The search for truth involves the possibility—even the inevitability—of error. The search cannot go on unless it proceeds freely in the minds and speech of all. This means, in the words of Justice Oliver Wendell Holmes, Jr., "not free thought for those who agree with us but freedom for the thought that we hate."[51]

Even though the First Amendment explicitly denies Congress the power to pass any law abridging freedom of speech, the amendment has never been interpreted in such absolute terms. Like almost all rights, the freedoms of speech and of the press are limited. In discussing the constitutional power of government to regulate speech, it is useful to distinguish among *belief*, *speech*, and *action*.

At one extreme is the right to *believe* as we wish, a right as absolute as any can be for people living in an organized society. Despite occasional deviations in practice, the traditional American view is that thoughts are inviolable. No government has the right to punish a person for beliefs or to interfere in any way with freedom of conscience.

At the other extreme is *action*, which is usually restrained. The Constitution protects from governmental regulation our right to believe we should drive our automobile through red lights, but we have no constitutional right to ignore traffic signals. As has been said, "The right to swing your arm ends where the other person's nose begins."

Speech stands somewhere between belief and action. It is not an absolute right as is belief, but neither is it as exposed to governmental restraint as is action. Some kinds of speech—obscenity, child pornography, libel, sedition, or speech that constitutes fighting words—although not "entirely invisible to the Constitution"[52] are not entitled, in most circumstances, to any constitutional protection. Many problems arise in distinguishing between what does and does not fit into these categories of "unprotected speech." All other speech is constitutionally protected from governmental regulation—but how much protection?

Historic Constitutional Tests

It is useful to start with the three constitutional tests developed earlier in this century, for they continue to reflect basic judicial and public attitudes toward governmental regulation of speech. These are the *bad tendency doctrine*, the *clear and present danger doctrine*, and the *preferred position doctrine*.

THE BAD TENDENCY DOCTRINE According to the adherents of the **bad tendency doctrine**, the Constitution authorizes legislative bodies to forbid speech that has a tendency to lead to illegal action. Moreover, "the legislature cannot reasonably be required to measure the danger from every . . . utterance in the nice balance of a jeweler's scale. . . . It may, in the exercise of its judgment, suppress the threatened danger in its incipiency."[53]

This doctrine, which stems from the common law, has not had the support of the Supreme Court since *Gitlow v New York* in 1925. Nonetheless, many legislators, city council members, and others (including some state courts as late as 1982) appear to hold this position.[54] It also seems to be the view of many college students who want to see their institution punish student colleagues or faculty who express "hateful" or "offensive" ideas.

Does the Constitution permit a city council or the trustees of a public university to ban public utterances of abusive racial remarks or insulting sexual taunts because they might lead to violence, or because they are so demeaning to some that such speech would interfere with their rights to an education or to a positive workplace? Those who hold to the bad tendency test contend that such a law or regulation would be constitutional because abusive racial or insulting sexual remarks can in fact provoke violence, do inflict injury on individuals, and create damaging racial divisions. These laws and regulations, they contend, are reasonable means to preserve the public order to protect the rights of persons not to be abused because of their race or sex. Empowering public officials to make such judgments, however, runs the risk that they may restrict speech merely because they dislike it.

THE CLEAR AND PRESENT DANGER DOCTRINE Justice Oliver Wendell Holmes, Jr., announced this celebrated doctrine in *Schneck v United States*: "The question in every case is whether the words are used in circumstances and are of such a nature as to create a clear and present danger that they will bring about substantive evils that Congress has a right to prevent."[55] Justice Louis D. Brandeis further elaborated in a later case, "No danger flowing from speech can be deemed clear and present, and unless the incidence of the evil" that will result from a speech "is so imminent that it may befall before there is opportunity for full discussion."[56]

Supporters of the **clear and present danger doctrine** concede that speech is not an absolute right. Yet they believe free speech to be so fundamental to the operations of a constitutional democracy that no government should be allowed to restrict any particular speech unless it can demonstrate that there is such a close connection between the speech and an illegal action that the speech itself takes on the character of the action. To shout "Fire" *falsely* in a crowded theater is Justice Holmes's famous example. A government should not be allowed to interfere with speech unless it can prove, ultimately to a skeptical judiciary, that the particular speech in question presented an immediate danger of a major evil—for example, speech leading to a riot, destruction of property, corruption of an election, or direct interference with recruitment of soldiers.

Consider our earlier example of public university hate-speech codes and city ordinances against abusive or insulting language. Advocates of the clear and present danger doctrine would argue that, even though a legislature had made it illegal to make abusive racial or insulting sexual remarks in public or the public university had made it grounds for disciplining a student, the regulation could not be applied constitutionally to any person for anything he or she said or wrote, unless the government or university presents convincing evidence that the particular remarks made by the particular individual might clearly and presently have led to a riot or to direct injury to specific individuals or be the direct cause of some other serious activity the government has a right to make illegal or the university to punish.

THE PREFERRED POSITION DOCTRINE Those who hold to the **preferred position doctrine,** such as the late Justice Hugo L. Black, come close to the position that freedom of expression, that is, the use of words and pictures, may never be curtailed. This does not mean that there is nothing left for judges to decide, for a line must still be drawn between speech and nonspeech.

The preferred position interpretation of the First Amendment gives these freedoms a preferred position in our constitutional hierarchy. Judges have a special duty to protect these freedoms and should be most skeptical about laws trespassing on them. Legislative majorities are free to experiment with and to adopt various schemes regulating our lives in general, but when they tamper with freedom of speech, they interfere with the channels of the political process. Only if the government can show that limitations on speech are absolutely necessary to avoid imminent and serious substantive evils are such limitations to be allowed.

If we apply the preferred position doctrine to our example of a law against abusive racial or insulting sexual remarks, the law itself would be declared unconstitutional. Restraints on such abusive speech are not absolutely necessary to prevent riots or other social disturbances. Whatever danger may come from such remarks does not justify restricting free comment. Moreover, supporters of the preferred position doctrine contend that the law itself, by imposing a *chilling effect* on speech and not merely its application, violates the Constitution.

Current Constitutional Tests

The three historic doctrines just discussed continue to provide the background for debates on freedom of speech. Today, however, the Supreme Court is more apt to use the following doctrines to measure the limits of governmental power.

PRIOR RESTRAINT Of all the forms of governmental interference with expression, judges are most suspicious of those that impose **prior restraint**—restraints prior to publication. Prior restraints include licensing requirements before a speech can be made, a motion picture shown, or a newspaper published. The Supreme Court has refused to declare all forms of prior censorship unconstitutional, but a "prior restraint on expression comes to this court with a 'heavy presumption' against its constitutionality. . . . The Government thus carries a heavy burden of showing justification for the enforcement of such a restraint."[57] Except as applied to motion pictures, most of the few examples of the Court's actual approval of prior restraints relate to military and security matters. The Court has also upheld the right of high school authorities to exercise "editorial control over the style and content of student speech" in school newspapers and other "school-sponsored expressive activities so long as their actions are reasonably related to legitimate pedagogical concerns."[58]

VAGUENESS Any law is unconstitutional if it "either forbids or requires the doing of an act in terms so vague that men of common intelligence must necessarily guess at its meaning and differ as to its application."[59] Laws touching First Amendment freedoms are required to pass even more rigid standards regarding vagueness. These laws must not allow those who administer them so much discretion that they could discriminate against those whose views they dislike. The law must also not be so vague that people are afraid to exercise protected freedoms. Such vague and overboard laws have a *chilling effect* on freedom of speech. The Supreme Court has struck down laws that condemn "sacrilegious" movies or publications of "criminal deeds of bloodshed or lust . . . so massed as to become vehicles for inciting violent and depraved crimes."[60]

OVERBREADTH Closely related to the vagueness doctrine is the overbreadth doctrine, the requirement that a statute relating to First Amendment freedoms cannot be so broad that it sweeps within its prohibitions protected speech as well as nonprotected activities, for example, a loyalty oath that endangers protected forms of association along with illegal activities. Because the very existence of overbroad statutes tends to repress protected speech, such statutes may be declared unconstitutional on their face, that is, entirely and not in some particular application of the law.

LEAST DRASTIC MEANS Even for an important purpose, a legislature may not choose a law that impinges on First Amendment freedoms if there are other ways to handle the problem. To illustrate, a state may protect the public from unscrupulous lawyers, but it may not do so by forbidding organizations to make legal services available to their members or by forbidding attorneys from advertising their fees for simple services. The state could adopt other ways to protect the public from such lawyers that do not impinge on freedom of association or speech; for example, providing for the disbarment of lawyers who misled their clients.

CONTENT NEUTRAL Content-neutral laws are much less likely to be struck down than those that restrict speech because of its content. As the Court wrote,

"Regulations which permit the Government to discriminate on the basis of the content of the message cannot be tolerated under the First Amendment."[61] For example, a law forbidding posting of handbills on telephone poles has been sustained. Yet a law prohibiting posting of handbills advocating racism or sexism would, in all probability, be declared unconstitutional because it would relate to what is being said rather than where and how it is being said.

The lack of content neutrality was the grounds for the Court striking down a St. Paul, Minnesota, ordinance that forbade burning crosses or displaying Nazi swastikas or other "fighting words" to arouse anger, alarm, or resentment on the basis of race, color, creed, religion, or gender because St. Paul did not forbid such displays to arouse anger on the basis of other matters, for example, political affiliation, union membership, or homosexuality. Said Justice Antonin Scalia for the Court, "Aspersions upon a person's mother . . . would seemingly be usable . . . in the placards of those arguing *in favor* of racial, color, etc., tolerance and equality, but could not be used by that speaker's opponents."[62]

CENTRALITY OF POLITICAL SPEECH   "Not all speech is of equal First Amendment importance. It is speech on 'matters of public concern that is at the heart of the First Amendment's protection.'"[63] There is some contradiction between content neutrality and centrality of political speech. Legislatures and city councils are supposed to pass laws that are content neutral, but in determining whether or not those laws violate the Constitution, judges may take into account what kind of speech is involved.

COMMERCIAL SPEECH   Commercial speech is speech that "proposes a commercial transaction."[64] The mere fact that it is uttered for a profit, for example, charitable solicitations, does not make it commercial speech. Even though commercial speech is constitutionally protected, common-sense differences exist between commercial and other kinds of speech. Commercial speech is, therefore, subject to much more regulation than other speech. For example, advertising the sale of anything illegal may be forbidden, as can false and misleading commercial advertising. However, a law forbidding false and misleading political speech or political advertising is clearly unconstitutional because government does not have the right to forbid anyone from expressing ideas because they are thought to be false or misleading.

Who Decides?

Plainly, neither doctrines nor constitutional tests decide cases; judges do. Doctrines are judges' starting points; each case requires a judge to weigh a variety of factors: What was said? Where was it said? How was it said? What was the intent of the person who said it? Which government is attempting to regulate the speech—a city council speaking for a few people, or the Congress speaking for many? Few acts of Congress have ever been struck down because of conflict with the First Amendment. How is the government attempting to regulate the speech? By prior censorship? By punishment after the speech? Why is the government acting? To preserve the public peace? To prevent criticism of those in power? These and scores of other considerations are involved in the never-ending process of determining what the Constitution permits and what it forbids.

FREEDOM OF THE PRESS

Freedom of the press is the same as freedom of speech, except that the clause relating to speech protects oral communications and the phrase relating to the press embraces written ones. When we speak of "the press," most people, including most journalists, think only of the print media.[65] Yet "the liberty of the press is not confined to newspapers and periodicals. . . . The press in its historic connotation comprehends every sort of publication which affords a vehicle of information and opinion."[66]

Although we still utilize street corner meetings and public rallies to communicate ideas and influence public policies, today most of us rely on television, newspapers, radio, movies—the mass media—to tell us what is happening in the world. The press thus includes electronic media—radio, television, E-mail, the World Wide Web. Differing constitutional rules apply, however, to each kind of media. Print media are largely unregulated; the electronic media are subject to limited regulation.

Some newspeople contend that the press, especially the written press, should have more freedom of speech than do nonjournalists. Former Chief Justice Warren Burger acknowledged that media representatives have a valid claim to function as "surrogates for the public and thus may be provided special seating and priority of entry [at trials] so that they may report what people in attendance have seen and heard."[67] "Media defendants" have more protection against libel suits than "nonmedia defendants."[68] The Supreme Court has been careful to protect the press from some kinds of tax burdens even when there is no evidence of any evil intent on the part of the taxing authorities.[69] And news corporations are not subject to the same kinds of limitations as other corporations on how they may spend corporate dollars to influence elections.

Still, the prevailing view is: "The First Amendment does not 'belong' to any definable category of persons or entities; it belongs to all who exercise its freedoms."[70] Representatives of the press continue to argue otherwise. They also claim not merely the constitutional right to publish but also a right of access, a right to protect their sources, and a right to secure their files against search warrants.

The Student Press

The First Amendment does not provide the same protection for the student press as it does for nonschool papers. The Supreme Court, although agreeing that the First Amendment was involved, nonetheless sustained the right of a St. Louis area high school principal to impose prior censorship upon a school newspaper written and edited by a journalism class. The paper was not a public forum, open by policy or practice "for indiscriminate use by the general public" or by student organizations. Rather, it was a school-sponsored paper and part of the school's educational program, and thus could be regulated by school authorities.[71] It is likely that the court would have a different view of the college press and would conclude that they are entitled to much the same protections as other newspapers, especially those university newspapers that have their own independent sources of funds and are operated by a corporation separate from the university.

Does the Press Have the Right to Know?

Courts have carefully protected the press's right to publish information, no matter how the journalists got it. But reporters, editors, and others argue that this is not enough. If reporters are excluded from places where public business is being conducted or denied access to information in government files, they are not able to perform their historic function of keeping the public informed. The Supreme Court has refused to acknowledge a right to know, although it did concede that there is a First Amendment right for the press, along with the public, to be presented at criminal trials.[72]

Although they have no constitutional obligation to do so, many states have adopted *sunshine laws* requiring public agencies to open their meetings to the

Thinking it Through

The Supreme Court has declared that reporters, and presumably scholars, have no constitutional right to ignore legal requests and withhold information from judicial authorities. If any privilege is to be given to newspeople, said the Court, it should be done by act of Congress and of the states.* Congress has not yet responded to this suggestion, but many states have passed so-called "shield laws" that provide some protection from state court subpoenas.

*Branzburg v Hayes, 408 US 665 (1972).

public and the press. Congress requires most federal executive agencies to open hearings and meetings of advisory groups to the public, and most congressional committee meetings are open to the public. Federal and state courtroom trials are also open, but judicial conferences, when the judges discuss how to decide the cases, are not.

Congress has authorized the president to establish a classification system to keep some public documents and governmental files secret, and it is a crime for any person to divulge such classified information. So far, however, although they have been threatened, no newspapers have been prosecuted for doing so.

EXECUTIVE PRIVILEGE Most presidents have claimed a constitutional right to withhold information not only from the press but from Congress and the courts if, in the president's judgment, its release would jeopardize national security or interfere with the confidentiality of advice. This claim is referred to as **executive privilege.** In the celebrated case of *United States v Nixon* (1974), the Supreme Court ruled that executive privilege does not shield a president from a judicial subpoena for material relevant to a criminal prosecution.[73] This historic decision, which marked the second time the Supreme Court decided a matter directly involving the president as a party to a case, rejected a claim of absolute executive privilege. The Court did, however, recognize that a president's "singularly unique role" gives the office a limited executive privilege to which judges should show the "utmost deference."

President Clinton, claiming lawyer-client confidentiality, at first refused to respond to a Senate subpoena to turn over to a Senate committee notes from a meeting he had had with his lawyers. The committee was investigating allegations about possible financial misconduct of the president when he was governor of Arkansas, what came to be known as the Whitewater investigation. President Clinton contended that the president, along with every other person, is entitled to have confidential conversations with his lawyers. The issue was complicated by the fact that at the meeting not only were the president's own private lawyers present but also lawyers from government agencies. When the Senate voted to go to court to try to enforce the subpoena, the president avoided a constitutional showdown and agreed to turn over the documents after investigators agreed not to use their release as a precedent to preclude the president from claiming lawyer-client privilege.[74]

Free Press versus Fair Trials

When newspapers and television report in vivid detail the facts of a crime, interview prosecutors and police, question witnesses, and hold press conferences for defendants and their attorneys, as in the O. J. Simpson case, they may so inflame the public that finding a panel of impartial jurors and conducting a fair trial is difficult. In England, strict rules determine what the media may report, and judges do not hesitate to punish newspapers that comment on pending criminal proceedings. In the United States, in contrast, free comment is emphasized. Yet the Supreme Court has not been indifferent to protecting persons on trial from inflammatory publicity. Its remedies have been to order new trials or to instruct judges to impose sanctions on prosecutors and police, not on reporters. "Lawyers representing clients in pending cases may be regulated under a less demanding standard than that established for regulation of the press."[75] They may be disciplined for their comments prior to or during a trial even if the comments do not present a clear and present danger but merely if they are "substantially likely to have a materially prejudicial effect."

Federal rules of criminal procedure forbid radio or photographic coverage of criminal cases in federal courts, but most states permit televising of courtroom proceedings. Such TV programs have become popular. People around the world followed the O. J. Simpson case, and it became one of the most publicized trials ever. Dissatisfaction with the results in some so-called "high profile" cases has led some judges in some states to exclude television coverage. Defendants always have the right to present evidence that television interfered with their trail, prevented fair hearings and deprived them of due process.[76]

OTHER MEDIA AND OTHER MESSAGES

When the Constitution was written, freedom of "the press" referred to leaflets, newspapers, and books. Today the Constitution also protects other media, such as the mails, motion pictures, billboards, radio, television, cable, telephones, fax machines, other electronic media, as well as expressive conduct. Because each form of communication entails special problems, each needs a different degree of protection.

The Mails

More than 75 years ago, Justice Oliver Wendell Holmes, Jr., wrote in dissent: "The United States may give up the Post Office when it sees fit, but while it carries it on, the use of the mails is almost as much a part of free speech as is the right to use our tongues."[77] In 1965, the Court adopted Holmes's views by striking down the first congressional act ever held to conflict with the First Amendment. That act had directed the postmaster general to detain foreign mailings of "communist political propaganda" and to deliver these materials only upon the addressee's request.[78] The Court has also set aside federal laws authorizing postal authorities to exclude from the mails materials they consider obscene.

Although government censorship of mail is unconstitutional, household censorship is not. The Court has sustained a law giving any householder the absolute right to ask the postmaster to order mailers to delete names in the household from all mailing lists and to refrain from sending any advertisements that householders, in their sole discretion, believe to be "erotically arousing or sexually provocative."[79] It makes no constitutional difference if a householder includes a mail order catalog in such a category. Moreover, Congress may forbid—and has forbidden—the use of mailboxes for any materials except those sent through the United States mails.

Motion Pictures and Plays

Films may be treated differently from books or newspapers, and prior censorship of films to prevent the showing of obscenity is not necessarily unconstitutional. However, laws calling for submission of films to a government review board are constitutional only if there is a prompt judicial hearing. The burden is on the government to prove to the court that the particular film in question is in fact obscene. Prior censorship of films through review boards used to be rather common in some places—for example, Massachusetts and Maryland and in some cities.

Live performances, such as plays and revues, are also entitled to constitutional protection.[80] Yet live theater is subject to greater regulation than either the printed page or the motion picture. The First Amendment, especially in view of the Twenty-first Amendment repealing Prohibition, does not protect liquor licensees from state regulations forbidding sexually suggestive performances in places where liquor is sold.[81]

The 1966 Freedom of Information Act

The Freedom of Information Act (FOIA) of 1966, as amended, liberalized access to nonclassified government records. This act makes the records of federal executive agencies available subject to certain exceptions, such as private financial transactions, personnel records, criminal investigation files, interoffice memoranda, and letters used in internal decision making. If federal agencies fail to move promptly on requests for information, persons are entitled to speedy judicial hearings. The burden is on an agency to explain its refusal to supply material, and if the judge decides the government has improperly withheld information, the government has to pay the legal fees. Since the inception of FOIA, more than 250,000 people have requested information, and more than 90 percent of these requests have been granted.

Some critics are concerned that FOIA has had an adverse effect on our ability to carry out confidential investigations and that its implementation costs too much. Others are concerned that FOIA may be used by businesses to obtain competitors' secrets. But most observers, especially newspaper reporters and scholars, believe that FOIA gives real meaning to the citizen's right to know.

SOURCE: Page Putnam Miller, "Status Report on the Freedom of Information Act," PS: Political Science and Politics (Winter 1988), pp. 87–90. See also Michael Moss, "Federal Service Gets Wider Use by Sleuths, Snoops—and Senators: Freedom of Information Act Offers Surprise Benefits for Business, Investors," Wall Street Journal, January 3, 1996, p. A1.

Handbills, Sound Trucks, and Billboards

Religious and political pamphlets, leaflets, and handbills have been historic weapons in the defense of liberty, and their distribution is constitutionally protected. So, too, is the use of their more contemporary counterparts—sound trucks and billboards. A state, for example, cannot restrain the distribution of leaflets merely to keep its streets clean[82] And the Supreme Court recently struck down an Ohio statue, similar to that found in all other states except California, that prohibited the distribution of campaign literature that did not contain the name and address of the persons or campaign official issuing the literature.[83] (The Court left open whether a state's interest in protecting the election process "might justify a more limited identification requirement.")

On the other side, the Supreme Court sustained a Tennessee statute prohibiting solicitation of votes and distribution of campaign literature within 100 feet of the entrance to a polling place. Even though this regulation applied to political speech, in a public forum, and was not content-neutral and thus was subject to strict judicial scrutiny, nonetheless the Court concluded that the 100-foot limit was narrowly drawn means to accomplish the state's compelling interest in protecting the integrity of the vote and the secrecy of the ballot.[84]

As for sound trucks, those that emit loud and raucous noises may be banned. Further, content-neutral regulations detailing the time, place, and manner in which amplification devices may be used for musical performances such as rock concerts are also acceptable. Billboards, too, are entitled to constitutional protection, especially those used for noncommercial purposes.

Radio and Television

Television today is the most important means of distributing news, as well as the primary forum for appealing for votes. Yet of all the mass media, broadcasting has received the least First Amendment protection. Congress established a system of commercial broadcasting, supplemented by the Corporation for Public Broadcasting, which provides funds for public radio and television. The entire system is regulated by the Federal Communications Commission (FCC). The FCC grants licenses for limited periods and makes regulations for their use. Broadcasters, using publicly owned airwaves, have no constitutional right to use these facilities without licenses.

The First Amendment would prevent censorship if the FCC tried to impose it. Yet the First Amendment does not prevent the FCC from imposing sanctions on stations that broadcast *filthy words,* as the FCC did in 1993 when it fined Infinity Broadcasting for allegedly indecent remarks by "shock jock" Howard Stern, even though such indecencies are not legally obscene. Nor does the First Amendment prevent the FCC from refusing to renew a license if in its opinion a broadcaster has not served the public interest.

The First Amendment did not prevent the FCC from adopting what came to be known as the **fairness doctrine,** requiring broadcasters to cover issues of public significance and to reflect differing viewpoints, as was done from 1949 to 1987. Thus, if licensees made editorial statements or endorsed candidates, they had to give persons representing a different point of view an opportunity to respond. Congress has imposed an additional **equal-time requirement,** requiring licensees to be sure that all candidates for public office had equal air time. Later Congress modified this requirement to make possible presidential debates between candidates of only the two major parties.[85]

The major argument in favor of allowing more government regulation of broadcasters than of newspaper and magazine publishers is that the public owns the limited number of airwaves, and those who have access to these airwaves have control over a limited resource. In a footnote to a 1984 decision, the Court noted, "The prevailing rationale for broadcast regulation has come under increasing criticism in recent years" because such technological changes as cable, direct-beam broadcast, and videotapes may be undermining the assumption that the scarcity of channels justifies government regulation. "We are not prepared, however," wrote Justice William J. Brennan, Jr., for the majority, "to reconsider our long-standing approach without some signal from Congress or the FCC that technological developments have advanced so far that some revision of the system of broadcast regulation may be required."[86]

In 1996, after years of debate, Congress gave that signal. Acknowledging that technological changes produced competition, Congress passed and the president signed the Telecommunications Act of 1996, which will allow phone companies, broadcasters, and cable TV to compete with one another. It will be years before the full impact of this law is realized, as many details are worked out by federal and state regulators and as the courts respond to Congress, making it clear that there is no longer the assumption of scarcity of channels to justify government regulation. However, adoption of the act did not mean that Congress abandoned all government regulation of the airways. On the contrary, the bill calls for many new regulations. It outlaws the transmission of "indecent material" over computer networks and requires that all new television sets sold in the United States be equipped with so-called 'v-chips' that allow viewers to block programs containing violent and or sexual material.

Cable Television and the Right of Access

New means of communication such as cable television raise old issues in new forms. The Supreme Court has decided that cable television is entitled to less constitutional protection than newspapers but more than broadcast television. The justices, however, are not in agreement on precisely how that protection applies. In 1996 the Court upheld in part and struck down in part a 1992 Act of Congress and FCC regulations implementing it that permit but do not require cable operators to forbid the transmission of "patently offensive" sex-related materials over both leased and public access channels. If operators, however, chose to permit such programming on leased channels, the act requires that it be scrambled and segregated into a single channel available only to viewers who file a written request 30 days in advance. The court upheld the provision permitting cable operators to refuse to allow leased channels to engage in this kind of programming, but struck down the provision allowing operators to impose such a ban on public access channels. Parents can block sexually oriented channels by calling their cable company, and the v-chip will soon enable parents to block offensive programs. The Court also struck down provisions requiring indecent programming on leased channels to be scrambled, segregated, and available only by written notice.[88]

Telephones, Fax, E-Mail, Internet, and Cyberspace

Now that fax machines are in widespread use, states are beginning to pass "junk fax laws," making it illegal to fax unsolicited advertisements. Similar legislation is proposed to restrict autodialers, which send computerized telephone messages into homes. A dozen states and Congress have either banned or restricted the use of autodialers, and these regulations are being challenged in the courts on First Amendment grounds.[89] Although federal laws protect against eavesdropping on telephone conversations, including those conveyed by cellular phones, these laws do not as yet extend to walk-around phones that transmit messages via radio waves. Moreover, enforcing laws against electronic eavesdropping on cordless phones is difficult, if not impossible.[90]

New technologies like the Internet have opened up the question of whether the government can constitutionally control or censor material aimed at children.

As Congress and the states begin to deal with these problems, they and the judges who will be reviewing subsequent lawsuits that are filed will have to apply traditional constitutional principles to new situations. For example, what about pornography and obscenity over telephones and E-mail? Congress, reflecting concern about "dial-a-porn," especially as directed to persons under age 18, imposed a total ban on obscene and indecent interstate commercial telephone messages to any person, whatever their age. The Supreme Court found no constitutional obstacles to the law as it relates to "obscene" messages but declared unconstitutional the provision relating to "indecent" messages. Justice Byron R. White wrote for the Court:

> It may well be that there is no fail-safe method of guaranteeing that never will a minor be able to access the dial-a-porn system, . . . but from all we know . . . the FCC's technological approach to restricting dial-a-porn messages to adults who seek them would be extremely effective, and only a few of the most enterprising and disobedient young people will manage to secure access to such messages.[91]

The Court also distinguished between the limited ban on indecent messages over the airwaves that it had previously sustained[92] and the ban on such messages over telephones. Because of the unique attributes of broadcasting, its messages are readily available to children and can intrude into the privacy of the home without prior warning. Telephone messages, on the other hand, are available only to people who want to hear them. It also may be possible, as the Court suggested, to deny minors access to indecent telephone messages more readily than to indecent broadcasting, excepting, of course, "enterprising and disobedient young people."

Following the Court's decision against allowing Congress to ban indecent telephone calls, Congress passed a law narrowly tailored to protect minors from exposure to such materials. Based on that law, the FCC adopted regulations requiring that telephone companies that bill customers for calls to a 900 number block pornographic services to all households except those that specifically request access. The Supreme Court, by refusing to review a decision of a court of appeals upholding the constitutionality of this law and implementing regulations, cleared the way for its enforcement.[93]

What of the thousands of electronic bulletin boards, news groups, and the World Wide Web on which people from all over the world communicate with each other by compute? May those who provide these services be held responsible for obscene and indecent messages, and do they have a right to exclude hate messages or racially or sexually offensive matter? And if government agencies are involved, to what extent do the First and Fourteenth Amendments limit the ability of the agencies to control the content of the messages?[94] These are some of the unanswered constitutional questions raised by the information superhighway.

Congress is struggling with issues of pornography and hate messages in cyberspace. In a provision known as the Communications Decency Act of 1996 in the 1996 Telecommunications Act, Congress made it a federal crime to use the Internet to knowingly transmit indecent material to minors. The act also imposes criminal penalties for transmitting or receiving certain *abortion-related information*. "Indecency" is defined in the law as communication that depicts patently offensive materials about sexual or excretory activies as measured by contemporary community standards. The law provides for expedited judicial review. A three-judge panel has unanimously ruled that this provision violates the First Amendment. The Internet "as the most participatory form of mass speech yet developed deserves the highest protection from governmental intrusion." Cyberspace, this court concluded, should be treated like books and magazines and thus subject to their broad constitutional protection.[95] This decision is being appealed directly to the Supreme Court.

Picketing

Picketing of employers is a normal trade union practice, and such picketing is constitutionally protected, as is picketing and protesting for various causes. A law forbidding all picketing would be an unconstitutional invasion of speech. However, "picketing involves elements of both speech and conduct, i.e., patrolling," and "because of this intermingling of protected and unprotected elements, picketing can be subject to controls that would not be constitutionally permissible in the case of pure speech."[96]

When picketing becomes coercive and interferes with the rights of customers to go into or out of a place of work, or keeps employees from going through a picket line, or interferes with people going into and out of places to which they are entitled to go, such as an abortion clinic, it may be regulated. Since First Amendment questions are involved, such regulations are subject to close judicial scrutiny. While indicating that it might not sustain a ban on all residential picketing, the Court upheld an ordinance that forbids picketing "before or about a single residence."[97] The Court also declined to adopt prior restraint analyses in reviewing the constitutionality of a state court injunction which restricted activities of antiabortion protesters where the protesters were simply prohibited from expressing their views within a 36-foot buffer zone around the property line of an abortion clinic and where the injunction was issued because of the prior unlawful conduct by the protesters.[98] On the other hand, while upholding a congressional prohibition on "hostile congregating" within 500 feet of a foreign embassy, the Court struck down a prohibition on "hostile picketing" in front of such embassies.[99]

Expressive Conduct

People express their views by many other means than just talking or writing. They raise flags, wave banners, march in parades, wear political buttons, carry signs. These various forms of expression, this symbolic speech (or, as it is coming to be called, expressive conduct), is constitutionally protected. This does not mean that people can claim exemption from otherwise valid laws merely by claiming that they are exercising their First Amendment rights. "We cannot accept the view," Chief Justice Earl Warren wrote, "that an apparently limitless variety of conduct can be labeled speech whenever the person engaged in the conduct intends thereby to express an idea."[100] Similarly, Chief Justice Warren Burger wrote:

> Conduct that the State police power can prohibit on a public street does not become automatically protected by the Constitution merely because the conduct is moved to . . . a "live theatre" stage, any more than a "live" performance of a man and woman locked in a sexual embrace at high noon in Times Square is protected by the Constitution merely because they simultaneously engaged in a political dialogue.[101]

Except when the government interest is directly aimed at the symbolic character of the conduct, such as laws forbidding flag burning, the burden is on those who engage in expressive conduct to show that the First Amendment applies. In reviewing laws that regulate expressive conduct, the Court uses a four-part test, first announced in *United States v O'Brien*.[102] The government may forbid or regulate expressive conduct if (1) the regulation is within the constitutional power of the government; (2) it furthers an important governmental interest; (3) the governmental interest is unrelated to the suppression of expression; and (4) the incidental restriction on alleged First Amendment freedom is no greater than is essential to the furtherance of the interest.[103]

Should the Bill of Rights be amended to prohibit flag burning?

The American flag arouses patriotic emotions in Americans, many of whom have fought or seen friends die under that banner. It is understandable that they will be angry to see that flag burned by protesters. Do you think flag burning should be prohibited by law, with appropriate punishments stipulated? Or do you think it is one of the aspects of free speech guaranteed by the Bill of Rights?

Applying these tests, the Supreme Court has concluded that the government cannot forbid the burning of the American flag as a form of political protest, for the interest of the government is directly aimed at the suppression of expressive conduct. Nor can a city make it a crime to burn a cross or display a Nazi swastika even if such displays create anger, alarm, or resentment based on racial, ethnic, gender, or religious bias. However, the Court has strongly hinted that a carefully drawn, content-neutral ordinance might be sustained.[104]

On the other side, burning a draft card in violation of a congressional regulation is not a constitutionally protected form of expressive conduct because Congress, when it made the protection and presentation of such cards a requirement was doing so for purely administrative reasons. It was not trying to prohibit conduct because of its communicative attributes. In the same fashion, the National Park Service was allowed to forbid persons from sleeping overnight in Lafayette Park across from the White House as a way to protest the government failure to protect the rights of the homeless.[105] And although acrobatic and ballroom dancing are not entitled to First Amendment protection, when nude dancing is performed as entertainment in order to express erotic thoughts, such dancing is "within the outer perimeters of the First Amendment." Said Chief Justice Rehnquist for the Court, "We view such dancing as only marginally so." (At least he did not say "barely so.") Nonetheless, the Court upheld the application of a state's public indecency statute to such dancing, requiring dancers to wear pasties and a G-string.[106]

NONPROTECTED SPEECH

As we have noted, some kinds of speech are not entitled to constitutional protection. This does not mean that the constitutional issues relating to these kinds of speech are simple. On the contrary, how we prove *libel,* how we define *obscenity,* and how we determine which words are *fighting words* are hotly contested issues.

Libel

At one time newspaper publishers and editors had to take considerable care about what they wrote, for fear they might be prosecuted for **libel**—written defamation—by the government or sued for money damages by individuals. Today, through a progressive raising of constitutional standards, it has become more difficult to win a libel suit against a newspaper or magazine.

In *The New York Times v Sullivan* and subsequent cases, the Supreme Court established the guidelines for libel cases. The Constitution severely limits a state's power to award damages in a libel action brought by a public official against critics of official conduct. Neither *public officials* nor *public figures* can collect damages for any comments made about them, unless they can prove with "convincing clarity" the comments were made with "actual malice."[107] *Actual malice* means not merely that the defendant had bad motives, but that the "statements were made with a reckless disregard for the truth," which in turn means that the defendant must have made the false publication with a "high degree of awareness of probable falsity."[108]

Public figures cannot collect damages even when subject to outrageous, clearly inaccurate, and false cartoons. Such was the case when *Hustler* magazine printed a cartoon parodying the Reverend Jerry Falwell; the Court held such cartoons cannot reasonably be understood as describing actual facts or actual events.[109] Nor does the mere fact that a public figure is quoted as saying something that he or she did *not* say amount to a libel. "Unless the alteration" in what the person has said "results in material change," the mere fact that the words were deliberately altered does not equate with the constitutionally required knowledge of falsity.[110]

Constitutional standards for libel charges brought by *private* persons are not so rigid. State laws may permit private persons to collect damages without having to prove actual malice if they can prove the statements made about them are false and negligently published.

Obscenity

Today, fears about obscenity and pornography have replaced seventeenth-century fears about heresy and 1950s fears about communism.[111] Obscene publications are not entitled to constitutional protection, but members of the Supreme Court, like everybody else, have great difficulty in defining obscenity. Almost 100 separate opinions have been written on the matter.

In *Miller v California* (1973), the Court was finally able to assemble a majority opinion. Speaking for five members of the Court, Chief Justice Warren Burger once again tried to clarify a constitutional definition of **obscenity.** A work may be considered legally obscene provided: (1) the average person, applying contemporary standards of the particular community, would find that the work, taken as a whole, appeals to a prurient interest in sex (that is, patently offensive interests "over and beyond those that would be characterized as normal"[112]); (2) the work depicts or describes in a patently offensive way sexual conduct specifically defined by the applicable law or authoritatively construed; and (3) the work, taken as a whole, lacks serious literary, artistic, political, or scientific value.[113] Chief Justice Burger specifically rejected part of the previous test—the so-called *Memoirs v Massachusetts* (1966) formula: No work should be judged obscene unless it is "utterly without redeeming social value."[114] He argued such a test would make it impossible for a state to outlaw hard-core pornography.

Does the *Miller* decision mean that local communities can ban whatever a prosecutor could persuade a jury is obscene? Many hoped they could; many others feared they would. But how far could a jury go? Could it decide to ban "Little Red Riding Hood"? After all, who really knows what went on in that bedroom? A year after the *Miller* decision, the Supreme Court warned: "It would be a serious misreading of *Miller* to conclude that juries have unbridled discretion in determining what is patently offensive." Appellate courts, said Justice Rehnquist speaking for the Court, should review jury determinations to ensure compliance with constitutional standards. And the Supreme Court itself, after such review, ruled that the movie *Carnal Knowledge* was not obscene, contrary to the conclusion of a jury in Albany, Georgia.[115]

Obscenity, then, is not entitled to constitutional protection. But governments must proceed under laws that specifically define the kinds of sexual conduct forbidden in word or picture. Moreover, it is not a crime for booksellers to offer obscene books for sale; they must be shown to have done so *knowingly.* Otherwise, booksellers would tend to avoid placing on their shelves materials that some authorities might consider objectionable, and the public would be deprived of an opportunity to purchase anything except some person's determination of the "safe and sanitary." The mere private possession of obscene materials is not a crime either.

What about X-rated movies that fall short of the constitutional definition of obscenity? They are entitled to some constitutional protection, but less protection than political speech, and they are subject to greater government regulation. "The state may legitimately use the content of these materials as the basis for placing them in a different classification from other motion pictures."[116] Cities may also regulate, by zoning laws, where so-called adult motion picture theaters may be located.

Thinking it Through

On June 21, 1989 the Supreme Court, in *Texas v Johnson*, decided by a 5 to 4 vote that the First Amendment protects the expressive act of burning the flag. President George Bush denounced the decision and called for a constitutional amendment that would nullify it. Congress responded by passing a federal law that would make it a crime to burn or to deface the flag—whatever one's purposes or intent. In June 1990, nine months after the first decision, the Supreme Court declared that law unconstitutional also in *United States v Eichman*.

The flag burning issue came up again in 1995, largely as a result of the 1994 elections that left Republicans in control of both the House and the Senate. In the summer of 1995 the House of Representatives readily approved such an amendment by a vote of 312 to 120. In the Senate the amendment was modified to take out the provision allowing states to act to avoid what Senator Joseph R. Biden, Jr. called "a potential patchwork of 50 idiosyncratic laws." In December 1995 the Senate came within three votes— 63 to 36—of the required two-thirds. With public opinion polls showing strong support for the amendment, the issue is clearly not dead. "This amendment is not going to go away," sponsor Orrin G. Hatch (R–Utah) said minutes after the final vote. "We will debate it in the next Congress."

Before you decide, you might want to read the opinions of the Supreme Court justices: *Texas v Johnson*, 491 US 397 (1989); *United States v Eichman*, 496 US 310 (1990).

The inflammatory and degrading messages in some popular records and on music television have aroused many groups to action. Starting several years ago with Tipper Gore's campaign for ratings on sexually explicit records to keep them out of the hands of children, protests were also heard from parent groups who asked television networks to monitor the violence in programs targeted for young children. "Gangster rap," and in particular a recording by Ice T calling for attacks on the police, brought out protests from police organizations and parents throughout the country and boycotts of the recording company. Women's groups voiced resentment of the portrayal of women as willing victims of brutal sex acts and the insulting language used to describe them in music videos.

Carol Moseley Braun, Illinois senator, presided over a hearing of the Juvenile Justice Subcommittee of the Judiciary Committee on the violent and vulgar lyrics of rap music. In their defense, music stations, recording companies, and rap singers cited the guarantees of free speech and maintained that they were speaking the truth as people in the ghettos saw it.

The rap group Ice T's records encourage killing cops and abusing women.

Senator Carol Moseley Braun looks on as young rappers prepare to testify before the Senate Judiciary Committee.

Sexually explicit materials either about minors or aimed at them are *not* protected by the First Amendment. Provided they act under narrowly drawn statutes, state and local governments can, for example, ban the knowing sale of "adult" magazines to minors, even if such materials would not be considered legally obscene if sold to adults. And governments can make it a crime to depict sexual conduct by children, even if the depicted behavior would not be considered obscene if performed by adults.

Pornography

Pornography used to be merely a synonym for *obscenity*. Pressure for regulating pornography came primarily from political conservatives and religious fundamentalists concerned that it undermines moral standards. More recently, many feminists have joined them, arguing that "pornography is central in creating and maintaining sex as a basis for discrimination."[117] They contend that pornography promotes sexual abuse of individual women and perpetuates social subordination of women as a class. Feminists define pornographic materials as sexually explicit pictures or words that depict women as sexual objects enjoying pain and humiliation or that present abuse of women as a sexual stimulus for men. Some have argued that the line should be drawn to permit regulation of "depictions of sexuality that involve rape and violence against women."[118]

Advocates of regulation of pornography argue that just as sexually explicit materials about minors are not entitled to First Amendment protection, so should there be no such protection for pornographic materials. They propose that civil penalties be imposed on pornographers, and that women—and others who have had pornography forced upon them—be given the right to file complaints and sue for damages. The Senate Judiciary Committee has proposed the Pornography Victim's Compensation Act allowing crime victims to sue producers, distributors, and exhibitors of a book, magazine, movie, or lyric "that the victim believes triggered the crime."[119]

Women and men have differed significantly in their attitudes about pornography (see Table 3-1). Men are less likely than women to think pornography damages adults who read it, and women are twice as likely to favor laws banning the sale of pornography, regardless of the age of the buyer, while men tend to favor restricting the sale of pornography to minors.[120]

Not all feminists favor antipornography ordinances, yet those who do have been joined by social conservatives, and thus a new era in the battle over pornography has begun. For this new antipornography coalition to be successful, a substantial alteration in constitutional doctrine will be required.[121] The Canadian Supreme Court has redefined obscenity to include materials that degrade women, and several cities in the United States have been considering the adoption of antipornography ordinances.[122] Only Indianapolis has passed such a law, which was declared unconstitutional in a decision affirmed by the Supreme Court without opinion.[123]

Censorship of films and books may be imposed by a variety of means other than formal action. In some cities, such local groups as the Legion of Decency may pressure authorities. Feminists, by threats of boycott, have pressured some stores to stop selling magazines they believe depict women in a demeaning and pornographic manner. Local police have been known to threaten booksellers with criminal prosecution if they persist in showing films or selling books of which some local people disapprove.

Fighting Words

Governments may punish certain well-defined and narrowly limited classes of speech that "by their very utterance inflict injury or tend to incite an immediate breach of peace."[124] These so-called **fighting words** "have a direct tendency to cause acts of violence by the person to whom, individually, the remarks are addressed."[125] That the words are abusive, harsh, or insulting, or that they create anger, alarm, or resentment based on racial, ethnic, gender, or religious basis is not sufficient. Thus, a four-letter word worn on a sweatshirt was not judged to be a fighting word in the constitutional sense, at least when it is not directed to any specific person.[126]

The "fighting words" category has taken on additional significance in recent years in view of the attempts by many state universities and colleges to regulate insulting racial, ethnic, and sexual slurs. The Constitution limits how public universities and colleges may punish students for what they say, and cases challenging these so called "hate codes" are working their way through the courts. That speech may be insulting or racially offensive or sexist does not mean that it lacks constitutional

TABLE 3-1

Attitudes Toward Pornography, 1994

	Yes	No	DK/NA*
Sexual materials lead to a breakdown of morals.			
Men	50%	43%	7%
Women	67	26	7
Sexual materials lead people to commit rape.			
Men	39%	50%	11%
Women	61	27	11

	Men	Women
There should be laws against the distribution of pornography, whatever the age.	26%	49%
There should be laws against the distribution of pornography to persons under 18.	66%	4%7
There should be no laws forbidding the distribution of pornography.	6%	3%
Don't know or No answer	2%	1%

SOURCE: National Opinion Research Center, University of Chicago, *General Social Surveys, 1972–1994.*

*Don't Know or No Answer.

protection. As the Court has said, "If there is a bedrock principle underlying the First Amendment, it is that the Government may not prohibit the expression of an idea simply because society finds the idea offensive or disagreeable."[127]

The Supreme Court has gone out of its way to warn governments and public universities against moving to punish fighting words by codes designed to protect people against insults solely because of their race, sex, or religion. "The First Amendment does not," wrote Justice Antonin Scalia for the Court, "permit [governments] to impose special prohibitions on those speakers who express views on disfavored subjects."[128] But in the role of landlord for residence halls, universities and colleges may have greater authority to impose reasonable time, place, and manner regulations against insulting racial, sexual, or religious slurs directed toward fellow residents.

The speech of faculty and staff at universities and colleges, public or private, is also protected by the Constitution from governmental regulation. What of the power of the university or college itself to regulate the speech of its employees, including faculty, and its students? As state agencies, public universities and colleges are subject to the restrictions of the Constitution. Nonetheless, a public university as an employer has some leeway in regulating the speech of its employees, more leeway than it has in regulating the speech of its students, especially student speech outside of the classroom or outside of residence halls. A university for example, has some discretion—in fact, under federal laws, some obligation—to control racially or sexually harassing speech by faculty and staff.

Private universities and colleges are not subject to these constitutional limitations on how they may regulate the speech of their students. However, state governments may protect the speech of students against undue regulation by these institutions, and colleges and universities that receive federal funds may find that their freedom to regulate the use of offensive speech by students is limited by federal laws and regulations. Federal and state laws regulating the responsibilities of employers to provide a workplace free from sexual harassment apply to universities, private and public.

RIGHT TO ASSEMBLE AND TO PETITION THE GOVERNMENT

Freedom of Assembly

In the winter of 1977, Frank Collins, "a self-avowed Nazi," threatened to lead his small band, dressed in brown shirts and carrying swastikas, in a jack-booted march through the streets of Skokie, Illinois, a Chicago suburb with a large Jewish population.[129] Skokie's citizens included survivors of Hitler's extermination camps; many of them had relatives who lost their lives in the Holocaust. Many people, including the officials of Skokie and a local judge, argued that Collins and his followers should not be allowed to march. They argued that this would be like shouting "Fire!" in a crowded theater, and that to permit such a use of the streets presented a clear and present danger of inciting people to violence. These same arguments were put forward to contend that Iranian followers of the late Ayatollah Khomeini should not be allowed to protest publicly in Washington, D.C., at a time when most Americans were angry about Khomeini's illegal and brutal treatment of innocent American hostages in Tehran. The right to assemble peaceably, they said, should not be extended to Iranian aliens who were abusing this right to provoke Americans to violence.

In both cases judicial authorities defended the rights of these unpopular minorities to demonstrate. (Collins never actually marched in Skokie, but he did march in another part of the Chicago area.[130]) But it is not always the "bad guys" whose rights have to be protected by the courts. It also took occasional judicial intervention in the 1960s to preserve for Martin Luther King, Jr., and for those who marched with him, the right to demonstrate in the streets of southern cities in behalf of civil rights for African Americans.

Such incidents present the classic free speech problem of the "heckler's veto," when the audience becomes so abusive that it is impossible for the speaker to be heard. It is almost always easier, and certainly politically more prudent, to maintain order by curbing public demonstrations of unpopular groups than by moving against those who are threatening them. On the other hand, if police did not have the right to order groups to disperse, public order would be at the mercy of those who resort to street demonstrations just to create tensions and provoke street battles.

Public Forums and Time, Place, and Manner Regulations

The Constitution protects the right to speak, but it does not give persons the right to communicate their views to everyone, every place, at any time they wish. No one has the right deliberately to incite others to violence, to block traffic, or to hold parades or make speeches in public streets or on public sidewalks whenever he or she wishes. Governments may not specify what can or cannot be said, but they can make reasonable *time, place, and manner* regulations for the holding of assemblies or protests or gatherings. The extent of government regulation varies with where the assembly takes place.

The Supreme Court has divided public property into three categories: public forums, limited public forums, and nonpublic forums. The extent to which governments may limit access depends on the kind of forums involved. *Public forums* are those public places historically associated with the free exercise of expressive activities, such as streets, sidewalks, and parks. Courts look closely at time, place, and manner regulations as they apply to these traditional public forums to ensure that they are being applied evenhandedly and that action is not taken because of what is being said rather than how and where or by whom it is being said.[131] Further, in these traditional public forums, no restrictive laws are permitted unless they are viewpoint neutral and the government in question can prove that they are necessary to serve a compelling government interest.

Other kinds of public property, such as designated rooms in a city hall or after-hour use of school buildings, may be designated as *limited public forums*, available for assembly and speech for limited purposes, a limited amount of time, and even for a limited class of speakers (such as only students, only teachers, or only employees), provided the distinctions between those allowed access and those not allowed access are viewpoint neutral.

Nonpublic forums include public facilities such as libraries, courthouses, schools, swimming pools, and government offices that are open to the public but are not public forums. As long as persons use such facilities within the normal bounds of conduct, they may not be constitutionally restrained from doing so. However, persons may be excluded from such places as a government office or a school if they engage in activities for which the facilities were not created. They have no right to interfere with programs or try to appropriate facilities—especially facilities such as a university president's office—in order to stage a political protest.

Does the right of peaceful assembly and petition include the right to violate a law nonviolently but deliberately? We have no precise answer. But in general, *civil disobedience*, even if peaceful, is not a protected right. When Dr. Martin Luther King, Jr., and his followers refused to comply with a state court's injunction forbidding them to parade in Birmingham without first securing a permit, the Supreme Court sustained their conviction, even though there was serious doubt about the constitutionality of the injunction and the ordinance on which it was based. Justice Potter Stewart, speaking for the five-member majority, said: "No man can be judge in his own case, however exalted his station, however righteous his motive, and irrespective of his race, color, politics, or religion." Persons are not "constitutionally free to ignore all the procedures of the law and carry their battles to the streets."[132] The four dissenting justices insisted that one does have a right to defy peacefully an obviously unconstitutional statute or injunction.

The First Amendment rights of anti-abortion protesters to picket in front of abortion clinics came into conflict with some women's rights of access to abortion clinics as a result of a campaign by anti-abortion protesters to shut down abortion clinics. The protesters often massed in front of clinics shouting at employees and patrons and sometimes blocked the entrance to the clinic. Congress responded with the Freedom of Access to Clinic Entrances Act of 1994, which makes it a federal crime and imposes severe fines, including prison terms, on persons who use force, threats, or physical obstruction to interfere with anyone providing or receiving abortions and other reproductive health services. It allows abortion clinic employees and clients or the Department of Justice to sue for damages and seek federal injunctions against violators. Although the act explicitly exempts conduct protected by the free speech and assembly clauses, such as peaceful picketing and passing out leaflets, opponents of the legislation contend that this act interferes with the anti-abortion movement's right to engage in picketing and protesting. They maintain that the act imposes punishment far more severe than state laws and city ordinances for blocking sidewalks and sit-ins.[133]

States too have tried to protect the patrons and employees of abortion clinics against coercive protesting, primarily via the issuance of injunctions. The Supreme Court, in trying to balance the legitimate speech rights of abortion protesters against the equally legitimate rights of access on the part of the partons and employees of these clinics, upheld some provisions of a state court injunction and struck down others. The Court upheld those provisions which prohibited protesters from congregating, picketing, patrolling, and demonstrating within a 36-foot buffer zone around the property line of an abortion clinic. The Court concluded this prohibition was a narrowly drawn limit on the protesters that was necessary to accomplish the legitimate governmental interest in protecting entrance and exit from the clinic. The Court also upheld those provision prohibiting singing, yelling, and using bullhorns within earshot of patients inside the clinic during specific hours as means to protect the health and well-being of the patients. On the other hand, the Court struck down provisions preventing protesters from picketing at the back of the clinic, the use of "images observable" to the patients, or prohibiting them from approaching within 300 feet of the clinic or of any person seeking services, and from using amplification devices within 300 feet. These provisions, the Court concluded, were too broad and therefore interfered with the protesters' First Amendment rights.[134]

Assembly on Private Property

The right to assemble does not include the right to trespass on private property. A state may protect property owners against those who attempt to convert property to their own uses, even if they are doing so to express ideas.

The profusion of large, privately owned shopping malls that cover many acres and are larger than some towns presents some difficult constitutional issues. The Supreme Court has set the following guidelines: Privately owned shopping malls are neither public streets nor places of public assembly; no one has a constitutional right to use such a mall to hand out political leaflets, to picket for political purposes, or otherwise to exercise First Amendment freedoms. On the other hand, states and cities may legally obligate the owners of such centers to permit their use for peaceful political purposes such as distributing handbills or getting people to sign petitions. In other words, although people have no constitutional right to engage in political action in a nonpublic shopping center, neither do the owners of such centers have a constitutional right to close them to political action in the face of reasonable state or local regulations providing for access that does not interfere with their primary commercial purposes.[135]

Freedom of Association

The right to petition the government for redress of grievances is specifically guaranteed by the Constitution. The right to organize to promote political and other causes is not expressly mentioned in the Constitution, but "it is beyond debate that freedom to engage in association for the advancement of beliefs and ideas is an inseparable aspect of the 'liberty' assured by the Due Process clause of the Fourteenth Amendment which embraces freedom of speech."[136]

The Supreme Court has written of freedom to associate in two distinct senses. In one line of decisions it has protected people's right to enter into and maintain "certain intimate human relationships" against "undue intrusion by the State. . . . In this respect, freedom of association receives protection as a fundamental element of personal liberty."[137] The other aspect relates to activities protected by the First Amendment: speech, assembly, petition, the redress of grievances, and the free exercise of religion.

Some troublesome constitutional questions arise from congressional and state regulation of the amount of money that candidates, political parties, and interest groups can raise and spend for political purposes. Is money speech? If so, then is government regulation of its use constitutionally suspect? Or is money more like action, and therefore open to governmental regulation?[138] In *Buckley v Valeo*, the Court sustained limits on the amount of money people may *contribute to candidates* and their campaign committees on the grounds that such limits only marginally restrict contributors' abilities to express political views.[139] But it struck down limits on the amounts that may be contributed to *associations* formed to support or oppose ballot measures submitted to popular vote.

Limits on what people can *spend*, in contrast to what they can contribute, have fared even less well. Governments may not set limits on the amounts that people (including candidates) can spend on political matters. Presidential candidates, such as Ross Perot in 1992 and Steve Forbes in 1996, who have access to their own wealth and who choose not to take federal funds for their campaigns may not be limited in what they spend. Limits on what presidential candidates can spend apply only to expenditures by the candidate's party organizations and "coordinated groups," not to "independent groups or committees," who have a constitutional right to spend as much as they wish to further the candidate's election.[140]

SUBVERSIVE CONDUCT AND SEDITIOUS SPEECH

"If there is any fixed star in our constitutional constellation," Justice Robert Jackson said, "it is that no official, high or petty, can prescribe what shall be orthodox in politics, nationalism, religion, or other matters of opinion."[141] Any group can champion whatever position it wishes: vegetarianism, feminism, sexism, communism, fascism, black nationalism, white supremacy, Zionism, anti-Semitism, Americanism.

It is one thing to punish persons for what they *do*; it is another to punish them for what they *say*. The story of the development of constitutional democracy is in large measure the story of making this distinction clear.

The Sedition Act of 1798

The adoption of the Constitution and the Bill of Rights did not result in a quick, easy victory for those who wished to establish free speech in the United States.[142] In 1798, only seven years after the First Amendment had been ratified, Congress passed the first national law aimed against **sedition**—attempting to overthrow the government by force or to interrupt its activities by violence. Those were perilous times for the young Republic, for war with France seemed imminent. The Federalists, in control of both Congress and the presidency, persuaded themselves that national safety required some suppression of speech.

The Sedition Act marked a considerable advance over English common law in that it made truth a defense and allowed the jury, not a judge, to decide the fact of sedition as well as the fact of publication. It did, however, make it a crime to utter false, scandalous, or malicious statements intended to bring the government or any of its officers into disrepute or "to incite against them the hatred of the good people of the United States."[143]

Popular reaction to the Sedition Act helped defeat the Federalists in the elections of 1800. They had failed to grasp the democratic idea that a person may criticize the government of the day, oppose its policies, and work for its downfall, but still be loyal to the nation.

The Smith Act of 1940

The first peacetime sedition law since the Sedition Act of 1798 was the Smith Act of 1940. The Smith Act forbids persons to advocate overthrow of the government with the intent to bring it about; to distribute, with disloyal intent, matter teaching or advising the overthrow of government by violence; and to organize knowingly or to help organize any group having such purposes.

In *Dennis v United States* (1950), the Court agreed that the Smith Act could be applied to the leaders of the Communist party, who had been charged with conspiring to advocate the violent overthrow of the government.[144] Since then the Court has substantially modified its holding. Congress may not outlaw the mere advocacy of the abstract doctrine of violent overthrow: "The essential distinction is that those to whom the advocacy is addressed must be urged to do something now or in the future, rather than merely to believe in something."[145] Moreover, advocacy of the use of force may not be forbidden "except where such advocacy is directed to inciting or producing imminent lawless action and is likely to incite or produce such action."[146]

In short, seditious speech, if narrowly defined to cover only the advocacy of immediate and concrete acts of violence, is not constitutionally protected. Such narrow interpretation of the sedition laws means people are free to work for their political objectives as long as they abandon the use of force—or its specific and immediate advocacy—as a means of bringing it about.

SUMMARY

1. First Amendment freedoms—freedom of religion, freedom from the establishment of religion, freedom of speech, freedom of the press, freedom of assembly and petition, and freedom of association—are at the heart of a healthy constitutional democracy.

2. Since World War I, the Supreme Court has become the primary branch of government for giving meaning to these constitutional restraints. And since 1925 these constitutional limits have been applied not only to Congress but to all governmental agencies—national, state, and local.

3. Clashes about First Amendment freedoms are not usefully thought of as battles between the "good guys" and the "bad guys" or as dramas in which judges rush to the rescue of liberty. Rather, these are arguments over conflicting notions of what is in the public interest.

4. Over the years, the Supreme Court has taken a practical approach to First Amendment freedoms. It has refused to make them absolute rights above any kind of governmental regulation, direct or indirect, or to say that they must be preserved at whatever price. But the justices have recognized that a constitutional democracy tampers with these freedoms at great peril. They have insisted upon compelling justification before permitting these rights to be limited. How compelling the justification is, in a free society, will always remain an open question.

FURTHER READING

STEPHEN BATES, *Battleground* (Poseidon, 1993).

LEE C. BOLLINGER, *Images of a Free Press* (University of Chicago Press, 1991).

JAMES MACGREGOR BURNS AND STEWART BURNS, *A People's Charter: The Pursuit of Rights in America* (Knopf, 1991).

T. BARTON CARTER, MARC A. FRANKLIN, AND JAY B. WRIGHT, *The First Amendment and the Fourth Estate*, 5th ed. (Foundation Press, 1991).

ZECHARIAH CHAFEE, JR., *Free Speech in the United States* (Harvard University Press, 1941).

JESSE CHOPER, *Securing Religious Liberty: Principles for Judicial Interpretation of Religion Clauses* (University of Chicago Press, 1995).

DONALD L. DRAKEMAN, *Church-State Constitutional Issues: Making Sense of the Establishment Clause* (Greenwood, 1991).

TERRY EASTLAND, ED., *Religious Liberty in the Supreme Court: The Cases That Define the Debate over Church and State* (Ethics and Policy Center, 1993).

IRA GLASSER, *Visions of Liberty: The Bill of Rights for All Americans* (Arcade, 1991).

MARK A. GRABER, *Transforming Free Speech: The Ambiguous Legacy of Civil Libertarianism* (University of California Press, 1991).

KENT GREENAWALT, *Fighting Words: Individuals, Communities, and Liberties of Speech* (Princeton University Press, 1995).

MARJORIE HEINS, *Sex, Sin and Blasphemy: A Guide to America's Censorship Wars* (New Press, 1993).

NAT HENTOFF, *The First Freedom: The Tumultuous History of Free Speech in America*, 2d ed. (Delacorte, 1988).

EUGENE W. HICKOK, JR., ED., *The Bill of Rights: Original Meaning and Current Understanding* (University Press of Virginia, 1991).

JAMES E. LEAHY, *The First Amendment, 1791–1991: Two Hundred Years of Freedom* (McFarland, 1991).

LEONARD W. LEVY, *The Establishment Clause: Religion and the First Amendment* (Macmillan, 1986).

ANTHONY LEWIS, *Make No Law: The Sullivan Case and the First Amendment* (Random House, 1991).

CATHARINE A. MACKINNON, *Only Words* (Harvard University Press, 1993).

JOHN STUART MILL, *Essay on Liberty* (1859), in *The English Philosophers from Bacon to Mill*, ed. Arthur Burtt (Random House, 1939), pp. 949–1041.

WILLIAM LEE MILLER, *The First Liberty: Religion and the American Republic* (Knopf, 1986).

MELVILLE B. NIMMER, *Nimmer on Freedom of Speech: A Treatise on the Theory of the First Amendment* (Mathew Binder, 1987).

J. W. PELTASON, *Understanding the Constitution*, 13th ed. (Harcourt Brace, 1994).

LUCAS A. POWE, JR., *The Fourth Estate and the Constitution: Freedom of the Press in America* (University of California Press, 1991).

JONATHAN RAUCH, *Kindly Inquisitors: The New Attacks on Free Thought* (University of Chicago Press, 1993).

NADINE STROSSEN, *Defending Pornography: Free Speech, Sex, and the Fight for Women's Rights* (Scribner's, 1995).

GEOFFREY R. STONE, RICHARD A. EPSTEIN, and CASS R. SUNSTEIN, EDS., *The Bill of Rights in the Modern State*, (University of Chicago Press, 1992).

CASS R. SUNSTEIN, *Democracy and the Problems of Free Speech* (Free Press, 1993).

ROBERT J. WAGMAN, *The First Amendment Book* (World Almanac, 1991).

RONALD C. WHITE, JR., AND ALBRIGHT G. ZIMMERAN, EDS., *An Unsettled Arena: Religions and the Bill of Rights* (Eerdmans, 1990).

EQUAL JUSTICE UNDER THE LAW

onsider again the ringing words of the Declaration of Independence: "We hold these truths to be self-evident, that all men are created equal, that they are endowed by their Creator with certain unalienable Rights, that among these are Life, Liberty, and the pursuit of Happiness." In this one sentence the Declaration affirmed the precious rights of *equality* and *liberty* and appeared to rate equality at least on a par with liberty. The Declaration does not talk about equality of white, Christian, or Anglo-Saxon men, but of *all* men. (Undoubtedly, if the Declaration were to be written today, the framers would speak of "persons" rather than "men.") This creed of individual dignity and equality is older than our Declaration of Independence; its roots go back into the teachings of Judaism and Christianity.

What about the Constitution that was signed eleven years after the Declaration? What was the framers' attitude toward liberty and equality? We know that the builders of our constitutional system cherished liberty as their highest ideal. And although you will not find any reference to the idea of equality (not even the word itself is in the Constitution or in the array of liberties that form the Bill of Rights), we know the framers believed that all men—at least all white men—were equally entitled to life, liberty, and the pursuit of happiness (the framers changed "pursuit of happiness" to "property" in the Bill of Rights). They felt strongly that there should be no noble or privileged class under the law. Like the Declaration, the Constitution refers to "men" or "him," not to women, and none of its lofty sentiments applied to slaves, who enjoyed neither liberty nor equality.

The framers resolved their ambiguity about what kind of equality and for whom by creating systems of government designed to protect what they called **natural rights**. Today we speak of **human rights**, but the idea is the same: All citizens are entitled to their dignity and worth. By equal rights the framers meant that every person has an equal right to protection against arbitrary treatment, an equal right to the liberties guaranteed by the Bill of Rights, and an equal right to protection by any laws passed by the new national government.

The Constitution itself provides two ways of protecting civil rights. First, it ensures that government imposes no discriminatory barriers; second, it grants national and state governments authority to protect civil rights against interference by private individuals. This chapter is concerned with both the protection of our rights from *abuse by government* and the *protection through government* of our right to be free from abuse by our fellow citizens. In this chapter we focus on the struggle to secure the basic civil rights to vote, to an education, to a job, and to a place to live on equal terms with our fellow citizens. We also examine the safeguards that protect these precious rights.

CITIZENSHIP RIGHTS

Citizenship as an Office

Who belongs to the body politic? Who is an American? Every nation has rules that determine nationality and define who is a member of, owes allegiance to, and is a subject of the nation-state. But in a democracy, citizenship is more than nationality, more than merely being a subject.[1] Citizenship is an office, and, like other offices, it carries with it certain powers and responsibilities. How citizenship is acquired and retained should therefore be a matter of considerable importance to everyone.

How Citizenship Is Acquired and Lost

This basic right of citizenship was not given constitutional protection until 1868, when the Fourteenth Amendment was adopted. The Fourteenth Amendment states: "All persons born or naturalized in the United States, and subject to the jurisdiction thereof, are citizens of the United States and of the State wherein they reside." This means that all persons born in the United States, except children born to foreign ambassadors and ministers, are citizens of this country regardless of the citizenship of their parents. (Congress has defined the United States for this purpose to include Puerto Rico, Guam, the Northern Marianas, and the Virgin Islands.) Although the Fourteenth Amendment does not make Native Americans citizens of the United States and of the states in which they live, Congress has done so.

The Fourteenth Amendment confers citizenship according to the principle of *jus soli*—by place of birth. In addition, Congress has granted, under certain conditions, citizenship at birth according to the principle of *jus sanguinis*—by blood. A child born to an American citizen living abroad is an American citizen if the American parent has lived in the United States for ten years, including two after age 14.

NATURALIZATION Citizenship may also be acquired by either collective or individual naturalization, a legal action conferring citizenship upon an alien. The granting of citizenship to the people of the Northern Marianas in 1977 by an act of Congress is an example of *collective* naturalization. Individual naturalization requirements are determined by Congress. Today, with minor exceptions, nonenemy aliens over age 18 who have been lawfully admitted for permanent residence and who have resided in the United States for at least five years and in the state in which they are residing for at least six months are eligible for naturalization, which is finally conferred by a court. Any state or federal court of record in the United States or the Immigration and Naturalization Service (INS) can grant citizenship. The INS makes the necessary investigations. Any person denied citizenship after a hearing before an immigration officer may seek a *de novo* (completely new) hearing before a federal district judge.

Citizenship is granted if the judge or hearing officer is satisfied that the applicant has met all the requirements, renounces allegiance to his or her former country, swears to support and defend the Constitution and laws of the United States against all enemies, and promises to bear arms on behalf of the United States when required to do so by law. Those whose religious beliefs prevent them from bearing arms are allowed to take an oath swearing that, if called to duty, they will serve in the armed forces as noncombatants or will perform work of

We The People

Foreign-Born Population of the United States

- Never have so many immigrants lived in this country, although the foreign-born proportion of the population was larger earlier in this century, when the U.S. population was smaller.

- The place of birth of most immigrants has shifted from Europe to Asia and Latin America.

- 19.7 million, or just under 8 percent of the U.S. population, are foreign-born.

- Nearly 32 million persons speak a language other than English at home, and more than 40 percent of them say they do not speak English very well.

- The number of immigrants from Mexico and from Asia has more than doubled in the last decade.

- Projected population percentages for Los Angeles County for the year 2000 are 40 percent Hispanic, 34 percent white, 16 percent Asian, and 10 percent black.

- The Los Angeles Unified School District (the second largest in the nation) serves more than 625,000 students speaking 80 different languages, more than 83,000 of them foreign-born.

SOURCES: U.S. Department of Commerce, Bureau of the Census, and Barbara Vobejda, "A Nation in Transition: Census Reveals Striking Stratification of U.S. Society," *The Washington Post*, May 29, 1992, pp. A1, A18–A19.

THE RIGHT OF CITIZENSHIP

Although natural-born Americans tend to take citizenship for granted, most naturalized citizens cherish it, for it represents hard work and a sincere commitment on their part. Would natural-born Americans appreciate citizenship more if they had to meet the same standards as foreign-born applicants?

Naturalization Requirements

An applicant for naturalization must:

1. Be over age 18.
2. Be lawfully admitted to the United States for permanent residence, and have resided in the United States for at least five years and in the state in which they are residing for at least six months.
3. File a petition of naturalization with a clerk of a court of record (federal or state) verified by two witnesses.
4. Be able to read, write, and speak English.
5. Possess a good moral character.
6. Understand and demonstrate an attachment to the history, principles, and form of government of the United States.
7. Demonstrate that he or she is well disposed toward the good order and happiness of the country.
8. Demonstrate that he or she does not now believe in, nor within the last ten years has ever believed in, advocated, or belonged to an organization that supports opposition to organized government, overthrow of government by violence, or the doctrines of world communism or any other form of totalitarianism.

Albert Einstein (1879–1955), his daughter *(right)*, and his secretary *(left)*, take the oath of American citizenship. A brilliant physicist known for formulating the theory of relativity, Einstein was born in Germany. Because he was Jewish, the Nazi government confiscated his property and revoked his citizenship in 1934, at which time he immigrated to the United States.

national importance under civilian direction. The court or INS then grants a certificate of naturalization.

Naturalized citizenship may be revoked by court order if the government can prove citizenship was secured by deception. In addition, citizenship, however acquired, may be renounced voluntarily. But citizenship cannot be taken from people because of what they have done—for committing certain crimes, for example, voting in foreign elections, or serving in foreign armies. Some actions, however, such as taking out citizenship in another country or swearing allegiance to another nation, may be taken into account as "highly persuasive evidence of a purpose to abandon citizenship." Even so, the government must prove that the citizen "not only voluntarily committed the expatriating act prescribed in the statute, but also intended to relinquish his citizenship."[2]

What Citizenship Means

We are in a period of growing public hostility toward aliens, so that the protection of American citizenship becomes even more precious. The Constitution protects many rights of all persons, not just citizens. For example, Congress and the states can no more deny to aliens than to citizens the right of free exercise of religion or the right of freedom of speech. Nor can any government deprive any person, alien or citizen, of due process of the law or equal protection under the laws. Other rights, however, are not so protected, and Congress can deny—and has denied—welfare and other kinds of benefits to aliens, especially to those who are not lawfully admitted.

What of states? Except for rights that flow from citizenship—such as the right to vote, to hold public office, or to work for the government—states may not deny to aliens who have been lawfully admitted any public benefits other than those permitted by Congress. Nor can states deny even to illegal aliens some rights that flow from the Fourteenth Amendment, such as the right to have your children educated in the public schools. In 1994 California challenged prevailing constitutional doctrine by adopting an amendment to its Constitution, Proposition 187, that denies illegal aliens the right to attend its public schools and colleges or to be admitted to any public hospital or clinic except for emergency treatment. In response to legal challenges, federal and state courts are now reviewing Proposition 187 to see which, if any, of its provisions are in violation of the equal protection clause of the Fourteenth Amendment.

THE RIGHT TO TRAVEL ABROAD Although the right of interstate travel is virtually unqualified, the right to international travel can be regulated within the bounds of due process. Under current law it is unlawful for citizens to leave or enter the United States without a valid passport (except for travel to Mexico, Canada, and parts of the Caribbean). The president, acting through the secretary of state, may refuse to grant or may revoke a passport if the government concludes that a holder's activities in foreign countries are causing, or are likely to cause, serious damage to our national security or foreign policy.

THE RIGHT TO LIVE IN THE UNITED STATES This right, which is not subject to any congressional limitation, is perhaps the most precious aspect of American citizenship. Aliens have no such right. They may be stopped on the high seas or at the borders and turned away if they fail to meet the terms and conditions stipulated by Congress for admission into the United States. Today millions of people around the world are begging to come and live in the United States, but only American citizens have a constitutionally guaranteed right to do so (see Figure 4-1).

When the Chinese ship *Golden Venture* ran aground in 1993 off Rockaway Beach, New York, its cargo of 350 illegal aliens swam ashore or died in the attempt. Their urge to come to the United States was so strong that they had agreed to work under slave labor conditions to pay back the smugglers who brought them here.

Equal Protection: Three Tiers of Tests

• **THE RATIONAL BASIS TEST** The traditional test to determine whether a law complies with the equal protection requirement places the burden of proof on those attacking it. If the facts justify a classification, the law will be sustained, even if it results in some inequality. If the Supreme Court chooses to apply this rational basis test, the law in question will usually be upheld.

• **SUSPECT CLASSIFICATIONS AND STRICT SCRUTINY** The most stringent test, the strict scrutiny test, is used when a suspect class or a fundamental right is involved. The normal presumption of constitutionality is reversed. When a law is subject to strict scrutiny, it is not sufficient that the law be a reasonable means to handle a particular problem. Rather, the courts must be persuaded that there is both a "compelling public interest" to justify such a classification and no other less restrictive way to accomplish this compelling public purpose.

A *suspect class* is a class of people subjected to deliberate unequal treatment in the past, or relegated by society to a position of such political powerlessness as to require extraordinary judicial protection. Classifications based on race and national origin are suspect and are subject to strict scrutiny. Laws that classify people by their religion would also create a suspect class, although there is no specific Supreme Court decision to this effect, probably because governments seldom classify people according to religion. State or local laws that impose political limitations on aliens also create suspect classifications, and thus are subject to strict scrutiny.

• **QUASI-SUSPECT CLASSIFICATIONS AND HEIGHTENED SCRUTINY** The intermediate test is called the heightened scrutiny test. It applies to what the court has called *quasi-suspect classes*. To sustain a law under this test, the burden is on the government to show that its classification serves "important governmental objectives" and is substantially related to these objectives. Gender classifications are subject to heightened scrutiny.

FIGURE 4-1 Coming to America

SOURCE: Steven Kearsley, *San Francisco Chronicle*, June 21, 1993, p. A7.

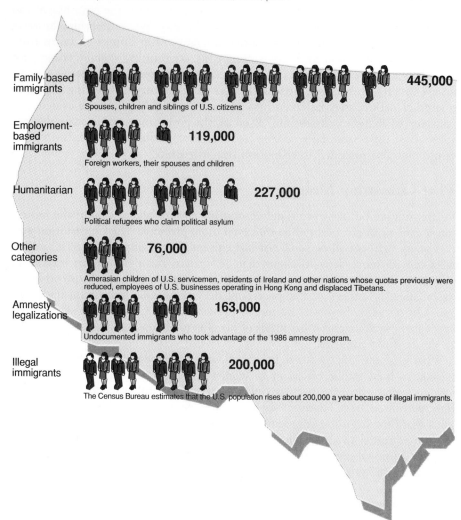

Family-based immigrants — 445,000
Spouses, children and siblings of U.S. citizens

Employment-based immigrants — 119,000
Foreign workers, their spouses and children

Humanitarian — 227,000
Political refugees who claim political asylum

Other categories — 76,000
Amerasian children of U.S. servicemen, residents of Ireland and other nations whose quotas previously were reduced, employees of U.S. businesses operating in Hong Kong and displaced Tibetans.

Amnesty legalizations — 163,000
Undocumented immigrants who took advantage of the 1986 amnesty program.

Illegal immigrants — 200,000
The Census Bureau estimates that the U.S. population rises about 200,000 a year because of illegal immigrants.

EQUALITY AND EQUAL RIGHTS

Equal Protection

The **equal protection clause** of the Fourteenth Amendment declares no state (including any subdivision thereof) shall "deny to any person within its jurisdiction the equal protection of the laws." Although there is no parallel clause limiting the national government, the Fifth Amendment's **due process clause**, which states that no person shall "be deprived of life, liberty, or property, without due process of law," has been interpreted to impose the same restraints on the national government. Note the restraints of equal protection apply only to the actions of governments, not to those of private individuals. Thus an important question is always: Is the action being challenged that of a government, that is, is it state action? Or is the challenged discriminatory action merely that of private persons, unsupported and detached from the actions of a government?

The equal protection clause does not prevent governments from making distinctions among people. Governments could not legislate without doing so. What the Constitution forbids is unreasonable classifications. In general, a classification is unreasonable when there is no relation between the classes it creates and permissible governmental goals. A law prohibiting redheads from voting, for example, would be unreasonable. On the other hand, laws denying to persons under 18 the right to vote, to marry without the permission of their parents, or to apply for a license to drive a car appear to be reasonable (at least to most persons over 18).

One of our most troublesome issues is how to distinguish between constitutional and unconstitutional classifications. The Supreme Court uses three tests for this purpose: (1) the traditional rational basis test for most laws; (2) the most stringent test of all, a strict scrutiny test for laws dealing with suspect classes and fundamental rights; (3) the heightened scrutiny test or, as it is sometimes called, middle tier or intermediate test for laws dealing with quasi-suspect classifications (see box).

The Court also strictly scrutinizes laws impinging on fundamental rights. What makes a right fundamental in the constitutional sense? It is not the importance or the significance of the right that makes it fundamental, but whether it is explicitly or implicitly guaranteed by the Constitution.[3] Under this test, the rights to travel and to vote have been held to be fundamental, as well as such First Amendment rights as the right to associate for the advancement of political beliefs. The rights to an education, to housing, or to welfare benefits have not been held to be fundamental. Important as these rights may be, they are not guaranteed by the Constitution, meaning that there are no constitutional provisions specifically protecting these rights from governmental regulation.

Proving Discrimination

Does the fact that a law or a regulation has a differential effect—what has come to be known as *disparate impact*—on persons of different race or sex by itself establish that it is unconstitutional? In one of its most important decisions, *Washington v Davis* (1976), the Supreme Court said no. "The invidious quality of a law claimed to be racially discriminatory must ultimately be traced to a racially discriminatory purpose."[4] "An unwavering line of cases" from the Supreme Court "hold that a violation of the Equal Protection Clause requires state action motivated by discriminatory intent; the disproportionate effects of state action are not sufficient to establish such a violation."[5] Or, as the Court said in another case: "The Fourteenth Amendment guarantees equal laws, not equal results."[6]

What do these rulings on disparate impact mean in practical terms? They mean, for example, that city ordinances that permit only single-family residences and thus make low-cost housing projects impossible are not unconstitutional—even if their effect is to keep minorities from moving into the city—unless it can be shown that they were adopted with the *intent to discriminate* against minorities. The rulings also mean that a preference for veterans in public employment does not violate the equal protection clause, even though its effect is to keep many women from getting jobs; the distinction between veterans and nonveterans was not adopted deliberately to create a sex barrier.

What is constitutional can nonetheless be made illegal. Things that are unconstitutional are always illegal, but what is illegal may not be unconstitutional. For example, there is no violation of the Constitution if a state adopts practices that may have the effect of depriving more African Americans of the right to vote than whites, unless the state adopted those practices with the intent to discriminate. However, in the Voting Rights Act of 1965, Congress intervened to make illegal some voting practices that were not necessarily unconstitutional. The act tests the legality of state voting laws and practices by their impact on the voting rights of African Americans and other minorities rather than by the intentions of those who passed them.

"Treat people as equals, and the first thing you know, they believe they are."

Drawing by Mulligan. © 1982 The New Yorker Magazine, Inc.

Should Congress forbid employment tests that have a disparate impact on ethnic minorities and women?

What if an employer requires a test that may be related to job performance, but nonetheless screens out more members of one race or sex than another? Does this disparate impact of the test, say, on women or African Americans, show indirect discrimination, and does it prove illegal discrimination?

You Decide!

One of the more hotly contested issues of recent years before the Supreme Court has been whether Congress intended various civil rights acts, especially Title VII of the Civil Rights Act of 1964, to forbid some employment tests that, even if adopted by employers without discriminatory intent, nonetheless screen out persons of one race or national origin or gender more than others (see You Decide box).

EDUCATION RIGHTS

Until the Supreme Court struck down such laws in the 1950s, southern states made it illegal for whites and blacks to ride in the same train cars, attend the same theaters, go to the same schools, be born in the same hospitals, or be buried in the same cemeteries. **Jim Crow laws**, as they came to be called, blanketed southern life.[7] Southern states and some places in the North enforced segregation in transportation, places of public accommodation, educational facilities, swimming pools, and parks. How could these laws stand in the face of the equal protection clause? This was the question raised in *Plessy v Ferguson.*

Segregation, Discrimination, and *Plessy v Ferguson*

In 1896 in *Plessy v Ferguson*, the Supreme Court endorsed the view that racial segregation did not constitute discrimination if "equal" accommodations were provided for the members of both races.[8] Equal accommodations were required only for public facilities such as schools and colleges and for a limited category of public utilities such as trains and buses. Although the *Plessy* decision required equality as the price for compulsory segregation, the "equal" part of the formula was meaningless. States segregated blacks into unequal facilities, and blacks lacked the political power to protest.

The passage of time did not lessen the inequalities. Beginning in the late 1930s, blacks started to file lawsuits challenging the doctrine. They cited facts to show that in practice, separate but equal always resulted in discrimination against blacks. At first the Supreme Court was not willing to upset the separate but equal doctrine, but started to undermine it.

The End of Separate but Equal: *Brown v Board of Education*

In the spring of 1954, in *Brown v Board of Education*, the Supreme Court finally reversed its 1896 holding as it applied to public schools. It ruled that "separate but equal" is a contradiction in terms. *Segregation is itself discrimination.*[9] A year later the Court ordered school boards to proceed with "all deliberate speed to desegregate public schools at the earliest practical date."[10] In the years following the *Brown* decision, federal judges struck down a whole battery of schemes designed to evade the Court's ruling. Beginning in 1963, the Supreme Court gradually reversed its decision that granted school districts time to prepare for desegregation. In 1969 the Court completed that reversal, stating: "Continued operation of racially segregated schools under the standard of 'all deliberate speed' is no longer constitutionally permissible. School districts must immediately terminate dual school systems based on race and operate only unitary school systems."[11]

In the 1960s Congress and the president joined even more directly in the battle against school segregation. Title VI of the Civil Rights Act of 1964 stipulates that federal dollars under any grant program or project must be withdrawn from an entire school or institution of higher education that discriminates "on the ground of race, color, or national origin" in "any program or activity receiv-

Thurgood Marshall (*center*), George E.C. Hayes (*left*), and James Nabrit, Jr., (*right*) argued and won *Brown v Board of Education of Topeka* before the Supreme Court in 1954.

ing Federal financial assistance." Congress in 1972 added sex discrimination to this list; other acts have added the handicapped, the aged, Vietnam veterans, and disabled veterans. Title VI also imposes a responsibility on schools to take affirmative action to ensure that persons in the protected categories are not denied access to any federally supported program or activity.

From Segregation to Desegregation But Not to Integration

School districts which prior to *Brown v Board of Education* operated two kinds of schools, one for whites and one for blacks, have a positive constitutional obligation to develop plans and programs to move from segregation to integration. Desegregation is not enough; they have a duty to bring about integration. If they fail to do so on their own initiative, federal judges or the Department of Justice are to supervise school districts to ensure that they are doing what is necessary and proper to overcome the evils of segregation. However, in 1995 Justice Clarence Thomas, in a concurring opinion in *Missouri v Jenkins*, argued that "racial isolation itself is not a harm: only state-enforced segregation is."[12] His view is picking up support among some African American leaders and scholars.[13]

Since school districts in most neighborhoods are racially homogenous, merely removing legal barriers to integration will not integrate the schools. To overcome residential clustering by race, federal courts have mandated school busing across neighborhoods, moving white students to once predominately black schools and vice versa. Busing students is not popular and has fostered widespread protest in many cities. The Supreme Court sustained the right of judges to order school districts to bus students to overcome racial imbalance *if and only if* it is to remedy the consequences of officially sanctioned or required segregation, that is, *de jure* segregation. The Court has refused to permit federal judges to order busing to overcome the effects of *de facto* segregation, segregation that arises from social customs or personal choice or as the result of residential segregation.[14] In other words, if judges find that authorities had in the past operated segregated schools or had caused segregation by systematic and purposeful actions, then judges may order a school district to bus pupils.[15] But judges may not, said the Supreme Court in a case involving the Detroit metropolitan area, order busing between suburbs and cities or any other interdistrict lines to overcome racial imbalances in schools where such segregation was not caused by official actions.[16] Since the Supreme Court's decision in the Detroit case, there has been little progress in school desegregation.[17]

After a period of authorizing federal judges to use a wide range of desegregation remedies, including even requiring school districts to raise taxes,[18] the Supreme Court has started to limit such remedies to those directly related to violation of the Constitution. For example, the Supreme Court denied a district judge the right to order school districts to create magnet schools (that is schools that are provided with good facilities, outstanding teachers, and comprehensive programs) to try to reverse "white flight."[19] Federal judges have been instructed to restore state and local authorities to the control of a school system "once the judge concludes that the authorities have done everything *practicable* to overcome the past consequences of segregation.[20] As a result, in many cities that used to operate legally compelled dual school systems, federal courts are ending their supervision of school boards' desegregation plans and releasing the districts from any busing obligations.[21]

Although the federal government intervened in more than 500 school desegregation cases in districts that once had governmentally mandated segregation, there has been no such judicial action for northern schools that have had *de facto*

Thinking it Through

In 1971, in *Griggs v Duke Power* concerning the requirement of a high school diploma for becoming a janitor, the Supreme Court held that showing the disparate impact of an employment practice was sufficient to shift the burden of proof to the employer to show that this practice or test was job related.* Eighteen years later, in *Wards Cove v Antonio*, the Supreme Court more or less gutted the *Griggs* test. The Court placed the burden on those charging discrimination to show that a challenged practice—say, a test—had a significantly disparate impact and was not connected with a business goal. Then, in the Civil Rights Act of 1991, Congress stepped in to provide that once those charging discrimination show that a test or a physical requirement for a job results in reducing the number of women, or minorities, or handicapped, or persons of a particular religion eligible for that job, then the employer must "demonstrate that the challenged practice is job related for the position in question and consistent with business necessity."

SOURCE: This discussion is based on a summary of the Civil Rights Act of 1991 prepared by David S. Tatel of Hogan & Hartson, December 18, 1991.

*Griggs v Duke Power, 401 US 424 (1971).

TABLE 4-1

Segregation Moves North and West

States with the largest percentage of Hispanic and black students attending schools that have 90 to 100 percent minority populations.

Blacks	
1. Illinois	59.3%
2. Michigan	58.5
3. New York	57.5
4. New Jersey	54.6
5. Pennsylvania	45.7
6. Tennessee	37.3
7. Alabama	36.8
8. Maryland	36.7
9. Mississippi	36.6
10. Connecticut	36.2

Hispanics	
1. New York	58.1
2. New Jersey	44.4
3. Texas	41.7
4. California	35.4
5. Illinois	33.7
6. Connecticut	33.7
7. Florida	28.0
8. Pennsylvania	27.4
9. Indiana	19.6
10. New Mexico	18.3
11. Arizona	16.2

SOURCE: Gary Orfield, "The Growth of Segregation in American Schools: Changing Patterns of Segregation and Poverty Since 1968," a report to the National School Boards Association, reported in *The New York Times*, December 14, 1993, p. A1.

segregation. As a result, southern cities now have more integrated schools than do large northern cities (see Table 4-1). In large metropolitan areas in the North and South, many school districts in central cities are predominantly black or Hispanic, partly as the result of "white flight" to the suburbs and private schools to escape court-ordered busing, but in more recent years due to higher birth rates and immigration. By the 1991-92 school year, "after decades of progress, schools in the South had rising concentrations of black students and those in the West had rising concentrations of Hispanic students," and two out of every three African American public school students attended schools where the enrollment was more than 50 percent black or Latino.[22]

The political support behind efforts to integrate the schools is fading.[23] School districts are beginning to eliminate mandatory busing, which according to one expert is "threatening to get us to a level of segregation we haven't seen since before the civil rights movement."[24] Some African American leaders, while still supporting desegregation efforts, are giving more attention to improving the quality of inner-city schools than to desegregating them. As Dr. Beverly P. Cole, director of education and housing for the NAACP, has said, "At the present time, we are more concerned with the quality of education, and this has to take precedence over whether schools are integrated."[25]

VOTING RIGHTS

Despite fierce opposition to the Nineteenth Amendment, no organized resistance to its implementation surfaced after its ratification gave women the right to vote. This was not so following ratification of the Fourteenth and Fifteenth Amendments. Black men were allowed to participate in the political life of southern states only when and because the federal government insisted upon it. As soon as federal troops were withdrawn from the South in 1877, southern Democrats regained control of state governments and set out to keep blacks from voting. They used social pressure and violence. Organized secret societies like the Ku Klux Klan engaged in such terrorist activities as midnight shootings, burnings, whippings, and lynchings to keep blacks from voting.

These measures worked. But toward the end of the nineteenth century, and for the first time since the Civil War, parts of the South had two strong political parties: the Democrats and the Populists. White supremacists were fearful the parties might compete for the black vote, and blacks might come to hold the balance of power. White supremacists also feared that continued use of excessive force and fraud to disenfranchise blacks might cause the president and Congress to intervene.

Southern leaders reasoned that if they could pass laws depriving blacks of the vote on grounds other than race, blacks would find it difficult to challenge such laws in the courts. Some whites protested that such laws could be used against whites as well as blacks. But keeping poor whites from voting did not disturb the conservative leaders of the Democratic party, for they were often just as anxious to undermine white support for the Populist party as they were to disenfranchise blacks. "The disenfranchisement movement of the 1890s gave the Southern states the most impressive system of obstacles between the voter and the ballot box known to the democratic world."[26]

In the 1940s the Supreme Court began to strike down one after another of the devices used to keep blacks from voting. In 1944 (*Smith v Allwright*) the Court declared the white primary unconstitutional.[27] In 1960 it held that **racial gerrymandering**—the drawing of election districts so as to ensure that blacks are a minority in all districts—is contrary to the Fifteenth Amendment.[28] In 1964 the Twenty-fourth Amendment eliminated the **poll tax**—payment required as a condition for voting—in elections including primary elections for members of Congress and presidential electors, and in 1966 the Court held that the Fourteenth Amendment forbade the poll tax as a condition in any election.[29] (The Court has suggested but not definitively decided that a filing fee to participate in a convention of a major political party that nominates candidates may be considered a poll tax.[30])

Those wishing to deny African Americans the right to vote were forced to rely on registration requirements. On the surface these requirements appeared to be perfectly proper; it was the way they were administered that kept blacks from the polls. They were often applied by white election officers while white police stood guard, with white judges hearing appeals from decisions of registration officials. These officials often seized on the smallest error in an application blank as an excuse to disqualify a voter. In one parish in Louisiana, after four white voters filed affidavits in which they challenged the legality of the registration of black voters on the grounds that these voters had made an "error in spilling" (sic) in their applications, registration officials struck 1,300 out of approximately 1,500 black voters from the polls.[31]

The Voting Rights Act of 1965

For two decades after World War II, under the leadership of the Supreme Court, federal judges carefully scrutinized voting laws and procedures in cases brought before them. Yet this approach did not open the voting booth to African Americans, especially those living in rural areas of the Deep South. Finally Congress began to act. The Civil Rights Act of 1964 set aside, for elections for members of Congress and the president, literacy tests for persons who had completed the equivalent of the sixth grade and prohibited denial of the right to vote because of minor errors on application forms.

The Civil Rights Act of 1964 had hardly been enacted when events in Selma, Alabama, dramatized the inadequacy of depending on lawsuits to prevent racial barriers in polling places. A voter-registration drive in that city, led by Martin Luther King, Jr., produced arrests, marches on the state capital, and the murder of two civil rights workers. Still there was no dent in the color bar at the polls. Responding to events in Selma, President Lyndon Johnson made a dramatic address to Congress and the nation calling for federal action to ensure that no person would be deprived of the right to vote in any election for any office because of color or race. Congress responded with the Voting Rights Act of 1965.[32]

Section 2 of the Voting Rights Act prohibits any voting qualifications, standards, or practices to be applied in any manner that results in a denial of the right of any citizen to vote on account of race and color. Section 5 requires those states that had a history of denying African Americans the right to vote to clear with the Department of Justice any changes in any voting practice or laws that might result in dilution of voting power.[33] Examples include changes in the location of polling places; changes in candidacy requirements and qualifications; changes in filing deadlines; changes in the composition of the electorate; changes from ward to at-large elections; changes in boundary lines of voting districts; changes that affect the creation or abolition of an elective office; and imposition by state political parties of fees to become delegates to nominating conventions.[34] The Court refused, however, to extend the act to cover changes in the distribution of power among officials after two Alabama counties altered the power of county commissioners in such a way as to reduce the authority of recently elected black commissioners.[35] It has also ruled that there is no prohibition in

Major Provisions of the Voting Rights Act of 1965 as Amended in 1974 and 1982 and Interpreted by the Supreme Court

Section 2

Forbids *any* government to use any procedures related to voting, regardless of intent, that result in the denial of vote to any person because of race or color or the *dilution* of the voting power of members of a protected class.

Sections 3, 6, and 7

In the areas covered by the law, those that have had a long history of discrimination against blacks, mostly but not exclusively in the South, federal courts and the United States attorney general may appoint federal examiners to register voters and to ensure that all persons' votes are counted.

Section 4

Abolishes English literacy requirements for any person who has gone beyond the sixth grade. In addition, in areas where more than 5 percent of the citizens are members of a single language minority, ballots and other written materials relating to the vote are to be printed in that language.

Section 5

Requires governmental units covered by the law, mostly southern states that prior to 1965 had a long history of discriminating against blacks, to submit for preclearance all proposed changes in their voting laws or practices to the United States attorney general or to the United States Court of Appeals for the District of Columbia. (Note that approval of the local federal district judge will not do. Congress did not want to entrust this responsibility to anyone who might be subject to local political pressures—even a federal judge.) These changes are not to be approved until reviewed to assure that the change has neither the *purpose* nor the *effect* of denying the vote to any person because of race or color or of *diluting* the voting power of any person because of race or color. The Department of Justice has up to 120 days to preclear any change in election procedure; it reviews an average of 17,000 electoral changes each year.* Sixteen states had to preclear part of and nine states had to secure approval for their entire redistricting plans following the 1990 census changes.

Section 10

Abolishes the poll tax as a precondition of voting in any governmental election.

*Clark v Roemer, 114 L Ed 2d 691 (1991).

"Five score years ago, a great American in whose symbolic shadow we stand, signed the Emancipation Proclamation. This momentous decree came as a great beacon light of hope to millions of Negro slaves who had been seared in the flames of withering injustice. It came as a joyous daybreak to end the long night of captivity. But one hundred years later, we must face the tragic fact that the Negro is still not free. One hundred years later, the life of the Negro is still sadly crippled by the manacles of segregation and the chains of discrimination. One hundred years later, the Negro lives on a lonely island of poverty in the midst of a vast ocean of material prosperity. One hundred years later, the Negro is still languishing in the corners of American society and finds himself an exile in his own land. So we have come here today to dramatize an appalling condition. . . .

I have a dream that one day this nation will rise up and live out the true meaning of its creed: "We hold these truths to be self-evident; that all men are created equal."

I have a dream that one day on the red hills of Georgia the sons of former slaves and the sons of former slave owners will be able to sit down together at the table of brotherhood.

I have a dream that one day even the state of Mississippi, a desert state sweltering with the heat of injustice and oppression, will be transformed into an oasis of freedom and justice.

I have a dream that my four little children will one day live in a nation where they will not be judged by the color of their skin but by the content of their character."

SOURCE: Martin Luther King, Jr., address at the Lincoln Memorial, August 28, 1963.

the act against operating a single commissioner form of county government, even if the consequence is to make it practically impossible for an African American to ever become the county commissioner.[36]

Following the 1990 Census, the Department of Justice refused to certify redistricting plans of southern state legislatures that failed to draw as many districts as possible in which minorities constitute a majority. Most of these districts tended to be Democratic, leaving the other congressional districts in these states heavily white and Republican The lower federal courts sustained the Department of Justice's interpretation. As a result there was a considerable increase in congressional districts represented by minorities and Republicans.[37]

The Supreme Court, however, in a series of cases beginning with *Shaw v Reno*,[38] announced that although states may take race into account, they may not make race the *sole* reason for drawing district lines. The Department of Justice, said the Supreme Court, was wrong in forcing states to create as many majority-minority districts as possible. North Carolina's legislatures created a majority-minority district 160-miles long and in some places only an interstate highway in width. "If you drove down the interstate," said one legislator about this district, "with both car doors open, you'd kill most of the people in the district."[39] The Supreme Court ruled that North Carolina's reapportionment scheme was so "irrational on its face that it can be understood only as an effort to segregate voters into separate voting districts because of their race."[40] In order to comply with the Voting Rights Act, the Supreme Court explained, states must provide for districts roughly proportional to the minority voters' respective shares in the voting-age population.[41]

The Court has expanded *Shaw* by clarifying that it "was not meant to suggest that a district must be bizarre on its face before there is a constitutional violation."[42] Legislatures may be aware of racial considerations when they draw district lines, but when race becomes the predominant factor, the state violates the equal protection clause. As a result of these decisions, the reapportionment plans of Texas, Georgia, and other southern state legislatures that have created the largest possible number of majority-minority districts have been set aside. As we approach the census of 2000, which will call for another round of redistricting by the states, it is clear that the Supreme Court is likely to declare unconstitutional the drawing of any districts if a "state substantially neglects traditional districting criteria such as compactness, and where there is evidence that race is the predominant factor motivating the legislature's redistricting decision."[43]

RIGHTS TO PUBLIC ACCOMMODATIONS, JOBS, AND HOMES

As we have noted, the Fifth and Fourteenth Amendments apply only to *governmental action*, not to private discriminatory conduct. Moreover, our Constitution creates "a zone of privacy which precludes government from interfering with private clubs or groups. The associational rights which our system honors permit all-white, all-black, all-brown, and all-yellow clubs to be established. They also permit all-Catholic, all-Jewish, or all-agnostic clubs. . . . Government may not tell a man or a woman who his or her associates must be. The individual may be as selective as he desires."[44]

Families, churches, or private groups organized for political, religious, cultural, social, or expressive purposes are constitutionally different from large associations such as the United States Jaycees (the Junior Chamber of Commerce) or a large law partnership. The Supreme Court has upheld the application of state and local laws forbidding sex or racial discrimination to organizations such as the Jaycees, the Rotary Club, and large (in this case more than 400 members) private eating clubs. Such associations and clubs are not small intimate groups. Nor were they able to demonstrate that allowing women or minorities to become members would change the content or impact of their purposes.[45]

Until recent decades the fact that the Fourteenth Amendment is inapplicable to private conduct hindered Congress's ability to legislate against non-state-sanctioned discriminatory conduct. In 1883 the Supreme Court declared unconstitutional an act of Congress that made it a federal offense for any operator of a public conveyance, hotel, or theater to deny accommodations to any person because of race or color on the grounds that the Fourteenth Amendment does not give Congress authority to legislate against discrimination by private individuals.[46]

Since the 1960s, however, the constitutional authority of Congress to legislate against discrimination by private individuals is no longer an issue. The Court has so broadly construed the commerce clause, which gives Congress the power to regulate interstate and foreign commerce, that it alone justifies almost any action that Congress might want to take against discriminatory conduct by individuals.

The Court has also reinterpreted the Thirteenth Amendment, at least as far as racial discrimination is concerned, to sustain congressional legislation against discrimination. In addition to the Thirteenth and Fourteenth Amendments, Congress has used the power to tax and spend to prevent not only racial discrimination but also discrimination based on ethnic origin, sex, disability, and age. It also used the power to regulate interstate commerce in the most important and sweeping Civil Rights Act—that of 1964.

"Thanks for coming in. It's such a relief to be able to deny someone a loan when there's no possibility of being charged with sex, race, age, or ethnic bias."

Drawing by Ed Fisher. © 1976 The New Yorker Magazine, Inc.

The Civil Rights Act of 1964

With this law, for the first time since Reconstruction, Congress authorized the massive use of federal authority to combat privately imposed racial discrimination.

TITLE II: PLACES OF PUBLIC ACCOMMODATION   Title II makes it a federal offense to discriminate against any customer or patron in a place of public accommodation because of race, color, religion, or national origin. It applies to any inn, hotel, motel, or lodging establishment (except establishments with fewer than five rooms and occupied by the proprietor—in other words, small boardinghouses); to any restaurant or gasoline station that serves interstate travelers or serves food or products, of which a substantial portion have moved in interstate commerce; and to any movie house, theater, concert hall, sports arena, or other place of entertainment that customarily presents films, performances, athletic teams, or other sources of entertainment that are moved in interstate commerce.

Title II has been vigorously enforced, and African Americans have organized programs to test it. The Department of Justice filed more than 400 lawsuits. Within a few months after its adoption, the Supreme Court, in *Heart of Atlanta Motel v United States*, unanimously sustained its constitutionality.[47] As a result, public establishments, including those in the South, opened their doors to all customers.

TITLE VII: EMPLOYMENT   The Constitution and numerous congressional laws forbid governments to deny persons employment because of race, color, religion, or sex. By Title VII of the Civil Rights Act, Congress has made it illegal for any employer or trade union in any industry affecting interstate commerce and employing 15 or more people (and, since 1972, any state or local agency such as a school or university) to discriminate in employment practices against any person because of race, color, national origin, religion, or sex.[48] Title VII forbids discrimination with respect to compensation, terms, conditions, or privileges of employment. The intent is to "strike at the entire spectrum of disparate treatment," which includes requiring people to work in a discriminatorily hostile or

Major Civil Rights Laws

Civil Rights Act, 1957: The first civil rights law since Reconstruction, PL 85-315 makes it a federal crime to prevent persons from voting in federal elections and authorizes the attorney general to bring suit when a person is deprived of his or her voting rights.

Civil Rights Act, 1964: The most sweeping antibias law, PL 88-352 bars discrimination in employment on the basis of race, color, religion, sex, or national origin and in public accommodations and federally funded programs on the basis of race, color, religion, or national origin. It also created the Equal Employment Opportunity Commission.

Voting Rights Act, 1965: PL 89-110 authorizes the appointment of federal examiners to register voters in areas found to have been discriminating and strengthens penalties for those who interfered with others' right to vote.

Age Discrimination in Employment Act, 1967: PL 90-202 prohibits job discrimination against workers or job applicants ages 40 through 65. It was amended in 1975 (PL 94-135) to bar age bias in federally assisted programs and in 1986 (PL 99-592) to prohibit mandatory retirement in most jobs.

Fair Housing Act, 1968: PL 90-284 prohibits discrimination on the basis of race, color, religion, or national origin in the sale or rental of most housing. It also includes provisions to protect civil rights workers from injury or intimidation and provides for federal penalties for those convicted of rioting or encouraging others to do so.

Title IX, Education Amendment of 1972: PL 92-318 provides that "No person . . . shall, on the basis of sex, be excluded from participation in, be denied the benefits of, or be subjected to discrimination under any education program or activity receiving Federal financial assistance."

Rehabilitation Act, 1973: Primarily a reauthorization of programs to rehabilitate the handicapped, PL 93-112 carries two little-noted provisions whose importance became clear only after the fact. Section 503 requires that recipients of federal grants greater than $2,500 institute affirmative action programs to hire and promote "qualified handicapped individuals," while Section 504 states, "No otherwise qualified handicapped individual . . . shall, solely by reason of his handicap, be excluded from the participation in, be denied the benefits of, or be subjected to discrimination under any program or activity receiving federal financial assistance."

Civil Rights Restoration Act of 1988: Overriding President Ronald Reagan's veto, Congress in PL 100-259 overturned a 1984 Supreme Court ruling that anti-sex discrimina-

abusive environment.[49] Employers have an obligation to create workplaces that avoid abusive environments. Other legislation makes it illegal to engage in discriminatory activities that affect those with physical handicaps, veterans, or persons over 40.

There are a few exceptions. Religious institutions such as parochial schools may use religious standards. Age, sex, or handicap may be considered where occupational qualifications are absolutely necessary to the normal operation of a particular business or enterprise.

In 1991, Congress amended Title VII to set aside several Supreme Court decisions and to make it easier to challenge employment practices—tests, qualifications, conditions—that, whatever the intent, have a disparate adverse impact on women and minorities.

Title VII was passed to protect minorities and women; nonetheless, employers who discriminate against white males also violate its provisions. Moreover, when Congress adopted Title VII, it stated that the act should not be used to require any employer to grant preferential treatment to any individual or to any group on account of racial or sexual imbalance that might exist in the employer's work force. Title VII, however, does not preclude employers, public or private, from adopting race-sensitive affirmative action programs designed to overcome past discrimination against minorities and women.

Title VII has several special features. Not only do aggrieved persons have a right of private action to sue for damages for themselves, but they can do so for other persons similarly situated in a **class action suit**. In addition, Congress created the Equal Employment Opportunity Commission (EEOC) to enforce its provisions. The commission, which consists of five members appointed by the president with the consent of the Senate, works together with state authorities to try to bring about compliance with the act and may seek judicial enforcement of complaints against private employers. The attorney general prosecutes Title VII violations by public agencies. The vigor with which the commission and the attorney general have acted has varied over the years, depending on the resources granted to enforcement by Congress and the commitment of the president in office.[50] Race-based cases make up about a third of the EEOC's case load, followed by claims based on gender discrimination and disabilities. Sexual harassment cases are also increasing.[51]

Title VII is supplemented, indeed in some instances even supplanted, by a 1965 presidential executive order requiring all contractors of the federal government, including universities, to adopt and implement affirmative action programs to correct for "underutilization" of women and minorities. Such programs may not establish racial or ethnic quotas for minorities or women, but they do call on contractors to establish timetables and goals; to follow open recruitment procedures; to keep records of applicants by race, sex, and national origin; and to explain why their labor force does not reflect the same proportion of persons in the covered categories that exist within the appropriate labor market pools. Failure of contractors to file and implement an approved affirmative action plan may lead to loss of federal contracts or grants.

Housing: The Civil Rights Acts of 1966, 1968, and 1988

Housing is the last frontier of the civil rights crusade, the area in which progress is slowest and genuine change most remote. In 1948, in *Shelley v Kraemer*, the Supreme Court held that judges could no longer enforce racially **restrictive covenants** (a provision in a deed to real property restricting its sale).[52]

In 1968 Congress passed the Fair Housing Act. This act, amended in 1988, excludes housing owned by private individuals who own no more than three houses, who sell or rent these houses without the services of an agent, and who do not indicate any preference or discrimination in their advertising; dwellings that have no more than four separate living units, in which the owner maintains a residence (so-called "Mrs. Murphy boardinghouses"); and religious organizations and private clubs housing their own members on a noncommercial basis. For all other housing, the act forbids owners to refuse to sell or rent to any person because of race, color, religion, national origin, sex (since 1974), and handicap or because a person has children (since 1988). Housing for older persons is exempted from this family provision. No discriminatory advertising is permitted.

The Department of Justice has filed hundreds of cases, especially those involving large apartment complexes. Yet African Americans and Hispanics continue to be discriminated against when they attempt to rent apartments or buy houses. Realtors continue to steer them toward neighborhoods that are not predominantly white, to require larger rental deposits for minorities than for whites, and even to refuse outright to sell or rent to minorities.[53] Very few of these discriminatory actions are complained about because they are often so subtle that victims are unaware that they are being discriminated against.

Yet the number of discrimination complaints received by the Department of Housing and Urban Development and local and state agencies has been increasing as the result of more aggressive enforcement. Complaints about discrimination in housing often center around denial of loans to minorities.

Voluntary segregation obviously also exists. "It's a fact of life that blacks like to live in black neighborhoods and whites like to live in white neighborhoods. . . . And real estate agents generally like to bring bring customers to places they will like and where the agent can make a sale."[54]

Whatever the reasons, housing segregation persists. "While blacks and other minorities have made strides in voting rights, education and jobs, the homes they return to each night are in communities still largely defined by race."[55]

Affirmative Action: Is It Constitutional?

Prior to 1954, when white majorities were using state power to segregate blacks and discriminate against them, civil rights advocates cited with approval the words of Justice John Marshall Harlan, dissenting in *Plessy v Ferguson*: "Our Constitution is color-blind and neither knows nor tolerates class among citizens."[56] It was not until 1954 that Justice Harlan's views triumphed. In *Brown v Board of Education*, the Court called racial classifications "odious to our system" and made race a suspect class. In the years immediately following, the Court also established that, although the Fourteenth Amendment was adopted to protect blacks, its provisions extend to other minorities, to women, and to white males. The Court emphasized that the rights protected belong to each and every individual, not to the group to which he or she may belong.

By the 1960s there was a new set of constitutional and national policy debates. People began to assert that government neutrality was not enough. If governments and universities and employers merely stop discriminating against blacks, Hispanics, and women, yet change nothing else, those previously discriminated against are still kept from equal participation in American life. They have been so handicapped by past discrimination that in the competition for openings in medical schools or for skilled jobs or for their share of government grants and contracts, they suffer disabilities not shared by white males.

Governments started to respond to these arguments. Presidents issued executive orders, Congress adopted programs, state legislatures created requirements, cities adopted ordinances, and university trustees issued policies. Although the details vary (and the details are constitutionally significant), these programs call

Major Civil Rights Laws (continued)

tion provisions of the 1972 Education Act Amendments applied only to the specific program or activity receiving federal aid and not to the entire institution. In reversing *Grove City College v Bell*, Congress also specified that antibias provisions of three other laws applied to entire institutions if any segment received federal funding. The three were the 1964 Civil Rights Act, Section 504 of the 1973 Rehabilitation Act, and the 1975 Age Discrimination Act.

FAIR HOUSING ACT AMENDMENTS, 1988: PL 100-430 gives the Department of Housing and Urban Development greater authority to enforce the 1968 law and prohibits housing bias against the handicapped and families with children.

AMERICANS WITH DISABILITIES ACT, 1991: PL 102-119 prohibits discrimination based on disability in employment, places of public accommodations, and public services and requires that facilities be designed to make them accessible and usable by those with disabilities and to the extent feasible be redesigned to do so.

THE CIVIL RIGHTS ACT OF 1991: PL 102-166 counters the effects of nine Supreme Court decisions. It places a greater burden on employers to justify practices that negatively affect women and minorities by requiring employers to justify such practices as being job related for the position in question, being a business necessity, or showing that there are no alternative practices which would have a less negative impact on the protected group. It authorizes limited compensatory damages for intentional discrimination and punitive damages if the defendant acted with malice or reckless indifference to the rights of the individual based on sex, religion, or disability. (Unlimited damages are allowed for racial or ethnic bias under a Reconstruction civil rights law.) It amends the 1866 civil rights law, now 42 USC 1981, to prohibit not merely racial discrimination in initial hiring but other forms of race bias in the workplace, for example, in promotions. It prohibits "race norming" of tests used for employment or promotion—that is, setting different cutoff scores on the bases of race or ethnic origin. The act also establishes a commission, appointed by the president and Congress, to examine the "glass ceiling" that seems to keep women from becoming executives and to make recommendations on how to increase promotion of women and minorities to management positions.

SOURCE: Adapted from *Social Policy*, May 13, 1989, p. 1122.

PL means Public Law, and the number following is the number of the Congress; thus PL 85-315 means it was enacted by the 85th Congress.

Alan Bakke, who won a historic affirmative action suit, is surrounded by reporters as he leaves class after his first day at the University of California medical school.

Affirmative Action or Affirmative Confusion?

In the spring of 1996 the Court of Appeals for the Fifth Circuit, in *Hopwood v Texas*,* set aside the University of Texas law school's affirmative action plan for the admission of students. The judges had concluded that Justice Powell's decision in the *Bakke* case no longer had the support of the Supreme Court, and that the use of race as one factor in the admission process violates the equal protection clause.

Following that decision, the university modified its plan and petitioned the Supreme Court to review the Court of Appeals decision. On the last day of the 1995–1996 term, the Supreme Court announced that it would not do so. Justices Ginsburg and Souter took the unusual step of explaining that the Supreme Court's refusal to review the decision should not be construed as indicating that they necessarily agreed with the Court of Appeals. Rather, since the law school had modified its plan, the issue of constitutionality was no longer before the courts. Justice Ginsburg noted, "Whether it is constitutional for a public college or graduate school to use race or national origin as a factor in its admission processes is an issue of great national importance." But, she concluded, "this Court reviews judgments, not opinions."

The result of this unusual combination of decisions is that, as far as the United States Constitution is concerned, race—and presumably gender—may no longer be considered as a factor for admission to public universities and colleges in the Fifth Circuit (Texas, Louisiana, and Mississippi) but may be considered in the rest of the nation.

Hopwood v Texas, 134 L Ed 2d 1095 (1996).

on governments, governmental contractors, and in some instances private employers to take **affirmative action** to redress imbalances in work forces and governmental contracts in order to reflect more accurately the racial, sexual, and ethnic diversity of employment pools and to give opportunities to minority and women contractors. These remedies to overcome the consequences of past discrimination against blacks, Hispanics, Native Americans, and women may be known as affirmative action programs by those who support them, but they are regarded as *reverse discrimination* by those who oppose them.

What of the constitutionality of affirmative action programs resting on race and sex classifications? The first major statement of the Supreme Court came in a celebrated case relating to university admissions. Allan Bakke, a white male and a top student at Minnesota and Stanford universities as well as a Vietnam War veteran, applied both in 1973 and 1974 to the medical school of the University of California at Davis. In each of those years the school admitted 100 new students, 84 in a general admissions program and 16 in a special admissions program created for African Americans, Chicanos, Asian Americans, and Native Americans—groups who had been underrepresented until the special admissions program was established. Bakke's application was rejected each year, but students with lower grade-point averages, test scores, and interview ratings were admitted under the special admissions program. After his second rejection, Bakke brought a suit in federal court claiming he had been excluded because of his race, contrary to requirements of the Constitution and Title VI of the Civil Rights Act of 1964.

In *University of California Regents v Bakke* (1978), the Supreme Court ruled the Davis plan unconstitutional.[57] But in an opinion by Justice Lewis Powell, which no other member of the Court completely shared, the Court also declared that affirmative action programs are not necessarily unconstitutional. In order to achieve a diversified student body, a state university may properly take race and ethnic background into account as one of several factors in choosing students. However, the university's goal may not be to redress past misconduct by society or to ensure that more minority members become doctors. The problem with the California plan was it created a category of admissions from which whites were excluded solely because of their race.

Following *Bakke*, the Court dealt with a variety of affirmative action programs, sustaining most, but not all of them. Yet as Justice Byron White said, "Agreement upon a means for applying the Equal Protection Clause to an affirmative-action program has eluded this Court every time the issue has come before us."[58] In *Richmond v Croson* in 1989, a Court majority struck down a plan of the city of Richmond requiring nonminority city contractors to subcontract at least 30 percent of the dollar amount of their contracts to one or more minority business enterprises. Said Justice Sandra Day O'Connor for the Court, in language that called into question the validity of most state and local government affirmative action plans, "Race-sensitive remedial measures are to be justified only after a strong basis in evidence has established that remedial action is necessary to overcome the consequences of past discriminatory action." Justice Thurgood Marshall in dissent contended that there is "a profound difference separating governmental actions that themselves are racist, and governmental actions seeking to remedy the effects of prior racism." The proper test, he wrote, for race-conscious classifications designed to further remedial goals is merely that they have to be justified as serving important governmental objectives and must be substantially related to the achievement of those objectives. The majority, he said, "sounds a full-scale retreat from the effort to deliver on the century-old promise of equality and scuttled the efforts of a city to surmount its discriminatory past."[59]

Although *Richmond v Croson* was interpreted to signal a hardened attitude by the Court toward affirmative action, on the last day of the 1989-90 term, to the surprise of most, Justice William J. Brennan, Jr., speaking for four other justices in *Metro Broadcasting v Federal Communications Commission*, maintained that the national government is not limited to using race-sensitive measures to overcome past discrimination but may use them for other legitimate governmental objectives. The Court upheld the right of the Federal Communications Commission under certain conditions to limit the transfer of certain existing radio and television broadcast stations only to minority-controlled firms. Justice O'Connor, the author of the *Croson* opinion, wrote in dissent, "'Benign' racial classification is a contradiction in terms. Governmental distinctions among citizens based on race or ethnicity, even in the rare circumstances permitted by our cases, exact costs and carry with them substantial dangers. To the person denied an opportunity or right based on race, the classification is hardly benign. The right to equal protection of the laws is a personal right."[60]

Two years later Justice O'Connor, speaking for the Court in *Adarand Construction, Inc. v Pena* overruled *Metro Broadcast*. The Court rejected the view that racial classifications, whatever their purpose, benign or hostile, should ever be subject to less than strict scrutiny by either the national or state and local governments and could be justified only if such a classification is precisely tailored to serve a compelling governmental interest. Although Justice O'Connor went out of her way to dispel the notion that strict scrutiny is "strict in theory, but fatal in fact,"[61] the *Adarand* decision calls into question the constitutionality of many affirmative action programs. It is worth noting that Justice Scalia, in concurring with Justice O'Connor, made clear that in his view "government can never have a 'compelling interest' in discrimination on the base of race in order to 'make up' for past racial discrimination in the opposite direction." Justice Thomas expressed a similar view.

The federal government is reviewing its various programs in light of the *Adarand* decision, especially those that relate to business contracting. President Clinton has said that affirmative action needs mending not ending. Republicans have attacked affirmative action programs as being unfair. The Regents of the University of California, who in 1978 carried the *Bakke* case to the Supreme Court, in July 1995, at the urging of Governor Pete Wilson, voted to eliminate race or gender as a factor in either admissions or in hiring except where federal law or regulations required contrary action. And the people of California in November of 1996 voted in favor of Proposition 209, which amends the California constitution to forbid state agencies—including schools, colleges, and universities—from discriminating against or giving any preferences based on race or gender for employment, admissions, contracting, or purchasing. There is likely to be considerable litigation to determine how Proposition 209 will relate to federally imposed affirmative action, as well as to how broadly it will be interpreted. It clearly forbids universities and other state agencies from taking race and gender into account. Does it also make unconstitutional state-supported outreach programs designed to recruit and encourage more women and minorities to become scientists and engineers?

Where does all this leave us, at least for the moment, with respect to the constitutionality of governmental affirmative action programs?

1. All racial classifications, including those justified for benign or remedial purposes, are suspect and are subject to the strict scrutiny test. "When a legislative body chooses to employ a suspect classification, it cannot rest upon a generalized assertion as to the classification's relevance to its goals."[62] Race-sensitive remedial measures are to be justified only after a strong basis in evidence has established that remedial action is necessary to overcome the consequences of past discriminatory action. Where there is evidence of past discriminatory conduct, it may justify a narrowly tailored race-based remedy.

Supreme Court Rulings on Sex Discrimination

Some Governmental Actions Declared Unconstitutional by the Supreme Court Because of Sex Discrimination

- Provisions of Social Security laws providing benefits to families with unemployed fathers but not unemployed mothers
- A state law giving sons child support from their fathers until they are 21, but daughters only until they are 18
- A state law prohibiting the sale of beer to males under 21, but to females under 18
- A state law providing that husbands, but not wives, may be required to pay alimony
- A state law excluding males from enrolling in a professional nursing program designed for women, offered by a public university
- The practice of giving prosecutors the right to have people disqualified from serving on a jury solely because of their gender

NOTE: The Constitution protects men as well as women from discrimination because of sex.

Some Governmental Actions Alleged to Be Unconstitutional Discrimination Against Persons Because of Sex but Sustained by the Supreme Court

- A state law granting a property tax exemption to widows but not to widowers
- A naval regulation giving female officers 13 years to be promoted or discharged but giving male officers only 9 years
- A provision giving larger Social Security retirement benefits to women than to men
- A federal law requiring registration for a possible draft for males but not for females

2. Congress has somewhat more discretion than do states or local governments in fashioning race-sensitive remedial measures because it is empowered by Section 5 of the Fourteenth Amendment to do what is necessary and proper to enforce equal protection guarantees. But even so, its action is also subject to strict judicial scrutiny, and any action based on race must be justified by compelling public necessity and be narrowly tailored to accomplish its purposes.

3. The Supreme Court's growing skepticism about the constitutionality of affirmative action programs is both cause and effect of a debate within the Congress and the states about the desirability of affirmative action.

PROPERTY RIGHTS

Constitutional Protection of Property

Property does not have rights. People do. **Property rights** are the rights of an individual to own, use, rent, invest in, buy, and sell property. Historically, the close connection between liberty and ownership of property, between property and power, has been emphasized in American political thinking and American political institutions.

A major purpose of the framers of the Constitution was to establish a government strong enough to protect people's rights to use and enjoy their own property. At the same time, the framers wanted to limit government so it could not endanger that right. As a result, the framers included in the Constitution a variety of clauses regarding property.

THE LEGAL TENDER AND CONTRACT CLAUSES Of special concern to the framers were the efforts of some state legislatures to protect debtors at the expense of their creditors by a variety of means, including issuing paper currency and setting aside private contracts. To prevent these practices, the Constitution forbids states from making anything except gold or silver legal tender for the payment of debts and from passing any "Law impairing the Obligation of Contracts."

Drug enforcement agents confiscate illegal substances during a drug bust and turn the money over to support drug prevention and treatment programs

The *contract clause*, Article I, Section 10, was designed to prevent states from extending the period during which debtors could meet their payments or otherwise get out of contractual obligations. The framers had in mind an ordinary contract between private persons. However, beginning with Chief Justice John Marshall, the Supreme Court expanded the coverage of the clause to prevent states from altering privileges previously conferred on corporations. In effect, the contract clause was used to protect property and to maintain the status quo at the expense of the power of the states to guard the public welfare. In the 1880s, however, the Court gradually began to restrict the coverage of the contract clause and to subject contracts to what in constitutional law is known as **police powers**—the power to protect the public health, safety, welfare, and morals. By 1934 the Supreme Court actually held that even contracts between individuals—the very ones the contract clause was intended to protect—could be modified by state law in order to avert social and economic catastrophe.[63] Although the contract clause is still invoked occasionally to challenge a state regulation of property, it is no longer a significant limitation on governmental power.

What Happens When the Government Takes Our Property?

Both the national and state governments have the power of **eminent domain**— the power to take private property for public use—but the owner must be fairly compensated.

What constitutes a "taking" for purposes of eminent domain?[64] This clause does not require compensation merely because government action may result in property loss. For example, if a zoning regulation restricts an area to single family homes and thus lowers the value of a particular property, no compensation is due. Ordinarily, but not always, the taking must be direct, and a person must lose title and control over the property. Sometimes, especially in recent years, the courts have found that a governmental regulation has gone "too far" and must be deemed a "taking" for which the government must pay compensation to its owners, even when title is left in the hands of the owners.[65] These are called **regulatory takings**. Thus, if a government creates landing and takeoff paths for airplanes over property adjacent to an airport, making the land no longer suitable for its prior use (say, raising chickens), compensation is warranted.

Nor is "just compensation" always easy to define. In case of a dispute, the final resolution is made by the courts. By and large, "the owner is entitled to receive what a willing buyer would pay in cash to a willing seller at the time of the taking."[66] An owner is not entitled to compensation for the personal value of an old, broken-down house that is loved dearly; it will still bring compensation only for an old, broken-down house.

The *taking clause* has received renewed judicial attention in the last several years as many state and local units strive to protect the environment and quality of life by regulating the terms and conditions under which land may be developed. In the late 1980s the Supreme Court began using the taking clause to review these governmental regulations. For example, the Supreme Court held that if a government has prevented a property owner from developing property by regulations that turned out to be unconstitutional, the owner is entitled to just compensation for the temporary taking, even if the government finally withdraws the regulation.[67] The Court also ruled that a government has engaged in a taking if it imposes an unrelated condition before issuing a building permit— requiring, for example, that the owner of a beach-front home allow the public to walk across the property to the beach as a condition for receiving a permit to enlarge the house.[68]

Due Process: New and Old

Perhaps the most difficult parts of the Constitution to understand are the clauses in the Fifth and Fourteenth Amendments that forbid national and state governments to deny any person life, liberty, or property without due process of law. These due process clauses have resulted in hundreds of Supreme Court decisions. Even so, it is impossible to explain due process precisely. In fact, the Supreme Court has refused to give due process a precise definition and has emphasized that "due process, unlike some legal rules, is not a technical conception with a fixed content unrelated to time, place and circumstances."[69]

The Pitfalls of Law Making

When faced with vexing social problems, we often mutter, "There ought to be a law." But devising clear laws and procedures in accordance with the Constitution and its guarantees of due process is easier said than done, as these examples show.

Some Statutes Declared Void for Vagueness

- A statute making it a crime to treat "contemptuously" the American flag.
- A vagrancy ordinance classifying vagrants as "rogues and vagabonds," "dissolute persons who go about begging," "common night walkers," and so on.
- An ordinance requiring persons who loiter or wander the streets to provide "credible and reliable" identification and to account for their presence when required by a police officer.

A Statute Not Considered Vague

- An ordinance requiring a license for businesses selling any items "designed or marketed for use with illegal cannabis or drugs"—what are commonly known as "headshops."

Some Laws Declared to Deny Substantive Due Process

- A school board regulation requiring teachers to cease teaching past the fourth month of pregnancy and barring them from returning to the classroom until three months after the birth of a child.
- A state law permitting confinement of nondangerous mentally ill persons against their wishes.

PROCEDURAL DUE PROCESS   There are two kinds of due process: procedural and substantive. **Procedural due process** generally refers to the methods by which a law is enforced. But a law itself, as enacted, may violate the procedural due process requirement if it is too vague or if it creates an improper presumption of guilt. A vague statute fails to provide adequate warning and does not contain sufficient guidelines for law enforcement officials, juries, and courts.

A statute that creates an improper presumption of guilt denies due process by shifting the burden of proof from the government to the accused person. Laws presuming, for example, that all marijuana or cocaine in a person's possession must have been obtained illegally have been declared unconstitutional. But the Court did uphold a presumption with respect to heroin. As virtually all heroin is illegally imported, it is therefore not unreasonable to presume that a person who possesses heroin obtained it illegally.[70]

Traditionally, however, procedural due process refers not to the law itself but to the way in which a law is applied. To paraphrase Daniel Webster's famous definition, it requires a procedure that hears before it condemns, proceeds upon inquiry, and renders judgment only after a trial or some kind of hearing. Originally, procedural due process was limited to criminal prosecutions, but it now applies to most kinds of governmental proceedings. It is required, for instance, in juvenile hearings, disbarment proceedings, proceedings to determine eligibility for welfare payments, revocation of drivers' licenses, and disciplinary proceedings in state universities and public schools.

Procedural due process has taken on new importance with the expanded interpretation of the words "liberty" and "property." The liberty that is protected is more than freedom from being thrown into jail, and the property that is secured goes beyond the mere ownership of real estate, things, or money. Rather, liberty includes "the right of the individual to contract, to engage in any of the common occupations of life, to acquire useful knowledge, to marry, to establish a home and bring up children, to worship God according to the dictates of his own conscience, and generally to enjoy those common law privileges long recognized as essential to the orderly pursuit of happiness by free men."[71] The property protected by due process includes a variety of rights that may be conferred by state law, such as certain kinds of licenses, protection from being fired from some jobs except for just cause (for example, incompetence) and according to certain procedures, protection from deprivation of certain pension rights, and so on.

This expansion of the meanings of liberty and property has blurred the distinctions between liberty rights and property rights. Moreover, it has lessened the difference between a right and a privilege. Today public welfare, housing, education, employment, professional licenses, and so on, are increasingly becoming matters of entitlement, that is, a legal right. Their denial thus may raise some due process questions.

Nevertheless, "the range of interests protected by procedural due process is not infinite." Not every "grievous loss visited upon a person by the State is sufficient to invoke the procedural protections of the due process clause."[72] Whether an interest is protected by due process depends on the nature of the interest, not its importance to the individual. Faculty members in public institutions, for instance, are not entitled to procedural due process before being denied tenure because they have no constitutional right to teaching jobs. However, if public employees, including teachers, are given tenure rights by law or institutional policies, they are entitled to due process before they may be deprived of property rights or jobs.[73] Since the due process clause applies only to the action of governments, faculty members at private institutions are not entitled to due process, but they, along with other employees, public and private, are protected by provisions of federal and state civil rights laws.

"Once it is determined that due process applies, the question remains what process is due." What is due varies with the kind of interest involved, the reliability of the procedures used, and the governmental purposes to be served.[74] In a federal courtroom, due process requires the careful observance of the provision of the Bill of Rights as outlined in Amendments Four through Eight. In a state courtroom, due process requires the careful observance of all provisions of the Bill of Rights except indictment by grand jury and jury trials in civil cases. The question of what is due in other kinds of proceedings is what must be done to ensure fundamental fairness. It is hard to generalize because many kinds of proceedings are involved, but at a minimum the person involved must have adequate notice and an opportunity to be heard.

SUBSTANTIVE DUE PROCESS Procedural due process places limits on *how* governmental power may be exercised; **substantive due process** places limits on *what* a government may do. Procedural due process pertains to the procedures of the law, substantive due process to the content of the law. Procedural due process mainly limits the executive and judicial branches; substantive due process mainly limits the legislative branch. Substantive due process means that an "unreasonable" law, even if properly passed and properly applied, is unconstitutional. It means that there are certain things governments should not be allowed to do, no matter how they do it.

Before 1937, substantive due process was used primarily to protect liberty of contract—that is, business liberty, or the right of employers to make contracts with employees freely, without government interference. Indeed, the adoption of the doctrine of substantive due process and the simultaneous expansion of the meaning of liberty and property made the Supreme Court, for a time, the final judge of our economic and industrial life. During this period the Supreme Court was dominated by conservative jurists who considered almost all social welfare legislation unreasonable. They used the due process clause to strike down laws setting maximum hours of labor, establishing minimum wages, regulating prices, and forbidding employers to fire workers for union membership.

The trouble with the substantive interpretation of due process is that what a person, including a judge, thinks is a "reasonable" law depends on economic, social, and political views rather than on legal doctrine. In democracies, elected officials are supposed to accommodate opposing notions of reasonableness and to decide what regulations of liberty and property are needed. When the Supreme Court substitutes its own ideas of reasonableness for those of the legislature, it acts like a superlegislature.

In response to this criticism, the Supreme Court since 1937 has largely refused to apply the doctrine of substantive due process in reviewing laws regulating the economy. The Court is now of the view that deciding what constitutes reasonable regulations of business and commercial life is a legislative, not a judicial, responsibility. As long as the justices find a conceivable connection between a law regulating business and the promotion of the public welfare, the Supreme Court will not interfere.

Substantive due process, resting on the notion that laws must be reasonable, has deep roots in concepts of natural law and a long history in the American constitutional tradition. For most Americans most of the time, it is not enough merely to say that a law reflects the wishes of the popular or legislative majority. We also want our laws to be just, and we continue to rely heavily on judges to decide what is just. In Chapter 12 we look again at the tensions between democratic procedures and judicial uses of substantive due process to review the constitutionality of the acts of elected officials.

PRIVACY RIGHTS

The most important extension of substantive due process in recent decades has been its expansion to protect the right of privacy, especially marital privacy. Although there is no mention of the right of privacy in the Constitution, the Supreme Court has put together some elements from the First, Fourth, Fifth, Ninth, and Fourteenth Amendments to recognize that personal privacy is one of the rights protected by the Constitution.

There are three aspects of this right: (1) the right to be free from governmental surveillance and intrusion, especially in marital matters; (2) the right not to have private affairs made public by the government; and (3) the right to be free in thought and belief from governmental compulsion.[75]

Congress showed concern about the first kind of privacy in the Family Educational Rights Act of 1974 and the Privacy Act of 1974. These laws limit record-keeping and record-disclosing activities of schools and universities that receive federal funds; place restraints on files kept by federal agencies; and, under certain conditions, give individuals access to government files in order to correct information about themselves. But privacy, although highly valued in the abstract, has often run afoul of other rights, such as freedom of the press. When in conflict with these other rights, it has not fared well before either Congress or the courts.

Abortion Rights

The most controversial aspect of constitutional protection for privacy relates to the extent of state power to regulate abortions. In *Roe v Wade*, decided in 1973, the Supreme Court ruled: (1) during the first trimester of a woman's pregnancy, it is an unreasonable and therefore unconstitutional interference with her liberty and privacy rights for a state to set any limits on her choice to have an abortion or on her doctor's medical judgments about how to carry it out; (2) during the second trimester, the state's interest in protecting the health of women becomes compelling, and a state may make a reasonable regulation about how, where, and when abortions may be performed; and (3) during the third trimester, when the life of the fetus outside the womb becomes viable, the state's interest in protecting the unborn child is so important that the state can proscribe abortions altogether, except when necessary to preserve the life or health of the mother.[76]

After two decades of heated public debate and attempts by both Presidents Ronald Reagan and George Bush to select Supreme Court justices who could be expected to vote to reverse *Roe v Wade*, on the final day of the 1991–92 court term the decision was reaffirmed. A bitterly divided Rehnquist Court, by a five-person majority (O'Connor, Kennedy, Souter, Blackmun, and Stevens), upheld the view that the due process clauses of the Constitution protect a woman's liberty to chose an abortion prior to viability. The Court, however, held that the

One controversial aspect of constitutional protection of privacy relates to government control of abortions.

right to have an abortion prior to viability is subject to state regulation that does not "unduly burden" it. In other words, states may make reasonable regulations on how a woman exercises her right to an abortion so long as "the State does not prohibit any woman from making the ultimate decision to terminate her pregnancy before viability."[77]

Applying the undue burden test, the Court held, for instance, that states can prohibit the use of state funds and facilities for performing abortions, that a state may make a minor's right to an abortion conditional on her first notifying at least one parent or a judge, that a state may condition an abortion on a 24-hour waiting period during which a doctor must inform the woman about alternatives in a state-prescribed talk. On the other hand, a state may not condition a woman's right to an abortion on her first notifying her husband.[78]

Sexual Orientation Rights

In 1986 by a 5 to 4 vote, the Supreme Court refused to declare unconstitutional a Georgia law that criminalized consensual sodomy as practiced by homosexuals. That homosexual conduct occurs in the privacy of the home, said the majority, does not affect the result. Justice Harry A. Blackmun, in dissent, wrote that the "Constitution embodies a promise that a certain private sphere of individual liberty will be kept largely beyond the reach of government," that the Court has long recognized that certain "decisions are properly for the individual to make," and that there are certain places, such as the home, where the government should intrude only in extreme circumstances.[79]

Without mentioning the 1986 decision, the Court in 1996, by a 6 to 3 vote, struck down a provision of the Colorado constitution that prohibited all legislative, executive, or judicial action at any level of state or local government designed to protect gays. This provision, declared the Court majority, violates the equal protection clause because it identifies persons by a single trait and then denies them protection across the board. Justice Scalia in dissent accused the Court of taking sides in "the cultural wars through an act not of judicial judgment but of political will."

Because of the strong emotions on both sides of this issue, the right of privacy as an element of substantive due process is one of the developing edges of constitutional law, one about which people both on and off the court have strong feelings. How the Supreme Court handles privacy issues is now front page news.

Drug Testing

In recent years Fourth Amendment questions have been raised about the constitutionality of testing blood and urine for drugs. Although agreeing that such tests intrude upon expectations of privacy and are searches within the meaning of the Fourth Amendment, the Supreme Court held that the federal regulations requiring such tests for railroad workers involved in accidents do not violate the Fourth Amendment, even as used without any warrant requirement. Justice Thurgood Marshall, bitterly dissenting, wrote, "The majority's acceptance of a dragnet blood and urine testing ensures that the first, and worst, casualty of the war on drugs will be the precious liberties of our citizens."*

Skinner v Railway Labor Executives, 489 US 602 (1989).

Freedom from Unreasonable Searches and Seizures

According to the Fourth Amendment "The right of the people to be secure in their persons, houses, papers, and effects, against unreasonable searches and seizures, shall not be violated, and no Warrants shall issue, but upon probable cause, supported by Oath or affirmation, and particularly describing the place to be searched, and the persons or things to be seized."

What is an unreasonable search and seizure? Despite what we sometimes see in television police dramas and read in the press, law enforcement officers have no general right to break down doors and invade homes. They are not supposed to search people except under certain conditions, and they have no right to arrest them except under certain circumstances.[80]

Seizures, or what we now call police detentions and arrests, are in fact given less protection than searches of our property. Police may arrest people without warrants in public places, provided there is *probable cause*—a fair probability that the persons in question have committed or are about to commit crimes. No later than two days after making an arrest, the police must take the arrested person to a magistrate so that the latter—not just the police—can decide whether probable cause existed to justify the warrantless arrest.[81] Probable cause, however, does not, except in extreme emergencies, justify a warrantless arrest of people in their own homes. Ordinarily, in order to enter a private dwelling to search or arrest persons in that dwelling, police need a search and arrest warrant, and before entering they must knock and announce their presence. To justify an unannounced entry, police have to show that they did so to preserve evidence, prevent persons from escaping, or that there is a threat of physical violence or some other justification to show the reasonableness of their unannounced entry.[82]

Not every time the police stop a person to ask questions or even to seek that person's consent to a search is there a seizure or detention requiring probable cause or a warrant. If all that happens is that the police ask questions or even seek consent to search that individual's person or possessions in a noncoercive atmosphere, there is no detention. "So long as a reasonable person would feel free 'to disregard the police and go about his business,' the encounter is consensual and no reasonable suspicion is required. The encounter will not trigger Fourth Amendment scrutiny unless it loses its consensual nature." But if the person refuses to answer questions or consent to a search, and the police, by either physical force or a show of authority, restrain the movement of the person, even though there is no arrest, the Fourth Amendment comes into play.[83] For example, if police approach people in airports and request identification, this act by itself does not constitute a detention. The same is true if police ask bus passengers for consent to search their luggage for drugs. But if the police do more, especially after consent is refused, then their actions create an "in-custody detention" that requires them to have some objective justification for the search beyond mere suspicion.

The Constitution does not forbid searches, only "unreasonable" ones. "It is a cardinal principle that searches conducted outside the judicial process, without prior approval by a judge or a magistrate, are unreasonable under the Fourth Amendment—subject only to a few specially established and well-delineated exceptions."[84] In fact, however, the number of exceptions keeps growing, and they are not well delineated. And there are various administrative searches by nonpolice government agents, such as teachers and health officials, not designed to uncover crimes. Rules governing the conduct of such administrative searches are more lenient than are those for searches by police investigating crimes.

Where the Fourth Amendment applies, the exceptions to the general rule against warrantless searches and seizures of what is found by police and customs officials are as follows:

1. *The Automobile Exception:* The exception is justified in part because of the mobility of automobiles and in part because persons are not entitled to the same expectations of privacy in their automobiles as in their homes or other places. If officers have probable cause to believe that an automobile is being used to commit a crime, even a traffic offense, or that it contains persons who have committed crimes, or that it contains evidence of crimes or contraband, they may stop the automobile, detain the persons found therein, and search them and any containers or packages found inside the car.[85]

2. *The Terry Exception:* First discussed in *Terry v Ohio*, these brief investigatory stops and searches were originally justified only when officers had reason to believe they were dealing with armed and dangerous persons, but they have subsequently been expanded to cover stops when the police have reason to believe that a person has committed or is about to commit a criminal offense. The intrusion permitted under a *Terry* search is limited to a quick pat-down to check for weapons that might be used to assault the arresting officer, to check for contraband, to determine identity, or to maintain briefly the status quo while obtaining more information.[86] If an officer stops and frisks a suspect to look for weapons and finds criminal evidence that might justify an arrest, then the officer can make a full search.[87] To illustrate: An officer, acting on an informer's tip, approached a man sitting in a car. The officer ordered the suspect to get out of the car, but the suspect merely rolled down the window. The officer saw a bulge on the suspect's waistband. He reached over into the car and removed a gun from the suspect's waistband. The officer arrested the suspect, although the mere possession of a weapon is not a crime, made a search, and found heroin.[88]

3. *Searches Subsequent to Valid Arrest:* When making a lawful arrest, either with an arrest warrant or because of probable cause, police may make a warrantless search of persons involved, the areas under their immediate control, and all the possessions they take with them to the place of detention. And police may make a protective sweep of the immediate area to be sure it does not harbor other dangerous persons.[89]

4. *Searches for Evidence:* When there is probable cause to make an arrest, even if one is not made, limited searches are permitted if necessary to preserve easily disposed of evidence, such as scrapings under fingernails.[90]

5. *Inventory Searches:* Searches that are part of the routine procedures of an arrest are permissible, provided there are established rules for inventory searches so that such a search does not become "a ruse for a general rumaging in order to discover incriminating evidence."[91]

6. *Consent:* Searches based on voluntary consent are allowed, even if the persons who give the consent are not told they have a right to refuse to grant permission.[92]

7. *Border Searches:* Searches of persons and the goods they bring with them are permissible at border crossings.[93] The border search exception also permits officials to open mail entering the country if they have "reasonable cause" to suspect it contains merchandise imported contrary to the law.[94] (The border search exception does not extend to searches by Puerto Rican

Police may detain and search cars and their passengers if they have probable cause to believe that the cars are involved in criminal activity, including even minor traffic offenses.

The Crime Control and Safe Streets Act of 1968

1. Makes it a crime for any unauthorized person to tap telephone wires or to use or sell, in interstate commerce, electronic bugging devices.

2. Empowers the United States attorney general to secure a warrant from a federal judge authorizing federal agents to engage in bugging in order to track down persons suspected of certain federal crimes.

3. Permits wiretaps without prior court approval for 48 hours in emergency situations involving certain crimes, such as child pornography, illegal currency transactions, offenses against crime witnesses, or immediate danger of death or serious injury.

4. Authorizes the principal prosecuting attorney of any state or political subdivision to apply to a state judge for a warrant approving wiretapping or other oral intercepts for felonies. (Most state and local jurisdictions allow such intercepts.)

5. Permits judges to issue warrants only if they decide probable cause exists that a crime is being, has been, or is about to be committed, and that information relating to that crime may be obtained only by wiretapping.

authorities of persons coming from the continental United States; such persons are not making an international crossing.[95])

8. *Plain-View Exception:* The plain-view exception permits officers to seize evidence without a warrant if: (1) they are lawfully in a position from which the evidence can be viewed; (2) it is immediately apparent to them that the items they observe are evidence of a crime or are contraband; and (3) they have probable cause—a reasonable suspicion will not do—that the evidence uncovered is contraband or evidence of a crime.[96]

9. *Exigent Circumstances:* Searches are permissible under "exigent circumstances," that is, when officers do not have time to secure a warrant before evidence is destroyed, or a criminal escapes capture, or when there is need "to protect or preserve life or avoid serious injury." An example of exigent circumstances is that fire fighters and police may enter a burning building without a warrant and may remain there for a reasonable time to investigate the cause of the blaze after the fire has been extinguished. However, after the fire has been put out, the emergency is not to be used as an excuse to make an exhaustive, warrantless search for evidence not in plain sight.[97] Films, books and other materials that might be protected by the First Amendment may be seized under the exigent-circumstances exception only if there are multiple copies of the seized materials, most of which are left undisturbed.

10. *Foreign agents:* Although never directly sustained by the Supreme Court, Congress has endorsed a presidential claim that the president can authorize warrantless wiretaps and physical searches of agents of foreign countries. Congress has created a special Foreign Intelligence Surveillance Court to approve of such requests. This Court, consisting of seven federal district judges, meets in secret. The attorney general submits annual reports to Congress, "reports that actually consist of a perfunctory one-paragraph letter."[98]

Outside these exceptions, a police search without consent is constitutionally unreasonable unless it has been authorized by a valid **search warrant**, issued by a magistrate after the police indicate under oath that they have probable cause to justify its issuance. Magistrates must perform this function in a neutral and detached manner and not serve merely as rubber stamps for the police.

The Constitution not only ordinarily requires a search warrant, but it also requires a specific one because *general search warrants*—warrants that authorize police to search a particular place or person without limitation—are unconstitutional. When a magistrate issues a warrant, the warrant must describe: (1) what places are to be searched, and (2) what things are to be seized. And a warrant is needed to search a person in any place he or she has an "expectation of privacy that society is prepared to recognize as reasonable," for example, in a hotel room, in a rented home, in a friend's apartment.[99] In short, the Fourth Amendment protects people, not places, from unreasonable governmental intrusions.

Wire Tapping and Electronic Surveillance

Scientific inventions have confronted judges with new problems in applying the Fourth Amendment. Obviously, the writers of the Fourth Amendment intended such physical objects as books, papers, letters, and other kinds of documents to be protected from seizure by the government except in cases in which magistrates had issued search warrants. But what of overhearing phone conversations by tapping phone wires, or using electronic devices to eavesdrop, or using secret video cameras to make videotapes? In *Olmstead v United States* (1928) a bare majority of the Supreme Court held there was no unconstitutional search unless seizure of physical objects or actual physical entry into a premise was involved. Justices Oliver Wendell

Holmes and Louis D. Brandeis, in dissent, argued that the Constitution should keep up with the times; the "dirty business" of wiretapping produced the same evil invasion of privacy the framers had in mind when they wrote the Fourth Amendment.[100]

Forty years later, in *Katz v United States* (1967), the Supreme Court adopted the Holmes-Brandeis position:

> The Fourth Amendment protects people—and not simply "areas"—against unreasonable searches and seizures. Wherever a man may be [subsequently modified and limited to those places where a person has a legitimate expectation of privacy that society is prepared to recognize as reasonable],[101] he is entitled to know that he will remain free from unreasonable searches and seizures.[102]

"The court finds itself on the horns of a dilemma. On the one hand, wiretap evidence is inadmissable, and on the other hand, I'm dying to hear it."
Drawing by Handelsman. © 1972 The New Yorker Magazine, Inc.

The Exclusionary Rule

Combining the Fourth Amendment prohibition against unreasonable searches with the Fifth Amendment injunction that persons shall not be compelled to be witnesses against themselves, the Supreme Court ruled, in *Mapp v Ohio* (1961), that evidence obtained unconstitutionally cannot be used in a criminal trial as part of the government's main case against persons from whom it was seized.[103] This is what is called the **exclusionary rule**. It was adopted in large part to prevent police misconduct. Because police are seldom prosecuted for making illegal searches and often can't afford to pay civil damages, the justices believed the exclusionary rule was the best—and maybe the only—sanction.

Critics of the exclusionary rule, including Chief Justice William H. Rehnquist, question why criminals should go free just because of police misconduct or ineptness. So far the Supreme Court has refused to abandon the rule. It has started making some exceptions to it, however, such as in cases in which police have relied in good faith on a search warrant that subsequently turned out to be improperly granted.[104]

The exclusionary rule covers only trials of those from whom the evidence was unconstitutionally seized, as one citizen, Jack Payner, found out. Internal Revenue Service agents, aided by a private investigator and operating in the best tradition of television police dramas, broke into Payner's banker's hotel room after a female undercover agent had lured the banker out to dinner. The agents "borrowed" the banker's briefcase, photographed documents, put the original documents back, and returned the briefcase. This "caper" was clearly a deliberate intrusion into the banker's privacy and a violation of his Fourth Amendment rights. Nonetheless, the evidence was allowed to be used to convict Payner, one of the banker's customers, of income tax evasion. Payner could expect neither privacy in his banker's briefcase nor any ownership of the documents taken from it.[105]

The Right to Remain Silent

During the seventeenth century, certain special courts in England forced confessions of heresy and sedition from religious dissenters. The British privilege against self-incrimination developed in response to these practices. Because they were familiar with this history, the framers of our Bill of Rights included in the Fifth Amendment the provision that persons shall not be compelled to testify against themselves in criminal prosecutions. This protection against self-incrimination is designed to strengthen a fundamental principle of Anglo-American justice: No person has an obligation to prove innocence. Rather, the burden is on the government to prove guilt.

The privilege against self-incrimination applies literally only in criminal prosecutions, but it has always been interpreted to protect any person subject to questioning by any agency of government, such as a congressional committee. It is not enough, however, to contend that answers might be embarrassing or might

The *Miranda* warning is read to suspects by a police officer before questioning them to inform them of their rights, such as the right to remain silent and the right to have an attorney present.

lead to loss of a job or even to civil suits; persons must have a reasonable fear that the answers might support a criminal prosecution or "furnish a link in the chain of evidence needed to prosecute" a crime.[106]

Sometimes authorities would rather have information from witnesses than prosecute them. Congress has established procedures so that prosecutors and congressional committees may secure a *grant of immunity* for such a witness. After immunity has been granted, a witness no longer has a constitutional right to refuse to testify. A person granted this immunity can still be prosecuted for crimes subject to such investigations, but the government cannot use the information directly derived from the compelled testimony in any subsequent prosecution. This grant of immunity can be a formidable bar to successful prosecution, as was indicated by the government's inability to prosecute successfully Oliver North and others involved in the Iran-Contra affair.

The Miranda Warning

Police questioning of suspects is a key procedure in solving crimes. It can, however, be easily abused. Police officers sometimes forget or ignore the constitutional rights of suspects, especially those who are frightened and ignorant. Unauthorized detention and lengthy interrogation to wring confessions from suspects, common practice in police states, until recently were not unknown in the United States.

What good is the presumption of innocence if, long before the accused are brought before the court, they are detained and forced to prove their innocence to the police? Judges have done much to stamp out such police brutality. The Supreme Court has ruled that admission into evidence of a coerced confession violates the self-incrimination clause, deprives a person of the assistance of counsel guaranteed by the Sixth and Fourteenth Amendments, deprives a person of due process, and undermines the entire proceeding.[107]

Federal and state laws require police officers to take those whom they have arrested before magistrates right away so that the magistrates may inform them of their constitutional rights and allow them to get in touch with friends and seek legal advice. Despite these requirements, police were often tempted to quiz suspects first, trying to get them to confess before a magistrate informed them of their constitutional right to remain silent.

To put an end to such practices, the Supreme Court, in *Miranda v Arizona* (1966), announced that no conviction—federal or state—could stand if evidence introduced at the trial had been obtained by the police during "custodial interrogation," unless suspects have been: (1) notified that they are free to remain silent; (2) warned that what they say may be used against them in court; (3) told that they have a right to have attorneys present during questioning; (4) informed that if they cannot afford to hire their own lawyers, attorneys will be provided for them; and (5) permitted to terminate any stage of the police interrogation. If suspects answer questions in the absence of an attorney, the burden is on the prosecution to demonstrate that suspects knowingly and intelligently gave up their rights to remain silent and to have their own lawyers present. Failure to comply with these requirements leads to reversal of a conviction, even if other evidence is sufficient to establish guilt.[108]

Critics of the *Miranda* decision believe the Court has unnecessarily and severely limited the ability of the police to bring criminals to justice. The importance of pretrial interrogations is underscored by the fact that roughly 90 percent of all criminal convictions result from guilty pleas and never reach a full trial. Nevertheless, despite sustained attack, the Supreme Court has refused to reverse *Miranda*, although it has modified its original ruling to some extent. In order to deter *perjury* (lying under oath), evidence obtained contrary to the

Miranda guidelines can be used to attack the credibility of defendants who offer contradictory testimony at their trials.

RIGHTS IN THE ORIGINAL CONSTITUTION

Even though most of the framers did not think a Bill of Rights was necessary, they considered certain rights important enough to be included in the original Constitution. These include the right of a writ of *habeas corpus* and protection against *ex post facto* laws and bills of attainder.

The Writ of Habeas Corpus

Foremost among constitutional rights is the guarantee that the **writ of habeas corpus** will be available unless suspended in time of rebellion or invasion. Literally meaning "produce the body," this writ is a court order directing any official having a person in custody to produce the prisoner in court and to explain to the judge why the prisoner is being held. Permission to suspend the writ is found in the article setting forth the powers of Congress so, presumably, only Congress has the right to suspend it.

As originally used, the writ was merely a court inquiry to determine whether a person was being held in custody as the result of an act of a court with proper jurisdiction. But over the years it has developed into a remedy "available to effect discharge from any confinement contrary to the Constitution or fundamental law."[109] Persons being held apply, usually through an attorney, for release and state why they believe they are being held unlawfully. The judge then orders the jailer to show cause why the writ should not be issued. If a judge finds a petitioner is being detained unlawfully, the judge may order the prisoner's immediate release. Although state judges lack jurisdiction to issue writs of *habeas corpus* to find out why national authorities are holding persons, federal district judges may do so to find out if state and local officials are holding people "in violation of the Constitution or laws or treaties of the United States."[110]

In recent years a controversy has erupted between those who believe federal judges should be given wide discretion to issue writs of *habeas corpus* in order to protect constitutional rights and those who believe the writ has been abused by state prisoners to touch off an endless and unessential round of reviews, which sometimes lead to convictions being set aside by a federal judge after the matter has been carefully reviewed by two or more state courts. Critics point to the many prisoners on death row who have successfully used *habeas corpus* to raise objection after objection, delaying the execution of their sentences for years.

Partly because of this criticism, partly from concern for maintaining the principles of federalism, and partly in response to a growing overload on federal courts, the Supreme Court has severely restricted the use of *habeas corpus* by federal judges.[111] In 1996 Congress, in the Anti-Terrorist and Effective Death Penalty Act, restricted state prison inmates' access to federal courts even further, especially those on death row. Congress placed time limits for filing petitions for *habeas corpus*, restricted the number of requests for such petitions, stopped appeals for most *habeas* petitions at the level of the U.S. courts of appeals, and called for deference by federal judges to the decisions of state judges on matters of fact and law, unless those decisions are clearly "unreasonable." The Supreme Court took the unusual step of expediting the review of that law, especially against the challenge that (1) the law violates the constitutional guarantee of Article I, Section 9 that the privilege of the writ of *habeas corpus* shall not be suspended unless in cases of rebellion or invasion, and (2) the challenge that the law unconstitutionally restricts the Supreme Court's jurisdiction by stopping most appeals at the court of appeals level.

The Minibill of Rights: Rights in the Original Constitution

1. Writ of *habeas corpus*
2. No bills of attainder
3. No *ex post facto* laws
4. No titles of nobility
5. Trial by jury in national courts
6. Protection for citizens as they move from one state to another, including the right to travel
7. Protects against use of crime of treason to restrict other activities and limits punishment for treason
8. Guarantee that each state has a republican form of government
9. No religious test oaths as a condition for holding a federal office.

At the end of the 1995–1996 term, the Court by unanimous vote held: (1) the added restrictions on second *habeas* petitions do not amount to a suspension of the writ contrary to Article I, Section 9; (2) although Congress had limited the Supreme Court's authority to review appeals from decisions of the Court of Appeals denying such *habeas* petitions, the act did repeal an earlier law giving the Supreme Court jurisdiction to entertain *habeas* petitions brought directly to it. Thus there can be no plausible argument that the act deprived the Supreme Court of its appellate jurisdiction in violation of Article III.

Ex Post Facto Laws and Bills of Attainder

The Constitution forbids both the national and the state governments from passing *ex post facto* laws and enacting bills of attainder (Article I, Sections 9 and 10).

An **ex post facto** law is a retroactive criminal law that works to the disadvantage of an individual. Examples would include a law making a particular act a crime that was not a crime when committed, increasing punishment for a crime after the crime was committed, or lessening proof necessary to convict for a crime after it was committed. The prohibition does not prevent the passage of retroactive penal laws that work to the benefit of an accused—a law decreasing punishment, for example. Nor does the prohibition prevent passage of retroactive civil laws. Income tax rates as applied to income already earned, for example, may be increased, as was done in 1993.

A **bill of attainder** is a legislative act inflicting punishment, including deprivation of property, without judicial trial on named individuals or members of a specified group. For example, Congress enacted a bill of attainder in conflict with this prohibition when it named three federal employees in an appropriations bill and declared they should receive no compensation from the federal treasury, other than for military or jury services, unless reappointed to office by the president with the consent of the Senate.

THE SHORT AND NOT TOO HAPPY LIFE OF JOHN CROOK

Evidence in the popular press affirms that many people consider the rights of persons accused of crime to be less important than other civil liberties. But, as Justice Felix Frankfurter observed, "The history of liberty has largely been the history of observance of procedural safeguards." Further, these safeguards have frequently "been forged in controversies involving not very nice people."[113]

The rights of persons accused of crime by the national government can be found in the Constitution and in the Fourth, Fifth, Sixth, and Eighth Amendments. To gain some idea of how these constitutional safeguards are applied, let us follow the fortunes and misfortunes of a fictitious character, John Crook, as he is prosecuted for a federal crime.

John Crook sent circulars through the mail selling shares in a nonexistent gold mine—an action contrary to dozens of federal laws. When postal officers uncovered these activities, they went to the district court and secured from a United States magistrate a warrant to arrest Crook and another warrant to search his home for copies of the circulars. They found Crook at home and read the *Miranda* warning to him, emphasizing especially *his right to remain silent and to have the assistance of counsel.* They showed him the warrant, arrested him for using the mails to defraud, and found and seized some of the circulars mentioned in the search warrant.

The Preliminary Hearing and Right to Counsel

Crook was promptly brought before a federal district judge (sometimes a magistrate acts for the judge), who again emphasized that Crook had a constitutional right to assistance of counsel. Judges have a positive obligation to ensure that all persons subject to any kind of custodial interrogation are represented by lawyers.[114] Unless the record clearly shows that the accused were fully aware of what they were doing and gave up the right to counsel, or intelligently exercised the right to represent themselves, the absence of counsel will render criminal proceedings unconstitutional. The right extends to all hearings for all offenses for which an accused could be deprived of liberty, whether or not a jury trial is required. Trials in which fines are the only penalty are exempt from the assistance-of-counsel requirement. This assistance is required at every stage of a criminal proceeding after the initiation of formal charges—preliminary hearings, bail hearings, trial, sentence, and first appeal. When Crook told the judge he could could not afford to hire his own counsel, the judge appointed an attorney paid for by the federal government to represent him.

At this point Crook had not been convicted of anything. In fact, he had not even been formally charged with any crime, and he was entitled to be free without having to pay excessive bail. (Note the Eighth Amendment does not require that bail be set, but forbids imposition of excessive bail.) Suspects are entitled to a hearing within five days, and judges or magistrates must explain in writing why they believe there is clear and convincing evidence that pretrial release might endanger the safety of other persons and the community.[115] The judge set Crook's bail at $5,000, and Crook was held over until the convening of the next federal grand jury. After hiring a professional bondsman, who posted the bail and collected a 10 percent fee, Crook was free as long as he remained within the judicial district.

The Indictment

Except for members of the armed forces, the national government cannot require anyone to stand trial for a serious crime except *on grand jury indictment*. Grand jurors are concerned not with a person's guilt or innocence but merely with whether there is enough evidence to warrant a trial. The **grand jury** has wide-ranging investigatory powers and "is to inquire into all information that might bear on its investigations until it is satisfied that it has identified an offense or satisfied itself that none has occurred."[116] The strict rules that govern jury proceedings do not apply. The grand jury may admit hearsay evidence, and the exclusionary rule to enforce the Fourth Amendment does not apply. If a majority of the grand jurors agree that a trial is justified, they return what is known as a *true bill*, or indictment.

When the next grand jury was convened, the United States district attorney brought evidence before the 23 jurors to indicate that Crook had committed a federal crime. In Crook's case the grand jury was in agreement with the United States district attorney and returned a true bill against Crook.

After a copy of the indictment was served on Crook, he was again ordered to appear before a federal district judge. The Constitution guarantees the accused *the right to be informed of the nature and cause of the accusation* so that he or she can prepare a defense. Consequently, the federal prosecutor took care that the indictment clearly stated the nature of the offense, and she saw to it that copies were properly served on Crook and his lawyer.

Actually, prior to his hearing, Crook's attorney discussed with the United States attorney's office the possibility of Crook's pleading guilty to the lesser offense of false representation, in return for which he would not have to stand trial for the more serious charge of using the mails to defraud. Prosecutors, faced with more cases than they can handle, like this kind of **plea bargaining**.

Does the Fourth Amendment protect against judicially ordered surgery?

At 1:00 A.M. on July 18, 1982, Ralph E. Watkinson was closing his shop for the night, when someone pointing a gun came toward him. Watkinson drew his own gun and fired, the fire was returned, and Watkinson was hit in the leg. He watched his assailant flee, apparently wounded on the left side. Later that night Rudolph Lee, Jr., suffering from a gunshot wound to his left chest, was identified by Watkinson as the man who shot him. Lee was charged with the crime. Shortly thereafter the Commonwealth of Virginia moved in a state court for an order directing Lee to undergo surgery to remove (in effect, search for) an object thought to be a bullet lodged under his left collarbone.

Does such a search violate the Fourth Amendment?

You Decide!

Likewise, defendants are often willing to "cop a plea" to a lesser offense to avoid the risk of more serious punishment.

When defendants plead guilty, they are usually forever prevented from raising objections to their convictions. That is why, before accepting guilty pleas, judges question defendants to be sure that their attorneys have explained the alternatives and that they know what they are doing. It never came to this in Crook's case, however. After discussing the matter with his attorney, Crook elected to stand trial on the charge and entered a plea of not guilty.

The Trial

After indictment, Crook's bail was raised to $20,000. Now the federal government was obligated to give him a *speedy and public trial.* Do not, however, take the word "speedy" too literally. Crook had to be given time to prepare his defense. Defendants, in fact, often ask for delays, because delay often works to their advantage. If, in contrast, the government denies the accused a speedy trial in a constitutional sense, the remedy is drastic. Not only is the conviction reversed, but the case must be dismissed outright.

Crook's lawyer pointed out that under the Sixth Amendment, Crook had a right to trial before an *impartial jury* selected from the state and district in which the alleged crime was committed because he was being tried for a serious crime, that is, one punishable by more than six months in prison or a $500 fine.[117] Although federal law requires juries of 12, the Constitution requires only that juries consist of at least six persons. Conviction in federal courts must be by unanimous vote. (The Constitution permits state courts to render guilty verdicts by nonunanimous juries, provided such juries consist of six or more persons. Only Louisiana and Oregon permit convictions by less than unanimous juries.[118])

An impartial jury, one that meets the requirements of due process and equal protection, consists of persons who represent a fair cross-section of the community. Although defendants are not entitled to juries on which there are necessarily members of their own race, sex, religion, or national origin, they are entitled to be tried by juries from which jurors have not been excluded because of these categories. Such discriminatory action also violates the civil rights secured by the equal protection clause of those denied the opportunity to serve on juries. Government prosecutors cannot strike persons from juries because of race or gender, and neither can defense attorneys use what are called *peremptory challenges* to keep people off juries because of race, ethnic origin, or sex.[119]

Crook told his lawyer he had dinner with George Witness on the night on which he was charged with sending the damaging circulars. The attorney took advantage of Crook's constitutional *right to obtain witnesses in his favor* and had the judge subpoena Witness to appear at the trial and testify. Although Witness could have refused to testify on the grounds that his testimony would tend to incriminate him, he agreed to appear. Crook himself, however, chose to use his constitutional right not to be a witness against himself and refused to take the stand. He knew that if he did so, the prosecution would have a right to cross-examine him, and he was fearful of what might be uncovered. To protect Crook's right against self-incrimination, the judge conducting the trial was required to caution the jury against drawing any conclusions from Crook's decision not to testify. All prosecution witnesses appeared in court and were available for defense cross-examination; the Constitution also insists that accused persons have the *right to be confronted with the witnesses against them.*

The Sentencing

At the conclusion of the trial, the jury brought in a verdict of guilty. The judge then raised Crook's bail to $50,000 and announced that she would hand down a sentence on the following Monday. The Eighth Amendment forbids the levying of excessive fines and the *inflicting of cruel and unusual punishments.*

The ban against cruel and unusual punishments limits government in three ways:

1. It limits the kinds and methods of punishment that may be imposed, prohibiting, for example, torture, intentional denial of medical care, inhumane conditions, unnecessary or wanton inflicting of pain, and deliberate indifference to medical and other needs of prisoners.[120] Recently challenges are being made that the use of the gas chamber is a cruel and unusual punishment.

2. It prohibits punishments grossly disproportionate to the severity of the crime. However, outside the context of capital punishment—where the Court has limited the death penalty to crimes in which a life has been taken—the Court has been "reluctant to review legislatively mandated terms of imprisonment,"[121] and "successful challenges to the proportionality of particular sentences will be exceedingly rare."[122]

3. It limits the power of the government to decide what can be made a criminal offense. For example, the mere act of being a chronic alcoholic may not be made a crime because alcoholism is an illness. However, being drunk in public may be a criminal offense.[123]

What of *capital punishment?* After much soul searching, and many cases, the Supreme Court has ruled that the death penalty is not necessarily cruel and unusual punishment when imposed for conviction of the crime of murder. The death penalty may, however, be imposed only on those convicted of crimes that have resulted in a victim's death. As more and more states have added the death penalty and the national government has increased the number of crimes for which the death penalty shall be imposed, the number of persons on death row has dramatically increased. In California alone there are almost 400 inmates on death row. Trial judges are imposing roughly 50 new death sentences per year, more than the Supreme Court has been able to process. It will take 10 years to process these cases at the existing rate.

Back to Crook. His case did not involve a capital offense. The judge, following the guidelines set down by the United States Sentencing Commission, gave Crook the maximum punishment of a $25,000 fine and three years in the penitentiary. Such a sentence could not be considered cruel and unusual. Crook could have appealed both his sentence and his conviction to the court of appeals, but he chose not to do so.

John Crook and the State Government

While still in the federal penitentiary, Crook was taken by federal authorities before the state courts to answer charges that when he solicited shares in his nonexistent gold mine, he had also violated several state laws. Through his state-appointed attorney, Crook protested he had already been tried by the federal government for using the mails to defraud. He pointed to the Fifth Amendment provision that no person shall be "subject for the same offense to be twice put in jeopardy of life or limb."[124] The judge answered: "The Supreme Court has said that **double jeopardy** prevents two criminal trials by the same government for the same criminal offense." Double jeopardy does not prevent punishment by the national and the state governments for the same offense or for successive prosecutions for the same crime by two states. Nor does it forbid civil prosecutions after criminal trials, as occurred when O.J. Simpson had to defend himself in a civil trial against a wrongful death suit after his acquittal in a criminal trial for the muder of his wife and a friend.

Thinking it Through

The Supreme Court previously sustained the right of a state, under proper circumstances and for proper reasons, to compel persons to submit to blood tests. In the Watkinson case, there was no question about lack of proper judicial and legal procedures: The state had more than a warrant for this "search"; it had a valid order of a state judge. Nonetheless, a unanimous Court found this to be an unreasonable search. The state failed, the Court concluded, to demonstrate such a compelling need for the bullet to justify so substantial an intrusion upon the suspect's privacy and security interests.*

In this rare example, a search was declared unconstitutional not because of improper procedures but because it intruded, under the circumstances, beyond the realm of the government's proper concerns.

What does such a case tell you about the guidelines for interpreting the Constitution? Did the Court follow the literal words of the Constitution, the intentions of the framers, or were the justices applying their interpretations of the current sense of justice? Which intentions of which framers? (Remember the framers did not intend the Fourth Amendment to apply to the states at all.) How is the Court to know which interpretation of the current sense of justice to follow?

*Winston v Lee, 470 US 753 (1985).

What constitutional rights can Crook claim in the state courts? First, every state constitution contains a bill of rights listing practically the same guarantees found in the national Bill of Rights. Until recently, most state judges were less inclined than federal judges to interpret the constitutional guarantees of their own state constitutions liberally in favor of those accused of crime. Although, as we noted in Chapter 3, some state judges now are being more liberal in using the bills of rights in their own state constitutions to protect the rights of persons accused of crimes, most cases still turn on the application of the provisions of the Bill of Rights of the U.S. Constitution.

To what extent does the U.S. Constitution protect courtroom procedures from state actions? As noted, the Bill of Rights does not directly apply to the states, but the Fourteenth Amendment does. As the result of a series of Supreme Court decisions interpreting the Fourteenth Amendment, it now imposes on the states all the provisions of the Bill of Rights except those of the Second, Third, Seventh, and the Tenth Amendments, and the grand jury requirements of the Fifth Amendment. No specific Supreme Court decision applies the excessive bail and fine limitation to the states. However, almost by definition, if a bail or fine is excessive, its imposition is likely to be considered a denial of due process.

The Supreme Court will probably not incorporate additional provisions of the Bill of Rights into the Fourteenth Amendment; most lawyers, political scientists, and other observers believe states should be allowed to continue, as many of them now do, to conduct civil trials before judges without juries and to indict persons for serious crimes by means other than grand juries. A number of states no longer require grand jury indictment for any except capital crimes; some do not require them for any crimes. Other provisions in the Second, Third, and Tenth Amendments not incorporated are really not applicable to the states.

HOW JUST IS OUR SYSTEM OF JUSTICE?

What are the major criticisms of the American system of justice? How have they been answered?

TOO MANY LOOPHOLES Some observers argue that by overprotecting the innocent and placing too much of a burden on the government not to make any mistakes, we delay justice, encourage disrespect for the law, and allow guilty persons to go unpunished. Justice should be swift and certain without being arbitrary. But under our procedures criminals may go unpunished because: (1) the police decide not to arrest them; (2) the judge decides not to hold them for a trial; (3) the prosecutor decides not to prosecute them; (4) the grand jury decides not to indict them; (5) the jury decides not to convict them; (6) the judge decides not to sentence them; (7) an appeals court decides to reverse the conviction; (8) a judge decides to release them on a *habeas corpus* writ; or (9) if retried and convicted, the executive decides to pardon, reprieve, or parole them. As a result, the public never knows whom to hold responsible when laws are not enforced. The police can blame the prosecutor, the prosecutor can blame the police, and they can all blame the juries and judges.

Others take a different view and point out that there is more to justice than simply securing convictions. All the steps in the administration of criminal laws have been developed over centuries of trial and error, and each step has been constructed to protect against particular abuses. History warns against entrusting the instruments of criminal law enforcement to a single officer. For this reason, responsibility is vested in many officials.

JURIES ON TRIAL

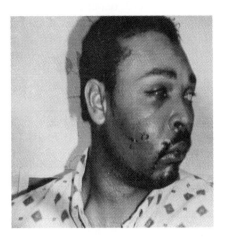

Criticism of the role of juries has increased in recent years as the general public learned the intimate details of some notorious trials because of around-the-clock television coverage and front-page newspaper attention. Resentment and bewilderment followed when juries failed to convict persons for what appeared to be obvious guilt. Examples include the 1992 acquittal of Los Angeles police officers whose extended beating of Rodney King had been videotaped and then witnessed by the entire nation (two officers were subsequently convicted of federal crimes); the 1993 trial of Damian Williams, whose brutal beating of truck driver Reginald Denny in the Los Angeles riots following the acquittal verdict in the King case was also captured on video, but who also received a relatively light sentence; and the repeated trials of the Menendez brothers, who confessed to killing both their parents but whose first trials resulted in hung juries that could not agree on the precise nature of their crime, and who were ultimately found guilty in a retrial. The 1995 acquittal of O. J. Simpson after the "trial of the century," whose televised details had dominated the news not only in the United States but throughout much of the world, divided the nation. A majority of whites believed that the jury—consisting of nine African Americans, two Hispanics, and one white—had ignored the evidence and had voted to acquit Simpson because of their resentment of the unfair treatment of African Americans at the hands of the Los Angeles Police Department. Most African Americans believed that the jury had done its duty. Contention about the Simpson trial added fuel to the demands to rewrite the rules for jury trials.

Marcia Clark, one of the best known lawyers in the country after appearing on TV screens for months, shows the "bloody glove" that was intended to prove O. J. Simpson's guilt.

TOO UNRELIABLE Critics who say that our system of justice is unreliable often point to trial by jury as the chief source of trouble. No other country relies as heavily on trial by jury as does the United States. Jury trials are also time consuming and costly. Trial by jury, critics argue, leads to a theatrical combat between lawyers who base their appeals on the prejudices and sentiments of the jurors. "Mr. Prejudice and Miss Sympathy are the names of witnesses whose testimony is never recorded, but must nevertheless be reckoned with in trials by jury."[125]

The jury system allows for what has come to be called *jury nullification* in which jurors ignore their instructions to consider only the evidence presented in court and by voting for acquittal express their displeasure with the law or the actions of prosecutors or police. There were many who accused the jury in the O. J. Simpson trial of voting to acquit him in order to express their displeasure with the Los Angeles Police Department and their belief that African Americans are routinely subject to police harrassment. Jury nullification has a long history. In colonial times juries refused to convict colonists of political crimes against the king as a way to protest British rule. Prior to the Civil War, Northern juries refused to convict persons for helping runaway slaves. Before the 1970s, white southern juries sometimes refused to convict police for actions of brutality against blacks.

Public cynicism about the effectiveness of the jury system, especially the belief that racial factors rather than the evidence were influencing juries, came to a head after a jury consisting largely of African Americans acquitted O. J. Simpson.[126] Most white Americans felt the jury had ignored the evidence. Most African Americans had similar feelings about the jury system when a jury consisting largely of whites had failed to punish white Los Angeles police officers for their beating of African American Rodney King. Responding to a growing public disenchantment with juries after a raft of unpopular verdicts "state legislatures and court systems across the nation are starting to rewrite the rules of the jury system."[127] These changes include making it more difficult for professionals to be excused from jury service, allowing for nonunanimous decisions, limiting the sequestration of jurors, and exerting more control over lawyer's statements to jurors.

Defenders of the jury system reply that trial by jury provides a check by nonprofessionals on the actions of judges and prosecutors.[128] There is no evidence that juries are unreliable. On the contrary, decisions of juries do not systematically differ from those of judges.[129] Moreover, the jury system helps to educate citizens and enables them to participate in the application of their own laws.

The grand jury has also come under attack. In theory, the grand jury has two functions: (1) to protect the innocent from having to stand trial by requiring prosecutors to demonstrate behind closed doors that they have enough evidence to justify trial; and (2) to provide an independent agency, not controlled by those in power, to investigate wrongdoing. Critics charge, however, that the grand jury has become a tool of the prosecutor. Said Justice William O. Douglas, "It is, indeed, common knowledge that the grand jury, having been conceived as a bulwark between the citizen and the Government, is now a tool of the Executive."[130]

During the 1960s critics on the left of the political spectrum charged that grand juries had become instruments to intimidate radicals, blacks, and antiwar militants. However, by the 1970s grand juries were being used to investigate the executive branch. In the Watergate investigation of the Nixon administration, it was through the use of the grand jury that the special prosecutor was able to present to the courts his contention that the president had no constitutional right to withhold information about wrongdoing.

In recent years, there are calls to reform the federal grand jury system and remove some of the limitations on the right of federal jurors to make public comments, so that such juries might more effectively investigate allegations of wrongdoing by federal officials and look into social problems. As one advocate of such a reform has written, "Federal grand juries with broad investigatory powers would give citizens a new tool and a new platform. The public would be far more likely to listen to what the grand jurors said than to what the experts said."[131]

TOO DISCRIMINATORY During the last several decades, the Supreme Court has worked particularly hard to enforce the ideal of equal justice under the law. Persons accused of crime who cannot afford attorneys must be furnished them at government expense. If transcripts are required for appeals, such transcripts must be made available to those who cannot afford to purchase them. If appeals are permitted, the government must provide attorneys for at least one appeal of the decision of the trial court. Poor people cannot be imprisoned because of inability to pay a fine. Nor, once sentenced, can poor persons be kept in jail beyond the term of the sentence because they cannot afford to pay a fine. Even for civil proceedings—divorce proceedings, for example—fees cannot be imposed that deny poor persons their fundamental rights, such as the right to obtain a divorce. A state has no obligation, however, to waive fees for those seeking to be declared bankrupt. The Court apparently believes that people have a constitutional right to be absolved of the ties that bind but not of their debts.

Despite all these protections, it remains true that racial and ethnic discrimination in the criminal justice system, especially outside the courtroom, persists. How much it persists is hard to measure. The editors of the *Harvard Law Review* believe it is significant. "Racism still pervades the United States criminal justice system," they charge, including police conduct, prosecutorial actions, among jurors, and in the sentencing process.[132] The editors blame the persistence of racism in the criminal justice system in part on the Supreme Court's requirement that, except in cases involving juror selection, litigants cannot legally prove racism through general evidence about racism in the system. They must show through direct evidence relating to their particular cases the discriminatory intent of the decision maker and the adverse consequence flowing from this intent to their case.[133]

Three Strikes and You're Out

Although the crime rate is actually going down, public concern about crime is going up. At both the national and state level, presidents, governors and legislators are vying with one another to show their toughness about crime. Laws have been proposed to require judges to impose lifetime sentences upon persons convicted of three felonies. In some states, the felonies have to be for violent crimes; in others any three felonies will do.

Some scholars are skeptical that "Three Strikes and You're Out " laws will reduce the crime rate; it will certainly require great expenditures of public funds to construct more jails and take care of aging felons.

"We find the defendant guilty as charged by the media."

Drawing by Chon Day. © 1978 The New Yorker Magazine, Inc.

One expert close to the subject comes to a different conclusion. He reports that about 80 percent of the black overrepresentation in prison can be explained by differential involvement in crime and about 20 percent by subsequent racially discriminatory processes.[134] "That is not at all to say that racial discrimination within the criminal justice system is unimportant; it certainly is important. What is suggested is only that it is relatively less important than other discriminatory pressures"[135] in society in general outside of the criminal justice system. Another scholar concludes: "While the reforms envisioned by Myrdal [a celebrated study by a Nobel Prize-winning Swedish social scientist] in *An American Dilemma*[136] may have eliminated the more obvious examples of racial discrimination in the criminal justice system, they have not produced an equitable, or color blind, system of justice. Fifty years after the publication of Myrdal's book, *An American Dilemma*, African Americans continue to suffer discrimination at the hands of the criminal justice officials in the United States."[137]

The American Dilemma

One of the more acute problems of our society is the tension between the police and the African American and Hispanic communities congregated in the ghettos and barrios of our large cities. Such tensions were evident in the Rodney King beating and the 1992 Los Angeles riots. Many members of minorities do not believe they have equal protection under the law. The revelations of detective Mark Furhman's racist remarks during the O. J. Simpson trial confirmed the view of many—especially, African Americans—that the police are instruments of white intolerance. "Even before the Simpson trial, 83 percent of blacks said in a poll. . .that they didn't trust the criminal justice system."[138] "Whether the stated belief is well founded or not is at least partly beside the point. The existence of the belief is damaging enough."[139]

Blacks consider the police to be enforcers of white law. Studies proving prejudice on the part of some white police officers and examples of rough, if not brutal, police treatment of blacks are ample evidence to support this viewpoint. The general pattern, however, is that minorities are shot by the police at rates approximately proportional to rates of minorities engaged in street crime, but "There is a slight added increment and all you can conclude is the data support what common observation and folk tales make very clear—there is an element of racial prejudice in police shooting at minorities."[140]

In recent decades action has been taken to recruit more African Americans, Hispanics, and women as police officers, including appointment to command posts, and community relations programs have been established. Considerable progress has been made, and relations between police and minority communities in some cities appear to be improving.

The Supreme Court and Civil Liberties

Clearly, judges—especially those on the Supreme Court—play a major role in enforcing constitutional guarantees. This combination of judicial enforcement and written guarantees of enumerated liberties is one of the basic features of the American system of government. As Justice Robert H. Jackson wrote:

> The very purpose of a Bill of Rights was to withdraw certain subjects from the vicissitudes of political controversy, to place them beyond the reach of majorities and officials and to establish them as legal principles to be applied by the courts. One's right to life, liberty, and property, to free speech, a free press, freedom of worship and assembly, and other fundamental rights may not be submitted to vote: they depend on the outcome of no elections.[141]

This emphasis on constitutional limitations and judicial enforcement is an example of the "auxiliary precautions" James Madison believed were necessary to prevent arbitrary governmental action. In other free nations citizens rely more on elections and political checks to protect their rights; in the United States we appeal to judges when we fear our freedoms are in danger.

Such reliance on judicial protection of our civil liberties focuses attention on the Supreme Court. Yet only a small number of controversies are actually carried to the Supreme Court, and a Supreme Court decision is not the end of the policy-making process. Lower-court judges as well as police, superintendents of schools, local prosecutors, school boards, state legislatures, and thousands of others give reality to the Court's doctrines.

The Supreme Court can do little unless its decisions over time reflect a national consensus. Judges by themselves cannot guarantee anything; neither can the First Amendment. As Justice Jackson once asked:

> Must we first maintain a system of free political government to assure a free judiciary to guarantee free government? It is my belief that the attitude of a society and of its organized political forces, rather than its legal machinery, is the controlling force in the character of free institutions. Any court which undertakes by its legal processes to enforce civil liberties needs the support of an enlightened and vigorous public opinion.[142]

Thus, the Bill of Rights—and the other procedural and substantive liberties of our Constitution—cannot rest on a foundation merely of tradition. The preservation of these rights depends on wide, continuing, and knowledgeable public support. Inevitably that public support will be tested—sometimes sorely tested—in the years to come.

SUMMARY

1. The Supreme Court uses a three-tiered approach to evaluate the constitutionality of laws challenged as violating the equal protection clause. Laws touching economic concerns are sustained if they are reasonably related to the accomplishment of a legitimate governmental goal. Laws that classify people because of sex are subject to the test known as heightened scrutiny and are sustained only if they serve important governmental objectives and are substantially related to achieving those objectives. Laws that touch fundamental rights or classify people because of race or ethnic origin are subject to strict scrutiny and will be sustained only if they are narrowly tailored to accomplish a compelling public interest.

2. The desirability and constitutionality of affirmative action programs that provide special benefits to those who have been subjected to past discrimination divide the nation and the Supreme Court. Remedial programs, especially those designed by Congress, closely tailored to overcome specific instances of disadvantage due to past discrimination, are likely to pass the Supreme Court's suspicion of race, national origin, and sex classifications. However, such programs are becoming subject to the more exacting strict scrutiny test, and fewer of them are likely to survive.

3. The Constitution protects the acquisition and retention of citizenship. It protects the basic liberties of citizens as well as aliens.

4. The Constitution imposes limits not only on the procedures government must follow but also on the ends it may pursue. Some actions are out of bounds no matter what procedures are followed. Legislatures have the primary role in determining what is reasonable and what is unreasonable. However, the Supreme Court continues to exercise its own independent and final review of legislative determinations of reasonableness, especially on matters affecting civil liberties and civil rights.

5. The framers knew from their own experiences that in their zeal to maintain power and to enforce the laws, public officials are often tempted to infringe on the rights of those accused of crimes. To prevent such abuse, the Constitution imposes detailed procedures federal officials must follow in making searches and arrests and in bringing people to trial.

6. The Supreme Court interprets the Constitution, especially the Fourteenth Amendment, to impose on state and local governments almost the same restraints in the administration of justice as it imposes on the national government.

JEFFREY ABRAMSON, *We, The Jury: The Jury System and the Ideal of Democracy* (Basic Books, 1994).

BARBARA R. BERGMANN, *In Defense of Affirmative Action* (Basic Books, 1996).

JANET K. BOLES, ED., "American Feminism: New Issues for a Mature Movement," *Annals of the American Academy of Political and Social Science* (May 1991).

STEPHEN L. CARTER, *Reflections of an Affirmative Action Baby* (Basic Books, 1991).

GEORGE F. COLE, *Criminal Justice: Law and Politics*, 6th ed. (Wadsworth, 1993).

CHANDLER DAVIDSON AND BERNARD GROFMAN, EDS., *Quiet Revolution in the South* (Princeton University Press, 1994).

JANET DEWART, ED., *The State of Black America* (National Urban League, published annually).

TERRY E. EASTLAND, *Ending Affirmative Action: The Case for Color Blind Justice* (Basic Books, 1996).

GERTRUDE EZORSKY, *Racism and Justice: The Case for Affirmative Action* (Cornell University Press, 1991).

BERNARD GROFMAN AND CHANDLER DAVIDSON EDS., *Controversies in Minority Voting: The Voting Rights Act in Perspective* (Brookings Institution, 1992).

ANDREW HACKER, *Two Nations: Black and White, Separate, Hostile, Unequal* (Charles Scribner's Sons, 1992).

RICHARD KLUGER, *Simple Justice* (Knopf, 1976).

LEONARD W. LEVY, KENNETH L. KARST, AND DENNIS J. MAHONE, *Criminal Justice and the Supreme Court* (Macmillan, 1990).

ROBERT E. LITAN, ED., *Verdict: Assessing the Civil Jury System* (Brookings, 1993).

PAULA D. MCCLAIN AND JOSEPH STEWART, JR., EDS., "The Voting Rights Act After *Shaw v. Reno*: A Symposium," *PS* XXVIII (March, 1995), pp. 24–55.

SUSAN GLUCK MEZEY, *In Pursuit of Equality: Women, Public Policy, and the Federal Courts* (St. Martin's Press, 1992).

GARY ORFIELD AND CAROLE ASHKINAZE, *The Closing Door: Conservative Policy and Black Opportunity* (University of Chicago Press, 1991).

J. W. PELTASON, *Fifty-eight Lonely Men: Southern Federal Judges and School Desegregation* (University of Illinois Press, 1971).

J. W. PELTASON, *Understanding the Constitution*, 13th ed. (Harcourt Brace, 1994).

JUDITH N. SHKLAR, *American Citizenship: The Quest for Inclusion* (Harvard University Press, 1991).

PETER SKERRY, *Mexican Americans: The Ambivalent Minority* (Free Press, 1993).

ROBERT W. TUCKER, CHARLES B. KEELEY, AND LINDA W. RIGLEY, EDS., *Immigration and U.S. Foreign Policy* (Westview Press, 1990).

MAURILIO E. VIGIL, *Hispanics in American Politics: The Search for Political Power* (University Press of America, 1987).

POLITICAL CULTURE AND IDEOLOGY

In 1995 the University of California Board of Regents voted to discontinue taking race or gender into account in making admissions decisions in hiring and contracting. As we noted in Chapter 4, this same Board of Regents had defended affirmative action before the U.S. Supreme Court in the *Bakke* case in 1978. By the mid-1990s, affirmative action had become an even more contentious issue as Californians debated a proposed ballot initiative to amend their state constitution to foreclose affirmative action by all state agencies, including the university.

The proposal to end affirmative action at the University of California was made by Ward Connerly, a land-use consultant and one of only three African Americans on the Board of Regents. The regents meeting was watched on television by students on all nine campuses of the university and by viewers throughout the state. Governor Pete Wilson, who had appointed Connerly to the Board of Regents, supported the Connerly proposal as a way to substitute a system of individual merit and student achievement for a system where some racial and ethnic groups receive preferential treatment.

Jesse Jackson spoke out against the proposal at the regents meeting; ten days earlier, he had criticized African Americans like Connerly and Supreme Court Justice Clarence Thomas, who were beneficiaries of affirmative action programs in education and employment but who now want to dismantle them. University President Jack Peltason spoke out in favor of affirmative action in a letter sent to the regents before the meeting. He said, "We are a public institution in the most demographically diverse state in the Union. Our affirmative action and other diversity programs, more than any other single factor, have helped us to prepare California for its future."[1]

Affirmative action in college admissions had been directed to minorities that are underrepresented at the University of California—primarily African Americans, Latinos, Native Americans, and women. Asian Americans are not underrepresented at the University of California and were not given preferential treatment in admissions, yet the population of Asian American students at the University of California nearly doubled between 1980 and 1994. During the same period, the percentage of white males in the student body declined from 40 to 24 pecent.

The major arguments by those who favored abandoning affirmative action were that it was an outmoded and unfair way to make decisions. Preferential treatment for racial and ethnic groups in admissions or hiring was also seen by some as stigmatizing all persons from that group, even those who obtained admission without preferential treatment.

Defenders of affirmative action argued that there is still not a level playing field in America, and minority groups are still at a disadvantage that needs to be redressed in admission and hiring decisions. Moreover, they argued, diversity of faculty and students is important and enriches the university environment.

In the end, the University of California Regents passed the Connerly proposal to bar the use of both race and gender as factors in admission decisions by a vote

Values We Share

Americans distrust government: 50 percent think "government regulation of business usually does more harm than good," and 69 percent think that "when something is run by the government, it is usually inefficient and wasteful"; 78 percent think "the federal government should only run those things that cannot be run at the local level."

Americans are patriotic and share a sense of civic responsibility: 91 percent say they are "very patriotic," 93 percent feel it is their "duty to always vote," and two out of three Americans (66 percent) think that voting gives them some say in how the government runs things.

Most Americans believe in providing equal opportunity: 91 percent of Americans believe that "our society should do what is necessary to make sure that everyone has an equal opportunity to succeed."

Americans believe that government should help those in need: 63 percent of Americans believe that "it is the responsibility of the government to take care of people who can't take care of themselves," and 59 percent think "the government should guarantee every citizen enough to eat and a place to sleep."

Americans are religious: 88 percent of Americans believe in the existence of God, and 78 percent see prayer as an important part of their daily life.

Americans see family and marriage as important: 84 percent of Americans say they have "old-fashioned values about family and marriage," and 75 percent think "too many children are being raised in day-care centers these days."

Americans distrust large corporations: 77 percent of Americans think "too much power is concentrated in the hands of a few big companies," and 53 percent think "business corporations make too much profit."

Americans are optimistic: 68 percent think that the United States "can always find a way to solve our problems and get what we want."

SOURCES: Times Mirror Center for the People and the Press, *The People, the Press, and Politics 1994: The New Political Landscape,* October 1994, pp. 132–165; Times Mirror Center for the People and the Press, *Voter Anxiety Dividing GOP: Energized Democrats Backing Clinton,* November 1995, pp. 84, 86; CBS News/New York Times Poll, October 25, 1995.

of 14 to 10, and also passed the proposal to bar racial preferences in contracts and hiring by a vote of 15 to 10. It should be noted that the Regents' action called for the university to comply with all federal law and executive orders that require the university to engage in affirmative action in hiring decisions.

The issues raised by this dramatic vote on affirmative action illustrate the longstanding tension in the United States between a standard for admission to college based on individual initiative and hard work, versus a standard that provides opportunities to groups that have suffered discrimination. The issue of affirmative action is being debated at other universities as well. In Texas, a federal appeals court ordered the University of Texas to abandon its affirmative action policy. It is likely that affirmative action policies will be reviewed again by the U.S. Supreme Court. How Americans resolve such conflicts tells us a lot about our political culture.

THE AMERICAN POLITICAL CULTURE

Political scientists use the term **political culture** to refer to a set of widely shared beliefs, values, and norms concerning the relationship of citizens to government and to one another. The American political culture is the sum of our most cherished shared values. American democratic values include liberty, equality, individualism, democracy, justice, the rule of law, and economic freedom. There is, however, no definitive listing of American political values, and, as we noted in Chapter 1, these widely shared democratic values overlap and sometimes conflict.

Shared Values

The values and beliefs described here as part of the American political culture are grounded in a philosophical tradition called **classical liberalism.** This tradition influenced the founders of our Republic and continues to be important to democratic movements around the world today. Classical liberalism, which is not the same as modern-day liberalism, stresses the importance of the individual and of freedom, equality, private property, limited government, and popular consent. All these elements, you will remember, are part of what we have described as the political culture of the United States.

Before the American and French Revolutions, these were radically new and different ideas. Europe had been dominated by aristocracies, had experienced centuries of political and social inequality, and had been ruled by governments that were unconstrained and often arbitrary in the exercise of power. Liberal political philosophers rebelled against these traditions and instead postulated the principles of classical liberalism. They claimed individuals have certain **natural rights,** and that the state (or government), as a primary threat to these rights, must be limited and controlled. At the same time, the economic system was changing from mercantilism to capitalism. People began to think they could improve their lot in life. The principles of a free market system were accepted and adopted, and these ideas clearly influenced the thinking of the founders of our nation.

The American Revolution, based on values like individual liberty and popular consent, has often served as a focal point of the American political culture. The Fourth of July celebrations held in every corner of the country salute freedom and liberty. The Constitution, like the Revolution, also defines our nation and its values.

LIBERTY Americans have always been united by a commitment to liberty or freedom. No value in the American political culture is more revered. "We have always been a nation obsessed with liberty. Liberty over authority, freedom over responsibility, rights over duties—these are our historic preferences," wrote the late Clinton Rossiter, a noted political scientist. "Not the good man, but the free man has been the measure of all things in this 'sweet land of liberty'; not national glory but individual liberty has been the object of political authority and the test of its worth."[2]

EQUALITY Jefferson's famous words in the Declaration of Independence express the primacy of our views of equality: "We hold these truths to be self-evident, that all men are created equal, that they are endowed by their Creator with certain unalienable rights, that among these are life, liberty, and the pursuit of happiness." We have always believed in social equality. In contrast to the Europeans, our nation shunned aristocracy. For example, we explicitly banned titles of nobility in our Constitution. Instead of having sharp distinctions between an upper and a lower class, our nation is characterized by its large middle class.

Equality also refers to *political equality*, the idea that every individual has a right to equal protection under the law and equal voting power. While political equality is a goal, it has not always been a reality. African Americans, Native Americans, and women have been denied political equality in the past.

Equality encompasses the idea of equal opportunity, especially with regard to improving economic status. Americans believe that social background should not limit our opportunity to achieve to the best of our ability, nor should race, gender, or religion. The nation's commitment to public education—programs like Head Start for underprivileged preschool children, state support for public colleges and universities, and federal financial aid for higher education—reflects our belief in equality. Yet, as the affirmative action debate at the University of California illustrates, how best to achieve equality of opportunity in admission to public universities is hotly contested. Other government programs motivated by the desire for equality include Medicaid and the Federal National Mortgage Association.

INDIVIDUALISM The United States is characterized by a persistent commitment to the individual. Under our system of government, individuals have both rights and responsibilities. The individual's importance and dignity are enhanced by our views of political equality.

Concern for preserving individual freedom of choice and what limits, if any, to place on individual choice often generate intense political conflict. The debate over legalized abortion is often framed in terms of individual choice versus limits on that choice prescribed by law. While we Americans agree with the idea of individual rights and freedom, we also understand that such rights often come into conflict with other rights or with the government's need to maintain order.

As Americans, we have faith in the common sense of the ordinary person. The tradition of Abraham Lincoln and Harry Truman, that anyone can become president, has been a bold one. We prefer action to reflection; we are generally antitheoretical, anti-expert, and indeed anti-intellectual. The emphasis on practicality and "common sense" has become part of our image. Poets like Walt Whitman, Stephen Vincent Benét, and Carl Sandburg, and storytellers like Mark Twain, Will Rogers, Eudora Welty, and Garrison Keillor have helped shape this idea into tradition. This reverence for the common man and woman helps to explain our ambivalence toward power, politics, and government authority. In the United States, government is often viewed as a necessary evil.

DEMOCRACY, GOVERNMENT, AND THE CONSTITUTION The American political culture includes attitudes and beliefs about principles of government, proce-

Rule of Law

For a government to adhere to the rule of law, its policies and laws should adhere to these five rules:

- *Generality*: Laws should apply generally, not singling out any group or individual.
- *Prospectivity*: Laws apply to the future, not to punish something done in the past.
- *Publicity*: Laws cannot be kept secret and then enforced.
- *Authority*: Valid laws are made by those with legitimate power; the people legitimate that power through some form of popular consent.
- *Due Process*: Laws must be enforced impartially with fair processes.

dures, documents, and institutions. A *democratic consensus*—a fairly widespread agreement on fundamental principles of governance and the values that undergird them—is essential to the maintenance of democracy and the other values we discuss here. We Americans have deeply rooted ideas about who has power to do what, how people acquire power, and how they are removed from power. These are fundamental "rules of the game" in which widespread consensus is important.

We believe in *majority rule,* yet we also believe that people in the minority should be free to try to win majority support for their opinions. Our institutions are based on the principle of representation and the consent of the governed. We believe in *popular sovereignty*—that the ultimate power resides in the people themselves. Government, from our perspective, should exist to serve the people rather than the other way around. The means by which the government learns the will of the people is through elections, perhaps the most important expression of popular consent. One of the most important jobs of government is to maintain order, something many of us take for granted.

Many of the limits on government are specified in the Constitution and the Bill of Rights. The Constitution is revered as a national symbol. Yet we often differ over what certain constitutional provisions require or over the precise meaning of the framers' language.

We Americans honor many of these rights more in the abstract than in particular situations (see Table 5-1). Just over half of us, for instance, think that books with dangerous ideas should be banned from public school libraries. Intolerance of dissenting or offensive views is amply demonstrated in many public opinion polls and is observed clearly on college and university campuses as well. Still, Americans can ordinarily be characterized as affirming support for democratic and constitutional values.

JUSTICE AND THE RULE OF LAW Inscribed over the entrance to the U.S. Supreme Court are the words "Equal Justice under Law." The rule of law means that government is based on a body of law applied equally and by just procedures (see box), as opposed to rule by an elite in which the whims of those in power decide policy or resolve disputes. Chief Justice John Marshall succinctly

TABLE 5-1

It Depends on What You Mean by Rights and Freedoms

	Agree	Disagree	Don't Know
The government ought to be able to censor news stories that it feels threaten national security.	62%	34%	4%
Books that contain dangerous ideas should be banned from public school libraries.	51	47	2
The police should be allowed to search the houses of known drug dealers without a court order.	51	48	1
School boards ought to have the right to fire teachers who are known homosexuals.	39	58	3

SOURCE: Times Mirror Center for the People and the Press, *The People, The Press, and Politics: A Times Mirror Political Typology,* October 11, 1990, pp. 126–27; Times Mirror Center for the People and the Press, *The People, The Press, and Politics: The New Political Landscape,* October, 1994, pp. 162–63.

summarized this principle: "The government of the United States has been emphatically termed a government of laws, not of men."[3] We Americans believe strongly in the principle of fairness: all individuals are entitled to the same legal rights and protections.

NATIONALISM, OPTIMISM, AND IDEALISM   Americans are also highly nationalistic. We are proud of our past and tend to deemphasize, or even forget, our nation's intolerance, diplomatic and military setbacks, the shame of slavery, and the denial of suffrage to women for more than a century. We are optimistic—about people, but not about government. We are also optimistic about opportunity, choice, options, individualism, and most of all, about freedom to improve ourselves and to achieve success with as little interference as possible from others or the government.

We know our system is not perfect. We grumble that our elected officials have lost touch with the common people. We are disgusted by too many scandals and impatient with the slowness of the system to solve problems like health care, crime, and balanced federal budgets. Yet we have an abiding faith in government by the people and in our ability to solve problems, as Table 5-2 indicates.

Despite our dissatisfactions, there remains a remarkable belief that our nation is better, stronger, and more virtuous than other nations. Doubtless this sense of mission is a source of discipline, a builder of morale, and a fortifier of nationalism. But an excessive or wrongheaded sense of mission can also cause problems. Like every country, the United States has interests and motives that are selfish as well as generous, squalid as well as idealistic. We, too, are part of human history. Still, our idealism persists, and our efforts in support of human needs and rights throughout the world are evidence of this idealism.

Political and Economic Change

Our political values are clearly affected by historical developments and by economic and technological growth. The Declaration of Independence and our Constitution identify such important political values as individual liberty, property rights, and limited government.[4] In the early years we also emphasized separation of powers, checks and balances, states' rights, and of course the Bill of Rights.

It took an additional generation or two before we also began to take seriously the ideal of democratic governance, the expansion of suffrage, and competitive nominations and elections. Notions of political equality and effective participation emerged during the presidency of Andrew Jackson and matured in the course of the nineteenth century. By the century's end, populists and suffragists turned ideals into action and formed large-scale movements to achieve more democratic forms of participation and more responsive forms of governance.

THE INDUSTRIAL TRANSFORMATION   By the late nineteenth century, the agrarian society the framers knew was largely replaced by industrial capitalism and the growth of large corporations. With these changes, American ideology was irreversibly transformed. We committed ourselves to encourage economic growth by fostering privately owned corporations. The changed economic order had profound consequences for our political values—for how we viewed the role of government and how we related to one another. No one captures the implications of this shift better than political scientist Robert A. Dahl:

> One of the consequences of the new order has been a high degree of inequality in the distribution of wealth and income—a far greater inequality than had ever been thought likely or desirable under an agrarian order by Democratic Republicans like Jefferson and Madison, or had ever been thought consistent with democratic or

TABLE 5-2

Satisfaction with Democracy

Question: How satisfied are you with the way democracy works in your country? Are you very satisfied, somewhat satisfied, neither satisfied nor dissatisfied, somewhat dissatisfied, or very dissatisfied?

	Satisfied	Dissatisfied
United States	64%	27%
Germany	55	27
Japan	35	32
United Kingdom	40	43
India	32	43
Venezuela	23	59
Hungary	17	50

SOURCE: Gallup Organization, "People's Satisfaction with their Lives and Government Poll," April 1995.

"Neither" responses are omitted, so totals do not equal 100 percent. "Very satisfied/dissatisfied" and "somewhat satisfied/dissatisfied" categories have been combined.

Randy Weaver, an avowed white-separatist, testified before a Senate subcommittee on the confrontation between his family and federal agents at Ruby Ridge, Idaho, in which a deputy U.S. marshal was killed along with Weaver's wife and son during an 11–day siege. After the standoff, Weaver was sentenced to 18 months in jail, and the FBI conducted an investigation into its policy for using deadly force.

CHAPTER 5 - Political Culture and Ideology   **139**

The use of child labor in factories was one aspect of the inequality between rich and poor in the industrial era.

republican government in the historic writings on the subject from Aristotle to Locke, Montesquieu, and Rousseau. Previous theorists and advocates had, like many of the framers of our own Constitution, insisted that a republic could exist only if the citizen body continued neither rich nor poor. Citizens, it was argued, must enjoy a rough equality of conditions.[5]

The success of the American industrial economy led to the accumulation of great wealth in the hands of a few—the robber barons or tycoons. Many had taken great risks and earned their fortunes through inventions and efficient production practices. As disparities of income grew, so did disparities in political resources. Economic resources can be converted into political resources, like time to spend on politics and money to contribute to parties and candidates.

The rise of the large corporation and concentrated individual wealth in the United States created divisions and fostered resentment. The growth of monopolies prompted passage of antitrust legislation, and unsafe work conditions led to regulation of the workplace. More important, at the turn of the century, muckraking journalists charged that the robber barons behind the huge corporations were using their power to exploit workers and limit competition. Only the national government, it seemed, had the power to ensure fair treatment in the marketplace. This sentiment not only gave rise to the nation's first antitrust legislation but also sowed the idea that government could—and should—as the Constitution asserts, "promote the general welfare" by doing more to regulate the workings of business.

THE GREAT DEPRESSION AND NEW DEAL Then came the Great Depression and the near-collapse of the capitalistic system. Unrestrained capitalism and the unregulated market were faulted by many as a cause of the Depression. In any event, when it came, it brought the nation to the brink of disaster. There was no unemployment compensation, no guarantee on bank savings, no federal regulation of the securities exchanges, no Social Security. Americans turned to government to improve the lot of the millions of jobless and homeless citizens. With Franklin D. Roosevelt's New Deal, the idea gained widespread acceptance that government should use its powers and resources assertively to ensure some measure of equal opportunity and social justice.

Today free enterprise is no longer unbridled; instead government regulations, antitrust laws, job safety regulations, environmental standards, and minimum wage rates all balance the freedom of enterprise against the rights of individuals. Most

TABLE 5-3

Attitudes on Business and Welfare, 1994

	Agree	Disagree	Don't Know
There is too much power concentrated in the hands of a few big companies.	73%	26%	1%
Business corporations make too much profit.	61	35	4
The government should help more needy people, even if it means going into debt.	41	56	3
We have gone too far in pushing equal rights in this country.	48	50	2
It is the responsibility of the government to take care of people who can't take care of themselves.	57	41	2

SOURCE: Times Mirror Center for the People and the Press, *The New Political Landscape*, October 1994, pp. 134–35, 152–53.

Americans support a semiregulated or mixed free enterprise system that checks the worst tendencies of capitalism while rejecting too much government intervention. Much of our politics centers on how to achieve this balance (see Table 5-3).

President Franklin Roosevelt's State of the Union Address in 1944 articulated an expanded "Second Bill of Rights" for all citizens. Roosevelt declared that this nation must make a firm commitment to "economic security and independence." Included in his Second Bill of Rights were:

- The right to a useful and remunerative job in the industries, shops, farms, or mines of the nation
- The right to earn enough to provide adequate food and clothing and recreation
- The right of every farmer to raise and sell his products at a return which will give him and his family a decent living
- The right of every businessman, large and small, to trade in an atmosphere of freedom from unfair competition and domination by monopolies at home or abroad
- The right of every family to a decent home
- The right to adequate medical care and the opportunity to achieve and enjoy good health
- The right to adequate protection from the economic fears of old age, sickness, accident, and unemployment
- The right to a good education.[6]

Roosevelt's proclamation and later efforts by Kennedy and Johnson in the 1960s to pass landmark civil and voting rights legislation and launch a War on Poverty have defined the ideological political fights of the last half of the twentieth century. Modern-day liberalism and conservatism turn, in large measure, on how much one believes in Roosevelt's Second Bill of Rights, how much government assistance one thinks is owed to minorities, women, or others who have suffered discrimination or have been left behind by the industrial or technological revolutions of the twentieth century. Passage of Johnson's Great Society programs of the 1960s gave renewed emphasis to this expanded view of rights. President Bill Clinton's efforts to provide health care to all Americans can be seen as an application of this approach to expanded rights. In calling for health care reform, Clinton referred to Roosevelt's Second Bill of Rights, asserting that "health care is a basic right all should have."[7]

THE BUDGET BATTLES OF THE '90S The agenda of American politics took an abrupt turn with the election of a Republican majority to both houses of Congress in 1994. Republicans, especially House Republicans, took very seriously their Contract with America, which promised to reverse the "welfare state" by balancing the budget, cutting taxes, passing procedural reforms, and reforming welfare. In the area of social welfare, Republicans proposed cutting spending for welfare programs, denying welfare benefits for additional illegitimate children born to women already on welfare, and enacting a two-years-and-out provision for welfare assistance in many cases. Newt Gingrich summarized their agenda as follows:

The greatest moral imperative we face is replacing the welfare state with an opportunity society. For every day that we allow the current conditions to continue, we are condemning the poor—and particularly poor children—to being deprived of their basic rights as Americans. The welfare state reduces the poor from citizens to clients. It breaks up families, minimizes work incentives, blocks people from saving and acquiring property, and overshadows dreams of a promised future with a present despair born of poverty, violence and hopelessness.[8]

Inside the cover of his best-selling book, *My American Journey*, it says "Colin Powell is the embodiment of the American Dream." In many ways this statement is true. Powell was born to immigrant parents from Jamaica. The army provided a chance for him to get an education and achieve career advancement. He rose to become a four-star general, a National Security Adviser, Chairman of the Joint Chiefs of Staff, and was viewed as a possible presidential candidate.

The Republican Congress passed and President Bill Clinton signed into law a far-reaching welfare reform law in 1996. Both Clinton and Congress ended up compromising on important provisions in order to get a law the president would sign. The new law includes a five-year lifetime limit on receiving welfare and a requirement that recipients begin working within two years after receiving benefits. The bill reduces federal spending for welfare by a projected $55 billion over six years, in part by reducing funding for food stamps and decreasing aid to legal immigrants.

Some Democrats, like former U.S. Senator Bill Bradley, envision a larger role for government in dealing with such issues as downsizing and corporate cutbacks. Bradley proposes that firms with more than one hundred workers be required to "pay a laid off employee's medical expenses for no less than a year."[9]

The American Dream

Many of our political values come together in the **American Dream**, a complex set of ideas about the economy and its relation to individuals. Whether we realize it or not, this American Dream speaks to our most deeply held hopes and goals. The essence of the American Dream can be found in our endorsement of **capitalism**, an economic system characterized by private property, competitive markets, economic incentives, and limited government involvement in the production and pricing of goods and services.

The concept of private property enjoys extraordinary popularity in our political culture. In many European democracies, the state owns and operates transportation systems, the media, and other businesses that are privately owned and operated in the United States. Americans cherish the dream of acquiring property; moreover, most of us believe that those who own property have the right to decide how it is to be used.

The right to private property is just one of the economic incentives that cement our support for capitalism and fuel the American Dream. We believe that this is the land of opportunity for the enterprising. Here the competitive, practical go-getter can make a fortune or build a dream home. People who have more ability or work extremely hard, we hold, should get ahead, should earn more, should enjoy economic rewards, and should be able to pass most of what they have earned along to their children and relatives. Even the poorest Americans oppose high inheritance taxes or limits on how much someone can earn. In fact, the widespread support of the American Dream is clearly more important than the number of people who actually achieve it.

We Americans believe our mixed free enterprise system gives almost everyone a fair chance, that this system is necessary for free government to survive, and that our freedom depends on it. We reject communism and even modified forms of socialism. Our faith in capitalism is enlarged by the fact that communism has not worked around the world, and most formerly communist nations are shifting toward free enterprise systems in the 1990s.

In the United States, both individuals and corporations have acquired great wealth and, at the same time, exercised great political clout. Their power has, in turn, bred a certain amount of resentment. An increasing number of people believe the political system too often favors the rich over the poor. It is widely believed that when it comes to taxes, corporations and wealthy people do not pay their fair share. In the continuing debate over tax reform, President Clinton has argued that taxing the rich at higher rates achieves greater fairness. Dick Armey, who became House majority leader with the Republican sweep to power in 1994, criticizes Clinton's changes in tax policy as "fake right, and run left." He contends that his proposed flat tax is fairer than the current system because "everybody pays a flat 17 percent rate on all income . . . and best of all, no tax attorneys, no lobbyists to plead your special case, no IRS to harass you."[10] Some candidates vying for the Republican nomination for president advocated variations on a flat tax in 1996, and the debate continues over how to make the federal tax system simple and fair.

This conflict in values between a *competitive economy*, in which individuals should be free to reap large rewards for their initiative and hard work, and an *egalitarian society*, in which everyone should be able to earn a decent living, carries over into our politics. How the public resolves this tension can change over time. For instance, social programs that sought to extend equality of opportunity enjoyed broad support in the 1960s. During the 1980s they were attacked and partially dismantled as Ronald Reagan sought to implement a more conservative, procapitalist policy.

As important as the American Dream is to our national consciousness, we must admit to certain realities. Many millions in this country are still denied equality of opportunity because of race, ethnic background, or gender. An underclass persists in the form of impoverished families, ill-nourished and ill-educated children, and people living in the streets. Many cities are actually two cities, in which some live in luxury while others live in squalor. The gap between rich and poor is growing.[11] The gap between rich farms and marginal farms has deepened. And a sharp difference between white and black income persists tenaciously. Far more than we want to admit, people's chances for success still depend on the neighborhood they grow up in or the college they attend.

IDEOLOGY AND PUBLIC POLICY

Ideology refers to the structure of a person's ideas or beliefs about political values and the role of government. It includes the views people develop as they mature about how government should work and how it actually works. Ideology links our basic values to the day-to-day operations or policies of government.

Two major, yet rather broad, schools of political thinking dominate American politics today: *liberalism* and *conservatism*. Two lesser, but more defined, schools of thought, *socialism* and *libertarianism*, also help define the spectrum of ideology in the United States. We turn now to a more detailed description of these approaches.

Liberalism

In the seventeenth and eighteenth centuries, classical liberals fought to minimize the role of government. They stressed individual rights and perceived of governments as the primary threat to these rights and liberties. Thus they favored a limited government and sought ample guarantees of protection from governmental harassment. Over time the emphasis on individualism has remained constant, but the perception of the need for government has changed. Nowadays, liberals view government as protecting individuals from being abused by a variety of governmental and nongovernmental forces such as market vagaries, business decisions, and discriminatory practices.

In its modern American usage, **liberalism** refers to a belief in the positive uses of government to bring about justice and equality of opportunity. Modern-day liberals wish to preserve the rights of the individual and the right to own private property, yet they are also willing to have the government intervene in the economy to remedy the defects of capitalism. Contemporary American liberalism has its roots in Franklin Roosevelt's New Deal programs, designed to aid the poor

"He's trustworthy, loyal, obedient, cheerful, and all that, but he leans to the left."

Drawing by Dedini. © 1988 The New Yorker Magazine, Inc.

The Family

One of the important sources of political culture in the United States and other nations as well is the family. Children are taught from an early age what it means to be an American. They are curious about why people vote, what the president does, and whether Grandpa fought in World War II. The questions may vary somewhat from family to family, but the themes of authority, freedom, equality, liberty, and partisanship are common.* Families are the most important reference groups, and compared to families in other cultures, American families are much more egalitarian.

The Schools

Public schools are another source of the American political culture. Children and teachers often begin the school day by saluting the flag, reciting the Pledge of Allegiance, or singing the National Anthem. Teaching American political and economic values is part of the curriculum. Not only are values taught in U.S. history class, but they are put into practice in school elections and newspapers and in encouraging students to participate in small-scale economic ventures.

Colleges and universities also play a role in fostering the American political culture. Students who attend college are often more confident than other persons in dealing with bureaucracy and politics generally, more likely to participate in politics and vote, and more knowledgeable about government. Many states, including large ones like California and Texas, require college students to take courses in American government or state government, in part to instill a sense of civic duty while imparting knowledge about state and national governments.

and to protect people against unemployment and bank failures. Today, liberals also seek protection against inadequate or deficient medical assistance and inadequate or deficient housing and education. They generally believe in affirmative action programs, regulations that protect workers' health and safety, tax rates that rise with income, and the right of unions to organize as well as to strike.

On a more philosophical level, liberals generally believe in the possibility of progress. They believe things can be made to work, that the future will be better, that obstacles can be overcome. This positive set of beliefs may explain some of their willingness to believe in the potential benefits of governmental action, a willingness to alter or even negate the old Jeffersonian notion that "government governs best when it governs least." Liberals contend that the character of modern technology and the side effects of industrialization cry out for at least limited governmental programs to offset the loss of liberties suffered by the less well-to-do and the weak. Liberals frequently stress the need for a compassionate and affirmative government.

Liberals contend that conservatives will usually rule in their own interest and are motivated by the maxim, "Let the government take care of the rich, and the rich in turn will take care of the poor." Liberals, on the other hand, prefer that government take care of the weak, for the strong can nearly always take care of themselves. "We have rejected the discredited theory that the fortunes of the nation should be in the hands of a privileged few," said President Harry Truman. "Instead, we believe that our economic system should rest on a democratic foundation and that wealth should be created for the benefit of all. . . . Every segment of our population and every individual has a right to expect from his government a fair deal."[12]

In the liberal view, all people are equal. Equality of opportunity is essential, and, toward that end, discriminatory practices must be eliminated. Some liberals favor the reduction of great inequalities of wealth that make equality of opportunity impossible. Most favor a certain minimum level of income. Rather than placing a cap on wealth, they want a floor placed beneath the poor. In short, liberals have sought "to lessen the harsh impact of oligarchical rule in economic life, to introduce a measure of democracy within or democratic controls over the industrial-technological process, to assure freedom from arbitrary command within the economic no less than within the political sphere."[13] They ask: How can citizens be equal and free if they are dependent on and necessarily servile to the powers that be?

TYPES OF LIBERALS Liberals, it should be emphasized, come in many varieties. Some stress civil rights or women's rights or high-quality public education. Others urge government to adopt a more progressive tax system and do more to help the homeless, the handicapped, and society's "have-nots." Still others decry militarism and crusade for treaties and alliances that might bring about a world without terrorism and war. And yet other liberals are preoccupied with environmental or consumer issues. Some liberals embrace all these issues, placing them on an equal plane.

In a sense, liberals who emphasize economic issues may be called *New Deal liberals*; others are *social liberals* or *peace liberals*. If this is not confusing enough, there are those who call themselves **neoliberals.** Neoliberals believe in liberty, justice, and a fair chance for everyone, and they argue that the truly down-and-out must have government assistance. Yet they do not automatically favor unions and big government, nor do they automatically criticize big business or the military. Neoliberals are best characterized as liberals who have lost faith in many welfare programs and are skeptical about the efficiency and responsiveness of large, Washington-based bureaucracies. They are better at diagnosing some of the deficiencies of old liberalism than they are at pointing out what should be done. A sample of neoliberal thinking regularly appears in *The Washington Monthly*.[14]

CRITICISMS OF LIBERALISM Not everyone, by a long shot, is convinced that liberals in whatever form have the answers for the problems of the 1990s. Critics of liberalism, old and new, say they place too much reliance on governmental solutions, higher taxes, and bureaucrats. Opponents of liberalism say that somewhere along the line liberals forgot that government, to serve our best interests, has to be limited. Power tends to corrupt, they add, and too much reliance or dependence on government can corrupt the spirit, can undermine self-reliance, and can make us forget about those cherished personal freedoms and property rights our Republic was founded to secure and protect. When we get too much government, it tends to start dictating to us, and then our rights and liberties are at risk. Further, too many governmental controls or regulations and too much taxation undermine the self-help ethic that has "made America great." In short, critics of liberalism contend that the welfare and regulatory state pushed by liberals will ultimately destroy individual initiative, the entrepreneurial spirit, and the very engine of economic growth that might lead to true equality of economic opportunities.

Some liberals admit that Ronald Reagan redefined the issues in the 1980s and 1990s in such a way that liberalism sounded unnecessary and dated, if not wholly harmful. Wrapping themselves in the symbols of nationalism and patriotism, conservatives took a strong stand in favor of business, the death penalty, and prayer in schools—issues popular with most voters. Liberals, on the other hand, wrapped themselves in the symbols of compassion, fairness, equality, and social justice, also popular issues, but perhaps more relevant in races for Congress than for the White House.

The 1992 election contest between Bill Clinton and George Bush centered on the economy. Clinton and the Democrats successfuly focused the campaign on the need for economic growth, jobs, and a lower federal budget deficit. In office, the major preoccupation of Clinton's first two years was health care reform. The proposal that finally evolved was comprehensive, complex, and costly, and it offended many entrenched interests. Republicans in Congress were able to defeat health care reform and claim in the 1994 election that they could do a better job of governing. The Republican Contract with America argued for less government and lower taxes. As Dick Armey, one of the primary architects of the contract argued, "The sheer mass of our federal government is simply inconsistent with a free society. If nearly half of what you make is spent by someone else, that means half your work time is spent working for someone else. . . The obvious solution frankly is to end many of these government programs and allow people to keep their own money, the better to provide for these benefits themselves."[15] This perspective reflects the laissez fair economics advocated by many Republicans for decades and raises a fundamental question about the role of the government in the economy and society. Politics in the late 1990s is more ideological, with Republicans especially unified in their conservative viewpoints.

Kevin Phillips believes that economic divisions will be the major theme of politics in the 1990s: "One could reasonably assume that the 1990s would be a time in which to correct the excesses of the 1980s, for the dangers posed by excessive individualism, greed and insufficient concern for America as a community went beyond the issue of fairness and, by threatening the ability of the United States to maintain its economic position in the world, created an unusual meeting ground for national self-interest and reform."[16] But Michael Barone, a well-regarded political observer, disputes the view that economics is the most important dimension of American politics. Rather, he says, cultural divisions matter most: "Civil rights,

Religious and Civic Organizations

Many other factors are also important to the formation and maintenance of the American political culture. Religious freedom and diversity have played a part. American churches and temples have long fostered "a common set of moral understandings about good and bad, right and wrong, in the realm of individual and social action."† Freedom, including freedom of religion, individualism, pluralism, and civic duty, have all been fostered by churches. As churches do not all take the same positions on political issues, their impact is sometimes mitigated, but they have been important to such major social and political movements as abolition of slavery, expansion of civil rights, and opposition to war. Other organizations like the Boy Scouts, 4-H, League of Women Voters, Rotary Club, and Chamber of Commerce encourage citizen participation and pride in community and nation.

The Mass Media

In modern times the mass media have taken over some functions previously performed by the family. By the time they are adults, children will probably have spent more time watching television than in conversation with their parents. They may have had more political instruction from MTV than from their parents or their schools.

Political Activities

Finally, Americans educate each other about political values in the workplace, at the PTA meeting, or in more expressly political activities.

* Fred I. Greenstein, *Children and Politics* (Yale University Press, 1965), p. 44.
† Robert N. Bellah, *The Broken Covenant: American Civil Religion in Time of Trial* (Seabury Press, 1975), p. ix. See also Charles W. Dunn, ed., *Religion in American Politics* (CQ Press, 1989) and Kenneth D. Wald, *Religion and Politics in the United States* (CQ Press, 1992).

Rush Limbaugh: A New Voice for Conservatism

Sixteen million Americans provide an audience for political commentator, talk show host, and former disc jockey Rush Limbaugh. His syndicated radio program earns him an estimated $5 million per year, and his total estimated income from his books, speeches, and broadcasting activities is about $20 million. Known for his outspoken attacks on Bill and Hillary Clinton, feminist groups, and other liberal groups, he has also become a best-selling author of books *The Way Things Ought to Be*, and *See, I Told You So*.

Some of Limbaugh's more memorable quotes include:

Limbaugh on the women's movement:
"I love the women's movement, especially when I'm walking behind it."

Limbaugh on the Clinton administration:
"America's latest hostage situation."

Limbaugh on himself:
"I'm the most dangerous man in America."

Limbaugh is so controversial that *Time/CNN* commissioned a poll of public opinion on the conservative commentator. Here are the words respondents used to describe him:

Intelligent	71%
Obnoxious	66
Tells it like it is	65
Offensive	59
Demeaning to women	47
Demeaning to blacks and minorities	34
Irresponsible	33

Conservative groups openly seek his endorsement and support. The National Rifle Association (NRA), for instance, hosted a banquet at which Limbaugh spoke. Seats were $125 each. The NRA sold 5,000 tickets, and another 5,000 people watched the speech on a televised hook-up.

Sources: Kurt Andersen, "Big Mouths," *Time*, November 1, 1993, pp. 60–66; Eric Morganthaler, "A Common Touch: Dittoheads All Over Making Rush Limbaugh Superstar of the Right," *The Wall Street Journal*, June 28, 1993, p. A-1; *Time/CNN* Poll, October 26, 1993.

the Vietnam War, drugs, abortion, policy toward the Soviets and the Third World tended to divide Americans more often on cultural than on economic lines."[17]

Is it possible to reconcile these two positions? Politics in the United States has several focal points. As those change, so do the electoral fortunes of liberals and conservatives. Still, elections often turn on how the economy is doing, with voters blaming the party of the president if it is doing poorly or responding positively if it is doing well. This tendency is true both in presidential elections and mid-term elections.

In his 1996 reelection victory, Bill Clinton capitalized on positive voter perceptions about the economy. At the same time, voters rejected Dole's promise of a 15 percent tax cut because they did not believe such a cut would be possible without deep cuts in popular programs such as Medicare or a large increase in the national debt. The Dole campaign attempted to use cultural issues like illegal immigration and rising drug use among teenagers to cast Clinton as too liberal. Clinton outmaneuvered the Republicans, however, by moving toward the center and taking over "Republican issues" like reforming welfare, putting more police on the streets to combat crime, and signing an act denying recognition to same sex marriages.

As the agenda of American politics changes, so does the popularity of liberal or conservative positions. With the collapse of communism many Americans are now less concerned about defense spending and more inclined to focus on solving problems at home. Yet the fiscal constraints imposed by the tax cuts of 1981 and the crushing budget deficit changed the debate about government solutions because few are willing to raise taxes to fund new programs or new ideas. Moreover, as the North American Free Trade Agreement (NAFTA) demonstrates, we live in a global economy, and our jobs and economic progress are linked to our neighbors and other countries around the world. The net effect of these changes is that our national government, while focusing on domestic issues like health care, crime, and welfare, does so in a context much more aware of the constraints of the budget deficit and the unpopularity of tax increases.

Conservatism

American **conservatism** has its roots in the political thinking of John Adams, Alexander Hamilton, and many of their contemporaries. They believed in limited government and encouraged individual excellence and personal achievement. Private property rights and belief in free enterprise are cardinal attributes of contemporary conservatism. In contrast to liberals, conservatives want to keep government small, except in the area of national defense. However, because conservatives take a more pessimistic view of human nature than liberals do, they maintain that most people need strong leadership institutions, firm laws, and strict moral codes to keep their appetites under control. Government, they think, needs to ensure order. Conservatives are also inclined to believe that those who fail in life are in some way the architects of their own misfortune and thus must bear the main responsibility for solving their own problems. Conservatives have a preference for the status quo and desire change only in moderation. A sample of conservative thinking can be found in *The National Review*, a weekly magazine.

Most conservatives opposed the New Deal programs of the 1930s and the War on Poverty in the 1960s, and they have seldom favored aggressive civil rights and affirmative action programs. Human needs, they say, can and should be taken care of by families and charities. Equal treatment can be achieved by encouraging citizens to be more tolerant. Conservatives place substantial faith in the private sector, and they consider social justice to be essentially an economic question. They dislike the tendency to turn to government, especially the national government, for solutions to societal problems. Government social activism, they say, has been highly inflationary and counterproductive. Conservatives also prize stability—stability of the dollar, stability in international affairs, and stability in political and economic affairs. They prefer private giving and individual voluntary efforts targeted at social and economic problems rather than government programs.

TRADITIONAL CONSERVATIVES Traditional conservatives recognize that government must exist, yet insist it should be limited in what it does, and that within its proper sphere of action, it should be strong and resolute. "The purpose of government is to maintain the framework of order within which other private institutions can operate effectively."[18] The traditional conservative applauds the heartfelt compassion implicit in Franklin Roosevelt's Second Bill of Rights but believes that to turn to the federal government to solve those problems is to guarantee a too powerful, intrusive, and expensive government.

Liberals favor national action and a stronger central government. Conservatives, however, contend that centralization means higher taxes, that the freedom of the majority would greatly diminish, and that the initiative and risk-taking entrepreneurial impulses of inventors, capital investors, and ingenious business leaders would be irreversibly discouraged.[19] As Newt Gingrich sees it:

> With the end of the cold war, the case for a strong central government has been dramatically weakened. The time has come for a reversion to first principles. In America, one of those first principles is that power resides first and foremost with the individual citizen. In America, individual citizens earn their bread, and the government had better have an overwhelming reason for taking it away from them.[20]

In addition to fighting the welfare state, traditional conservatives, in the name of freedom, have been emphatically pro-business. Thus, they oppose higher taxes and resist all but the most necessary antitrust, trade, and environmental regulations on corporations. The functions of government should be, say conservatives, to encourage family values, protect us against foreign enemies and criminals, preserve law and order, enforce private contracts, foster competitive markets, and encourage free and fair trade.

Traditional conservatives have customarily favored dispersing power broadly throughout the political and social systems, precisely to avoid concentration of power at the national level. They favor having the market, rather than the government, distribute goods. Traditional conservatives subordinate economic and social equality to liberty and freedom. To allow the worst-off to take advantage of the best-off is to hurt both groups in the end, they maintain.

THE NEW RIGHT Another brand of conservatism—sometimes called the New Right, ultraconservatism, or even the Radical Right—emerged in the past generation. The New Right shares the love of freedom shown by the traditional conservatives and, during the 1980s, backed an aggressive effort to combat international communism, especially in Central America. It has also developed an activist public policy agenda that it would like implemented by conservatives in Congress and in the White House. The New Right favors the return of organized prayer in the public schools and renewal of covert operations by the Central Intelligence Agency. It wants strict limits on abortion; it opposes policies like job quotas, busing, and any tolerance of pornography. In short, a defining characteristic of the New Right is a strong desire to impose various social controls.

One driving force in the New Right is the Religious Right. Leaders of this group include Pat Robertson, a candidate for the presidency in 1988, and Jerry Falwell, who founded and promoted the Moral Majority in the 1980s. Much of the Religious Right's agenda overlaps that of the New Right—a concern with

The 1996 presidential primaries came down to a battle between moderate and conservative candidates "for the soul of the Republican party." Bob Dole gained the support of party moderates to win the nomination. Despite strong support from the religious right, economic isolationists, and gun advocates, Pat Buchanan was seen by many as too extreme in his views.

HOW AMERICANS DEFINE THEIR IDEOLOGY

Most Americans are not deeply "ideological." They lack an internally consistent and coherent set of beliefs about politics and public issues. The average citizen does not spend a lot of time thinking about government and public policies. Still, many Americans have ideological moorings, and some hold them fiercely. Politically, Americans are often said to be moderate and pragmatic rather than ideological. The most common measure of ideology is simply to ask people where they would place themselves on a liberal/conservative scale.

Ideology Curve

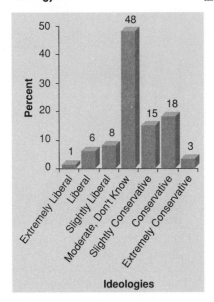

SOURCE: Center for Political Studies, University of Michigan, *1994 National Election Study.*

What the Public Thinks It Means to Be a Liberal or a Conservative

Q: What sort of things do you have in mind when you say someone's political views are Liberal? (top five responses)

Accept change	38%
Favor social programs	20
Favor government spending/spend freely	17
Favor abortion	14
Favor freedom to do as one chooses/ not interested in setting moral standards	11

Q: What sort of things do you have in mind when you say someone's political views are Conservative? (top five responses)

Resist change or new ideas	44%
Spend less freely/tight economic policy	18
Are slow or cautious in response to problems/do nothing	14
Support free enterprise/capitalism	13
Oppose abortion	11

SOURCE: Center for Political Studies, University of Michigan, *1994 National Election Study.*

Ideology over Time

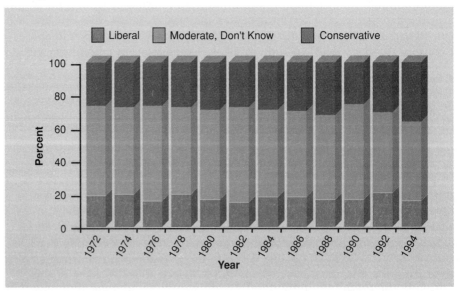

SOURCES: Center for Political Studies, University of Michigan, *1994 National Election Study; 1952–1992 Cumulative Data File.*

moral issues like abortion, homosexuality, and prayer in public schools and public meetings. Adherents of the Religious Right have been especially active at the state and local levels, in political parties and initiative campaigns and on school boards. The 1992 initiative in Colorado to overturn ordinances protecting gays and lesbians from discrimination was placed on the ballot largely through their efforts.[21] The Colorado law was later declared unconstitutional by the state supreme court.

The Christian Coalition, which grew out of Pat Robertson's 1988 presidential supporters, has come to be a major organizational force of the religious right in the 1990s. Led by Ralph Reed, the group has been very active at organizing at the local level. Reed claims that the coalition has more than 1.7 million members in 1,700 local chapters distributed across 50 states. As *The Washington Post* reported, "An outpouring of religious conservatives helped trigger the political upheaval of 1994."[22] The coalition's conservative agenda on issues like abortion and family values appealed primarily to Protestants, but in late 1995 a Catholic auxiliary was formed.[23]

Some conservatives question the moralistic tone of the New Right. For example, Barry Goldwater, the Republican presidential candidate in 1964, worries that too much prominence and influence have been granted to the New Right, especially the Moral Majority and those he calls the "checkbook clergy." Our Constitution, Goldwater says, seeks to allow freedom for everyone, not merely those professing certain moral or religious views of ultimate right. Goldwater points to the bloody divisions in Northern Ireland, the holy wars in Lebanon, and the pernicious religious righteousness in Iran as examples of the politicalization of churches. "The Moral Majority has no more right to dictate its moral and political beliefs to the country than does any other group, political or religious," says Goldwater. "The same is true of pro-choice, abortion, or other groups. They are free to persuade us because this land is blessed with liberty, but not to assign religious or political absolutes—complete right or wrong."[24] Goldwater fears that the great danger of the New Right is that instead of broadening its base, it will tear his beloved Republican party apart. He also, one gathers, opposes moral absolutes—the kind the Moral Majority thrives on.

NEOCONSERVATIVES The past generation has also witnessed the emergence of people who call themselves **neoconservatives.** Many are former Democrats who admired FDR and Harry Truman but left the Democratic party over Vietnam, busing, and the decisions of the liberal (overly liberal in their view) Earl Warren Supreme Court. They want to continue programs that work and are truly necessary, but reject the rest. An example of a successful program they would be inclined to keep is Head Start, the federally funded program for disadvantaged preschool children. Neoconservatives believe that too many government programs will lead to a paternalistic state. Though willing to interfere with the market for overriding social purposes, neoconservatives prefer finding market solutions to social problems. An example of neoconservative writing can be found in *Commentary*, a monthly magazine.

Neoconservatives favor larger military expenditures than do liberals. They remain skeptical of the intentions of some nations or terrorist groups. Conservatives also favor sufficient military spending to permit the United States to play a role in mediating conflicts around the world, especially in settings where U. S. interests are involved. But conservatives are not always united in their support for the use of military force, as indicated by the opposition of some conservatives to the use of American troops in Somalia, Bosnia, and Haiti in the 1990s. They also favor the death penalty and are more worried about crime than about the homeless. Neoconservatives say the courts have gone too far in protecting the

We The People
Differences in Political Ideology

	Conservative	Moderate	Liberal
Sex			
Male	43%	41%	15%
Female	30	54	16
Race			
White	39	46	15
Black	14	70	15
Age			
18–24	27	64	9
25–34	25	39	36
35–44	30	50	20
45–54	26	55	18
55–64	38	50	13
65–74	38	50	12
75+	29	66	4
Religion			
Protestant	41	52	7
Catholic	33	55	12
Jewish	26	21	53
Education			
Less than high school	23	71	7
High school diploma	31	60	9
Some college	39	42	19
Bachelor's degree	49	27	24
Advanced degree	46	21	33
Party			
Democrat	19	61	20
Independent	52	43	6
Republican	64	31	4

SOURCE: Center for Political Studies, University of Michigan, *1994 American National Election Study.*

Note: We have combined with the moderates persons who do not know their ideology or had not thought much about it. For the party identification, we have combined Independent leaners with their respective parties. Numbers may not add up to 100% due to rounding.

rights of the criminals and are too little concerned about the rights of the victims of crime.

Neoconservatives are credited with various original writings on social policy, supply-side economics, education, and the role of "national interest" in foreign affairs. *Supply-side economics* (which during the 1980s was often called "Reaganomics") is the belief that lower taxes will encourage economic growth, new jobs, and ultimately new tax revenues. The United States, in the neoconservative view, should use its power to shape events; it cannot retreat into isolationism.

CRITICISMS OF CONSERVATISM   Not everyone agreed with Ronald Reagan's statement that "government is the problem."[25] Indeed, critics of conservatism before and during the Reagan-Bush era saw hostility to government as counterproductive and inconsistent. Conservatives, they argued, have a selective opposition to government. They want more government when it serves their needs—by regulating pornography and abortion, for example—but are opposed to it when it serves somebody else's. Critics point out that government spending, especially for defense, grew during the 1980s when the conservatives were in control. Conservatives are often criticized for insensitivity to the social needs of the homeless and mentally ill.

Conservatives place great faith in our market economy—critics would say too much faith. This posture often puts them at odds with labor unions and consumer activists and in close alliance with business people, particularly large corporations. Hostility to regulation and a belief in competition are some of the reasons conservatives pushed deregulation in the 1980s. These changes did not always have the intended positive effects, as the collapse of many savings and loans revealed.[26] During the same decade, according to some critics, the Reagan administration's decision not to pursue antitrust actions encouraged a flurry of mergers and acquisitions that diverted our economy from more productive economic activity.[27] Conservatives counter that relying on "market solutions" and encouraging the free market are still the best course of action in most policy areas.[28]

Consistent with the conservative hostility to government was the policy of the Reagan years of lowering taxes. In his 1981 address to the nation on the state of the economy, Reagan likened government to children who spend more than their parents can afford. He mentioned that such extravagance could be cured by "simply reducing their allowance."[29] Implied was the idea that government spending could be controlled by reducing the amount government was allowed to spend. Many conservatives embraced the idea that if we lower taxes on the rich, their economic activity will "trickle down" to the poor. This view was criticized by many Democrats in the 1992 election campaign, who pointed out that the growth in income and wealth in the 1980s was largely concentrated among the well-to-do.[30]

Conservatives are also criticized for their failure to acknowledge and endorse policies that deal with racism and sexism in the United States. Their opposition to the civil rights laws in the 1960s and their opposition to affirmative action in the 1990s are examples of this perspective. Not only have conservatives opposed new laws in these areas, they have hampered the activity of the executive branch when in power, and have sought to limit the activity of the courts in these matters as well.

Socialism and Libertarianism

Our review of American political ideology would not be complete without a brief comment on socialism and libertarianism.

SOCIALISM **Socialism** is an economic and governmental system based on public ownership of the means of production and exchange. Karl Marx once described socialism as a transitional stage of society between capitalism and communism. In a capitalist system, the means of production and most of the property are privately owned, whereas in a communist or socialist system, property is "owned" by the state in common for all the people. In the ultimate socialist country, justice is achieved by having participants determine their own needs and take what is appropriate from the common product of society. Marx's dictum was, "From each according to his ability, to each according to his needs."[31]

In one of the most dramatic transformations in recent times, Russia, its sister republics, and its former European satellites abandoned their version of socialism—communism—and are now attempting to establish free markets. These countries had previously rejected capitalism, preferring state ownership and centralized government planning of the economy. But by the 1990s the disparities in economic well-being between capitalist and communist nations produced a tide of political and economic reform that left communism intact in only a few countries, such as Cuba. Former communists have had some success in elections, and others have been appointed to important positions in formerly communist East European countries.

American socialists—of whom there are very few outspoken or prominent examples—favor a greatly expanded role for the government. They would nationalize certain industries, institute a public jobs program so that all who want work would be put to work, and place a much steeper tax burden on the wealthy. In short, American socialists favor policies to help the underdog by means of income redistribution programs. They also favor stepped-up efforts toward greater equality in property rights. American socialists would drastically cut defense spending as well.[32] Most of the democracies of Western Europe are far more influenced by socialist ideas than we are in the United States, but they remain, like the United States, largely market economies.

LIBERTARIANISM **Libertarianism** is an ideology that cherishes individual liberty and insists on a sharply limited government. It carries some overtones of anarchism, of the classical English liberalism of the past, and of a 1930s-style conservatism. The Libertarian party has gained a modest following among people who believe that both liberals and conservatives lack consistency in their attitude toward the power of the national government. Libertarians preach opposition to government and just about all its programs. They favor massive cuts in government spending, an end to the Federal Bureau of Investigation and the Central Intelligence Agency and most regulatory commissions, and a minimal defense establishment (one that would defend the United States only if directly attacked). They oppose *all* government regulation, including, for example mandatory seat-belt and helmet laws. A poster at one of their recent national conventions read, "U.S. out of Latin America; U.S. out of North America!" Libertarians favor eliminating not only welfare programs but also programs that subsidize business, farmers, and the rich. They opposed government-backed guaranteed loans for Chrysler and other businesses and would turn the functions of the Postal Service over to private companies. Unlike most conservatives, libertarians would repeal laws that regulate personal morality, including abortion, pornography, prostitution, and recreational drugs.

A Libertarian party candidate for president has been on the ballot in every state in recent presidential elections, although never obtaining more than 1 percent of the vote. The Libertarian candidate for president in 1996, Harry Browne, ran on a platform that declared "government doesn't work" and proposed to solve the country's problems by eliminating government programs instead of reforming old programs or creating new ones. Libertarians would eliminate federal programs in education, crime control, welfare, housing, transportation, health care, agriculture, and overseas military bases. Libertarians would also repeal the income tax and all other direct taxes, decriminalize drugs, and pardon prisoners convicted of nonviolent drug offenses. Libertarian positions are rarely timid; at the very least they prompt intriguing political debates.

A Word of Caution

Political labels have different meanings across national boundaries as well as over time. To be a liberal in certain European nations is to be on the right; to be liberal in the 1990s in the United States is to be on the left. In recent elections, "liberal," which back in FDR's day had been popular, became "the L-word," a label most politicians sought to avoid. George Bush found it helpful in his 1988 campaign to charge Michael Dukakis and congressional Democrats with being "liberal," which he equated with supporting high taxes, being "soft on crime," and advocating too much government interference in the economy.

During the 1992 election, Bill Clinton attempted to define himself as a "New Democrat," someone more in the country's political mainstream than some past Democratic candidates had been. Republicans ridiculed this idea when Clinton unveiled his health care reform proposal, which they blasted as too costly and prescribing more big government. Following the stunning congressional election defeat in 1994, Clinton again attempted to redefine himself as a moderate. He was aided in this task by some of the rhetoric of House Speaker Gingrich and by the dispute with House and Senate Republicans on passing a balanced budget based on Congressional Budget Office (CBO) figures. The different ideological interpretations of Bill Clinton teach us that labels are rarely static, and that the game in politics is to define the opposing party as extreme and your own party as moderate and sensible.

It is also important to appreciate that ideology both causes events and is affected by them. Just as the Great Depression resulted in almost a tidal wave of ideological change, so did our involvement in World War II, Korea, and Vietnam, each in its own way. World War II, with its positive example of how government can work to defend freedom, strengthened positive views about the role of the national government. The Vietnam War probably had the opposite effect—disillusionment with government. The antigovernment sentiment in recent presidential elections is undoubtedly related to Vietnam, the Watergate scandal, and the endless wrangling between the president and Congress.

Debates about communist expansionism are increasingly dated and irrelevant in American politics. In the 1990s there is little fear that the United States will become communist, and the communist threat around the world is greatly diminished. But people of varying ideologies do indeed worry about whether the United States is becoming too soft and losing ground in the global economy. Today we are more likely to debate what will make us beat, or at least compete with, "those capitalists from Japan" and other Pacific Rim nations. Ideological controversy centers on how we can improve our schools, encourage a stronger work ethic, and stop the flow of drugs into the country; whether to permit openly gay people into the military or sanction gay marriages; and the best ways to instill religious values, build character, and encourage cohesive and lasting families.

Do social programs and job-training programs make things better or worse? Is reliance on the marketplace or on government planners a better way to make long-term policy decisions for the nation? What is the best way to balance the budget and curb inflation? Are foreign investors and international conglomerates shaping our lives as well as our economic policy decisions? Ideological debate and differences are always with us, but the nature of the issues changes.

IDEOLOGY AND THE AMERICAN PEOPLE

Despite the twists and turns of American politics, the distribution of ideology in our nation has been remarkably consistent in the past 20 years (see the Closer Look box on page 148). There are more conservatives than liberals, but the proportion of conservatives did not increase substantially with the decisive Republican presidential victories of the 1980s. Survey questions used to ascertain ideology permit respondents not only to answer "moderate" but also to indicate that they "don't know" their ideology or "have not thought much about it." The combined "moderate" and "don't know" categories are consistently much larger than either the conservative or liberal group and constitute a cluster more interested in pragmatism than ideology. These people vote for liberals in some races and conservatives in others because they simply prefer one candidate over another. Indeed there are more who indicate no ideology than indicate liberal and conservative combined. In sum, most Americans are unconstrained by a consistent ideology.[33]

One other important fact about ideology in the United States is that very few people see themselves as extreme conservatives or extreme liberals. In 1994, only 3 percent of the population saw themselves as extreme conservatives, and an even smaller percentage, 1 percent, saw themselves as extreme liberals. These percentages have changed very little over time. When given the option to describe themselves as "conservative" or "slightly conservative," 15 percent say "slightly conservative" and 18 percent say "conservative."[34] The same tendency is true of liberals. (We analyze party identification in Chapter 7, but it is important to note here that there are liberal and conservative wings in both parties.)

For those who have a liberal or conservative preference, ideology provides a lens through which to view politics. It helps simplify the complexities of politics, policies, personalities, and programs. An ideology may be an accurate or an inaccurate description of reality, yet it is still the way a person thinks about people, power, and society. For these reasons, it is important to understand how people view candidates, issues, and public policy. Among legislators, lobbyists, and party activists, ideology is even more important. Their ideologies shape our social and political institutions and help determine public policies and constitutional change.

An alternative to the liberal/conservative self-identification measure of ideology is to ask people about their attitudes toward politicians and public policies. Most Americans do not organize their attitudes systematically. A voter may want increased spending for defense but vote for the party that is for reducing defense spending because he or she has always voted for that party or prefers its stand on the environment. Or a person may favor adoption of the North American Free Trade Agreement and government-financed health care for all and still support Ross Perot.

Consistency among various attitudes and opinions is often relatively low. Much of the time people view political issues as isolated matters and do not apply a

"There's no justice in the world, Kirby, but I'm not convinced that this is an entirely bad thing."

Drawing by Handelsman. © 1986 The New Yorker Magazine, Inc.

general standard of performance in evaluating parties or candidates. Indeed, many citizens find it difficult to relate what happens in one policy situation to what happens in another. This problem becomes worse as government gets into more and more policy areas. Hence, most people, not surprisingly, have difficulty finding candidates who reflect their ideological preferences across a range of issues.

The absence of widespread and solidified liberal and conservative positions in the United States makes for politics and policy-making processes that are markedly different from those in many European and other nations. Our policy making is characterized more by coalitions of the moment than by fixed alignments that pit one set of ideologies against another. And our politics is marked more by moderation, pragmatism, and accommodation than a prolonged and strained battle between two, three, or more competing philosophies of government. Elsewhere, especially in countries where a strong Socialist or Christian Democratic party exists, things are different.

By no means, however, does this mean that policies or ideas are not elements in our politics. Such issues as affirmative action, the budget deficit, how to fund welfare, the Supreme Court's abortion rulings, and options for health care reform, gun control, and environmental protection have aroused people who previously were passive about politics and political ideas.

IDEOLOGY AND TOLERANCE

Is there a connection between support for civil liberties and tolerance for racial minorities and the ideologies of liberalism and conservatism? Some political scientists assert that conservatives are generally less tolerant than liberals. This view is stoutly contested by conservatives, who have charged liberals with trying to impose a "politically correct" position on universities and the media. "Conservatives," observe Herbert McClosky and Alida Brill, "have repeatedly shown their fear of political and social instability. With rare exceptions, the conservatives have been the party of tradition, stability, duty, respect for authority, and the primacy of 'law and order' over all competing values."[35]

Liberals share many of these views but place a different emphasis on the interpretation. They have more faith in government and readily turn to government to help achieve greater equality of opportunity. Liberals are usually more tolerant of dissent and the expression of unorthodox opinions. However, some liberals can be intolerant—of antiabortion forces, for example, or the National Rifle Association, or the views of Rush Limbaugh.

Most liberals are strongly opposed to crime and lawbreaking, yet they are as concerned about the roots or causes of crime as they are about the punishment of criminals. Perhaps for this reason, liberals exhibit somewhat greater concern than conservatives for the rights of the accused and are more willing to expand the rights of due process. Conservatives usually take a harder line and, in recent years, have won widespread popular support for their greater concern for the victims of crime than for the rights of the accused.

Such differences are most evident in the responses of liberals and conservatives to questions of civil rights and civil liberties. Research in the early 1980s found that, despite our common political culture and despite our widespread allegiance to constitutionalism and the Bill of Rights, many Americans sharply disagree on some basic political matters. Liberals are ordinarily more willing than conservatives to defend the rights of those who are in the minority, who may be wrong, or who take unorthodox or unpleasing stands.

In the area of free speech, conservatives were once seen as less willing to permit speech that was out of the political or cultural mainstream. Perhaps conservatives were less tolerant because those who claimed to be exercising the right of free speech often attacked established values. Now the argument that liberalism is correlated with tolerance is more complicated and the evidence less persuasive.

Conservatives believe that the United States has become too permissive. Many conservatives, especially in the New or Religious Right, are highly critical of homosexuals, drug users, prostitutes, unwed mothers, and pornography. They worry about what they claim has been a decline in moral standards and, interestingly, call on government to help reverse these trends. Liberals, on the other hand, generally accept nonconformity in conduct and opinion as an inescapable by-product of freedom.[36] In this regard, liberals are like libertarians.

It is these sharp cleavages in political thinking that stir opposing interest groups into formation and action. Groups such as the Moral Majority, the American Civil Liberties Union, Amnesty International, Mothers Against Drunk Driving, Queer Nation, and countless others promote their views of what is politically desirable. It is also these differences in ideological perspectives that reinforce party loyalties and that divide us at election time. Policy fights in Congress, between Congress and the White House, and during judicial confirmation hearings also have their roots in our uneasily coexisting ideological values.

Ideologies have consequences. Although Americans share many ideas in common, we as a people also hold many contradictory ideas. Our hard-earned rights and liberties are never entirely safeguarded; they are fragile and are shaped by the political, economic, and social climate of the day. In Chapter 7 we examine the interest groups and political parties that are ever-present to advance their values and compete in the always-evolving American political culture. Before turning to those topics, we will examine the social and economic diversity of the American political landscape in Chapter 6 and see why agreement on shared democratic values is all the more remarkable.

SUMMARY

1. The United States, like every other nation or society, has a distinctive political culture. It consists of a widely held set of fundamental political values and accepted processes and institutions that permit us to manage conflict and resolve problems. In the United States, there is, at least in the abstract, a widespread reverence for the Constitution, the Bill of Rights, a two-party system, and the right to elect officials on the basis of majority rule. Our belief in social equality has fostered acceptance of the notion that government should guarantee equality of opportunity through programs like education and job training.

2. Americans share a widespread commitment to classical liberalism, which embraces the importance of the individual and of freedom, equality, private property, limited government, and popular consent.

3. Perhaps the most notable tension in the American political culture is that we simultaneously believe in free market economics and a democratic society based on political equality. We want our economy to be relatively free from government controls and want major economic decisions to be shaped by the marketplace; yet we also want every American to enjoy the possibility of an equal voice in shaping our laws and policies, an ideal that may require government intervention.

4. American political values have been affected by the industrial transformation, the development of large corporations and other large institutions, the Great Depression, the rights revolution, and a global economy.

5. The sources of the American political culture include the family, the schools, religious and civic organizations, the mass media, and political activities.

6. Although many Americans are nonideological and are guided primarily by moderate pragmatism, a significant segment of Americans are conservatives or liberals.

7. In addition to the liberal and conservative traditions, there are subgroups such as neoliberals, neoconservatives, New Right, libertarians, and socialists, with most Americans favoring moderate rather than extreme ideologies.

8. Our ideological orientation has a bearing on how tolerant we are of the views and conduct of others. Liberals tend to be more permissive, whereas conservatives generally favor tradition, stability, and greater levels of "law and order." These differences have consequences for electoral contests, judicial interpretation, and policy development in our political system.

FURTHER READING

DICK ARMEY, *The Freedom Revolution: The New Republican House Majority Leader Tells Why Big Government Failed, Why Freedom Works, and How We Rebuild America* (Regnery, 1995).

LEON P. BARADAT, *Political Ideologies: Their Origins and Impact*, 5th ed. (Prentice Hall, 1993).

BILL BRADLEY, *Time Present, Time Past: A Memoir* (Knopf, 1996).

WILLIAM F. BUCKLEY AND CHARLES R. KESLER, *Keeping the Tablets: Modern American Conservative Thought* (Harper & Row, 1988).

JAMES MACGREGOR BURNS, *Uncommon Sense* (Harper & Row, 1972).

E. J. DIONNE, JR., *They Only Look Dead: Why Progressives Will Dominate the Next Political Era* (Simon & Schuster, 1996).

JOHN EHRMAN, *The Rise of Neoconservatism: Intellectuals and Foreign Affairs, 1945–1994* (Yale University Press, 1995).

LOUIS HARTZ, *The Liberal Tradition in America* (Harcourt, Brace, 1955).

NEWT GINGRICH, *To Renew America* (HarperCollins, 1995).

IRVING KRISTOL, *Neoconservatism: The Autobiography of an Idea* (Free Press, 1995).

ROBERT KUTTNER, *The End of Laissez-Faire: National Purpose and the Global Economy after the Cold War* (Knopf, 1991).

HERBERT MCCLOSKY AND JOHN ZALLER, *The American Ethos: Public Attitudes Toward Capitalism and Democracy* (Harvard University Press, 1984).

KEVIN PHILLIPS, *Boiling Point: Democrats, Republicans, and the Decline of Middle-Class Prosperity* (Random House, 1993).

COLIN POWELL WITH JOSEPH E. PERSICO, *My American Journey* (Random House, 1995).

THE AMERICAN POLITICAL LANDSCAPE

6

A recent state court decision in Texas is a good example of the continuing national debate over issues of language and culture among immigrants to the United States. During a child custody hearing in the summer of 1995, State District Judge Samuel C. Kiser, who is bilingual and minored in Spanish as a college student, ordered Marta Laureano to speak only English to her daughter at her home. Until the hearing, Ms. Laureano spoke only Spanish to her daughter, who is enrolled in her school's bilingual education program. During the hearing Judge Kiser accused Laureano of abusing her daughter because the family spoke only Spanish at home. He said, "There's lots of abuse and in my opinion, Ms. Laureano, you're abusing your child. If she starts first grade with the other children and cannot even speak the language that the teachers and the other children speak and she's a full-blood American citizen, you're abusing the child and you're relegating her to the position of a housemaid."

Judge Kiser's remarks were both criticized and defended. Texas Attorney General Dan Morales said Kiser's remarks were "way off base," and further criticized him for "trivializing legitimate child abuse." Other critics went so far as to label Kiser a racist. Ms. Laureano, who has five children, defended her practice of speaking only Spanish at home because she wants her children to be bilingual so that they can communicate with Mexican relatives and have a competitive edge in two cultures. After the controversial hearing Judge Kiser defended his statement, saying, "This is not a race issue. If you don't give your child as much help to get along in society as you possibly can, it is a form of abuse or neglect, one or the other." Ms. Laureano countered by saying, "This is a free country, and everybody who comes here brings something with them—their memories, their language, their culture. Nobody can take that away from us."[1]

The Texas case raises important issues involving language, culture, and politics. During the 1980s, voters in Arizona, Colorado, California, and Florida enacted initiatives to make English the official language. Nearly three out of four Californians voted for this measure. In Florida the result was even more decisive—84 percent approved. All but three states have considered similar measures.

The controversy over language reflects our long history as a nation of immigrants. From the Germans in the 1700s and 1800s to the Hispanic and Asian newcomers of the 1980s and 1990s, the nation has had to accommodate many cultures and languages, and the controversy persists today over whether to encourage bilingual education in American schools. Bilingual education raises many of the same issues as the effort to designate English as the official language.

It is difficult for political scientists—and for college students and everyone else—to overcome the tendency to generalize from their own experience. Most of us do not stop to consider how people from other backgrounds might see things differently. This **ethnocentrism**—selective perception based on individual background, attitudes, and biases—is not uncommon among college students, who often assume that others share their economic opportunities, social attitudes, sense of civic responsibility, and self-confidence.

Albert Einstein once said few people are capable of expressing opinions that differ much from the prejudices of their social upbringing.[2] In this chapter we examine Einstein's view that the social environment explains or at least shapes our opinions and prejudices. It would be a mistake to contend that a person's social environment and background define his or her political behavior in totality. People change, learn, and grow. Yet, as we will see, the impact of social and economic factors is powerful.

Politics and government involve more than laws and legal institutions; they involve *people*, and while people in this nation have many things in common, they can also be very different. This chapter describes American diversity and the implications of geographic, social, and economic divisions for politics and government. Specifically, it explores the effects of regional or state identity on political perspectives; the implications of differences in race, ethnicity, gender, sexual orientation, religion, wealth and income, occupation, and social class for opinions on issues and voting choices; and the relationship between age and education and political participation.

WHERE ARE WE FROM?

You may have often been asked, "Where are you from?" In certain settings you answer the United States; in others, you may say Illinois, California, or Idaho; and in still others, Dallas, Brooklyn, or North Las Vegas. Where you are from can be important to your personal political identity, attached at the levels of town, city, state, and nation. Where you are from is also important to politics, because the history, economy, and social makeup of cities, states, and regions differ.

Geography and National Identity

The United States is a geographically large and historically isolated country. As Alexis de Tocqueville observed in 1830, the country has no major political or economic powers on its borders "and consequently [has] no great wars, financial crises, invasions, or conquests to fear."[3] Geographic isolation from the major powers of the world during our government's formative period helps explain American politics. The Atlantic Ocean served as a barrier to foreign meddling, giving us time to establish our political tradition and develop our economy.

In our entire history we have fought only one foreign enemy on our own soil—England in the War of 1812. (The war with Mexico of 1846–48 was fought on Mexican land, some of which became American land as a result of the war. The only other war fought on our soil was, of course, the Civil War.) In contrast, during the same period, Poland was invaded and eventually partitioned by Austria, Prussia, and Russia. The difference is largely explained by location: Poland was surrounded by Europe's great powers. Had the United States been closer to Europe, it may have been overrun like Poland, and our Constitution and institutions repeatedly changed to suit the invaders. Having powerful and aggressive neighbors makes it difficult for relatively weak nations to nurture democracy.

The United States is a large country. Its land mass exceeds that of all but three nations in the world. In contrast, India has a population more than three times larger than the United States on a land mass one-third the size. Geographic space gave the expanding population of the United States room to spread out. This meant that some of the political conflicts arising from religion, social class, and national origins were diffused because groups could isolate themselves from one another. (See James Madison, *The Federalist*, No. 10, in the Appendix, for a development of the large republic idea.) Moreover, the large and accessible land

Part of our national identity is bound up with the physical isolation many families endured as pioneers. This family was seeking a new home in Custer county, Nebraska, in 1886.

mass helped foster the perspective that the United States had a **manifest destiny** to be a continental nation with coasts on both the Atlantic and Pacific oceans. This notion that the United States was "destined" to expand all the way to the Pacific was used to justify taking land once occupied by Native Americans and to justify our entry into the Mexican American War.

The United States is a land of abundant natural resources. We have rich farmland, which not only feeds our population but makes us one of the three major exporters of food in the world. We are rich in such natural resources as coal, iron, uranium, and many precious metals. All these resources enhance economic growth, provide jobs, and stabilize government. "The physical causes, unconnected with laws, which can lead to prosperity are more numerous in America than in any other country at any other time in history," observed Alexis de Tocqueville. "In the United States not legislation alone is democratic, for Nature herself seems to work for the people."[4]

Geography also helps explain our diversity. Parts of the United States are wonderfully suited to agriculture, others to mining or ranching, and still others to shipping. These differences produce different regional economic concerns, which in turn influence politics. For instance, a person from the agricultural heartland may have a different perception of foreign trade than an automobile worker in Detroit. In addition, that automobile worker may be African American, a fact that may be more important than what he does or where she lives. To understand American politics, we must recognize these differences.

In the United States—unlike Canada, Eastern Europe, and India—geography does not define an ethnic division. All the Serbs do not live in one place, all French-speaking Catholics in another, and all German immigrants in another. Sectional differences in the United States are primarily geographic, not ethnic or religious.

Sectional Differences

The most distinct section of the United States remains the South, although differences from other regions are diminishing. From the beginning of the Republic, the agricultural South differed from the industrial North, but the most important difference between the regions was the southern institution of slavery. Northern opposition to slavery, which grew increasingly intense in the middle of

TABLE 6-1

**Voting Patterns in the Eleven
Former Confederate States**

Average Republican Vote for President	
1980	50%
1984	62
1988	59
1992	43
1996	46

Average Republican Vote for U.S. Representative	
1980	40%
1982	39
1984	42
1986	41
1988	42
1990	43
1992	48
1994	58

Proportion of Republicans in State Legislatures		
	House	*Senate*
1980	18%	17%
1982	22	14
1984	23	17
1986	24	20
1988	27	24
1990	28	26
1992	31	31
1994	37	37

SOURCE: U.S. Bureau of the Census, *Statistical Abstract of the United States, 1995* (Government Printing Office, 1995), pp. 273, 275; U.S. Bureau of the Census, *Statistical Abstract of the United States, 1993* (Government Printing Office, 1993), p. 279; U.S. Bureau of the Census, *Statistical Abstract of the United States, 1989* (Government Printing Office, 1989), p. 254; U.S. Bureau of the Census, *Statistical Abstract of the United States, 1987* (Government Printing Office, 1987), p. 239.

the nineteenth century, reinforced the sectional economic interests that divided the nation. The eleven Confederate states, by virtue of their decision to secede from the Union, reinforced a common political identity that persists more than a century after the Civil War.

Sectional differences were strengthened by the policy of Reconstruction, the region's common economic interests, and especially the problems of race relations. The Civil War was fought over the issue of state self-determination in such matters as slavery. When the North won the war, African Americans were emancipated, but they were not politically, socially, or economically integrated. They did not, for example, have equal voting rights; as recently as 1960, only 5 percent of African Americans in Mississippi were registered to vote.[5]

Things have changed in the last 35 years, and as a result the South is becoming less distinct today. The large migration of persons from outside the region who have moved to the sun belt has diminished somewhat the sense of regional identity. But the South has also undergone tremendous change. The civil rights revolution gave African Americans the right to vote, opened up new educational opportunities, and helped to integrate the South into the national economy. African Americans still lag behind whites in voter registration, but the gap is now no wider in the South than elsewhere and is explained more by differences in education than by race.[6] In economic terms, the South still falls below the rest of the country in per capita income and education, but much less so than 50 years ago. The religious and moral conservatism of the South remain notable.

Until recently, political observers spoke of the "solid South," a region that voted for Democrats at all levels. The reason for the connection between the South and Democrats is simple: "The Civil War made the Democratic party the party of the South, and the Republican party, the party of the North."[7] The Democratic "solid South" was to remain a fixture of American politics for more than a century. The region has become more competitive over the past several elections, and in most recent presidential elections Republicans have carried most of the region.

During the last month of the 1996 campaign, Bill Clinton visited Southern states frequently to boost his own chances and to campaign for Democratic congressional candidates. In 1996, Clinton carried Arkansas, Florida, Louisiana, and Tennessee; four years earlier, Bush had carried Florida while Clinton won in Georgia.

Republican success at the presidential level was slow to reach contests for the U.S. House of Representative and even less evident in state legislative races. The 1994 Republican landslide saw Republicans win 58 percent of southern votes for the House (see Table 6–1) and swept them to governorships in six of the eleven former confederate states. Republicans picked up another southern governship in 1995 in Louisiana. Despite these dramatic gains, Republicans had risen to only 37 percent of southern state legislative seats in 1995. Republicans won majorities in the state senate of Florida and the state assemblies of North Carolina and South Carolina, but Democrats continued to carry a two-to-one majority in both houses of the state legislature in Alabama, Arkansas, Louisiana, and Mississippi. At the state legislative level in several southern states, the remnants of the old "solid South" remain, yet Republicans have made major inroads, and the region is now much more competitive.

Other sectional differences have political importance. Alexis de Tocqueville saw the New England Puritan spirit as significant.[8] More recently, the West has developed an identity of individualism, hostility to government intervention, and belief in self-sufficiency. It was especially fertile ground for Ronald Reagan, who seemed to personify western values.

Another common sectional division is the sun belt/frost belt (see map). Sun belt states have been growing in population much more rapidly than the rest

From Coast to Coast

Sun Belt/Frost Belt States

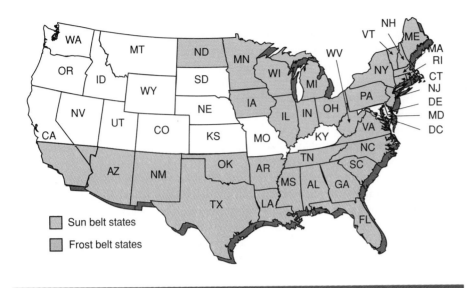

Sun belt states

Frost belt states

of the country, in part because they are attractive places for retirees. As a result of population shifts revealed by the 1990 census, the sun belt states gained 17 seats in the U.S. Congress, while frost belt states lost 15 seats. However, population growth in the South and West is occurring in different age groups. In the South population growth is largest among those over 65, while in the West it is younger persons who provide the growth. Sun belt states have also experienced greater economic growth as industries headed south and southwest, where land is cheaper and more abundant, and where labor is cheaper as well (see Figure 6-1).

State and Local Identity

Americans move often, and they quickly become identified with the politics of the state in which they now live. Mention Wyoming, Mississippi, Oregon, New York, or Kansas, and it brings to mind a certain type of politics. The same is true for many other states. Like most stereotypes, these images are often misleading, but they reflect the fact that there is a sense of identity to states as political units that is supported by recent empirical evidence. States have distinctive political cultures that go beyond demographic characteristics, and this culture affects public opinion and policy outcomes of each state.[9] These state identities are reinforced by our electoral rules and other laws.

In American politics today, one state—California—stands out. One out of nine Americans is a Californian.[10] In terms of economic and political importance, California is in a league by itself; its 52 members of the House of Representatives exceed the total number of representatives in the smallest 20 states. No presidential candidate can afford to lose California's 54 electoral votes.[11] Californians like Richard Nixon and Ronald Reagan have helped deliver these electoral votes to the Republicans in several elections since 1952. Hard hit by the recession, California went solidly for Clinton in 1992, helping to push him to victory.

FIGURE 6-1
Population Gains by Region, 1970–1990.

SOURCE: U.S. Bureau of the Census, *Statistical Abstract of the United States, 1992* (Government Printing Office, 1993), p. 48.

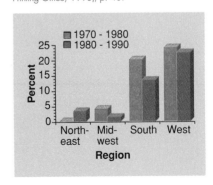

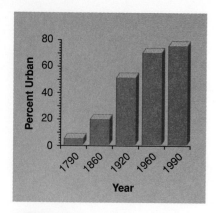

FIGURE 6-2
A Changing Landscape as America Becomes Urban

SOURCE: U.S. Bureau of the Census, U.S. Population Reports P 23. no.185, *Population Profile of the United States, 1993* (Government Printing Office, 1993), p. 8.

Clinton also carried California in 1996, having visited often and claiming credit for California's economic recovery. Bob Dole stressed his midwestern roots when he campaigned throughout that region, but to no avail.

Americans live in four types of places—central cities, suburbs, smaller communities, and rural areas. Most Americans, 80 percent of them, now live in central cities and their suburbs—what the Census Bureau calls *metropolitan areas*. During the early twentieth century, the movement of population was from rural areas to central cities, but the movement since the 1950s has been to the suburbs. During the 1970s and 1980s Americans kept moving farther and farther out from the central cities to new suburbs. Today the most urban state is California (92.6 percent); Vermont is the least urban, with only 32.2 percent living in cities or suburbs. Regionally, the West and Northeast are the most urban, the South and Midwest the most rural. The 75 percent of the population that now lives in cities and suburbs occupies only 2.5 percent of the nation's land (see Figure 6-2). Nine of the largest 25 cities lost population over the previous decade,[12] a continuation of a trend since World War II.

There are many reasons people left the cities to move to the suburbs—better housing, new transportation systems that made it easier to get to work, the desire for cleaner air and safer streets, and "white flight," the movement of whites away from the central cities so that their children could attend predominantly white schools and avoid being bused for racial integration. The white, middle-class migration to the suburbs has meant that American cities have become increasingly poor, increasingly African American, and increasingly Democratic (see Table 6-2). Half of all African Americans now live in central cities, as opposed to only about one-quarter of whites. The proportions are very nearly reversed for suburbs, where more than half of all white Americans reside. Almost one-third of American suburbanites are now African Americans, up from one in five in 1980.[13]

In such large cities as Washington, D.C., Detroit, Baltimore, Atlanta, and New Orleans, the city population is now more than 50 percent African American. Hispanics comprise nearly two-thirds of the population of El Paso, Texas,

TABLE 6-2

Cities with Populations of 100,000 or More That Are at Least 50 Percent African American, 1992

City	Total Population	African American
Atlanta, Georgia	395,000	67%
Baltimore, Maryland	726,000	59
Birmingham, Alabama	265,000	63
Detroit, Michigan	1,012,000	76
Gary, Indiana	117,000	81
Inglewood, California	111,000	52
Jackson, Mississippi	196,000	56
Macon, Georgia	107,000	53
Memphis, Tennessee	610,000	55
Newark, New Jersey	268,000	59
New Orleans, Louisiana	490,000	62
Richmond, Virginia	202,000	55
Savannah, Georgia	139,000	51
Washington, D.C.	585,000	66

SOURCE: U.S. Bureau of the Census, *Statistical Abstract of the United States, 1995* (Government Printing Office, 1995), pp. 44–46.

and Santa Anna, California, and more than half of the population of Miami and San Antonio.[14] As population shifts occur, the tax base of cities declines because the richer people have gone to the suburbs, where they now pay local sales and property taxes. At the same time, service needs in the cities have grown as the remaining less affluent population must pay for education, police protection, and health care.

Metropolitan areas are much larger than central cities. More than four times as many people live in metropolitan Los Angeles than actually live in the city.[15] Half the nation's population live in the 32 largest metropolitan areas of more than 1 million in population.[16] While people from the Chicago metropolitan area have some things in common—like an affinity for the Chicago Bulls basketball team—the characteristics of metropolitan areas as a whole can be quite different from the characteristics of the city.

Suburbs vary in relative affluence. Many older ones now face the same problems as the inner cities, but their populations typically have higher per capita income, have fewer minorities, and are typically more Republican. Companies employing professionals or engaging in high-tech or service activities frequently relocate in the suburbs to avoid city congestion and to be closer to the bedroom communities of their workers. Political boundaries, which define local governments and delineate responsibility for services, create understandable tensions among cities, suburbs, and rural areas. Tax revenues, legislative representation, zoning laws, and governmental priorities are hotly contested issues on the local level.

A LAND OF DIVERSITY

Most nations consist of groups of people who have lived together for hundreds of years and who speak the same language, share the same concept of deity, and share a common history. Japan, for example, has some people from other nations, but most of its citizens are Japanese in the fullest sense of the word, and it is the same in Germany, Sweden, Saudi Arabia, China, and France. The United States is different. We are largely a land of immigrants. We attract the poor and oppressed from all over the world, and we have been more open to accepting these people than have other nations.

One reason so many people want to come to the United States is because it is a land that holds a promise of religious, political, and economic freedom. It is also a place of opportunity for the enterprising. Our economic system has provided widespread (but not universal) opportunity for individuals to improve their economic standing. The American Dream—that everyone can "make it big"— is widely shared.

Some elements of our diversity become traditions that have political significance. Sectional differences persist between the South and the rest of the country, in part because of tradition. Third- or fourth-generation Americans may retain an identity with the native land of their ancestors, even though their spouses and neighbors do not share that identity. Holding onto our differences is often the result of socialization in our families, churches, and other closely knit groups.

Because where we live and what we are in terms of our religion and occupation affect how we vote, many who study voting and make predictions about it do so in terms of these factors—what are called **demographics.** A political predisposition is a characteristic of individuals that is predictive of political behavior. While demographics can be important, as this chapter and those that follow will demonstrate, there are large individual differences within socioeconomic and demographic categories.

We The People

Percent of the Population by Race and Hispanic Origin

	1990	1995	2000	2025	2050
White	83.9%	82.9%	81.9%	77.3%	72.8%
African American	12.3	12.6	12.8	14.2	15.7
American Indian, Eskimo, Aleut	0.8	0.8	0.9	1.0	1.1
Asian and Pacific Islander	3.0	3.7	4.4	7.5	10.3
Hispanic	9.0	10.2	11.3	16.8	22.5

Source: U.S. Bureau of the Census, *Statistical Abstract of the United States, 1995* (Government Printing Office, 1995), p. 14.

Percentages do not equal 100 because Hispanics can be of any race.

When social and economic differences coincide, they reinforce each other and make the differences more important. Social scientists call these differences **reinforcing cleavages**, and experience predicts that when these happen, political conflict becomes more intense and there is greater polarization in society. Nations can also have **cross-cutting cleavages**, instances when differences do not reinforce each other. To illustrate, let's look at religion and income. If in a society all the better-off individuals were of one religion and the poor another, we would have reinforcing cleavages and political conflict would be intensified. But if there were rich and poor in all religions, and if people sometimes voted on the basis of their religion and sometimes on the basis of their wealth, then we would say the divisions are cross-cutting. American diversity has generally been more of the cross-cutting type than the cleavage type, lessening political conflict because individuals have multiple allegiances.

In some societies, politics centers largely around passions over economic and religious differences. In Northern Ireland, for instance, the religious differences between Catholics and Protestants are a violent division. Although socioeconomic differences are important to understanding American government and politics, they are not as central to the form and structure of politics as religion is in Bosnia or race is in South Africa. Understanding this distinction is also important.

Americans, in the past as well as today, are not always tolerant of those from a different religion, class, or race. We often associate only with people "like us" and are suspicious of people "like them." From hostility toward German-speaking immigrants in the early colonies, to the anti-immigration movements of the late 1800s and early 1900s, to attempts to restrict assistance to immigrants in the 1990s, Americans have sometimes exhibited ethnocentrism. For much of our history, minorities have been excluded from full participation in American political and economic life. Recently, Americans have begun to take greater pride in their racial, ethnic, and religious traditions and cultures. As discussed at the beginning of this chapter, language is increasingly seen as part of a group's identity, an identity that minorities want to protect legally. Conflict over the extent to which a group seeks assimilation or maintenance of a strong group identity continues to mark American politics.

Race and Ethnicity

Among the most important distinctions in American politics are race and ethnicity. Our history as a nation of immigrants and our struggle with race relations have reinforced the importance of these differences, and they have become part of our political debate. **Race** can be defined as a grouping of human beings with common characteristics presumed to be transmitted genetically. **Ethnicity** is a social division based on national origin, religion, and language, often within the same race, and includes a sense of attachment to that group. In the United States, race issues focus on African Americans, Asians, and Hispanics, although Hispanics can be of any race. What are the racial divisions?

About four out of five Americans are white, according to census estimates. The largest nonwhite racial group is African Americans. There are more than 33 million African Americans in the United States, roughly 13 percent of the population. Asian Americans constitute just under 4 percent of the population, and Native Americans just under 1 percent. Most American Hispanics are classified as white by the Census Bureau. The Census Bureau estimates that there are 26.8 million American Hispanics, constituting over 10 percent of the population.[17]

The racial and ethnic diversity of the American polity will only increase over time, due to different birth rates across different groups as well as different immigration rates. Between 1981 and 1991 the white population experienced a natural increase (births minus deaths) of just under 5 percent, while American Indians, Asians and Pacific Islanders, and Hispanics all had natural increase rates of around 20 percent. African Americans were in between, at 14 percent.[18] The Census Bureau has projected that by the year 2050, whites will decline from over 83 percent of the total population today to about 73 percent. Hispanics will grow from 10 percent in 1995 to 23 percent in 2050. The political system will have to accommodate this transformation.

AFRICAN AMERICANS   Folklore tells us that people came to this country because it was a land of freedom and opportunity. For many it was, but for most African Americans it was the opposite. They came as slaves. African Americans were freed as a result of the Civil War, but race relations and racial divisions have been enduring issues of American politics.[19] (Many of the important civil rights cases and controversies are described in Chapter 4.)

Until 1900, more than 90 percent of all African Americans lived in the South;[20] in 1995 the figure was 52 percent.[21] Put another way, about 20 percent of the people in the South are African American. South Carolina, Alabama, Mississippi, and Louisiana are more than 30 percent African American. Two-thirds of the citizens of the District of Columbia are African American.

Many African Americans left the South after the turn of the century, hoping to improve their lives by settling in the large cities of the Northeast, Midwest, and West. The migration from the South was substantial: 4.5 million more left the South than migrated to it between the mid-1940s and late 1960s.[22] By the 1960s, many African Americans were living in poverty in large cities, without the economic and social resources to take advantage of recently won legal opportunities. More recently, African Americans have been returning to the South, especially to its urban areas.

In economic terms, African Americans are much worse off than whites in the United States. African American median family income in 1994 was $21,550, compared to $39,300 for whites. Nearly one-third of African Americans are below the poverty level, compared to 12 percent of whites.[23] Another way to measure economic well being is in terms of assets or wealth. African American's net wealth is only one-tenth that of whites, and Hispanics have only slightly more wealth than African Americans (see Figure 6-3). As a result, African Americans and Hispanics have fewer resources to fall back on in hard times, and they are less likely to have the savings to help a child pay for college.[24] Some African Americans have become relatively prosperous: 14.5 percent of African American households had earnings in 1993 of over $50,000, a proportion still less than half of that for whites of non-Hispanic origin.[25] Some African Americans have risen to the top in earnings in their fields of endeavor. Athletes like Michael Jordan

FIGURE 6-3   Wealth Distribution in the United States by Race, 1993

SOURCE: U.S. Bureau of the Census Home Page, http://www.census.gov/ftp/pub/hhes/wealth/wlth93f.html, May 1996.

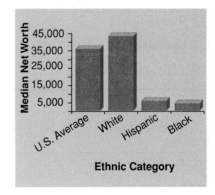

and Barry Bonds and entertainers like Bill Cosby, Whitney Houston, and Oprah Winfrey are examples. Oprah Winfrey, who earned $98 million during 1991–92, was the highest paid entertainer in the world during this time, more than doubling the income of her closest competitor.

Middle-class African Americans provide role models and leadership to the civil rights movement, yet their comparatively small number in the past serves as a reminder that most African Americans remain behind whites in an economy that relies more and more on education and job skills. About 23 percent of whites graduate from college, whereas only about 13 percent of African Americans do.[26] For 18-to-21-year-old high school graduates, 45 percent of whites went on to college, only 29 percent of African Americans.[27] Finally, the African American population is much younger than the white population; the 1994 median age for whites was 33.2, compared to 29.1 for African Americans.[28] The combination of the younger African American population, the lower level of education among African Americans, and the concentration of African Americans in economically hard-pressed urban areas has resulted in a much higher unemployment rate for young African Americans; unemployment, in turn, leads to social problems like crime and drug abuse.

African Americans have had limited rights and little political power for most of the period since emancipation. Owing their freedom to the "party of Lincoln," most African Americans initially identified with the Republicans.[29] This loyalty started to change with Franklin Roosevelt, who insisted on equal treatment for African Americans in his New Deal programs.[30] In the period after World War II, African Americans came to see the Democrats as the party of civil rights. This perception was reinforced by the 1964 presidential campaign, in which the Democratic nominee, Lyndon Johnson, took credit for the Civil Rights Act of 1964, which his Republican opponent, Barry Goldwater, had voted against. The 1964 Republican platform position on civil rights espoused states' rights—then the creed of southern segregationists—in what appeared to be an effort to win the support of Southern white voters.[31] Virtually all African Americans voted for Johnson in 1964; and in presidential elections since 1964, their Democratic vote has averaged over 91 percent.

Recently, African Americans have become much more important politically because of their increased level of voter participation and their concentrated population. African Americans now constitute .2 percent of the population in Montana and .4 percent in Idaho, Maine, and South Dakota, but 66 percent in Washington, D.C., 36 percent in Mississippi, 31 percent in Louisiana, and 30 percent in South Carolina.[32] Southern senators and representatives, for instance, can no longer afford to ignore the African American vote.[33] Evidence of growing African American political power is the dramatic growth in the number of African American state legislators, a number that rose from 168 in 1970 to 575 in 1995.[34]

Black representation in the U.S. House of Representatives was enhanced by some states drawing congressional districts to improve the chances of blacks winning election. As we discussed in Chapter 4, that practice has been restrained by the U.S. Supreme Court. Longstanding suspicions that the criminal justice system is stacked against blacks and other minorities have been reinforced by such publicized trials as the Rodney King beating and O.J. Simpson murder trials.

ASIAN AMERICANS Asian Americans are a heterogeneous group classified together by the census for statistical purposes but with significant differences in culture, language, and political experience in the United States. The group includes persons of Chinese, Japanese, Korean, Vietnamese, and Filipino origin, as well as persons

TABLE 6-3

The Ethnic Asian Population in the United States

	1980	1990
	(thousands)	
Japanese	715	848
Chinese	810	1,645
Indian	385	815
Korean	355	799
Filipino	780	1,406
Vietnamese	245	615

SOURCE: U.S. Bureau of the Census, *Statistical Abstract of the United States, 1993* (Government Printing Office), p.18.

from the Pacific Islands (see Table 6-3). In 1994, the United States was home to approximately 9 million Asian Americans and Pacific Islanders residing primarily in the western states, especially Hawaii, California, and Washington.[35] Asian Americans are the most successful racial group economically and educationally. More than two out of every five Asian Americans have graduated from college, compared to just over one of every five white Americans.[36]

The numbers of Asian Americans grew during the 1970s and 1980s, largely as a result of Southeast Asian immigration. In the 1990 census, persons from Asia had climbed to one of four of all foreign-born persons living in the United States, and the Philippines was surpassed only by Mexico as the country of birth for foreign-born persons living in this country. Immigrants from the Pacific Islands more than doubled during the 1980s, and most persons in this group reside in three states—California, New York, and Hawaii. Pacific Islanders are also a diverse group in terms of language and culture. In states with heavy concentrations of Asian immigrants, these groups are now becoming more politically important and visible in politics.

NATIVE AMERICANS Centuries ago, explorers sailed west looking for another passage to India. Colonists followed, often holding grants of land from their own government—grants they believed gave them a right to land in the New World. However, by virtue of prior usage the land belonged to "Indians," the tribal peoples who had long inhabited the land. As settlers moved west, colonial leaders dealt with Indian representatives to obtain land for colonists and to reserve certain lands for these Native Americans.

The Native American population today is more than 2 million.[37] Native Americans have incomes well below those of other Americans, and Native American families are generally twice as likely to be below the poverty level as African Americans or whites.[38] Native Americans are below the rest of the nation in the proportion of persons completing high school; and the proportion completing college is roughly half that of the rest of the population.[39]

HISPANICS/LATINOS Hispanics (persons of Spanish-speaking descent) are defined by the U.S. Census Bureau as an ethnic group, and they can be of any race. For example, the president of Peru, Alberto Fujimori, is Hispanic of Japanese ancestry. Even if the Spanish-speaking descent is one or more generations removed (grandparents or great grandparents), that person is still considered Hispanic.

The terms "Latino" and "Chicano" are preferred by some persons of Spanish-speaking descent, in part because they lack association with Spain, a colonial power against which many in Latin America fought wars of independence. "The term 'Hispanic' emphasizes the white European culture of Spain because it refers to lovers of Spanish culture."[40] "Hispanic" is a term most widely used by government agencies and the media, while "Latino" appears more popular to leaders of the group. "Chicano" is often associated with the politically active Mexican-American movement of the 1960s and 1970s. Most Mexican Americans, Puerto Rican Americans, and Cuban Americans prefer to be called American rather than Latino or Hispanic.[41] Ross Perot's derogatory references to Mexicans in his campaign against NAFTA in 1993 angered many Hispanics and created anti-American feeling in Latin America.

Latinos are not a monolithic group, and while they share a common linguistic heritage, they often differ from one another, depending on which country they immigrated from (see Table 6-4). Cuban Americans, for instance, tend to be Republicans, while Mexican Americans and Puerto Ricans are disproportionately Democrats.[42] Socioeconomically, Cuban Americans approximate the white population, while Puerto Rican Americans and Mexican Americans are generally

TABLE 6-4

Persons of Hispanic Origin in the United States, 1994

	Number	Percent
Mexican	17090	64.1%
Puerto Rican	2776	10.4
Cuban	1111	4.2
Central and South American	3725	14.0
Other	1944	7.3
Total	26646	100.0

SOURCE: U.S. Bureau of the Census Home Page, http://www.census.gov/ftp/pub/population/socdemo/hispanic/hnatvy94.txt.

TABLE 6-5

Origin of Foreign-Born Population: 1980 and 1990

	1980	1990
European	36.6%	22.0%
Asian	18.0	25.2
Mexican	15.6	21.7
Caribbean	8.9	9.8
Central American	2.5	5.7
South American	4.0	5.2
African	1.4	1.8
Other	13.0	8.6

SOURCE: U.S. Bureau of the Census, *Population Profile of the United States, 1993* (Government Printing Office, 1993), p. 40.

at the lower end of the scale.[43] Socially, Latinos divide up along these lines as well, and there can be intense rivalry among Hispanic groups. Politically, Latinos can differ on their levels of support, depending on whether the candidate is from Puerto Rico, Cuba, or Mexico. A recent study of Latinos found differences between Latinos of Mexican, Puerto Rican, and Cuban descent in partisanship, ideology, and rates of participation but widespread support for a liberal domestic agenda, including increased spending on health care, crime and drug control, education, the environment, child services, and bilingual education.[44] Given the overall growth of the Latino population, it is not surprising that both major parties have aggressively sought to cultivate Hispanic candidates.

The divisions within Latinos became more important because of the tendency of the groups to settle in different areas. Nearly two-thirds of Cuban immigrants live in Florida, especially greater Miami. Puerto Rican immigrants are concentrated in or around New York City, and Mexican American immigrants in the Southwest and California. The Census Bureau estimated in 1995 that more than 9.1 million Hispanics live in California alone.[45] The issue of illegal aliens became the focus of a much publicized ballot initiative in California in 1994—Proposition 187. California voters, by a margin of 59 percent to 41 percent, adopted the measure, which would deny most state welfare and educational benefits to illegal immigrants. The constitutionality of the initiative was immediately challenged in court.

The Ties of Ethnicity

Except for Native Americans, all Americans are immigrants or are descended from immigrants. The largest number of immigrants came between 1900 and 1924, when 17.3 million people relocated to the United States—by far the largest immigration to one country in any quarter-century in human history. From 1991–1993, there were more than 3.7 million immigrants.[46] This new wave of immigrants came primarily from Latin America, especially the Caribbean and Mexico, and Asian countries such as the Philippines, Vietnam, and China. The foreign born proportion of the U.S. population increased during the 1980s, rising from 14 million in 1980 to 20 million in 1990, the largest number of foreign-born in U.S. history. Table 6-5 shows the origin of foreign-born population in 1980 and 1990. Note that among U.S. foreign born, the proportion of Asian and Mexican immigrants has pulled even with or surpassed the number of Europeans.

Having large numbers of immigrants can pose challenges to any political and social system. They are often the source of social conflict as they compete with more established groups for jobs, rights, political power, and influence.

Among the most prominent ethnic groups in the United States are Irish Americans, Italian Americans, German Americans, Polish Americans, Hispanics, and Greek Americans. The country's early settlers were generally English-speaking Protestants; in fact, people of English, Scottish, and Welsh background make up the largest ethnic group in the United States. Irish immigrants, largely Catholics, started coming before the potato famine in the 1840s and came in even larger numbers after it. They experienced economic exploitation and religious bigotry. The Irish American response was often to retreat among themselves, forming a strong ethnic group consciousness. Other ethnic groups that followed—Italians, Greeks, Chinese—each experienced a similar cycle: flight from their homeland and happy arrival here, discrimination, exploitation, residential clustering, and the formation of a strong group identity.

Ethnic group identity is often persistent. In certain ethnic sections of large cities, people still converse in their native languages. Ethnic groups gain in political importance as they become more affluent; eventually they support candidates "of their own kind," ultimately electing mayors, governors, or even presidents. Irish Americans understandably were proud of the election to president of John

F. Kennedy; and most Greek Americans identified with Michael Dukakis, the Democratic presidential nominee in 1988.

Gender

For most of U.S. history, politics and government were men's business. Women gained the right to vote primarily in the western territories, beginning with Wyoming in 1869 and Utah in 1870, and then in Colorado and Idaho before the turn of the century.[47] The right was extended nationally with passage of the Nineteenth Amendment in 1920. The fears of some opponents of woman suffrage—that women would form their own party and vote largely for women or fundamentally alter our political system—have not been realized. During Susan B. Anthony's suffrage campaign, Jonas H. Upton, editor of the *Democratic Salem Monitor* in Salem, Oregon, contended that women, if given the right to vote, would combine to vote for war because they were exempt from the draft.[48] Others said women would unite to vote for prohibition.[49]

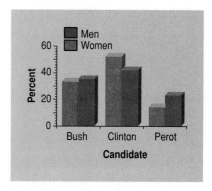

FIGURE 6-4
Gender and the Vote for President, 1992

SOURCE: *1992 American National Election Study*, Center for Political Studies, University of Michigan.

Instead of voting as a bloc, women have typically divided their vote between the two major political parties. However, in 1992, women were more likely than men to vote for Clinton and less likely to vote for Perot (see Figure 6-4). For most of the period since gaining the right to vote, they have voted at a lower rate than women in other Western democracies, but this trend appears to be changing.[50] Since 1976, women have voted at nearly the same rate as men, meaning that in recent elections, because females in the population outnumber males, the female vote has outnumbered the male vote.[51] Women have chosen to work within the existing political parties and do not overwhelmingly support female candidates, especially if they must cross parties to do so. The numbers of women elected to public office have been low; since 1917, less than 6 percent of representatives in the House have been women. The high point so far came after the 1992 election, when the number of women elected to the House of Representatives reached 47, and the number of women in the U.S. Senate rose to six. The success of so many women in the 1992 elections led some to label the election the "Year of the Woman."[52] The number of women in the House remained at its all-time high after the 1994 elections, and the number of women serving in the Senate rose to eight.

In 1996, two women were elected to the U.S. Senate. The number of women in the U.S. House following the 1996 elections was 49 (a net gain of two), and the number of female governors following the 1996 elections was two.

Barbara Burrell contends women win office as often as men when they run under similar circumstances. The reason there are now more women members of Congress is that in recent elections more women have chosen to run for office, especially open seats.[53]

One of the groups that has most aggressively promoted women as candidates is EMILY's List, a group that funds pro-choice, Democratic candidates. EMILY is an acronym for *Early Money Is Like Yeast,* meaning that campaign contributions given to candidates early in their campaigns can help raise more money, just as yeast helps dough to rise. Republicans have duplicated EMILY's List with their own political action committee, Wish List, which gives to female candidates who are pro-choice on abortion.

The women's movement in American politics encompasses a comprehensive agenda, including voting and political rights but also extending to other basic liberties of the Bill of Rights and Fourteenth Amendment. In addition to rights and liberties, women seek equal opportunity, education, jobs, skills, respect, and self-esteem in what has been a male-dominated system.[54] There are serious inequalities between men and women in areas such as income. About 30 percent more women than men work for the minimum wage.[55] In 1993, 46 percent of

Charges of sexual harassment by women employees of Senator Bob Packwood eventually led to his resignation one day after the Senate ethics committee had unanimously recommended expulsion.

women earned less than $10,000, compared to only 24 percent of men.[56] While women earn on average only about 70 cents for every dollar earned by men, this figure has improved from the 60 cents for every dollar in 1980.[57] Because an increasing number of women today are the sole breadwinners for their families, the implications of this low income level are even more significant. The problem of lower pay for women is not restricted to working mothers. Among college graduates ages 25 to 34, women earn an average of 79 cents for every dollar earned by men of the same age and education. As age increases, the earnings gap widens, so that 55-to-64-year-old college-educated women earn only 64 cents for every dollar earned by men of the same age and education.[58] Increasing women's income is an important issue to the women's movement.

There is a **gender gap**—significant differences between men and women—in public opinion and voting. Women are more likely to oppose violence in any form—death penalty, new weapons systems, or the possession of handguns. Evidence suggests that women as a group are more compassionate than men, and so are more likely to favor government that provides health insurance and family services. Women are more concerned about women's rights, enforcement of child support, sexual abuse and rape, unequal treatment of women in the legal system, the environment, peace, and pornography than men. These so-called gender issues are becoming increasingly important. American women identify such work and family issues as day care, prenatal and postnatal leave policy, and equality of treatment on the job as important.[59] Other gender issues, some of them focal points in recent U.S. Senate elections, include reproductive rights and sexual harassment.[60]

Providing a workplace in which people are not subject to sexual harassment came to the top of the political agenda after being raised during the confirmation of Supreme Court Justice Clarence Thomas and again because of charges raised against U.S. Senator Bob Packwood. Former staff workers had accused Packwood of sexual harassment after his reelection in 1992. After a protracted dispute with the Senate Ethics Committee, including a dispute over his personal diaries, the committee unanimously recommended that Packwood be expelled from the Senate. Packwood resigned rather than face a vote by the full Senate on his expulsion. He was replaced by Democrat Ron Wyden in a special election early in 1996.

The Supreme Court and Congress, as we noted in Chapter 4, have provided legal protections against such harassment, and the number of lawsuits filed is on the increase (see Table 6-6).

Sexual Orientation

The 1990s have seen a growing visibility and increased awareness of diversity in sexual orientation. Gays and lesbians have more aggressively pursued their political agenda of antidiscrimination laws, access to legally sanctioned homosexual

TABLE 6-6

Sexual Harassment in the Workplace

	1990	1991	1992	1993	1994	1995
Cases Filed	6,127	6,883	10,532	11,908	14,420	15,549
Cases Resolved	5,671	6,718	7,484	9,971	11,478	13,802
Compensation (in millions)	$7.7	$7.1	$12.7	$25.1	$22.5	$24.3

SOURCE: U.S. Equal Employment Opportunity Commission, Office of Communications and Legislative Affairs, *Sexual Harassment Statistics: FY 1990-FY1995* and personal communication.

marriages, rights to custody of children and the ability to adopt children, and access to employee benefits for homosexual partners. Groups like Queer Nation, Act Up, and the National Gay and Lesbian Task Force have organized marches and otherwise sought to heighten gay awareness.

During the 1992 election, the question of gays in the military became an issue. Candidate Bill Clinton promised to drop the ban on homosexuals, and early in his administration he set out to fulfill this campaign promise. However, military leaders, including the Joint Chiefs of Staff, opposed the idea, as did key members of the congressional committees dealing with the armed forces. A slight majority of the public did not approve of "Bill Clinton's decision to ease the ban on homosexuals in the armed forces."[61] In the face of the intense and well-organized opposition and a possible defeat in Congress, the Clinton administration abandoned its original proposal and settled for a compromise policy of "don't ask, and don't tell"—meaning that the military will no longer ask recruits if they are homosexual, and military personnel are under no obligation to divulge their sexual orientation. Some remnants of the old policy remain, however, including an understanding that practicing homosexuals will be discharged from the military if their homosexuality is discovered.

One focal point of the politics of sexual orientation has been AIDS. Acquired Immune Deficiency Syndrome, or AIDS, has disproportionately affected the homosexual community and motivated gays and lesbians to become more politically active, visible, and well organized. Public fear of AIDS was behind a 1986 California ballot initiative to quarantine all persons with the disease, a measure that was defeated.

As the homosexual rights movement has grown in visibility and power, an opposition movement has also become part of American politics. During the 1970s, voters in some cities and states voted on measures targeted either to protect or limit homosexual rights. One unsuccessful measure in California, for instance, would have removed suspected homosexuals from the public school classroom until a hearing could be held. In 1992 and 1993, voters in Colorado, Oregon, and scattered cities, including Cincinnati, Ohio, voted on ballot measures to remove special protections previously granted to homosexuals. Similar measures were on the ballot in several states in 1994. These plebiscites reflect a backlash against what their sponsors see as laws legitimizing homosexuality. Not surprisingly, the campaigns and debates over these votes become heated. The consequence of these votes has been to put gays and lesbians on the defensive, fighting to hold onto the advances they had made in the 1980s.

Religion

In some parts of the world, religious differences can be a source of violent conflict. In Northern Ireland, Protestants and Catholics have been at war for more than four hundred years. The war in Bosnia-Herzegovina was a religious and ethnic battle among Muslims, Serbs, and Catholics. Countries like Lebanon, India, and Sri Lanka have also experienced intense religious conflict. Jews have often been the target of religious discrimination and persecution (anti-Semitism), including the holocaust, which murdered or displaced an estimated 6 million Jews.[62] The United States has not been immune, despite its principle of religious freedom. In 1838, Governor Lilburn W. Boggs of Missouri issued an extermination order against the Mormons.[63]

Although the intensity of religious conflict varies, it can become especially strong if there is one predominant or official faith. This is one reason why the framers did not sanction a national church in the United States. In fact, James Madison wrote in *The Federalist*, No. 51, "In a free government the security for

A Closer Look

At one time we thought a Catholic could not be elected president. With the election of 1960 that issue was resolved. John F. Kennedy directly confronted the question of whether a Catholic would put aside religious teachings if they conflicted with constitutional obligations. He said, "I am not the Catholic candidate for President. I am the Democratic Party's candidate for President who happens also to be Catholic. I do not speak for my church on public matters, and the church does not speak for me." A candidate's religion may still become an issue if religious convictions on sensitive issues such as abortion threaten to conflict with public obligations.

John F. Kennedy

Jewish 1.9%
Other Christian 2.6%
Secular 16.9%
White Evangelical Protestants 26.1%
Roman Catholic 25.6%
Black Protestants 7.2%
White Mainline Protestants 19.8%

Religious Denominations of Americans

Note: Religious divisions based on Kellstedt/Green Index. See Lyman A. Kellstedt and John C. Green, "Knowing God's Many People: Denominational Preference and Political Behavior," in David C. Leege and Lyman A. Kellstedt, eds., *Rediscovering the Religious Factor in American Politics*, (M.E. Sharp, 1993). p. 70.

SOURCE: *1994 American National Election Study*, Center for Political Studies, University of Michigan.

civil rights must be the same as that for religious rights. It consists in the one case in the multiplicity of interests, and in the other in the multiplicity of sects."

The absence of an official American church does not mean that religion is unimportant in American politics. Indeed there were established state churches until the 1830s. Politicians frequently refer to God in their speeches or demonstrate their piety in other ways. And many share John Conway's view that "at the root of American political and social values . . . is the distinctive Puritanism of the early New England settlers."[64] Many Americans take their religious beliefs seriously, more so than peoples of other industrial democracies.[65] Nearly two-thirds of Americans attend houses of worship several times a year, more than half attend church or synagogue at least once a month, and more than one-third attend nearly every week.[66] Religion, like ethnicity, is a shared identity—people identify themselves as Baptist, Catholic, Buddhist, and so on. Sometimes church attendance or nonattendance is more important than differences between religions in explaining attitudes. "Among both Catholics and Protestants, frequent churchgoers are less likely to support abortion than those who rarely or never attend."[67]

Religion can be an important catalyst for social change, as it was in the overthrow of communism in Central Europe[68] and in the leadership of the black church in the American civil rights movement. As writer Taylor Branch explains, the black church "served not only as a place of worship but also as a bulletin board to a people who owned no organs of communication, a credit union to those without banks, and even a kind of people's court."[69] African American ministers, like the Reverend Martin Luther King, Jr., became leaders of the civil rights movement; others, like the Reverend Jesse Jackson, have run for office. Hence religion can be important not only as a source of personal values and attitudes but as a means of political activity and organization.

In recent years there has been an increase in political activity among fundamentalist Christians. Led by ministers like Jerry Falwell and Pat Robertson, they have supported political organizations like the Moral Majority and the Christian Coalition. Throughout the 1980s and 1990s they sought to influence the national agenda, and Robertson ran for president in the Republican party in 1988. More recently, they have focused attention at the local level—school boards, city councils, mayorships, and local GOP leadership.[70] Their agenda includes the return of school prayer, the outlawing of abortion, restrictions on homosexuals, and opposition to gun control. They achieved some successes in the elections of 1993 and 1994 and are seen as an important political force in some parts of the country.

One defining characteristic of religion in the United States is the tremendous variety of denominations. About half the people in the United States describe themselves as Protestant. The largest Protestant denomination is Baptist, followed by Methodists, Lutherans, Presbyterians, and Episcopalians. Because there are so many different Protestant churches, Catholics have the largest single membership in the United States, constituting more than one-quarter of the population. Jews constitute less than 2 percent of the population. Protestants came to the United States first; most Catholics and Jews immigrated after the 1840s. It was not until 1960, however, that Americans elected a Catholic president.

In recent presidential elections, most Protestants voted Republican, while most Catholics and Jews voted Democratic.[71] The perception among many Catholics and Jews that the Democratic party is more open to them partly explains the strength of their Democratic identification. The Democrats won the loyalty of many Catholics by their willingness to nominate Al Smith for the presidency in 1928 and John Kennedy in 1960. Southern Protestants are Democrats for different reasons, largely having to do with the sectional issues discussed earlier. Religious groups vary in their rates of participation. Jews have the highest rate of reported voter turnout, 79 percent in 1992, while those who claim no religious affiliation have the lowest, 62 percent. Catholics voted at a slightly higher rate than Protestants.[72]

Religion is especially important in American politics because of the clustering of populations. Hence Catholics make up only 26 percent of the U.S. population, yet they are more than 50 percent of the population of Rhode Island, Massachusetts, and Connecticut. Baptists represent 19 percent of the U.S. population, yet they are more than 50 percent of the population of Mississippi, Alabama, and Georgia. Mormons are only 2 percent of the U.S. population, yet they are more than 70 percent of the population of Utah. The South is the most Protestant—61 percent. The state of New York has the highest percentage of Jews, 7 percent; New York City is 14 percent Jewish.

Religious differences can be related to other politically important characteristics. For instance, Jews are the most prosperous and best educated of any ethnic or religious group. More than 46 percent graduated from college, compared to 22 percent of Protestants and 20 percent of Catholics.[73] In this example, as in others, religion is a cross-cutting cleavage in American politics; the differences do not reinforce one another. On the basis of income and education, Jews predictably would be Republicans, but 79 percent of American Jews are Democrats,

INCOME DISTRIBUTION IN THE UNITED STATES

The bar chart on the left demonstrates that most of the population is what we might call middle class, with 64 percent of American families having incomes ranging from $15,000 to $75,000, with the median income $31,241. Political scientists term such a distribution "normal" because it bows out in the middle. In some societies, notably developing countries, most people are either in the high or low income ranges, giving two "peaks" to the distribution. Though the bar chart shows a large middle class, the pie chart on the right indicates that the richest 20 percent earn twelve times more than the poorest 20 percent, or nearly half of all income.

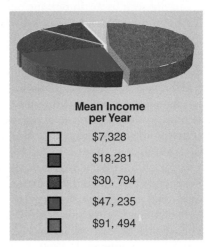

Mean Income per Year

☐	$7,328
☐	$18,281
☐	$30, 794
☐	$47, 235
☐	$91, 494

Share of Aggregate Income Received by Fifths of Households, 1992

SOURCE: U.S. Bureau of the Census, *Money Income of Households, Families, and Persons in the United States, 1992* (Government Printing Office, 1993), p. B-6.

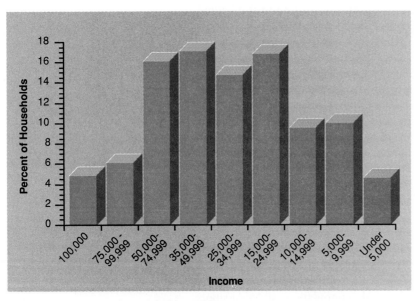

Total Money Income of Households, 1993

Source: U.S. Bureau of the Census, *Statistical Abstract of the United States, 1995* (Government Printing Office, 1995), p. 472. Number (thousands) 97,101; median income $31,241.

"To the rich, the very rich, and the super rich! Have I left anybody out?"

Drawing by Mirachi. © 1988 The New Yorker Magazine, Inc.

while only 15 percent are Republicans. In contrast, more than 55 percent of all white Protestants are Republicans.[66]

Wealth and Income

The United States is a wealthy nation in a world of scarcity and intense economic conflict over the distribution of wealth. Indeed, to some knowledgeable observers, "the most striking thing about the United States has been its phenomenal wealth."[74] A large proportion of the people in the United States lead comfortable lives in terms of housing, nutrition, and medical care and enjoy a standard of living beyond the reach of many who live in other countries. But even in affluent societies, the distribution of wealth and income can result in important political divisions and conflicts. *Wealth* encompasses the things of economic value (savings, stocks, property) you possess; *income* is how much money you make from your job or investments. "The most common and durable source of factions has been the various and unequal distribution of property," wrote James Madison, in *The Federalist*, No. 10. He continued, "Those who hold, and those who are without property, have ever formed distinct interests in society" (see Appendix). Madison was right: economic differences often lead to conflict, and Americans remain divided politically along economic lines. Aside from race, income may be the single most important factor in explaining views on issues, partisanship, and ideology. Most rich people are Republicans, and most poor people are Democrats, and this has been true since at least the Great Depression of the 1930s.

The distribution of income within a society can have important consequences for democratic stability. If there is a perception that only the few at the top of the economic ladder can hope to earn enough for an adequate standard of living, then domestic unrest and revolution may follow. Income is related to participation in politics. Poor people who need the most help from government are the least likely to participate. They are also the most likely to favor social welfare programs.

Income has been rising in the United States. Even after adjusting for inflation, income doubled in the period between 1952 and 1991,[75] but the tendency for income to rise has slowed down. Economists debate the causes for this change; some cite higher energy costs, low levels of personal savings, and the worldwide slowdown in productivity growth.[76] In terms of income, the Northeast is the most prosperous region and the South the least prosperous. Compared to other nations, our purchasing power is higher than that of any other advanced democracy, including Japan.[77]

Most college students come from the top quarter of American families in income—those earning $50,000 a year or more. In fact, students from these families graduate from college at nearly twice the rate as those from the bottom 75 percent of the socioeconomic ladder.[78]

At the other end of the economic continuum are the poor. For twenty-five years, roughly one in every ten Americans comes from a family whose income is below the poverty line. In 1995 the official poverty level for a family of four was income below $15,150.[79] Most persons classified as below the poverty line are in families in which adults of working age either do not have jobs or work in jobs with low pay. Families headed by a female have three times the chance of falling below the poverty line, and nearly 39 percent of all households headed by females fall below the poverty line.[80] African Americans are three times as likely to be poor than whites, and Hispanics are two and a half times as likely to be poor than whites. Thirty-nine percent of the poor are children, and many appear trapped in a cycle of poverty.[81]

Missing Persons

The 1990 census was surrounded by charges of a severe undercount. President George Bush's secretary of commerce admitted that real population in 1990 was about 259 million, instead of the 254 million reported by the Census Bureau. Still, he resisted calls to revise the count to reflect more accurately the distribution of the population among states, cities, and neighborhoods, saying that such adjustments were "unreliable."

Why is undercounting so controversial? Federal funding to cities and states totaling $59 billion is often allocated on the census population counts. The undercounting appears to have been most pronounced among minority populations and in central cities. New York's former mayor, David N. Dinkins, called the undercounting nothing less than "statistical grand larceny," because it resulted in a substantial loss in federal funds to the city.

Undercounting also has important political consequences. If the estimates had been adjusted upward, Arizona and California would have each gained another congressional seat, while Pennsylvania and Wisconsin would have each lost one.

In 1995 the controversy was heard before the U.S. Supreme Court in *New York v Wisconsin*. The case put President Clinton's Secretary of Commerce, Ronald Brown, in the uncomfortable position of defending a decision made by his Republican predecessor, Robert Mosbacher, that Brown had heavily criticized when he was chairman of the Democratic Party during the Bush administration. The legal question centers on whether the Supreme Court decides to defer to the judgement of the Department of Commerce on census adjustment decisions or instead evaluate and possibly mandate controversial statistical techniques used in census adjustment. In March 1996, the Supreme Court decided that the Constitution leaves the matter to the discretion of Congress and the president.

SOURCE: Adapted from Felicity Barringer, "U.S. Won't Revise 1990 Census, Says Chief of Commerce," *New York Times*, July 16, 1991, p. A1. Copyright ©1991 by The New York Times Company. Reprinted by permission.

The definition of poverty is itself political. The poverty-level figure of $15,150 for a household of four identifies those who cannot meet a minimum standard in such basics as housing, food, and medical care. Regardless of how one defines poverty, however, the poor are a minority who lack political power. During the Reagan years of the 1980s there was increasing inequality between rich and poor, a trend quite different from the 1960s, when the gap between rich and poor narrowed.[82] While there are even fewer persons over the age of 65 than there are poor people, older Americans are a much more potent force in American politics.[83] The poor vote less and are less confident and organized in dealing with politics and government.

Following the 1994 elections, one of the priorities that President Clinton and the Republican Congress agreed upon was welfare reform. Welfare as a broad public policy has long been unpopular with the American people, but specific welfare programs like aid to the blind and disabled, support for mentally retarded, and unemployment compensation have been widely supported. Unlike other public policy programs the beneficiaries of welfare are not politically well organized.

The far-reaching welfare reform bill signed into law by President Clinton in 1996 permits states to exclude up to 20 percent of current welfare recipients like the blind, disabled, or mentally handicapped from the work requirements and lifetime limit. Some advocacy groups for poor people fought against the changes, but they were politically ineffective.

Wealth is more concentrated than income. The wealthiest families hold most of the property and other forms of wealth like stocks and savings. Traditionally, one of the problems with concentrated wealth has been that it fosters an aristocracy. Jefferson sought to break up the "aristocracy of wealth" by changing from laws based on *primogeniture* (the eldest son's exclusive right to inherit his father's estate) to laws that encouraged people to divide their estates equally among all their children, the result being smaller landholding. He sought to foster an "aristocracy of virtue and talent" through a public school system open to all for primary grades and for the best students through the university level.[84] Education has been one of the most important means for Americans to achieve economic and social mobility. Those with an education are wealthier, and those with wealth are more inclined to get an education.

Occupation

Americans at the time of Thomas Jefferson and for several generations after worked primarily in agriculture. In 1800, 83 percent of the entire U.S. labor force was engaged in farming.[85] The agrarian period was characterized by a large number of independent, landowning farmers with little formal schooling.

By 1920, the United States had become the world's leading industrial nation. This dramatic transformation also resulted in the expansion of American cities as large numbers of workers moved there to find jobs. Labor conditions, including child labor practices, became important political issues. The invention and application of technology, such as Henry Ford's assembly line, when combined with abundant natural and human resources, meant that the U.S. gross domestic product (GDP) rose by more than 550 percent in real terms over the 65-year period from 1929 to 1994.[86]

The United States has now entered what Daniel Bell, a noted sociologist, has labeled the "post-industrial phase of our development." "A post-industrial society, being primarily a technical society, awards less on the basis of inheritance or property . . . than on education and skill."[87] Knowledge is the organizing device of the post-industrial era. Post-industrial societies have greater affluence and a class structure less defined along traditional labor versus management lines.

FIGURE 6-5
Occupational Distribution in the United States, 1900-1990

SOURCE: Data for 1900–70: U.S. Bureau of the Census, *Bicentennial Statistics, Pocket Data Book, USA* (Government Printing Office, 1976), pp. 386–87; data for 1910: U.S. Bureau of the Census, *Historical Statistics of the United States: Colonial Times to 1970,* (Government Printing Office, 1976), p. 139; data for 1980: U.S. Department of Labor, *Employment and Earnings,* vol. 28, no.1 (Government Printing Office, January 1981), p. 42; data for 1990; U.S. Department of Labor, *Employment and Earnings,* vol. 38, no.1 (Government Printing Office, January 1991), p. 36.

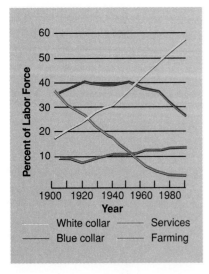

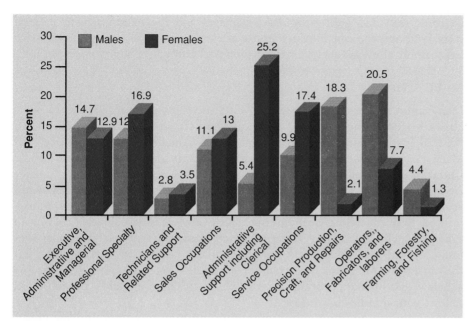

FIGURE 6-6
Occupational Distribution by Gender, 1991

SOURCE: U.S. Department of Labor, *Employment and Earnings* (Government Printing Office, November 1995), p. 27.

The changing dynamics of the American labor force can be seen in Figure 6-5, which shows the percent of the U.S. labor force in various occupations since 1900. As it demonstrates, there has been tremendous growth in the white-collar sector of our economy, rising from under 20 percent of the work force at the turn of the century to more than half by 1980. The white-collar sector includes managers, accountants, and lawyers as well as professionals and technicians in such rapid growth areas as communications, finance, insurance, and research. This shift has been accompanied by a dramatic decline in the number of people engaged in agriculture and a more modest decline in the number of people who produce goods (the manufacturing sector). Today less than one in three working Americans produces goods, and only 3 percent work on farms.

Governments are among the biggest employers. About one-sixth of our GDP is produced by federal, state, and local governments.[88] Indeed, education is one of our largest industries; there are 3.5 million teachers.[89] The Department of Defense employs nearly 3 million civilian and military personnel.[90]

Women and racial minorities have distinct occupational patterns (see Figure 6-6). Women are much less likely than men to work in blue-collar jobs and more likely to work as professionals and technicians in white-collar jobs. More than one in four working women are employed as clerical workers, and another 18 percent are in service occupations. As noted earlier, women generally earn less than men of the same age and education. Occupations in which women predominate, like teaching and clerical work, are generally lower paying than industrial or management jobs.

Like women, African Americans and Hispanics tend to have occupations different from those of white males. African Americans are more likely than whites or Hispanics to be engaged in clerical work or service sector jobs. Large numbers of Latinos work as operators and laborers, in service jobs, and on farms. Even in occupations in which African Americans or Hispanics have done better at finding jobs, they run into barriers. The courts and Congress have confronted some of these barriers.[91] The 1991 Civil Rights Act gives workers more protection against

"It's like this. If the rich have money, they invest. If the poor have money, they eat."

Drawing by Dana Fradon. ©1992 The New Yorker Magazine.

discrimination and greater monetary damages and the reimbursement of legal costs for those who can convince courts of employment bias.[92] See Chapter 4 for a discussion of employment discrimination and affirmative action issues.

Social Class

Many commentators have questioned why Americans are not divided into social classes in the European sense. American workers have not formed their own political parties, nor does class help to explain much about our political life. Marxist categories of *proletariat* (those who sell their labor) and *bourgeoisie* (those who own or control the means of production) are not as important here as they are in Europe. But we do have social classes and what social scientists call **socio-economic status (SES)**—a division of the population based on occupation, income, and education. Such measures help explain some citizen behavior in American politics, but these categories have some obvious inconsistencies. For instance, some individuals perform working-class tasks (such as plumbing), but their income is middle class or even upper middle class. A schoolteacher's income is below that of many working-class jobs, but in terms of status, the job ranks at least with middle-class fields.

Most Americans, when asked what class they belong to, say "middle class." The second most frequently mentioned category is "working class." Very few Americans see themselves as lower class or upper class. But what constitutes "middle class" is highly subjective. George Bush once defined "middle class" as persons making over $50,000.[93] Actually, only 5.7 percent of Americans had that much income.[94] In many other industrial democracies, large proportions of the population think of themselves as working class instead of middle class.[95] In England, nearly three out of five persons see themselves as working class.[96] But to many Americans there is something undesirable about the label "working class."

One explanation for Americans' responses may be the elements of the American Dream that involve upward mobility. Or this may reflect the hostility many feel toward organized labor, which solidifies workers. European labor unions are stronger than American labor unions. In any case, compared to many countries, class divisions in the United States are less defined and less important to politics. As political scientist Seymour Martin Lipset has written, "The American social structure and values foster an emphasis on competitive individualism, an orientation that is not congruent with class consciousness, support for socialist or social democratic parties, or a strong union movement."[97]

Age

Americans are living longer, a phenomenon that has been called the "graying of America." Not only are we living longer, but fewer babies are being born proportionate to the population. This demographic change will eventually have important consequences; it will increase the demand for medical care, retirement benefits, and a host of other age-related services. The growing population of older persons was most pronounced in the West during the 1980s, but Florida remains the state with the largest proportion of persons over age 65. Persons over the age of 65 constitute 13 percent of the population but account for 43 percent of the total medical expenditures.[98]

Older Americans as a group have a political agenda, and they vote. Figure 6-7, which plots voter turnout rate by age, shows a clear relationship: as age increases, so does the propensity to vote. In recent presidential elections, less than half of all 18- and 19-year-olds voted. In contrast, four out of every five 68- and 69-year-olds turned out to vote.[99] As a group, they fight to ensure that Social Security is

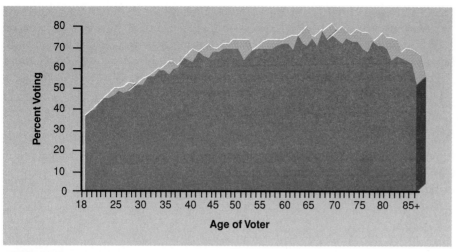

FIGURE 6-7
Percent Voting in the 1992 Presidential Election by Age

SOURCE: U.S. Bureau of the Census, *Voting and Registration in the Election of November 1992* (Government Printing Office, 1993).

protected; they value Medicare and favor catastrophic health insurance. Despite their desire for services that benefit themselves, they also are the group most in favor of tax cuts. Past legislative victories have changed the lives of older citizens. For instance, the poverty rate among this age group dropped from 35 percent in 1959 to 12 percent in 1993, a change partly due to improved medical benefits passed during the 1960s.[100]

The "gray lobby" not only votes in large numbers but also has four other political assets that make it politically powerful—disposable income, discretionary time, a clear focus on issues, and effective organization—factors not found in any other age group. When older Americans compete for their share of the budget pie, the young, minorities, and the poor often lose out to the "gray lobby." During his prolonged budget fight with Congress, President Clinton vetoed Republican budget proposals in part, he said, because they cut too deeply into Medicare, the health care program for the elderly. The popularity of this program and the importance of this group bolstered Clinton's standing in the polls and forced the Republicans to back down.

President Clinton had sought the support of older Americans for his health care reform package by promising no reduction in benefits for older Americans and reduced overall costs.[101] The American Association of Retired Persons (AARP), the largest and most powerful arm of the "gray lobby," disappointed President Clinton by refusing to endorse his health care reform bill. Instead, they, like other interested groups, sought to make their own case before the Congress.

Age is important to politics in two additional ways: life cycle and generation. Examples of life-cycle effects are that as people become middle-aged they become more politically conservative, less mobile, and more likely to participate in politics. As they age further and become senior citizens who rely more on the government for services, they tend to grow more liberal.[102]

There are also *generational effects* in politics that arise when a particular generation has had experiences that make it politically distinct. An example is the experience of the Great Depression, which, for those who lived through it, shaped lifelong views of parties, issues, and political leaders. Some of this generation saw Franklin Roosevelt as the person who saved the country by pulling it out of the Depression, while others felt he sold the country down the river by launching too many government programs. A more recent generation that shared a common and distinctive political experience is the Vietnam generation. Americans who came of age politically during the Vietnam War experienced not only an unpopular war but also the civil rights movement. As with the Great Depression, not everybody saw the Vietnam War and related issues in the same way. Such differences do not diminish the importance of the issue in shaping a generation's perspective on politics and government.

Education

Education has long been linked to citizenship and civic virtue. Thomas Jefferson wrote of education, "Enlighten the people generally, and tyranny and oppressions of body and mind will vanish like evil spirits at the dawn of day."[103] The vast majority of people in the United States are educated in public schools. Nine out of every ten students in kindergarten through high school attend public schools, and four out of five students in college are in public institutions.[104]

The U.S. population has a wide range of number of years of school completed. Only recently did the number of college graduates in America surpass the number of persons who had not graduated from high school.[105] High school dropout rates have declined in the last decade, yet African Americans, Hispanics, and individuals from low income families still have higher than average dropout rates. Roughly two-thirds of Americans have not gone to college, though many college students assume that the college experience is widely shared.

Americans are becoming more educated. In a 50-year period, the number of Americans 25 years and older with four or more years of college has gone from only 5 percent in 1940 to more than 22 percent in the mid 1990s.[106] Impressive gains have been made by all groups in the proportion graduating from high school, yet racial and ethnic minorities still lag behind whites in completing four or more years of college. African Americans have increased their rate of completion of four or more years of college tenfold since 1940, and Hispanics have almost doubled their college attendance since 1974, when data were first collected. To compete for jobs in a post-industrial society, more education, especially technical education, is necessary.

Compared to persons in other industrial democracies, Americans and Canadians are more likely to go to college.[107] But the experience of higher education has not been uniformly shared. The proportion of whites who are college graduates is nearly double that for African Americans or Hispanics; roughly 35 percent of African Americans and nearly half of all Hispanics stopped their schooling before completing high school. Part of the difference among whites, African Americans, and Hispanics in years of school completed is a function of age. Older African Americans and Hispanics are much less likely to have completed high school. One in five African Americans and 27 percent of Hispanics over the age of 65 stopped school before the fifth grade. In contrast, younger African Americans (those under the age of 29) are more likely than whites to have stayed in school through the eighth grade, but they then have a higher dropout rate than whites in high school. Hispanics, on the other hand, have high rates of dropout, even in the lower grades. Twelve percent did not go beyond the fourth grade, and one in three did not go to high school.[108] These differences in education affect not only economic well-being but political participation and involvement.

Education is one of the most important variables in predicting political participation, confidence in dealing with government, and awareness of issues. Education is also related to the acquisition of democratic values. Those who have failed to learn the "prevailing norms" of American society are far more likely to express opposition to democratic and capitalist ideals than those who

We The People

Distribution of Education in the United States

	4 Years of High School	1–3 Years of College	4+ Years of College	Total
Total	34.4%	24.4%	22.2%	81.0%
Male	32.3	23.6	25.1	81.0
Female	36.2	24.9	19.6	80.7
White	34.5	24.6	23.0	82.1
African American	36.2	23.8	12.9	72.9
Other	26.0	20.6	32.4	79.0
Hispanic	26.2	18.0	9.1	53.3
Non-Hispanic	35.1	24.9	23.4	83.4
Age				
25–34	34.5	28.4	23.4	86.3
35–44	33.2	28.5	27.1	88.8
45–54	34.0	25.0	26.2	85.2
55–64	37.2	19.5	18.8	75.5
65–74	36.6	17.5	13.6	67.7
75+	30.6	13.3	10.9	54.8

SOURCE: U.S. Bureau of the Census, *Statistical Abstract of the United States, 1995* (Government Printing Office, 1995), p. 158.

are well educated and politically knowledgeable.[109] Education is, in short, a factor we will return to again and again in subsequent chapters as we study government by the people.

UNITY IN A LAND OF DIVERSITY

As remarkable as American diversity is, the existence of a strong and widely shared sense of national unity and identity may be even more remarkable. Writing about the United States some years ago, a famous reporter, John Gunther, summarized his extensive travels across the United States by saying:

> Whoever invented the motto E Pluribus Unum [one out of many] has given the best three-word description of the United States ever written. The triumph of America is the triumph of a coalescing federal system. Complex as the nation is almost to the point of insufferability, it interlocks. Homogeneity and diversity— these are the stupendous rival magnets. . . . Think of the United States as an immense blanket or patchwork quilt solid with different designs and highlights. But, no matter what colors burn and flash in what corners, the warp and woof, the basic texture and fabric is the same from corner to corner, from end to end.[110]

Americans have always been united by their commitment to liberty. Equally important has been the belief that government should exist to serve the people, rather than the reverse. What shapes our political culture is the persistent commitment to the individual. One author recently concluded that "equality, individualism and openness are the crucial values of American politics in the 1990s."[111]

Part of the explanation for our unity is the unifying effect of the American Dream—the belief that this is the land of opportunity for enterprising individuals. Unity in the midst of diversity has also been enhanced by a sense of a common fate, often highlighted by a crisis. Social and economic differences become less important, for example, when we fight wars. World War II drew many Americans to experience life in different parts of the country and confirmed the patriotism of diverse groups. One question for the late 1990s will be: Can we maintain the same degree of unity in a world with fewer foreign enemies and only one military super-power? Finally, the United States has achieved a measure of unity through residential mobility, intermarriage, the mass media, and a common culture.

Social scientists sometimes speak of the *melting pot*, meaning that as minorities, especially ethnic groups, associate with other groups, they are assimilated into the rest of American society and come to share democratic values like majority rule, individualism, and the notion that America is the land of opportunity. Recently the melting pot idea has been criticized as assuming that differences between groups are to be discouraged. In its place, critics propose the notion of the *salad bowl*, in which "though the salad is an entity, the lettuce can still be distinguished from the chicory, the tomatoes from the cabbage."[112] As we have seen, important differences persist among groups, and in that sense the salad bowl analogy is accurate. Divisive issues like immigration, affirmative action, and programs for the poor have reinforced our differences. But in another way, our society has achieved a unity of commitment to democratic values and processes—a political culture—that is at least in part a consequence of such elements of the melting pot theory as public schools, a common language, and hope for a better life for one's children. While ethnic divisions in the United States have posed challenges to the institutions and processes of government, the public has generally accepted diversity in political appointments, government jobs and contracts, and other aspects of policy. This is a sharp contrast to the problems of ethnicity in Canada, India, Bosnia, and Russia. But what is the appropriate balance among recognition, preservation, and representation of ethnic groups and the needs for assimilation, common commitments, and a shared identity?

The United States is part of a global political landscape in which many of the same variables are important—race, religion, wealth, and the distribution of income. The changing world landscape has served, and will serve, to remind us of the challenges that diversity poses to governments. Racial, religious, and ethnic strife and historical divisions in many of the new democracies of Central Europe and the Commonwealth of Independent States have fostered insecurity within and between many nations. Other countries that are not yet democratic, like most in the Middle East, face similar challenges. While our effort to meld a single nation out of many diverse groups has not been without its failures, achieving some measure of unity is one of our governmental system's most important accomplishments.

SUMMARY

1. The character of a political society, its social and economic divisions, its traditions, and its sectional and local identifications are important to understanding public opinion, participation, voting, interest groups, political parties, and the communications process. It is often a mistake to generalize solely from one's own experience, background, beliefs, and values.

2. Geography, room to grow, abundant natural resources, our wealth, and our relative isolation from "foreign entanglements" help to explain American politics and traditions, including the notions of manifest destiny, ethnocentrism, and isolationism.

3. The South has been the most distinct region in the United States, in large part because of the issue of slav-

ery and race relations. Other important sections include the frost belt/sun belt division.

4. Americans moved from farms to cities and more recently from cities to suburbs. Population movements were largely responses to economic opportunities, including the large migration of African Americans from the South. Today, large cities are increasingly poor, African American, and Democratic, surrounded by suburbs that are primarily middle class, white, and Republican.

5. The United States is a land of tremendous diversity in race, ethnicity, religion, wealth and income, occupation, social class, age, and education. Divisions by gender and sexual orientation have recently become more important. This diversity is often important to our politics.

6. Race has been among the most important of the differences in our landscape. We fought a civil war on the issue of freedom for African Americans, and the issue of racial equality was largely postponed until the latter half of this century. Race remains an important issue in our politics and government. Ethnicity, including the rising numbers of Hispanics, continues to be a factor in politics, as demonstrated by the controversy over English as the official language. Religion is a difference that helps explain political behavior both in terms of persons from different religions behaving differently, but also differences between those who are religious and those who are not.

7. Gender is important in American politics. Women have gradually acquired political rights, they now play important roles in our government, and they differ from men in their attitudes on some issues. Sexual orientation is also a distinction increasingly important to politics and policy.

8. While the United States is a land of wealth and is known for its large middle class, not everyone has an adequate share in the American economic success. Poverty has grown over the past decade, and it is most concentrated among African Americans, Native Americans, Hispanics, and single-parent households. Women as a group continue to earn less than men, even in the same occupations. Differences in income and wealth remain important.

9. Age and education are important to understanding American politics. Our aging population poses important challenges to public policy. Because they participate so much more than young voters, older Americans are a potent political force. Education not only opens up economic opportunities in America but also explains many important aspects of political participation.

10. Despite our diversity, Americans share an important unity. We are united by our shared commitment to democratic values, economic opportunity, the work ethic, and the American Dream. Our national experiences like wars, olympic teams, and global economic competition have also unified us.

FURTHER READING

DANIEL BELL, *The Coming of Post-Industrial Society: A Venture in Social Forecasting* (Basic Books, 1973).

DAVID H. BENNETT, *The Party of Fear* (University of North Carolina Press, 1990).

SARAH H. EVANS, *Born for Liberty: A History of Women in America* (Free Press, 1989).

RODOLFO O. DE LA GARZA ET AL., *Latino Voices: Mexican, Puerto Rican, and Cuban Perspectives on American Politics* (Westview Press, 1992).

ANDREW HACKER, *Two Nations: Black and White, Separate, Hostile, Unequal* (Charles Scribners, Sons, 1992).

LOIS LOVELACE DUKE, ED., *Women in Politics: Outsiders or Insiders?* (Prentice Hall, 1993).

SEYMOUR MARTIN LIPSET, *Continental Divide: The Values and Institutions of the United States and Canada* (Routledge, 1990).

SEYMOUR MARTIN LIPSET, *Political Man* (Doubleday, 1963).

NANCY E. MCGLEN AND KAREN O'CONNOR, *Women, Politics, and American Society* (Prentice Hall, 1995).

PETER NABOKOV, ED., *Native American Testimony: A Chronicle of Indian-White Relations from Prophesy to the Present, 1492–1992* (Viking, 1991).

KEVIN PHILLIPS, *The Politics of Rich and Poor: Wealth and the American Electorate in the Reagan Aftermath* (Random House, 1990).

STEVEN J. ROSE, *Social Stratification in the United States: The American Profile Poster Revised and Expanded* (New Press, 1992).

ARTHUR M. SCHLESINGER, JR., *The Disuniting of America* (W.W. Norton, 1992).

PAUL M. SNIDERMAN, *The Scar of Race* (Harvard University Press, 1993).

STUDS TERKEL, *Race: How Blacks & Whites Think and Feel About the American Obsession* (W. W. Norton, 1992).

ALEXIS DE TOCQUEVILLE, *Democracy in America*, ed. J. P. Mayer, trans. George Lawrence (Doubleday and Company, 1969).

KENNETH D. WALD, *Religion and Politics in the United States*, 3rd ed. (Congressional Quarterly Press, 1996).

POLITICAL PARTIES AND INTEREST GROUPS

I magine you are voting in an election for the junior college board of trustees for your area. The board has seven members, all to be determined in the election. The election is to be nonpartisan, each voter having seven votes. All registered voters can run if they pay the $50 filing fee and gather 500 valid signatures on a petition supporting their candidacy; 133 candidates have qualified for the ballot. On what basis would you determine how to cast your votes?

Such an election actually happened in Los Angeles for a community college board in April 1969, and it is a useful case study of what politics is like without political parties, which generally narrow the field of candidates and thereby simplify the voting choice. In this election a second voting cue was absent: incumbency. Because the junior college board of trustees was newly created, none of the candidates were incumbents.

What explained voting behavior in this unusual context? First, ballot order. Candidates were listed alphabetically, and those whose names began with the letters A to F did better than those who came later in the alphabet. Being well known helped. One of the candidates, E. G. ("Jerry") Brown, Jr., was the son of a former governor and benefited from his father's popularity. Political scientist John Mueller found that endorsements by the *Los Angeles Times* influenced the outcome, as did the activity of a conservative campaign group and having a Mexican-American surname.[1]

Rarely are American voters asked to choose from among 133 candidates because political parties facilitate voting by organizing elections and simplifying choices. E. E. Schattschneider, a noted political scientist, once said, "The political parties created democracy, and modern democracy is unthinkable save in terms of the parties."[2] This provocative statement is true.

Political parties have sometimes been called **factions**—groups organized around common interests. One of the important roles of political parties is to build coalitions among interests or factions. We all have many interests, and our interests are often affected by government.

This chapter begins by examining the purposes parties serve that make them so vital to the functioning of democracy. We then examine the evolution of political parties in our democratic experience. Later in the chapter we explore the range of interest groups, their activities, and the challenges they pose for democracy. We also examine the strength of parties today and the prospects for party reform and renewal.

WHAT PARTIES DO FOR DEMOCRACY

The view that parties are essential to democracy runs counter to the long-standing and deep-seated American distrust of parties. Yet few of us would prefer a democracy in which we were asked to choose from among 133 candidates for each office on the ballot. To most Americans, parties are a "necessary evil."

Although political parties have changed over time, they remain important in three quite different settings: as institutions, in government, and in the electorate. It is important to understand how parties facilitate government and democracy in all three settings.

Party Functions

Political parties in our democratic system serve a wide variety of political and social functions, some obvious and some not so obvious. In this section we examine some of the most important.

NOMINATE CANDIDATES From the beginning, parties have been the mechanism for choosing candidates for public office. For several decades after the United States was established, party groups in the national and state legislatures served as a caucus for nominating candidates. Then, during the 1830s and 1840s, a system of party conventions was instituted. Delegates, usually chosen directly by party members in towns and cities, chose the party nominees, debated and adopted a platform, and built party spirit. But the convention method was soon criticized for being controlled by the party bosses and their machines.

To involve more voters and reduce the power of the bosses to pick party nominees, states adopted the **direct primary** election in which people vote directly for the party's nominees for office. By 1920, direct primaries were used for at least some offices in almost all states. Today the direct primary is the typical method of picking party candidates. However, primaries vary significantly from state to state. They differ in terms of: (1) who may run in a primary and how one qualifies for the ballot; (2) whether the party organization can or does endorse candidates before the primary; (3) who may vote in a party's primary— that is, whether a voter must register with a party in order to vote; and (4) how many votes are needed for nomination—a plurality, a majority, or some other number determined by party rule or state law. The differences among primaries are not trivial; they have an important impact on the role played by party organization and on the strategy used by competing candidates.[3]

In states with **open primaries**, any voter, regardless of party, can participate in whichever primary he or she chooses. This kind of primary permits **crossover voting**—Republicans and Independents helping to determine who the Democratic nominee will be, for example. Some states use **closed primaries**, in which only persons registered in a party may participate.

A central and distinct feature of the American party system is that party leaders no longer control party nominations. Party officials may participate in the process, as they do in caucuses or even as delegates to national nominating conventions. And doubtless they influence others, but they do not dominate the process. The spread of the direct primary took this important function out of the hands of the party organization.

The campaign of H. Ross Perot in 1992 demonstrated that candidates with sufficient volunteers or resources can get on the ballot without a party; this was a major effort, and by 1996 Perot chose to use his resources to create a new party. Nonparty candidates can do this in most states by circulating petitions that voters sign to place the name of the candidate on the ballot. Should this become a trend for the future, it could lead to a longer ballot and a crowded general election field, something like the situation in the Los Angeles Community College board elections.

ORGANIZE THE COMPETITION One of the most important functions of parties is to organize the competition by choosing the candidates to run under their label. We often take for granted this important simplification of democracy until

Party Functions

1. Recruit and nominate candidates for office.
2. Organize the competition within elections by registering and activating voters and by providing resources to candidates.
3. Simplify the choices facing the electorate.
4. Unify the electorate and moderate conflicts.
5. Translate public preferences into policy.
6. Bridge the separation of powers and foster coordination and cooperation in our system of checks and balances.
7. Provide a loyal opposition to elected officials at the national, state, and local levels.

we think about the alternative of having to do the sorting ourselves, as voters did in the Los Angeles case cited above. Parties do much more than nominate candidates. They register and activate voters. They also provide resources to candidates, including training, campaign funds, research, and expertise. In many states, ballots are organized into party columns, permitting voters to vote for all party candidates in that column, or a **straight ticket**. This type of ballot is called the **party column ballot** or *Indiana ballot*. Other states permit voters to do the same thing by flipping one switch on the voting machine. Even though many voters are **split-ticket** voters—casting votes for candidates in more than one party—the party label of the candidates means something to most voters and is important in their voting decision. Parties simplify the choices for the electorate.

UNIFY THE ELECTORATE Parties also serve to unify the electorate and bring together groups, sections, and ideologies, thus moderating conflicts within the body politic. When the parties failed to bring the sections together in 1860, the very fabric of the nation was torn apart by the vehemence of the North-South rupture over slavery. For more than a century since that break, however, Republicans and Democrats have held domestic conflict within acceptable bounds. Party leaders and candidates for public office appeal to diverse groups and sections if only because these groups represent a large number of votes. Groups such as women, African Americans, and Jews have seen parties as allies in their fight for social justice and equality. Even when parties are intensely divided on controversial social issues—as they have been in recent years on civil rights, the Equal Rights Amendment, affirmative action, and abortion—the conflict has stayed within the limits of tolerance.

TRANSLATE PREFERENCE INTO POLICY Elections make a difference. Winning parties carry out their promises as they translate public preferences into policy. The election of a Republican majority in both houses of Congress in 1994 transformed the agenda of American politics from one dominated by Bill Clinton and the Democrats to the Republican Contract with America. Clinton and the Democrats in Congress were put on the defensive. Clinton had to resort to presidential vetoes, and Democrats in the House had to be the opposition for the first time in forty years. Republicans quickly cut all committee staff by one-third, required members to vote in committee in person and not by proxy, and applied the same laws about discrimination and the workplace to Congress that already applied to all other employers. Committees in both houses began lengthy investigations of the Clinton administration and Bill and Hillary Clinton's handling of the Whitewater investigation.

Parties help organize the machinery of government and influence the men and women they have helped put into office. The president serves as party leader; Congress is organized on party lines; even bureaucrats are supposed to respond to new party leadership. In the states, governors and legislative majorities serve in the same way. Thus parties may help bridge the separation of powers and foster cooperation in our system of constitutional checks and balances.

PROVIDE A LOYAL OPPOSITION Another function of parties is to provide a loyal opposition. Indeed, this role was first played by the Jeffersonians during the Washington administration. After a polite interval following an election, sometimes called the **honeymoon**, the opposition party begins to criticize the party in the White House, especially when the opposition party controls one or both houses of the Congress.[4] Bill Clinton's honeymoon with the Republicans and even some Democrats was rocky as he faced early opposition on permitting gays in the military and had to abandon most of his proposals to stimulate the economy through tax cuts and federal spending. Clinton did get over 80 percent of his bills through Congress in 1993, much better than the 36 percent he got in 1995.

Why Two Parties?

What would a different system look like? Most other democracies in the world have *multiparty systems*. In a typical multiparty system the legislature is the most important branch of the government, and the most important individual in the government (often called the *prime minister* or *premier*) is the leader of one of the major parties in the legislature. Frequently, individual districts elect more than one member of the legislature. Parties run slates of candidates for those positions. The winners are determined by **proportional representation**—the parties receive the proportion of the legislators corresponding to their proportion of the vote. Under such a system an incentive exists for third, fourth, or additional parties to run because they may win some seats. Further, if no party wins a majority of seats in the legislature, as frequently happens in countries such as Italy and Israel, the leading parties must form a coalition in order to govern. Minor parties can gain concessions—cabinet posts or particular policies they want implemented—in return for their participation in a coalition. Major parties need the minor parties in order to form governing coalitions and therefore are willing to bargain. Thus the system favors the existence of minor parties by giving them incentives to persevere. No such incentives exist for minor parties in the United States.

In our system the winner of the most popular votes typically wins the office or, in the case of presidential elections, receives all of a state's electoral votes. This practice is called **winner take all**. In Maine and Nebraska, electoral votes are distributed so that the popular-vote winner in each congressional district receives the electoral vote for that district, and the popular-vote winner statewide receives two additional electoral votes. Because a party does not gain any offices by finishing second, minor parties can rarely overcome the assumption that a vote for them is a wasted vote.[5] Even if a third-party candidate can keep each major party candidate from receiving more than 50 percent (a majority) of the vote, the candidate with the most votes wins (a plurality).

In multiparty systems more parties form on the extremes. This means that voters' views are more accurately reflected, but it also means that the parties that reflect them tend to be more doctrinaire and do not appeal to great masses of people. Minor parties outside the governing coalition of parties have little say in setting government policy. In a two-party system, on the other hand, parties tend to be centrist, appealing to moderate elements but not closely reflecting the views of those with stronger positions.

Another consequence of multiparty systems is that they make governments unstable, as coalitions form and collapse. In addition, the swings in policy when party control changes can be quite dramatic. Two-party systems lead to majority governments, which tend to be stable and centrist. As a result, policy shifts occur more incrementally, except in rare situations.

Minor Parties: Persistence and Frustration

Two-party politics has been the American norm, but **minor parties**—temporary parties that often arise during presidential elections—have also played a role. Minor parties are sometimes persistent and generally composed of ideologues. Minor parties have occasionally been important: the abolitionists, the populists, the prohibitionists, Theodore Roosevelt's Bull Moose party, the Communist party and its ideological offshoots, George Wallace's American Independent party in 1968, John Anderson's National Unity party in 1980, Ross Perot's "United We

---

Straightening Out the Terms

Major parties: Democrats and Republicans, the two parties that win almost all American elections at the national, state, and local levels.

Minor parties: Parties that are often based on a single idea or principle. Many have been around for decades but only win occasionally at the state or local levels. Examples include the Libertarian party, which was on the ballot in all 50 states and the District of Columbia in 1992, the Socialist party, and the Conservative party of New York.

Minor parties often solicit a protest vote against one or both of the major parties. This occurs most often at the presidential level but may also arise occasionally in gubernatorial elections. Examples include Theodore Roosevelt's Bull Moose party in 1912 and George Wallace's American Independent party in 1968.

Independent candidates: It is possible to become a candidate by petition without a political party. It happens occasionally at the state and local level, and in 1992 it happened at the national level when Ross Perot made much of the fact that his United We Stand, America, was not to be considered a party. John Anderson's National Unity party in 1980 is another example of a party organized to promote a candidate.

A minor party currently active on the national scene is the Libertarian party. Founded in 1972, this party wants to turn all, or nearly all, government services over to the private sphere. In compliance with its anti-Big Government platform, the Libertarian party would end the welfare state, do away with all federal taxes, reduce the military to a bare minimum, terminate all foreign commitments (including membership in the United Nations), and abolish all laws legislating morality, such as those dealing with prostitution, drugs, gambling, gay rights, and abortion. (Libertarians are, however, divided on the abortion issue.) In 1980 the party polled more than 1 million votes, but by the late 1980s its strength had slipped, leading some to think that Ronald Reagan had partially stolen some of its support and agenda. In the 1996 elections their presidential candidate was Harry Browne.

Stand, America" in 1992, and Ralph Nader's 1996 candidacy with the Green party, to name but a few. Some parties arise around a single issue like the States Rights party that split with the Democratic party in 1948 over President Harry Truman's civil rights policies.

Minor parties often revolve around a particular political personality. The Bull Moose party of Theodore Roosevelt and George Wallace's American Independent party (AIP) exemplify this type of third party; AIP polled more than 13 million votes and won 46 electoral votes after Wallace broke with the Democratic party over desegregation and conservative social issues. In 1980, John Anderson split from the Republican party, favoring many of its economic stands but taking liberal positions on social issues; he garnered 6.6 percent of the national vote but no electoral votes (see Closer Look box). Had Pat Buchanan decided to run as an independent in 1996, his campaign would have attempted to build on his personal popularity.

Before the primary elections had run their course in 1992, H. Ross Perot, a wealthy Texas businessman, made known his interest in running for president. Perot was initially "interested" yet "not committed" to running; if citizens were successful in getting his name on the ballots of all fifty states, then he would run. Perot demonstrated that you can run for president without any party behind you. Until 1996, his "United We Stand, America" was more a movement than a party, and in any event was his creation. On election day, Perot did not win a single state, but he did secure 19 percent of the popular vote and came in second in Maine and Utah.

In October 1995, Ross Perot formed a new third party, called the Reform party, in time for the 1996 elections. Originally Perot said the Reform party would find its own presidential candidate. A few months later, however, he defeated the only other Reform party candidate, Richard Lamm, for his party's nomination.

Ross Perot's low standing in the polls meant he was excluded from the 1996 presidential debates, and voters and the news media did not give him nearly as much attention in 1996 as they did in 1992. In what Perot called a "weird and inconsequential" meeting, Dole's campaign manager had flown to Texas to ask Perot to withdraw from the race and endorse Dole. Perot refused, and the move only served to embarrass the Dole campaign. Perot accepted $29 million in federal matching funds, much of which he used to buy television time. Despite these expenditures, his vote total dropped by half from 1992, and he again did not win the electoral votes of a single state. Exit polls indicated that roughly half of 1992 Perot voters cast their 1996 ballots for Dole, with the remainder evenly divided between Clinton and Perot. Whether the Reform Party survives as a factor in the years ahead remains to be seen.

AMERICAN PARTIES TODAY

What is the current state of political parties in the United States? It is hard to generalize, and we must make distinctions between party organizations as they operate inside the government and in the electorate. Rather curiously, at the same time that political parties are becoming more significant in Congress and state legislatures, party organizations are becoming less significant in managing and influencing elections. Party leaders no longer make the most crucial decision in national party politics—the choice of the presidential nominee. This choice is made by voters in primary elections and precinct caucuses. At state and local levels, direct primaries are also typically used to determine the party nominees. Parties have also been weakened by the loss of patronage.

Most Americans, although partisans themselves, are largely indifferent about our political parties. If anything, most people are critical toward the main parties. Some see the parties as corrupt institutions, interested in the spoils of politics and

MINOR PARTIES IN AMERICAN POLITICS

Minor parties have succeeded in calling attention to controversial issues by organizing groups such as the antislavery and anti–civil rights movements. They boast, sometimes correctly, that they are champions not of lost causes but of causes yet to be won. But they have never won the presidency or more than a handful of congressional seats. They have never shaped national policy from *inside* the government. And their influence on national policy in general and on the platforms of the two major parties has been limited.

Theodore Roosevelt.

Eugene Debs.

George Wallace.

Year	Party	Candidate	Percent of Vote	Electoral Votes
1832	Anti-Masonic	William Wirt	8	7
1856	American (Know-Nothing)	Millard Fillmore	22	8
1860	Democratic (Secessionist)	J.C. Breckinridge	18	72
1860	Constitutional Union	John Bell	13	39
1892	People's (Populist)	James B. Weaver	9	22
1912	Bull Moose	Theodore Roosevelt	27	88
1912	Socialist	Eugene V. Debs	6	0
1924	Progressive	Robert M. La Follette	17	13
1948	States' Rights	Strom Thurmond	2	39
1948	Progressive	Henry A. Wallace	2	0
1968	American Independent	George C. Wallace	14	46
1980	National Unity	John Anderson	7	0
1992	United We Stand, America	Ross Perot	19	0

primarily concerned with keeping their incumbents in office. At the same time, Americans see the parties as necessary. Most Americans want party labels kept on the ballot, think of themselves as Democrats or Republicans, and typically vote for candidates from their party. They contribute millions of dollars to the two major parties. More individual contributions go to the Republicans than to the Democrats.[6]

Both our two major parties, the Democratic and Republican parties, are moderate in their policies and leadership.[7] Each party usually takes its extremist supporters more or less for granted and seeks out the voters in the middle. However, to win party nominations it is often necessary to appeal to the most ideological party members, and then in the general election, appeal to moderates in both parties. This is why Republican candidates are often more conservative during the nomination campaign than they are during the general election. Similarly, Democratic candidates must appeal to the more liberal members of their party to win the party nomination and then shift their focus to moderates for the general election. Successful party leaders must be group diplomats; to win presidential elections and congressional majorities, they must find a middle ground among sometimes hostile groups so that they can reach agreement on general principles.

The major parties are decentralized, organized around the units of competition—elections in states, cities, or congressional districts. Like the government itself, they have national, state, and local organizations.

Parties as Institutions

Political parties are institutions that seek political power by electing people to office so that their positions and philosophy become public policy. Like Congress, the presidency, and the courts, parties have rules, procedures, and organizational structure, and they help shape policy.

NATIONAL PARTY LEADERSHIP Supreme authority in both major parties is the **national nominating convention**, which meets every four years to nominate candidates for president and vice-president, to ratify the party platform, and to elect officers and adopt rules. Delegates have only four days to accomplish their business, and many key decisions have been made ahead of time. The convention now typically ratifies the presidential aspirant already chosen in the presidential primaries and caucuses.

More directly in charge of the national party is the *national committee*. In the past the national committee gave large states only a little more representation than small ones. Committee members were usually influential in their states but had little national standing, and the committees rarely met. Both parties have made their national committees more representative. Democrats, for instance, enlarged their national committee to make it more responsive to areas that tended to be more populous and more Democratic and to groups that have traditionally supported Democratic candidates. But such changes in both national committees have not necessarily brought stronger leadership.

PARTIES AT THE GRASS ROOTS Party organization at the state and local levels is structured much like that at the national level. Each state has a *state committee*, headed by a state chair. State law determines the composition of the state committees and sets rules regulating them. Members of the state committees are usually elected from local areas, yet party auxiliaries such as the Young Democrats or the Federation of Republican Women are sometimes represented as well. In many states these committees are dominated by governors, senators, or coalitions of local elected business and ethnic leaders. State chairs are normally elected

Haley Barbour, Republican national committee chair.

by the state committees, although approximately one-quarter are chosen at state conventions. When the party controls the governorship, chairs are often agents of the governor, but some can be independent.[8]

Some powerful state parties have developed in recent years. Despite much state-to-state variation, the trend is toward stronger state organizations, but with Republicans typically much better funded.[9] Third, and in some states fourth, parties play a role in elections. New York, for instance, has both a Liberal and a Conservative party in addition to the Democratic and Republican parties. The role these parties play in statewide elections can be important even though they rarely win office.

Below the state committees are *county committees*, which vary tremendously in function and power. The key role of these committees is recruiting candidates for such offices as county commissioner, sheriff, and treasurer; the recruiting job often involves finding a candidate for the office, not deciding among competing contenders. For the party that almost never wins an election, the county committee works just to find someone willing to run. When the job is valued by those seeking it, however, primaries, not the party leaders, usually decide the winner.[10]

Despite this organizational structure, party politics tends to be organized around the candidates. Candidate organizations often supersede the party organization. They have been especially prevalent in campaigns for major offices—the mayor in a large city, a governor, a member of Congress or the U.S. Senate.

Senator Christopher Dodd, Democratic national committee chair.

PARTY PLATFORMS AND PARTY DIFFERENCES The typical **party platform**, the official statement of party policy, is often a vague and ponderous document that hardly anyone reads. Platforms are ambiguous by design, giving voters few substantive reasons to vote *against* their party. This generalization could be overstated. Many voters see their own party as well as the opposition party as standing for something. Thus most business leaders and conservative Christians believe the Republican party best represents their interests, while workers and liberals tend to look to the Democrats as more helpful. The proportion of voters discerning important differences increased sharply during the Reagan years, when parties seemed to become more polarized.[11]

Party platforms in 1996 were largely designed to minimize problems for the candidates in their election campaigns. The Democratic platform, for example, stressed opportunity, responsibility, security, freedom, peace, and community—issues delegates and voters were not likely to oppose—along with the Democrats' commitment to improving education, guaranteeing economic security for families, fighting crime, and strengthening national security. The Republican platform was also intended to reinforce broad areas of political consensus but was more explicit in its discussion of social issues. The GOP platform opposed same-sex marriages, supported California's Proposition 209 to eliminate affirmative action programs in the public sector, and called for the abolition of the Department of Education.

The most contentious issue in the 1996 Republican platform was abortion. Between 1976 and 1992 Republican platforms had endorsed a constitutional amendment making abortion illegal. Pro-choice governors like William Weld of Massachusetts, Pete Wilson of California, and Christine Todd Whitman of New Jersey pressed the party to moderate this language. Bob Dole wanted to meet the concerns of these powerful party moderates, so rather than modify the language of the platform, the Republicans added an appendix to the platform that expressed "tolerance" for differing views on abortion.

Many politicians say platforms rarely help elect anybody, yet platform positions can hurt a presidential candidate. Because the platform-writing process is not always controlled by the nominee, it is possible for presidential candidates to disagree with their own party platform. It has been fashionable to scoff at political party platforms as meaningless and of little consequence in elections. Yet to party

Thinking it Through

It is naive to believe that the removal of parties will negate conflict, self-interest, or ambition. A political system without parties would be a society without the means to deal with disagreements over policies, economics, or social values. Americans expect legislatures to be partisan, to be contentious, and to make the most of partisan opportunities. Divided government may be less efficient, but it clearly has not bothered voters, who routinely have elected legislators from one party and governors or presidents from another. Finally, people with judicial or administrative ambitions understand the role that parties play in appointments, giving them an incentive to get involved in a party. This is not all bad because, as we have seen, it is possible for idealistic individuals to redefine and reshape a party.

activists, especially issue activists, they are seen as very important. Party leaders also take them seriously. One of the best examples of such a party document serving as a road map for party leaders was the 1994 Contract with America, which Republican House leaders initiated and then worked hard to implement after being elected to House and Senate majorities. Platforms also serve to identify the most important values and principles upon which the two parties are based.

Parties in Government

Despite the organizational weakness of political parties, they remain central to the operation of government.

IN CONGRESS   Members of Congress take their partisanship seriously, at least while they are in Washington. Their power and influence are in part determined by whether their party is in control of the House or Senate. They also have a stake in which party controls the White House. The chairs of all standing committees come from the majority party. The presiding officials of both chambers come from the majority party, except when the vice-president is in attendance at the Senate. Members of both houses sit with fellow partisans on the floor and in committee, leading to the expression often heard in floor debate, "the other side of the aisle."

Members of the congressional staff are also partisan. From the volunteer intern to the senior staffer, members of Congress expect their staff to be loyal first to them and then to their party. Should you decide to work for a representative or senator, you would be expected to identify yourself with that person's party and would have some difficulty working for persons from the other party later. Patronage still prevails for the employees of the House and Senate. With few exceptions, congressional jobs, from elevator operators to the Capitol Hill police and even including the chaplain, go to persons from the party that has a majority in the House or the Senate.

IN THE EXECUTIVE BRANCH   The presidency is no less partisan. Senior White House aides are almost always from the president's party. Presidents often surround themselves with advisers and political appointees at the cabinet and subcabinet levels who have campaigned with them and proven their loyalty.[12] Sometimes it is not enough to have been a good partisan; you must also be acceptable to a particular wing of the party. Conservative Republicans in the Reagan and Bush administrations attempted to influence political appointments in an ideological as well as partisan direction.

IN THE JUDICIAL BRANCH   The judicial branch of the national government, with its lifetime tenure and political independence, operates in an expressly nonpartisan manner (see Chapter 12). Judges, unlike Congress, do not sit together by political party. But the appointment process for judges has been partisan from the beginning, and party affiliation remains an important consideration in the naming of federal judges today.[13]

AT THE STATE AND LOCAL LEVELS   The importance of party to the operation of government varies somewhat among states and is even more divergent at the local level. In some states and cities, partisanship remains important; in others, like Nebraska, the state legislature is expressly nonpartisan. But for most states and many cities, the same generalizations about the importance of party to the operation of the legislature and governor or mayor apply. Judicial selection in most states is a partisan matter.

We The People

Portrait of the Electorate

	Republican		Democratic		Independent	
	1992	**1994**	**1992**	**1994**	**1992**	**1994**
Sex						
Male	42%	35	45%	31	13	34
Female	34	31	54	42	11	28
Race						
White	42	36	46	33	12	31
Black	8	6	79	65	13	30
Hispanic	27	*	61	*	11	*
Age						
18–24	36	32	46	32	17	36
25–34	40	34	46	33	14	33
35–44	38	35	51	33	11	32
45–54	40	31	50	33	11	36
55–64	36	29	54	42	10	29
65+	39	31	53	47	8	22
Income						
Less than $10,000	28	14	56	51	16	35
$10,000–$19,999	30	25	59	47	11	28
$20,000–$29,999	30	31	56	40	14	29
$30,000–$39,999	42	37	48	35	10	28
$40,000–$59,999	45	40	47	28	8	32
$60,000+	54	44	37	22	10	35
Religion						
Jewish	9	11	86	53	5	37
Catholic	33	24	55	43	11	33
Protestant	44	41	45	35	11	24
Ideology						
Liberal	14	20	77	63	9	17
Moderate/Don't Know	31	21	53	54	16	25
Conservative	65	30	28	61	7	9
Region						
Northeast	32	24	55	37	13	39
Midwest	43	33	45	33	12	34
South	34	31	53	39	13	29
West	44	41	49	36	8	23
Total	38	46	50	44	12	10

SOURCE: Center for Political Studies, University of Michigan, 1992 and 1994 American National Election Studies.

Note: We have classified Independents who lean toward a party with that party.

*Indicates that the number is too small for an accurate breakdown by party for that category.

In short, political parties are important to the operation of American government. They play an important role in filling senior executive branch and judicial positions. They organize the legislature. And for the party of the president or governor, they provide a bridge that spans the separation of powers between the executive branch and legislative branches.

Parties in the Electorate

Political parties would be of little significance if they did not have meaning to the electorate. Despite the fact that parties have little to say about who runs under their label, parties remain important. Parties organize the competition, simplify the voting choices, and provide a link between the people and their government.

HOW THE PARTIES DIFFER   Democrats, as a rule, are ideologically more diverse than Republicans. The two major parties accommodate all kinds of people who take all kinds of views. There are conservative Democrats and liberal Republicans; there are rich Democrats and poor Republicans; there are African Americans, Jews, and Catholics who are Democrats; and there are African Americans, Jews, and Catholics who are Republicans. That is why Democrats and Republicans are major parties. Nevertheless, there is a group dynamic to partisan choice, and party labels do have content. Democratic leaders are more liberal than Republicans. Democrats are more likely to be pro-government in the sense that they believe government can and should have a role in civil rights, social programs, and economic fairness. Increasingly, southern conservatives like Alabama's Richard Shelby and South Carolina's Strom Thurman are finding their home in the Republican party; a most apt example is Texas senator and 1996 presidential candidate Phil Gramm, who switched from the Democratic party to the Republican party. This movement of white southern Democrats into the Republican party is one of the largest shifts in allegiance of any demographic group since African Americans left the Republican party for the Democrats during the Great Depression and New Deal in 1932 and 1936.

Adherents of the two parties are drawn to them by a combination of factors: stands on particular issues; personal or party histories; religious, racial, or social peer groupings; attraction of candidates. The emphases among these factors change over time, but they are remarkably consistent with those identified by political scientists more than 35 years ago.[14]

Party activists fall into three broad categories: party regulars, candidate activists, and issue activists. Party regulars value the party first. They value winning elections and understand that compromise and moderation are often important to that objective. They also realize that in our system it is important to keep the party together as much as possible, because a fractured party only helps the opposition.

Candidate activists are followers of a particular candidate who see the party as the means to place their candidate in power. Politicians often generate followings, and these persons correctly see the political party as the means to achieve their electoral objective. Candidate activists are often not concerned with the other operations of the party—with nominees for other offices, for example, or with raising money for the party.

Issue activists see politics from a focused perspective. They wish to push their party in a particular direction on a single issue or narrow range of issues like abortion, taxes, school prayer, the environment, or civil rights. To issue activists, the party platform is an important battleground because they seek the party endorsement for their position. Issue activists are also often candidate activists if they can find a candidate willing to embrace their position.

PARTY REGISTRATION   For citizens in many states, "party" has a particular legal meaning—**party registration**. In these states at the time voters register to vote they are asked to state their party preference; thus they become registered Democrats, Republicans, Libertarians, and so on. Voters can subsequently change their party registration. Why do some states have party registration? One reason is to limit the participants in primary elections to persons from that party; such elections are called *closed primaries.* Hence, in states like New York, only registered Republicans can vote in the Republican primary. States that have *open primaries* generally do not have party registration; they permit voters to choose which party primary they wish to vote in on election day. Closed primaries tend to help more ideological candidates who want the party "to stand for something."

Political parties work to register workers before election, and then get them out to vote on election day.

In 1996 California voters approved an initiative (Proposition 198) establishing an open primary system patterned after those in Washington and Alaska. Under the new system all candidates from all parties are randomly listed by office, and voters have one vote per office. Proponents of the change contend it will benefit moderates in both parties and give Independents a say in who the nominees will be in the general election. Opponents fear that some voters will vote for the weakest candidate in the other party as a way of helping their own party.

Party Identification

Party activists include a diverse group of people who come to the political party with different objectives. It is not surprising, then, that some of the most interesting politics you will observe are over candidate selection and issue positions within the political parties. These fights over strategy and party position are conducted in open meetings and under democratic procedures. Political parties foster democracy not only by competition between the parties but through competition within the parties as well.

The vast majority of Americans are mere spectators to this kind of party activity. They lack the partisan commitment and interest needed for this level of involvement. This is not to say parties are irrelevant or unimportant to Americans. Partisanship is what political scientists call **party identification**—the subjective affiliation with a political party that most people acquire in childhood.[15] In many ways it is a standing preference for one party over another. Yet in particular contests for president, governor, or some other office, the voter will not vote for a candidate from the other party. But in the absence of a compelling reason to do otherwise, most Americans vote their party identification.

Party identification is the single best predictor of the vote. Unlike candidates and issues, which come and go, party identification is a long-term element in voting choice. The strength of party identification is also important in predicting participation and political interest. Strong Republicans and Strong Democrats participate more actively in politics than any other groups and are generally more knowledgeable and informed. Pure Independents, on the other hand, are just the opposite: They vote at the lowest rates and have the lowest levels of interest and awareness of any of the categories of party identification. This evidence runs counter to the notion that people who are strong partisans are unthinking party adherents.[16]

Party identification is something generally acquired in childhood from parents and often reinforced by peers and early political experiences. It is part of the political socialization process described in Chapter 5. To say that most persons have the same partisan preferences as their parents is not to say that some individuals do not form their own identification with a party. In either case, once established, party identification is more stable than attitudes on issues or support for well-known candidates. To define party identification as a stable, long-term force in voting is not to say that there cannot be change in the underlying support for the parties or a major realignment.

The current system of party identification is built on a foundation of the New Deal and the critical election of 1932, events that took place more than sixty years ago. How can events so removed from the present still be important in shaping our party system? As Table 7-1 on page 198 demonstrates, the partisan identification has been quite stable for the past forty years. Although new voters have been added to the electorate—blacks and 18- to 21-year-olds—the basic character of the party system has not changed dramatically. While people may not be changing their underlying party preference, they seem willing to vote for

PARTY IDENTIFICATION

Party identification is measured by the answers to the following question:

> Generally speaking, in politics do you usually think of yourself as a Republican, a Democrat, an Independent, or what?

Persons who answer Republican or Democrat to this question are then asked:

> Would you call yourself a strong or a not very strong Republican/Democrat?

Persons who answered Independent to the first question are asked this follow-up question:

> Do you think of yourself as closer to the Republican or the Democratic party?

The party identification question thus produces seven categories of persons: Strong Democrats, Weak Democrats, Independent-leaning Democrats, Pure Independents, Independent-leaning Republicans, Weak Republicans, and Strong Republicans. Over the 40-year period during which political scientists have been asking these questions, the partisan preferences of the American public have been remarkably stable. The following table presents the party identification breakdown for the period from 1952 to 1994.

Party Identification, 1952–1994

	Strong Democrat	Weak Democrat	Independent-leaning Democrat	Pure Independent	Independent-leaning Republican	Weak Republican	Strong Republican	Apolitical
1952	22%	25%	10%	6%	7%	14%	14%	3%
1956	21	23	6	9	8	14	15	4
1958	27	22	7	7	5	17	11	4
1960	20	25	6	10	7	14	16	3
1962	23	23	7	8	6	16	12	4
1964	27	25	9	8	6	14	11	1
1966	18	28	9	12	7	15	10	1
1968	20	25	10	11	9	15	10	1
1970	20	24	10	13	8	15	9	1
1972	15	26	11	13	11	13	10	1
1974	18	21	13	15	9	14	8	3
1976	15	25	12	15	10	14	9	1
1978	15	24	14	14	10	14	8	2
1980	18	23	11	13	10	14	9	3
1982	20	24	11	11	8	14	10	2
1984	17	20	11	11	12	15	12	2
1986	18	22	10	12	11	15	11	2
1988	18	18	12	11	13	14	14	2
1990	17	19	12	11	13	17	11	2
1992	18	18	14	11	12	14	11	1
1994	15	19	13	10	12	14	16	0

SOURCE: Center for Political Studies, University of Michigan, 1952–1992 cumulative data file and 1994 American National Election Studies.

Public Confidence in the Parties

I'm going to read a few phrases about the political parties. For each, tell me whether you think the phrase better describes the Republican Party or the Democratic Party.

	Republican	Democratic
Well organized	55%	25%
Able to manage the federal government well	52	30
Can bring about the kinds of changes this country needs	46	39
Cares about the middle class	36	55
In touch with what most Americans think	37	49
Cares about people like you	35	51

Which political party, the Democrats or the Republicans, do you trust to do a better job on...

	Republican	Democratic
Handling the nation's economy	43%	38%
Handling the crime problem	34	36
Handling foreign affairs	45	36
Improving education and schools	30	45
Maintaining a strong national defense	53	31
Helping the middle class	33	48
Holding taxes down	42	37
Helping the poor	22	58
Providing affordable health care	29	46
Encouraging high moral standards and values	41	31
Creating jobs	36	43
Reducing the federal budget deficit	38	36
Making American industry competitive with Japan and other countries	45	30
Keeping the United States out of war	37	38

Do you think political parties make democracy work better in this country?

Yes, better	49%
No, not better	45
No opinion	6

SOURCES: *Washington Post* Poll, October 27–30, 1995, of 839 adults nationwide; ABC News/*Washington Post* Poll, October 20–23, 1994, of 1,011 adults nationwide; CNN/*USA Today* Poll, October 22–25, 1994, of 1,007 adults nationwide.

Percentages do not equal 100 because responses like "Both equally," "Neither" or "Don't know" were omitted.

"Very Republican. I love it."
Drawing by Tobey. © 1986
The New Yorker Magazine, Inc.

How to Tell 'em Apart

- Republicans usually wear hats. Democrats usually don't.
- Democrats buy banned books. Republicans form censorship committees and read them.
- Democrats eat the fish they catch. Republicans hang them on the wall.
- Republicans study the financial pages of the newspaper. Democrats put them on the bottom of the bird cage.
- On Saturday, Republicans head for the golf course, the yacht club, or the hunting lodge. Democrats get a haircut, wash the car, or go bowling.
- Republicans have guest rooms. Democrats have spare rooms filled with old baby furniture.
- Republicans hire exterminators. Democrats step on the bugs.
- Republicans sleep in twin beds—some even in separate rooms. That is why there are more Democrats.

SOURCE: Adapted from the National Republican Congressional Committee newsletter.

TABLE 7-1

Voting Behavior of Partisans and Independents, 1990-1994

	Percent of Democratic Vote		
	U.S. House (1990)	President (1992)	U.S. House (1994)
Strong Democrats	90%	93%	88%
Weak Democrats	79	68	73
Independent-leaning Democrats	79	70	68
Pure Independents	61	41	55
Independent-leaning Republicans	32	11	25
Weak Republicans	39	14	21
Strong Republicans	17	3	7

SOURCE: Center for Political Studies, University of Michigan, 1990, 1992, 1994 American National Election Studies.

candidates from the other party. Democrats have supported Republicans, and persons from both parties defected to vote for Ross Perot in 1992. The dramatic victory of the Republicans in 1994 may be the harbinger of a deeper and more lasting party shift. Following 1994, the Republicans could lay claim to being a dominant party, controlling both houses of Congress, thirty governorships including states like New York, California, and Texas, and having made major strides in state legislatures.

Bill Clinton's substantial 1996 victory defeated Republican claims that their 1994 victories were a harbinger of a long-term Republican trend. However, Clinton's coattails were ineffective, and the Republicans retained control of both congressional chambers, giving some credence to Republican claims that the .country has moved to the right. Neither party can make a claim for a strong mandate from the voters. Clearly, the electorate has no qualms about divided government; in fact, they may even prefer it. Theories of realignment often assume important differences between the parties on major issues. Clinton's move to the center muted issue differences in 1996, as did his claiming credit for a strong economy. The voters' choice of divided government also means a realignment has not yet happened.

Another variant of the realignment debate is the **dealignment** argument, which contends that instead of people changing from one party to another or new voters joining one party in large numbers, what we have experienced is a rejection of the parties and a move toward Independent status. There has been an increase in numbers of persons who characterize themselves as Independents. One noted observer, Hedrick Smith, expresses a widespread view when he says, "The most important phenomenon of American politics in the past quarter century has been the rise of independent voters who have at times outnumbered Republicans."[17]

The dealignment argument would be more persuasive were it not for the fact that two-thirds of all Independents are really partisans in their voting behavior and attitudes. One-third of the people who claim to be Independents actually lean toward the Democratic party and vote Democratic election after election; another one-third of Independents lean toward the Republican party and vote just as predictably Republican. The remaining one-third appear to be genuine

Independents who are without partisan preferences and do not vote predictably for one party or another. As it turns out, these are individuals with little interest in politics; they are the least likely to vote of any category of party identification.[18] There are, in short, at least three types of Independents, and most of them are predictably partisan.

Political parties, as we have seen, have enjoyed something of a resurgence in organization and activity during the past decade. Moreover, the claim that Americans do not consider partisanship when voting is largely false, and the reported growing role of Independents is a myth. Parties remain important in government. They are in all these respects vital to democracy.

INTEREST GROUPS AND SOCIAL MOVEMENTS

One of the challenges of democracy is to assimilate the large number of interest groups and social movements that arise. We turn to the topic of interest groups and social movements.

The Mischiefs of Faction

What we call **interest groups** today—groups based on ethnic, religious, economic, sectional, and ideological differences—James Madison called **factions**. Madison also thought of political parties as factions. Madison included groups based on ethnic, religious, economic, sectional, and ideological differences. Interest groups today continue to reflect these differences but also include such disparate groups as the League of Women Voters, the Sierra Club, and the National Organization for Women. For Madison and the other framers of the Constitution, the daunting problem was how to establish a stable and orderly constitutional system that at the same time would respect the liberty of free citizens. Madison warned of the tendency of popular government toward the "vice" of faction, toward "instability, injustice, and confusion." Still, he would not sacrifice the liberty that led to the formation of factions. How could this dilemma be resolved?

Madison, a good practical politician and a brilliant theorist, offered both a diagnosis and a solution. The solution had already taken concrete form in the new Constitution that Madison firmly believed would control the effects of factionalism; Madison summarized this solution in *The Federalist*, No. 10 (reprinted in the Appendix).

The genius of *The Federalist*, No. 10, lies in the manner in which Madison describes the factions of the day. He begins with a fundamental proposition: "The latent causes of faction are thus sown in the nature of man." Madison does not take a simplistic approach to faction: Factions are not merely religious, economic, or political, but a combination of these; and factions can be divided into subfactions. Thus property owners can be divided into landed, manufacturing, mercantile, and moneyed subfactions. Madison demonstrated that Americans lived in a maze of group interests. Yet he went on to argue that the "most common and durable source of factions, has been the various and unequal distribution of property."

One of the enduring features of democracy is the interplay of interests. Freedom and democracy seem to go hand in hand, with individuals acting on their perceived interests. Concern about what to do to limit the tendency of self-interested persons to seek more and more social and economic power is also enduring. From the founding of our Republic to our own time, students of government have debated how to limit zealous interests without damaging essential freedom.

Different from interest groups—but often shading into them—are movements. A **movement** is a large body of people who are interested in a common

Groups: Straightening Out the Terms

Categories: People with certain characteristics in common: country music lovers, 16-year-olds, women, blacks, the aged.

Groups: People who share common goals and who interact with one another: union leaders, your family, the senior class of your college.

Interest groups: People who share common goals, interact with one another, and are organized to press claims on government, veterans, soybean growers, bankers.

Associations: Formal organizations created by interest groups: the National Association for the Advancement of Colored People (NAACP), National Organization for Women (NOW), American Federation of Labor and Congress of Industrial Organizations (AFL-CIO), National Rifle Association (NRA).

Political action committees (PACs): The political arms of interest groups, which are legally entitled to raise and spend campaign contributions.

Movements: People united but loosely organized around a central idea whose goal is to change attitudes or institutions, not just policy: the civil rights movement, women's movement, antiabortion movement.

Factions: A term used by James Madison and other founders of this country to refer to political parties as well as what we now call interests or interest groups.

Some Movements in the United States

- Abolitionist
- Suffragist
- Temperance
- Single tax
- Populist
- Civil rights
- Anti-Vietnam War
- Gay rights
- Moral Majority
- Nuclear freeze
- Animal rights
- Term Limits

issue, idea, or concern that is of continuing significance and who are willing to take action on that issue. Examples of movements include civil rights, environmental, antitax, the so-called Militia groups, and women's rights. Each of these movements represented or represents groups who felt "left out" of government. They often arise at the grass-roots level and evolve into national groups. Movements tend to see their causes as morally right and the positions of the opposition as morally wrong. To illustrate the dynamics of movements we will briefly examine the women's movement.

The Women's Movement

American women in the 1770s, like their sisters in Western Europe, were dependents of fathers and husbands. Women could not make legal arrangements or contracts, earn wages separate from those of their husbands, or vote. By marrying, they forfeited to their husbands legal custody of themselves as well as custody of all property and children.[19] Lacking the right to vote, women could not turn to electoral politics to overcome discrimination. Rather, they "determined to ferment a rebellion," in Abigail Adams's words, for "we would not hold ourselves bound by any laws in which we have no voice or representation."[20] Formal education for women was restricted to female academies in which daughters of the wealthy were taught social graces and other "female arts." Women began to gain a sense of group consciousness when they worked so their husbands could fight in the Revolutionary War and the War of 1812 and when they worked in New England textile mills.[21]

The women's movement grew in response to this sense of powerlessness, as well as in response to social problems of concern to women, such as illiteracy, slavery, and liquor. An 1848 convention in Seneca Falls, New York, called for equal rights in marriage, property, contracts, trades, professions, and universities; the convention also called for the adoption of female suffrage. The right to vote was gradually extended to women and was finally included in the Constitution with the passage of the Nineteenth Amendment in 1920. (See the We The People box on pages 202–203 showing women's role in history.)

Women in the United States have been involved in a long struggle for their rights, from the time of the suffragettes who campaigned for the right to vote to rallies and marches in recent years for the Equal Rights Amendment.

Having achieved the vote, the women's movement shifted its attention to other issues, like child welfare, voter education, prison reform, anti-lynching measures, and peace. One continuing issue of importance has been women's rights. But the women's movement, like all movements, has competing concerns and interests. Should it focus on women's rights only or on the needs of other disadvantaged groups like African Americans, children, and low-paid workers? Which right should be most aggressively pursued: the right to an education, to legal protection, to equal pay, to a decent job? The answer is that the women's movement is not just one movement but several movements that share some, but not all, concerns. Those who see themselves as part of the movement sometimes disagree on tactics even though they may agree on goals.

One of the most important women's issues in the 1970s and 1980s was the Equal Rights Amendment. This proposed amendment sought to guarantee "equality of rights under the law" regardless of gender. While most women's groups, most women, and the Democratic party remain committed to the ERA, despite its failure to become part of the Constitution, the amendment has not been the driving concern it once was. In its place have come issues like abortion, affirmative action for women, and the changing of particular laws that discriminate against women.

Abortion has been seen as a women's issue because it is women, more than men, whose bodies and lives are affected. As Justice Harry A. Blackmun said in *Roe v Wade*, "Freedom of personal choice in matters of marriage and family life is one of the liberties protected by the due process clause of the Fourteenth Amendment. . . . That right necessarily includes the right of a woman to decide whether or not to terminate her pregnancy."[22] But both women and men are divided on the issue of abortion, and there are women's groups on both sides of the issue.

The story of women's movements in the United States is the story of groups whose members originally lacked political power, developed a sense of group consciousness, entered politics despite countless frustrations and setbacks, and, after long struggles, achieved some of their major political goals. The story continues, as the movement still faces important unresolved issues.

The abortion issue has brought out emotionally charged protests in front of clinics and in the nation's capital. In some instances the protests turned violent, even resulting in deaths.

Movements and Democracy

New movements constantly form as people discover new needs and the old ones become satisfied. A movement that has recently become increasingly vocal and militant, for example, is the animal rights movement. In 1996 a movement stimulated by the leadership and funds of Ross Perot became a political party. Although it has many "movement qualities," like members who feel deeply that they have been wronged and for whom being right is as important as being successful, it entered national politics as a party.

In the future, will our more than 200-year-old constitutional democracy be able to cope with a tide of larger, more activist political and social movements, each proclaiming some essential cause? Or will the movements engulf and endanger our slow-moving, often deadlocked governmental system? Social movements polarize opinion, but they also persuade many people to change their attitudes and raise public consciousness about social issues that government might otherwise ignore.[23] In many countries movements are viewed as a threat to the existing government, as indeed they may be, as the governments of South Africa, China, and others have learned.

To a marked degree, our Constitution continues to protect the liberties and independence of political movements. The Bills of Rights guarantees movements—whether popular or unpopular—free assembly, free speech, and due process. Hence

We The People

Women's History Is Half of History

Timeline 1840–1860

		Sewing machine invented	Women's Rights Convention		Clara Barton, Mother Bickerdyke, nurses
Lucretia Mott, Elizabeth Cady Stanton barred from this convention	Declaration of Sentiments, Seneca Falls	Harriet Beecher Stowe, *Uncle Tom's Cabin*	Sojourner Truth	Women's Loyal League	Harriet Tubman leads rai...

1840 ——————————————— **1860**

World Antislavery Convention	Irish imigration begins			*Dred Scott* decision	Lincoln elected	Emancipation Proclamation
	Texas admitted to the Union			Harper's Ferry	Fort Sumter	

Timeline (1900)

			Women's Trade Union League	Brandeis brief, protective legislation	
International Council of Women	Ladies' Home Journal	Jane Addams, Hull House			
General Federation of Women's Clubs	National American Women Suffrage Association	Susan B. Anthony	Florence Kelley. reformer	Charlotte Perkins Gilman, Women and Economics	Comstock laws	National Woman's Party

1900

	Samuel Gompers, American Federation of Labor	Immigration from Southern Europe		Progressive Era	Panama canal begun	
		Populists	Battle of Wounded Knee	Theodore Roosevelt		Woodrow Wilson

Timeline 1940–1960

	WACS, WAVES, WASPS. women's service corps			Dr. Spock			Title VII prohibits sex discrimination in employment	Executive Order mandates affirmative action
Rosie the Riveter		800,000 women fired by aircraft companies	Suburbia		Mary McCarthy, *The Group*	Betty Friedan, *The Feminine Mystique*		The "Pill

1940 ——————————————— **1960**

Pearl Harbor	Atomic bomb	Television			The New Frontier	Kennedy assassinated	The Great Society	Vietnam
	World War II ends		Korea	Eisenhower	March on Washington, Martin Luther King Jr.	Civil Rights Act		Peace moveme...

Timeline (Reagan era)

	ERA deadline passed without ratification	Geraldine Ferraro, first woman nominated as vice-presidential candidate of a major political party (the Democratic party)	State of Washington adopts comparable worth for some State employees	Congress reverses impact of *Grove* decision that had limited federal civil rights laws	
Sandra Day O'Connor, first woman Supreme Court justice appointed	ERA reintroduced in Congress				Sup... restrict...

Reagan			*Challenger* explodes	Reagan-Gorbachev talks, INF Treaty	Bush

"Battle Hymn of the Republic," Julia Ward Howe

Equal Rights Association

Frances Willard Woman's Christian Temperance Union

Clara Barton, Red Cross

Evaporated milk available

Radcliffe, Bryn Mawr founded

Mother Mary Jones, labor organizer

Emily Dickinson

1880

...ee surrenders to Grant

14th Amendment makes blacks citizens and adds the word "male" to the Constitution

15th Amendment (provides for black male suffrage)

Reconstruction

Custer, Little Big Horn

Civil service reform

Transcontinental railroad completed

Women's Joint Congressional Committee National Council of Defense

...ffragists jailed ...r White House ...emonstration

Women get the vote

League of Women Voters

Alice Paul introduces Equal Rights Amendment (ERA)

Margaret Mead, *Coming of Age in Samoa*

The flapper

Frances Perkins, secretary of labor

Frozen foods introduced

Claire Booth Luce, *The Women*

1920

U.S. enters World War I

Treaty of Versailles

19th Amendment (Women's Suffrage) ratified

Prohibition

Herbert Hoover

Stock market crash

Depression

FDR, New Deal

Eleanor Roosevelt

National ...rganization ...or Women (NOW)

Gloria Steinem, *Ms. Magazine*

National Women's Strike

ERA passed by Congress

Title IX prohibits sex discrimination in education

International Women's Year

Supreme Court legalizes abortion in *Roe v Wade*

Women's Educational Equity Act passed

Episcopalians ordain women

National Women's Conference, Houston

ERA ratification deadline extended

Nancy Kissebaum elected to Senate

1980

...ent ...est

Resurrection City

Cambodia

Watergate

Carter

Nixon

Moon landing

...e Court ...oe v Wade

Clarence Thomas Supreme Court confirmation hearings

54 women elected members of Congress in "The Year of the Woman"

Supreme Court reaffirms core holding of *Roe v Wade*

Ruth Bader Ginsburg appointed to the Supreme Court

1992

Middle - East Peace talks

1993

What's So Special About "Special Interests"?

When social scientists call something an "interest group" or a "special interest," they are not calling it names. These are analytic terms to describe a group that speaks for some but not all of us. Much of our politics focuses on what is in the national interest. The democratic process exists to decide upon those national interests. If it were possible to know the national interest without the give and take of politics, we could, as Plato argued, put the philosophers in charge, since presumably they would know. Interest groups are important because they help sort out the needs and priorities of the moment.

Interest groups are sometimes called "special interests." Presidents and presidential candidates often use this term to describe those interest groups that disagree with them and do not support their programs. But what makes an ordinary interest group a "special" one? The answer is highly subjective. One person's special interest is another's national interest. Special interests often claim to be "public interests." Even so-called "public interest groups" like Common Cause or the Center for Responsive Politics, which presume to speak for the entire public, are also special interests.

In a democracy there are many interests and many organized interest groups. Part of the politics of interest groups is to persuade the public that your group's interest is better, broader, more beneficial, and more general, and at the same time to label groups that oppose yours as "special interests." For this reason we choose to use the neutral term "interest groups" in the textbook discussion. The definition of "special interest" can be highly subjective: "The specialness of an interest lies in the eye of the beholder."*

*Paul E. Peterson, "The Rise and Fall of Special Interests," *Political Science Quarterly* 105 (1990-1991), p. 540

militant groups do not have to engage in terrorism or other violent activities in the United States, as they do in some countries, and they need not fear persecution for demonstrating. In a democratic system that restricts the power of those in authority, social movements have considerable room to operate *inside* the constitutional system.

A NATION OF INTERESTS

In the late eighteenth century, James Madison was concerned about religious, political, and economic "factions." What are the key interest groups and issues today? What are the sources of the groups' strengths and weaknesses? How do these interests seek to influence government? Are they as dangerous to the public interest now as Madison feared they were in his time? If so, what has been done about it, and what else may be done?

The United States has been described as a nation of joiners. Europeans sometimes make fun of us for setting up all sorts of organizations, and we ourselves are often amused by the behavior of our groups—the noisy conventions of veterans' associations, the solemn rites of great fraternal organizations, and the oratory of patriotic societies. Yet most of these groups have serious goals and play an important role in politics.

Some scholars have recently questioned the extent to which Americans engage in groups and build up *social capital*—features of social organization that foster social interaction.[24] Robert Putnam theorizes that the decline in membership in organizations in America negatively influences democracy. As an illustration, Putnam points out that more and more Americans are bowling alone. The significance of this observation lies in the "social interaction and even occasionally civic conversations over beer and pizza that solo bowlers forgo."[25]

Interest groups vary widely from business organizations to public interest groups. Some are formal associations or organizations; others have no formal organization at all. Some are organized primarily to lobby; some have other goals, such as securing wage increases, conducting research, or broadly influencing public opinion by publishing reports and mass mailings.

Interest groups can be categorized into several broad types: (1) economic, including both business and labor; (2) social and ideological; (3) public interest; (4) government itself; and (5) other. Obviously these categories are not mutually exclusive; some business groups are also ideological and economic. The variety and overlapping nature of interest groups in the United States has been called *interest group pluralism*, meaning that competition among open, responsive, and

Movements in support of religious freedom have appeared frequently in this country. Here members of the Hare Krishna religion demonstrate against a court order to sell six of their temples.

diverse groups helps preserve democratic values and limits the concentration of power in any single group.

Economic Interest Groups

Madison pointed out that some of the most common and durable factions derive from property interests, or how we make our living and manage what we own. There are thousands, even tens of thousands, of economic interests—agriculture, skilled laborers, plumbers, northern businesses, southern businesses, labor unions, the airplane industry, landlords, developers, bondholders, savings and loan investors, and so on.

BUSINESS The most familiar business institution is probably the large corporation. Corporations range from small, one-person enterprises to large, multinational entities. Large corporations—General Motors, AT&T, and Fortune 500 companies—exercise considerable political influence, as do hundreds of smaller corporations.

In the last century, both the national and state governments began to regulate business practices. Antitrust legislation was adopted to limit monopolies; labor laws were enacted to protect workers. The 1980s brought the need to regulate business and financial institutions back to the forefront as a result of leveraged buyouts and savings and loan scandals. In the 1990s, questions about such corporate practices as work force reductions ("downsizing"), government subsidies for big business ("corporate welfare"), and disproportionately high salaries for top management became political issues. As we move into the next century, the implications of a changing domestic and global economy will keep corporations and their practices important issues.

TRADE AND OTHER ASSOCIATIONS Trade associations bring together businesses with similar interests. They are as diverse as the products and services they provide. In addition, businesses of all types are organized into large, nationwide business associations such as the Conference Board, the Business Roundtable, the Business Higher-Education Forum, and the Chamber of Commerce.

LABOR The American work force is the least unionized of almost any industrial democracy, but many employees belong to some kind of job-related association. These workers' associations have a range of interests, from professional standards to wages and working conditions. Labor unions are one of the most important groups representing workers.

Probably the oldest "unions" in the United States were farm organizations. Other workers, too, have long been organized. Throughout the nineteenth century, workers organized political parties and local unions. Their most ambitious effort at national organization, the Knights of Labor, claimed 700,000 members. By the beginning of this century, the American Federation of Labor (AFL), a confederation of strong and independent-minded national unions mainly representing craftsworkers, was the dominant organization. During the ferment of the 1930s, unions more responsive to workers organized by industry, broke away from the AFL, which was seen as more responsive to workers organized by trade, and formed a rival national organization organized by industry, the Congress of Industrial Organizations (CIO). Later the AFL and CIO reunited in the organization that exists today.

Some industrial union leaders contend that the AFL-CIO has become too conservative, and that this political "machine" has sputtered and faltered. Because the AFL-CIO is a federation of powerful and independent national unions, state

---

We The People

Some Facts About Interest Groups

In the United States there are
- 68,490,000 families (1994)
- 77 religions with at least 50,000 adherents (1995)
- 257,648 religious congregations (1991)
- 4,016 political action committees (1995)
- 3,869,000 corporations (1992)
- 16,740,300 labor union members (1994)

In Washington, D.C., there are approximately
- 15,000 individual representatives of groups working to influence government policies
- 5,000 representatives of 2,200 trade and professional associations and labor unions
- 1,500 representatives of individual corporations
- 2,500 advocates for public interest groups, representing interests from the environment to abortion to gun control
- 3,000 lawyers registered as lobbyists or who represent clients before the government
- 2,500 public and government relations consultants and professional managers of interest groups
- 200 officers of political parties or political action committees
- 300 advocates for policy think tanks
- 30 religious lobbies
- 40 groups dedicated to preserving Alaska's environment

SOURCES: U.S. Bureau of the Census, *Statistical Abstract of the United States, 1995* (Government Printing Office, 1995), pp. 57, 69, 444, and 547; *World Almanac of Books and Facts, 1996* (Funk & Wagnalls, 1995), pp. 644–45; Federal Election Commission home page, http://www.fec.gov/press/012396.htm; Arthur C. Close, J. Valerie Steele, and Michael E. Buckner, eds., *Washington Representatives, 1995*, 19th ed. (Columbia Books, 1995), pp. 3–8.

A three-week strike of workers at General Motors shut down most of the company's plants in 1996 for lack of parts. Workers were protesting the use of outside nonunion labor to produce cheaper parts.

and local groups or federations of unions have sometimes been politically divided. Leadership of the AFL-CIO had been in the hands of only a few men who, once elected, hold office for a long time. Moreover, the AFL-CIO by no means speaks for all workers; union labor represents only about 16 percent of the nation's work force, and AFL-CIO membership amounts to about 80 percent of the total number of those organized.[26]

Organized labor's political and lobbying muscle is obviously limited, and the prospects for increasing influence in the future are dim. Figure 7-1 demonstrates that organized labor's membership is dwindling relative to the increase in the national work force. Union membership is optional in states whose laws permit the **open shop**. In states with the **closed shop**, union membership may be required as a condition of employment. In both cases the unions conduct negotiations with management, and the benefits the unions gain are shared with all workers.

An individual who does not join an interest group representing his or her interests yet receives the benefit of the influence of the group is known as a **free rider**. It is understandable in open-shop states that many workers choose not to affiliate with the union when they can secure the same pay without incurring the costs associated with union membership. The decline in the proportion of union membership is explained in part by the shift from an industrial to a service economy. Only a small fraction of the work force in the South and sun belt is unionized. Closely identified with the Democratic party, unions have not enjoyed the same relationship with Republican administrations. Given its limited resources, one option for labor is to form temporary coalitions with consumer, public interest, liberal, and sometimes—especially when faced with the issue of foreign imports—even with industry groups. But labor pays a price for such collaboration; it must water down or even give up some of its own goals. Few of labor's recent legislative initiatives have been successful, and, with the Reagan and Bush appointments, labor faces a much less sympathetic Supreme Court.

FIGURE 7-1
Labor Force and Union Membership, 1930–1994

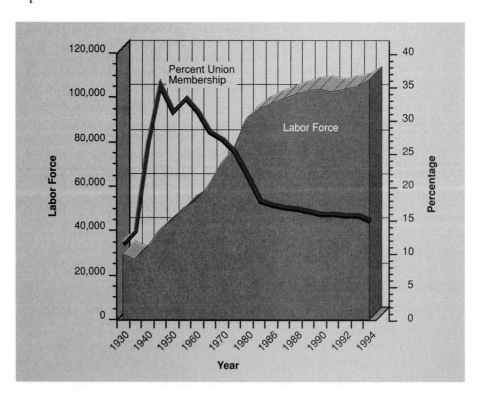

PROFESSIONAL ASSOCIATIONS Professional people have organized some of the strongest "unions" in the nation. Some are well known, such as the American Medical Association and the American Bar Association. Others are divided into many subgroups. Teachers, for example, are organized into large groups such as the National Education Association, the American Federation of Teachers, and the American Association of University Professors, as well as into subgroups based on specialties, such as the Modern Language Association and the American Political Science Association. Many professions are dependent on and regulated by government, especially on the state level. Lawyers, for example, are licensed by states, which, often as a result of pressure from lawyers themselves, have set up certain standards of admission to the state bar.

"There's getting to be a lot of dangerous talk about the public interest."
The Herblock Gallery (Simon & Schuster, 1968).

Ideological Interest Groups

Virtually all interest groups convince themselves that they are devoted to the public welfare and not merely to their own self-interests; their cases are usually presented in terms of their value to the "public interest." Countless groups have organized around specific issues, such as civil liberties, birth control, abortion, environmental protection, nuclear energy, and nuclear arms.[27] One of the best-known ideological groups is the American Civil Liberties Union (ACLU), with 275,000 members committed to the protection of civil liberties.[28] Some highly ideological groups are thriving in the otherwise pragmatic, pluralistic politics of the 1990s.[29]

Public Interest Groups

So-called "public interest" groups arose out of the political ferment of the 1960s. Common Cause, founded in 1970 by independent Republican John W. Gardner and later led by noted Watergate prosecutor Archibald Cox, campaigns for electoral reform and for making the political process more open. Its Washington staff raises money through direct mail campaigns, oversees state chapters, issues a flood of research reports and press releases on current issues, and lobbies on Capitol Hill and in major government departments. Ralph Nader started a conglomerate of consumer organizations that investigates and reports on governmental and corporate action—or inaction—relating to consumer interests. Public Interest Research Groups (PIRGs), founded by Ralph Nader, today number among the largest interest groups in the country. PIRGs have become important players on Capitol Hill and in several state legislatures, promoting environmental issues, safe energy, consumer protection, and good government. Nader was a presidential candidate for the Green party in 1996.

Foreign Policy Interest Groups

Issues of domestic policy are not the only matters of concern to interest groups. More and more, groups are organizing to promote or oppose certain foreign policies. Among the most prestigious (although not uncontroversial) foreign affairs groups is the Council on Foreign Relations in New York City. Other groups, devoted to narrower areas of American foreign policy, exert pressure on legislators to enact specific policies. Among these are interest groups concerned with the Arab-Israeli conflict and the abolition of the apartheid system of segregation in South Africa. Formal lobbies for both Israel and the Arab nations—the American Israel Public Affairs Committee and the National Association of Arab-Americans, respectively—compete to influence policy makers in Washington. Both organizations make their cases on the basis of U.S. national interests. Interest group pressure has also influenced U.S. policy toward South Africa and played a role in South Africa's decision to abandon apartheid. Groups ranging from student organizations to national lobbies like the American Committee on Africa urged divestment, sanctions, or other policy measures in seeking to promote change in South Africa from the outside.

Government and Other Interest Groups

Government itself is a source of important interest groups. Some may think that odd, but as the size of government has grown and the scope of its activity has expanded, so has governmental lobbying. Many cities and states retain Washington lobbyists, and cities in turn hire lobbyists to represent them at the state legislature. Governors are organized through the National Governors' Association, cities through the National League of Cities, and counties through the National Association of Counties. Public employees form a large and well-organized group. The National Education Association (NEA), for example, claims more than 2.75 million members. Public employers are also important to organized labor. The fastest growing unions in the AFL-CIO are public employee unions.[30]

In recent years there has been a virtual explosion in the number and variety of interests and associations.[31] This is especially true for single-issue interest groups. These groups crusade tirelessly for or against politically "hot" issues such as abortion or the sale of firearms. Numerous environmental protection groups press for legislation at all levels of government.

CHARACTERISTICS AND POWER OF INTEREST GROUPS

The United States has long been known for the number and diversity of its interest groups. Most Americans belong to a number of interest groups, some of which they are aware of and others of which they may not be. Groups vary in their goals, methods, and power. Among the most important group characteristics are size, resources, cohesiveness, leadership, the political and social system in which they operate, and how they activate members. Interest groups also differ in the ways they attempt to influence government.

Size and Resources

Obviously size is important to political power; an organization representing five million voters has more influence than one speaking for five thousand. Perhaps even more important than size is the extent to which members are actively involved and focus on the attainment of policy objectives. Often people join an organization for reasons that have little to do with its political objectives. They may want to secure group insurance, take advantage of travel benefits, participate in professional meetings, or get a job.

While the size of an interest group is often important, so, too, is its *spread*—the extent to which membership is concentrated or dispersed. Automobile manufacturing is concentrated in Michigan and a few other states, and as a result its influence does not have the same spread as that of the American Medical Association, which has an active chapter in virtually every congressional district. An association consisting of three million supporters concentrated in a few states will usually have less influence than another group consisting of 3 million supporters spread out in a large number of states. Most interest groups cultivate specific and recognizable identities.[32]

Groups also differ in their *resources*, which include money, volunteers, expertise, and reputation. Some groups have the ability to influence many centers of

Organized groups have been active on all sides on health care reform. The perceived threat to Medicare funding brought out these union members, but the medical profession, hospitals, and older persons also made their views known.

power—both houses of Congress, the White House, federal agencies, the courts, and state and local governments—while others cannot.

Cohesiveness

Because many Americans are members of many associations, their loyalties are divided. This *overlapping membership* largely determines the *cohesiveness* of an association and can create problems for organizational leaders. For example, suppose a union official asks a dozen members to come to a meeting. Several may say they will come, but two belong to a club that bowls that night, two others may have to stay home with their families, and another may have to attend a church supper. Even those who attend the meeting may not be 100 percent supporters. Perhaps they are asked to vote for a particular candidate in a coming election. Some will. But one may decide to vote for the other candidate because she is a neighbor, and another will vote for her because they are both Italian Americans. Political party loyalties or American Legion membership may also interfere with a union request. Or perhaps one union member will not know what to do and will not vote at all.

Obviously, the *unity* of the membership is a key element, as is the ability to act quickly and decisively. Unity, however, is easier to achieve in a small group that focuses on a relatively specific and concrete concern that does not noticeably affect others, such as a tariff on steel pins.

Usually a mass membership organization is made up of three types of members.[33] The first type comprises a relatively small number of formal leaders who may hold full-time, paid positions or at least devote much of their extra time, effort, and money to the group's activities. The second includes persons intensely involved in the group, organizationally and psychologically. They identify with the group's aims, attend meetings, faithfully pay dues, and do a lot of the legwork. The third type comprises people who are members in name only. They do not participate actively, do not look on themselves as Teamsters or Rotarians or Legionnaires, and cannot be depended on to vote in elections or otherwise act as the leadership wants.

Another factor in group cohesiveness is its organizational structure and its ability to commit its members to action. Some associations have no formal organization. Others consist of local organizations that have joined together in some sort of loose state or national federation. The local organizations retain a measure of separate power and independence, just as the states did when they entered the Union. A sort of separation of powers may be found as well. The national assembly of an organization establishes, or at least ratifies, policy. An executive committee meets more frequently. A president or director is elected to head and speak for the group, and permanent, paid officials form the organization's bureaucracy. Power may be further divided between the organization's main headquarters and its Washington office. An organization of this sort tends to be far less cohesive than a centralized, disciplined group, such as the National Rifle Association or some trade unions.

Leadership

Closely related to cohesion is the nature of the leadership. In a group that embraces many attitudes and interests, leaders may either weld the various elements together or sharpen their disunity. The leader of a national business association, for example, must tread cautiously between big business and small business, between exporters and importers, between chain stores and corner grocery stores, and between the producers and the sellers of competing products. Yet leaders must not be at the mercy of different interests, for above all they must lead. They must show how to achieve organizational goals. The group leader is in the same position as a president or a member of Congress; he or she must know when to lead followers and when to follow them.

Techniques

Interest groups seeking to wield influence choose from a variety of political weapons and targets. As a result, they carefully monitor federal agencies and departments, both houses of Congress, the White House staff, and state and local governments. They also become involved in litigation. Other techniques include persuasion, rule making, election activities, and lobbying.

PUBLICITY AND MASS MEDIA APPEALS   Interest groups exploit the communications media—television, radio, newspapers, leaflets, signs, direct mail, and word of mouth—to influence voters during elections and to motivate constituents to contact their representatives between elections. Business enjoys a special advantage in this arena, and businesspeople have the money to use propaganda machinery. As large-scale advertisers, they know how to deliver their message effectively or to find an advertising agency to do it for them. Most important, they generally have easy access to the means of disseminating propaganda, such as the press.

MASS MAILING   New technologies have increased the reach and effectiveness of interest groups. One of these new technologies is computerized and targeted *mass mailing*.[34] For many decades interest groups have been sending out huge mailings to people whose names are on lists culled from telephone directories and other sources. Some of these mailings are sent out indiscriminately. Mass mailing is used by all kinds of interest groups, but it has been especially refined by public interest groups, which are sometimes accused of being a small headquarters with a good mailing list. Today's technology can produce personalized letters targeted to specific groups, called *targeted direct mail*. Speaking of the National Rifle Association, Congressman William J. Hughes (D.-N.J.) said, "It's a lobby that can put 15,000 letters in your district overnight and have people in your town hall meeting interrupting you."[35] Such targeted letters are also used to raise money from people who share a common concern, such as environmental groups.

LITIGATION When groups find the usual political channels closed to them, they may turn to the courts.[36] The Legal Aid and Defense Fund, allied with the National Association for the Advancement of Colored People (NAACP), for example, has initiated and won numerous court cases in its efforts to improve legal protection for African Americans. In recent decades, urban interests and environmental groups, feeling underrepresented in state and national legislatures, have also turned to the courts to influence the political agenda.[37]

INFLUENCE ON RULE MAKING Groups have ready access to the rule-making process, in which executive and regulatory agencies write the rules that implement laws. Agencies publish proposed regulations in the *Federal Register* and invite responses and reactions from all interested persons before the rules are finalized. (The *Federal Register* is published every weekday. You can find it in your school or public library.) Well-staffed associations and corporations peruse the *Register*, ever alert for proposed agency actions that will affect their interests.

ELECTION ACTIVITIES Although nearly all large organizations say they are nonpolitical, almost all are politically involved in some way. What group leaders usually mean when they say they are nonpolitical is that they are *nonpartisan*. A distinguishing feature of organized interest groups is that they often try to work through *both* parties; usually this means working for individual candidates.

Labor usually, but not always, favors Democrats. The AFL-CIO supported Democrats Hubert Humphrey, Jimmy Carter, Walter Mondale, Michael Dukakis, and Bill Clinton. The Teamsters Union during this period endorsed Richard Nixon, Gerald Ford, Ronald Reagan, and George Bush. But in 1992 the Teamsters reversed this pattern and endorsed Democrat Bill Clinton. Clinton also benefited from the endorsement and support of the National Education Association, a group with over 2 million members, most of them teachers.

Business groups generally endorse the incumbent but favor Republicans when no incumbent is running. Some organizations are prevented from taking a firm position by the diversity of their members. A local retailers' group, for example, might be composed equally of Republicans and Democrats, and many of its members might refuse to take a position on a candidate for fear of losing business. In such cases more subtle means may be equally effective: word may be passed around at meetings that candidate *X* is sound from the organization's point of view; that candidate may also receive a campaign contribution from the organization's political action committee.

FORMING A POLITICAL PARTY Another interest group strategy is to form a political party. Such parties are organized less with the intent to win elections than to publicize a *cause*. The Free Soil party was formed in 1848 to propagandize against the spread of slavery, and the Prohibition party was organized 20 years later to ban the sale of liquor. Farmers have formed a variety of such parties. In 1991 the National Organization for Women (NOW) announced it was forming a political party to call attention to issues of concern to its membership. NOW's party ended up without candidates or votes in the 1992 election. More often, however, interest groups prefer to work through existing parties.

The most recent example of a movement becoming a political party is Ross Perot's United We State America becoming the Reform Political Party in 1996.

Why Are They Called Lobbyists?

Lobbyists, as noted, are individuals, groups, and organizations that seek to influence legislative and administrative actions. Ever since governments existed, individuals and groups have petitioned their rulers. And this is an especially cherished right in constitutional democracies such as the United States.

The terms "lobbying" and "lobbyist" were not generally used until around the middle of the nineteenth century in the United States. The root in these words refers to the "lobby" or "anteroom" outside chambers in the U.S. Capitol. It was also used to refer to hotel lobbies in Washington, where the petitioners and agents of influence also congregated. Thus a senator coming out of the Senate chamber might be approached politely by several lobbyists seeking to influence his vote on some measure. Or a president might be dining at the Old Willard Hotel, a few blocks from the White House, and make reference to the number of "lobbyists" hanging around in the hotel lobby.

Nowadays we have turned the noun "lobby" into a verb as we use it in this political context. Thus "to lobby" is to seek to influence legislators and government officials, and we call this lobbying even if there is no lobby in sight. It has become a generic term even though it originally took its meaning from the place where the activity occurred.

"Please understand. I don't sell access to the government. I merely sell access to the guys who *do* sell access to the government."

Drawing by Ed Lieber. © 1986 The New Yorker Magazine, Inc.

Whether the Reform Party can become a significant party or simply remains an instrument of Perot's ego remains to be determined by the events of the years ahead and the willingness of Perot to continue to invest his own money in the party.

COOPERATIVE LOBBYING   Interest groups often form alliances. An example is the Food Group, a 30-year-old informal conference group in Washington that has represented more than 60 business and trade associations. In addition, it spawned an Information Committee on Federal Food Regulations to fight truth-in-packaging legislation. Although the Food Group has been fairly effective, it does run into the predictable problem of differences among constituents over goals and priorities, and has found it difficult to put strong and unified pressure on Congress and government agencies.

THE INFLUENCE OF LOBBYISTS

The typical image of interest groups in action is that of powerful, hard-nosed lobbyists who skillfully employ a combination of knowledge, persuasiveness, personal influence, charm, and money to influence legislators and bureaucrats. Who are the lobbyists and what do they do?

Lobbyists are the employees of associations who try to influence policy decisions and positions in the executive and, especially, in the legislative branches of our government. They are experienced in the ways of government, often having been public servants before going to work for an organized interest group or association or corporation. They might start as staff in Congress, perhaps on a congressional committee. Later, when their party wins the White House, they gain an administration post. After a few years in the administration, they are ready to move on to lobbying, either by going to work for one of the interests they dealt with while in the government or by obtaining a position with a lobbying firm.

The political information provided by lobbyists includes such matters as who supports or opposes legislation and how strongly they feel.[38] The legislator gains important facts and figures on the impact of proposed laws that might not be available from any other source. Lobbyists often provide technical assistance on the drafting of bills and amendments, identify persons to testify at legislative hearings, and formulate questions to ask of administration officials at oversight hearings. The salary for such a lobbyist, who has extensive contacts in Congress and the administration, can be two to three times a government salary.

This employment cycle from government to interest group is known as the **revolving door**. Contacts gained during government service are crucial to effective lobbying, and many former members of Congress make good use of their congressional experience as full-time lobbyists. For example, former Senators Dennis DeConcini (D-Ariz.) and Dave Durenberger (R-Minn.), as well as numerous former House members and congressional staff currently lobby Congress on the same issues they dealt with in Congress.[39] A 1989 reform prohibits members of Congress from lobbying Congress for one year after leaving office. Congressional staff are also prohibited from lobbying the member, office, or committee they served for one year.

This revolving door between government and interest groups is one of the reasons why networks are formed of people who care about such issues as energy policy or child welfare. These networks have been called **iron triangles**—meaning a mutually supporting relationship among interest groups, congressional committees and subcommittees, and the government agencies that share a common policy concern. Sometimes these relationships become so strong and mutually beneficial that the issue network becomes very powerful.

INTEREST GROUP MONEY AND POLITICS

Technically, a **political action committee (PAC)** is simply the political arm of a business, labor, or trade association or other interest group that is legally entitled to raise funds on a voluntary basis from members, stockholders, or employees in order to contribute funds to favored candidates or political parties.[40] Because PACs link two vital techniques of influence—giving money and other political aid to politicians and persuading officeholders to act or vote "the right way" on issues— we look now at PACs more broadly as the means by which interest groups seek to influence who the legislators are and what they do once they take office.[41]

PACs can be categorized according to the type of interest they represent: corporations; trade, membership, and health organizations; labor unions; non-connected (primarily ideological) organizations; cooperative organizations; and corporations without stock. Figure 7-2 represents the total of campaign contributions to congressional candidates for each type of PAC since 1978.

In 1978 there was little difference in the level of campaign activity of PACs representing corporations, labor unions, or trade associations.[42] But now that has changed, with corporate PACs spending more than the others and ideological PACs at roughly half the level of spending of trade and labor PACs. In the 1993-1994 election cycle, corporate PACs spent $116.9, nearly $29 million more than labor PACs and $23 million more than trade association PACs.[43]

The Growth of Political Action Committees (PACs)

Ironically, considering that the explosion of PACs has occurred mainly in the business world, it was organized labor that invented this device. In the 1930s John L. Lewis, president of the United Mine Workers, set up the Non-Partisan Political League as the political arm of the newly formed Congress of Industrial Organizations.

The 1970s brought a near-revolution in the role and influence of PACs, ironically as the result of the post-Watergate reforms. The number of PACs increased dramatically, from about 150 to more than 4,000 today. Corporations and trade associations contributed most to this growth; today their PACs constitute the majority of all PACs. Labor PACs, on the other hand, increased only slightly in number, representing less than 10 percent of all PACs. But the increase in the number of PACs is less important than the intensity of recent PAC participation in elections and in lobbying.

How PACs Invest Their Money

In response to reporters' questions concerning the influence of money in politics, Charles Keating once said, "One question, among the many raised in recent weeks, [has] to do with whether my financial support in any way influenced several political figures to take up my cause. I want to say in the most forceful way I can: I certainly hope so."[44] PACs take part in the entire election process, but their main influence lies in their capacity to contribute money to candidates. Candidates today need big money to wage their election or reelection campaigns. It is no longer uncommon for House candidates to spend more than a million dollars, and for many senators or would-be senators to spend ten times that amount[45] (see Table 7-2).

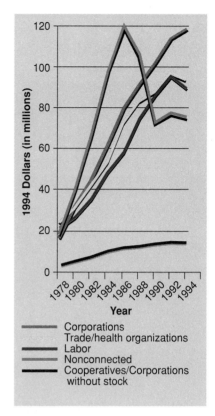

FIGURE 7-2
PAC Contributions to Congressional Candidates (1994 dollars, in millions)

SOURCE: Howard W. Stanley and Richard G. Niemi, *Vital Statistics on American Politics*, 5th ed. (Congressional Quarterly Press, 1995), p. 164.

TABLE 7-2

PACs That Gave the Most
to Federal Candidates

1992	Dollars (Millions)
Realtors Political Action Committee	2.9
American Medical Association Political Action	2.9
Democratic Republican Independent Voter Education Committee	2.4
Association of Trial Lawyers of America Political Action Committee	2.3
National Education Association Political Action Committee	2.2
United Auto Workers Voluntary Community Action Program (UAW-V-CAP)	2.3
American Federation of State, County, and Municipal Employees (AFSCME)	1.9

1994	
United Parcel Service Political Action Committee (UPSPAC)	2.6
American Federation of State, County, and Municipal Employees	2.5
Democratic Republican Independent Voter Education Committee	2.5
American Medical Association Political Action Committee	2.4
National Education Association Political Action Committee	2.3
Association of Trial Lawyers of America Political Action Committee	2.2
UAW-V-CAP (UAW Voluntary Community Action Program)	2.1
NRA Political Victory Fund	1.9
Realtors Political Action Committee	1.9
Dealers Election Action Committee of the National Automobile Dealers Association (NADA)	1.8

SOURCE: Federal Election Commission.

As corporate, industry, and labor PACs increase in number and dollars contributed, their influence grows accordingly. What counts is not only the amounts they give but also to whom they give: the more influential incumbents. In 1994, top PAC recipients in the House included Speaker Newt Gingrich, Tom Foley (former Speaker of the House), Richard Gephardt (former majority leader), and Dan Rostenkowski (former chair of the Ways and Means Committee).[46]

CURING THE MISCHIEFS OF FACTION

If James Madison were to return today, more than 200 years after writing *The Federalist*, No. 10, he would not be surprised by the existence of interest groups. Nor would he be surprised by their variety. He *might* be surprised, however, by the intense expression of *factionalism*—the varied weapons of group influence, the deep involvement of interest groups in the electoral process, and the vast number of lobbyists in Washington and the state capitals. And doubtless, Madison, were he alive today, would be concerned about the power of faction, especially its tendency toward instability and injustice.

Concern about the evils of interest groups has been a recurrent theme throughout U.S. history. Americans today are also worried about the power of faction, and for somewhat the same reasons. Specifically, they fear that

1. The struggle among factions is not a fair fight; narrower, more highly organized, and better-financed single-issue groups hold a decided advantage over more general groups.

2. The interest-group battle leads to great inequities, because lower-income people are grossly underrepresented among interest groups as compared to richer, more highly organized people, many of whom are represented by a multitude of organizations and lobbyists.

3. Even though the organization of hundreds of single-issue groups has reinforced the diffusion of power and fragmentation in government that the Constitution's framers so desired, it has led to incoherent policies, waste and inefficiency, endless delays, and the inability to plan ahead and anticipate crises.

4. The role of interest groups in elections has made incumbents more secure (diminished electoral competition) and enhanced the power of these groups in relation to Congress and state/local government.

What should be done, if anything? For decades Americans have tried to find ways to keep interest groups in check. They have agreed with James Madison that the "remedy" of suppressing factions would be worse than the disease. It would be absurd to abolish liberty simply because it nourished faction. And the existence and activity of interest groups and lobbies is solidly protected by the Constitution. But by safeguarding the value of *liberty*, have Americans allowed interest groups to threaten *equality*, the second great value in our national heritage? The question remains: How can interest groups be regulated in a way that does not threaten their constitutional liberties?

Lobbying Regulation and Campaign Finance Reform

Americans have generally responded to this question by seeking to regulate lobbying in general and political money in particular. Lobbying is dealt with by registration and disclosure. Recently, there has been a renewed desire to regulate not only lobbyists but those who may someday become lobbyists. Bill Clinton required top appointees to his administration to agree "not to lobby their former agencies for five years after leaving the government . . . [and] never to become lobbyists for foreign governments or foreign political parties." The White House Staff pledged "not to lobby any agency for which they have had 'substantial personal responsibility' for five years after leaving office."[47]

Concern over the use of money—especially corporate funds—to influence politicians goes back well over a century, to the Credit Mobilier scandals during the administration of Ulysses S. Grant. During the Progressive Era, Congress legislated against corporate contributions in federal elections and required disclosure of the use of money.

Federal legislation regulating campaign finance, including the 1925 Federal Corrupt Practices Act and the 1946 Federal Regulation of Lobbying Act, was not very effective. It was, in fact, largely unenforced. Many candidates filed incomplete reports or none at all. The reform mood of the 1960s brought basic changes, "nurtured by the ever-increasing costs of campaigning, the incidence of millionaire candidates, the large disparities in campaign spending between various candidates and political parties, some clear cases of unique influence on the decision-making process by large contributors and special interests, and the apparent disadvantages of incumbency in an age of mass communications with a constant focus on the lives and activities of officeholders."[48] The upshot was the Federal Election Campaign Act (FECA) of 1971, which supplanted the earlier legislation.

The FECA, which has been amended three times, establishes reporting or disclosure requirements for all candidates for the U.S. House of Representatives, the Senate, and the presidency, as well as their political parties and campaign committees. It also requires disclosure of the amounts spent to influence federal elections by others, including individuals and political action committees. The act established partial public financing for presidential candidates, financed by a voluntary check-off on federal income tax forms. Candidates may spend an unlimited amount of their own money; however, contributions by others to their campaigns are limited. Some candidates for Congress spend or loan their campaigns millions of dollars. Steve Forbes declined federal funds in his 1996 presidential campaign, permitting him to spend more than $32 million of his own money.

There have been notable problems with the act, including the **soft money** loophole—money that can be given to parties for party-building activities that does not have the same limitations as other money given to parties. Other problems were nondisclosure of some money that goes to state and local parties and an ineffective Federal Election Commission. The act has had its critics, and Congress has frequently debated reforming campaign financing.

In his 1995 State of the Union Address, President Clinton challenged the new Republican Congress to send him bills on campaign finance and lobby reform—two elements Republicans had been criticized for leaving out of their Contract with America. The 104th Congress did not address campaign finance reform but it did produce the first major overhaul of lobbying laws since 1946.

The new law, which took effect January 1, 1996, expands the definition of lobbyist. Previously, only lobbyists who spent a majority of their time dealing with members of Congress were required to register. Now anyone who lobbies part time, as well as lobbyists who deal with congressional staff or executive branch agencies, also must register. This bill is expected to increase the number of registered lobbyists from three to ten times its current level.[49] Under the new law lobbyists must disclose twice each year the issues they lobbied on, whom they contacted in their lobbying efforts, and the amount of money they spent. This reporting requirement goes well beyond any previous disclosure requirements.

What have been the effects of campaign-finance and lobbying reforms on interest groups? Ironically, one has been to increase the number and importance

Lobbying Disclosure Act of 1995

After a long battle, a new law restricting lobbying took effect January 1, 1996. The major provisions of the bill make the following changes in existing law:

1. *Covered Officials.* While the 1971 Federal Election Campaign Act covered only those who lobby members of Congress, the new bill covers lobbyists who seek to influence congressional staff members and policy-making officials of the executive branch, including the president, top White House officials, Cabinet secretaries and their deputies, and independent agency administrators and their assistants.

2. *Disclosure Requirements.* Lobbyists have to register within 45 days of being hired or within 45 days of making their first contact, either oral or written, to a covered official, whichever came first. Lobbyists who expected to receive $5,000 or less in a six-month period, or organizations that expected to spend $20,000 or less in a six-month period on lobbying with their own employees, do not have to disclose their activities. After registering, lobbyists are required to file semiannual reports detailing their activities during each six-month period.

3. *Information Requirements.* The registration forms have to include the name, address, principal place of business, and phone number of the registrant, plus a general description of the registrant's business or activities, as well as the same information about any client. The semiannual reports have to list the specific issues lobbied on, a list of the chambers of Congress and the executive agencies contacted, the lobbyists involved, and the involvement, if any, of a foreign entity. The lobbyists does not have to disclose the names of the lawmakers, staff members, executive branch officials, or congressional committees contacted. The semiannual reports also have to include an estimate of the cost of the lobbying campaign.

4. *Foreign Agents.* The bill requires representatives of a U.S. subsidiary of a foreign-owned company and lawyer-lobbyists for foreign entities to register. Both groups were previously exempt from registration requirements.

5. *Exceptions.* The bill exempts all grassroots lobbying and that of all tax-exempt religious organizations, such as churches, from disclosure requirements.

SOURCE: Adapted from Jonathan D. Salant, "Highlights of Lobby Bill," *Congressional Quarterly Weekly Report* 53, no. 47 (December 2, 1995), p. 3632.

of such groups. The growth in numbers and contributions from corporate and trade association PACs (like doctors and realtors) has been great.[50] There has been no significant increase in labor PACs. Another effect is that there is greater disclosure of how politicians fund campaigns. With the important exception of soft money, we have a much better idea now of how much money candidates raise and how they spend it. Disclosure permits the press and the public to assess the implications of how candidates finance their campaigns.

Candidates and some appointed officials must also disclose their personal finances, which permits voters and the press to see what investments and resources candidates have that may affect their ability to be impartial. Such public disclosure of personal worth, the value of property owned, and outstanding debts no doubt discourages some persons from entering public life, but it also makes officeholders accountable for certain obligations and actions once they enter office.

Should We Reform the Reforms?

Do we need to reform further how campaigns are financed? Do PACs have too much influence? There are many who argue that we have done enough; others contend that our present arrangements for financing our parties and running campaigns still give too much influence to powerful and wealthy interest groups. Moreover, it is doubtful that Congress really *wants* reform. Many members of Congress thrive on the present arrangements, and the leaders and members of both parties actually compete for PAC dollars. The natural alliance between Republicans and business PACs that had been disrupted by Democrats running Congress ended with the 1994 election. As the 1996 elections demonstrated, business-related PACs gave to Republican incumbents in record-setting amounts. Republicans who only a few years earlier had been calling for the abolition of PACs were now the beneficiaries of the same system that had long benefited Democratic incumbents.

There are other arguments for keeping hands off the lobbyists. PACs support both Democratic and Republican candidates and hence do not favor just one party. Another argument is that the increase in corporate PAC spending is not as great as it appears; in fact, much of the PAC money may be "old wine in new bottles"— that is, money given publicly that used to be given in the form of legal or illegal personal campaign contributions by business chiefs.[51] One argument against reform is that it is impossible in a free society to restrict the flow of money. Laws can be passed to limit or regulate the flow of money in politics, but money will find an alternative way to accomplish its purpose of influencing elections. Finally, in the spirit of the Bill of Rights, whatever the evils, no action should be taken that may threaten the liberties and autonomy of individuals or interest groups in general.

One's attitudes toward an interest group often depend on one's political values and goals. Union leaders believe business PACs enjoy too much financial power; business leaders believe that labor has too much electoral power. Groups defined by race and sex argue that a system so grounded in economic interests discriminates against citizens with little access to economic power. Is a more fair solution possible?

As the efforts of the 1970s should teach us, reforming interest groups and regulating campaign money often lead to unintended consequences. Those laws written to protect labor unions helped promote nonunion PACs. Some believe efforts to limit the cost of campaigns often serve to protect incumbents, because the "return on campaign expenditures is much greater for challengers than incumbents."[52] But it is important to remember the consequences of doing nothing at all about our current system: continued dependence by candidates on PACs and other forms of interested money, uncontested races, and, in contested races, challengers who are often grossly underfunded.

Some observers favor wider regulation of political money and publicly financed congressional elections. Others call for no regulation of the political arms of interest groups, hoping that the groups will find a natural and proper balance. Still others believe the balance must be righted between the intense activity of corporate PACs and the far less influential role of PACs for consumer groups, women's groups, environmental groups, and civil rights groups.[53]

A different school of thought holds that none of these solutions will work because the problem lies outside interest groups and PACs. This school cites James Madison, who concluded that while the *causes* of faction could not be removed, the *effects* could be controlled only by fundamental changes in the whole political system. His solutions were to extend the sphere of government to take in "a greater variety of parties and interests," create federal-state-local tiers of government, and fragment the power of government so no majority or minority could control it.

Finally, some believe the main problem lies not in interest groups but in the way public opinion is formed, managed, and manipulated—above all, by the barons of the electronic media in a new age of communications politics. These observers urge Congress to limit what commercial television stations can charge for political advertising and to discourage so-called "negative targeting" of candidates in political advertising. Strengthening political parties would be one way to reduce the power of special interests. If campaign contributions were directed more to parties than to candidates, then candidates would be more accountable to the parties and less tied to any particular interest. Parties are also more likely to invest in challengers than PACs are. Finally, because parties must seek to broaden their appeal, they cannot risk becoming captive of a particular narrow interest.

SUMMARY

1. Political parties are essential to democracy by organizing the competition, simplifying choices, unifying the electorate, translating public preferences into policy, bridging the separation of powers by fostering cooperation among branches of government, providing loyal opposition, and recruiting and nominating candidates for office.

2. American parties are moderate, and they are organized around elected offices at the state and local levels. Parties bring factions and interests together in coalitions broad enough to win the presidency and other elections. Parties have declined both in organizational strength and in the esteem they command among many Americans since the days in which they were described as strong political forces. Sometimes parties are seen as corrupting and are often feared. Yet, at the national level and within state and local governments, both parties have shown renewed signs of vitality. Third parties have not been notably successful.

3. Parties are vital in the operation of government. Congress is organized around parties, and judicial and many executive branch appointments are based in large part on partisanship.

4. The dominant interest groups in the United States are economic or occupational, but a variety of other groups—religious, racial, ideological, ethnic—have memberships that cut across the big economic groupings; thus their influence is both reduced and stabilized.

5. The sources of interest-group power are size, unity, singleness of purpose, organization, leadership, and the ability to contribute to candidates and political parties as well as the ability to fund lobbyists. But the actual power of an interest group stems from the manner in which these elements relate to the political and governmental environment in which the interest group operates.

6. For many decades, interest groups have engaged in lobbying, but these efforts have become far more significant as groups become more deeply involved in the electoral process, especially through the expanded use of political action committees (PACs). Concern for PACs centers on their ability to raise money and spend it on elections in behalf of endorsed candidates, typically incumbents. This concern has led to proposals to ban PACs or to more strictly limit their spending. Yet their existence and rights are protected, many believe, by our First Amendment.

7. Reforms of interest-group excess often include strengthened political parties or regulations that seek fairness, disclosure, and balance between interest groups. All reform efforts must operate in such a way as not to take away basic constitutional rights of individuals.

FURTHER READING

DAN BALZ AND RONALD BROWNSTEIN, *Storming the Gates: Protest Politics and the Republican Revival* (Little, Brown, 1996).

MICHAEL BARONE, *Our Country: The Shaping of America from Roosevelt to Reagan* (Free Press, 1990).

JOHN F. BIBBY, *Politics, Parties and Elections in America* (Nelson-Hall, 1992).

JEFFERY H. BIRNBAUM, *The Lobbyists: How Influence Peddlers Get Their Way in Washington* (Times Books, 1992).

MARY C. BRENNAN, *Turning Right in the Sixties: The Conservative Capture of the GOP* (University of North Carolina Press, 1995).

ALLAN J. CIGLER AND BURDETT A. LOOMIS, EDS., *Interest Group Politics*, 4th ed. (Congressional Quarterly Press, 1994).

STEPHEN C. CRAIG, ED., *Broken Contract: Changing Relationships Between Americans and Their Government* (Westview, 1996).

LEON EPSTEIN, *Political Parties in the American Mold* (University of Wisconsin Press, 1986).

PAUL S. HERRNSON, *Party Campaigning in the 1980s: Have the National Parties Made a Comeback as Key Players in Congressional Elections?* (Harvard University Press, 1988).

ALLEN D. HERTZKE, *Representing God in Washington: The Role of Religious Lobbies in the American Polity* (University of Tennessee Press, 1988).

RONALD J. HREBENAR AND RUTH K. SCOTT, *Interest Group Politics in America*, 2d ed. (Prentice Hall, 1990).

LARRY JOHNSTON, *Ideologies: An Analytical and Contextual Approach* (Broadview, 1996).

WILLIAM J. KEEFE, *Parties, Politics, and Public Policy in America*, 7th ed. (Congressional Quarterly Press, 1994).

BRUCE E. KEITH, DAVID B. MAGLEBY, CANDICE J. NELSON, ELIZABETH ORR, MARK WESTLYE, AND RAYMOND E. WOLFINGER, *The Myth of the Independent Voter* (University of California Press, 1992).

DAVID B. MAGLEBY AND CANDICE J. NELSON, *The Money Chase: Congressional Campaign Finance Reform* (Brookings, 1990).

SIDNEY M. MILKIS, *The President and the Parties: The Transformation of the American Party System Since the New Deal* (Oxford University Press, 1993).

MANCUR OLSON, *The Logic of Collective Action* (Harvard University Press, 1965).

MARK P. PETRACCA, ED., *The Politics of Interests: Interest Groups Transformed* (Westview, 1992).

STEVEN J. ROSENSTONE, ROY L. BEHR, AND EDWARD H. LAZARUS, *Third Parties in America: Citizen Response to Major Party Failure* (Princeton University Press, 1984).

MICHAEL J. SANDEL, *Democracy's Discontent: America in Search of a Public Philosophy* (Harvard University Press, 1996).

JAMES SUNDQUIST, *Dynamics of the Party System: Alignment and Realignment of Political Parties in the United States*, rev. ed. (Brookings, 1983).

JACK L. WALKER, JR., *Mobilizing Interest Groups in America: Patrons, Professions, and Social Movements* (University of Michigan Press, 1991).

MARTIN P. WATTENBERG, *The Decline of American Political Parties, 1952–1992* (Harvard University Press, 1994).

HERBERT F. WEISBERG, ED., *Democracy's Feast: Elections in America* (Chatham House, 1995).

CLYDE WILCOX, *Risky Business? PAC Decisionmaking in Congressional Elections* (Sharpe, 1994).

PUBLIC OPINION, VOTING, AND ELECTIONS

8

I n January 1996, Oregon voters elected a United States senator in the first-ever election for federal office conducted entirely through the mail. After the ballots were mailed out, voters had 22 days to return them. Advocates of this new voting process, especially state elections officials, argue that it dramatically reduces cost and administrative burden and increases turnout. Opponents worry about party leaders, union bosses, spouses, or others exercising undue influence because the privacy of the voting booth is eliminated. Opponents also feel that the effort required by voting in person is an essential part of democracy, and they fear that many voters will send in their ballot long before the campaign is over, thus leaving the deliberative process incomplete. Political scientist Norman Ornstein claims, "The mail ballot turns that sacred experience [of voting in person] into the equivalent of filling out a Publishers Clearinghouse ballot."

Early studies of the Oregon vote-by-mail experiment show little evidence of manipulation or fraud and a higher turnout than would normally be the case for a special election to replace a U.S. senator. Some cite the Oregon data as evidence that we should change our voting system to permit elections by mail—maybe even by telephone or computer. Telephone and computer voting are being used with success in some university and municipal elections. Should voters be given a Personal Identification Number like millions of Americans use at automated teller machines? Americans vote more often and for more offices than do the citizens of any other democracy. Given the frequency of our elections, some election officials may urge that we move to vote-by-mail elections.

In this chapter we look at the nature of public opinion and how to measure it, how we formulate our political beliefs, the factors that affect the formation of our opinions, the nature and level of political participation in the United States, and why people vote as they do. We also examine the importance of rules of our constitutional democracy and the role of campaigns for Congress and the presidency. Finally, we examine some possible reforms of campaigns and elections.

PUBLIC OPINION

All governments in all nations must be concerned with public opinion, for widespread public unrest and protest can topple them. But in a constitutional democracy like ours, public opinion plays an especially large role. As we discussed in earlier chapters, our widely shared values include belief in popular sovereignty, political equality, and majority rule. Individuals have opinions, and they express those opinions in a variety of ways, including protest demonstrations, letters to newspaper editors, and voting in free and regularly scheduled elections. Elected officials refer often to public opinion as a basis for their actions. In short, democracy and public opinion go hand in hand.

What Is Public Opinion?

We define **public opinion** as the distribution within a population of individual views about a given issue, candidate, or institution. **Distribution** means the proportion of the population that holds a particular opinion. When a substantial percentage of a sample agrees on an issue—for example, that schools should be racially integrated—there is a *consensus*. But on most issues, people's opinions are divided, and when a large portion of each side feels intensely about an issue, voters are said to be *polarized*. The Vietnam War in the late 1960s and abortion today are polarizing issues. In the last pre-election poll done by Gallup in 1996 the distribution was Clinton 52 percent, Dole 41 percent, Perot 7 percent, and undecided 0 percent. *Individual preference* means that we are asking *individuals*—not groups, elected officials, or journalists—about their opinions. The *universe*, or *population*, is the relevant group of people for the question.

The factor that produces the brightest and deepest hues in the fabric of public opinion is **intensity**. The fervor of people's beliefs varies greatly: some individuals mildly favor public financing of congressional elections; others mildly oppose it; still others are emphatically for or against it; some people may have no interest in the matter at all; still others may not even have heard of it. Intensity is typically measured by asking people to indicate how strongly they feel on an issue or politician. Such a question is often called a *scale*.

Latency refers to political opinions that exist merely as a potential. They may not have crystallized yet, but they are still important, for they can be evoked by leaders and converted into action. Latent opinions set rough boundaries for leaders, who know that if they take certain actions they will trigger opposition or support from millions of people. If leaders have some understanding of people's real wants, needs, and hopes, they will know how to motivate and mobilize them to go to the polls on election day.

What causes opinions to be stable or fluid, intense or latent? A major factor is salience. By **salience** we mean the extent to which people believe issues are relevant to them. Your next-door neighbor may feel intensely about abortion or gun control or Bill Clinton, whereas you may get excited about health care or unemployment. Most people are more concerned about personal issues like paying the bills and keeping their jobs than about national issues. But if their personal concerns are connected with national issues, salience rises sharply. Salience may change over time.

How Do We Get Our Political Beliefs, Opinions, and Values?

No one is born with political views. We learn them from many teachers. The process by which we develop our political attitudes and values is called **political socialization**. This process starts in childhood, and the family and the schools are probably the two most important political teachers. Children not only learn the content of their culture in childhood and adolescence, but they in turn reshape it as they live their lives. Socialization also lays the foundation for political beliefs, values, ideology, and partisanship.

Nationalism, a common element of political socialization in all cultures, is a consciousness of the nation state and of belonging to that entity.

As soon as we are born, in most places on this earth, we acquire a nationality, a membership in a community. . . . A royal doll, a flag to wave in a parade, coins with their engraved messages—these are sources of instruction and connect a young person to a country. The attachment can be strong, indeed even among children yet to attend school, wherever the flag is saluted, the national anthem sung. The attachment is as parental as the words imply—homeland, motherland, fatherland. . . . Nationalism works its way into just about every corner of the mind's life.[2]

The sources of political attitudes are immensely varied in the pluralistic political culture of the United States. But we can make at least one generalization safely: We form our attitudes in groups, not only in groups such as schools and social organizations, but especially in close-knit groups like the family. When we identify closely with the attitudes and interests of a particular group, we tend to see politics through the "eyes" of this group.[3]

Children in the United States at an early age adopt common values central to American society that provide continuity with the past and legitimize the political system. Young children know what country they live in, and their loyalty to the nation develops early. Although the details of our political system may still elude them, most young Americans acquire a respect for the Constitution and for the concept of participatory democracy, as well as an initially positive view of the most visible figure in our democracy, the president.

FAMILY American children typically show political interest by the age of ten or even earlier, and by the early teens their interest may be fairly high. Learning experiences gradually shape the values and beliefs they acquire in childhood. Consider your own political development. You probably formed your picture of the world by listening to your parents at dinner or absorbing the tales your older brothers and sisters brought home from school. Perhaps you heard about politics from grandparents, aunts, and uncles. You, in turn, influenced your family, if only by bringing some of your own hopes and problems home from school. What we first learn in the family is not so much specific political opinions as basic *attitudes* that shape our opinions—attitudes toward our neighbors, political parties, other classes or types of people, particular leaders (especially presidents), and society in general.

There is a high correlation between the political party of parents and the partisan choice of their children. This relatively high degree of correspondence continues throughout life. Such a finding raises some interesting questions: Does the direct influence of parents create the correspondence? Or are parents and children equally influenced by living in the same social environment—neighborhood, church, socioeconomic groups? The answer is both, and one influence often strengthens the other. For example, a daughter of Democrats, growing up in a small southern town with strong Democratic leanings, will be affected by friends, by other adults, and perhaps by youngsters in a church group, all of whom may reinforce the attitudes of her parents.[4]

What happens when a young person's parents and friends disagree? It seems that when high school students are pressured this way, they tend to go along with parents rather than friends on party affiliation, with friends rather than parents on an issue like giving the right to vote to 18-year-olds, and somewhere in between on their actual votes in presidential elections.[5]

SCHOOLS Schools also mold young citizens' values and attitudes. American schools see as part of their purpose to prepare students to be citizens and active participants in governing their communities and nation. At an early age, schoolchildren begin to pick up specific political values and acquire basic attitudes toward our system of government. Education, like the family, prepares Americans to live in society.

From kindergarten through college, children generally develop political values that will enhance their citizenship and legitimize the American political system. In their study of American history, schoolchildren are introduced to our nation's

"It should be a 'yes' or 'no' or 'undecided'—we don't accept a 'don't give a damn answer!'"

The Wall Street Journal, December 12, 1990.

The Influence of the Mass Media

The mass media serve as agents of socialization by providing a link between individuals and the values and behavior of others. For example, the mass media present information about our society, and when we watch, listen, and read, we discover which values and role models are considered important. Events that get intensive media coverage often focus our attention on certain issues, as, for example, the televised Senate hearings of the Clarence Thomas confirmation for the Supreme Court. Those hearings directed widespread attention to the issue of sexual harassment in the workplace.

heroes and heroines, the important events in our history, and the ideals of our society. Other aspects of the student's experience, such as the daily Pledge of Allegiance, reinforce respect of country. Children also gain practical experience in the workings of democracy through elections for class or school officers and student government. In some colleges, state legislatures or college trustees have made courses in U.S. history or American government a graduation requirement.

How does college influence political opinions? There is some evidence that students planning to attend college are more likely to be knowledgeable about politics, more in favor of free speech, and more likely to talk and read about politics.[6] Reflecting national trends, campus conservatism and Republicanism increased in the 1980s, but college students in the 1990s were again more liberal.[7] Is this the influence of the professors, the curriculum, or the students? It is difficult to generalize. Parents sometimes fear professors have too much influence on their college-age children; however, most professors doubt that they have significant influence over students. The debate about students being pressed to conform to certain acceptable ideas—so-called *political correctness* (PC)—highlights the role higher education can play in shaping attitudes and values.

OTHER INFLUENCES Family and school are not the only influences on children and adolescents. The mass media also serve as agents of socialization by providing a link between individuals and the values and behavior of others. For example, news broadcasts present information about our society, and media figures can be important trend setters and role models.

Religious and ethnic attitudes may also serve to shape opinions, both within and outside the family. Historically, Protestant families tend to be more conservative than Catholics on economic and welfare issues, whereas Jewish families tend to be more liberal on both economic and noneconomic issues than either Catholics or Protestants. Protestants express varying opinions ranging from conservative to liberal on certain social issues, and all persons are subject to **cross-pressures**, situations in which individuals feel pulled in different directions because of their racial, religious, ethnic, union, or other group pressures. Evangelicals, whose numbers include a small percentage of Catholics but are mainly made up of Protestants from the more fundamentalist sects, tend to be more socially conservative than nonevangelicals. For a discussion of the most important social and economic divisions in American politics, see Chapter 6.

Stability in Public Opinion

Adults are not simply the sum of all their early experiences, however. Political analysts are becoming more interested in the ways in which adults modify their views *after* completing school or college. A major factor may be a harsh experience, such as a war, economic depression, or loss of a job. A clear example of how change in public opinion can lead to change in policy is the issue of troop withdrawal from Vietnam. During the course of the war public support declined, and as that change occurred, so did the rate of troop withdrawals.[8]

In the Persian Gulf War, opposition to the use of U.S. forces was greatly reduced after a few days of success in the air and ground war. A few days before the war, 48 percent favored continued sanctions and 47 percent wanted intensified actions, but after President Bush began the air and ground war, 76 percent said he was right.[9] When American forces were dispatched to Somalia in Operation Restore Hope in January 1993, 79 percent approved of the use of our troops to ensure the delivery of humanitarian aid, food, and medical provisions. But when U.S. soldiers were killed and dragged through the streets of Mogidishu, support fell to only 17 percent in October of the same year.[10]

Sometimes even the strongest and most stable opinions are subject to change. One of the "sacred cows" of American politics in the 1950s and 1960s was nonrecognition of the People's Republic of China. A powerful lobby composed of leaders of both major parties carried on an intense campaign against admitting mainland China to the United Nations. Then President Richard Nixon, who had earlier opposed the recognition of the People's Republic, made his dramatic trip to China and promoted a policy of conciliation with Chinese leaders in Beijing. Many Americans, responding to Nixon's leadership, shifted their own position toward friendlier relations with China. But with the massacre of students in Tiananmen Square in June 1989, American attitudes toward the government of China hardened again.

Some of our opinions change very little because they are part of our basic values. Thus our views on abortion and the death penalty remain basically stable over time. On issues that are less central to our values, such as our view of how a president is performing his job, opinions can show substantial change over time.

Awareness and Interest

For most people, politics is of secondary importance to earning a living, raising a family, and having a good time. Americans are often more concerned about which team wins the Super Bowl than they are about who wins the school board elections, who gets to be mayor, even who gets to be the president of the United States. Most people find politics complicated and difficult to understand. And they should, for democracy is complicated and difficult to understand.

The general adult public fares poorly when quizzed about the name of their member of Congress; only 60 percent can name even one of their U.S. senators[11] (see Table 8-1). Not surprisingly, "On even hotly debated congressional issues, few people know where their Congress member stands."[12] Knowledge of important public policy issues is no better. After years of debate over ratification of the Equal Rights Amendment, nearly one-third of the adults in the United States said they had never heard of it. In late August 1993, several weeks before the vote in Congress on the North American Free Trade Agreement (NAFTA), 6 out of 10 Americans reported they were not following the NAFTA story at all.[13]

Fortunately, not all Americans are uninformed or uninterested. Figure 8-1 presents varying levels of interest in politics. Since 1960, about 25 percent of the public has indicated it is interested in politics most of the time. We call these persons the **attentive public**. They know and understand how the government works, vote in most elections, read a daily newspaper, and "talk politics" with their family and friends. They tend to be better educated and more committed to democratic values than other Americans.

At the opposite end of the spectrum are *nonvoters*, people who have little interest in politics and rarely vote. Since 1960, about 35 percent of Americans have indicated that they have little interest in politics or are only occasionally interested.[14] Between the attentive public and nonvoters are people who might be called *part-time citizens*, roughly the other 40 percent of the American public. These individuals selectively participate in elections, voting in presidential elections but usually not in others. Politics and government do not greatly interest them; they pay only minimal attention to the news, and they rarely discuss candidates or elections with others.

Democracy can exist even with a large number of citizens who are passive and uninformed, as long as there is a substantial number of people who serve as opinion leaders and who are interested and informed about public affairs. But obviously, opinion leaders will have much greater influence than their less active fellow citizens.

TABLE 8-1

Political Participation and Awareness in the United States

Vote in presidential elections	50%
Vote in congressional elections	36
Know name of U.S. representative	28
Sign a petition	48
Write congressman or state representative	30
Vote in local elections	10–30
Try to persuade vote of others	23
Display campaign button, sticker, or sign	7
Attend dinner, meeting, or rally for candidate	6
Contribute to candidate	5
Contribute to a party	4

SOURCES: U.S. Bureau of the Census, *Statistical Abstract of the United States: 1995* (Government Printing Office, 1995), p. 290; Center for Political Studies, University of Michigan, *1994 American National Election Study;* CBS News/New York Times Poll, October 29–November 1, 1994 of 1,429 adults nationwide; Institute for Social Inquiry, Roper Center Poll, August 22–29, 1994 of 1,053 adults nationwide.

FIGURE 8-1 Level of General Interest in Politics, 1994

SOURCE: Center for Political Studies, University of Michigan, *1994 American National Election Study.*

Question: Would you say that you are very much interested, somewhat interested, or not much interested in following the political campaigns this year?

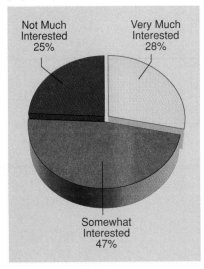

Not Much Interested 25%

Very Much Interested 28%

Somewhat Interested 47%

ELECTION FORCASTING

The use of polls to predict how an election will turn out has not always been accurate. On the whole, the record of leading forecasters in "day before" polling has been good, but the most sensational slip occurred in the 1948 presidential battle between President Harry Truman and New York Governor Thomas E. Dewey. Most polls indicated that Truman was running far behind, and most pollsters held to that prediction to the very end. Gallup gave the president only 45 percent of the popular vote in his final forecast, and Roper predicted 37 percent. *The Chicago Tribune* even ran their early edition with a headline to that effect. When all votes were tallied, Truman had won the election with 48 percent of the popular vote, and the pollsters were subjected to much ridicule.

Presidential Winners Forecast by the Pollsters

Year	Actual Democratic Vote	Roper Poll	Gallup Poll	Harris Poll
1944	54%	54%	53%	—
1948	49	37	45	—
1952	45	43	46	—
1956	42	40	40	—
1960	49	47	49	—
1964	61	—	61	—
1968	43	—	40	43
1972	38	—	35	35
1976	51	51	46*	46*
1980	41	—	44	41
1984	41	45	41	44
1988	46	—	45	48
1992**	43	—	44	44
1996	49	—	52	48

*In 1976 both Gallup and Harris said it was a "toss-up" and refused to make a prediction. They also reported that more people than usual had not made up their minds.

**In 1992, CBS/*New York Times*, *The Washington Post*, *USA Today*/CNN, and *Wall Street Journal*/NBC all predicted Bill Clinton would win with 44 percent of the vote; ABC predicted his vote as 43 percent.

1996 Final Election Forecasts

	Clinton	Dole	Perot
NBC/Wall Street Journal	52	35	6
CNN/USA Today	51	35	8
ABC/Washington Post	51	35	10
CBS/New York Times	53	35	9

PARTICIPATION: TRANSLATING OPINIONS INTO ACTION

Americans can influence their government's actions in different ways. They may vote in elections, join interest groups, go to political party meetings, ring doorbells, place calls to friends urging them to vote for issues or candidates, sign petitions, write letters to the editors of newspapers, and make calls to radio talk shows. But the most common and most important way in which Americans can translate their opinions into government policy is by voting.

Turnout

In part because there are so many elections, American voters tend to pick and choose which elections to vote in. Americans elect officeholders in *general elections*, determine party nominees in *primary elections*, and conduct *special elections* to replace senators who have died or left office. **Turnout**—the proportion of the voting-age public that actually votes—is highest in presidential general elections (see Figure 8–2). It is higher in general elections than in primary elections, and higher in primary elections than in special elections. Turnout is higher in presidential general elections than in midterm general elections (elections held midway between presidential elections), and higher in presidential primary elections than in midterm primary elections.[15] Turnout is higher in elections in which candidates for federal office are on the ballot (U.S. senator, member of the House of Representatives, president) than in state elections in years when there are no federal contests. Some states elect their governor and other state officials in odd-numbered years to separate state from national politics. The result is generally lower turnout. Finally, local or municipal elections have lower turnout than state elections, and municipal primaries have an even lower rate of participation. In Pasadena, the 1992 general election saw a 46 percent turnout, as opposed to only 34 percent for the 1990 statewide general election and 6 percent for the local school board election (see Table 8–2).

Registration

Voting laws can also affect turnout. One peculiarly American legal requirement—**voter registration**—discourages voting. Most other democracies have automatic voter registration. Average turnout in the United States is more than

TABLE 8-2

Voter Participation in Pasadena, California, 1990–1996

	Number	Percent
1996 voting age population	106,911	
1990 statewide primary election	24,692	24%
1990 statewide general election	34,909*	34
1991, March, school board primary election	8,112**	8
1991, April, school board general election	6,397**	6
1992 statewide primary election	23,193	22
1992 statewide general election	47,346	45
1993, March, school board primary election	9,064**	9
1993, April, school board general election	6,588*	6
1993 statewide special election	18,303	17
1994 statewide primary election	17,236	16
1994 statewide general election	31,225	30
1995, March, school board primary election	10,735**	10
1995, April, school board general election	8,692**	8
1996 statewide primary election	20,842	19
1996 statewide general election	36,943	35

SOURCES: Los Angeles County Registrar, Election Information Office; Pasadena, City Clerk Department; census data from Department of Finance, California State Data Center.

Note: All percentages were calculated using an estimated voting age population for each year. Nationwide turnout in 1996 as a percentage of voting age population was 49 percent.

*Absentee ballots not counted at city level; countywide average of 14 percent added for estimate of in-person and absentee voting.

**Pasadena turnout on the basis of 62 percent of registered voters in school district residing in Pasadena.

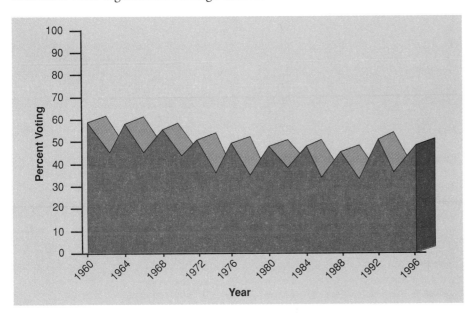

FIGURE 8-2 Voter Turnout in Presidential and Midterm Elections, 1960–1996

SOURCE: U.S. Bureau of the Census, *Statistical Abstract of the United States, 1995* (Government Printing Office, 1993) p. 290. For 1996, Committee for the Study of the American Electorate.

30 percentage points lower than in countries like Australia, Austria, Belgium, Denmark, Italy, and West Germany; only Switzerland has lower average turnout[16] (see Table 8–3). This was not always the case. In fact, in the 1800s, turnout in the United States was much like that of Europe today; roughly 80 percent or more of those eligible voted. Turnout began to drop significantly around the turn of the century, in part as a result of election reform (see Figure 8–3).

American elections in the 1800s were quite different from those of today. Ballots were prepared by the parties, often using different colors of paper which allowed them to monitor how people had voted. In some areas there were charges of multiple voting because there was no system of voter registration. These problems led to a reform movement that substituted the **Australian ballot**, a secret ballot printed by the state, for the party ballots, and a system of voter registration to reduce multiple voting and to limit voting to those who had previously established their eligibility. These reforms were implemented by states and not by the federal government, which accounts for different registration requirements and ballot forms across states.

TABLE 8–3

Registration and Voting in the World's Democracies, 1980s and 1990s

	Turnout as Percent of Eligible Vote	Compulsion Penalties*	Automatic Registration**
Australia	94%	Yes	No
Austria	91	No	Yes
Belgium	93	Yes	Yes
Canada	76	No	Yes
Denmark	86	No	Yes
Finland	78	No	Yes
France	66	No	No
Germany	84	No	Yes
Greece	85	Yes	Yes
Iceland	90		
Ireland	69	No	Yes
Israel	80	No	Yes
Italy	91	Yes	Yes
Japan	71	No	Yes
Luxembourg	87		
Malta	96		
Netherlands	86	No	Yes
New Zealand	87	No	No
Norway	84	No	Yes
Portugal	73		
Spain	71	No	Yes
Sweden	86	No	Yes
Switzerland	46	No	Yes
United Kingdom	75	No	Yes
United States	53	No	No

SOURCE: Thomas T. Mackie and Richard Rose, *The International Almanac of Electoral History*, 3d ed. (Congressional Quarterly, 1991). G. Bingham Powell, Jr., "American Voter Turnout in Comparative Perspective," *American Political Science Review* 80 (March 1986), p. 38.

*Compulsion penalties are fines or other possible state actions against nonvoters.

**Automatic registration utilizes other forms of citizen identification like a driver's license.

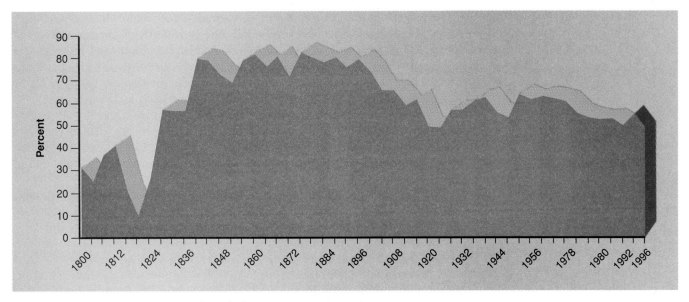

FIGURE 8-3 Voter Turnout in Presidential Elections, 1800–1996

SOURCE: For 1800–1986, Walter Dean Burnham, "The Turnout Problem," in *Elections American Style*, ed. A. James Reichley (Brookings, 1987), pp. 113–114; for 1988–1992, U.S. Bureau of the Census, *Current Population Reports, Studies in the Measurement of Voter Turnout* (Government Printing Office, 1990, 1992). For 1996, Committee for the Study of the American Electorate.

Voter registration places a responsibility on voters to take an extra step—usually filling out a form at the county courthouse or with a roving registrar—some days or weeks before the election. Registration laws vary by state, but in every state except North Dakota, registration is required in order to vote. Three states permit election day voter registration. The most important provision regarding voter registration may be the closing date; some years ago it was not uncommon for closing days to be 180 days or six months before the election. In elections for members of Congress and president, no state can now stop registration more than 30 days before an election.[17]

MOTOR VOTER In 1993 Congress passed and President Clinton signed into law the National Voter Registration Act, a law requiring states to allow citizens to register when they apply for or renew drivers' licenses, request public certificates, or make contact with welfare or disability assistance offices. States also have the option to include public schools, libraries, and city and county clerks' offices as registration sites. The law also requires states to permit registration by mail using a standardized form.

The "Motor Voter" law took effect with the 1996 election cycle. Motor Voter was supported by most Democrats and opposed by most Republicans, consistent with the assumption that Republicans are more likely to register without Motor Voter. Proponents of the reform argue that it will reach the 49 million Americans who are of voting age with driver's licenses or identification cards but are not registered to vote. Opponents claim that the law is another federal mandate that does not appropriate money to pay for the costs involved. They also contend that it will increase election fraud because of the difficulty of removing names from voting rolls.

It appears that the law has been successful, at least in terms of numbers of new voters registered. Nearly one million people per month have registered or updated their voting addresses since January 1995. By the 1996 election there will be 20 million new voters and an estimated 20 million more by 1998.[18] Early data on the impact of Motor Voter suggest that neither Democrats nor Republicans are the primary beneficiaries because most who have registered claim to be Independent.

States may continue to make voter registration even easier than Motor Voter. Six states permit registration on election day, and North Dakota, as noted, has no voter registration at all. Motor Voter requires a questionnaire be mailed to registered voters every four years in order to purge for death and change of residence, but forbids purging for any other reasons, such as nonvoting. Making registration easier, as was done with Motor Voter, should increase turnout.

Although Americans can hardly avoid reading or hearing about political campaigns, almost 90 million Americans fail to vote in presidential elections! Voting turnout peaked in 1960, when 63 percent of the voting age population voted.[19] Turnout is even lower in years when there is no presidential election or in local elections.[20]

The fact that the percentage of Americans who vote has been going down since 1960 is even more significant because since then the number of Americans eligible to vote has been going up. The Voting Rights Act of 1965 added large numbers of African Americans to the pool of registered voters. Women, another historically underrepresented group, have also increased their voting levels to the point where, in 1988, 1992, and again in 1996, turnout among women actually exceeded that of men. Finally, our electorate has grown richer and more educated since the 1960s, and since wealth and education are related to voting, we should have seen an increase instead of a decrease in voting. Turnout in 1996 dropped to 49 percent, just under the percentage that voted in 1988 (50 percent) and well below the 55 percent who voted in 1992. Minnesota led the country with more than two-thirds of the voting age population voting, while turnout was lowest in Georgia and South Carolina (41 percent).

Why Is Turnout So Low?

Cynicism about politics is widespread and has grown in recent years, as this photo shows.

Half of all eligible voters do not vote. Who are they? Why do they not vote? Is the fact that so many Americans chose not to vote a cause for alarm? If so, what can we do about it? Some people do not vote because they are lazy, and some people do not vote because they have no interest in matters political. But lack of interest in politics does not appear to be a satisfactory explanation of why Americans have such a bad voting record, for we compare favorably with other nations in political interest and awareness.[21] But for a variety of institutional and political reasons we fail to convert our political interest into votes.

The "cost" of voting is higher in the United States than in other industrial democracies, while the perceived benefits are lower.[22] By "cost" we mean the expenditure of time and effort required to vote. In our system, individuals face tough institutional obstacles to voting and must make sense out of political alternatives that do not necessarily meet their interests. In the United States, the two major parties have drawn closer together on many issues, and their concurrence, it can be argued, makes the voting choice of lesser consequence. But voter registration, already examined, appears to be the major block to voting.[23]

In other large industrialized democracies, the political parties shoulder much of the burden of persuading people to vote. American parties are too weak to take on this task; in particular, the Democratic party, which has an enormous stake in a heavy voter turnout from lower-income Americans, seldom achieves the voting participation it wants. Another factor is the absence of real competition in many election contests. There is also a psychological factor. Some Americans believe it makes no difference who wins.

Some critics also say the reason people do not vote is that our political leaders do not appeal to them. Some of the reasons elections are characterized as unappealing or uninteresting are that the candidates do not offer "real choices." Candidates are not exciting, or parties and candidates avoid taking positions on

From Coast to Coast

Average Turnout Percentage in General Elections by State, 1980–92

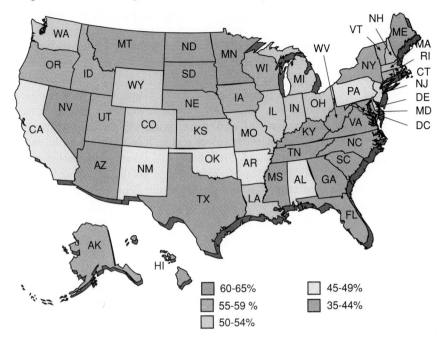

Legend:
- 60-65%
- 55-59 %
- 50-54%
- 45-49%
- 35-44%

SOURCE: Royce Crocker, "Voter Registration and Turnout: 1948–1990," *Congressional Research Service*, August 11, 1992, pp. 20–31; and Royce Crocker, "Voter Turnout in the Presidential Election of 1992: The States," *Congressional Research Service*, January 26, 1993.

the most important issues. Yet in several recent elections, there have been important differences between the parties on such salient issues as the size and role of government, health care reform, taxes, and how to achieve a balanced budget.

During the 1992 election campaign there was much discussion of voter anger and frustration with government. The candidacy of H. Ross Perot was seen as appealing to this anger and frustration. Widespread concern with the economy and the perception that there was a need for change in the government motivated a record number of Americans to vote in the 1992 elections. More than 10 percent of the people who voted in 1992 were voting for the first time, and these new voters mainly supported Bill Clinton. Turnout rose by 5 percentage points over the 1988 election; in some states, the increase was as much as 10 percent.

In the 1994 midterm elections, 36 percent of the voting age population voted. This figure was higher than in the preceding midterm elections of 1986, when turnout was 33.5 percent, and 1990, when it was 33.1 percent.[24] According to exit polls, voters in 1994 were about twice as likely to be conservative as liberal. Although Republicans won both houses of Congress, there were more Democrats than Republicans among voters in 1994, and a plurality said they had voted for Clinton in 1992. Turnout may have been a partial explanation for the defeat suffered by Democrats in 1994, but it is not the primary explanation.

Reforms like the Motor Voter law and efforts to register younger voters through programs like "Rock the Vote" fostered increases in voter registration in 1996. But turnout declined in 1996 to 49 percent. What explained this drop in turnout? One among many plausible explanations is that voters decided there was no point in voting because of Clinton's large lead in preelection polls.

	1992	1994
Sex		
Male	60.2%	44.4%
Female	62.3	44.9
Age		
18–20	38.5	16.5
21–24	45.7	22.3
25–34	53.2	32.2
35–44	63.6	46.0
45–64	70.0	56.0
65+	70.1	60.7
Education		
8 Years or less	35.1	23.2
Some High School	41.2	27.0
High School Graduate	57.5	40.5
Some College	68.7	49.1
College Graduate	81.0	63.1
Race		
White	63.6	46.9
Black	54.0	37.0
Hispanic	28.9	19.1

SOURCE: U.S. Bureau of the Census, *Statistical Abstract of the United States: 1995* (Government Printing Office, 1995), p. 289.

Who Votes?

The extent of voting varies widely among different groups. The amount of education individuals have especially helps predict whether or not they will vote. "Education increases one's capacity for understanding complex and intangible subjects such as politics, as well as encouraging the ethic of civil responsibility. Moreover, schools provide experience with a variety of bureaucratic problems, such as coping with requirements, filling out forms, and meeting deadlines."[25] The data are convincing: as education increases, so does the propensity to vote.[26]

Income and age are also important factors. Those with higher family incomes are more likely to vote than those with lower incomes. Income, of course, corresponds to occupation, and those with higher-status careers are more likely to vote than those with lower-status jobs. Poor people are less likely to feel politically involved and confident, and their social norms tend to de-emphasize politics.[27] Older people, unless they are very old and perhaps infirm, are more likely to vote than younger people. People 18 to 24 years of age have a poor voting record; so do those over 78.[28] Women's recent higher turnout is generally attributed to increasing levels of education and employment; black women in particular are influenced by their party identification and by attitudes on gender issues.[29]

To sum up, the poor, the young, the uneducated, African Americans, Hispanics, and the homeless are still seriously underrepresented among voters. College graduates, high-income persons, farmers, and public employees are overrepresented.

Other Forms of Participation

Aside from voting, most people participate in politics and government infrequently and sporadically. For most people, politics is a private activity. Some books on manners still advise it is impolite to discuss politics at dinner parties. To say that politics is private does not mean people do not have opinions or will not discuss them when asked by others, including pollsters. But often politics is avoided in discussions with neighbors, work associates, even friends and family, as too divisive or upsetting. Typically, less than one person in five attempts to

College students have comparatively low rates of voting, perhaps because they are busy with other matters. Older citizens are more likely to vote and participate in the political process.

influence how another person votes in an election. An even smaller number actually work for a candidate or party. Only 5 percent of the public in 1994 made a contribution to a candidate, and only one in four designated one dollar of their taxes to the fund that pays for presidential general elections.[30] Despite concern about whether there would be enough money in the presidential campaign fund to cover the 1996 election, it turned out that the amount was sufficient.

Few individuals attempt to influence others by writing letters to elected officials or to editors of newspapers for publication. Even smaller numbers participate in protest groups or activities. Despite the small number of persons who engage in these activities, it would be a mistake to assume that small numbers of individuals cannot make a difference to politics and government. Often an individual or small group can generate media interest in an issue and expand the impact. Peaceful protests for civil rights, environmental issues, and abortion generate public attention and perhaps even change public opinion.

New democracies are often founded on protest or revolution—a form of participation that involves substantial risk for the participants. The 1991 attempted coup in the former Soviet Union collapsed in part because of the participation of more than 100,000 people who formed a human barricade between President Boris Yeltsin and those who would have arrested him. Such participation is not always successful; the protest in 1989 of Chinese students in Tiananmen Square failed to stop the onslaught of tanks and the repression that followed. Americans sometimes forget that democracy is often born of protest or revolution, and the continued existence of a constitutional democracy is much less difficult and demanding of public participation than its creation.

VOTING BEHAVIOR IN THE UNITED STATES

Why do people vote as they do? Political scientists have identified three main elements of the voting choice: partisan identification, candidate appeal, and issues. These elements overlap.

Partisan Identification

Partisan identification is the subjective sense of identification or affiliation that a person has with a political party, a long-standing preference for one party over the other. Partisan identification has a lot to do with one's evaluation of the candidates and often predicts a person's stand on issues. It is part of our national mythology that Americans vote for the person and not the party because, as we will see, the person we vote for is most often from our party.

Partisanship is typically acquired in childhood or adolescence as a result of the socialization process in the family, then reinforced by peer groups in adolescence. In the absence of reasons to vote otherwise, people depend on this preference or identification to simplify their voting choices. Partisan identification is not party registration, the device used in several states to restrict voting in party primaries to persons who register with that party. It is not party membership in the sense of being a dues-paying, card-carrying member, as in some European parties. Rather it is a psychological sense of attachment to one party or another.

Partisan identification remains more stable than people's attitudes on issues or political ideology. Fluctuations in partisan identification appear to be in response to economic conditions and political performance, especially of the president.[31] The more information voters have about their choices, the more likely they are to defect from their party and vote for a candidate from the other

especially when we recognize that two-thirds of all Independents are, in fact, partisans in their voting behavior. There were only 11 percent pure Independents, people with no party preference in 1994, and the average from 1952 to 1994 was only 13 percent.[32] Party identification is discussed in greater detail in Chapter 7.

Although long-term partisan identification is important, it clearly is not the only factor; otherwise the Democrats should have won every presidential election since the last realignment in 1932. In fact, Republicans have been quite successful in winning the White House during this period. The answer to this puzzle is largely found in a second major explanation of voting choice—*candidate appeal*.

Candidate Appeal

The focus on candidates and their strengths or weakness is not new, but the greater weight given to these candidate evaluations is an important development in American politics.[33] Candidate appeal or the lack of it—in terms of leadership, experience, good judgment, integrity, competence, strength, and energy—is often more important than party or issues. Dwight Eisenhower had great candidate appeal. He was a legendary five-star hero of the Allied effort in the World War II. Yet not all generals are successful in politics. Rather, it was Ike's unmilitary manner, his moderation, his personal charm, and his lack of a strong party position that made him appealing across the ideological spectrum. Ronald Reagan generated positive candidate appeal, in part by asserting mainstream values the public found lacking in Jimmy Carter—leadership and strength. Reagan also attempted to broaden his appeal in his acceptance speech in 1980 by conspicuously quoting Franklin D. Roosevelt, the leader of the modern Democratic party.

George McGovern in 1972, like Barry Goldwater in 1964, had negative appeal. Many of his supporters who appeared on television and in the newspapers, by their dress and manner, appeared not to be part of mainstream America. McGovern raised doubts about his judgment and leadership by how he handled his choice of a vice-president. McGovern named Missouri Senator Tom Eagleton as his running mate, only to discover that Eagleton had been hospitalized previously for treatment of emotional exhaustion and depression. McGovern initially stood behind Eagleton, but as press coverage and criticism of McGovern's lack of investigation into Eagleton's past grew, McGovern dropped Eagleton and named a new running mate. To the public, the episode reflected poorly on McGovern's judgment and his consistency in the face of opposition. In the end, "only about one-third of the public thought he could be trusted as president."[34]

Candidate appeal can thus have positive or negative components; increasingly, our politics focuses on the negative elements of candidates. Opponents and the media are quick to point out the limitations or problems of any given candidate. The 1996 primary campaigns in the Republican party were often negative in tone, with candidates claiming that Bob Dole had been in Washington too long and was too old, that Pat Buchanan had never held public office and was an extremist, that Steve Forbes lacked experience and was attempting to buy the election.

Bob Dole and Bill Clinton brought very different styles to the 1996 campaign. Clinton's skill in thinking on his feet, establishing rapport with his audience, and in articulating his position were important parts of his candidate appeal. Dole emphasized his war record and having overcome serious injuries as evidence of his strength of character.

For most of the general election campaign, Dole was unwilling to attack Bill Clinton's character: his rumored extramarital affairs, disputed honesty, the ethical problems associated with Whitewater, and FBI files of Republicans requested by his White House staff.

What did Americans make of the character issue in 1996? On dimensions of candidate character like "keeps his promises" and "honest and truthful," people found Dole more appealing. Exit polls demonstrate that more than half the voters did not see Bill Clinton as honest, and 60 percent said he had not told the truth about Whitewater. But to most voters in 1996, issues like the economy and jobs mattered more than a candidate's character. Polls also demonstrated that candidate character includes such dimensions as "has new ideas" or "cares about people like me," and on these dimensions voters preferred Clinton to Dole.

Voting on the Basis of Issues

Analysts of voting behavior heatedly debate the role of issues in voters' choices; yet most scholars agree that issues, while important, are not as central to the decision-making process as partisanship and candidate appeal.[35] Part of the reason is that candidates often intentionally obscure their positions on issues, an understandable strategy.[36] Richard Nixon said he had a plan to end the Vietnam War in 1968, clearly the most important issue at the time, but he would not reveal the specifics of his plan. By not detailing his plan, he stood to gain votes from those who wanted a more aggressive war effort as well as those who wanted a cease-fire.

Voting on the basis of issues presumes a level of voter interest and awareness found in only a few voters. For issue voting to occur, the issue must be important to voters, opposing candidates must take different stands on the issues, and voters must know the candidates' positions and vote accordingly. Rarely do candidate elections focus on only one issue. Voters will often agree with one candidate on one issue and with the opposing candidate on another. In such an instance, issues will likely not be the determining factor. This view of issues does not mean candidates can take any issue position they wish.[37]

Issue voting can be *prospective issue voting*, voting based on what a candidate pledges to do about an issue if elected, or *retrospective issue voting*, voters holding the incumbent administration responsible for its performance with the economy and foreign policy.[38] Voter dissatisfaction with the economy was important to the outcome of the 1992 and 1996 presidential elections. More than two-thirds of Americans responding in exit polls described the economy in 1992 in negative terms. Bill Clinton had sought to focus the 1992 campaign on the economy, and his success in doing so was essential to Democratic victory. The economic issue included concern about the recession, uncertainty about jobs, and the threat of foreign competition.

Bill Clinton was successful again in making the economy the focus of the 1996 election, pointing to job creation, low inflation, and progress in lowering the federal budget deficit.

The state of the economy is often the central issue in midterm elections as well as in presidential elections. Several studies have found a positive relationship between the state of the economy and "out" party gains (and "in" party losses) in congressional seats.[39] Voters tend to vote against candidates of the "in" party, including incumbents, if the voters perceive a decline in their personal financial situation.[40] Voters see responsibility for the economy resting more with the president and Congress than with governors or local officials.[41]

Socioeconomic status is also important. Less-educated and low-income voters tend to judge a candidate on the basis of their personal financial condition. Upper-status voters, who personally tend to suffer less when economic conditions decline, are more likely to watch the overall performance of the economy and to judge candidates on that basis.[42]

The Clinton campaign won the battle of issues in 1996. He made the economy and job creation a centerpiece of his reelection bid, and voters rewarded him with a second term in office. Exit polls indicated that voters, by a margin

What Do You Think Is the Most Important Issue Facing the Country Today?

Balancing the Budget/ Budget Deficit	19%
Crime	13
The Economy	9
Unemployment	8
Welfare	4
Ethics/Morality	4
Homelessness	4
Health Care	3
Medicare	3
Drugs	3
Congress	2
Race Relations	2
Education	2
Taxes	2
Youth	2
Politicians/Government	2
Foreign Policy	2
Other	8
Don't Know/No Answer	8

SOURCE: © The Roper Center for Public Opinion Research, University of Connecticut, Storrs, CT. Reprinted by permission.

of three to two, saw the condition of the nation's economy as excellent or good compared to those who saw it as poor or not so good. The Dole campaign countered that the economy was not growing fast enough and tried to revive one of the themes of the Republican presidential primaries that there was uncertainty about the stability of employment and the economy.

Dole, Clinton, and Perot all stressed deficit reduction. Voters, however, by a margin greater than two to one, rejected Dole's supply-side argument that he could lower taxes by 15 percent and still reduce the federal budget deficit.

Foreign and defense policy were rarely mentioned by voters as important problems. While Clinton and Dole disagreed occasionally over how much money to spend on defense or when to commit U.S. forces as peacekeepers, the issue did not matter to many voters.

Both Bob Dole and Ross Perot attempted to make Bill Clinton's character an issue in the general election campaign. His first term had been plagued with controversies surrounding the dismissal of the White House travel staff, whether confidential FBI reports had been improperly obtained, whether the president or first lady had broken any laws in their failed Whitewater business venture, and whether the campaign contributions on behalf of the Indonesian business interests had been proper. Both of Clinton's opponents raised the possibility of multiple investigations against the president in his second term, but most voters saw issues affecting their lives—the economy, jobs, and medical leave—as more important.

ELECTIONS: THE RULES OF THE GAME

The rules of the electoral game make a difference. Although the Constitution sets certain conditions and requirements, and Congress has been exercising this power with greater frequency, most electoral rules remain matters of state law.

Regularly Scheduled Elections

Elections in the United States are set in advance and at fixed intervals. General elections in which members of Congress and presidential electors are chosen—*federal elections*—occur the first Tuesday after the first Monday in November of even-numbered years. While there are some exceptions (special elections or peculiar state provisions), we know in advance just when the next election will be. In most parliamentary democracies, such as Great Britain and Canada, the time of the election is open, as long as an election is held every five years; elections can be called by the existing government at a time of its choosing.

Fixed, Staggered, and Sometimes Limited Terms

Our electoral system is based on *fixed terms*, meaning that the length of a term in office is set, not indefinite. The Constitution has set the term of office for the U.S. House of Representatives at two years, the Senate at six years, and the presidency at four years. Fixed terms of office mean that politicians can anticipate the next election for a given office and plan for it.

Our system also has *staggered terms* of office, meaning that not all offices are up for election at the same time. Although all House members are up for election every two years, only one-third of the senators are up for election at the same time. House members find themselves in a perpetual campaign, and many have expressed support for lengthening their terms to four years. House members must also give up their seats to run for the Senate; with a four-year term they could run for the Senate at the middle of their term and, if they lost, still retain their House seat. Senators strongly oppose this change, even though the same concern affects those senators who think of running for the presidency. If the presidential election occurs two or four years into their six-year term, senators can run for the presidency without fear of losing their seat. But if their Senate term expires the same year as the presidential election, they must give up their Senate seat to run for president or vice-president. Texas is an exception. Lyndon Johnson had state law changed to permit him to run for both vice-president and the Senate in 1960.[43]

Term limitation is another electoral rule with important consequences. The Twenty-second Amendment to the Constitution, adopted in 1951, limits persons elected president to two terms. Knowing that a president cannot run again changes the way the Congress, the opposing party, and the press regard a president. A politician who cannot, or has announced he or she will not, run again is called a **lame duck**. Efforts to limit the terms of other politicians have become a major issue in several American states. The most frequent targets have been state legislators.

Term limits are very popular. They have only been defeated in three states (Washington, Utah, and Mississippi); 22 states have enacted them.[44] Three-fourths of all voters favor term limits; as do nine out of ten Strong Republicans and seven out of ten Strong Democrats. Still, despite their popularity and the Contract with America's promise to bring them to a vote, term limits failed to pass in the 104th Congress.

The Supreme Court, by a vote of five to four, declared that a state has no power to impose limits on the number of terms for which its members of Congress are eligible either by amending its own constitution or state law.[45] If term limits are to be imposed on Congress, it will have to be done either by an amendment to the United States Constitution or a change in the decisions of the Supreme Court.

Winner Takes All

One of the most important features of our electoral system is the **winner-takes-all** rule.[46] In most American electoral settings, the candidate with the most votes wins. The winner does not necessarily need to have a *majority* (more than half); in a multicandidate race, the winner may have only a *plurality* (the largest number of votes), as Bill Clinton did in 1992.

Most American election districts are *single-member districts*, meaning that for any given election—senator, governor, U.S. House, state legislative seat—the election is to choose only one representative or official.[47] An important consequence of the winner-takes-all rule and the single-member district rule is our moderate two-party system. The only way to win power is to assemble a large coalition that leads to a majority or at least a plurality.

The single member district system is very different from **proportional representation** systems, in which political parties secure legislative seats and power in proportion to the number of votes they receive in the election. Let's assume a hypothetical state with three representatives up for election. In each of the three contests the Republican defeats the Democrat, but in one district by only a very narrow margin. If you add up the statewide vote, the Republicans get 67 percent and the Democrats 33 percent. Under our winner-takes-all and single-member district rules, the Republicans get all three seats. But under a system of proportional representation, the Democrats would receive one seat because they got roughly one-third of the vote. Proportional representation

"Yes, I think some officials should be limited to one or two terms, and others to none."

Dunagin's People by Ralph Dunagin. Reprinted with special permission of NAS, Inc.

When there are only two major candidates for the presidency, the chances of an election being "thrown into the House" are remote. But twice in our history the House has had to act: in 1800, before the Twelfth Amendment came into existence, the House had to choose in a tie vote between Thomas Jefferson and Aaron Burr; in 1824 the House picked John Quincy Adams over Andrew Jackson, William Crawford, and Henry Clay.

The 1824 vote in the House was especially contentious. Jackson, the popular vote winner, was passed over when the vote went to the House. This infuriated the supporters of Jackson, who won the electoral college vote by a wide margin four years later.

thus rewards minor parties and permits them to go their separate ways. Countries that practice some form of proportional representation include Germany, Israel, and Japan. Other examples of election practices that make a difference include determining party nominees by primary election rather than by party elites, electing U.S. senators by a vote of the people rather than in the state legislature (as of 1913 prohibited by the Seventeenth Amendment), and the form of the ballot adopted by the state.

The Electoral College

When it comes to electing our president and vice-president, we do so by a clumsy device known as the **electoral college**, a system the framers devised to remove the choice from a direct vote by the people.

Each state has as many electors as it has representatives plus senators. California, for instance, has 54 electoral votes, and Vermont has three. Electors are often long-time party workers appointed by the parties. They pledge, if elected, to cast their electoral votes for the party's candidates for president and vice-president. Electors vote separately for president and vice-president. If you voted for Bill Clinton for president in 1996, you were actually voting for electors pledged to vote for Clinton and Albert Gore. If you voted for Bob Dole and Jack Kemp, you were in fact voting for electors pledged to them. Candidates who win a plurality of the popular vote in a state secure *all* of that state's electoral vote except in Nebraska and Maine, which allocate electoral votes to the winner in each congressional district plus two electoral votes for whoever carried the state as whole. If no candidate gets a majority of the electoral votes for president, the U.S. House of Representatives chooses among the top three candidates, with each state delegation having one vote. If no candidate gets a majority of the electoral votes for vice-president, the Senate chooses among the top two candidates, with each senator casting one vote.

Interest in the electoral college is renewed every time there is a serious third party candidate for the presidency, as was the case in 1992 when Ross Perot ran for president. Third-party candidacies evoke lots of questions about the process of electing the president: Which Congress casts the vote, the one now serving or the new one just elected? The answer is the new one, the one elected in November and taking office the first week in January. But what happens if a state's delegation cannot agree on a candidate? Its vote doesn't count. Would it be possible to have a president of one party and a vice-president of another? Yes, if the election were thrown into the House and Senate.

The operation of the electoral college influences presidential politics. In order to win a presidential election, a candidate must appeal successfully to big states such as California, Texas, Ohio, and Illinois.[48] California's total electoral vote of 54 exceeds the combined electoral votes of the fourteen least-populated states plus the District of Columbia. Figure 8–4 provides a visual comparison of state size according to electoral votes. Presidential candidates ordinarily do not waste time campaigning in a state unless they have at least a fighting chance of carrying that state; nor do they waste time in a state in which their party is a sure winner. The contest usually narrows down to the medium-sized and big states, where the balance between the parties tends to be fairly even.

Our electoral college system makes it possible for a person to receive the most popular votes but not enough electoral votes. This has happened three times: in

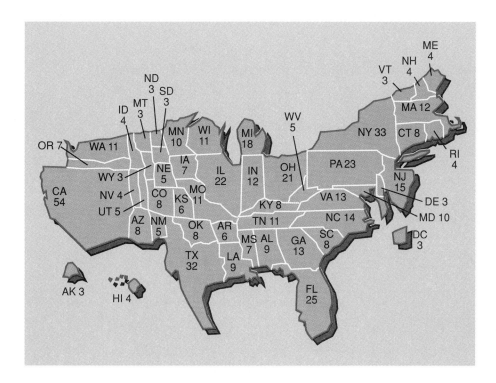

FIGURE 8-4 State Size Based on the Number of Electoral Votes, 1990

SOURCE: Holly Idelson, "Count Adds Seats in Eight States," *Congressional Quarterly Weekly Report* 48 (December 29, 1990), p. 4240.

1824, when Andrew Jackson won 12 percent more of the vote than John Quincy Adams; in 1876, when Samuel Tilden received more popular votes than Rutherford B. Hayes; and again in 1888, when, despite his large popular vote, Grover Cleveland received fewer electoral votes than Benjamin Harrison. It has almost happened in recent history, particularly in the close elections of 1960 and 1976, when the shift of a few votes in a few key states would have resulted in the election of a president without a popular majority. In a year with a serious minor party candidate, the result could be the election of a president without a plurality of the vote.

RUNNING FOR CONGRESS

How candidates run for Congress depends on the nature of their district or state, on whether candidates are incumbents or challengers, on the strength of their personal organization, on how well known they are, and on how much money they have to spend on their campaign. We can, however, note five similarities in House and Senate elections:

1. Most congressional elections are not even close, and incumbents enjoy a substantial advantage in congressional campaigns.
2. Presidential popularity, or its absence, affects both House and Senate elections (see Figure 8–5).
3. Congressional campaigns are increasingly run by professionals skilled in the new campaign technologies: opinion pollsters, direct-mail fund raisers, computer experts, and media specialists.
4. Campaigns often use negative campaigning—focusing on an opponent's alleged failings or previous record.

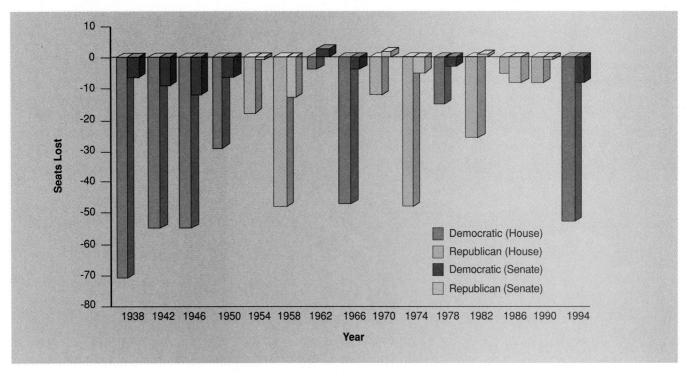

FIGURE 8-5 Seats Lost by the President's Party in National Midterm Elections to Congress, 1938–1994

SOURCE: Harold W. Stanley and Richard G. Niemi, *Vital Statistics of American Politics*, 5th ed. (Congressional Quarterly Press, 1995), p. 189.

Congressional elections in the 1990s are candidate-centered, as opposed to issue-centered or party-centered, and increasingly involve use of the mass media. Politicians essentially nominate themselves for office by winning votes in the primary election. To do this, candidates must rely on the building blocks of name identification and raising funds for advertising.[49] Once elected, politicians are driven by the desire for reelection.[50] Concern with governing becomes less important than winning reelection or positioning oneself for a run at a higher office.

The House of Representatives

Every two years, as many as 1,000 candidates—including approximately 400 incumbents—campaign for Congress. After deciding to take the plunge, candidates must first plan a primary race, unless they face no opponents for their party's nomination. Incumbents are rarely challenged for renomination from within their own party, and when they are, the challenges are rarely serious. Challengers running against entrenched incumbents are least likely to encounter primary opposition.[51] In 1988 and again in 1990, for example, only one House incumbent was defeated in a primary election. In 1992 more candidates lost in the primaries or chose not to seek reelection than had been the case for many years; in large part this was because the redistricting after the 1990 census placed some incumbents in the same district as a fellow incumbent. In 1994 only four incumbents seeking reelection were not renominated, reinforcing the long-standing pattern that once elected, representatives are almost always renominated.

MOUNTING A PRIMARY CAMPAIGN   For would-be challengers in contested primaries or for those seeking open seats, the first step is to build a *personal organization*, because the party organization usually stays neutral until the nomination is decided. A candidate can build an organization while holding a lesser office, such as a seat in the state legislature, or by deliberately getting to know people, serving in civic causes, helping other candidates, and being conspicuous without being controversial.

The next step is to raise funds, to hire campaign managers and technicians, buy television and other advertising, conduct polls, and pay for a variety of other activities. But few candidates are able to do this effectively in primaries. Most primary campaigns are run on low budgets with limited funds.

A candidate's main hurdle is gaining visibility. Candidates work hard to be mentioned by the media. But in large metropolitan areas where print and broadcast journalists cover many campaigns simultaneously, congressional candidates are frequently lost in the media "noise." In rural areas the press often plays down political news. Candidates rely on personal contacts, on hand shaking and door-to-door campaigning, and on identifying likely supporters and courting their favor—the same techniques used in campaigns for lesser offices. Turnout in primaries tends to be very low, except in campaigns in which large sums of money are expended on advertising.

CAMPAIGNING FOR THE GENERAL ELECTION   Campaigning for Congress becomes more sophisticated in the general election. General election campaigns can be divided into three types: incumbent campaigns with serious challenger campaigns; incumbent campaigns with weak challenger campaigns; and open-seat campaigns.

Most incumbent members of Congress successfully seek reelection.[52] Since 1970, over 95 percent of incumbent House members seeking reelection have won. Even in 1994, which is often seen as a year of major change in the U.S. House, over 90 percent of incumbents seeking reelection were returned to office. Incumbents tend to win reelection because they are popular, and those who run against them run weak campaigns and are underfunded.[53] Potential challengers, knowing the advantage of incumbency, choose not to challenge and thereby help the incumbent further.[54] In House elections incumbents outspent challengers by roughly 3 to 1, although this narrowed in 1994; in the Senate the difference is typically closer to 2 to 1.[55] Most challengers spend little money, run campaigns that are not significantly more visible than primary campaigns, contact few voters, and lose badly.

Why is keeping a House seat so much easier than gaining it? Incumbents have a host of perquisites. These "perks" include free mailings to constituents (the franking privilege), the free use of broadcast studios to record radio and television tapes to be sent to local media outlets, and perhaps most important of all, a large staff to perform countless favors and send a stream of press reports and mail back to the home district. All these advantages help a House member build name recognition and a positive image.[56] Representatives also try to win committee posts, even on minor committees, that relate to the needs of their districts and build connections with constituents.[57]

If incumbents win so often, how do we get any significant turnover in the House of Representatives at all? Turnover comes when incumbents die, decide to retire, or seek some other office. Redistricting, which happens once each decade, can lead to high turnover, as it did in 1992 when incumbents were forced to run against each other in new districts. The number of House members retiring has been high in the last three elections—65 retired in 1992, 48 in 1994 and 36 in 1996. Reasons for retirement vary, but the effect has been

"My former opponent is supporting me in the general election. Please disregard all the things I said about him in the primary."

Dunagin's People by Ralph Dunagin. Reprinted with special permission of NAS, Inc.

to reinforce the partisan and ideological shift in the House to greater conservatism and Republicanism. Incumbents may decide that the new district is less friendly to them and may either run for another office or retire. Potential candidates for the House as well as political action committees and political party committees all watch open seat races closely. Hence open-seat races tend to be more competitive.

The Senate

Running for the Senate is big-time politics. The six-year term and the national exposure make a Senate seat a glittering prize, so competition is usually intense. A race normally costs millions of dollars.[58]

Although Senate races tend to be like those for the House, Senate candidates are far more visible, they take positions on national problems, and they cannot easily duck tough issues. The essential tactics are to get good people involved, make as many personal contacts as possible (especially in the states with smaller populations), avoid giving their opposition any positive publicity, and have a simple campaign theme. Incumbent senators are less able to influence media coverage and generally face tougher competition from their challengers.[59] Not surprisingly, incumbent senators still benefit from their incumbency, but not as much as House candidates.[60]

RUNNING FOR PRESIDENT

Presidential elections are major media events, with candidates seeking as much television as possible and seeking to avoid negative news coverage. The formal election process involves seeking the nomination and then amassing enough votes in November to win a majority in the electoral college. The formal campaign has three stages: winning the nomination, campaigning at the convention, and mobilizing support in the general election.

Winning the Nomination

Presidential hopefuls must make a series of critical tactical decisions. The first is when to start campaigning. Some candidates begin almost as soon as the last presidential election is over. Early decisions are increasingly necessary for candidates in order to raise the money and assemble the organization to be competitive. The problem with having to decide on a race for the presidency years before the next election is that circumstances change. A president who is popular can suffer a dramatic loss of popularity, and a front runner who appears invincible may stumble.

The hardest job for candidates and their strategists is calculating how to deal with the complex maze of presidential primaries and caucuses that constitutes the delegate selection system. This complex system varies from state to state and often from one party to the other in the same state. Although the process is influenced somewhat by federal regulation of campaign financing and national party rules, within broad limits states can set up the systems they prefer.

PRESIDENTIAL PRIMARIES State presidential primaries, unknown before this century, have become the main method of choosing delegates. Voters in states like Iowa and New Hampshire bask in media attention for weeks and even months before they cast the first ballots in the presidential sweepstakes.

Because these early contests have had the effect of limiting the choices of voters in states that come later in the process, there has been a tendency for states to move their primaries up. California, which traditionally held its primary in June, moved it to March in 1996 so that their voters would play a more important role in selecting the nominee. Other states did the same thing. As a result, the 1996 primary season was compressed into a few weeks of intense activity, and even with the change, Bob Dole emerged as the winner before Californians voted.

Today more than three fourths of the states use presidential primaries. In 1996 primaries selected 78 percent of the Democratic delegates and 88 percent of the Republican delegates.[61] The rest of the states use caucuses or conventions.

Presidential primaries have two main features: the "beauty contest," in which voters indicate their choice for president but do not actually elect delegates to the convention, and primaries in which they elect delegates pledged to a candidate. Different combinations of these two features have produced the following systems:

1. *Proportional representation.* Delegates to the national convention are allocated on the basis of the votes candidates win in the "beauty contest." This system has been used in most states, including several of the largest ones, and in 1992 Democrats mandated that all primaries be proportional.[62] In some states Republicans use this same system, but Republicans are much more varied in their delegate selection processes.[63]

2. *Winner takes all.* The results of the presidential preference poll bind all the delegates, so that the winner gets all the delegates in that state or congressional district. To win all the delegates of a state like California is an enormous bonus to a candidate. (Bob Dole won all of California's delegates in 1996.) Only the Republicans still use the winner-takes-all system at the state level, and in 1996 about half of all states used this rule at either the state or congressional district levels.

3. *Delegate selection.* In some states voters choose delegates who may or may not have indicated how they will vote at the national nominating convention. The names of the presidential hopefuls do not appear separately on the ballot; there is no presidential preference. Under this arrangement, delegates are more likely to feel free to exercise their independent judgment at the convention. Again, this system is used only by the Republicans; in 1996 it was used most prominently in New York and Illinois.

CAUCUSES AND CONVENTIONS   About eight states use a caucus and/or convention system for choosing delegates. There are many variations of the caucus and convention system, because they are regulated by each state's parties and legislature. The most significant variation may be Iowa's, because Iowa has held the earliest caucuses in most recent presidential nominating contests. This is the oldest method of choosing delegates. It is fundamentally different from the primary system because it centers on the *party organization.* Delegates to the national nominating conventions are chosen by delegates to state or district conventions, who themselves are chosen earlier in county, precinct, or town meetings of party members and supporters of various candidates. These meetings are open to all party members.

STRATEGIES   Strategies for gaining delegates to the national convention through primaries and caucuses have changed over the years. Some candidates

Nomination by Petition

There is a way to run for president of the United States that avoids the grueling process of primary elections and conventions—if you are rich enough or well known enough. H. Ross Perot took this route in 1992. Independent candidates Perot in 1992 and John Anderson in 1980 met the various state petition requirements or paid the $500 filing fee in Louisiana and made it onto the ballot in all fifty states. The petition process can be as simple as submitting the signatures of 200 registered voters in Washington state, or as difficult as getting the signatures of 3 percent of registered voters (63,000 signatures) in Maryland.

Perot and Anderson demonstrated that you do not need a political party to run for president. They also demonstrated that you do not need a political party to run a visible campaign that is taken seriously by your opponents and the American people. In 1992 Perot and his running mate, James Stockdale, got nearly one-fifth of the popular vote. Perot was not nominated by any political party, did not run in any primaries, and had not sought any office before. How did he do it?

He did it by spending about $65 million of his own money to promote himself as a candidate. His candidacy was unusual because it generated so much media attention; he skillfully used free media, like the television program *Larry King Live* on which he opened his 1992 campaign and appeared many times during its course. Perot's anti-politician, anti-Washington, and anti-deficit message struck a responsive chord in the American public. His folksy and often humorous manner of communicating reinforced his appeal.

Despite some early mistakes and difficulties with his staff, Perot ran a respectable campaign and played an important role in defining the issues. In fact, there was the possibility that he might come in second in the race or win enough electoral votes to throw the election into the House of Representatives. Perot did come in second in two states—Utah and Maine—and he garnered almost 20 million votes. However, he won no electoral votes.

Following the 1992 election, Perot continued to be courted by both Republicans and Democrats, who hoped to win back his supporters for the 1994 and 1996 elections. His influence fell after the televised debate over the North American Free Trade Agreement (NAFTA) with Vice-President Al Gore, in which Perot was widely seen as testy, whiney, and a "bossy, old billionaire bully."*

*William Safire, "Gore Flattens Perot," *The New York Times,* November 11, 1993, p. A27.

The Republican primary battle of 1996 started with a large field of eager candidates, who killed each other off as the primaries moved through the states, leaving only Bob Dole still standing at the end.

think it wise to skip some of the earlier contests and enter where their strength lies. This strategy was challenged by a "go everywhere" strategy that Jimmy Carter pursued in winning the 1976 Democratic nomination. Most candidates choose to run hard in Iowa and New Hampshire, which receive a great deal of media attention, hoping early showings in these states will move them into the spotlight. In 1996 Steve Forbes spent approximately $37 million of his own money in a few selected states early in the process, and as a result he won in Arizona and Delaware. Forbes, however, was not able to sustain his strong showing and dropped out of the race soon after the New York primary.

During this early phase, candidates win or lose by their ability to adapt their own strengths to changing circumstances: the number of candidates running, their standing in the polls, the ideological splits among the candidates, the calendar of events, the amount of resources available for various aspects of the campaign, the ways in which the media cover a particular state, and how much money they have to spend. Especially important is the ability of candidates to manage media expectation of their performance. Lyndon Johnson actually won the New Hampshire primary in 1968, but because Eugene McCarthy did better than the press expected, McCarthy was interpreted as the "winner." Winning in the primaries thus becomes a game of expectations, and candidates intentionally downplay their expectations so that doing better than expected might generate momentum for their campaign. Pat Buchanan made the most of his early victories in Alaska, Louisiana, and New Hampshire in 1996 and generated a lot of free publicity. As the field of candidates narrowed, however, Bob Dole picked up supporters and handily defeated Buchanan.

Campaigning at the Convention

National nominating conventions are the national meeting of the delegates elected in primaries, caucuses, or state conventions who assemble to pick the party's presidential and vice-presidential candidates. The first convention was held in 1808, when a few Federalist leaders met secretly in New York to nominate candidates for president and vice-president. Historically, delegates arrived at national nominating conventions with differing degrees of commitment to pres-

identical candidates. Some delegates were pledged to no candidate at all, others to a specific candidate for one or two ballots, and others firmly to one candidate only. Since 1952, both parties' conventions have seen the nominee chosen on the first ballot. Recent reforms require delegates to pledge themselves to a definite presidential hopeful, and delegates are often required to stick to the person to whom they are pledged for at least the first two ballots.

Despite being a foregone conclusion, conventions attract national attention. It is a chance to focus attention on the nominee, party luminaries, and the spectacle of the convention, not to mention the excitement generated by the selection of a vice-presidential running mate. National nominating conventions compress into four days in July or August all the excitement of the preceding six or seven months of preconvention politics.

THE PARTY PLATFORM Delegates to the national nominating conventions decide upon the platform, which sometimes involves a divisive fight. Why? Critics have long pointed out that the party platform is binding on no one, and overly specific promises are more likely to hurt than help a candidate. But presidential politicians take the platform seriously. It gives a good indication of the general direction a party wants to take. Also, despite the charge that the platform is ignored, most presidents make considerable efforts to implement their party's platform.[64]

THE VICE-PRESIDENTIAL NOMINEE The choice of the vice-presidential nominee has become increasingly important. Rarely does a person actually "run" for vice-president because only one vote counts, but there is a good deal of maneuvering to capture that one vote. The presidential nominee generally dictates the choice of a running mate, but this practice is not taken for granted. Sometimes the choice of a running mate is made by the presidential nominee at the convention—not a time conducive to careful and deliberate thought. More often the choice is made before the convention, yet the announcement is delayed until the convention, as speculation about the choice often adds drama. However, presidential contender Ronald Reagan announced his choice in 1976 before the convention, as did Bill Clinton in 1992 and Bob Dole in 1996. Dole's choice of Jack Kemp helped energize the Republicans at their convention and reinforced Dole's promise of a 15 percent tax cut, but it also meant that Kemp needed to reverse field on such issues as immigration and affirmative action.

Traditionally the presidential nominee chooses a running mate who will "balance the ticket." Walter Mondale raised this tradition to a dramatic new height in 1984 by selecting a woman, Representative Geraldine A. Ferraro, to run with him. Mondale's bold decision was an effort to strengthen his appeal to women voters. Presidential candidates sometimes ignore the idea of a balanced ticket, as Bill Clinton did in 1992 when he chose another southern white male, Al Gore, to be his running mate.

Mobilizing Support in the General Election

The national nominating convention adjourns immediately after the presidential and vice-presidential candidates deliver their acceptance speeches to the delegates and the national television audience. Traditionally, the time between the conventions and Labor Day was a time for resting, binding up post-convention wounds, gearing the party for action, and planning campaign strategy. In recent elections, however, the campaigns have hardly paused after the convention.[66] This

Jack Kemp, former professional football player, congressman, and secretary of Housing and Urban Development, was chosen by Bob Dole as his vice-presidential candidate.

was especially the case in 1996 because both parties held their conventions in August so as not to conflict with the Olympic games.

Strategy differs from one election to another, but politicians, pollsters, and political scientists have collected enough information in recent decades to agree broadly that a number of basic factors affect election outcomes. Most people vote for their party's candidate because of a candidate's appeal, yet how the economy is doing is also a factor.[66] Much depends on voter turnout as well.

THE MEDIA AND THE IMAGE   Candidates and their campaign staff devote considerable attention to defining themselves positively and the opposition negatively. For example, there was a highly effective effort by the 1968 Nixon campaigners to shed his old image of divisive campaigning and failure.[67] In 1992 Clinton's campaign team, led by political strategist James Carville, succeeded in keeping the focus of the campaign on the economy rather than on foreign policy or elements of Clinton's background like his Vietnam era draft status or his involvement with a failed real estate development in Arkansas.

In 1996 Clinton used the media to highlight his moderate positions on welfare reform, gun control, and the government shutdown. He used campaign ads that linked Bob Dole to the unpopular House Speaker Newt Gingrich, and that labeled the Republican positions on guns, the budget, and tobacco as extreme.

PRESIDENTIAL DEBATES   Televised presidential debates are now a major feature of presidential elections. The 1960 debate between John Kennedy and Richard Nixon boosted Kennedy's campaign and elevated the role of television in our politics.[68] The 1992 debates generated a large viewing audience, averaging over 80 million viewers for each debate (around 110 million people watch the Super Bowl).

Fewer viewers watched the 1996 debates than in the past. Perot was excluded because he failed to meet one of the criteria, a plausible chance of winning any electoral votes. The two presidential and one vice-presidential debate were informative and helped clarify differences between the candidates. None of the candidates made any major mistakes. Still, the debates changed a few voters' minds, and most viewers had their opinions about the candidates reinforced.

IMPROVING ELECTIONS

Concern over how we choose presidents now centers on two main issues: 1) the number, timing, and representativeness of presidential primaries, and 2) the role of the electoral college, including the real possibility that a presidential election might be thrown into the House of Representatives.[69] Electoral reform also focuses on encouraging greater turnout and changing the way we finance elections.

Reforming the Nominating Process

What would the critics substitute for state presidential primaries? Some are in favor of a *national presidential primary*. This could take the form of a single nationwide election, probably held in May or September, or of separate state primaries held in all the states on the same day. Supporters contend that a one-shot national presidential primary (though a runoff might be necessary) would be simple, direct, and representative. It would cut down the wear and tear on candidates, and it would attract a large turnout because of intense media coverage.

Opponents argue that such a reform would make the present system even worse. It would enhance the role of media showmanship and candidate gamesmanship; in addition, being enormously expensive, it would hurt the chances of candidates who lacked strong financial backing.[70]

A more modest proposal is to hold *regional primaries*, possibly at two- or three-week intervals across the country; in other words, expand on the South's Super Tuesday idea. But such primaries would retain most of the disadvantages of the present system—especially the emphasis on money and media. Clearly, regional primaries would give an advantage to candidates from whatever region held the first primary, and this advantage might encourage regional candidates and might increase polarization among sections of the country. Another proposal is to cut down drastically on the number of state presidential primaries and make more use of the caucus system. By centering delegate selection in party meetings, the caucus system would also, some say, enhance the role of the party.[71]

Still another idea—used by Colorado for nominations to state offices and by Utah for nominations to federal and state offices—would turn the process around. Beginning in May, local caucuses and then state conventions would be held in every state. These meetings would send delegates—a certain percentage of whom would be unpledged to any presidential candidate—to the national conventions, which would be held in the summer. Deliberations at the national conventions would result in the selection of two or three candidates to compete in a national primary to be held in September. In this Colorado plan, or *national preprimary caucus and convention* plan, voters registered by party would be allowed to vote for their party nominee in the September primaries.[72]

Reforming the Electoral College

Many people have been concerned about the nature and workings of the electoral college. Direct popular election of the president is the most frequently proposed reform of the electoral college. Presidents would be elected directly by the voters, just as governors are. The electoral college and its individual electors would be abolished. This kind of proposal usually provides that if no candidate receives at least 40 percent of the total popular vote, a *runoff election* would be held between the two contenders with the most votes. Supporters say this plan would give every voter the same weight in presidential balloting, in accordance with the one-person, one-vote doctrine. Winners would take on more credibility or "legitimacy" because of their clear-cut popular victories. The dangers and complications of the present electoral system would be replaced by a simple, visible, and decisive method. Opponents say the plan would further undermine federalism; it would encourage unrestrained majority rule and hence political extremism; and it would hurt the smaller states, which would lose some of their present influence. Some also fear that the plan would increase the reliance of presidential campaigns on television.

Some scholars and political analysts have worked out a "national bonus plan" that retains the electoral college but would be heavily weighted toward the winner of the popular vote. A pool of 102 electoral votes (two for each state and the District of Columbia) would automatically be granted to the candidate who gained the most popular votes. These bonus votes would be added to that candidate's electoral college vote. If these votes totaled a majority in the electoral college, the candidate would be elected. If not, a runoff would be held between the two candidates who won the most popular votes. The largely ceremonial position of elector would be formally eliminated. Proponents contend the plan

Michael Huffington spent over $25 million of his own money in an unsuccessful race to represent the state of California in the U.S. Senate in 1994. His opponent, incumbent Dianne Feinstein, also spent heavily and defeated him by a slim margin in the most expensive Senate campaign in history.

The costs of congressional elections have risen dramatically over the past fifteen years, while the rates of reelection have risen. Part of the explanation for the success incumbents have enjoyed is their "special" relationship with Political Action Committees (PACs). Between 1980 and 1990 over 90 percent of House incumbents seeking reelection have been returned to office, leading critics to charge that what we have in Washington is "the permanent Congress."

1. The Permanent Congress

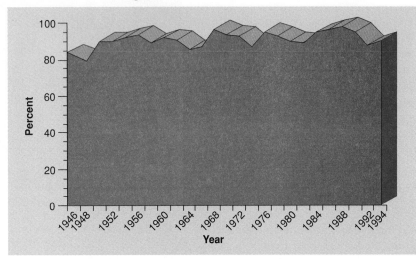

SOURCE: Congressional Quarterly Press, 1995.

2. Rising Campaign Costs (General Elections in 1994 Dollars)

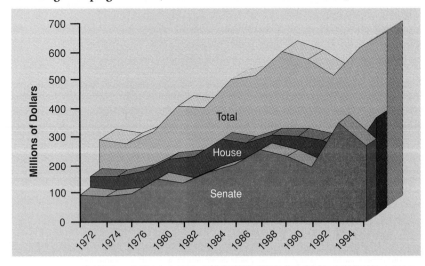

SOURCE: David B. Magleby and Candice J. Nelson, *The Money Chase: Congressional Campaign Finance Reform* (Brookings, 1990), p. 29; Federal Election Commission, "1994 Congressional Fundraising Sets New Record."

3. Incumbents' Dependence on PAC Money

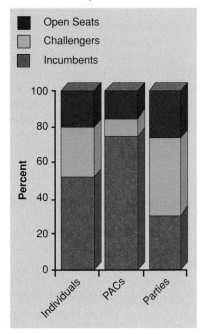

SOURCE: Federal Election Commission, "1994 Congressional Fundraising Sets New Record."

"THE VOTE THAT REALLY COUNTS."
By permission of Bill Mauldin and Wil-Jo Associates.

would ensure that the popular-vote winner would also be the electoral-vote winner. They also claim the plan would encourage increased voter turnout and two-party competition in one-party states and do away with the elector who votes against the decision in his or her state.[73] Opponents say minor parties and independent candidates would be discouraged by such a system.

No plan for reforming the electoral college has garnered much public support. The possibility of three viable presidential candidates in 1992, with the prospect of throwing the election into the House of Representatives, once again put the issue of reform of the electoral college on the national agenda. But when such a prospect did not materialize, interest in such a reform again waned. Americans apparently find it hard to focus on procedural reform.

Reforming Campaign Finance

Election campaigns cost money, and the methods of obtaining the money have long been controversial. Campaign money can come from a variety of sources: the candidates themselves, the political parties, interested individuals, or interest groups. Money is contributed to candidates for a variety of reasons ranging from altruism to self-interest. Concern about campaign finance stems from the possibility that candidates, in their pursuit of campaign funds, will decide that it is more important to represent their contributors rather than their conscience or the views of the voters. The potential corruption that results from politicians' dependence on "interested money" concerns many observers of American politics. **Interested money** is given by persons or groups with interests in government decisions in the hopes of influencing the outcome of an election and subsequently influencing policy.

The higher costs of campaigns have diminished the ability of challengers to mount visible campaigns. Declining competition in elections is at least in part explained by the difficulty challengers have in raising money. Incumbents have a substantial advantage in raising interested money from wealthy individuals and political action committees (PACs), the political arms of interest groups that are allowed to make political contributions. Hence it is not only the source of campaign money that is a problem but the pattern of unequal distribution as well.

INTERPRETING THE 1994 AND 1996 ELECTIONS

Even though he won election by a margin of only 5 percent of the total popular vote in 1992, Bill Clinton swept to a landslide victory in the electoral college. Clinton ran as a "different kind of Democrat" in 1992, arguing that he was different from Walter Mondale and Michael Dukakis. Part of his strategy was to avoid the "liberal Democrat" label that Bush and Reagan had attached to Democratic nominees. Exit polls demonstrated that Clinton succeeded in recapturing more than half of the Democrats who voted for George Bush in 1988.[74]

The glue holding this Clinton coalition together was agreement on the need for change and a stronger economy. Try as George Bush did to shift attention from this topic, he was unable to do so. Attacks on Clinton's lack of experience in foreign policy, his explanation of his draft record, or the Republican party's commitment to "family values" did not overcome the bad news about the economy. Ross Perot's insistence that the candidates talk about the federal deficit, the national debt, and the stagnant economy only made it more difficult to change the focus of the campaign.

In 1994 Republicans turned the table on Clinton and captured the "change" issue for themselves. They won stunning victories in contests for Congress, governor, and state legislatures across most of the country. Democrats lost control of both houses of Congress for the first time since 1954. Tom Foley was the first sitting Speaker to be defeated since 1860, and prominent Democrats like Dan Rostenkowski, Jack Brooks, and Jim Sasser were defeated. The Republicans won control of governorships that had been Democratic in New York, Texas, Pennsylvania, Tennessee, Alabama, and Idaho. Republicans gained an additional 450 seats in state legislatures and achieved control of 15 state legislative chambers.

The shift to Republicans was especially pronounced in the South, which had tended to vote Republican for president in recent elections but remained Democratic in Congress. Republicans changed that in 1994, picking up a net gain of two Republican senators and 16 House members in the eleven confederate states. Republicans also enjoyed a net gain of three governors in this once solidly Democratic region.

Part of the explanation for the Republican success is a very good set of candidates, often well financed. Two sons of former President George Bush ran for governor in 1994; George W. Bush was elected in Texas and Jeb Bush narrowly lost in Florida. Other examples of strong Republican candidates included Mitt Romney, who gave Ted Kennedy a race in Massachusetts, and Olympia Snowe, who won a Senate seat in Maine.

Republicans also captialized on the strong antigovernment sentiment in the country. Much of this anger was directed to the Congress, because of the check-cashing scandal, corruption in the House Post Office, and a sense that the institution was not working. Republicans were successful in arguing that change was needed because of the 10-year period of Democratic dominance in Congress.

In a remarkable turnaround, Bill Clinton recovered from an overwhelming rejection of his party in the 1994 election to win a landslide victory in 1996 by seizing the middle of the political spectrum and isolating Gingrich and Dole as extremists. The issue that helped him most in this objective was the protracted budget battle in which the government was shut down twice by Republicans in Congress. The Republicans also committed the error of proposing Medicare cuts that were deeper than any proposed by Clinton, an issue used by Clinton to mobilize senior citizens to vote for him. Clinton also used gun control to demonstrate the extreme position of Gingrich's House majority, who had voted to overturn the ban on assault rifles. In a move that angered the liberal elements of his own party, Clinton then compromised with the Republicans in Congress on welfare reform.

Bob Dole's campaign failed to generate much momentum, so he reversed his long-held view that deficit reduction is more important than tax cuts and promised an across-the-board 15 percent tax cut. None of his moves changed the polling numbers much.

Both parties spent large amounts of soft money in 1996, raising questions about whether the post-Watergate campaign finance reforms were of any consequence. Clinton's fund raising was more controversial than Dole's beacause of charges that he had accepted large sums from foreign nationals.

As the 1996 campaign closed, Republicans openly used the prospect of a second Clinton term to motivate voters not to "give Clinton a blank check." Voters chose to keep divided government and, as a result, both parties have a foothold for the 1998 and 2000 elections.

SUMMARY

1. Public opinion is a complex combination of views and attitudes individuals acquire through various influences from childhood on. Public opinion takes on qualities of stability, fluidity, intensity, latency, consensus, or polarization—each of which is affected by people's feelings about the salience of issues.

2. The American public has a generally low level of interest in politics, and most people do not follow politics and government closely. The vast majority of Americans do not engage in such forms of participation as working in campaigns, writing letters to newspaper editors or elected officials, or even attempting to influence how another person will vote.

3. Better educated, older, and party- and group-involved people tend to vote more; the poor tend to vote the least. Voter turnout tends to be higher in national than in state and local elections, and higher in presidential than in midterm elections.

4. Party identification remains an important element in the voting choice of most Americans. It represents a long-term attachment and is a "lens" through which voters view candidates and issues as they make their voting choices. Campaigns are important in defining candidates for the public. Voters decide their vote less frequently on the basis of issues.

5. Our system is based on winner-takes-all rules, with typically single-member district or single-officeholder arrangements. These rules encourage a moderate two-party system.

6 Many House, state, and local races are not seriously contested. The extent to which a campaign is likely to be hotly contested varies with the importance of the office and the chance a challenger has of winning. Senate races are more likely to be contested, though most incumbents win.

7. The race for the presidency actually takes place in three stages: winning delegate support in presidential primaries and caucuses, gaining the formal party nomination at the presidential convention (usually predetermined by the first stage), and winning a majority of the electoral college.

8. Conventions are important in setting the party's direction, unifying its ranks, and firing up enthusiasm.

9. The present presidential selection system is under criticism because of its length and expense and because it seems to test candidates for media skills less needed in the White House than the ability to govern, including the capacity to form coalitions and make hard decisions.

10. Because large campaign contributors are suspected of improperly influencing public officials, Congress has long sought to regulate political contributions. The main approaches of reform have been: (1) imposing limitations on giving, receiving, and spending money; (2) requiring public disclosure of the sources and uses of political money; and (3) giving governmental subsidies to presidential candidates, campaigns, and parties, including incentive arrangements.

FURTHER READING

HERBERT ASHER, *Polling and the Public: What Every Citizen Should Know*, 3d ed. (Congressional Quarterly Press, 1995).

EARL BLACK AND MERLE BLACK, *The Vital South: How Presidents Are Elected* (Harvard University Press, 1992).

M. MARGARET CONWAY, *Political Participation in the United States*, 2d ed. (Congressional Quarterly Press, 1991).

ALAN EHRENHALT, *The United States of Ambition: Politicians, Power, and the Pursuit of Office* (Times Books, 1991).

ROBERT S. ERIKSON AND KENT L. TEDIN, *American Public Opinion: Its Origins, Content, and Impact*, 5th ed. (Allyn and Bacon, 1995).

WILLIAM H. FLANIGAN AND NANCY H. ZINGALE, *Political Behavior of the American Electorate*, 8th ed. (Congressional Quarterly Press, 1994).

PAUL S. HERRNSON, *Congressional Elections: Campaigning at Home and in Washington* (Congressional Quarterly Press, 1995).

GARY C. JACOBSON, *The Politics of Congressional Elections*, 3d ed. (HarperCollins, 1992).

BRUCE E. KEITH, DAVID B. MAGLEBY, CANDICE J. NELSON, ELIZABETH ORR, MARK C. WESTLYE, AND RAYMOND E. WOLFINGER, *The Myth of the Independent Voter* (University of California Press, 1992).

JOHN KESSEL, *Presidential Campaign Politics*, 4th ed. (Brooks Cole, 1992).

V. O. KEY, JR., *Public Opinion and American Democracy* (Alfred A. Knopf, 1961).

JONATHAN S. KRASNO, *Challengers, Competition, and Reelection: Comparing Senate and House Elections* (Yale University Press, 1994).

ROBERT D. LOEVY, *The Flawed Path to the Presidency, 1992: Unfairness and Inequality in the Presidential Selection Process* (State University of New York Press, 1994).

DAVID B. MAGLEBY AND CANDICE J. NELSON, *The Money Chase: Congressional Campaign Finance Reform* (Brookings Institution, 1990).

RICHARD G. NIEMI AND HERBERT F. WEISBERG, *Classics in Voting Behavior* (Congressional Quarterly Press, 1993).

RICHARD G. NIEMI AND HERBERT F. WEISBERG, *Controversies in Voting Behavior*, 3d ed. (Congressional Quarterly Press, 1993).

FRANK R. PARKER, *Black Votes Count: Political Empowerment in Mississippi after 1965* (University of North Carolina Press, 1990).

NELSON W. POLSBY AND AARON WILDAVSKY, *Presidential Elections: Contemporary Strategies of American Politics*, 9th ed. (Chatham House, 1995).

GERALD M. POMPER, et al., *The Election of 1992* (Chatham House, 1993).

SAMUEL L. POPKIN, *The Reasoning Voter: Communication and Persuasion in Presidential Campaigns* (University of Chicago Press, 1991).

FRANK J. SORAUF, *Inside Campaign Finance: Myths and Realities* (Yale University Press, 1992).

JAMES A. THURBER AND CANDICE J. NELSON, eds., *Campaigns and Elections American Style* (Westview Press, 1995).

STEPHEN J. WAYNE, *The Road to the White House, 1996: The Politics of Presidential Elections*, 5th ed. (St. Martin's Press, 1996).

JOHN ZALLER, *The Origins and Nature of Mass Opinion* (Cambridge University Press, 1992).

See also *Public Opinion Quarterly, The American Journal of Politics*, and *The American Political Science Review*.

THE MEDIA AND AMERICAN POLITICS

9

The question of what role the United States should play in mediating or ending the protracted civil war in what was once Yugoslavia concerned policy makers for years. News reports of innocent civilians being killed had become routine. One such atrocity occurred at midday on February 5, 1994, when a Serb artillery unit fired a 120-millimeter shell into the crowded central marketplace of Sarajevo, Bosnia. An ABC television news crew recorded the scene of death and destruction in the marketplace. Peter Jennings summarized the event to millions of American viewers: "It was a disaster. . . .The dead—and many of them were in pieces—were eased onto trucks and taken to the morgue at one of the two city hospitals. . ."

News reports on this incident also communicated the bitter frustration felt by the residents of Sarajevo toward the unsuccessful efforts of the United Nations and the United States to mediate the conflict or bring peace to the troubled region. One bystander shouted, "Thank you Boutros-Ghali! Thank you, Clinton! All the world killed these people."[1] Some, like this man, placed blame for the carnage on an international arms embargo and efforts by the UN and U.S. government to negotiate peace.

Public opinion here in the United States appeared consistent with a policy of not directly engaging U.S. forces in this dispute. In a poll a week before the bombing, 68 percent of Americans were opposed to U.S. military involvement in Bosnia.[2] The day after the bombing, President Clinton denounced the attack but his statement carried no immediate threat of retaliation.[3] Perhaps in response to the public outcry against the marketplace bombing, two days later Clinton changed his mind and announced he favored bombing, saying, "I very much welcome the request that authority be given to our commanders there on the ground to take appropriate action."[4] Clinton appeared to accurately read the public mood, because one week after the bombing, public opinion had shifted to 72 percent expressing support for U.S. involvement.[5]

Coverage for this and other acts against innocent civilians result in changes of public opinion and policy in the United States. The news media can have a dramatic impact on public policy when they bring American public immediate access to events around the world.

Americans have more ways to find out what is going on in the world than do citizens of any other democracy. We have widespread access to television. We get constant around-the-clock news. Our magazines reflect all kinds of opinions and perspectives and promote every conceivable cause. We have some of the world's greatest newspapers. Although during wartime we have had some censorship of the news, with very few exceptions people are free to say or write whatever they wish.

Television brought the pain of the war in Bosnia into American livingrooms with scenes of the carnage in a Sarevejo marketplace following a Serbian mortar attack. As a result, President Clinton ordered the bombing of Serbian gun emplacements around the city and the withdrawal of all heavy weapons outside a safety zone.

This is not to say that press coverage of politics and government in the United States is without problems. Our Constitution guarantees a free press, not a responsible one. People often blame the media for many of our ills—for increasing tension between the races, for biased attacks upon public officials, for sleaze and sensationalism, and for being more interested in making money than in conveying information. Media bashing has become something of a national pastime, and there is considerable merit to all these charges. But "the media" at times is simply an abstraction for those who prefer criticizing the messenger to avoid dealing with the message. Comments like, "It is the media's fault that we have lost our social values," or "The media's preoccupation with negative traits of candidates turns Americans off to politics" are overly broad assertions. The media do have certain tendencies that affect American politics and public policy, but, as we shall see, far more problems are blamed on the media than they deserve.

No discussion of American politics today is complete without assessing the role of the media. The media provide the major source of information, even for the most important policy makers. A free press is also essential for the maintenance of democracy. This chapter examines the media's role in American politics, beginning with the factors promoting the rise of the media as an independent force, continuing with a discussion of the media's influence on each of us as citizens and on our election campaigns, and culminating in an appraisal of the media's influence on the governance of our nation.

THE INFLUENCE OF THE MEDIA

Is the influence of the media in politics real or a myth? The media, in particular the print media, have been called "the other government," "the fourth estate," and "the fourth branch of government."[6] Evidence that the mass media influence our culture and politics is plentiful. Before we can examine that influence, however, we must define some terms. The **mass media** are means of communication that reach the mass public; they include newspapers and magazines, radio, television (broadcast, cable, and satellite) and films, recordings, and books.[7] The news media emphasize news, but the distinctions are not clear-cut. Some media critics contend there is now a combination of the two—a medium called "infotainment" that uses entertainment techniques to present the news. As evidence, they point to evening news programs featuring "happy talk" between news anchors and to prime-time programs such as *60 Minutes, Primetime, 20/20*, and talk shows with hosts like Rush Limbaugh, Larry King, and Oprah Winfrey.

By definition, the mass media disseminate their message to a large and often heterogeneous audience at the same moment. Because they must have broad appeal, their messages often are simplified, stereotyped, and formulaic. Certainly the mass media are big business. They live off high audience ratings and substantial advertising revenues, which are essential to their "bottom line" of big profits. But does profit spell political clout? Two factors are important here: the media's pervasiveness and their role as a linking mechanism.

The Pervasiveness of Television and Radio

Almost all Americans see television every day, and most homes have at least two sets, each turned on for an average of seven hours per day. While television is primarily an entertainment medium, most Americans use it for news as well. Three out of four Americans watch television news regularly.[8]

For several decades the three network evening news programs captured more than 90 percent of the audience for television news, and national news was available only at set times in the morning and early evening hours. Today, many options exist for broadcast news information, and Americans rely more and more on these alternative sources. One-quarter of Americans say they are regular viewers of CNN, while two out of five say they regularly watch network prime-time newsmagazine shows like *60 Minutes.*[9]

Television has not displaced radio. On the contrary, radio continues to reach more American households than does television. Only one household in a hundred does not have a radio. Nine out of ten Americans listen to the radio every day.[10] Cars and radios seem to go together.

Americans get more than "the facts" from radio and TV. They also get analysis of the news. Following major speeches or news events, on talk shows and on magazine programs like *60 Minutes*, media personalities provide interpretations and assessments of the news. Many people will not decide "what to think" before they have heard from their favorite commentators. Radio commentators and talk show hosts like Rush Limbaugh, Jerry Brown, and G. Gordon Liddy have committed followings. Some commentators themselves become important political figures, as Patrick J. Buchanan did in 1992 and 1996; his regular participation on CNN's *Crossfire* increased his public visibility before he ran for the presidency.

The Continuing Importance of Newspapers

Recent technological advances have created intense competition for advertising revenues and have contributed to sweeping changes in the manner in which news is transmitted and received. Satellites, cable television, computers, the Internet, and videocassette recorders (VCRs) make vast amounts of political information available 24 hours a day; satellites eliminate the obstacles of time and distance; computers increase the volume of information that can be stored and retrieved; and cable channels and VCRs increase viewing options.

Despite vigorous competition from the broadcast media, many Americans still read newspapers. Newspaper circulation has held steady at about 63 million

Some Key Terms

When we refer to "the media," what do we mean? Years ago the only means of communication to large numbers of people was through the press. With the advent of radio and television, we adopted the term "mass media," a general term that refers to television, newspapers, and magazines.

- *Media*—a general term that refers to all forms of communication. The term "the media" is an abstraction that often lacks precision.
- *Mass media*—communication by the media on a large scale.
- *Media event*—activity undertaken to generate news coverage and publicity that would not be done if news reporters or cameras were not present.
- *The press*—the news media, in popular language often limited to print media.
- *News media*—print and broadcast coverage of the news.
- *Journalist*—a news reporter who writes news for the press or broadcasts news via electronic media.
- *Fourth estate*—the press and news media in general. In medieval Europe the three estates were nobility, clergy, and commons; the news reporters have been called the fourth estate.
- *Fourth branch of government*—the news media are sometimes referred to as supplementing the three traditional branches of government—executive, judicial, and legislative.

TABLE 9-1

Top Newspapers in Circulation, 1995*

1. USA Today	1,966,355
2. Wall Street Journal	1,823,207
3. New York Times	1,185,614
4. Los Angeles Times	1,065,440
5. Washington Post	842,244
6. New York Daily News	725,849
7. Chicago Tribune	693,668
8. New York Newsday	670,150
9. Detroit Free Press	533,702
10. Dallas Morning News	516,793

SOURCE: *USA Today Research,* July 5, 1995, p. B7.

*Total Monday-through-Friday circulation for six-month period ending March 31, 1995.

nationwide—or about one copy for every four people—for the past 20 years. Another indication of the media's pervasiveness is the rise of national newspapers. *The Wall Street Journal,* with a circulation of nearly 2 million, has long acted as a national newspaper with a specialization in business and finance. Other newspapers with more general interests have emerged. *USA Today,* created in 1982 by the Gannett Corporation, now has a circulation of nearly 2 million. In addition, *The New York Times* has a national edition and is read by more than 1 million people (see Table 9–1).

A Linking Mechanism

The pervasiveness of the media alone does not prove their political influence. But it does place the media in a position to be influential because they can reach so much of the American public so quickly. With a large population scattered over a continent, both the reach and speed of the modern media elevate their importance.

The media have become the primary linking mechanism in American politics—a way of connecting policy makers, candidates, and the public in a national, largely electronic, communication network. Candidates talk to voters. Voters respond to candidates. Policy makers and constituents interact. And policy makers and other elite groups—such as interest groups and policy experts—communicate with each other through the media. The media do more than pass along information. The information transmitted can change voters' perceptions of social reality, and it affects their responses to those perceptions. Candidates also may tap voter sentiment from media polls. Policy makers assess policy effectiveness in part through media coverage. And the people rely on the media to evaluate governmental performance and policy.

The Rise of an Autonomous Press

Back in the eighteenth century, not only was there no television or radio, there were only a few newspapers, and those that did exist were run by political parties. Their purpose was not to distribute the news but to defend their own party and attack the other party. The framers relied heavily upon pamphlets and essays to get their messages to the public.

POLITICAL MOUTHPIECE At the time of the ratification of the Constitution, newspapers consisted of a single sheet, often printed irregularly by store owners to hawk their services or goods. Newspapers rarely lasted more than a year, due to delinquent subscribers and high costs.[11] But the framers understood the important role the press should play as a watchdog of politicians and government.

The new nation's political leaders, such as Alexander Hamilton and Thomas Jefferson, recognized the need to reach the people. Political party organizations as we know them did not exist, but the active role of the press in supporting the Revolution had fostered a growing awareness of the political potential of newspapers. Hamilton recruited staunch Boston Federalist John Fenno to edit and publish a newspaper in the new national capital of Philadelphia. Jefferson responded by attracting Philip Freneau, a talented writer and editor and a loyal Republican, to do the same for the Republicans. (Jefferson's Republicans later became the Democratic party.)

Although the two newspapers competed in Philadelphia for several years, their lasting significance was as a model for future partisan newspapers. They became the nucleus of competing partisan newspaper networks throughout the nation. Federalist and Republican newspapers in the various states relied on the national newspapers for national government news and editorials. The free mailing of newspapers among editors allowed by the U.S. Post Office encouraged this usage.

The linkage between newspaper editors and politicians was maintained through several methods. Politicians loaned or gave money to partisan editors to set up newspapers. Hamilton and other prominent Federalists gave $1,000 each for the start-up of the *New York Evening Post*[12] and helped solicit subscriptions from party supporters. Government patronage appointments were extended to favorite editors. John C. Calhoun, for example, while serving as secretary of war, hired his favorite editor as federal superintendent of Indian trade. One means of financial support was designation as a government newspaper duly authorized to print the text of laws, reports, speeches, and treaties.[13]

The early American press served as a political mouthpiece for political leaders. Its close connection with politicians and political parties offered the opportunity for financial stability, but at the cost of journalistic independence.

FINANCIAL INDEPENDENCE The Jacksonian era of the 1820s and 1830s was characterized by increased mass participation in American politics through rallies, bonfires, and local political clubs. As the vehicle for communication with the public, the press began to shift its appeal away from elite readers and toward large masses of less educated and less politically interested readers. This movement was reinforced by rising literacy rates that supported greater circulation for newspapers. These two forces—increased political participation by the common people and the rise of literacy among Americans—began to alter the relationship between politicians and the press.

Some newspaper publishers began to experiment with a new financing structure. They charged a penny a paper, paid on delivery, instead of the traditional annual subscription fee of eight to ten dollars, which was beyond the ability of most readers to pay. Through expanded circulation and more emphasis on advertising, newspapers could become financially independent. The plan for a new "penny press" not only worked, it became a common model for the press thereafter.

The effect of this new independence on the political role of the press was not immediate; in keeping with the strong partisanship of the nineteenth century, many publishers continued to promote partisan causes and candidates anyway. However, some began to criticize their own party. Republican Horace Greeley, editor of the *New York Tribune*, felt at liberty to criticize Abraham Lincoln during the Civil War. Several Republican newspapers abandoned their party's candidate for president in 1884.[14]

The changing finances of newspapers also affected the definition of what constituted news. Before the "penny press," news was political—speeches, documents, editorials—directed at a politically interested readership. The "penny press" reshaped the definition of news as it sought to appeal to the less politically aware with human interest stories, sports, crime and public trials, and social activities.

As news about politics began to constitute a smaller proportion of the newspaper, politicians searched for alternative ways to communicate with the public. In the 1850s, members of Congress used their mail privileges—the franking privilege—to distribute copies of their speeches. During the first half of 1858, for example, members of Congress mailed 800,000 copies of their speeches without charge.[15]

"OBJECTIVE JOURNALISM" The death knell of the partisan press sounded with the rise of "objective journalism." Many journalists began to argue that the press should be independent of the political parties. *New York Tribune* editor Whitelaw Reid eloquently expressed this sentiment:

Independent journalism! That is the watchword of the future in the profession. An end of concealments because it would hurt the party; an end of one–sided

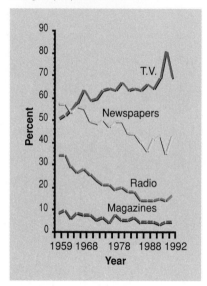

FIGURE 9-1   Where Americans Get Most of Their News

Source: Surveys by the Roper Organization for the Television Information Office, 1959–1992.

expositions…; an end of assaults that are not believed fully just but must be made because the exigency of party warfare demands them…that is the end which to every perplexed, conscientious journalist a new and beneficent Declaration of Independence affords.[16]

Journalists also began to view their work as a profession and established professional associations with codes of ethics and publication of journals. This professionalization of journalism reinforced the notion that journalists should be independent of partisan politics—a notion that still pertains today. The rise of the wire services as the primary source for national news (they were politically neutral in order to attract more customers) further strengthened the trend toward objectivity.

THE IMPACT OF BROADCASTING   Radio and television changed the media's role in politics by nationalizing and personalizing the news. Radio did it first, beginning with the creation of networks in the 1920s. Radio dominated national politics until the rise of television after World War II.

President Franklin Roosevelt showed how to use radio effectively. Before 1933 most radio addresses were treated like commencement speeches and major orations, but Roosevelt spoke to his audience on a personal level and showed that radio could be used as a one-to-one conversation. Roosevelt's "fireside chats" established a standard for presidential use of the broadcast media still followed today. Frances Perkins, secretary of labor, recalled that when Roosevelt began speaking over the microphone, he would visualize the average citizen in front of him. "His face would smile and light up as though he were actually sitting on the front porch or in the parlor with them."[17]

Radio was also used for political speeches, campaign advertising, and coverage of political events such as national nominating conventions. Members of Congress used radio extensively. During the 1930s, more than one thousand speeches were made by members of Congress on one network alone.[18]

Radio provided a means to bypass the editorial screening of the press, since politicians could speak directly to listeners without editing. It also contributed to increased interest in national and international news, since activities outside a listener's local area could be heard as if one were actually there.

Television added a visual dimension, which greatly contributed to rising audience interest in national events. Audience interest grew to the point that by 1963, two major networks doubled the length of their evening news broadcast from 15 to 30 minutes. Today the amount of time devoted to local news by most stations has also grown, with many providing as much as 90 minutes in the evening and a half hour at noon. With the advent of cable television, the coverage of news expanded as well as the range of possible programs. Viewers now can watch news programs 24 hours a day. Specialized cable stations give substantial coverage to Congress and the courts, and some local cable stations provide live coverage of city councils and other public meetings. As we learned during the Persian Gulf War and later in Bosnia, American cable news coverage is watched around the world for instantaneous coverage of news stories. Coverage of news-related issues in the prime evening hours is provided in programs like *60 Minutes, 20/20,* and *Crossfire.*

MOST IMPORTANT NEWS SOURCE   What is the most important source of news for most Americans? In 1959, when this question was first asked, the proportion who answered newspapers was 6 percent higher than television; the remaining group said they used both television and newspapers. Today, television is the most important source of news by a margin of 3 to 2 (see Figure 9–1). Television is now the most trusted source of the news. Generally about two-thirds of Americans indicate that television is one of their most important news sources. This number climbed to over 80 percent in early 1991, when television coverage of the Persian Gulf War kept the nation glued to their TV sets night after night. Newspapers have dropped and are most trusted by about 1 in 4 Americans. Newspapers are the preferred news sources for local candidates.

MEDIA CONGLOMERATES   Television can be profitable. One reason is that governmental limitations on competition permit monopoly ownership of broadcast licenses. Radio networks and newspapers were the first to purchase the new medium and establish cross-ownership patterns that persist today. For example, in 1996 the Gannett Corporation owned 92 daily newspapers, 15 television stations, 11 radio stations, and cable television systems in 5 states. Media conglomerates with large financial resources now dominate the media business and have contributed to the centralization of news. The Federal Communications Commission in 1992 relaxed ownership rules permitting one owner to control up to 30 AM and 30 FM radio stations.

Are a few media conglomerates likely to provide sufficient competition of ideas to support a democratic system?[19] And without them, can local populations scattered around the country, depending only on local media, find out what is happening in the nation's capital? Why not have government-owned media carry out educational and information functions as well as entertainment functions, as they do in Great Britain and France?[20] The answer is that Americans put great stock in an independent press and news media; Americans find centralized government-owned media unacceptable.

Another concern has been the gobbling up of American communication assets by large corporations and by foreign interests. Local newspapers, radio, and television stations used to be owned primarily by local firms; today this is not the case. Large firms, many of them foreign, have acquired ownership of many newspaper and broadcasting stations. The merger of the Disney organization with ABC/Capital Cities that was finalized early in 1996 cost Disney $19 billion. It gave them control not only of the ABC television network but also ESPN, the cable television sports station. Months later the Westinghouse Company bought the CBS television network for $7.5 billion.[21] In this instance an industrial corporation expanded to include a communications/entertainment company. A national press—*USA Today*, *The Wall Street Journal*, and *The New York Times*—has also developed. The remaining local outlets depend heavily on news that is gathered, edited, and distributed by national organizations like United Press International and Associated Press. As a result, some people contend that information these days is more diluted, homogenized, and moderated than it would be if the newspapers and broadcast stations were locally owned and the news was gathered and edited locally.[22]

THE NEW JOURNALISM   A new sense of professionalism among news reporters has given the press greater autonomy. By the 1960s, schools of journalism were attracting students who wanted to contribute to social change.[23] Press autonomy was enhanced by a press corps self-confident enough to feel equal to politicians. A consequence of objective journalism was the creation of a press that acted as a "common carrier" of information between government and the public. Some journalists, however, challenged this role by arguing they should be more than mere conduits of official information; they should provide their own analysis and interpretation of events to balance the government's position. Others went so far as to advocate that journalists should side with those who are less powerful in society and unable to speak for themselves—a practice termed *advocacy*

Rupert Murdoch and His Media Empire

There's a new player in the high stakes game of television networks and media companies—Rupert Murdoch. Murdoch is the owner of the Fox empire, including Fox network, Fox movie studios, Fox television production company, *TV Guide* magazine, HarperCollins publishing, British Sky Television, Star TV in Asia, and News Corp (an Australian-based company). Murdoch has established an international media empire that spans the globe. Some of his recent actions have included adding at least 12 stations to Fox early in 1995, outbidding CBS for television rights to the National Football League, and creating a global news team that could rival Ted Turner's CNN.

Murdoch and his Australian-based subsidiary News Corp took some heat a few years back when NBC brought charges with the Federal Communications Commission (FCC) that News Corp owned more than 90 percent of the television station equity, when the legal limit for foreign firms is 25 percent. The charges and allegations were dropped by NBC when Murdoch stopped negotiating on NBC programming services in Asia via Murdoch's Asian satellite broadcast company, Star Television.

Murdoch's flavor is definitely international. He receives licenses from the British government to own British Sky Television, a specialized satellite server; the FCC gives News Corp a waiver so it can maintain equity and ownership of Murdoch's 12 original stations; and with the Star Television satellite in Asia, Murdoch is planning on global influence and coverage.

SOURCE: Walt Belcher, "Murdoch's Moves Make Many Shake," *Tampa Tribune*, December 11, 1994, p. 1; David Lieberman, "NBC Drops Complaints Against Fox, Murdoch," *USA Today*, February 20, 1995, p. 2B.

journalism.[24] A related trend was toward *adversarial journalism*—the practice of challenging government and serving as the opposition to public officials, particularly the president.[25] Notable examples include the reporting of Seymour Hersh of *The New York Times,* who exposed secret documents which came to be known as the *Pentagon Papers* on how the United States became involved in the Vietnam War; Robert Woodward and Carl Bernstein of *The Washington Post,* who played an important role in uncovering the Watergate conspiracy; and Nina Totenberg of National Public Radio, whose reporting on sexual harassment charges helped force the Senate Judiciary Committee to extend the hearings on the confirmation of Clarence Thomas to the U.S. Supreme Court. The growth in this type of journalism was in part a consequence of the types of people choosing journalism as a profession.

A New Mediator in American Politics

Political parties and interest groups have long been seen as political mediators between private individuals and the government—mediators who help to organize the world of politics for the average citizen. This is less so today because the media now serve that function, and political parties have lost their exclusive control over the nominating process. Moreover, there is much greater attention given today to judging candidates not so much in terms of party affiliations and platforms, but in terms of character and competence. The press, not the parties, is performing this evaluative function.

News media have taken over the role of "speaking for the people." Journalists tell politicians what "the people" want and think, and then they tell the people what politicians and policy makers are doing. Politicians understand this, and they know how dependent they are on the media in getting their message out to voters. They know a hostile press can hurt them. Clearly, today's politicians have to spend much of their time cultivating the press. President Clinton, after a rocky start with the White House press corps, hired David Gergen to help him improve his press relations and coverage. Gergen had previously worked for Republican presidents, most notably Ronald Reagan, and was credited with improving Clinton's performance in this area.

Presidents experience both positive and negative news coverage. When the news is likely to be good, they are happy to spend time with the media; when it is likely to be bad, they limit their contact as much as possible. Bill Clinton experienced positive news coverage as he helped orchestrate the Middle-East and Bosnian peace processes, but he became testy with the media over their coverage of Whitewater and the role of Hilary Rodham Clinton in the firing of the White House travel office employees. Press coverage of Mrs. Clinton also went through highs and lows. She received positive coverage for her mastery of the complexities of health care reform in 1993, but in 1996 her statements about Whitewater prompted *New York Times* columnist William Safire to call her a "congenital liar."[26] President Clinton's response was that he wished he could "deliver a more forceful response . . . on the bridge of Mr. Safire's nose."[27]

Journalists now contend they have a proper function of screening candidates and looking into their characters—a function that once belonged to party leaders. Thus in recent presidential elections, candidates have been subjected to investigative reporters looking into their sex and drug practices as well as going through their records all the way back to college to see if there is anything that might be considered "improper." During the 1992 campaign as well as after his election, the media reported charges of President Clinton's alleged extramarital affairs and his business dealings with the Whitewater Development Corporation.

THE MEDIA AND PUBLIC OPINION

Scholars, journalists, politicians, and political pundits have long debated the power of the media over public opinion. Do the media shape opinions? Do they alter people's behavior? Can they even affect our core values? For a long time, analysts tended to play down the influence of the news media in American politics as compared with the influence of use of the media by political leaders. The impact of Franklin D. Roosevelt's "fireside chats" symbolized the power of the politician against that of the news editor. Roosevelt spoke directly to his listeners over the radio in a way and at a time of his own choosing, and no network official was able to block or influence that direct connection. President John Kennedy's use of the television press conference represented a similar direct contact with the public. President Ronald Reagan was nicknamed the "Great Communicator" because of his ability to take an issue directly to the people through television. Ross Perot emerged on the national scene because of his skill in using television talk shows.

The news media are now so important that elected officials and politicians spend considerable time trying to learn how to use them. Presidential events and "photo opportunities" are planned with the evening news and its format in mind.[28] Members of Congress use Capitol Hill recording studios to tape messages for local television and radio stations. And the media often respond positively to these activities by politicians. White House press briefings are frequently included in the evening news, and Congress has excellent access to local media. How government officials use the press, how the press uses government officials, and to what extent the press and television can and should be regulated are critical questions for study.

In recent years many entertainment shows have broken the stereotypes about women and minorities and shown them as major figures in their own persona. In the past such shows tended to show African Americans, Hispanics, and gays and lesbians in stereotypical gender and race roles that subtly reinforced cultural values of sexual and racial inequality. Subtle political messages are found in all types of programming; for example, every sports event begins with the National Anthem, which encourages people to be proud of their country. Many entertainers feature jokes about political figures and institutions like the Congress. Clearly the media play an important role in reinforcing norms and attitudes.

Audience

People are not just empty vessels into which politicians pour information and ideas. How we interpret political messages depends on a variety of factors: political socialization, selectivity, needs, and the individual's ability to recall and comprehend the message.

POLITICAL SOCIALIZATION Although we would like to believe we consume the news with an open mind, the reality is that we employ a set of filters or screens to help us interpret and integrate the information. When we watch television or read newspapers, magazines, and books, we bring with us values and attitudes that have been shaped by family, peers, school, and the groups to which we belong.[29] We develop our political attitudes, values, and behavior through an education process that social scientists call **political socialization**. (See Chapter 8 for more detail on this process.) The media, particularly television, may influence our values and attitudes, but they are not as important in the formation of our political attitudes as is our family.[30] Face-to-face contacts often have far more impact on us than the more impersonal television or newspaper. Strong

Thinking it Through

In a free society, the media are the judge of what is newsworthy. The videotape of the Rodney King beating clearly constituted news. The fact that it reinforced perceptions in the African American community of unfair treatment by police could not be avoided. It may be possible that some people engaged in looting and violence in other cities as a result of what they saw on television, but the media were only reporting important events. People's responses to such events are much more likely to be driven by previous beliefs, attitudes, and values than by media coverage. Months later in a second trial the media also reported convictions under federal civil rights statutes against the police officers involved in the beatings.

"VALUES" AND THE MEDIA

For decades conservatives have claimed that the mass media in this country are too liberal—advancing a liberal agenda and attacking traditional values. The issue surfaced again in the 1996 presidential campaign, when all the Republican candidates stressed the need for a return to "family values"; President Clinton picked up on the theme in his State of the Union address. Hearings in Congress proposed the use of a V-chip to allow parents to screen out violent or sexually explicit programs they did not want their children to see.

Studies show that moviemakers are more liberal than the general public. A survey of 104 top television writers and executives found that many of their attitudes toward moral and religious questions are not shared by their audience.

TV talk shows feature an array of dysfunctional families and eccentric individuals who tell about their outrageous and sometimes vicious exploits.

Believe adultery is wrong	
Hollywood	49%
Everyone else	85
Have no religious affiliation	
Hollywood	45%
Everyone else	4
Believe homosexual acts are wrong	
Hollywood	20%
Everyone else	76
Believe in a woman's right to an abortion	
Hollywood	97%
Everyone else	59

SOURCE: "Newsweek, The Center for Media and Public Affairs." ©1992 Newsweek, Inc., All rights reserved. Reprinted by permission.

identification with a party also acts as a powerful filter.[31] A conservative Republican from Arizona might watch the "liberal Eastern networks" night after night and year after year and complain about the biased news coverage while sticking to his or her own opinions.

SELECTIVITY People practice **selective exposure**—screening out those messages that do not conform to their own biases. They subscribe to newspapers or magazines that already support their views. People also practice **selective perception**—perceiving what they want to in media messages and disregarding the rest.[32] One dramatic example is viewers' varying responses to Professor Anita Hill and Judge Clarence Thomas in the 1991 Senate hearings on Thomas's nomination to the Supreme Court. Those who believed Anita Hill's testimony on sexual harassment perceived Thomas as untruthful, while those who believed Thomas's denials discounted Hill's testimony. A similar example of selective perception was the supportive way conservatives generally responded to Paula Jones's charge that Bill Clinton had made sexual advances, as compared to the defensive reactions of Clinton's liberal supporters.

Needs Another mitigating factor in how the media influence opinions is the use to which people put media messages. People read newspapers, listen to the radio, or watch television for very different reasons—sometimes because they are bored, tired, or have nothing better to do, sometimes to get information.[33] People who want to gain information and cultivate an interest in politics are affected differently from those who use media primarily for entertainment.[34] For those who are most interested in entertainment, gossip about President Clinton's alleged affairs, Senator Bob Packwood's diary entries, or Phil Gramm's financing of an x-rated movie is more important than Clinton's, Packwood's, or Gramm's political opinions or deeds. Thus, events like rape trials of prominent individuals are likely to draw more attention than foreign policy speeches by presidential candidates. Members of the broader audience will also more likely follow news that directly affects their lives, such as interest rate changes.[35]

Recall and Comprehension Still another limitation on media influence on public opinion is the extent to which the audience can recall the stories or comprehend their importance. Candidates and officials send out tons of information designed to influence what people think and do, especially how they vote. But people forget or fail to comprehend much of it.[36] The fragmentary and rapid mode of presentation of television news contributes to the problem.

Given all the information available to people about politics and government, it is not surprising most people pick and choose which media source—television, radio, newspapers—to pay attention to and which news stories are important. One scholar who studied the process of selecting which news to pay attention to and remember found that comprehension varied widely, "depending on the nature of stories, the use of visuals, and the concerns and lifestyles of the audience."[37] The best predictor of retention of news stories was political interest. People tend to fit today's news stories into more general assumptions or beliefs about government, politicians, or the media itself.

Bias

There is continuous debate over whether newspapers, radio commentators, television reporters, magazine writers, and especially the mass media are biased. Americans believe they are.[38] Conservatives complain the media are too liberal; liberals claim the media represent the interests of the establishment; and politicians complain they cannot get their messages across. People in general blame many things either on the politicians or on the media.

How can we assess the political bias of the news media? Some contend that television networks are large corporations whose first and foremost concern is profit.[39] For many critics of the media, this observation defines the peculiar nature of the press. It is dedicated, on the one hand, to the impartial reporting of "fact" and, on the other, to boosting ratings and pleasing circulation managers, advertisers, sponsors, and stockholders. Somewhere along the line, the search for truth may get lost, although news organizations pride themselves on their objectivity.[40]

It is becoming more and more difficult to distinguish news from entertainment. Political jokes abound on late-night comedy shows, and we get pungent political messages from the cartoon pages and prime-time network shows. Hollywood actors have become politicians, and politicians have become media commentators. Political analysis creeps onto the front pages of most papers, and many fear that the politics of the editorial page influences coverage of the news.

David Broder of *The Washington Post* voices similar concerns about the confusion of roles by journalists who have served in government (see Table 9–2). According to Broder, a line must divide objective journalism from partisan politics, but many in the print and television media have crossed this line. Broder opposes the idea of journalists becoming government officials and vice versa.[41] Others argue that, because of their government service, journalists with close working relationships with politicians can give us a valuable perspective on government without losing their professional neutrality.

Equally disturbing to some observers is the media's alleged political bias, whether liberal or conservative. But to whom are these critics referring? To reporters, writers, editors, producers, or owners of TV and newspapers? Do they assume a journalist's personal politics will be translated into biased reporting? And does the public think so?

Conservatives say the press is too liberal. They criticize the press for advocating liberal social causes and ignoring the conservative viewpoint.[42] Rush Limbaugh, an influential conservative talk show host, speaking of the media argues, "they all just happen to believe the same way. . . . They are part of the same culture as Bill Clinton."[43] Journalists usually are more liberal than the population as a whole, while editors tend to be a bit more conservative than their reporters, and media owners are more conservative still. Twenty-three percent of the public describe themselves as liberal, compared to 38 percent of college-educated professionals, from whose ranks most journalists are drawn. But even among the professionals, journalists' liberalism stands out. Fifty-five percent describe themselves as liberals.[44]

The far left also accuses the media of bias. Leftist critics contend the mainstream press is purely a propaganda device of the ruling class, creating the boundaries of acceptable thinking and thereby shutting out left-wing viewpoints. Leftist critics see the mass media as capitalist enterprises that dislike airing anticapitalist

TABLE 9-2

Samples of the Revolving Door between Journalism and Government Service

	Media Job	Government Job
Ken Bode	TV news reporter ◄———	Press secretary
Patrick Buchanan	TV commentator ◄———►	Speechwriter and presidential candidate
Hodding Carter	TV commentator ◄———►	Assistant secretary of state
John Chancellor	TV news anchor ◄———►	Director, U.S. Information Agency
Leslie Gelb	Newspaper columnist ◄———	Assistant secretary of state
David Gergen	Newsmagazine editor ———► and TV commentator	Presidential communications counselor
Chris Matthews	Newspaper columnist ◄———	Press secretary
Bill Moyers	Newspaper editor ◄——— and TV commentator	Press secretary
William Safire	Newspaper columnist ◄———	Speechwriter
Pierre Salinger	TV news reporter ◄———	Press secretary
Diane Sawyer	TV news anchor ◄———	White House aide
Carl Stern	TV reporter ◄———	Director of Public Affairs, Justice Department
John Sununu	TV commentator ◄———	White House chief of staff
Strobe Talbott	Newsmagazine editor ◄——— and reporter	Deputy secretary of state
Mary Matalin	TV talk show host ◄———	Republican National Committee staff and 1992 Bush campaign staff
Dee Dee Myers	TV talk show host ◄———	Clinton White House press secretary

sentiments. As well as being a tool of the business class, according to these critics, the media are also a tool of government propaganda that seeks to distort the facts. Others see this "conspiracy theory" as merely a rationalization by leftists who are disgruntled over the failure of their views to take hold with the American people.[45]

Another theory of bias has to do with the possible cultural bias of journalists. Elite journalists—those who work for national news media organizations—tend to share a similar culture—cosmopolitan, urban, upper class. Their approach to the events and issues they cover is governed by their common world view. Part of this bias may be derived from their professional training.[46] The result is an almost unconscious perspective that produces bias because elite journalists give greater weight to the side of issues that corresponds to their own version of reality.[47] Newspapers and television news often set a tone of dissatisfaction with the performance of the national government and a cynicism about politics and politicians. A critical tone may be an inevitable element in the mind set of the press.

But to whose benefit does that critical tone work? Conservatives and the far left are not the only ones who perceive bias. Liberals point to newspaper endorsements of Republican presidential candidates to support their claim that newspapers are biased toward conservative policies and candidates. Daily newspapers tend to endorse Republicans over Democrats for president by a ratio greater than 2 to 1.

The critical question is not how the press is biased but whether the press bias, whatever the direction, seeps into the content of the news. The answer to that question is still not settled. Some empirical studies of news content have failed to find the expected bias.[48]

Public Opinion

The media can make a big difference in what Americans believe. Television, because of its visual dimension, is especially important in shaping opinion, and television news exposure cuts across age groups, educational levels, social classes, and races. Television, with all its concreteness and drama, has an emotional impact that print cannot hope to match.[49] Newspapers, on the other hand, provide more detail about the news and often contain contrasting points of view, at least on the editorial pages, that help inform the public more substantially. Both print and broadcast media are a potent influence in agenda setting and issue framing.

AGENDA SETTING   The power to set the public agenda is significant, and by calling public attention to certain issues, the media help to determine what topics will become the subject of public debate.[50] However, the agenda-setting function of the media is not uniformly pervasive. It is limited by the audience and the nature of the issue.[51]

One politician who effectively used the media for agenda setting was Ronald Reagan. More than any other president before him, Reagan and his advisers carefully crafted the images and scenes of his presidency to fit the role of television. Thus television became an "electronic throne." According to former Vice-President Walter Mondale, "If I had to give up...the opportunity to get on the evening news or the veto power,...I'd throw the veto power away. [Television news] is the President's most indispensable power."[52]

Agenda setting has significant political consequences. It focuses public attention on certain aspects of American politics and ignores others.[53] In assessing governmental or candidate performance, the media can affect the ultimate choice of policy or candidate.[54] Politicians often attempt to use the media to promote their own political or policy agenda. Indiana Senator Richard Lugar carefully timed the announcement of his 1996 presidential candidacy for a Monday, typically a slow news day on which he was likely to get greater coverage. However,

The Infomercial

In the final days of the 1992 presidential campaign, Ross Perot turned to a form of advertising used infrequently in previous presidential elections. He purchased television time in 30-minute segments and used it to talk about the deficit, the national debt, and governmental reform—especially term limits and the elimination of political action committees. Perot also used this "infomercial" format to introduce himself to the American public. One infomercial was essentially a video biography of Perot, replete with testimonials from Perot family, friends, and employees.

The infomercials were successful. One infomercial had almost 20 million viewers and captured an audience share greater than one of the two competing networks. The novelty of these advertisements attracted viewers, which in turn generated media attention and elevated Perot to a serious contender in the presidential election.

TALK SHOWS:
THE NEWEST FORUM

Every day, around the clock, in homes all over the United States, talk shows provide a kind of 1990s American town meeting. With an audience of millions, hosts, hostesses, and their guests analyze the day's news events and vent their feelings from all political perspectives. Radio and television are today's major political arenas.

Presidential candidates appeared frequently on television and radio talk shows during the 1992 campaign, and televised talk shows continued to be major media events after the election. Vice-President Al Gore and Ross Perot debated the merits of the North American Free Trade Agreement (NAFTA) on a special 90-minute edition of *Larry King Live*. The debate was watched by 11.2 million people. In the 1996 tug-of-war between Congress and the president over balancing the budget, leaders of both sides appeared frequently on the *McNeil Lehrer News Hour* and the Sunday morning news panels. Throughout the primary and the election campaigns that year, the airwaves were filled with talk, talk, talk. Phone-in radio and TV shows gave ordinary citizens a way to react to events and offer advice to the candidates, providing a give-and-take of political opinion reminiscent of the direct democracy of the town meeting.

on that Monday the bombing of the Oklahoma City federal building occurred, and Lugar's announcement was barely noticed.

ISSUE FRAMING The context given an issue or event in a news story can affect public perceptions.[55] For example, when United States involvement in Bosnia was framed in news stories as a repetition of Vietnam, Clinton administration officials were understandably anxious about vanishing public support for U.S. involvement. When George Bush sought support for the Persian Gulf War, he compared Suddam Hussein to Adolf Hitler so as to frame the conflict in stark terms. The same kind of framing has been part of the abortion debate, with those favoring abortion defining their position in terms of freedom of choice as a positive way to frame the issue. Similarly, when voters decide ballot questions, the side that most effectively defines the issue generally wins.[56] Bill Clinton won the protracted battle with Congress over issue definition on balancing the budget. He broadened the issue to include the need to protect Medicare, Medicaid, education, and the environment from severe budget cuts.

Regulation

The charges of media bias and the importance of agenda setting and issue definition are only some of the reasons why some urge government to regulate the media. Traditionally, newspapers have not been regulated because of our First Amendment guarantee of freedom of the press and because competition among newspapers has been seen as a way to limit bias. Critics of the growth of media conglomerates propose that newspaper chains be broken up through antimonopoly legislation.

Regulation of the broadcast media has existed in some form since its inception. Because of the limited number of television and radio frequencies, government has overseen matters like licensing, financing, and even content. One such regulation required "fairness" in news programming.[57] As written into law and interpreted by the Federal Communications Commission, the **fairness doctrine** imposed on radio and television license holders an obligation to ensure that differing viewpoints were presented about controversial issues or persons. With the advent of cable television and the Reagan administration's antiregulatory perspective, the doctrine was repealed in 1987.

The media are criticized for sensationalism, overemphasis on "theater" and spectacles, obsession with violence, lack of self-criticism, lack of objectivity, and superficial reporting. They have been urged to provide more explanation, interpretation, and analysis; to look at how they report on activities of the government; to depend less on "packaged" news handed out by government bureaucracies; to be more aggressive in covering the White House; and to become better educated themselves about what really goes on in the Congress.[58]

Critics hesitate to propose harsh or sweeping remedies for the failures of press, television, and radio—lest controls threaten First Amendment liberties. But critics are also uncertain about how serious the problem really is and how improvement can best be accomplished.[59] Moreover, the seriousness of the problem varies widely with the situation. For example, in closely balanced election races, in which media influence or bias might be strong enough to tilt the outcome one way or the other, the opinions put forth by major press and networks may be crucial. But others argue that in our pluralistic nation, which comprises an enormous variety of groups and movements, Americans have so many "filters" through which to observe events that it is extremely difficult to influence public opinion.

THE MEDIA AND ELECTIONS

Do news stories determine who wins or loses elections, who gets nominated for office, or which referenda get passed? News stories probably have more influence today because of the shift to greater direct democracy in our political system by which primaries nominate candidates, with little role left for parties. In addition, voters decide many important issues directly through initiatives and referendums.

While the influence of the media may be greater due to these changes, there is little evidence such influence controls elections. Generally, the more visible the campaign, the less likely voters are to be swayed by any one source. Hence, news coverage is more likely to be important in a city referendum than in an election for president or the Senate.

Diversification of the news media also lessens the ability of any one medium to dominate politics. Newspaper publishers who were once seen as very important in state and local politics now know that politicians and their media advisers can communicate their message through television, radio, direct mail, videocassettes, and cable television. Hence, while the news media remain an important means of communication, there is now more competition among the various media, and politicians and candidates can get their message out regardless of what the editor of the state's largest newspaper may think.

The Electoral Campaign

Campaigns are run differently today than they were a generation ago. During the 1960 election, John Kennedy's effort to attract media attention by winning early primaries was considered novel; today it is standard operating procedure.

CHOICE OF CANDIDATES   The role of the media begins with the decision of who will run. Television greatly affects the list of preferred traits for presidential candidates. A hundred years ago, successful candidates needed a strong pair of lungs. Today it is a "telegenic" appearance, a pleasing voice, and no obvious physical impairments. Back in the 1930s, the press chose not to show Franklin Roosevelt in his wheelchair or using braces, whereas today the country knows every intimate detail of the president's health.

The importance of the public's perception of these traits is evident in the ridicule directed at candidates who lack them. In 1988, Michael Dukakis was derided for his boring speaking style and Richard Gephardt for his blond eyebrows that vanished on television screens. Paul Tsongas, in 1992, was criticized for his dull speaking. The emergence of candidates like Tsongas, who lack the preferred traits, suggests that not having them has not deterred "unmedia" types from running. But the absence of these characteristics has become a formidable obstacle for a candidate.

Republican and Democratic contenders for the presidency, Bob Dole and Bill Clinton, face moderator Jim Lehrer during the televised debate on October 6, 1996. Despite the smiles and courteous demeanor, each tried to tear down the other's positions on Medicare, taxes, affirmative action, and other key issues of the campaign.

If the news media pay no attention to a candidate, he or she is not likely to win any elections. Although the media insist that they pay attention to all who have a chance to win, they also influence who has such a chance. Some candidates have come up with creative ways to generate media attention. Lawton Chiles, running for the U.S. Senate from Florida, captured media attention by walking across the state. The novelty of the idea meant that reporters gave Chiles lots of free media coverage. Sometimes candidates can make their advertisements generate news coverage. Paul Wellstone used creative advertisements in his Minnesota Senate campaign in which he said that he did not have much money to pay for ads, so he would have to talk fast to cram what he had to say into fewer commercials. The witty way he did this became a news event itself—and got Wellstone additional coverage.

CAMPAIGN EVENTS   Because of the importance of media attention for communicating with voters, candidates schedule media events—talk shows, press conferences, interviews, and "photo opportunities" with various groups and in visual settings that reinforce the verbal message. Even the national party conventions have become less focused on the responsibility of actually choosing the nominee than on serving as the first media event of the general election campaign.[60] In the wake of declining viewership of the conventions, the political parties have sought to regain audience interest by reliance on "movie stars, entertainment routines, and professionally produced documentaries in their convention proceedings."[61] Coverage of national political conventions was scaled back to key personalities a few hours each night on the major networks, and only C-SPAN broadcast the entire proceedings of both conventions.

MEDIA TECHNOLOGY   Thanks to new media technology, candidates finally can be in more than one place at a time. Satellites allow candidates to conduct local television interviews without actually traveling to the area or to communicate with party workers across the country. Specific voter groups can be targeted through cable television systems or low-power television stations that reach homogeneous neighborhoods or small towns. Videocassette tapes with short messages from the candidates further extend the campaign's reach.[62] Many candidates for Congress and president in 1996 made themselves and their positions available through a home page on the World Wide Web.

The expense associated with media technology has contributed to the skyrocketing costs of campaigning (discussed in Chapter 8). Candidates wonder if they are really getting "the bang for their buck." Political scientist Michael J. Robinson concludes that paid advertising has little effect on voters in primary contests. It is most useful as a means to respond to other candidates' advertisements and as a measure of candidate viability to the press.[63]

Technology permits campaign staffers to cover their own candidate, following the candidate around with cassette recorders and minicams and taping anything he or she does that resembles news. These tapes are then delivered to radio and television stations and cable systems. Speed and low cost permit campaign staffs to make these electronic actualities, or *soundbites*, available to the media, and these reports are often broadcast intact and, in many instances, without much editorial comment.[64]

Image Making

Do the media tend to prefer image over issues? Actually, image has always been an important part of presidential campaigns.[65] Themes such as "Tippecanoe and Tyler Too" and "Abe the Rail Splitter" were not issue oriented. The new kinds of media have expanded this "defining" role, which in turn has affected candidates'

Thinking it Through

In the spring of 1994 a congressional hearing solicited testimony from parent groups, psychologists, and law enforcement representatives on the effects of viewing murders, rapes, beatings, and torture on the minds of both children and adults. Experts showed a correlation between aggressive behavior and the depiction of violent acts in movies and TV. "Copycat" killings were also attributed to seeing such crimes portrayed. TV violence, it was agreed, fosters attitudes of indifference to violence and social acceptance of violent behavior.

In response, representatives of the movie, TV, and cable industries maintained that they could police themselves and establish standards to moderate the amount of violence in their programs. They proposed a grading system for TV shows that would indicate to parents what ages the shows were suitable for. Attorney General Janet Reno warned the industry that if they did not clean up their act, the government would step in to set limits on what could be shown.

Some object to the idea of censorship because it is contrary to the ideals of a democratic society and places too much power in the hands of the government. Should the cruelty of the wicked stepmother in Hansel and Gretel be considered objectionable? Whose standards should be applied? If some movies are too vicious for children to see, should adults also be denied the right to see them? The situation is complex and does not lend itself to simple solutions.

vote-getting strategies and the ability to communicate messages. Television is especially important here because of the power of the visual image. Edmund Muskie crying while defending his wife's reputation in 1972, Ronald Reagan taking charge of a debate against George Bush in 1980, and Ross Perot speaking in down-home language in 1992 and 1996 are all examples.

Candidates recognize that their messages about policy are often ignored or given little attention. The press tends to emphasize goofs and gossip, or tensions within the campaign or among party leaders. In the 1996 elections, for instance, the press reported on a $1,000 campaign contribution given to Bob Dole by the Log Cabin Republicans, a gay and lesbian group, that was initially returned by the Dole campaign. Dole later reversed the decision of his campaign staff and said they had not consulted him in the decision.[66] Another 1996 Republican candidate, Texas Senator Phil Gramm, was characterized as having invested in X-rated movies, which raised doubts with conservatives. But Gramm then showed a sense of humor that also became news. Larry King asked Gramm if he would consider a women running mate. Gramm replied, "Sophia Loren is not a citizen."[67]

Media Consultants

Attention to image making has been a contributing factor in the rise of a new player in campaign politics—the consultants, media campaign professionals who provide candidates with advice and services such as media relations, advertising strategy, and opinion polling.[68] In the 1992 election, for instance, consultants attempted to counter the impression that Hillary Clinton was too assertive by having her discuss her cookie-making skills, drop her maiden name in campaign references, and play the role of the supportive spouse.[69]

Some media consultants have been credited with propelling candidates to success. Republican consultants like Roger Ailes and Stuart Spencer, and Democratic consultants like Patrick Caddell and Robert Squier, have acquired powerful reputations among political activists. But media consultants also have been blamed for the negative themes of recent presidential campaigns. The classic example is a 1988 ad linking Michael Dukakis to Willie Horton, a convicted murderer who murdered again while on a prison furlough program.

Media consultants have taken over the role formerly played by party politicians. Before World War II, candidates for office at all levels from president to dog catcher were advised by party professionals. Such leaders made their judgments about possible candidates on the basis of long observation of the candidates' performances under fire, decisiveness, conviction, political skill, and other "presidential" qualities (in addition to their chances of victory). Party professionals told candidates which party and interest-group leaders to placate, which issues to stress, and which topics to avoid. Today, candidates are more interested in the advice of a media consultant. Consultants think more in terms of the candidates' images, television techniques, flexibility, "salability," and the like. Consultants report the results of *focus groups* (small sample groups of people who are asked questions about candidates and issues in a discussion setting) and public opinion polls, which in turn determine what the candidate says and does. Some critics allege that political consultants have become a new "political elite" who can virtually choose candidates by determining in advance which men and women have the right images, or at least images that can be restyled for the widest popularity.[70]

Political consultants who specialize in media advertising and image making realize their own limitations in packaging candidates. As one media consultant put it, "It is a very hard job to turn a turkey into a movie star; you try instead to make people like the turkey."[71] Media consultants have even attempted to cre-

"Hey, do you want to be on the news tonight or not? This is a sound bite, not the Gettysburg Address. Just say what you have to say, Senator, and get the hell off."

Drawing by Ziegler. © 1989 The New Yorker Magazine, Inc.

ate antipackaging images for their candidates. Michael Dukakis and Paul Simon in 1988 and Ross Perot in 1992 ran campaigns based on the image that they were not creatures of their media consultants.

Voter Choice

The media play an especially important role during political campaigns because they are seen as the most important source of news by the public. Candidates accordingly court the media and develop a media strategy. The media in turn provide information about candidates, help set the agenda of important issues, and provide cues on how to vote.

INFORMATION ABOUT CANDIDATES   What voters know about candidates is largely based on media coverage. If the media have not covered a candidate, the voters generally do not know him or her. The images voters acquire from the media tend to be more stylistic than issue oriented. Journalists are more likely to comment on a candidate's personal background, style of campaigning, or standing in the polls compared to other candidates—in what is sometimes called the "horse race"[72] (see Table 9–3). "Many stories focus on who is ahead, who is behind, who is going to win, and who is going to lose, rather than examining how and why the race is as it is."[73] Reporters focus on the tactics and strategy of campaigns because they perceive that the public is interested and influenced by such coverage.[74] The media also seem to alternate between a kind of "gee whiz" attitude toward their current hero and a tendency to pounce on a candidate's ill-chosen remarks.

INFORMATION ABOUT ISSUES   The media's propensity to focus on the "game" of campaigns displaces coverage of issues. When there is a scarcity of issue information on television news, voters tend to learn more about issue positions from televised political advertisements or newspapers.[75] Such advertising is becoming increasingly negative in tone. A rule of thumb in the "old politics" was to ignore the charges of the opposition, thus according one's rival no importance or standing. That practice seems to be changing, however, as candidates trade charges and countercharges increasing in viciousness and character assassination.

Political advertising may be even more important to campaign workers, contributors, and the reporters and analysts who cover the election.[76] Recent evidence suggests that expensive media campaigns fostering negative impressions of the candidates contribute to lower turnout.[77] In referendum elections, advertising is the most important source of information in voter decision making.[78]

THE DECISION   Newspapers and television seem to have more influence in determining the outcome of primaries than of general elections.[79] This is probably because voters are less likely to know about the candidates and have fewer clues about how they stand in a primary. By the time of the November general election, however, party affiliation, incumbency, and other factors moderate the impact of media messages. The mass media are more likely to influence undecided voters, voters who in a close election can determine who wins and who loses.

ELECTION NIGHT REPORTING   Does election night reporting affect the outcome of elections? Election returns from the East come in three hours before the polls close on the West Coast. As major networks often project the presidential winner well ahead of poll closings in western states, some western voters have been discouraged from voting. As a result, voter turnout in congressional and local elections has been affected. In a close presidential election, however, such early reporting may well stimulate turnout because voters will know their vote could determine the outcome. In short, it is only in elections in which one candidate

TABLE 9-3

Themes of Election News Coverage

Horse race: winning and losing, strategy and tactics, fund raising	32%
Campaign issues: facts and rumors of scandals, allegations of dirty or low-level campaigning	13
Campaign images: candidates' style of campaigning, posturing, likability	15
Governing images: leadership ability, trustworthiness	7
Policy issues: foreign policy and domestic economy	17
Candidates' orientation: personal and political background, ideology, group support	16
Total	100%

SOURCE: Thomas E. Patterson, "The Press and Its Missed Assignment," in *The Elections of 1988*, ed. Michael Nelson (Congressional Quarterly Press, 1989), p. 98.

TABLE 9-4

Presidential News Conferences
with White House Correspondents

President	Average per Month	Total Number
Herbert Hoover (1929–33)	5.6	268
Franklin D. Roosevelt (1933–45)	6.9	998
Harry Truman (1945–53)	3.4	334
Dwight Eisenhower (1953–61)	2.0	193
John Kennedy (1961–63)	1.9	64
Lyndon Johnson (1963–69)	2.2	135
Richard Nixon (1969–74)	0.5	37
Gerald Ford (1974–77)	1.3	39
Jimmy Carter (1977–81)	0.8	59
Ronald Reagan (1981–89)	0.5	44
George Bush (1989–93)	3	142
Bill Clinton (1993–96)	2.7	129

SOURCE: Samuel Kernell, *Going Public* (Congressional Quarterly Press, 1986), p. 69; *Public Papers of the Presidents, Ronald Reagan,* Book II, 1988–89 (Government Printing Office, 1991), p. C-8; *Public Papers of the Presidents, George Bush,* Book II, 1992–93 (Government Printing Office, 1993), p. C-7; *Weekly Compilation of Presidential Documents,* Vol. 31, Annual Index, p. C-12.

appears to be winning by a large margin that television reporting makes voters feel their vote is meaningless.[80]

THE MEDIA AND GOVERNANCE

Walter Lippmann termed the media's influence on public affairs the "beam of a searchlight that moves restlessly about, bringing one episode and then another out of darkness into vision."[81] The searchlight lands on a policy issue because of a combination of factors, including "the efforts of political actors who seek to illuminate the process for their own purposes, as well as the particular news values of the media."[82]

The press serves as both observer and participant.[83] As observer, the press records and transmits information to and from actors in policy making. But as participant, the press acts as watchdog or critic and serves as the "eyes and ears" of the general public. It helps set the agenda of policy issues and serves as a check on the abuse of power.

But the press's role as participant is limited by its own news values. The policy stage at which the press is most powerful is that of agenda setting. The press brings problems to the fore and challenges policy makers to address them but rarely follows the policy process to its conclusion. Rather, it leaves the issue at the doorstep of public officials. By the time the issue reaches the stages of policy formulation and implementation, the press has moved on to another issue. While policies are being formulated and implemented, decision makers are at their most impressionable;[84] yet the press has little impact at this stage.

Lack of media interest in policy implementation explains the lack of coverage of the bureaucracy. Bureaucratic activities rarely constitute news. Only in the case of a scandal, such as the savings and loan debacle in the early 1990s or the Housing and Urban Development disclosures of abuse in 1989, does the press take notice. Some agencies, however, prefer bureaucratic anonymity. After his study of government press offices, Stephen Hess wrote, "Most executives would be satisfied with a press strategy of no surprises. All their press officers need do to be doing their job is provide a rudimentary early warning system [for crises] and issue routine announcements."[85] But the assumption of most policy makers, even those handling classified national security information, is that their actions will leak out sooner or later.

Some media critics contend a negative consequence of the media's searchlight approach to policy coverage is the media's pressure on policy makers to resolve a problem once the searchlight is focused on it. Foreign policy may be in particular danger from such quick responses due to media attention. Presidential adviser Lloyd Cutler asserts the press's pressure on a president can be difficult to resist:

> If an ominous foreign event is featured on TV news, the president and his advisers feel bound to make a response in time for the next evening news broadcast....If he does not have a response ready by the late afternoon deadline, the evening news may report that the president's advisers are divided, that the president cannot make up his mind, or that while the president hesitates, his political opponents know exactly what to do.[86]

Political Institutions and the Press

The president has become a star of media coverage, particularly television, and has made the media his forum for setting the public agenda and achieving his legislative aims. Presidential news conferences command attention (see Table 9–4). Every public activity, both professional and personal, is potentially newsworthy. A presidential cold or sickness can become front page news.

A president attempts to manipulate news coverage to his benefit. Speeches are used to set the national agenda or spur congressional action. Travel to foreign countries usually boosts popular support at home, thanks to the largely favorable news coverage. Better yet for the president, most coverage of the president—either while at home or abroad—is favorable or at worst neutral.[87]

Congress, on the other hand, has suffered at the hands of the media. News coverage of Congress is typically negative and portrays a badly fragmented body unable to act quickly on much of anything.[88] Congress's problem is that it does not meet news imperatives. Unlike the presidency, it lacks an ultimate spokesperson—a single individual who can speak for the whole institution.[89] A good example of the disadvantage Congress faces in a political battle with the White House is the budget deadlock of 1995 and 1996, which resulted in much of the federal government being shut down for several weeks. The most visible spokesperson for Congress during this political battle was Speaker Newt Gingrich, but at times Bob Dole broke away from Gingrich, once again demonstrating the inability of Congress to speak with one voice. Polls showed that the public blamed Congress more than the president for the shutdown. Congress does not organize its work for the press. While the White House engages in the "care and feeding" of the press corps, Congress does not arrange its schedule to suit the media; floor debates, for example, might compete with both committee hearings and press conferences.[90] By its nature, Congress does not act quickly. Singularly dramatic actions are nearly impossible for the Congress, but such actions constitute news for the press. The press, therefore, turns to the president to describe federal government activity on a day-to-day basis and treats the Congress largely as a foil to the president. Most coverage of the Congress is of its reaction to the initiatives of the president.[91]

The federal institution least dependent on the press is the Supreme Court, which relies little on public communication for political support. Rather, it relies indirectly on public opinion for continued deference and compliance with its decisions.[92] The Court has strong incentives to avoid the perception of direct manipulation of the press, so it retains an image of aloofness from politics and public opinion. Thus, manipulation of press coverage of the Court is far more subtle and complex than for the other two institutions.[93]

The news media's greatest role as a participant in the governing process may be at the local level. Most of us have multiple sources for finding out what is happening in Washington that act as a check on the biases and limitations of reporters who cover national government and policy. But when it comes to finding out about the city council, the school board, or the local water district, most of us are dependent on the work of a single reporter. Consequently the media's influence is much greater when there are fewer news sources.

Presidents use the news conference to get certain information out to the public, but run the risk of having to respond to criticism and challenges by reporters.

THE MEDIA AND CONSTITUTIONAL DEMOCRACY

Indisputably, the media have acquired a role as a major, highly autonomous force in American politics. They mold political attitudes and behavior, organize debate, affect electoral outcomes, help shape policy, and influence the behavior of institutions. The question for our constitutional democracy is: Are the news media doing a good job of bringing information to the citizens and providing a forum in which to debate complex issues?

Scholars, politicians, media critics, and even some journalists have chided the press for failure to fulfill adequately certain roles in a democratic society. There is no shortage of critics with suggestions as to how newspeople might do better, such as greater specialization by journalists by policy area and more stringent separation between the entertainment and news functions of a network, newspaper, or magazine. Others, chiefly political scientists, have suggested that journalists should show less interest in the "game" aspect of campaigns. However, Thomas Patterson, a political scientist, does not think these reforms will work or make any significant difference. The problem, according to Patterson, is that the news business cannot, no matter how hard it tries, perform the functions once carried out by our political parties. It is not that the journalists are not doing their job, but that political parties no longer function as the chief connection between candidates and voters.[94] Newspeople now play that role and have made parties less necessary.

Other critics believe that the influence of the press has been vastly overstated. They claim parties, interest groups, and the personalities of politicians are more important influences. City, state, and federal governments, they assert, have far more impact on a person's politics than does television or the press. Religion, friends, family, teachers, wars, depressions, and assassinations are all more important than the media, which can only reflect the nation's wants, cater to its needs, and sometimes illuminate its troubles or successes.

Not all those who think the media are powerful agree that their power is harmful. After all, they argue, the media perform a vital educative function. Further, they continue, almost 70 percent of the public think the press is a watchdog that keeps government leaders from doing bad things[95] (see Table 9–5). At the very least, the media have the power to mold the agenda of the day; and at most, in the words of the late Theodore White, they have the power to "determine what people will talk and think about—an authority that in other nations is reserved for tyrants, priests, parties, and mandarins."[96]

TABLE 9-5

Confidence in Institutions

Question: I am going to read you a list of institutions in American society. Please tell me how much confidence you, yourself have in each one—a great deal, quite a lot, some, or very little?

	Great Deal	Quite a Lot	Some	Very Little	None/ Don't know
Church or organized religion	32%	25%	28%	11%	4%
The military	33	31	27	7	2
The U.S. Supreme Court	20	24	39	14	4
Banks	18	25	42	12	3
Public schools	18	22	36	20	4
Newspapers	13	18	44	24	2
Congress	9	12	49	28	3
Television news	13	21	41	23	3
Organized labor	11	15	46	24	5
Big business	8	13	50	24	5
The presidency	21	24	34	19	2
The police	26	32	30	10	2
The medical system	18	23	38	19	3
The criminal justice system	9	11	37	37	6

SOURCE: *CNN/USA Today*, Gallup Poll, April 1995.

SUMMARY

1. The news media include newspapers, television, radio, magazines, and books in all of their forms. These means of communication have been called "the fourth branch of government."

2. The news media are a pervasive feature of American politics, and the popular media more generally help to define our culture. Moreover, the rise of new communications technologies has made the media more influential throughout American society. The news media provide a "linking" function between politicians and government officials and the public, and vice versa.

3. The influence of the mass media over public opinion is significant yet not overwhelming. People may not pay much attention to the media or believe all they read or see or hear. They may be critical or suspicious of the media and hence resistant to it. People tend to "filter" the news in part through their political socialization, their selectivity, their interest and attention, and their ability to recall or comprehend the content of the news.

4. Presidential campaigns are dominated by media coverage during both the pre– and postconvention stages. One effect of media influence is that most people seem more interested in the contest as a "game" or "horse race" than as an occasion for serious discussion of issues and candidates.

5. A major effect of mass media news is agenda setting, that is, determining what problems will become salient issues for people to form opinions about and to discuss. The media are also influential in defining issues.

6. The media are criticized as biased both by conservatives (who charge that reporters are too liberal) and by liberals (who claim that the media are captive of corporate interests). The mass media are big business, but their product is information, which is protected under the First Amendment. Little evidence exists of actual, deliberate bias in news reporting.

7. The media are under attack for sensationalism, superficial reporting, biased coverage, and overemphasis on the "theatrical." Any efforts at comprehensive reform will be frustrated, however, by at least two factors: reformers do not agree on what course to follow; and they, and virtually all other Americans, fear taking any action that might threaten the freedom of the press.

FURTHER READING

STEPHEN ANSOLABEHERE AND SHANTO IYENGAR, *Going Negative: How Attack Ads Shrink and Polarize the Electorate* (Free Press, 1996).

LANCE W. BENNETT, *Governing Crisis: Media, Money, and Marketing in American Elections* (St. Martin's 1992).

TIMOTHY COOK, *Making Laws and Making News: Press Strategies in the U.S. House of Representatives* (Brookings Institution, 1990).

RICHARD DAVIS, *The Press and American Politics: The New Mediator* (Prentice Hall, 1996).

RICHARD DAVIS, ED., *Politics and the Media* (Prentice Hall, 1994).

JAMES FALLOWS, *Breaking the News: How the Media Undermine American Democracy* (Pantheon Books, 1996).

CAROL FELSENTHAL, *Power, Privilege and "The Post": The Catherine Graham Story* (Putnam, 1993).

SUZANNE GARMENT, *Scandal: The Culture of Mistrust in American Politics* (Time Books, 1991).

LAWRENCE K. GROSSMAN, *The Electronic Republic: Reshaping Democracy in the Information Age* (Viking, 1995).

STEPHEN HESS, *Live from Capitol Hill! Studies of Congress and the Media* (Brookings Institution, 1991).

KATHLEEN HALL JAMIESON, *Dirty Politics: Deception, Distraction, and Democracy* (Oxford University Press, 1992).

PHYLISS KANISS, *Making Local News* (University of Chicago Press, 1991).

S. ROBERT LICHTER AND RICHARD E. NOYES, *Good Intentions Make Bad News: Why Americans Hate Campaign Journalism* (Rowman and Littlefield, 1995).

S. ROBERT LICHTER, STANLEY ROTHMAN, AND LINDA S. LICHTER, *The Media Elite* (Adler and Adler, 1986).

JOHN ANTHONY MALTESE, *Spin Control: The White House Office of Communications and the Management of Presidential News* (University of North Carolina Press, 1992).

RUSSELL W. NEWMAN, *Common Knowledge: News and the Construction of Political Meaning* (University of Chicago Press, 1991).

THOMAS E. PATTERSON, *Out of Order* (Knopf, 1993).

TOM ROSENSTEIL, *Strange Bedfellows: How Television and the Presidential Candidates Changed American Politics, 1992* (Hyperion, 1993).

SIMON SEFATY, *The Media and Foreign Policy* (St. Martin's Press, 1990).

DARRELL M. WEST, *Air Wars: Television Advertising in Election Campaigns, 1952-1992* (Congressional Quarterly Press, 1993).

CONGRESS: THE PEOPLE'S BRANCH

American voters reelected a Republican Congress in 1996 as they sent Democrat Bill Clinton back to the White House for a second term. Republican leaders politely congratulated Clinton and talked about finding "common ground" with the White House. Both Clinton and Republican leaders Speaker Newt Gingrich and Senate Majority leader Trent Lott agreed that "We don't have to live in a world of confrontation." Clinton noted that he and the Republicans had set aside differences and achieved impressive legislative victories in the second session of the 104th Congress, which included welfare reform, a minimum-wage increase, expansion of pension opportunities and health insurance coverage, and increased amounts for college student loans.

In the presidential election campaign, Clinton signaled that he wanted Congress to work on balancing the budget, giving our children the world's best education, opening the doors of college to everyone willing to work hard, finishing the job of welfare reform, and passing real campaign reform. Republicans, not surprisingly, pressed for a constitutional amendment requiring a balanced budget, Medicare reform, and tax cuts.

Republicans in 1997 were not claiming a sweeping mandate—as they had in 1995—yet they were plainly not shirking their responsibility to their voters. Clinton knew from the start of his second term that he would face relentless opposition on many of his policy initiatives, as well as the predicted hearings and investigations on Whitewater and Democratic party campaign finances.

"Most elections confer power," observed political analyst David Broder. "This one divided it. None of the victors tried to claim a mandate—and a good thing, too."[1] Voters chose to extend the Clinton presidency because of the good economic times, making him a lame duck on a short leash held by a Congress far more conservative than his inclinations.

CONGRESSIONAL ELECTIONS

Members of Congress get their job by winning an election, the outcome of which depends on many factors. By far the most important is the nature of the state or district in which the candidate runs. Is it a **safe seat**—one that is predictably won by one party or the other—or is it a highly competitive one? Other factors affecting winning elections are personal appeal of the candidate, whether the opponent is an incumbent or a newcomer, local issues, campaign strategies, the fundraising abilities of the candidate, and occasionally, national tides, such as the 1964, 1974, and 1994 elections.[2]

Incumbents have traditionally enjoyed a great advantage over challengers. In recent years, however, incumbency has become less of an advantage, if not a handicap. Critics like Ross Perot, Ralph Nader, Steve Forbes, and Rush Limbaugh have targeted the "Washington insiders" and helped to create a climate of antagonism toward Congress as an institution. Still, about 90 percent of incumbents who run for reelection to Congress win their elections over their challengers.

Districting and Apportionment

Congress has given state legislatures control over the drawing of congressional districts. Senators, of course, represent entire states, but House seats are distributed among the states according to population; each state receives at least one seat. State legislatures, subject to a gubernatorial veto, draw the district lines for the House of Representatives. The party in control of the state legislature traditionally draws the lines to enhance their political fortunes.[3] This is known as **gerrymandering**, after Governor Elbridge Gerry of Massachusetts, who, in 1811, reluctantly signed a redistricting bill that created a distinctly partisan district shaped like a salamander.

The word *gerrymandering* comes from the name of a governor of Massachusetts, Elbridge Gerry, and the salamander-shaped district that was created to favor his party.

State legislatures are free to draw congressional districts pretty much as they wish, subject to some constitutional limitations. First, each district must be equal in population, or as equal as possible.[4] To accommodate population shifts, **redistricting** occurs once a decade, after each national census. Because population shifts also occur between states, it is necessary once a decade to reapportion seats for the U.S. House of Representatives. Thus, in 1990, 13 states lost representatives and 8 gained new seats in the House.

A state legislature must not be overzealous in favoring one party at the expense of another. The Supreme Court has held that grossly partisan gerrymandering is, under certain circumstances, unconstitutional.[5]

Finally, although a state legislature may design congressional districts to virtually guarantee the election of a member of a particular minority, it must be careful not to do so in a fashion that focuses only on racial considerations and ignores such matters as county lines and city boundaries.[6] Indeed, the Supreme

The new members of the 104th Congress reflected greater diversity in the large number of women, African Americans, Hispanics, and other ethnic groups who came to Washington in recent years.

Why Do Incumbent Members of Congress Usually Win?

- *They enjoy better name recognition,* and to be known at all is generally to be known favorably. Challengers are almost always less well known.

- *They enjoy free mailings* (called the franking privilege) to every household in the state or district. These mailings—which often resemble campaign brochures—portray members as hardworking and influential.

- *They have greater access to the media.*

- *They raise campaign money more easily than challengers,* because lobbyists and political action committees (PACs) seek their ears and their favors. Also, many campaign contributors know that incumbents are more likely than challengers to get reelected, so they give to those they know will win.

- *They usually have had more campaign experience,* and they can claim to have had more experience in Congress and in Washington.

- *They have staffs* to help with casework and constituency services for the folks back home.

- *They take credit for federal monies* that get allocated to their regions.

- *They are in a better position than challengers to take advantage of government research staffs,* new government studies, and even classified information.

No one of these factors can guarantee a member's reelection, yet skillful use of them makes it difficult to unseat a healthy incumbent.

"Please, Senator Fairchild, you have to leave. You lost."

Drawing by Sauers. © 1983 The New Yorker Magazine, Inc.

Court ruled that making race "the predominant factor" while ignoring traditional redistricting principles such as compactness was unconstitutional.

A Profile of Members of Congress

The entire membership of the House of Representatives (435) is elected to two-year terms in even-numbered years. Elections for the six-year Senate terms are staggered, so that one-third of the Senate's 100 members are chosen every two years. Members of the House of Representatives must be 25 years old and have been citizens for seven years. Senators must be at least 30 and have been citizens for nine years.

Nearly 90 percent of our national legislators are male. Most are well-educated, middle-aged, and come from upper-middle or upper income backgrounds. Until recently, they were also mainly white Anglo-Saxon Protestants (WASPs). Larger numbers of Roman Catholics and many Jews now bring Congress's religious makeup closer in line with the general population.[7] But there are still far fewer African Americans and women in Congress than in the general public, and only a handful of Asian Americans and Hispanics, as well as one Native American. Nearly 40 percent of our national legislators are lawyers. There are also some farmers, teachers, clergy, business people, a veterinarian, and even a few former college professors. Few members come from blue-collar occupations. That most members are the products of middle- and upper-class families does not necessarily mean they are interested only in improving the position of that portion of the population. Senators like Edward Kennedy (D.-Mass.) and Jay Rockefeller (D.-W.Va.) for instance, are affluent white males but strong advocates of legislation to protect women, minorities, and poor people.

Issues of special interest to women have received increased attention in Congress lately, no doubt due in part to the doubling of the number of women in Congress in the 1990s. Thus, Congress has enacted laws to combat violence against women and to improve medical research on diseases that affect women. Congress has also made it a crime to block access to abortion clinics by force.

THE STRUCTURE AND POWERS OF CONGRESS

The most important fact about Congress is it is **bicameral**, that is, made up of two houses. Few national legislatures are genuinely bicameral. Many have two houses, but one is usually largely ceremonial. In the United States, the Senate and the House each have an absolute veto over the other's law making. Each chamber runs its own affairs, sets its own rules, and conducts its own investigations. The law-making role, however, is shared. Each must be seen as a separate institution, even though both houses reflect similar political forces and share common organizational patterns.

As James Madison explained in *The Federalist*, No. 51, the protection against giving too much power to the legislature "is to divide the legislature into different branches; and to render them, by different modes of election and different principles of action, as little connected with each other as the nature of their common functions, and their common dependence on the society will admit." (*The Federalist*, No. 51, is reprinted in the Appendix.) The House of Representatives was expected to reflect the popular will of the average citizen, whereas the Senate was to provide for stability, continuity, and in-depth deliberation. Many of the framers hoped the Senate would stem any rash populist impulses of the other chamber.

In Article I, the Constitution outlined the structure, powers, and responsibilities of Congress, giving it "All legislative Powers herein granted": the power to spend and tax in order to "provide for the common Defense and general Welfare of the United States"; the power to borrow money; the power to regulate commerce with foreign nations and among the states; the power to declare war, raise and support armies, and provide and maintain a navy; the power to establish post offices; and the power to set up the federal courts under the Supreme Court. As a final catchall, the Constitution gives Congress the right "to make all Laws which shall be necessary and proper for carrying into Execution" the powers set out. Several nonlegislative functions were also granted, such as participating in the process of constitutional amendment and impeachment (given to the House) and trying an impeached federal officer (given to the Senate).

The Constitution confers additional responsibilities on the Senate. The Senate has the power to confirm many presidential nominations—sometimes as many as 500 key executive and judicial nominees a year. In a two-year Congress there may be more than 5,000 civilian nominations and 90,000 military nominations needing senatorial approval. The Senate must also ratify, by a two-thirds vote of the senators present, before a president may sign a treaty.

Although the Seventeenth Amendment to the Constitution (1913), which provides for direct election of U.S. senators, altered the character of the Senate's membership, the two chambers still have many differences (see Table 10-1). However, the two houses are more similar today in their membership and operations than they were two hundred or even one hundred years ago.

The House has some distinctive responsibilities, yet these have not proved to be as important as those given to the Senate. For example, although all revenue bills must originate in the House, this practice does not give the House much advantage, as the Senate has freely amended these bills, sometimes changing everything except the title.

The framers did not intend Congress to be all-powerful. They reserved certain authority for the states and for the people and gave other powers to the

TABLE 10-1

Differences between the House of Representatives and the Senate

House of Representatives	Senate
Two-year term	Six-year term
435 members	100 members
Smaller constituencies	Larger constituencies
Fewer personal staff	More personal staff
Equal populations represented	States represented
Less flexible rules	More flexible rules
Limited debate	Unlimited debate
More policy specialists	Policy generalists
Less media coverage	More media coverage
Less prestige	More prestige
Less reliance on staff	More reliance on staff
More powerful committee leaders	More equal distribution of power
Very important committees	Less important committees
19 standing committees	16 standing committees
Nongermane amendments (riders) not allowed	Nongermane amendments (riders) allowed
Important Rules Committee	Special treaty ratification power
Some bills permit no floor amendments (closed rule)	Special confirmation power
	Filibuster

We The People

A Profile of the 105th Congress (1997–1999)

SENATE:
55 Republicans
45 Democrats

Sex:
9 women
91 men

Race:
1 African American
2 Asian-Pacific
1 Native American

Average Age: 58

Religion:
24 Catholic
11 Episcopalian
13 Methodist
10 Baptist
9 Jewish
8 Presbyterian
4 Lutheran
3 Mormon

HOUSE:
227 Republicans
207 Democrats
1 Independent

Sex:
49 women
386 men

Race:
38 African American
18 Hispanic
4 Asian-Pacific

Average Age: 52

Religion:
125 Catholic
57 Baptist
50 Methodist
47 Presbyterian
34 Episcopalian
24 Jewish
15 Lutheran
10 Mormon

Senator Ben Nighthorse Campbell (R.-Colo) and Senator Carol Moseley Braun (D.-Ill), elected in 1992, were, respectively, the first Native American and the first African American woman to win seats in the U.S. Senate.

executive and judicial branches of the national government. As time passed, Congress gained power in some respects and lost it in others. The power of Congress also changes with the times and the president. For example, Clinton was more effective in getting legislation passed in his first two years in office but was largely thwarted by Congress after the Republican takeover in 1995. Despite the comparatively high number of his measures adopted, Clinton struck out on the issue that mattered most to him—health care reform. Clinton's inability to deliver any legislation on this issue he had made so central to his presidency hurt his party with 1994 midterm elections. As the role and authority of the national government have expanded, so, too, have the policy-making and oversight responsibilities of Congress. Still, Congress has difficulty keeping pace with its great rival, the presidency. The president's national security responsibilities, preparation of the budget, media visibility, and agenda-setting influence have all enhanced the position of the presidency. The growth of executive authority may be part of a worldwide trend. Legislative bodies almost everywhere have become subordinate to the executive at all levels of government.

Despite its sometimes secondary role in recent decades, however, Congress still performs these seven important functions:

1. *Representation* involves expressing the diversity and conflicting views of the regional, economic, social, racial, religious, and other interests in the United States.
2. *Law making* is enacting measures to help solve substantive problems.
3. *Consensus building* is the bargaining process by which these interests are reconciled.
4. *Overseeing the bureaucracy* means ensuring that laws and policies approved by Congress are faithfully carried out by the executive branch and that they accomplish what was intended.
5. *Policy clarification* (or policy incubation, as it is sometimes called) is the identification and publicizing of issues.
6. For the Senate, *confirming* presidential appointees and ratifying treaties.
7. *Investigating* the operation of government agencies or other problems.

The House of Representatives

The organization and procedures in the House are different from those in the Senate, if only because the House is more than four times as large as the Senate. *How* things are done affects *what* is done. The House assigns different types of bills to different calendars. For instance, finance measures—tax or appropriations bills—are put on a special calendar for quicker action. The House has other ways to speed up law making, including electronic voting. Ordinary rules may be suspended by a two-thirds vote, or immediate action may be taken by unanimous consent of the members on the floor. By sitting as the *committee of the whole*, the House is able to operate more informally and more quickly than under its regular rules. A quorum in the committee of the whole is composed of only 100 members, rather than a majority of the whole chamber, and voting is quicker and simpler. Members are limited in how long they can speak, and debate may be cut off simply by majority vote.

THE SPEAKER AND OTHER LEADERS   The **Speaker** is the presiding officer in the House of Representatives.[8] The Constitution mandates that the House of Representatives shall choose its Speaker, yet it does not say anything about duties or powers of the office. This officer is formally elected by the House yet is actually selected by the majority party; it is usually someone with broad appeal in the party. Revolts in 1910 by the rank-and-file Progressives stripped Speakers of much of their power, including control over who served on which congressional committees. As the highest-ranking officer in Congress, the Speaker represents it on ceremonial occasions. Third in line of succession to the presidency (in case of death, resignation, or impeachment), the Speaker must keep the White House informed about his whereabouts.

The routine powers of the Speaker include recognizing members who wish to speak, ruling on questions of parliamentary procedure, and appointing members to select and conference committees—that is, temporary committees, not standing committees. In general, the Speaker directs business on the floor of the House. More significant, of course, is a Speaker's political and behind-the-scenes influence. When the Republicans won control of the House in 1994, they elected Newt Gingrich as Speaker. As the first Republican Speaker in forty years, he was a novelty in Washington. "I had set out to do a very unusual job," said Gingrich, "which was part revolutionary, part national political figure, part Speaker, part intellectual."[9]

Gingrich established his authority right from the start—naming committee chairs, bypassing the seniority rule, reorganizing House committees, and reducing perks and committee staffs. He delegated considerable power to his fellow Republican leaders, yet he claimed for himself the main role as spokesman for major policy initiatives. He published a book detailing his ideas about government, and he cheerfully took on the White House and the liberal press.[10]

Gingrich won enormous attention for his positions and eventually for himself and sometimes seemed to be performing the role of an American prime minister. But he admitted that he found it demanding to perform the many roles his speakership provided. He soon found it difficult to control the often ideologically oriented Republicans, especially the 73 Republican freshmen elected in 1994. He also sometimes lost his temper with the press. He had become as much of a lightning rod for the public's discontent with Congress as many of his Democratic predecessors had been in the 1980s and early 1990s.

Gingrich's negative public opinion ratings forced most Republican candidates in 1996 to distance themselves from his views as they ran for reelection. Yet despite Clinton's reelection to the White House, most of Speaker Gingrich's allies won reelection. These Republicans continued to oppose many of Clinton's policies.

The Speaker is assisted by a **majority leader,** who helps plan party strategy, confers with other party leaders, and tries to keep members of the party in line. The minority party elects a **minority leader,** who usually steps into the speakership when his or her party gains a majority in the House. These positions are also sometimes called *majority and minority floor leader.* Assisting each floor leader are the party **whips.** (The term comes from the "whipper-in," who in fox hunts keeps the hounds bunched in a pack.) The whips serve as liaison between the House leadership of each party and the rank-and-file. They inform members when important bills will come up for a vote, prepare summaries of the bills, do nose counts for the leadership, exert mild pressure on members to support the leadership, and try to ensure maximum attendance on the floor for critical votes.

At the beginning of the session and occasionally afterward, each party holds a **caucus** of all its members (called a **conference** by Republicans) to elect party officers, approve committee assignments, elect committee leaders, discuss important legislation, and perhaps try to agree on party policy.

THE HOUSE RULES COMMITTEE   The House, unlike the Senate, has a Rules Committee that helps regulate the time of floor debate for each bill as well as limitations on floor amendments. In the normal course of events, a bill does not

The Gingrich Speakership: How Powerful?

House Speaker Newt Gingrich is seen by most political scientists as the most influential Speaker in generations. He has a "vision" both on policy issues and on how the U.S. House of Representatives should be run. He is effective in capturing media coverage for himself and his party. On assuming the speakership, he boldly centralized power in the hands of the Speaker and the committee chairs. He insisted on cohesiveness in voting by Republicans in the House, and he bypassed or cajoled them to work with him on top priority issues.

Gingrich brings enormous energy to his work, and he quickly became a tough opponent of President Bill Clinton. He and his Republican leadership team helped defeat the Clinton health care reform, and in the 104th Congress Gingrich and his allies clearly became the equal of the executive branch in initiating legislation and forcing compromises on the budget by their intransigence on continuing resolutions that keep the government running.

Gingrich aroused strong feelings, both positive and negative, with proposals to cut Medicare, college loans, education, welfare, and environment programs. Most people felt that Gingrich overestimated the "mandate" voters gave the Republican Contract with America. Controversy also swirled about his book contract and about the House Ethics Committee investigation of his use of campaign funds. In any event, Gingrich's articulate and vigorous leadership as Speaker earned him high visibility and acclaim, along with high negatives in the polls.

Republican leaders Robert Dole and Newt Gingrich brief the press on their budget proposals. Their threat to shut down the government to force President Clinton to agree to a seven-year balanced budget was carried out in December 1995 and January 1996.

come up for action on the floor without a *rule* from the Rules Committee; the rule sets the length of debate and specifies whether the bill can or cannot be amended. By failing to act or refusing to grant a rule, the committee can delay consideration of a bill. A **closed rule** prohibits amendments altogether or provides that only members of the committee reporting the bill may offer amendments; closed rules are usually reserved for tax and spending bills. An **open rule** permits debate within the overall time allocated to the bill.

Until the mid-1960s, the Rules Committee was dominated by a coalition of Republicans and conservative Democrats. Liberals denounced it as unrepresentative, unfair, and dictatorial. More recently, the Rules Committee membership has come to reflect the views of the total membership of the majority party. The Rules Committee today is an arm of the leadership, and rather than block legislation, it offers a "dress rehearsal" on procedural issues like time allotted for debate to those trying to press for new measures.

The Senate

The Senate has the same basic committee structure, elected party leadership, and decentralized power as the House, but because the Senate is a smaller body, its procedures are more informal, and it permits more time for debate. Television has made the Senate an even more visible and key political forum. It has become more open and outward looking, and its members today share influence more equitably than in the past. The Senate now addresses a wider range of issues than ever before.[11]

The president of the Senate (the vice-president of the United States) has little influence over Senate proceedings. A vice-president can vote only in case of a tie and is seldom consulted when important decisions are made. The Senate also elects from among the majority party a **president pro tempore**, usually the most senior member, who is official chair in the absence of the vice-president. Presiding over the Senate on most occasions is a thankless chore, so the president pro tempore regularly delegates this responsibility to junior members of the chamber's majority party.

Party machinery in the Senate is somewhat similar to that of the House. There are party caucuses (conferences), majority and minority floor leaders, and party whips. Each party has a *policy committee*, composed of the leaders of the party, which is theoretically responsible for the party's overall legislative program. In the Senate the party steering committees handle only committee assignments. Unlike the House party steering committees, the Senate's party policy committees are formally provided for by law, and each has a regular staff and a budget. Although the Senate party policy committees have some influence on legislation, they have not asserted strong legislative leadership or managed to coordinate policy.

The Senate *majority leader*—the elected leader of the majority party in the Senate—is an influential person within the Senate and sometimes nationally. As the Senate's major power broker, the majority leader has the right to be the first senator heard on the floor. In consultation with the *minority leader*, the majority leader determines the Senate's agenda and has much to say about committee assignments for members of the majority party. The position confers somewhat less authority than the speakership in the House, and its influence depends on the person's political and parliamentary skills and on the national political situation.[12]

Senator Trent Latt of Mississippi was selected by his fellow Republicans to assume the job of Senate majority leader when Bob Dole resigned to campaign for the presidency.

POLITICAL ENVIRONMENT Senators have more diverse policy interests than do members of the House, serve on more committees, and are more likely to wield power in their state parties. For these reasons, the Senate has a character different from that of the House. Even first-term senators can become visible and politically significant. This possibility for prominence is due to the smaller size of the Senate, its greater access to the media, and the larger staffs that senators enjoy.[13]

The contemporary Senate is individualistic. With the expanding role of subcommittee chairs and enlarged staff, the influence of committee chairs has declined, and key decisions are often made on the Senate floor. The Senate is a more open, fluid, and decentralized body now than it was a generation or two ago. Indeed, it is often said that the Senate has one hundred separate power centers and is so splintered that the party leaders have difficulty arranging the day-to-day schedule.

THE FILIBUSTER A major difference between the Senate and the House is that debate is much less limited in the Senate. A senator who gains the floor may go on talking until he or she relinquishes the right to talk voluntarily or through exhaustion. This right to unlimited debate may be used by a small group of senators to **filibuster**—delay Senate proceedings in order to delay or prevent a vote. At one time the filibuster was a favorite weapon of southern senators intent on blocking civil rights legislation. More recently the filibuster has been used for a wider range of issues. The Senate in 1987 had, for instance, a week-long filibuster opposing a congressional campaign finance reform bill. And in 1993, Republicans used a filibuster to kill President Clinton's economic stimulus package. A filibuster, or the threat of a filibuster, is typically most potent at the end of a congressional session, when there is a fixed date for adjournment, because it could mean that many bills that have made it to the end of the legislation process will die for lack of a floor vote. The knowledge that a bill might be subject to a filibuster is often just enough to force a compromise satisfactory to its opponents. Sometimes the leaders, knowing that a filibuster will tie up the Senate and keep it from enacting other needed legislation, do not bring a bill to the floor.

A filibuster can be defeated. Until 1917 the Senate could terminate a filibuster only if every member agreed. That same year, however, the Senate adopted its first debate-ending, or **cloture**, rule. Now, as long as the senators who are doing the talking stay on their feet, debate can be stopped only by a cloture vote. The rule of

"Listen pal, I didn't spend seven million bucks to get here so I could yield the floor to you."

Drawing by Dana Fradon. © 1987 The New Yorker Magazine, Inc.

cloture specifies that two days after 16 members sign a petition, the question of curtailing debate must be put to a vote. If three-fifths of the total number of senators (60 of the 100 members) vote for cloture, no senator may speak for more than one hour. A final vote must be taken after no more than 30 hours of debate, including all delaying tactics, such as quorum calls and roll call votes on procedure. After the 30 hours of debate, the motion before the Senate must be brought to a vote.

The tactic or the threat of a filibuster is available to Senate minorities to force the majority to compromise and modify its position, and both parties have learned to use it well when they are in the minority. Cloture votes are relatively rare, yet they are more common today than in earlier years, in part because the Senate reduced the number of votes needed from 67 to 60.

THE POWER TO CONFIRM   The Senate has the constitutional power to confirm presidential appointments to such positions as the cabinet, the U.S. Supreme Court and other federal courts, all ambassadorial positions, and many executive branch positions. As with other legislative business, the confirmation process starts in committees, with the relevant standing committee having jurisdiction. The Judiciary Committee considers judges and Supreme Court nominees; the Foreign Relations Committee considers all ambassadorial appointments. Nominees now routinely appear before the committee to answer questions, and they typically have met individually with key senators well before the hearing.

The framers of the Constitution regarded the confirmation process and its advice and consent by the Senate as an important check on executive power. Alexander Hamilton viewed it as a way for Congress to prevent the appointment of "unfit characters." Today the U.S. Senate and the president often struggle over control of top personnel in the executive and judicial branches.

The Constitution leaves the question somewhat ambiguous: "The President . . . shall nominate, and by and with the Advice and Consent of the Senate, shall appoint Ambassadors, other public Ministers and Consuls, Judges of the Supreme Court, all other officers of the United States." Presidents, however, have never enjoyed exclusive control over hiring and firing in the executive branch. The Senate jealously guards its right to confirm or reject major appointments; during the period of strong Congresses after the Civil War, presidents had to struggle to keep their power to appoint and dismiss. But for most of the twentieth century, presidents gained a reasonable amount of control over top appointments, in part, because a growing number of people in and out of Congress believe that chief executives without compatible cabinet-level appointees of their choice cannot be held accountable.

In recent years the Senate has taken a somewhat tougher stand on presidential appointments. Time spent evaluating and screening presidential nominations has increased. The Senate rejected several nominees of presidents George Bush and Ronald Reagan, including turning down Bush's choice for secretary of defense, John Tower. President Bill Clinton has had to withdraw nominees for attorney general and several lesser posts because of Senate opposition.

The Senate's role in the confirmation process was never intended to eliminate politics but rather to use politics as a safeguard. Some conservatives in recent years object that the Senate has occasionally rejected nominees because of their political beliefs and thus interfered with the executive power of presidents. In such instances, so this complaint goes, the Senate's decision is not a reflection of the fitness of a nominee but rather of the political strength of the president and certain interest groups.

By the tradition called **senatorial courtesy**, a president confers with the senator or senators from the state where an appointee is to work. A nomination is less likely to secure Senate approval against the objection of these senators, especially if these senators are members of the president's party, even if his party does not control the Senate. Thus, for nearly all district court judgeships and a variety of other positions, senators can exercise what is, in fact, a veto that can be overridden only with difficulty. Further, it is usually exercised in secret and subject to little accountability. But this form of patronage is sufficiently important to senators that senatorial courtesy is likely to continue.

It is useful to note a distinction between *judicial appointments*, especially those to the Supreme Court, and *administration appointments*. The Senate plays a greater role in judicial appointments because judges serve for life and constitute an independent and, as we discuss in Chapter 12, vital branch of the government.[14] There is an argument that when it comes to cabinet-level positions in the executive branch, a president ought to be able to choose those who will carry out the general views of the White House. In contrast, a president is not expected to enjoy partisan loyalty from those nominated to the bench.

The confirmation provisions in the Constitution have fulfilled most of the intentions of the framers. The Senate has been able to use its power to reject unqualified nominees. It has sometimes also been able to prevent those with serious conflicts of interest from taking office. In addition, senators have been able to use the confirmation process to make their views known to prospective executive officials. Indeed, the very existence of the confirmation process generally deters presidents from appointing weak, questionable, or "unfit characters."

THE JOB OF THE LEGISLATOR

Congress as a Place to Work

The elegant U.S. Capitol building is the working center of our nation's legislative process. It is flanked by a half a dozen House and Senate office buildings, the sprawling Library of Congress, and a number of other annex office buildings that help Congress do its work. Although staff size has been cut in recent years, members of Congress employ nearly 20,000 staff aides who work directly with them in Washington, D.C., or in their districts. Nearly another 16,000 work for the General Accounting Office, the Government Printing Office, the Library of Congress, the Architect of the Capitol, and smaller agencies that work under the control of Congress.

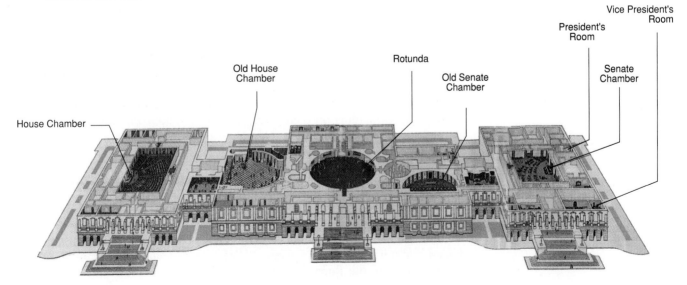

HOUSE OF REPRESENTATIVES

SENATE

Old House Chamber

Rotunda

Old Senate Chamber

President's Room

Vice President's Room

Senate Chamber

House Chamber

Congressional staffs grew enormously in the 1960s and 1970s. But in more recent years critics as well as several elected officials have called for major reductions in the number of both staffs and committees. Bill Clinton, Newt Gingrich, Ross Perot, and Ralph Nader differ on many things, yet they have all favored cutting committee staffs and shrinking the size of the legislative branch.[15]

Legislators as Representatives

Congress has a split personality. One Congress is a *law-making institution* that writes laws and makes policy for the entire nation. In this capacity, all the members are expected to set aside their personal ambitions and perhaps even the concerns of their own constituencies. Yet Congress is also a *representative assembly*, made up of 535 elected officials who serve as links between their constituents and the national government. The dual roles of *making laws* and *responding to constituents' demands* have forced members to balance national concerns against the specific interests of their states or districts.

For whom does a representative speak? The geographical district and its immediate interests? The party? The nation? Some special interest? His or her conscience? Congress was intended to serve as a forum for registering the interests and values of the nation. It was never intended that the legislative branch represent views identical to those of the executive. But to whom does the individual representative listen?

Members of Congress perceive their roles differently. Some believe they should serve as **delegates** from their districts. These legislators believe it is their duty to find out what "the folks back home" want and act accordingly. This orientation is often assumed by Republicans, nonleaders, nonsoutherners, or members with low seniority.

Other members see their role as that of **trustee**. Their constituents, they contend, did not send them to Congress to serve as mere robots or "errand-runners." They act and vote according to their own view of what is best for their district or state as well as the nation. As one member explained, "I have a responsibility not only to follow [my constituents], but to inform them and lead them. I'm not going to betray my responsibility to my constituents. I owe them not only my industry but my judgment. That's why they sent me here."[16] In this view a legislature is a place for deliberation and learning, not a mere gathering of ambassadors from localities. The trustee focus is more common among Democrats, House leaders, southerners, and high-seniority members.

Although the question of *delegate* versus *trustee* is an old one, it poses a false dichotomy. Representatives cannot follow detailed instructions from their constituents, because such instructions seldom exist. On many important policy questions, members hear nothing from their constituents. They hear most often only from those who agree with them. Still, a legislator should be able to define, or help define, the national interest, and this means trying to understand the needs and aspirations of millions of people. Most legislators shift back and forth in their role, depending on their perception of the public interest, their standing in the last and next elections, and the pressures of the moment. Overall, however, most members of Congress view themselves more as free agents than as delegates for their districts.

Legislators as Lawmakers

Members of Congress cast hundreds of votes each year. In 1995 House members voted on a record high 867 "yea" or "nay" roll call votes. The Senate had a more modest yet still a record 613 votes. Members voted 96.5 percent of the time. "One reason for the flurry of votes [in 1995] in the House was the vow of

Republican leaders to allow legislation to be considered whenever possible under open rules that allowed all amendments."[17] The House had to vote on numerous Democratic amendments to Republican bills. When voting, members of Congress are influenced by their perceptions of the problem addressed by the legislation, their perceptions of their constituents' interests, and the views of their trusted colleagues, staff, party leaders, lobbyists, and the president.

POLICY AND PHILOSOPHICAL CONVICTIONS Most of the time, members vote their own ideological beliefs, knowing that constituents tend to grant them considerable leeway. A liberal on social issues is also likely to be a liberal on tax and national security issues. Thus, on controversial issues such as national health insurance, taxes, or defense spending, knowing the general philosophical learnings of individual members provides a helpful guide both to how they make up their minds and how they will vote.

One voting pattern, described as the **conservative coalition**, cuts across party lines. It consists of southern Democrats and Republicans who vote together against other Democrats. In the 1950s and 1960s, the coalition formed on about one-quarter of the important roll call votes. From the mid 1980s to the mid 1990s, the coalition came together on roughly a dozen votes a year, and when it did, it won more than 80 percent of the time in the House and did even better in the Senate.[18] The conservative coalition generally forms around domestic issues, especially social welfare legislation. The conservative coalition became less of a factor after the Republicans gained control of Congress in 1995. Some Southern Democrats switched and became Republicans; others were replaced by Republicans at the polls. But more important, the conservatives would have won most of the major votes anyway because Republicans enjoyed majorities in both chambers.

VOTERS Legislators pay attention to the views of their constituents on issues as well as their "potential views" as issues become more important.[19] Party and executive branch pressures also play a role, but when all is said and done, the members' political futures depend on how most voters in their districts feel about their performance. Rarely does a legislator consistently and deliberately vote against the wishes of the people back home. Legislators might pay more attention to voter attitudes on controversial or heavily publicized matters than on less-known issues.

A paradox is evident here. Members of Congress sometimes think that their individual law-making actions have considerable impact on constituents. Yet constituents' general ignorance of how their representatives vote implies the impact can be small. Members may think their constituents like (or dislike) what they are doing, when actually the voters have little idea of what is going on in Congress. This misperception is explained in part by the tendency of legislators to overestimate their visibility; most citizens do not even know the names of their senators and representatives.[20] Aside from periodic polls, members hear most often from the **attentive public**—those who follow public affairs carefully—rather than the general public. Still, members of Congress must constantly be concerned about how they will explain their votes, especially around election day. Even if only a few voters are aware of their stand on a given issue, this group might make the difference between victory and defeat.

COLLEAGUES Voting decisions are also affected by the advice members obtain from other representatives. Severe time limitations and the frequency with which members must make decisions force them to depend on the advice of like-minded colleagues. In particular, they look to respected members of the

This photo, taken from a television monitor on the floor of Congress, shows the final tally on a proposed congressional pay raise. Defeated here, the pay raise was later passed by Congress.

Bill Bradley on What Influences a Senator's Decisions and Votes

"Every day, an effective Senator calculates the interaction of substance, procedure, and personality in his dealings with his fellow Senators. To have command of only one of these and not the other two dooms one to failure. The skillful Senators know what they're talking about and have mastered the substance of at least two or three subject areas... The skillful Senators use procedures to further their goals. They don't let Senate leadership arrange their procedural lives. The skillful Senators are at home with their colleagues...

Finally, the behavior of every Senator, be that Senator collegial or not, is affected by the quest for re-election. Senators running for re-election do not act normally. They justify an egregious legislative position or their sudden support of the other party's amendment or their participation in outrageous pandering to special interests as being absolutely necessary for re-election."

SOURCE: Bill Bradley, *Time Past, Time Present: A Memoir:* (Knopf, 1996). pp. 88–89.

committee who worked on a bill, especially the committee chair or ranking member of the minority party.[21]

Unlike voters back home, other members usually have detailed knowledge about issues before Congress. Their views are often public; they may have voted on the matter in previous sessions or in committee, and their public statements may have been placed in the *Congressional Record.* Members are sometimes influenced to vote one way merely because they know a colleague is on the *other* side of the issue. On occasion, in recent years, members say they have been impressed by watching a member's speech on C-SPAN while working in their office. More often, legislators find out how their friends stand on an issue, listen to the party leadership's advice, and take into account the various committee reports. If they are still in doubt, they consult other friends and staff. The members most often consulted are those who represent similar districts or the same region or state, like-minded members of the same party or faction, and those on the committee from which the legislation has come.

For some legislators, the **state delegation**—senators and representatives from the same state—reinforces a common identity. Texas Democrats have long been a strong and cohesive delegation. Other states, like California, have less cohesive state delegations.

A member may also vote with a colleague in the expectation that the colleague will later vote for a measure about which the member is concerned (*log rolling*). Some vote trading takes place to build coalitions so that members can "bring home the bacon" to their constituents. Other vote trading reflects *reciprocity* in congressional relations or deference to colleagues' superior information or expertise.

Many forces—regional, local, ties of friendship—can override party influence. Members are sometimes influenced by informal groups (ideological groups, ethnic caucuses, regional groupings, and even the class of colleagues with whom they were elected—for example, "the class of 1994"). Social groups in Congress ranging from the Congressional Progressive Caucus to the more conservative Family Concerns or New Federalists groups also can provide voting cues.

CONGRESSIONAL STAFF Congress is the only legislature in the world with a huge staff, and its staff is one of its chief sources of power. For years, political scientists urged Congress to strengthen its staff. Without additional help, they said, representatives and senators were at a disadvantage in dealing with the executive branch and were overly dependent on information supplied by the White House or lobbyists. Complexity of issues and increasingly demanding schedules, too, created pressures for additional staff. Congress responded, some would say, with a vengeance. About 20,000 staff members, researchers, budget analysts, and others now work for Congress. This number had increased threefold in the 1960s and 1970s, but leveled off in the 1980s, and was reduced in the mid and late 1990s when all of the federal government was cut back.

Every congressional committee, however, and every subcommittee is now at least minimally staffed. In addition, all members of Congress have increased the number of personal staff members working for them both in their Washington and home district offices. About one-third of the House of Representatives staff and one-fourth of the Senate staff are based back home. These staff members help members of Congress communicate with the voters back home and provide constituency services and casework. Much of the work done in district offices is akin to a continuous campaign effort: generating favorable publicity, arranging for local appearances and newspaper interviews, scheduling, and contacting important civic and business leaders in the region.

Because of the complexity of their responsibilities, members of Congress must delegate all kinds of tasks to their staffs. As a result, some members occasionally wonder whether they or their staffs are in charge. This is especially true of senators, who tend to have a wider range of subject matter specialties than do representatives. At congressional hearings, it is often a staff member who tells the legislator what to ask. Congressional staffers become knowledgeable about special policy areas and deal on a day-to-day basis with their counterparts in the executive departments and interest groups. Indeed, some observers say that some of the most powerful people in Washington are congressional staffers. Staffers draft bills, conduct research, and often do much of the parliamentary negotiating and coalition building. Professional staffers often have the opportunity to influence legislative decisions. And certainly there is some truth to the notion that the more staffers there are, the more they look for things to do, such as preparing more legislation, suggesting more investigations, and in general making more work for themselves.

We should not exaggerate the independent power base of staffers, who can be summarily fired at the whim of those they serve. Although they cannot be dismissed because of their race, sex, or national origin, they know that if they wander too far from the views of the one person who can fire them, they will quickly be called back into line.

PARTY Another source of influence on legislative behavior is the political party. Naturally, there is a fair amount of agreement among party colleagues, and friendships tend to develop within the party. On some issues the pressure to conform to a party position is immediate and direct, even when a member does not believe in the party position. Members most often vote with their party; whether as a result of party pressure or natural affinity, on major bills there is a tendency for *most* Democrats to be arrayed against *most* Republicans.

Partisan voting has been increasing in the House since the early 1970s and has been especially cohesive among Republicans since the 1994 elections. Republicans in the Class of 1994 voted together in impressive numbers. House Democrats from districts outside the South also voted together nearly 90 percent of the time in recent years. Party differences are stronger over domestic, regulatory, and welfare reform measures than over foreign policy or civil liberty issues.

On the Party Connection

"Party cohesion and control in the House of Representatives falls short of what is to be found in parliamentary systems or even in many state legislatures. . . . But the parties retain a central role in both the present functioning of the Congress and in periodic efforts to improve its performance.

The party structure is the most important mechanism we have to contain those excesses and impose a measure of collective responsibility on ourselves. The precise rewards and costs of party loyalty will differ for members who are differently situated, but for all, I believe, there ought to be a presumption that enables a House of disparate parts to function."

SOURCE: David E. Price, *The Congressional Experience: A View from the Hill* (Westview Press, 1992), pp. 73 and 90.

Party leaders in both chambers try to promote loyal party voting. Speaker Gingrich claimed cohesive voting was the only way Republicans could implement their Contract with America and satisfy the majorities who elected them. Party leaders in the Senate generally have a harder time encouraging party discipline.

In 1995, Republicans managed "to hold an average of 91 percent of their caucus in line in the House and 89 percent in the Senate."[22] Democrats stuck together in the House and Senate only about 80 percent of the time. Still, this level of party cohesion is the highest in recent times. Much of it may be due to decline of the liberal wing of the Republican Party and a similar decline of the conservative wing in the Democratic party.

INTEREST GROUPS Lobbyists represent interest groups in the legislative process. Interest groups, acting through their political action committees (PACs), make substantial contributions to congressional elections, giving largely to incumbents. In addition to their role as financiers of elections, interest groups (through their lobbyists) are important participants in the legislative process because they provide information.

THE PRESIDENT Presidents and executive branch officials also influence how legislators vote, particularly on foreign policy or national security issues.[23] President Bush benefited from a bipartisan coalition that passed the resolution authorizing the use of military force in the Persian Gulf. President Clinton benefited from strong Republican support in Congress to help win approval for the North American Free Trade Agreement, even when large numbers in his own party opposed this measure. Congress is sometimes overwhelmed by the greater public relations and persuasive abilities of a president.

Through effective use of their constitutional and political powers, presidents have become full-time partners in the legislative process. Still, members of Congress are reluctant to admit that they are influenced by pressures from the White House. On key domestic issues, legislators are more likely to be influenced by their constituents and by their own policy convictions than by what the White House wants.

THE LEGISLATIVE OBSTACLE COURSE

Congress operates under a system of multiple vetoes. The framers dispersed powers so they could not be accumulated by any would-be tyrant. In addition to the checks of bicameralism, Congress has also developed an elaborate set of customs to accompany these constitutional features that serve to distribute power. Follow a bill through the legislative process, and you clearly see this *dispersion of power* (see Figure 10-1). Procedures and rules of the Senate differ somewhat from those of the House, but in each chamber power is fragmented and influence is decentralized.

Every bill, including those drawn up in the executive branch, must be *introduced* in the House and the Senate by a member of that body. Bills are then *referred* by the leadership to the appropriate standing committee. Roughly 90 percent of the bills introduced every two years die in a subcommittee for lack of support. For bills that have significant backing, a committee or subcommittee holds *hearings* to receive opinions. It then meets to *mark up* (discuss and amend) and vote on the bill. If the subcommittee and then the parent committee vote in favor of the bill, it is *reported*—that is, sent—to the full chamber, where it is debated and voted on. In the House the bill must go first to the Rules Committee for a *rule* that sets the time limit for debate and indicates whether floor amendments are allowed.

FIGURE 10-1 How a Bill Becomes a Law

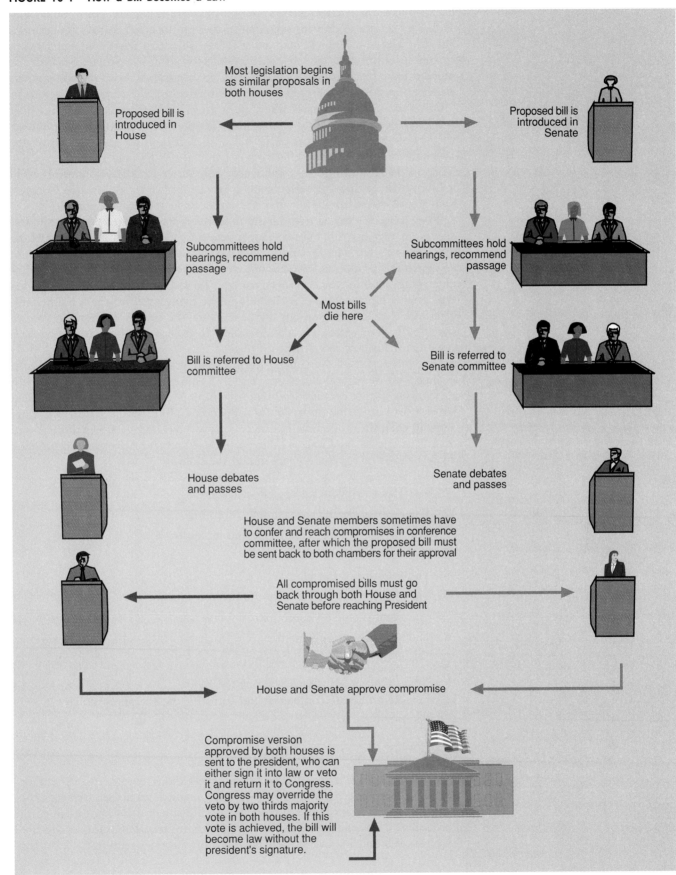

Most legislation begins as similar proposals in both houses

Proposed bill is introduced in House

Proposed bill is introduced in Senate

Subcommittees hold hearings, recommend passage

Subcommittees hold hearings, recommend passage

Most bills die here

Bill is referred to House committee

Bill is referred to Senate committee

House debates and passes

Senate debates and passes

House and Senate members sometimes have to confer and reach compromises in conference committee, after which the proposed bill must be sent back to both chambers for their approval

All compromised bills must go back through both House and Senate before reaching President

House and Senate approve compromise

Compromise version approved by both houses is sent to the president, who can either sign it into law or veto it and return it to Congress. Congress may override the veto by two thirds majority vote in both houses. If this vote is achieved, the bill will become law without the president's signature.

In the Senate, it is not uncommon for legislators to attach **riders**—provisions that may have little relationship to the bill they are riding on. For example, riders that have little to do with spending money can be attached to appropriations bills. The House of Representatives has stricter rules that require amendments to be relevant to the bill, but no such rule is enforced in the Senate. Senators use riders to force the president to accept legislation attached to a bill that is otherwise popular, because the president must either accept the entire bill or veto it.

On most important topics (aside from taxes), both chambers consider their own bills, often at roughly the same time. There is no requirement that one act first. If only one chamber passes the bill, it dies. If both houses pass bills on the same subject but there are differences between the bills—and there often are—the two versions must go to a conference committee for reconciliation. If a bill does not make it through both chambers in identical form in the same Congress (two-year term), it must begin the entire process in the next Congress.

When a bill has passed both houses in identical form, it then goes to the president, who may sign the bill into law or veto it. If Congress is in session and the president waits ten days (excluding Sundays), then the bill becomes law without his signature. If Congress has adjourned and the president waits ten days without signing the bill, it is then defeated by a **pocket veto**. Except for the pocket veto, when a bill is vetoed it is returned to the chamber of its origin by the president with a message explaining the reasons for the veto. Congress can vote to **override** the veto with a two-thirds vote in each chamber, but assembling such an extraordinary majority is often difficult.

The complexity of the congressional system provides a tremendous built-in advantage for the opponents of any measure. Those who sponsor a bill must win at every step; opponents need to win only once. Multiple opportunities to kill a bill exist because of the dispersion of influence, and because at a dozen or more points in committee or in the House or Senate, a bill may be stopped or allowed to die (inaction is the same as killing a bill). Whether good or bad, a proposal can be delayed or rejected by any one of the following:

1. The House subcommittee and its chair
2. The chair of the House standing committee
3. The House standing committee and its leaders
4. The House Rules Committee
5. The majority of the House
6. The chair of the Senate subcommittee
7. The Senate standing committee
8. The majority of the Senate
9. The floor leaders in both chambers
10. A few senators, in the case of a filibuster
11. The House-Senate conference committee, if the chambers disagree
12. The president (by veto)

Authorization and Appropriation

Congress acts by a two-step process; it *authorizes* and it *appropriates*. After Congress and the president authorize a program, Congress, with the president's concurrence, has to appropriate the funds to implement it. Appropriations are processed by a separate committee and its subcommittees. For example, the 1992 Education Act and its several titles reauthorize a variety of programs for a five-year period, including those for federal loans and grants for college students. The authorization act sets the limits on the amount that students may borrow and the conditions under which they must pay back the loan. But the authorization is useless until Congress appropriates funds and the president signs the appropriations bill into law each year. Congress is often likely to appropriate less money for student loans and grants than it has authorized.

The Importance of Compromise

Clearly, a bill does not become law unless its sponsors are willing to compromise to get the votes necessary for its passage. One tactical decision at the start is whether to push for action in the Senate first, in the House first, or in both. For example, if a bill is expected to be opposed in the Senate, its sponsors may seek passage in the House and hope that a sizable victory there will spur the Senate into action. Another decision concerns the committee to which the bill is assigned. Normally, referral to a committee is automatic. Sometimes, however, a bill involves more than one jurisdiction and can be written in such a way that it may go to a committee that will look more kindly on it.

Getting a bill through Congress requires more than a majority at any one time or place. Majorities must be mobilized over and over again—in subcommittee, in committee, in chamber, and possibly again in chamber to override a presidential veto. These majorities shift and change, and they involve different legislators in different situations at different points in time. New coalitions must be built again and again.[24]

Effective legislators are good at building coalitions, overcoming the objections of legislators who are undecided or only slightly opposed to the bill, and reciprocating when colleagues' bills are put forward. The job of a legislator, in sum, requires the ability to compromise and to work well with others.

COMMITTEES: THE LITTLE LEGISLATURES

It is sometimes said that Congress is a collection of committees that come together in a chamber every once in a while to approve one another's actions. There is much truth in this. Congress has long relied on committees to get much of its work done. Woodrow Wilson, a teacher of political science before he became president, expressed a similar thought: "Congress in session is Congress on display. Congress in committee is Congress at work."[25] Today we would say that Congress in subcommittee is Congress at work. The initial struggle over legislation takes place in subcommittees.[26] Congress also utilizes **joint committees** whose members are selected from both houses to oversee such institutions as the Library of Congress or to investigate issues like the Iran-Contra affair in the Reagan administration. Some committees organized to conduct investigations are also called **select or special committees**.

The House Democratic caucus divides standing committees into three categories. The first category is *exclusive committees* and includes Appropriations, Ways and Means, and Rules. Members who serve on one of these committees may not serve on any other standing committee. The second category is *major committees*, which include committees like National Security; members can serve on only one of these but can add assignments to two *nonmajor committees*, such as Small Business. House members rarely serve on more than three standing committees.

Standing committees and their subcommittees are where most of the legislative work is done. Bills can be pigeonholed for weeks, amended beyond recognition, or kept in committee forever. Or a bill can go through the committee in

A Closer Look

COMMITTEES: CONGRESS AT WORK

The 19 standing committees of the House of Representatives each have an average membership of about 46 representatives. These committees have a total of about 85 subcommittees. Committees are "the eye, the ear, the hand, and very often the brain of the House."

What Senate and House Committees Do

- Study legislative proposals
- Consider communications from the executive branch
- Confirm or reject federal appointees
- Conduct hearings and investigations
- Review ongoing executive operations
- Prepare reports and surveys
- Make recommendations about corrective legislation
- Review reports, documents, and research related to committee policy
- Meet informally with public and private-sector leaders about their committee domain
- Conduct on-site visits and inspections

Standing Committees of the House of Representatives

- Agriculture
- Appropriations
- Banking and Financial Services
- Budget
- Commerce
- Economic and Educational Opportunity
- Government Reform and Oversight
- House Oversight
- International Relations
- Judiciary
- National Security
- Resources
- Rules
- Science
- Small Business
- Standards of Official Conduct (Ethics)
- Transportation and Infrastructure
- Veterans' Affairs
- Ways and Means

Standing Committees of the Senate

- Agriculture, Nutrition, and Forestry
- Appropriations
- Armed Services
- Banking, Housing, and Urban Affairs
- Budget
- Commerce, Science, and Transportation
- Energy and Natural Resources
- Environment and Public Works
- Finance
- Foreign Relations
- Governmental Affairs
- Judiciary
- Labor and Human Resources
- Rules and Administration
- Small Business
- Veterans' Affairs

a hurry. A committee reports out favorably only a small fraction of all the bills that come to it. Although a bill can be forced to the floor of the House through a **discharge petition** signed by a majority of the membership, legislators are reluctant to bypass committees. They regard committee members as experts in their fields. Sometimes, too, they are reluctant to risk the anger of committee leaders. And there is a strong sense of *reciprocity:* "You respect my committee's jurisdiction, and I will respect yours." Not surprisingly, few discharge petitions gain the necessary number of signatures.

The Senate has 16 standing committees, each composed of 12 to 29 members, and more than 85 subcommittees. While members of the House hold relatively few committee assignments, each senator normally serves on three standing committees and at least seven subcommittees. Senators are more likely to serve on choice committees (committees that have clout).

Among the most important Senate committees are Foreign Relations, Budget, Finance, and Appropriations. Senate committees have the same powers over the framing of legislation as do those of the House, but they have somewhat less power to keep bills from reaching the floor.

Choosing Committee Members

Control and staffing of standing committees are partisan matters. The chair and a majority of each standing committee come from the majority party. The minority party is represented on each committee roughly in proportion to its membership in the entire chamber, except on some powerful committees on which the majority may want to enhance its position. Getting on a politically advantageous committee is important to members of Congress. A representative from Kansas, for example, would much rather serve on the Agriculture Committee than on the Education and Labor Committee. Members usually stay on the same committees from one Congress to the next, although less senior members who have had less desirable assignments often seek better committees when places become available.

How are committee members chosen? In the House of Representatives, a Committee on Committees of the Republican membership allots places to Republican members. This committee is composed of one member from each state having Republican representation in the House; the member is generally the senior member of the state's delegation. Because each member has as many votes in the committee as there are Republicans in the delegation, the group is dominated by senior members from the large state delegations. On the Democratic side, assignment to committees is handled by the Steering and Policy Committee of the Democratic caucus in negotiation with senior Democrats from the state delegations. In the Senate, veterans also dominate the assignment process; each party has a small Steering Committee that makes committee assignments. In making assignments, leaders are guided by various considerations: how talented and cooperative a member is, whether his or her region is already well represented on a committee, and whether the assignment will aid in reelecting the member. Senator Bill Bradley, who retired in 1997, said "there were fierce battles" within the Democratic Committee on Committees, which is charged with assigning members to committees. "The battles are generally drawn along classic lines—liberal/conservative, environment/industry, rural/urban, East/West."[27]

One reason Congress can cope with its huge workload is that its committees and subcommittees are organized around subject matter specialties. This specialization allows members to develop technical expertise in specific areas and to recruit skilled staffs. Thus Congress is often able to challenge experts from the bureaucracy. Interest groups and lobbyists realize the great power a specific committee has in certain areas and focus their attention on its members. Similarly, members of executive departments are careful to cultivate the committee and subcommittee chairs and members of "their" committees. One powerful Senate committee chair reminded his constituents of the amount of federal tax money being spent in their state: "This does not happen by accident," the senator's campaign pamphlet said. "It takes power and influence in Congress."

Committees are not all alike. Some are powerful, others are less important. Because of the Senate's special role in foreign policy, for example, the Senate Foreign Relations Committee is usually more influential than the House Committee on National Security. For the two Appropriations Committees, however, the reverse is true; the House Appropriations Committee plays a more significant role than the Senate committee, although these differences are less than they used to be. We should also note that committees differ not only for institutional reasons but also according to the goals and abilities of their members.[28]

How Congress uses committees is critical in its role as a partner in policy making. In recent years progress has been made in opening hearings to the public and improving the quality of committee staffs, but it is difficult to restructure committee jurisdictions so that they do not overlap. Thus, a dozen different committees deal with energy, education, and the war on drugs. Efforts to make the committee system more efficient are often considered threats to the delicate balance of power within the chamber.

Seniority Rule

Forty years ago committee chairs determined the total workload of committees, hired and fired staff, and formed subcommittees and assigned them jurisdictions, members, and aides. Chairs also managed the most important bills assigned to their committees. Since the mid-1970s, however, less senior members have insisted they be given more authority. Subcommittee chairs have also become more independent. It is not uncommon these days for a member of Congress after only one or two terms to be the chair of an important subcommittee, and indeed such placement is the tradition in the Senate. In recent years there have also been moves to strengthen the powers of the party leaders and caucuses at the expense of the committee chairs.

Most chairs are still selected on the basis of the **seniority rule**; the member of the majority party with the longest continuous service on the committee becomes chair upon the retirement of the current chair or a change in which party controls the Congress. The seniority rule gives power to representatives who come from **safe districts**—one where one party dominates and a member can build up years of continuous service. Conversely, the seniority rule lessens the influence of states or districts where the two parties are more evenly matched, and where there is more turnover.

In the 104th Congress, Speaker Newt Gingrich ignored the seniority tradition, assigning chairmanships in some cases to younger committee members who would provide the kind of support and energy he expected. But both Democrats and Republicans have occasionally passed over the most senior committee member in order to place someone with more energy or with a more compatible policy perspective in a committee chair position. In 1975 Democrats removed a few aging committee chairs and appointed younger members to chair several committees. In 1995 Speaker Gingrich and his allies appointed several committee chairs who did not have the most seniority on the committee. Thus Republicans Bob Livingston, Tom Bliley, and Henry Hyde became chairmen of Appropriations, Commerce, and Judiciary, respectively, even though they did not have seniority. "In each case," said Gingrich, "I thought they would bring a level of aggressiveness and risk taking that we would need in these very important positions."[29]

Still, the practice of elevating the senior member of a committee to serve as committee chair remains the general rule. It has long been respected in Congress for several reasons: it encourages members to stay on a committee; it encourages specialization and expertise; it also reduces the interpersonal politics that would arise if several members of a committee "ran" for election to become chair.

Investigations and Oversight

The power to investigate is one of Congress's most important functions; some think it even more important than its power to legislate. Congress conducts investigations to determine if legislation is needed, to gather facts relevant to legislation, to assess the efficiency of executive agencies, to build public support, to expose corruption, and to enhance the image or reputation of its members.[30] Hearings by standing committees, their subcommittees, or special select committees are an important source of information and opinion. They provide an arena in which experts can submit their views, and statements and statistics can be entered in the record.[31] Congress's investigations are controversial, especially such well-publicized open hearings as those of the Senate Foreign Relations Committee during the Vietnam War and more recently the "Whitewater" hearings examining the Clinton family investments.

There are various kinds of investigations or hearings: routine ones conducted in the ordinary work of committees and subcommittees, and special ones conducted by special or select committees. These latter tend to be the most publicized, such as the 1987 Joint Senate-House Committee on the Iran-Contra affair. The Senate Watergate Committee's televised investigation into election practices and campaign-finance abuses in 1973 was intended less to obtain new information than to arouse citizens and promote support for electoral reforms.

Among the more important functions of congressional hearings is the oversight function—the responsibility to question executive branch officials to see whether their agencies are complying with the wishes of the Congress and conducting their programs efficiently. Authorization committees regularly hold oversight hearings, and appropriations committees, exercising "the congressional power of the purse," often use appropriations hearings to communicate committee members' views about how agency officials should carry out their business. Cabinet members and agency heads have been known to dread the loaded questions of hostile members of Congress and to hate having to watch themselves on the evening news trying to explain why their agencies made some mistakes.

Conference Committees

When the framers created a two-house national legislature, they anticipated the two chambers would represent sharply different interests. The Senate was to be a small chamber of persons elected indirectly by the state legislatures to hold long, overlapping terms. It was to be a chamber of scrutiny, a gathering of wise leaders who would counsel and sanction a president—whether that president liked it or not. The House of Representatives, elected anew every two years, was to be a more direct instrument of the people.

The Senate did serve as a conservative check on the House, especially in the late nineteenth and early twentieth centuries, when it was extremely conservative and something of a rich man's club. But some factors—chiefly political—have altered the character of both the House and the Senate. Today the House is more conservative than the Senate. Executive departments and agencies, for instance,

Discouraged by bickering and gridlock, an unusually large number of key Democratic members of Congress decided not to run for reelection in 1996. Among them were Senator Bill Bradley, Representative Pat Schroeder, and Senator Sam Nunn.

occasionally consider the Senate to be a court of appeals for appropriations that have been shot down by the House.

Given the differences between the House and the Senate, it is not surprising that the version of a bill passed by one chamber may differ substantially from the version passed by the other. Only if both houses pass an absolutely identical measure can it become law. Most of the time one house accepts the language of the other, but at least 15 percent of all bills passed (usually major ones) must be referred to a **conference committee**—a special committee of members from each chamber—that settles the differences between versions. Both parties are represented, but the majority party has more members.

The proceedings of a conference committee are usually an elaborate bargaining process. When the proposed bill is brought back to the two chambers, the conference report can be accepted or rejected (often with further negotiations ordered), but it cannot be amended. Each set of conference members must convince its colleagues that any concessions made to the other chamber were on unimportant points and that nothing basic to the original version of the bill was surrendered.

How much leeway does a conference committee have? Ordinarily members are expected to stay somewhere between the different versions. On matters for which there is no clear middle ground, members are sometimes accused of exceeding their instructions and producing a new bill. The conference committee has even been called a "third house" of Congress, one that arbitrarily revises policy. Conference committees are also criticized on the ground that they are not representative, even of the committees approving the bill, and that they disproportionately represent senior committee leaders. Critics also complain little can be done about the subtle new features that might be slipped into a bill by a conference committee. Despite such criticism, some kind of conference committee is needed for a two-house legislature to work. Conference committees integrate a bill as it comes from the two chambers.

Which chamber, House or Senate, wins more often in conference committees? On the surface it appears that the Senate's version wins more often, but this is partly because the Senate more often than not acts on its legislation after the House. Political scientist David J. Vogler concludes that "by creating the original bill and setting the agenda for debate on the issue, the House is judged to have the more real impact on the final shape of legislation as it passes through conference than does the Senate."[32] In effect the House plays a dominant law-making role, while the Senate plays a key representational role through amendments.

CONGRESS: AN ASSESSMENT AND A VIEW ON REFORM

More than two hundred years after its creation, Congress is a much larger and very different kind of institution. Yet most of its major functions remain the same, and their responsible exercise is crucial to the health of our constitutional democracy. We still look to Congress in the late 1990s to make laws, raise revenues, represent citizens, investigate abuses of power, and oversee the executive branch, and the Senate still confirms top administrative and judicial appointees. Congress is still a bicameral organization, and its chambers still check one another as together they check and balance the executive and judicial branches of government. The interests of states and regions are still represented, debated, and brokered.

Today most members engage in continual electioneering to stay in office. So many members appear driven by their desire to win reelection that much of what takes place in Congress seems mainly designed to promote reelection. These efforts usually pay off. At the same time, this concern with reelection is generally healthy because it fosters accountability; the desire to please the voters is the link that keeps the system democratic. Congress is also characterized by internal fragmentation and diffusion of power. More and more of the work these days is done in committees or subcommittees. Multiple, successive decision points make it much easier to prevent than to pass legislation.

Senator William S. Cohen (R.-Maine) retired early in 1997 after an impressive career in Congress. He admired the institution's deliberative practices yet feared its paralysis. His concerns are widely shared.

> Our republic, we know, was designed to be slow-moving and deliberative. Our founding fathers were convinced that power had to be entrusted to someone, but that no one could be entirely trusted with power. They devised a brilliant system of checks and balances to prevent the tyranny of the many by the few. They constructed a perfect triangle of allocated and checked power.... There could be no rash action, no rush to judgment, no legislative mob rule, no unrestrained chief executive.
>
> The difficulty with this diffusion of power in today's cyberspace age is that everyone is in check, but no one is in charge.
>
> But more than the constitutional separation of powers is leading to the unprecedented stalemate that exists today. There has been a breakdown in civil debates and discourse. Enmity at times has become so intense that members of Congress have resorted to shoving matches outside the legislative chambers.[33]

How does such a Congress make any progress? In an institution where most members act as individual entrepreneurs and consider themselves leaders, the task of providing institutional leadership is increasingly difficult. This is particularly true in the Senate, which prides itself on extended debate and deliberation. With limited resources, and only sometimes aided by the president, congressional leaders are asked to bring together a diverse, fragmented, and independent institution. The congressional system requires majority action and acts only when majorities can be achieved. That the framers accomplished their original objective—creating a Congress that would not move with undue haste—has been generally well realized.

Americans often characterize Congress as a bickering, timid, ignorant, selfish, or narrow-minded body. Yet we also admire the stamina and civic responsibility of members of Congress we know. Individual members of Congress are more popular than the institution. Perhaps this is because we expect Congress to solve most of our national ills, yet we judge individual members primarily on how well they serve the interests of their states and districts and on their personal appeal (see Figure 10-2).

Some of the criticism of Congress is justified. Yet critics usually forget that our national legislature is particularly exposed, and some of our expectations of it are unrealistic. First, Congress does nearly all its work directly in the public eye. Unfortunate incidents—quarrels, name calling, evasive actions, inaccurate statements, and ethical lapses—that might be hushed up in the executive or judicial branches are almost always observed and duly reported by the news media. Second, Congress by its nature is controversial and argumentative. Its 535 members are found on both sides, sometimes on half a dozen sides, of every important question. The average citizen who holds one opinion is likely to be intolerant of other views and of the legislators holding them. There is also a considerable difference between holding an opinion and writing legislation. Moreover, during the 1990s Congress has both raised taxes and cut services, closed military bases, reduced student loans, and shut down the government—not a recipe for popularity!

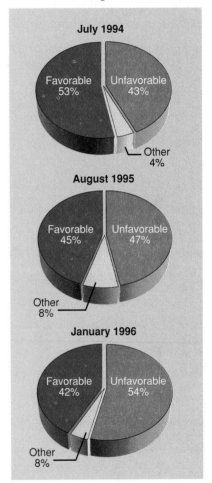

The Public Is Still Unhappy About Congress

The American public continues to look unfavorably on Congress, according to the latest in a series of polls by the Pew Research Center for The People and The Press. Poll respondents were asked: "Would you say your over-all opinion of Congress is very favorable, mostly favorable, mostly unfavorable or very unfavorable?" The chart below combines the two favorable and the two unfavorable categories.

July 1994
Favorable 53%
Unfavorable 43%
Other 4%

August 1995
Favorable 45%
Unfavorable 47%
Other 8%

January 1996
Favorable 42%
Unfavorable 54%
Other 8%

SOURCE: "Congressional Facts and Figures," *National Journal*, February 3, 1996, p. 268.

Criticisms of Congress

How would you "reform" Congress?

Which of these proposed reforms do you think should be adopted to improve Congress?

- Move to a European-style parliamentary system
- Extend House terms to four years
- Limit House and Senate tenure to 12 years
- Provide for public financing of campaigns and ban campaign contributions
- Permit only people who live in a district or state to contribute to candidates for Congress
- Radically reduce the number of committees and subcommittees
- Strengthen the power and resources of the party leaders
- Reduce the size of congressional staffs
- Set and abide by an agenda agreed to at the beginning of each session
- Have shorter sessions for Congress, so members can spend more time in their districts

You Decide!

CONGRESS IS INEFFICIENT House and Senate procedures are, some charge, simply not suited to the needs of a modern industrial nation. Too much time is required to get bills through the complicated legislative process, and bills are often buried or defeated by procedural devices. Members are not as well informed as they should be. The dispersion of power guarantees slowness.

Some of this criticism is exaggerated. Evaluating procedure and structure is difficult to separate from evaluating policy, about which everyone has an individual preference. From the White House's vantage point, for example, Congress is inefficient when it does not process the president's bills quickly.

Congress deals with an enormous number of complex measures. Many procedures in both houses expedite handling of bills, and the committee and subcommittee system is a reasonable device for hearing arguments and compiling information. Still, the question of efficiency remains. Many members feel defeated by the system. Study groups inside and outside Congress have urged the chambers to reduce the number of committee assignments, establish better information systems, centralize more power in their leadership positions, and strengthen majority rule. Congress has done many of these things recently, yet the pace of legislation has not improved.

Some of the paralysis in Congress is caused by the proliferation of subcommittees, the overlapping jurisdictions of these committees, and a congressional staff seeking to advance the agenda of individual members or subcommittees. A complicated budget process also adds to the paralysis. Better-educated and more independent-minded people are being elected to Congress. These younger and more independent members sometimes make it difficult for party leaders to build coalitions and to maintain an efficient agenda for Congress.

CONGRESS IS UNREPRESENTATIVE The complaint is often made that Congress represents regional or constituents' interests over the national interest. Defenders of Congress respond that representing their districts is precisely what Congress was designed to do. Legislators are described as being obsessed with staying in office—indeed, as concentrating solely on winning reelection—often at the expense of critical national issues such as the deficit, drug abuse, foreign policy, and trade. Former House Republican leader John Rhodes was perhaps too harsh

FIGURE 10-2 Presidential, Congressional, and Own House Member Approval Ratings, 1975–1996

SOURCES: The Gallup Poll, CBS News/New York Times Poll, ABC/Washington Post Poll, NBC News/Wall Street Journal Poll.

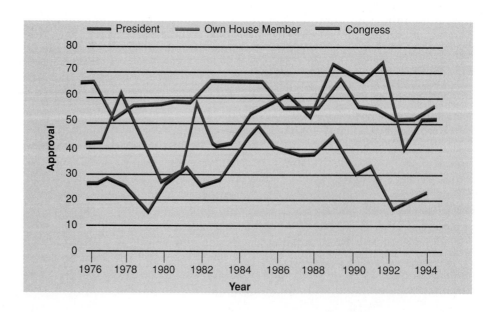

when he said that "the majority of congressional actions are not aimed at producing results for the American people as much as perpetuating the longevity and comfort of the men who run Congress."[34]

Can the members of Congress, who are so much the products of upper- or upper-middle-class backgrounds, really speak for the needs of low-income groups? Can a Congress that has only 9 percent women and 5 percent African American membership truly represent our female and minority populations? Moreover, the seniority system, even with its modifications, biases both houses toward conservatism. Defenders of Congress respond that there should be a strong institution to guarantee minority rights and to act as a check on mindless majority rule. Critics answer by arguing that minorities should have a right to publicize and delay what the majority proposes to do but not to defeat it.

In fact, we have a system of dual representation in which both Congress and the president can and do claim to speak for the people. But because "the people" seldom, if ever, speak with a single voice, the structure and character of the two systems tend to give us a Congress that speaks for one majority and a president who often speaks for another. Between the two, sometimes we get a balance—and sometimes deadlock.

CONGRESS IS UNETHICAL   Some critics claim we have "the best Congress money can buy." Many people allege that special interests and single-issue groups are stronger than ever and that they are able to fragment and often delay or block proceedings in Congress. The current system of financing congressional elections has been called a scandal. It forces members of Congress to beg for money from wealthy individuals and political action committees representing interest groups whose primary purpose is to seek support for pet legislation.

Critics complain that some members of Congress are tied to the economic interests they are asked to regulate and are beholden to the political action committees that increasingly fund their campaigns. Others charge that members of Congress get too many personal privileges and that there have been too many abuses of these so-called fringe benefits. One such benefit—the House Bank's no penalty for bounced checks—became a major issue in 1992.

In response to occasional scandals, both houses have passed ethics codes and have created ethics subcommittees. These codes require public disclosure of income and property holdings by legislators, key aides, and spouses. They also ban most gifts to a legislator, a staff member, or a legislator's family from a registered lobbyist, an organization with a political action committee, a foreign government, or a business with an interest in legislation before Congress. In 1995 the House made it impossible for a lobbyist to take a member out to dinner and pay for it. But even these actions have apparently not improved the image of Congress.

CONGRESS LACKS COLLECTIVE RESPONSIBILITY   Others wonder if the problems of Congress arise because each branch can blame the other for inaction or mistakes in policy. Some suggest, for example, that we might be better served by having four-year terms for members of the House and permitting members of Congress to serve simultaneously in the president's cabinet, on the model of the British parliamentary system. A few scholars even propose that we elect presidents and members of Congress on a team ticket, that is, send a partisan team to Washington and prevent split-ticket voting. These reformers also seek means to strengthen partisan ties and efforts to link Congress and the president.[35]

Some critics see the main problem in Congress as the dispersion of power among committee and subcommittee leaders, elected party officials, factional leaders, informal caucus leaders, and other legislators. It is a "nobody's-in-charge" system. This dispersion of power means that to get things done, congressional

Reforming the Lobbying Process

Members of Congress have become painfully aware that the general public thinks they have too many "perks" and too cozy a relationship with powerful Washington lobbyists. But lobbying enjoys First Amendment protection that guarantees the right to try to influence Congress.

In the 1995 Lobbying Disclosure Act, Congress redefined who is a lobbyist or lobbying organization. Lobbyists are required to register and disclose what legislation they are working on, and also how much they are spending on their lobbying. The new law sets tough limits on gifts to legislators and their aides. The Senate passed a $50 limit on any gift of a meal or entertainment that lobbyists provide; the House passed an even more restrictive measure calling for a total ban on such gifts. Although the act has loopholes, it will help inform the public about the nearly twenty thousand professional lobbyists who are regularly at work influencing Congress.

Thinking it Through

No "reform" is neutral in terms of effects. Some groups will benefit more than others from the passage of a reform proposal. Most reforms also have unanticipated consequences that may create more problems. Still, the search goes on for practical ways to improve Congress's ability to do the people's work. Congress spent a lot of time in the mid 1990s trying to come up with procedure and fundraising reforms—but despite great public pressure to reform, Congress did little to alter its old ways.

They did, however, require lobbyists to register and limited the kind and amount of gifts members could receive from lobbyists.

Vocal critics of congressional fiscal irresponsibility are former presidential candidate Paul Tsongas (*left*) and former Senator Warren Rudman (*right*), who joined together to form the Concord Coalition to work for reform of Congress.

leaders must bargain and negotiate. The result of this "brokerage" system is that laws may be watered down, defeated, delayed, or written in vague language. According to some critics, too much leeway is given to unknown bureaucrats to develop the regulations that will enforce the legislation. Accountability is confused, responsibility is eroded, and well-organized special interests that know how to work the system have an unfair advantage.

Critics worry that if Congress responds to so many single interests, it cannot speak for the great majority or for the nation as a whole. It cannot anticipate problems, plan ahead, and put together political coalitions to deal with critical problems. Some of those concerned about congressional irresponsibility do not blame the special interests alone. They argue that brokerage is mainly the result of a constitutional system that divides authority, checks power with power, and disperses political leadership. Yet other factors making it difficult for Congress to act as a unified branch arise from the fact that each chamber may be controlled by a different political party.

CONGRESS DELEGATES TOO MUCH TO THE EXECUTIVE BRANCH Because of the complexity of modern problems and the inability to work out coalitions and compromises, there is a tendency for Congress to say to the executive branch: "Do something" about drugs; or "Do something" about AIDS and acid rain. If Congress turns a matter over to an administrative agency, the result may be that the rules and regulations issued by the administrators effectively become the law.

CONGRESS IS TOO RESPONSIVE TO ORGANIZED INTERESTS It is also charged that the committee system is *too* responsive to organized special interests. Both houses, critics hold, overrepresent well-organized economic power structures at the expense of the average citizen. This final charge suggests that even though members of Congress are rarely bought by campaign contributions, the way Congress conducts its business—and who gets heard at its hearings and in its corridors—is influenced to a great extent by those who can raise and disburse large sums of money as campaign contributions through political action committees.

Defenders of Congress insist these charges are overstated. They say money would hardly influence the three dozen or more millionaires who are members of the Senate and the one hundred or so members of the House who are well-off financially. Defenders of Congress also point out that some members of Congress regularly turn down certain types of campaign contributions. Because of various campaign reform laws, candidates for Congress must now report all major campaign contributions to the Federal Election Commission. Thus, who gives what to whom is at least part of the public record. Still, the criticism is valid, and a large number of Americans are perplexed or disturbed about the degree of influence seemingly associated with campaign contributions from political action committees and wealthy individuals.

A Defense of Congress

Some criticize Congress for being both imperial and lazy—criticisms that contradict one another yet are nonetheless widespread. For example, the Bush and Reagan administrations often said Congress interfered with the president's conduct of foreign policy, was tied to parochial interests, and was too slow, too unwieldy, and too captured by sectional and special interests. Unlike the presidency, they added, Congress was more like a lawyer representing special clients than like a judge weighing the larger picture and the longer-term interests of the entire nation.

Supporters of Congress say that a president and Congress are given co-equal responsibility for shaping *both* foreign and domestic policy. The challenge that confronted the framers—how to reconcile the need for executive energy with republican liberty—is still with us. The history of constitutional democracy has always been the search for limitations on absolute power and for techniques of sharing power. Our American style of constitutionalism and separation of powers, especially in the absence of a major crisis, often means a slow-moving and sometimes inefficient decision-making system. It means a system that often hinders rather than facilitates leadership. It is a system that invites contention, division, debate, delay, and political conflict. Critics often call this *gridlock* or *deadlock* or even *paralysis*. Defenders of the Congress prefer to call it the world's greatest deliberative body.

Plainly, however, members of Congress are rarely lazy. For instance, a typical day for a senator might begin with an early morning breakfast with constituents or a visiting group of businesspeople, students, or foreign dignitaries. This meeting is followed by subcommittee and committee meetings, a working lunch, several trips to the Senate floor to vote, and interviews with journalists, professors, and prospective staff in the afternoon. Then there is a dinner with other committee members to work out the details of a bill, interrupted by votes on the Senate floor. Often a senator will finish the day around 10 P.M. or later.

Some members are criticized for taking so-called "junkets," that is, trips abroad in connection with the work of their committee assignments. But most of the travel of members of Congress is hard work. They have to travel back home, generally once a month, where they speak from morning to night and meet with students, public officials, and constituents, including a few irate ones. Then they get back on the plane and head for Washington, D.C. It is a demanding schedule.

Although several scandals in the early- and mid-1990s brought attacks on Congress to the forefront of American politics, attacking Congress has been a national pastime for generations. Will Rogers told some of his best jokes at the expense of Congress, as Jay Leno and David Letterman do today. Cartoonists love Congress for its unfailing ability to put its worst foot forward. Even members of Congress often "run" against Congress when they are at home in their districts.

Criticism of Congress—its alleged incompetence, its overresponsiveness, its inefficiencies—are difficult to separate from the context of policy preferences and democratic procedures. Sometimes criticism tells us more about the critic than it does about the effectiveness of Congress. Constitutional democracy is not the most efficient form of government. Congress was never intended to act swiftly; it was not created to be a rubber stamp or even a cooperative partner for presidents. Its greatest strengths—its diversity and deliberative character—also weaken its position in dealing with the more centralized executive branch. Its members will rarely be fast on their 1,070 feet. The 535 members, divided into two houses, two parties, dozens of committees, and hundreds of subcommittees, will almost always have a difficult time arriving at a common strategy to combat a president determined to use executive powers to the fullest.

Congress is supposed to reflect geographical and narrow interests, to register the diversity of the United States. In *The Federalist*, No. 57, James Madison wrote: "Who are to be the electors of the Federal Representatives? Not the rich more than the poor; not the learned more than the ignorant; not the haughty heirs of distinguished names, more than the humble sons of obscure and unpropitious fortune."[36] Yet as the costs of campaigning increase, and as the body of elected officials continues to come from essentially upper or upper-middle class, we must question whether ours is the open, representative, responsive, and responsible legislative system we can point to with pride as a model for those in other parts of the world who yearn for constitutional democracy.

Why One Senator Left

"There was no one moment when I decided to leave the Senate. As I worked through my decision, I remembered 14-hour days: running from one room to another and one office building to another because four of my committees were meeting at the same time; lunching just off the Senate floor while waiting for my amendment to come up; dashing to the Capitol steps for photos with three groups from home and back to my offices for five appointments on pending legislation or projects—all followed by three or four hours of returning new phone calls, answering dozens of new letters, and reading a pile of urgent action memos from staff members asking directions on issues or constituent problems. Those days usually ended at 10 P.M. with dinner at my desk.

There was no time for reflection, no time to exchange ideas with fellow senators. . . . My family life and personal friendships paid a stiff price. There were only three weekends last year when I was not airborne. . . . One month it took 27 days before my wife and I could have dinner together and an unscheduled evening at home. At the end of certain days, I sometimes asked myself what I had really done to help solve the major problems facing our country. My honest answer was: not much."

SOURCE: Adapted from David L. Boren, "Why I Am Leaving the Senate," *The New York Times*, May 13, 1994, p. A15.

The 105th Congress (1997–1999) has again proved that ours is a system of separated powers and that Congress cherishes its independence and its ability to differ as well as cooperate with the White House. Congress may defer to the White House on sensitive foreign policy matters, but it insists on a major role in shaping economic, budgetary, tax, and social programs.

As Congress prepares for the twenty-first century, the following questions have to be raised: Can Congress overcome partisan bickering and agree on legislation that will solve problems? Can it have a long-range view, staying power, the span of attention, and the ability to make sensible laws for the whole nation? A real question is whether Congress is operating effectively enough most of the time to deal with crime, welfare, health, economic development, the creation of jobs, and other issues the general public believe require national action. Although our answers would differ, all of us would agree that a vital, responsive, and effective Congress is essential if we would make our constitutional democracy live up to its ideals.

SUMMARY

1. Members of Congress are largely driven by the desire to seek election and win reelection. Much of what Congress does is in response to this motive. Members work hard to get favors for their districts, to serve the needs of constituents, and to maintain a high visibility in their districts or states. Incumbents have advantages that help explain their success at reelection: they have greater name recognition; they have large staffs; they are better able to raise campaign money; and they have greater access to the media. Partisanship, candidate appeal, and important issues contribute to the voters' choice for Congress.

2. Senators and representatives come primarily from upper- and middle-class backgrounds. They are better educated than Americans as a whole. The typical member of Congress is a middle-aged, white, male lawyer.

3. Congress performs these functions: representation, law making, consensus building, overseeing, investigating, policy clarification, and legitimizing. Congress as a collective body must attempt to perform these tasks even as most of its members serve as ombudsmen for their constituents and work for their own reelections.

4. Most of the work in Congress is done in committees and subcommittees. Congress has attempted in recent years to streamline its committee system and modify its methods of selecting committee chairs. Seniority practices are still generally followed, yet the threat of removal forces committee chairs to consult with younger members of the majority party.

5. Subcommittees are important. They can prevent or delay legislation from being enacted. But there are numerous other stages where bills can be killed, making it easier to stop legislation than to enact it.

6. The workload for Congress is exhausting. Much could be done to make our national legislature perform its functions more effectively. Some improvements have been made in recent years: redistricting and reapportionment have shaped a Congress that somewhat more accurately reflects the population. The filibuster in the Senate and the Rules Committee in the House are less obstructive than they once were. The role of the Speaker and of party steering committees has been enhanced. Congress has made itself subject to the same laws it passes for corporations, universities, and other organizations. Congress has also passed measures that require lobbyists to register and to disclose how they spend their money, and they have limited gifts and entertainment by lobbyists.

FURTHER READING

JOEL D. ABERBACH, *Keeping a Watchful Eye: The Politics of Congressional Oversight* (Brookings Institution, 1990).

DICK ARMEY, *The Freedom Revolution* (Regenery, 1995).

BARBARA BOXER, *Strangers in the Senate* (National Press, 1993).

BILL BRADLEY, *Time Present, Time Past: A Memoir* (Knopf, 1996).

STEPHEN L. CARTER, *The Confirmation Mess: Cleaning Up the Federal Appointment Process* (Basic Books, 1994).

GARY COX AND MATTHEW MCCUBBINS, *Legislative Leviathan: Party Government in the House* (University of California Press, 1993).

ROGER H. DAVIDSON AND WALTER J. OLESZEK, *Congress and Its Members*, 4th ed. (Congressional Quarterly Press, 1994).

Lawrence C. Dodd and Bruce J. Oppenheimer, eds. *Congress Reconsidered*, 5th ed. (Congressional Quarterly Books, 1993).

Richard F. Fenno, Jr., *Home Style: House Members in Their Districts* (Little, Brown, 1978).

Morris Fiorina, *Congress: Keystone of the Washington Establishment*, 2d ed. (Yale University Press, 1989).

Newt Gingrich, *To Renew America* (HarperCollins, 1995).

Fred Harris, *Deadlock or Decision: The U.S. Senate and the Rise of National Politics* (Oxford University Press, 1992).

Gary C. Jacobson, *The Electoral Origins of Divided Government: Competition in U.S. House Elections, 1946–1988* (Westview Press, 1990).

Gary C. Jacobson, *The Politics of Congressional Elections*, 3d ed. (HarperCollins, 1992).

Victor Kamber, *Giving Up on Democracy: Why Term Limits Are Bad for America* (Regenery, 1995).

John W. Kingdon, *Congressional Voting Decisions*, 3d ed. (University of Michigan Press, 1989).

Burdette A. Loomis, *The Contemporary Congress* (St. Martin's Press, 1996).

Thomas Mann and Norman Ornstein, eds., *Renewing Congress: A Second Report* (American Enterprise Institute and Brookings Institution, 1993).

Janet M. Martin, *Lessons from the Hill: The Legislative Journey of an Education Program* (St. Martin's Press, 1993).

David R. Mayhew, *Congress: The Electoral Connection* (Yale University Press, 1974).

Walter J. Oleszek, *Congressional Procedures and the Policy Process,* 4th ed. (Congressional Quarterly Press, 1995).

Timothy Penny and Major Garrett, *Common Cents* (Little, Brown, 1995).

Ronald M. Peters, Jr., ed. *The Speaker: Leadership in the U.S. House of Representatives* (Congressional Quarterly Books, 1995).

David E. Price, *The Congressional Experience* (Westview Press, 1993).

David Schoenbrod, *Power Without Responsibility: How Congress Abuses the People Through Delegation* (Yale University Press, 1994).

Paul Simon, *Advice and Consent: Clarence Thomas, Robert Bork and the Intriguing History of the Supreme Court's Nominating Battles* (National Press Books, 1992).

Barbara Sinclair, *The Transformation of the U.S. Senate* (Johns Hopkins University Press, 1989).

Steven S. Smith, *Call to Order: Floor Politics in the House and Senate* (Brookings Institution, 1989).

Carol M. Swain, *Black Faces, Black Interests: The Representation of African-Americans in Congress* (Harvard University Press, 1993).

Steven Waldman, *The Bill: How Legislation Really Becomes Law: A Case Study of the National Service Bill* (Penguin, 1996).

Students of Congress also should consult, *Congressional Quarterly's Weekly Report, National Journal, Role Call,* and *The Hill.*

THE PRESIDENCY: THE LEADERSHIP BRANCH?

As he traveled slowly up the east coast from Mount Vernon to New York (the temporary seat of government) in 1789, newly elected President George Washington was showered with parades and fireworks. His whole trip was one long ovation, a celebration of the people's yearning for a strong individual who could provide continuity and leadership for the nation.

Yet Washington and his compatriots were of two minds about the power of the presidency. The framers both admired and feared leadership. They realized the country needed a more effective, centralized government, yet they were suspicious of the potential abuses of power, especially the power vested in a single individual. Given what they had lived through in the preceding decades, they had every right to these fears. Moreover, they hardly wanted to jeopardize the rights and liberties they had fought so hard to win in the recent revolution.

Americans still have not resolved their ambivalence toward the presidency. Should a president be "above politics" and merely wait for a consensus to emerge from the people and Congress? Or should the institution be clearly political, *leading* the people and *leading* Congress? Should its powers be narrowly defined, or should it be granted broad authority to respond to national and international emergencies? Is an office created over two hundred years ago in an agrarian society adequate for the post-cold war era in which the United States is challenged to play a leading role in global trade, diplomacy, peacekeeping, and environmental conservation? Can any person meet such high expectations of the presidency? And does the greatly enlarged role of the presidency under today's circumstances alter and perhaps undermine some of the fundamental checks and balances in our constitutional democracy? We try to answer these questions as we take a closer look at the central role of the American presidency.

WHAT WE LOOK FOR IN PRESIDENTS

The framers conceived their president in the image of George Washington, the man they expected would first occupy the office. Like Washington, the American executive was to be a wise, moderate, dignified, nonpartisan leader of all the people. Washington had served his country in a variety of ways, most notably as commander in chief of the Continental Army for eight years and as an instigator of, and later presiding officer at, the Constitutional Convention of 1787. No one commanded the trust and respect that Washington did, and he was unanimously elected as the first president of the new republic in 1789. George Washington knew the people needed to have confidence in their fledgling government, a sense of continuity with the past, a time of calmness and stability, free of emergencies and crises. He knew, too, that the new nation faced many foreign dangers.

Article II of the Constitution outlined the nature and scope of presidential power. It responded to Washington's calls for vigorous executive leadership. Washington's misgivings about his qualifications and about the scope of presidential power faded as he set precedents and fulfilled the hopes of the people.[1] He was sensitive to the fine line between providing stronger leadership and infringing on the individual rights and liberties of the people. He knew then, as every president after him has either known or learned, that Americans have a strong streak of anti-government and even anti-authority sentiment. We want strong presidential leadership when the times demand it or when it serves our favorite causes, yet we insist that no elected official or governmental agency dare infringe on our rights.

We are not at all clear about how much power we want to vest in the president. When presidents take charge and try to run the country, they are often criticized for trying to impose their will on the nation. If they are not activist leaders, however, they are going to be criticized because they do nothing and, even more likely, to be blamed for whatever happens to the country—for our not having a proper health policy, for an unfair tax system, for a recession, for inflation, for the homeless, for corporate downsizing and loss of jobs, or for ethnic warfare in remote nations. People who like what the president is doing are champions of presidential leadership, but people who disapprove of what a president is doing point to the dangers of dictatorship.

What kind of person does it take to perform this delicate balancing act? Our Constitution establishes only three qualifications for the office: a president must be at least 35 years of age, have lived in the United States for 14 years, and be a natural-born citizen. Our "unwritten presidential job description"—the one we carry around in our heads—says a president has to be many things to many people. Every four years Americans search the national landscape for a potential heroic leader who is blessed with the judgment of a Washington, the mind of a Jefferson, the steadfastness of a Lincoln, the calm of an Eisenhower, and the grace of a John F. Kennedy.

Americans want leadership, but what kind of leadership? We want someone who can provide a sense of purpose, someone who can remind us of our shared aspirations as a constitutional democracy and a pragmatic, hardworking, generous nation. Yet we also want someone who can pay close attention to our immediate needs—jobs, peace, prosperity.

Voters sometimes place more emphasis on a presidential candidate's character and integrity than they do on a candidate's stands on social and economic issues (see Table 11-1). This emphasis is not misguided. Presidents have enormous power, especially in times of crisis. They also select the people who run the executive departments and serve on our courts, and thus they have much to do with the standards of governmental performance and ethics. Hence it is important to weigh their character and their allegiance to democratic values and to the spirit of the Constitution.

We also pick our candidates in terms of their personalities. Can they get along with members of Congress, the press, fellow party leaders, and leaders of other nations? We also ask whether the would-be president displays vision, judgment, a grasp of history, a sense of proportion, and a sense of humor. To be sure, people prefer candidates whose views on issues accord with their own; if they like a person's personality, they trust that individual's policy ideas to be acceptable. A candidate's character and policy preferences sometimes get blurred—if not reversed—in the voter's mind.

In addition, even in a democracy the public wants a president to be tough, decisive, and competent. Voters recognize the need for strong leadership. They yearn for a leader with foresight and personal strength. Moreover, people want

George Washington was unanimously elected as the first president and was inaugurated in New York City on April 30, 1789.

TABLE 11-1

The One Quality Voters Said They Wanted Most in a President

Honesty/integrity	43%
Leadership/ability to make decisions	11
Sense of responsibility to people	6
Believes United States rates first	5
Understanding of the poor	4
Sound economic program	4
Intelligence	2
Good judgment	2
Self-confidence	2
Experience	2
High moral standards	2
Accessibility	1
Other	3
No answer/don't know	12

SOURCE: CBS News–New York Times Poll, April 1996.

Recent presidents George Bush, Ronald Reagan, Jimmy Carter, Gerald Ford, and Richard Nixon are generally not classified among the best or the worst we have had. How would you rate them? What criteria would you use?

someone who will simplify politics, symbolize the protective role of the state, and yet be concerned with them. We want *effectiveness* but also *fairness*. Do we ask too much? The novelist John Steinbeck thought so: "We give the President more work than a man can do, more responsibility than a man should take, more pressure than a man can bear. We abuse him often and rarely praise him. We wear him out, use him up, eat him up. . . . He is ours and we exercise the right to destroy him."[2]

Americans applaud presidents when things go well and blame them when things go wrong. Disasters as well as triumphs are credited to presidents—Wilson's League of Nations, Hoover's Depression, Roosevelt's New Deal, Johnson's Vietnam War, Nixon's Watergate, Bush's Persian Gulf War, Clinton's Bosnia. An exaggerated sense of presidential wisdom and power sometimes causes us to forget there are limits to what presidents can accomplish. Although the tragedies of American involvement in Vietnam and of presidential involvement in the Watergate scandal deglamorized the presidency, the vitality of our constitutional democracy still depends in large measure on creative presidential leadership.

The Original Intent

The framers of the Constitution created a presidency of limited powers. They wanted a presidential office that would steer clear of parties and factions, enforce the laws passed by Congress, handle relations with foreign governments, and help states put down disorders. They wanted a presidency strong enough to match Congress but not so strong that it would overpower Congress. They seemed to have in mind that the president should be an elected king with substantial personal authority, who serves the common good and minimizes the negative influence of the worst factions. They combined the ceremonial head of government with the actual head of government. The term of office would be four years, and presidents would be indefinitely eligible to succeed themselves (the two-term limit would be added to the Constitution much later, in 1951).

Although independent from the legislature, presidents would still *share* considerable power with Congress. The essence of the arrangement would be in intermingling powers with Congress. To enact government business, the separate branches would have to cooperate and consult with one another. A president's major appointments would have to be approved by the Senate; Congress could

override the chief executive's veto by a two-thirds vote of each chamber; and the president could make treaties only with the advice and consent of two-thirds of the senators. All appropriations (the power of the purse) would be legislated by Congress, not the president. But even a presidency with such limited powers, hemmed in by the system of checks and balances, worried some Americans in 1787. The framers deliberately outlined the powers of the president broadly. The president, they thought, should have discretionary power to act when other governmental branches failed to meet their responsibilities or to respond to the urgencies of the day.

"If George Washington never told a lie, how did he get to be president?"

© Edgar Argo.

The Politics of Shared Power

Our constitutional democracy was designed to be one of both shared powers and division. The framers wanted disagreement as well as cooperation because they assumed that the checks and balances within the government would prevent the president and Congress from "ganging up" against the people's liberties. The framers actually made disagreements inevitable by providing that the president, Senate, and House of Representatives would be elected by different constituencies and for different lengths of service.

The United States is unique among major world powers because it is neither a parliamentary democracy nor a wholly executive-dominated government. Our Constitution plainly invites both Congress and the president to set policy and govern the nation. Leadership and policy change are implemented only when two, and sometimes all three, branches of government concur on the desirability of new directions.

A president and members of Congress are legitimate participants in a whole range of policy activities. Triumphs for a president acting alone in a system of separated powers are rare. "Whenever powers are shared, attention must be devoted to the other decision makers," writes political scientist Charles O. Jones "How do they view the problem? What are their present commitments? On what basis will they compromise? The test in a separated system is not simply one of presidential success. It is rather one of achievement by the system, with presidents and members of Congress inextricably bonded and similarly judged."[3]

The politics of shared power has often been stormy, as the Persian Gulf War, Iran-Contra affair, and the Whitewater investigations illustrate. The politics of shared power is characterized by changing patterns of cooperation and conflict depending on the partisan and ideological makeup of Congress, the popularity and skills of the president, and various events that shape the politics of the times.

The Roots of Divided Government

We can point to numerous roots of divided government in the United States, yet these factors are most clearly at work: constitutional ambiguities, different constituencies, varying terms of office, divided party control of the branches (much of the time in recent years), weak political parties, and fluctuating power.

CONSTITUTIONAL AMBIGUITIES Article I of the Constitution grants to Congress "all legislative Powers" but limits them to those "herein granted." It then sets forth in some detail the powers vested in Congress. In contrast, Article II vests in the president "the executive Power" without limiting it to such powers as are "herein granted" and then proceeds to describe those powers in very general terms. Is this difference in language between Articles I and II significant? Some scholars and most presidents have argued that a president is granted by Article II a general and undefined power to act to promote the well-being of the United

Should we have a six-year nonrenewable term for presidents?

Several presidents (Lyndon Johnson, Richard Nixon, Jimmy Carter) have favored amending the Constitution to provide for a single, nonrenewable six-year term for president. Most experts on the presidency oppose this proposal. What are the merits and disadvantages of this proposed amendment?

States, subject only to precise constitutional limits. Therefore, they contend, a president is not limited to the specific powers spelled out in the Constitution, as is Congress, but has all the executive powers of the United States.[4] Other scholars and many members of Congress say the president either has no such inherent power or has it only in extraordinary circumstances.[5]

Whatever the language of the Constitution, the president has often exercised powers not expressly defined in it. These powers have been given a variety of names: *implied, inherent, or emergency powers.* For example, George Bush sent troops into Panama to help overthrow its government and capture General Manuel Noriega, and he did so without asking for a declaration of war and largely without consulting Congress. Bush was criticized by Congress for acting without congressional approval. Yet even the most faithful defenders of congressional prerogatives recognize that in extraordinary emergencies a president "may have to act promptly without clear constitutional or statutory support."[6] This difference between Capitol Hill and the White House over a president's general executive powers is merely one of several ambiguities in our constitutional arrangements.

DIFFERENT CONSTITUENCIES Another root of divided government comes from the different constituencies Congress and the president represent. Members of Congress represent state and local districts, and hence reflect specific geographic, ethnic, and economic interests. James Madison and other framers of the Constitution anticipated legislators would often be pressured by local and state interests.

Presidents and their aides often think members of Congress are captives of sectional interests and local pressures. Members of Congress, of course, see sensitivity to state and local concerns as essential to their job as representatives. As a result, members of Congress—even those from a president's own party and own region—may look at problems and solutions somewhat differently from the way a president does, as a president represents a national perspective.

There is an old saying in Washington, D.C., that "where you stand depends on where you sit." President Lyndon Johnson, for example, viewed the importance of civil rights legislation differently when he was in the White House from the way he viewed it when he represented Texas in the U.S. House and Senate. And President Gerald Ford quipped, "When I was in the House for 25 years, I almost always looked down Pennsylvania Avenue at the White House, regardless of whether Democrats or Republicans were there, and wondered why they were so arrogant. Then, when I was in the White House myself, I looked up at the Congress and wondered how there could be 535 irresponsible members of Congress."[7]

VARYING TERMS OF OFFICE Presidents serve for four years with a chance of reelection to a second term; senators have the luxury of six-year terms; members of the House of Representatives are elected for two-year terms. Different constituencies and lengths of service make these national offices responsive to different moods and points of view. Different electoral forces may have been at work in the election that elected them. A majority of the voters can win control over only part of the national government at a time—and this arrangement, too, was by design.

Presidents often act quickly to shape national priorities in their first year following the flush of their electoral victories. They act to win support for their agendas before the almost inevitable decline in public approval. Congress, on the other hand, moves more slowly; as President Bush once joked, "The way to slow down old age is to move it through Congress." Congress is inefficient in part "because it represents a vast array of local interests. Congress passes new laws

Roots of Presidential-Congressional Conflict

- Varying terms of office
- Diverse geographical constituencies
- Conflicting responsibilities and constitutional ambiguities
- Different partisan ties
- Constitutional provisions requiring extensive sharing of power
- Congress seen as disorganized and inefficient by the president and by the public
- The White House viewed as arbitrary and insensitive by Congress
- Each wants the credit for successes, and each seeks to blame the other when things go wrong

slowly and reviews old ones carefully." The decision-making pace of Congress and of the president is not the same because of their different terms of office. The result is often conflict and deadlock.[8]

Moreover, members of Congress may have been in office for 10 or 15 years and perhaps look forward to serving more terms. Some members of Congress are, in effect, career politicians and stay in office a long time. Hence they assume they will outlast the president, who has a limited term of service and is a **lame duck** in the second term. Presidents, however, think mainly about today and tomorrow.

DIVIDED PARTY CONTROL OF THE BRANCHES Since 1952 there has been a split in partisan control of the presidency and Congress for about two-thirds of the time. Republican Presidents George Bush, Gerald Ford, and Richard Nixon had to deal with a Congress that was entirely under the control of Democrats. Bill Clinton has had a Congress controlled by the Republicans. And Republican Presidents Ronald Reagan and Dwight Eisenhower had to deal with Congresses that most of the time were under the control of Democrats. Only Presidents John Kennedy, Lyndon Johnson, and Jimmy Carter enjoyed majority control by their own party in Congress, and even then they had considerable trouble getting support for their legislative programs.

In the days, weeks, and sometimes months following their inauguration, presidents usually enjoy what has been called the **honeymoon**, a period of generally positive relations with the press and Congress, which is often thought to last about six months. Franklin Roosevelt, Lyndon Johnson, Ronald Reagan, and Bill Clinton all enjoyed legislative success in their first years in office.

The opposition party in Congress regularly mounts its own programs. It will, when possible, defeat a president's policy initiatives and substitute its own. This effort becomes all the more troublesome for a president when Congress is controlled by the opposition party—as Bill Clinton clearly learned when the Republicans swept into power in Congress following the 1994 elections.

WEAK POLITICAL PARTIES Political parties in the United States, as we noted in Chapter 8, are organizationally weak and highly decentralized when it comes to managing elections. Moreover, they are also weak in giving the president and the national party leaders any power to discipline party members.

Most members of Congress run and finance their elections with only minimal assistance or even ties to their national party. They customarily respond to local conditions and run their campaigns independently of their party's presidential candidate or national platform. Thus they feel few obligations to go along with the president of their own party, unless whatever measure is at stake is in the interest of their home district or state. Parties, however, have become somewhat stronger inside Congress. Party discipline has not weakened the president's ability to influence how members of Congress will vote. It has helped him with his own party and hurt him with the opposing party.

FLUCTUATING POWER The American public's waxing and waning support for Congress complicates the problems of divided government. We often like our own members of Congress while being highly critical of the Congress as a whole. In recent years Americans have generally held presidents in higher esteem than Congress as an institution, and this fluctuating prestige has consequences. Greater prestige for the presidency often gives the incumbent in the White House a slight edge in battles with Congress.[9]

Congress is viewed by most people as inefficient, in part because it has to represent local interests and respond (some think too much) to narrow-minded

Favor a Six-Year Term

- It might help take politics out of the presidency and thereby lessen the likelihood of scandals like Watergate.
- Four years is too short a time to get the job done.
- Budgets are already cast for about two years ahead when a president gets into office.
- Presidents could concentrate on the job rather than on reelection.
- During wartime a president would not waste time campaigning.
- Six years is enough even for the healthiest of presidents.
- Few second terms have been successful (for example, Wilson, Nixon, and Reagan).

Against a Six-Year Term

- A six-year term would give us two more years of the "clunkers" and two fewer years of the great ones.
- Four years is long enough to tell whether a president is doing the job.
- The best way to be reelected is to do the job well, maintain majority support, and be an effective leader.
- The four-year term forces presidents to be accountable for their promises and platforms.
- Some of our great presidents served ably for more than six years: Washington, Jefferson, FDR, and Eisenhower.
- A healthy, democratic country needs a politician in the White House, one who can bargain, persuade, build crucial political coalitions, and get diverse political factions to work together.
- We should not surrender a hard-won democratic right: to kick a leader *out* of office.

Factors that Influence a President's Success in Congress

- Same party in control of Congress
- Similar ideological interests in control of Congress
- National emergencies
- The "honeymoon" effect experienced during the first year in office
- High public approval ratings for the president
- Effective presidential lobbying of the Congress
- Threat of presidential veto
- Presidential bargaining with use of patronage powers
- Clear presidential priorities that win consensus in the nation
- President's "bully pulpit" publicity efforts, including addresses and news conferences

"Bully Pulpit"

This term was used and made popular by President Theodore Roosevelt (TR), who believed the office of president provided an enormous opportunity to inspire and even preach to a national constituency as if it were a national congregation. "Bully" is a term of approval and affirmation. TR used it as in "Bully for you," meaning terrific, great, or well done! Presidents like Woodrow Wilson, Franklin Roosevelt, John Kennedy, and Ronald Reagan have been noted for their use of the presidential "bully pulpit."

constituencies. Yet when presidents decline in popularity, such as after the Watergate scandal, Americans turn to Congress to hold the president and the presidency accountable. At such times the public insists Congress be strengthened and asks it to play a more equal role in governing the nation. Americans often remind themselves that they do not want presidents unilaterally dictating policies and laws. They want a Congress that does more than just rubber-stamp presidential decisions.

Although separation of powers and divided government are obstacles, they are not insurmountable barriers to good public policy making. Presidents and Congress can legislate when the leaders of both institutions bargain and compromise in ways that overcome the roots of division discussed here. In fact, while the Constitution disperses power and invites a continual struggle between these two branches, it also requires the two branches to integrate the fragmented parts of the system into a workable government. And usually these two branches of government do work together. Even when the relationship is regarded as hostile, "bills get passed and signed into law. Presidential appointments are approved by the Senate. Budgets are enacted and the government is kept afloat. This necessary cooperation goes on even when control of the White House and the Capitol is divided between the two major parties."[10]

The presidential record of dealing with Congress in recent decades is mixed. Presidents enjoy considerable success in getting most of their nominations confirmed by the Senate. Relatively few presidential vetoes are overturned by Congress. Also, most presidential budget requests eventually win approval, although Congress jealously guards its right to modify them, especially in certain areas such as defense and agriculture. On the other hand, Congress approves only about 50 percent of the president's major policy recommendations. And Congress is, in fact, the source of a fair percentage of the laws identified as part of the president's program.

The battle between the president and Congress over the 1996 budget illustrates another power struggle between the legislative and executive branches. Republicans in Congress hoped to force acceptance of their proposed spending cuts and tax relief by threatening a government shutdown when the federal spending authorization expired. To keep the government running, Congress had to pass and the president had to sign a **continuing resolution**, which allows the federal government to continue paying its bills until a new budget is passed. Because the resolution Congress sent to the president contained terms that Clinton would not accept, he vetoed the resolution shortly before Christmas of 1995, and thousands of federal workers were sent home without pay. A second shutdown that lasted three weeks occurred later in January until Congress, smarting under the negative publicity generated by their actions, finally passed a continuing resolution that allowed time for negotiations to settle the impasse. A budget for Fiscal 1996, which started October 1, 1995, was finally agreed to in April 1996.

A relatively unified Congress can make life pretty miserable for a president. It can, for example, refuse to confirm a president's vital nominations, reduce funds for key programs, and reject treaties. It can also override the chief executive's vetoes. Bill Clinton certainly learned what an opposition Congress was all about, especially when he had to face Speaker Gingrich's relatively cohesive House Republicans in 1995 and 1996. Yet the historical record suggests most presidents have enjoyed greater cooperation from Congress than Clinton's difficulties might imply, and modern-day presidents are more powerful than those of the last century, even though their constitutional powers have not changed.

The Extension of Executive Power

After two centuries, our presidential track record is good. Perhaps in no other nation have leaders with so much power at their command so carefully followed the restraints imposed on them by a written Constitution. The exact dimensions of executive power at any given moment are partly the consequence of the incumbent's character and energy, combined with the needs of the time, the party balance in Congress, the values of the citizenry, and the challenges to our nation's survival. By and large, the history of presidential power is one of steady, if uneven, growth. Of the individuals who have filled the office, about one-third have enlarged its powers. Andrew Jackson, Abraham Lincoln, and both Roosevelts, for example, redefined both the institution and many of its powers by the way they set priorities and responded to crises.

In this extension of the executive power, Congress and the courts have sometimes been willing partners. In emergencies Congress often delegates discretion to the executive branch; and the legislature sometimes seems incapable of dealing with matters that are highly technical or that require immediate response and constant management. Some people think what Congress lacks most is the will to use the powers it already has. But this explanation is hardly satisfactory as the weakness of Congress is not unique among legislative bodies. During the last two centuries in all democracies, and at all levels, power has drifted from legislators to executives. The English prime minister, the French president, governors of our states, and mayors of our cities all play more dominant roles than they did, generally speaking, one hundred years ago.

Several factors have strengthened the presidency. The danger of war plainly increases a president's influence on the nation's affairs. The cold war—with its enormous standing armies, nuclear weapons, and widespread intelligence and alliance operations—invited presidential dominance in national security matters. Television also contributes to the growth of presidential influence. With access to prime time, presidents take their cases directly to the people. This invitation to bypass and sometimes to ignore Congress, the Washington press, and even party leaders weakens the checks once imposed on the presidency.

Growth of the federal role in domestic and economic matters has also increased presidential responsibility and contributed to an enlarged presidential establishment. Problems not easily delegated to any one department often get pulled into the White House. When new programs involve several federal agencies, someone near the president is often asked to set a consistent policy and reconcile conflicts. White House aides, with some justification, claim the presidency is the only place in government where it is possible to establish and coordinate national priorities. And presidents constantly set up central review and coordination units that help formulate new policies, settle jurisdictional disputes among departments, and provide access for the well-organized interest groups who want their views to be given weight in decision making.

The growth of the presidency is also encouraged by public expectations. Although we may dislike or condemn individual presidents, popular attitudes toward the institution of the presidency remain positive. We want very much to believe in our presidents, perhaps because we have no royal family, no established religion, and no common ceremonial leadership. Sometimes, in an effort to live up to exaggerated expectations, presidents overextend themselves. Wanting to maintain popularity encourages them to make frequent appeals to the general public. These television appeals become bargaining chips that may help presidents temporarily improve their public images and even win occasional fights in

Congress. If used too often, though, these appeals can undermine a president's relations with Congress and render the parties less important in supplying policy ideas and in keeping presidents accountable. Also a president risks wearing out his or her welcome with the public.

Today a president is asked to play several roles that are not carefully spelled out in the Constitution. We want the chief executive to be an international peacemaker as well as a national morale builder, a politician in chief as well as a commander in chief, and a unifying representative of all the people. We want the president to be the architect of "a new world order" and to negotiate favorable trade pacts with major trading partners. We want every new president to be virtually everything all our great presidents have been, and then some.

THE JOB OF PRESIDENT

In addition to the obvious leadership responsibilities a president has in foreign policy, economics, and domestic policy, six broad functional kinds of leadership are expected of a president. These policy areas and functions permit us to develop a job profile of an American president (see Table 11-2).

Presidents as Crisis Managers

"The President shall be Commander in Chief of the Army and Navy of the United States," reads Section 2 of Article II of the Constitution. Even though this is the first of the president's powers listed in the Constitution, the framers intended the military role to be a limited one—far less than a king's. Congress would declare war and call up the army and navy. Congress would also control the power of the purse and hence the funding of wars. Yet it was important, the framers insisted, that the people's elected representative—the president—be in charge of the military. This principle of *civilian* control over the military is a central element in our constitutional democracy.

TABLE 11-2

A Presidential Job Description

| Functional Leadership | Examples of Policy Responsibilities | | |
	Foreign Policy	Economics	Domestic Policy
Crisis management	Liberating Kuwait (Persian Gulf War)	FDR's handling of the Depression, 1930s	Response to urban riots
Symbolic and morale-building leadership	Clinton's trip to Europe on 50th anniversary of D-day	Being bullish on American productivity	Visiting flood and disaster victims; helping Alaska clean up oil spill
Recruitment of top officials	Selecting Joint Chiefs of Staff chair	Hiring wise economic advisers	Nominating a chief justice
Priority setting and problem clarification	Working with United Nations on peacekeeping priorities	Outlining tax-cut or revenue-producing programs	Setting priorities in environmental protection and health care
Legislative and political coalition building	Negotiating with Congress on aid to Eastern European nations	Clinton's efforts to pass welfare reform	Fighting for domestic spending programs
Program implementation, administration, and oversight	Making Middle East peace accords work	Monitoring Internal Revenue Service performance	Appraising the impact of federal social programs

This principle has meant that in the United States today we do not worry, as do people in many nations around the world, whether the military establishment will accept the outcome of elections. General Douglas MacArthur tested this principle of American constitutionalism late in the Korean War when he challenged President Harry Truman. Truman, an unpopular president at the time, had to tell the popular general to leave his command—and the general went. Many people consider this civilian supremacy over the military one of our most significant contributions to the survival of constitutional democracy. We put the president, a civilian, on top.

When crises and national emergencies occur, Americans instinctively turn to the chief executive, who is expected to provide not only executive and political leadership but also the appearance of a confident, "take-charge" executive who has a steady hand at the helm. Public necessity forces presidents to do what Lincoln and Franklin Roosevelt did during the national emergencies of their day: provide the stability and continuity needed to protect the union and safeguard vital American interests.

Two centuries of national expansion and recurrent crises have increased the powers of the president beyond those specified by the Constitution. The complexity of Congress's decision-making procedures, its unwieldy numbers, and its constitutional tasks make it a more public, deliberative, and divided organization than the presidency. When major crises occur, Congress traditionally holds debates and, almost as predictably, delegates authority to a president, charging that official to take whatever actions are deemed necessary. This is essentially what Congress in the 1990s has done in response to presidential calls for U.S. involvement in Kuwait, Haiti, and Bosnia.

The primary factor underlying this transformation in the president's function as commander in chief has been the changed role of the United States in the world, especially since World War II. In the postwar years every president from Truman to the present argued for and won support for the use of U.S. troops overseas as part of NATO or various UN peacekeeping forces. Nations grew dependent on our assistance, which often became translated into treaties, pacts, and diplomatic agreements. These commitments, plus the fear of nuclear war and the importance of deterrence, prompted Congress to give presidents flexibility in this area. This does not mean Congress will always agree with a president. Congress may set detailed limits of time and scope for the use of U.S. troops, as when Congress agreed in 1995 to our participation in Bosnia, yet specified it was for one year and only under U.S. command.

President Clinton took a leadership role in bringing an end to the fighting in Bosnia. At the signing ceremony in Paris on December 14, 1995, Serbian President Slobodan Milosevic shakes hands with Croatian President Franjo Tudjman as Bosnian President Alija Izetbegovic and other heads of government look on.

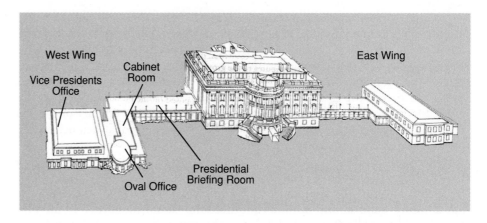

The White House is an executive office, a ceremonial mansion, and a home. Some presidents have viewed it almost as a jail, preferring to spend as much time as possible at other retreats outside Washington, but most Americans view the rather elegant White House as the center of political and social activity in the nation's capital. It is also something of a national shrine and draws millions of people from the United States and around the world to visit it each year.

West Wing

Vice Presidents Office

Cabinet Room

East Wing

Oval Office

Presidential Briefing Room

Presidents are expected to be crisis managers in the domestic sphere as well. Whenever things go wrong, we demand presidential-level planning and problem solving. When terrorists attack U.S. citizens, people assume their president will retaliate. When a disastrous oil spill occurs, as it did off the Alaskan coast a few years ago, people expect the head of state to step in and assist. When riots occur in our cities, we ask what the president is going to do about it. In many crises, however, presidents are little more than victims of fast-breaking events and forces outside of their control. They are sometimes surprised, overtaken by developments, and placed on the defensive.

Presidents as Morale Builders

Presidents are the nation's number-one celebrities; almost anything they do is news. Presidents command attention merely by jogging, fishing, or going to church. By their actions they can arouse a sense of hope or despair, honor or dishonor.

The framers of the Constitution did not fully anticipate the symbolic and morale-building functions a president must perform. Certain magisterial functions, such as receiving ambassadors and granting pardons, were conferred. But over time the presidency has acquired enormous *symbolic* significance. People turn to national leaders just as tribespeople turn to shamans—for meaning, healing, empowerment, assurance, and a sense of purpose. Many people find comfort in an oversimplified image of the president as a warrior-captain at the helm of the great ship of state—liberator, prophet, defender of liberty and democracy, and spokesperson for the American Dream.

Presidential head-of-state duties often seem trivial and unimportant; for example, throwing out the ceremonial first baseball of the season, promoting Easter seals, or pressing buttons that start big power projects. Yet a president is continuously asked to champion our common heritage, unify the nation, and create an improved climate within which the diverse interests of the nation can work together.

In 1996, as one example, President Clinton travelled to Egypt and Israel to attend an anti-terrorist summit of heads of state and to express our nation's opposition to terrorist attacks that upset the Middle East peace process.

The morale-building job of the president involves much more than just ceremonial, cheerleading, or quasi-chaplain duties. Presidential leadership, at its finest, radiates confidence and empowers people to give their best, to unlock the possibility for good that exists in the nation. Our best leaders have been able to provide this special and often intangible element.

A PRESIDENTIAL DILEMMA Some expectations for presidents are inconsistent with one another. On the one hand, the president is a representative of a segment of the population loosely identified with a particular party. As such, the president not only directs the national party organization, but as chief legislator, also takes specific positions on issues for or against some groups. On the other hand, as ceremonial leader and chief of state, the president attempts to act for *all* the people. A chief executive must faithfully administer the laws, whether passed by Democratic or Republican majorities in Congress. Yet in making appointments and in applying the law, presidents often understandably think first of the interests of those who elected them.

Presidents as Recruiters

Often a single appointment may have a lasting impact, more so than scores of presidential policy initiatives. President Eisenhower's nomination of Earl Warren to be chief justice of the United States may have been the single most significant decision of his administration in the area of domestic policy. Warren served for more than 15 years and presided over vast changes in civil rights and civil liberties. President Clinton's nominees Ruth Bader Ginsburg and Stephen Breyer are also likely to have long-term impacts. In a similar way, selection of a secretary of state, top economic advisers, a secretary of the interior, or top White House aides can have an enormous impact on long-term national policy.

President Clinton has won both praise and criticism for his performance as a recruiter. He won praise for appointing cabinet members like Interior Secretary Bruce Babbitt and Treasury Secretary Bob Rubin. Yet he was faulted for his appointments at Agriculture, Energy, and the CIA. His Surgeon General, Jocelyn Elders, was forced out of office for her liberal statements on birth control education. Although his management style has been criticized, Clinton succeeded in making the cabinet and his administration "more like America." More women and more minorities have served than under previous presidents.

Presidents control more than 4,000 appointments, including hundreds of federal judgeships and top positions in the military and diplomatic service. (Note, however, that many appointments must be made with the approval of the Senate.) Effective presidents shrewdly use their appointment powers not only to reward campaign supporters and enhance ties to Congress, but also to communicate priorities and policy directions. The chief executive needs the best possible managers and motivators in these crucial positions because the top appointees are also a major link between the White House and the millions of people who serve in the federal and military career services.

Besides identifying and recruiting them, the president must also try to keep the most talented of these officials in government as long as possible.[11] The turnover problem is acute. Many able people come to top positions—say in the cabinet or subcabinet—and stay for just two years; less than one-third stay for more than three years. These top federal posts do not pay as much as similar positions in the private sector, and living in Washington is expensive. Moreover the White House in recent decades has often placed loyal campaign aides in key deputy positions to ensure cabinet member loyalties.[12]

Various financial disclosure and conflict-of-interest requirements, imposed on presidential appointees as a result of the Ethics in Government Act of 1978, discourage some potential appointees from accepting government jobs. They must fill out many forms, and they must testify at sometimes complicated, time-consuming, confusing, and embarrassing congressional hearings. Media scrutiny of citizen-leaders called to government service has also become more intensive. Recruiters for recent presidents report they often go to their second or third choice before they find someone willing to accept an appointment. "No other nation relies so heavily on noncareer personnel for the management

The Job of President
Constitutional Responsibilities

Act as commander in chief
Negotiate treaties
Receive foreign ambassadors
Nominate top federal officials, including federal judges
Veto bills
Faithfully administer federal laws
Pardon persons convicted of federal offenses
Address Congress and the nation

Informal Roles

Crisis manager
World leader
Legislative leader
Party leader
Morale builder
Personnel recruiter
Priority setter
Budget setter
Conflict resolver
Coalition builder
Bargainer and persuader

of its government. . . . If talented Americans decline the opportunity for public service, if they endure it only for brief periods, or if they are ill-prepared for the challenges they will face in the public sector, the system will not deliver on its promise."[13]

A president must strengthen the hand of the ablest people working in the bureaucracy and promote them to higher positions at the senior reaches of the executive branch. In short, the personnel responsibilities of a president are great and require much time.

Presidents as Priority Setters

Presidents, by custom, have become responsible for proposing initiatives in the areas of foreign policy, economic growth and stability, and the quality of life in the United States. This was not always the case. But beginning with Woodrow Wilson, and especially since the New Deal, a president is expected not only to promote peace, but also to prevent depressions and propose reforms to ensure domestic progress. New ideas to improve national policies are seized upon by a president searching for campaign issues or legislative program material, and they are refined by the executive office staff, by special presidential task forces, and by Congress.

NATIONAL SECURITY POLICY The framers foresaw a special need for speed and unity in our dealings with other nations. As a result, presidents generally have more leeway in foreign policy and military affairs than they have in domestic matters. For example, President Clinton sent troops to Haiti and Bosnia despite widespread public opposition and grudging acceptance in Congress. The Constitution vests in a president command of the two major instruments of foreign policy—the diplomatic corps and the armed services. It also gives the chief executive responsibility for negotiating treaties and commitments with other nations, although Congress usually gets to vote on these matters.

Congress has also granted presidents discretion in initiating foreign policies, for diplomacy frequently requires quick action. A president can act swiftly; Congress usually cannot. The Supreme Court has upheld strong presidential authority in this area. In *United States v Curtis Wright* in 1936, the Court referred to the "exclusive power of the president as the sole organ of the federal government in the field of international relations—a power which does not require as a basis for its exercise an act of Congress, but which, of course, like every other governmental power, must be exercised in subordination to the applicable provisions of the Constitution."[14] These are sweeping words.[15] Yet a determined Congress that knows what it wants to do and can agree on action does not lack power in foreign relations. Congress must authorize and appropriate the funds that back up our policies abroad.

ECONOMIC POLICY Ever since the New Deal, presidents have been expected to keep unemployment low, fight inflation, keep taxes down, and promote economic growth and prosperity. The Constitution did not specify these duties for the executive, yet presidents know that when the nation is not prosperous and jobs are scarce, they may suffer the fate of Herbert Hoover, who was denounced for his alleged inaction during the Great Depression. The growth and complexity of economic problems since the Depression of the 1930s have placed even more initiatives in the president's hands. The delicate balancing required to keep a modern economy operating means that presidents must regularly make key fiscal and budgetary policy decisions. Recent elections have turned largely on economics, or as Bill Clinton's staff aides put it, "It's the economy, stupid!"[16]

THE PRESIDENTIAL WAR POWER

The Constitution delegates to Congress the authority to declare the legal state of war (with the consent of the president), but in practice the commander in chief often starts the fighting or initiates actions that lead to war. This power has often been used by the president. From George Washington's time until Clinton's, the president, by ordering troops into battle, has often decided when Americans will fight and when they will not. When the cause has had political support, the president's use of this authority has been approved. In 1846, James K. Polk ordered American forces to advance into disputed territory; when Mexico resisted, Polk informed Congress that war existed by act of Mexico, and a formal declaration of war was soon forthcoming. Abraham Lincoln called up troops, spent money, set up a blockade, and fought the first few months of the Civil War without even calling Congress into session. William McKinley's dispatch of a battleship to Havana harbor, where it blew up, helped precipitate war with Spain in 1898. The United States was not formally at war with Germany until late 1941, but prior to the Japanese attack on Pearl Harbor, Franklin Roosevelt ordered the navy to guard convoys to Great Britain and to open fire on submarines threatening the convoys. Since World War II, presidents have sent forces without specific congressional authorization to Korea, Berlin, Vietnam, Lebanon, Grenada, Cuba, Libya, Panama, Kuwait, Somalia, and Rwanda—in short, around the world.

In 1973, Congress overrode Richard Nixon's presidential veto and enacted the War Powers Resolution, which declared that henceforth the president can commit the armed forces of the United States only: (1) after a declaration of war by Congress; (2) by specific statutory authorization; or (3) in a national emergency created by an attack on the United States or its armed forces. After committing the armed forces under the third circumstance, the president is required to report to Congress within 48 hours. Unless Congress has declared war, the troop commitment must be ended within 60 days. The president is allowed another 30 days if the chief executive claims the safety of the United States forces requires their continued use. A president is also obligated by this resolution to consult Congress "in every possible instance" before committing troops to battle. Moreover, at any time, by concurrent resolution *not subject to presidential veto*, Congress may direct the president to disengage such troops.

Not everyone was pleased by the passage of the War Powers Resolution of 1973. Nixon vetoed it because he said it encroached on presidential powers. Others said it gave away a constitutional power plainly belonging to Congress—namely, the war-making or war-declaring power—for up to 90 days. Still other observers, however much they may have thought this resolution was defective, believed nonetheless that war powers legislation was of symbolic and institutional significance because it reflected a new determination in Congress at the time. Presidents from Nixon to Clinton have not changed their behavior much, yet they have been put on notice that the commitment of American troops is subject to congressional approval. According to the resolution, presidents have to persuade Congress and the nation that their actions are justified by the gravest of national emergencies. Presidents in the future will, at least occasionally, hold back from conflict until they get what, in effect, might be a congressional declaration of war.

President Franklin D. Roosevelt signed the declaration of war against Japan on December 8, 1941 as leaders of Congress looked on. It was the last time a president of the United States signed a formal declaration of war.

Although presidents sometimes get their economic advice elsewhere, their chief advisers on economic policy are the secretary of the treasury, the three members of the Council of Economic Advisers, and the director of the Office of Management and Budget. The chair of the Federal Reserve Board of Governors is often also a key White House adviser on the economy.

DOMESTIC POLICY A leader is one who knows where the followers are. Lincoln did not invent the antislavery movement. Kennedy and Johnson did not begin the civil rights movement. Clinton was hardly the first leader to notice the unfairness of health care and welfare policies. But they all, in their respective times, became embroiled in these controversies, for a president cannot long ignore what divides or inspires a nation.

The essence of the modern presidency lies in its potential to resolve societal conflicts. To be sure, much of the time a president will try to avoid conflict, seeking instead to defer, delegate, or otherwise delay controversial decisions. An effective president, however, will clarify the major issues of the day, define what is possible, and organize the governmental structure so that important goals can be realized. Clearly, a president has the ability to focus the legislative agenda on administration priorities, whatever their origins.

A president—with the cooperation of Congress—can set national goals and propose legislation. Close inspection indicates, however, that in most instances "new initiatives" in domestic policy are measures that have been under consideration in previous sessions of Congress. Just as the celebrated New Deal legislation had a fairly well-defined history extending back several years before its embrace by Franklin Roosevelt, many of Clinton's initiatives—health care and "the end of welfare as we know it"—are the fruits of long campaigns by congressional activists and certain interest groups.

Presidents as Legislative and Political Coalition Builders

The Constitution provides that the president "shall from time to time give to the Congress information on the State of the Union, and recommend to their Consideration such Measures as he shall judge necessary and expedient." From the start, strong presidents have exploited this power. George Washington and John Adams went in person to Congress to deliver information and recommendations. Thomas Jefferson and many presidents after him sent written messages, but Woodrow Wilson restored the practice of delivering a personal, and often dramatic, message. Franklin Roosevelt used radio talks and personal appearances to draw the attention of the whole nation to his program, as have most subsequent presidents. Bill Clinton visited Congress soon after he was elected and went back on several occasions to mingle with members of Congress or to give major reports to the nation. Clinton has also held numerous television forums in attempts to win public support for his legislative programs.

Less public, yet equally important, are the frequent written policy messages dispatched from the White House to the members of Congress on a range of public problems. These messages are important in defining the administration's position and in giving assistance to friendly legislators. Moreover, these messages are often accompanied by detailed drafts of legislation that members of Congress may sponsor with little or no change. These White House proposals, the products of bill-drafting experts on the president's staff or in the executive departments and agencies, may be strengthened or diluted by Congress, but many of the original provisions survive.

An effective president is an effective politician—the most visible and potentially the strongest mobilizer of influence in the American system of power.

"Politician" is a nasty word to many Americans; it often connotes a scheming, evasive, self-interested person. Little wonder many politicians claim they are "above politics." There is, however, a more constructive definition of "politician": one who helps manage conflict; one who knows how to negotiate, bargain, and help reconcile different views in order to make the difficult and desirable become reality. Presidents cannot escape political coalition-building tasks.[17] As candidates, they have made promises to the people. To get things done and to be reelected, they must work with many people and countless interest groups who have differing loyalties and responsibilities. Inevitably, presidents become embroiled in legislative, bureaucratic, and lobbying politics, and their approval ratings suffer as a consequence (see Figure 11-1).

Presidents make good on more of their promises than the general public appreciates. Most presidents enjoy at least partial success on most of the initiatives they favored during their campaigns or soon after they came to the White House. Although presidents control much of what they recommend to Congress, other institutions and realities—especially the leaders in Congress, the health of the economy, and budget deficits—shape what presidents can achieve. President Clinton enjoyed moderate success with his program in Congress in his first two years, but in 1995 his success rate with Congress dropped to the lowest point, about 36 percent, since *Congressional Quarterly* began measuring presidential success with Congress in 1953.[18]

Despite their formal powers, presidents can rarely command; they spend most of their time *persuading* people. Potentially, presidents have enormous persuasive power, but in a government of separated institutions that share powers, some congressional, bureaucratic, and military leaders are beyond the president's political reach. They have their own constituencies—a House committee, for example, or a powerful interest group. Presidents cannot simply give orders like a first sergeant.

From a president's vantage point, it is seldom helpful or wise to punish legislators from one's own party who, for whatever reason, decide not to support

Why Presidential Approval (in Polls) Usually Declines the Longer Presidents Are in Office

Political scientists are not exactly sure of the precise relationships among the following factors; different studies produce different findings. These factors are, however, plainly some of the more important ones, and some of them are doubtless interrelated.

- Expectations that are raised in campaigns are dashed as time forecloses resources and options.
- Things that go wrong get blamed, rightly or wrongly, on presidents, whether or not presidents have the power to deal with these matters.
- Rising disapproval of incumbent presidents is often influenced by inflation and unemployment.
- Major negative events, such as the Vietnam War, Watergate scandal, Iranian hostage crisis, or Whitewater investigation, influence how people evaluate presidents.
- Press and media criticism accumulates over time and sharpens the public's dissatisfaction with a president. Perhaps, too, time in office simply wears out our welcome for a president.

FIGURE 11-1   Presidential Approval Ratings, 1945–1996

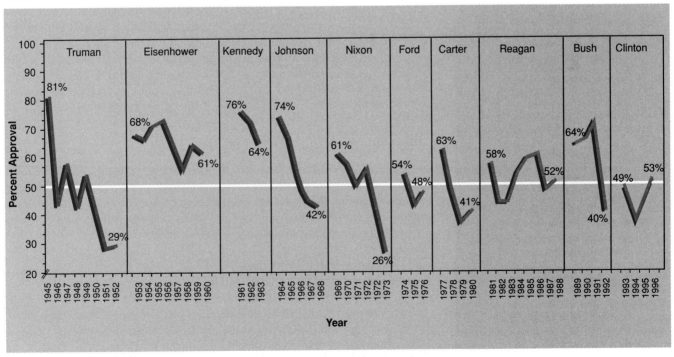

SOURCE: The Gallup Organization.

part of the president's legislative program. With power dispersed and decentralized in Congress, it is just too risky for a president to single out a few party "disloyalists" for retribution. White House congressional relations aides abide by the motto of "No permanent allies, no permanent enemies." Someone whose vote is lost today may cast the crucial supportive vote on some other measure next week.

This is also true of a president's dealings with interest groups. Thus Clinton and the leaders of organized labor were on opposite sides of the North American Free Trade Agreement (NAFTA) vote in 1993, yet they were able to patch things up and work together on several issues thereafter.

Presidents are sometimes in a better position to bargain and trade for votes with members of Congress than are the members themselves. In addition to receiving presidential help in their reelection campaigns, members of Congress also want federal projects for their districts, patronage for their supporters, help with their own pet legislative measures, and defense contracts and benefits for major industries in their districts or states. Then, too, "among the currencies in the president's trading system are negative sanctions—threats to withhold favors from members who fail to go along."[19]

The White House has a number of resources with which to influence most members of Congress. Presidents can make stirring appeals for party unity—if their parties enjoy majorities in Congress. They can also try to educate and rally the public around their programs. Much of the time, however, a president must deal with a Congress that moves according to its own pace and that responds to a variety of constituent and organized interests above and beyond the requests and appeals coming from the White House.

Many students of the presidency think the power to persuade is the president's chief resource and that such power comes through bargaining. Bargaining, in turn, comes primarily through getting others to believe it is in their self-interest to cooperate. Hence the skill of a president in communicating and winning others over is the necessary energizing factor in moving the institutions of the national government to action. This school of thought also holds that a president cannot be above the battle or above politics. Rather, a president must enjoy the give and take of congressional-presidential relations as well as between the parties and between the White House and the press. Classic examples of effective presidential coalition building are Franklin Roosevelt's winning public support for his New Deal programs, Lyndon Johnson's getting his Great Society legislation passed, and Clinton's mobilizing public and congressional support to win approval for the North American Free Trade Agreement.

The Presidential Veto

A president can veto a bill by returning it, together with specific objections, to the house in which it originated. Congress, by a two-thirds vote in each chamber, may **override** the president's veto. Another variation of the veto is known as the **pocket veto**. In the ordinary course of events, if the president does not sign or veto a bill within ten weekdays after receiving it, it becomes law without the chief executive's signature. But if Congress adjourns within the ten days, the president—by taking no action—can kill the bill.

The veto's strength lies in the difficulty Congress has in getting a two-thirds majority of both houses. From 1789 through 1996, presidents have exercised their regular veto power 1,437 times; only 105 of these vetoes have been overridden by Congress. However, when scholars separate out the vetoes of private bills (bills dealing with individual claims against the government, or land titles, or matters such as immigration and naturalization) from public bills, they find that about 19 percent of the public bill vetoes have been overridden by Congress. Still, writes Robert Spitzer, "a presidential success rate of more than 80 percent for important legislation poses a daunting challenge to anyone seeking to overturn a veto."[20]

In short, there is little Congress can do when confronted with a veto. It must either get enough votes to override the veto or modify the legislation and try again (see Table 11-3). Presidents are able to make the vast majority of their regular vetoes stick. Although Congress overrode 23 percent of Reagan's vetoes, it was only able to override one of George Bush's 46 vetoes.

Congress often manipulates legislation to reduce the chance of a presidential veto. It attaches irrelevant but controversial provisions, called **riders**, to legislation the president considers vital. In one appropriations bill, for example, lawmakers may combine badly needed funds for the armed forces with costly **pork-barrel** items. "Pork-barrel" refers to government benefits or programs that help the economy of a member's district—as in "bringing home the bacon."

Presidents can also use the veto power in a positive way. They can announce that bills under consideration by Congress will be turned back unless certain changes are made. They can use the threat of a veto against a bill Congress wants badly in exchange for other bills that they want. A presidential veto can also protect a national minority from hasty, unfair legislation passed in the heat of the moment. But the veto is essentially a negative weapon of limited use to a president like Clinton, who is pressing for action.

The Politics of the Item Veto

President Clinton in 1996 signed into law a bill passed by Congress authorizing an **item veto**, which he said would allow future presidents to fight "special interest boondoggles, tax loopholes, and pure pork."[21] Clinton was the most recent in a list of modern-day presidents who called for the right to veto subsections or items within major appropriation bills passed by Congress. Presidents, as noted above, already had the constitutional authority to veto an entire bill.

The item veto approved in 1996 to take effect in 1997 applies to discretionary spending, new direct spending, and items of limited tax benefit. The president has five calendar days after enactment of the law to notify Congress of his decision to "rescind." Congress has thirty days to act and does not require a two-thirds vote to override, merely a majority vote of each house. Item veto authority is granted to presidents for eight years, from 1997 through the year 2005, after which Congress would have to decide whether or not to extend it.

Adoption of the item veto was a victory for both Bill Clinton and for the Republicans, who had listed it as a key provision of their Contract with America. But the item veto will almost certainly be challenged as unconstitutional. Senator Robert C. Byrd of West Virginia had long campaigned against the item veto, saying it was a colossal mistake that upsets the balance of powers laid out in the Constitution. He and other critics charged it gave away too much of the congressional control over the purse strings. Said Byrd: "This so called line-item veto act should be more appropriately labeled 'The President Always Wins Bill.' From now on, the heavy hand of the president will be used to slap down congressional opposition wherever it may exist."[22]

Some constitutional scholars agree with Byrd and believe enacting an item veto should have gone through the complex process of amending the Constitution rather than by legislative statute. Other experts believe Congress can voluntarily

TABLE 11-3

Presidential Vetoes, 1933–1996

President	Vetoes
Franklin D. Roosevelt	635
Harry S. Truman	250
Dwight D. Eisenhower	181
John F. Kennedy	21
Lyndon B. Johnson	30
Richard M. Nixon	43
Gerald R. Ford	66
Jimmy Carter	31
Ronald Reagan	78
George Bush	46
Bill Clinton	17

SOURCE: *Congressional Quarterly* and Office of Executive Clerk, The White House.

delegate this kind of authority to a president. The Supreme Court will have to settle this one way or another.

The pros and cons about the item veto are rather clear. Presidents wanted it to fight deficit spending and to cut expenditures whose main purpose is to help members of Congress win reelection. Such items are often added to necessary appropriations bills at the last minute, and the president is forced to sign the bill, including these wasteful provisions. But with the item veto, wasteful measures would be unlikely to win support for an override in both chambers of Congress.

Proponents of the item veto have regularly noted that 43 state governors have the item veto authority, and it has worked reasonably well in the states. They add that the American people endorse giving this additional authority to the presidents.

Perhaps the most compelling argument of those who have supported the item veto is the enduring concern over the national debt and federal deficits. Congress has not been able to balance the budget—even with Republican majorities in control of both chambers. If Congress can't balance the budget, supporters say, why not give the president this additional clout?[23]

Presidents and Public Opinion

The press conference is an example of how a president can employ the machinery of communication in an influential manner. Years ago press conferences were rather casual affairs. Franklin Roosevelt ran his get-togethers informally and was a master at withholding information as well as giving it. Under Truman the conference became an institutionalized part of the presidential communications apparatus. Kennedy authorized regular live telecasts of press conferences and used them frequently for direct communication with the people. Reagan effectively used five-minute Saturday afternoon radio chats to communicate his views, ask

President Clinton's visit to the troops in Bosnia generated good will and good publicity. Although public opinion was divided on the Bosnia action, most people wanted to show support of our men and women in service.

for support, and win Sunday morning media coverage. Clinton occasionally uses the press conference, which has aided him in his efforts to deal with Congress and the media, and he too speaks directly to the public on his Saturday morning radio broadcasts.

Presidents commission private polls to gauge public opinion; they want to be able to distinguish the public's whims, estimate the strength and direction of its thinking, and respond to its impatience. Presidents must know not only *what* to do but *when* to do it. Public opinion can be unstable and unpredictable. Lyndon Johnson recognized that his wide popular support of the mid-1960s had melted away by 1968, when he decided not to run again. Nixon's dramatic drop of nearly 45 percentage points in public opinion polls, a result of the Watergate scandal, helped force his resignation. Bush won unusual public approval during and after the successful military efforts in the Persian Gulf in early 1991, but his popular approval sharply diminished during the economic downturn that followed. Most presidents lose support the longer they are in office. Dissatisfaction sets in; interest groups grow impatient; unkept promises must be accounted for; and the president gets blamed for many of the things that go wrong.

Both as a candidate and in the White House, Bill Clinton has had especially testy relations with the press. Clinton used every available means to get his message out to the American public. He was the first president to appear on MTV, and he turned up on town meetings and talk shows with regularity. Both he and Hillary Clinton have had to deal with the press in an era of "in your face journalism," where many of the old rules and courtesies about the separation of public and private life have disappeared, especially those having to do with marital and extramarital relations. We have to remember, however, that Jefferson, Lincoln, and Franklin Roosevelt were all vilified by the press and rarely shown much reverence in their lifetimes. Presidents are always fair game for media critics.[24]

PARTY LEADERSHIP Another potential source of influence for the president is the political party. Most presidents since Jefferson have been party leaders, and generally the more effective the presidents, the more use they have made of party support. Wilson, the two Roosevelts, and Reagan fortified their executive and legislative influence by mobilizing support within their party. Yet presidents are led by their party as much as they lead it; no president has ever wholly dominated his party.

Presidents as Administrators

The Constitution charges the president to "take Care that the Laws be faithfully executed." Presidents, however, must delegate much of their administrative authority. Because their other responsibilities demand most of their attention, presidents are very often dependent on their subordinates. Theoretically, at least, orders flow *down* an administrative *line*: from president, to cabinet members, to bureau chiefs, to smaller offices. Like all top executives, a president is assisted by a *staff*, who advise the chief executive. This line and staff organization is typical of every large administrative entity, whether it be the army, General Motors, or the United Nations.

Presidents have come to rely heavily on their personal staffs. Nowhere else—not in Congress, not in the cabinet, not in the party—can presidents find the loyalty and single-mindedness that often develop among their closest White House aides. Presidents often come to see many cabinet heads as staunch advocates of their departments and the constituencies they serve. Presidents assume, however, that their aides will provide them with neutral and objective advice, but there are substantial costs to listening only to one's closest aides. The White House can usually be thought of as a palace court in which strong presidents create an environment that weeds out any assistant who persists in presenting irritating or opposing views.[25]

The number of employees in the presidential entourage has grown steadily since the early 1900s, when only a few dozen people served a president at a cost of less than a few hundred thousand dollars annually. Today a White House staff of about 400 operates at the cost of several million dollars a year, a reduction from previous years, as Clinton had promised in his election campaign. This staff makes up just one part of the Executive Office of the President.

THE INSTITUTIONALIZED EXECUTIVE OFFICE Approved by Congress in 1939, the Executive Office of the President was the recommendation of Franklin Roosevelt's Committee on Administrative Management. Its intention was to provide presidents the help they obviously needed to carry out the growing responsibilities imposed by the Great Depression and by the enlarged role of government. The Executive Office of the President consists of the Office of Management and Budget, the Council of Economic Advisers, and several other staff units (see Figure 11-2).

The staff of the White House office can be categorized by their primary functions: (1) domestic policy; (2) economic policy; (3) national security or foreign policy; (4) administration and personnel matters (as well as personal paperwork and scheduling for the president); (5) congressional relations; and (6) public relations.

Presidential aides sometimes insist they are simply the eyes and ears of the president, that they make few important decisions, and that they never intrude between the chief executive and the heads of departments. But the White House staff and the inevitable emergence of a few strong White House advisers have made this traditional picture nearly obsolete. Some White House aides, impatient with bureaucratic and congressional bottlenecks or even political sabotage, come to view the presidency as if it alone were the whole government.

The **Office of Management and Budget (OMB)** continues to be the central presidential staff agency. Its director advises the president in detail about the hundreds of government agencies—how much money they should be allotted in the budget and what kind of job they are doing. The OMB seeks to improve

FIGURE 11-2 Executive Office of the President

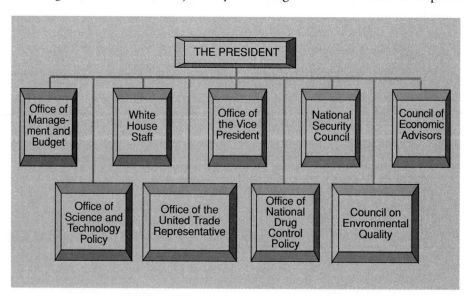

the planning, management, and statistical work of the agencies. It makes a special effort to see that each agency conforms to presidential policies in its dealings with Congress; each agency has to clear its policy recommendations to Congress through OMB first.

A budget is more than just a financial plan, because it reflects power struggles and indicates national priorities (and wishful thinking).[26] To the president, the budget is a means of control over administrators who may be trying to join ranks with politicians or interest groups to thwart presidential priorities. Through the long budget preparation process, presidents use the OMB as a way of conserving and centralizing their own influence.

THE CABINET It is hard to find a more unusual institution than the president's cabinet. The cabinet is not specifically mentioned by name in the Constitution (but see the Twenty-fifth Amendment). Yet since George Washington's administration, every president has had one. Washington's consisted of his secretaries of state, treasury, and war, plus his attorney general.

Today the selection of cabinet members is the first major job for the president-elect. The cabinet consists of the president, the vice-president, the officers who head the 14 executive departments, and a few others a president considers cabinet-level officials. The cabinet has always been a loosely designated body, and it is not always clear who belongs in it. In recent years, certain executive branch administrators and White House counselors have been accorded cabinet rank.

Presidents need strong and creative aides to sift through the competing advice that comes to the White House, and a staff to help them monitor the implementation of policies in the sprawling federal executive departments. But presidents also need a strong cabinet and counselors in Congress and elsewhere to provide alternative views to help ensure that they do not become isolated by an overly protective entourage.[27]

Cabinet government as practiced in parliamentary systems—where the voice and the vote of the cabinet members count for a lot—simply does not exist in the United States. In fact, an American president is not required by the Constitution to form a cabinet or to hold regular meetings. Kennedy, Johnson, and Nixon all preferred small conferences with individuals specifically involved in a problem. Kennedy saw no reason to discuss defense department matters with his secretaries

The Cabinet

Vice-President
Secretary of State
Secretary of Treasury
Secretary of Defense
Attorney General
Secretary of Interior
Secretary of Agriculture
Secretary of Commerce
Secretary of Labor
Secretary of Health and Human Services
Secretary of Housing and Urban Development
Secretary of Transportation
Secretary of Energy
Secretary of Education
Secretary of Veterans Affairs
Chief of Staff at the White House
Director of the Office of Management and Budget
U.S. Trade Representative
U.S. Representative to the United Nations
Chairman, Council of Economic Advisors
Administrator, Environmental Protection Agency
Director, Drug Control Office

The cabinet that Bill Clinton selected when he took office is sworn in by Supreme Court Chief Justice Rehnquist.

Ceremonial duties of the vice president include representing the United States at events such as this commemoration of the end of World War II. Vice President Albert Gore shakes hands with French President Jacques Chirac.

of agriculture and labor, and he thought cabinet meetings wasted valuable time for too many already busy people. Both Carter and Reagan tried to revive the cabinet, and both met often with their cabinets during their first two years. But the longer they remained in office, the less frequently they met with their cabinets as a whole. Some of Clinton's cabinet complain of too little contact with the president and of too many calls from young White House aides. This is an old problem.

Presidential advisers and the heads of various White House-based cabinet-level councils or review units, such as the National Security Council and the Office of Management and Budget, have gained equal or even superior status to many of the department and cabinet secretaries. This has occurred in part because these people are physically located in or next door to the White House. Further, presidents believe some department heads often adopt narrow "advocate" views: the agriculture cabinet officer as a strident advocate for the farmers; the Housing and Urban Development cabinet officer as an ambassador for the housing industry and, to some extent, also for big city mayors; and so on through much of the cabinet, especially those preoccupied with domestic policy matters. As good relations between presidents and cabinet members weaken, presidents, in frustration, turn more often to trusted senior White House staff aides to settle conflicts and coordinate policy. Tension almost always builds between senior White House aides and their counterparts in the cabinet. Personal staff members remain close to the president's ear and are more influential as a result.

Recent presidents have formed various committees of certain cabinet or subcabinet members, such as Clinton's National Economic Council, in an attempt to integrate key departmental and White House advisers around major policy matters. Such committees or councils are patterned after the **National Security Council**, established in 1947 to confer with the president on matters relating to national security. These initiatives are aimed at decentralizing policy discussions while giving cabinet members a genuine feeling that they are being consulted and involved in important policy developments.

THE VICE-PRESIDENT

Although the vice-presidency is now a part of the presidential establishment, it has not been so for long. Most vice-presidents served mainly as president of the Senate. Up to the 1950s, the vice-president was at best a "fifth wheel" and at worst a political rival who sometimes connived against the president. The office was often dismissed as a joke. One reason for the vice-president's posture as an outsider was that presidential nominees prior to Clinton usually chose running mates who were geographically, ideologically, demographically, and in other ways likely to "balance the ticket." Clinton ignored the desire to balance the ticket and picked another white, male, progressive southerner.

As the Clinton-Gore example suggests, recent presidential candidates have selected more like-minded persons as their running mates and have also made more use of them. Today the vice-presidency brings both advantages and liabilities to a person who aspires to the presidency. The job surely provides exposure to the issues and challenges of the office, but it is hard to appear "presidential" while at the same time avoiding the appearance of being disloyal to or upstaging the president.[28]

Bob Dole said he wanted someone who he could work closely with and someone with demonstrated party loyalty who wouldn't hurt the ticket. Because of both Dole's age (73) and his poor showing in the polls, he definitely needed a running mate who looked presidential and would boost Dole's ratings. His surprise pick of former congressman and cabinet member Jack Kemp did give him a boost in the polls and reassured the party faithful. Kemp, however, was never known for his closeness to Dole. He had run against him in 1988 and had endorsed Steve Forbes in the 1996 primary season.

Ideally, a vice-president serves several roles in addition to the ceremonial function of acting as president of the Senate. A vice-president gets to cast the tie-breaking vote if the Senate has a tie vote, but this situation usually occurs less than once a year. The vice-president is also a member of the National Security Council. Vice-president Al Gore headed a national review of the federal bureaucracy for Clinton, a temporary yet highly visible presidential assignment. In addition, Gore effectively debated Ross Perot in a widely viewed TV debate on the North American Free Trade Agreement. Gore also spearheaded various "information superhighway" initiatives for Clinton.

The real test of the role of vice-president is whether he or she is fully integrated into the decision-making process in the White House. All vice-presidents are "back-up equipment" in case something happens to the president. They can head up any number of councils, visit any number of countries, and still not be much involved in the day-to-day operations of the presidency. President Carter included Walter Mondale in the daily processes of decision making in the White House; President Reagan sometimes included George Bush in a similar way; President Clinton used Al Gore as an important adviser and confidant on domestic as well as foreign policy matters.

Tensions sometimes develop between presidential aides and vice-presidents and their staffs. Part of the problem arises because most presidents seldom wish to give up any ceremonial duties for which they themselves can win credit. Neither do cabinet members like to share their responsibilities with vice-presidents, making it hard for vice-presidents to gain administrative experience. Presidents often delegate unpleasant political chores to their vice-presidents. The importance of the vice-presidency is underscored, however, by the fact that nine presidents have not been able to finish their terms. Four presidents have been assassinated, four have died naturally, and one has resigned. One-third of our presidents were once vice-presidents, including Truman, Lyndon Johnson, Nixon, Ford, and Bush.

The vice-presidency has been significantly affected by two post-World War II constitutional amendments. The Twenty-second Amendment, ratified in 1951, imposes a two-term limit on presidents; consequently vice-presidents have a better chance of moving up to the Oval Office. The Twenty-fifth Amendment, ratified in 1967, confirms the prior practice of making the vice-president not an acting president, but president, in the event of the death of a president. Also of significance, this amendment provides a procedure to determine whether an incumbent president is unable to discharge the powers and duties of the office and establishes procedures to fill a vacancy in the vice-presidency. For a few hours in 1985, George Bush became the first "acting president" when President Reagan underwent a minor cancer operation. The amendment also provides that in the event of a vacancy in the office of vice-president, the president nominates a vice-president, who takes office upon confirmation by a majority vote of both houses of Congress. This procedure generally ensures the appointment of a vice-president in whom the president has confidence. Thus vice-presidents who have to take over the presidency can be expected to reflect most of their predecessor's policies.

Now that presidents are choosing as their vice-presidential running mates persons of like minded views rather than somebody just to balance the ticket, tensions between president and vice-president are not as normal a pattern as was the case in the past. Still, the tension between a president and a vice-president is natural. After all, except for the vice-president, everybody who works closely with a president can be fired. It is almost certain that vice-presidents will continue to have an undefined ad hoc set of assignments, subject more to the good will and mood of the president than to any fixed description.[29]

First Lady: A Search for the Appropriate Role

A president cannot by law appoint a spouse to a federal job. Yet Hillary Rodham Clinton became an influential and important adviser to President Bill Clinton. She headed up the Clinton administration's planning for national health care; however, these efforts failed to win majority support in Congress. She also took an active role in the selection of various nominees for cabinet and judicial posts.

Political spouses have often influenced their husbands or wives. Earlier presidential spouses—including Eleanor Roosevelt, Edith Wilson, and Dolly Madison—counseled and lobbied their presidential husbands. Every "first spouse" defines responsibilities differently. Bess Truman and Pat Nixon chose to remain in the background.

Hillary Clinton was as controversial as she was influential. Her role as an advocate of health care initiatives and women's rights attracted criticism as well as praise. Her role in the Whitewater real estate development and her alleged failure to answer specific questions about it caused additional concerns. She became the first First Lady to be subpoenaed to testify before a grand jury, and she, along with her husband, was questioned by a federal independent counsel.

Hillary Clinton has been hailed as a first lady for our times and a model for contemporary women who choose to have both a career and a family. She has also been seen as a political liability. She was criticized in the press, satirized in the novel *Primary Colors*, and ridiculed by opposition politicians and pundits—especially William Safire, Alfonse D'Amato, Rush Limbaugh, and Pat Buchanan.

It is unlikely that future presidential spouses will revert to the traditional supporting role. The question also arises of whether the husband of our first woman president will continue with his career.

CONSTRAINTS ON THE PRESIDENT

Should presidents be limited to two terms in office?

Before he left office, former President Ronald Reagan called for the repeal of the Twenty-second Amendment to the Constitution, the one that limits a president to two terms. Why do you think he opposed the amendment? What additional reasons could be put forth to persuade people to repeal this relatively new (1951) provision in the Constitution? What are the best reasons for retaining the Twenty-second?

Factors that Constrain Presidents

The Constitution
Federalism
Separation of powers
Congress
Federal courts
News media
Public opinion
Opposing party
Opposing factions in president's party
Interest groups
Editorial opinion (and cartoonists)
Bureaucratic resistance
Opposing world powers and the international economy
World public opinion and U.N. policies
World leaders
Presidential advisers
Regularly scheduled elections
Unrealistic expectations
Party platforms
Independent counsels
The shape of the economy and the imperatives of economic development
Fear of losing next election for self or party

Presidential power may be greater today than ever before. It is misleading, however, to infer from a president's capacity to begin a nuclear war that the chief executive has similar power in most policy-making areas. Seldom are presidents free agents in bringing about basic social change. As priority setter, politician, and executive, a president shares power with members of Congress, bureaucrats, and interest-group elites. The ability to set priorities is not the same as the ability to enforce laws and administer them properly. Presidents who want to be effective in implementing policy changes must know they face a number of constraints. Besides the formal system of checks and balances, effective presidents must learn to deal with media criticism, cultural challenges, and international pressures. Presidents are also shaped by their times, by the ideological leanings of the people, and by the successes and failures of their immediate predecessors.[30]

Media Criticism

Ronald Reagan once walked away from one of his news conferences and, turning to an aide, blasted the reporters, not realizing a microphone was picking up his every word. John F. Kennedy once canceled more than 50 White House subscriptions to the *New York Herald Tribune* because he was furious about the way the paper treated his decisions. Lyndon Johnson regularly planted "softball questions" (questions he could easily answer) among friendly reporters at presidential press conferences. Bill Clinton complained about "gotcha journalism," and was especially upset at the media's rough treatment of his wife. All recent presidents have complained that the modern media misrepresent them and disproportionately report bad news.

Enjoying enormous First Amendment rights in this country, reporters usually go about their business of analyzing and criticizing presidents with gusto. Scores of media representatives are regularly stationed at the White House, and they travel everywhere the president goes, reporting on every move. Reporters from all the major networks and newspapers are assigned to be with the president 24 hours a day; they call this "the death watch." Presidential statements—even on trivial matters—are sent back to the newsrooms and immediately printed or aired. Major statements and policy initiatives are reported and subjected to analysis. The media, at the White House and elsewhere, call attention to subjects that might never have been discussed publicly in earlier times and that seldom are discussed in other countries.

Presidents, of course, want all their initiatives printed and praised as much as possible. But media people believe they should provide a context in which presidential statements can be understood; hence, they not only tell people what a president said but often try to explain what the statement means. This interpretation is offered primarily by columnists, editorial writers, and commentators. Those who manage newspapers and radio and television stations also want to balance their stories about what presidents say—especially in presidential speeches—with an equal amount of time for the spokespersons of the opposition party or persons who hold different points of view.

In recent years this kind of *adversarial* media coverage has often left the impression that a president's influence is more divisive than unifying. Except when a president attends a baseball game or welcomes some noted sports or arts hero to the White House, media coverage involves interpretation. No reporter has ever won a Pulitzer Prize for writing a story favorable to an administration. The journalism profession invariably honors those who uncover wrongdoing.

What have presidents done about this? Typically they have been patient and respected the critical dialogue so essential in a democracy. However, presidents and their aides have also engaged in extensive public relations efforts aimed at winning admiration and support for the president and White House policies.[31] Out-of-town editors are invited in for special briefings, and extra effort is made to get the president out of Washington for meetings with local and regional media representatives, who are generally viewed as less critical than Washington-based media. White House media experts devise ways to get the president's point of view out to the public, to get the president on prime-time television, or to arrange for flattering action photos.

The modern media are indeed a formidable adversary of the modern presidency. But the presidency is not being brutally wounded, and its capacity for leadership is not being sapped because of aggressive coverage by the media. Defenders of the press like to quote Thomas Jefferson, who, although angered by the press when he was president, said: "Were it left to me to decide whether we should have a government without newspapers or newspapers without a government, I should not hesitate to prefer the latter."

Defenders of the media say presidents have often lied or manipulated the public's understanding of the issues. The media, they contend, are obligated to cover opposition views, especially when they think a president is wrong. Even though journalists may have political sympathies, they prize their independence and seldom play the role of cheerleader. "Their fault may be the opposite: seeing politicians and their handlers up close, they have no faith in any of them and are carriers, as well as recorders, of the prevailing disenchantment."[32]

No matter who is in the White House, presidents and the media will be in conflict. This ongoing struggle is inherent in a constitutional democracy. The Watergate scandal fortified the media through their important role in bringing the scandal to public attention. Further, because the media—especially television—are viewed as more trustworthy and believable than some other national institutions, most Americans, most of the time, believe what they hear and see on television. But the resources of the White House and the amount of free media coverage given presidents—especially communicators like Franklin Roosevelt, John Kennedy, Ronald Reagan—provide an effective counterpoint to the media.

Cultural Challenges

Because all presidents face cultural dilemmas (for example, attitudes and values toward gay rights or abortion), they need to understand the cultural contexts and cultural values of those they would lead. Political scientists Richard Ellis and Aaron Wildavsky contend presidents can be evaluated in terms of dilemmas confronted, evaded, created, or overcome. The "great" presidents, like Washington, Jefferson, Jackson, and Lincoln, provided solutions to the cultural and societal dilemmas of their day. Borrowing from anthropologists, Ellis and Wildavsky suggest three competing political cultures: *hierarchical, egalitarian,* and *individualistic.* "The type of leadership preferred and feared, and the kinds of support given to and demands made upon leaders, we hypothesize, vary by political culture."[33]

In a hierarchical culture, characterized by respect for authority and acceptance of formal hierarchical relations (for example, the marines or a college basketball team), leadership is relatively easy to exercise. On the other hand, those who try to provide leadership in a society that yearns for equality are invariably frustrated, for egalitarians (lovers of equality) are dedicated to diminishing differences among people. "Would-be egalitarian leaders are thus in trouble before they start," for authority and leadership inherently create inequalities.[34]

Thinking it Through

Reagan said the people should be able to reelect a president as many times as they want, just as they now reelect House and Senate members. He also hinted that the Twenty-second Amendment might weaken a president late in his second term by making him a lame duck, less powerful because everyone knows he will not be around in a year or so. Advocates of repeal also say we may sometimes need to keep a veteran president in office during a crisis period, much as we retained Franklin Roosevelt in 1940. Others say eight years may not be enough time to resolve certain major problems.

The Twenty-second Amendment is not only a limit on the incumbent but also on the electorate, the first since the ratification of the Constitution to restrict the power of the electorate rather than expand it. It is based, advocates of repeal suggest, on the assumption that the voters cannot be trusted.

Those who favor keeping the Twenty-second Amendment cite these reasons: First, the presidency is so powerful today that we need the Twenty-second Amendment as an additional check and balance against abuse of this power. Second, the amendment encourages both parties to seek out quality candidates to succeed to office and discourages dependence on a single ruler. Third, few leaders are likely to have the health, the intellectual energy, and the new ideas needed to perform the demanding responsibilities of the presidency beyond eight years in office. Finally, Americans have always believed in citizen-leaders rather than career politicians, and this amendment encourages this ideal.

Unrealistic Expectations?

The presidency will surely remain one of our nation's best sources for creative policy change. Americans will continue to expect presidents to do more, not less. The presidency will almost certainly continue to be a hard-pressed office, laden with the cumulative weight of contradictory expectations. Thus, we want our presidents to be:

- Gentle and kind, but also forceful, cunning, and decisive
- A common person who can give an uncommon performance
- Above politics, yet a skilled political coalition builder
- An inspirational leader who never promises more than he or she can deliver
- A programmatic but also pragmatic and flexible leader
- Innovative and inventive, ahead of the times, yet always responsive to popular majorities
- A moral leader, yet not too preachy or moralizing
- A bipartisan leader of all the people but also a leader of one political party
- A "take charge" leader yet someone who listens a lot

In the individualist culture, Ellis and Wildavsky see governance organized to maximize individual freedom and thus minimize the need for governmental authority. Citizens in such a culture perform a delicate balancing act between permitting leaders to arise when they are needed and getting rid of them whenever possible.

These authors note that the United States is a nation rightly characterized by its strong individualism, weak hierarchies, and only occasional bursts of egalitarianism. Thus, "with egalitarians rejecting authority, individualists desiring to escape it, and hierarchical forces too weak to impose it, presidents seeking to rely on formal authority alone are in a precarious position."[35]

One of the contributions of George Washington's leadership was his commitment to central government yet wise appreciation for the limits of authority in the United States. Abraham Lincoln is credited with skillfully exercising executive leadership in a notably antileadership system, but doing so in a way that showed a government could provide emergency leadership in times of total war without allowing this power to lead inexorably to permanent dictatorship in peacetime. Lincoln delicately balanced the need for leadership with the need for assurances that the circumstances were extraordinary.

At their best, presidential leaders are individuals who perceive what is needed and understand how to mobilize people and resources to accomplish mutual goals. Effective presidents build on strengths—their own as well as those of their followers and colleagues—and on the opportunities afforded by their culture and situation.

International Pressures

Many writers call attention to the growing number of international pressures facing any president. Historian Paul Kennedy bluntly observed that the task facing American leaders over the next few decades must be to recognize that broad trends are under way on a global scale and that "there is a need to 'manage' affairs so that *relative* erosion of the United States' position takes place slowly and smoothly."[36] Our presidents and leaders, he and others are saying, have to learn to cooperate with and persuade allies, and they must have the ability to win the support of leaders elsewhere as well.

Presidents today are forced to deal with a much stronger European Community and with the increasingly powerful economic force of Japan and other Pacific Rim nations. Multilateral action usually makes far more sense than unilateral action. Presidents have to secure not only the support of Congress and the American people; they must also win the cooperation of foreign nations. It is increasingly clear, as Bill Clinton has surely learned, that the international system, especially the international economy, is stronger than any president or prime minister.[37]

Most other nations long ago learned that to succeed in an international system requires understanding other nations as well as one's own. Current and future presidents will have to be even better prepared than in the past to take global needs, aspirations, and politics into account.

LEADERSHIP IN A CONSTITUTIONAL DEMOCRACY

Some people worry about "imperial presidents" and about the possible alienation of the people from their leaders, especially as complex issues continue to centralize responsibilities in the hands of the national government and the executive.

Those who are concerned about these matters will not content themselves—nor should they—with the existing safeguards against misuse of presidential powers. It is not easy, however, to contrive devices that will check a president who would misuse powers without hamstringing a president who would use those same powers for appropriate purposes and democratically acceptable ends.

James Madison warned that our country could never trust "parchment barriers" to halt the encroaching abuse of power. In the end, constitutions live only if they embody the spirit, values, and deeply held civic beliefs of the people. As the poet Walt Whitman reminded us, tyranny is always a possibility—if the people lose their supreme confidence in themselves and their spirit of defiance. Tyranny may always enter; there is no bar or charm against it. The only bar against it is a large, resolute breed of citizens.

Too much has been made by too many presidents and too many scholars of the view that only the president is the representative of all the people. Members of Congress do not represent the people exactly as a president does, but the two houses collectively represent the people in ways a president cannot and does not.

In the end, the issue is not so much whether the presidency should be stronger than Congress or vice versa. The real issue is that Congress and the presidency must *both* be strengthened to do the pressing work required for the well-being of the American people.

The most compelling restraint on presidential power is the opinion of the American people. Citizens have more power than they realize. Presidents listen when citizens are "sending a message." Citizens can also "vote" between elections in innumerable ways—by changing parties, by organizing protests, by voting for the opposition party in off-year elections, by voting for or against issues in state referenda.

We need a healthy skepticism toward presidential decisions. A lesson learned from the Watergate period in the 1970s is not that the powers of the presidency should be lessened, but that other institutions—parties, Congress, the courts—need constantly to be revitalized. Unless we can find ways to renew and reinvigorate our political parties to achieve some measure of responsiveness to the electorate and party control over public policy, we might develop an American version of how General Charles de Gaulle governed in France—a highly personalized and centralized system overly dependent on a charismatic individual.

One of the persisting paradoxes of the American presidency is that, on the one hand, the institution is always too powerful, and on the other, it is always too weak. It is too strong because in many ways it is contrary to our ideals of government by the people and the decentralization of power. It is too weak because presidents seldom are able to keep the promises they make. Of course, the presidency is always too strong when we dislike the incumbent. And the presidency is always too constrained when we believe a president is striving to serve the public interest—as we define it!

Americans' mixed views of the job often put our presidents in a "no-win" situation. History suggests there is no foolproof way to guarantee our presidents will possess the appropriate administrative skills as well as the moral character the job requires. On balance, voters have chosen well. Still, James Madison's advice remains useful: "A dependence on the people is, no doubt, the primary control of the government; but experience has taught mankind the necessity of auxiliary precautions" (see *The Federalist*, No. 51 in the Appendix). We must maintain the effectiveness of these "auxiliary precautions"—Congress, parties, the courts, the press, the Bill of Rights, and concerned citizens' groups—if we are to ensure a properly balanced and constitutional presidency.

Thinking it Through

People who believe a president should be immune from civil suits contend that a president's responsibilities are unique, and therefore a president should be protected from distractions such as civil lawsuits until he or she leaves the White House. If a president were subject to such suits, Clinton's lawyer held, this could lead to a flood of frivolous lawsuits that would distract the president from effectively conducting the nation's business. In effect, he maintained, a president should be treated as special, at least while in office, because otherwise his ability to serve the public could be seriously compromised.

The Supreme Court ruled in 1982 that presidents are immune from lawsuits for official acts, yet the court has never granted immunity to a public official for unofficial acts. Lawyers for Paula Jones argue that a president shouldn't be treated differently from any other citizen.

A U.S. Court of Appeals panel in 1996 ruled that the president can be forced to stand trial. In effect they said no citizen, even a president, is above the law. Their decision will be reviewed by the U.S. Supreme Court.

How would you settle the matter? Are the responsibilities of a president different from those of other elected or appointed officials? This complicated and politically explosive case will eventually be settled in the federal courts.

SUMMARY

1. Presidents must act as crisis-managing, morale-building, personnel-recruiting, priority-setting, coalition-building, and managerial leaders. No president can divide the job into tidy compartments. Ultimately, these responsibilities overlap.

2. The office of the president combines a huge presidential establishment, a president's personality, the cultural dilemmas of the day, high popular expectations, and the heavy demands on the chief executive. It is still being reshaped as new presidents with ideas and styles of their own move into the White House.

3. The expansion of presidential powers has been a continual development during the past several decades. Crises, both foreign and economic, have enlarged these powers. When there is a need for decisive action, presidents are asked to supply it. Congress, of course, is traditionally expected to share in the formulation of national policy. Yet Congress is often so fragmented that it has been a willing partner in the growth of the presidency. At the same time, Congress is constantly setting boundaries on how far presidents can extend their influence. Every president must learn anew the need to work closely with the members of Congress.

4. The separation of powers and necessity of sharing decision making, especially in foreign affairs, produce a creative tension between the White House and Congress. Both presidents and Congress have occasionally overstepped their roles in recent years; the process is never neat and tidy; complete accord is only sometimes achieved. Yet the two branches do cooperate, and somehow the business of government does get done.

5. Several factors can cause conflict in our system of divided government. Among them are constitutional ambiguities, different constituencies, varying terms of office, divided party control of the different branches, weak party discipline, and fluctuating support for Congress or the president.

6. Presidents generally exercise more leadership in foreign and national security policy than does Congress, and generally, though not always, Congress is more supportive of presidential requests in these areas. These tendencies have led to the notion that there are "two presidencies"—a stronger, more successful one in foreign affairs and a weaker, less successful one in domestic policy.

7. The overriding task of American citizens is to bind presidents to the majority's will without shackling them. To expect too much of our presidents may be to weaken them in the leadership tasks we need them to perform. To require immediate accountability might paralyze the presidency. Presidential leadership, properly defined, must be more than the power to persuade and less than the power to coerce. It must be the power to achieve by democratic and constitutional means results acceptable to the people.

FURTHER READING

DAVID GRAY ADLER AND LARRY N. GEORGE, EDS., *The Constitution and the Conduct of American Foreign Policy: Essays on Law and History* (University Press of Kansas, 1996).

JAMES DAVID BARBER, *The Presidential Character*, 4th ed. (Prentice Hall, 1992).

JON R. BOND AND RICHARD FLEISHER, *The Presidents in the Legislative Arena* (University of Chicago Press, 1990).

PAUL BRACE AND BARBARA HINCKLEY, *Follow the Leader* (Basic Books, 1992).

THOMAS E. CRONIN, *The State of the Presidency*, 2d ed. (Little, Brown, 1980).

THOMAS E. CRONIN, ED., *Inventing the American Presidency* (University Press of Kansas, 1989).

TERRY EASTLAND, *Energy in the Executive* (Free Press, 1992).

LOUIS FISHER, *Constitutional Conflicts Between Congress and the President*, 3d ed. (University Press of Kansas, 1991).

LOUIS FISHER, *Presidential War Power* (University Press of Kansas, 1995).

MICHAEL GENOVESE, *The Dilemmas of Presidential Leadership* (HarperCollins, 1995).

CHARLES O. JONES, *The Presidency in a Separated System* (Brookings Institution, 1994).

SAMUEL KERNELL, *Going Public: New Strategies of Presidential Leadership* (Congressional Quarterly Press, 1986).

THOMAS S. LANGSTON, *With Reverence and Contempt: How Americans Think About Their President* (Johns Hopkins Press, 1995).

LEONARD W. LEVY AND LOUIS FISHER, EDS., *Encyclopedia of the American Presidency* (Simon & Schuster, 1994).

JOHN A. MALTESE, *Spin Control: The White House Office of Communications and the Management of the Presidential News* (University of North Carolina Press, 1992).

SIDNEY M. MILKIS, *The President and the Parties: The Transformation of the American Party System Since the New Deal* (Oxford University Press, 1993).

MICHAEL NELSON, ED., *Guide to the American Presidency* (Congressional Quarterly Press, 1989).

RICHARD E. NEUSTADT, *Presidential Power and the Modern Presidents* (Free Press, 1991).

MARK A. PETERSON, *Legislating Together: The White House and Capitol Hill from Eisenhower to Reagan* (Harvard University Press, 1990).

JAMES P. PFIFFNER, *The Strategic Presidency: Hitting the Ground Running*, 2d ed. revised (University Press of Kansas, 1996).

GLENN A. PHELPS, *George Washington and American Constitutionalism* (University Press of Kansas, 1993).

JOHN PODHORETZ, *Hell of a Ride: Backstage at the White House Follies, 1989–1993* (Simon & Schuster, 1993).

DAN QUAYLE, *Standing Firm* (Harper Paperbacks, 1995).

MARK J. ROZELL, *Executive Privilege: The Dilemma of Secrecy and Democratic Accountability* (Johns Hopkins Press, 1994).

ARTHUR M. SCHLESINGER, JR., *The Imperial Presidency* (Houghton Mifflin, 1973).

JEAN REITH SCHROEDEL, *Congress, The President and Policymaking* (M.E. Sharpe, 1994).

ROBERT SPITZER, *The President and Congress: Executive Hegemony at the Crossroads of American Government* (McGraw-Hill, 1993).

KENNETH T. WALSH, *Feeding the Beast: The White House versus the Press* (Random House, 1996)

THOMAS J. WEKO, *The Politicizing Presidency: The White House Personnel Office, 1948–1994* (University Press of Kansas, 1995).

BOB WOODWARD, *The Agenda: Inside the Clinton White House* (Simon & Schuster, 1994).

THE JUDICIARY: THE BALANCING BRANCH

I t was not an inspiring occasion. The few people present could hardly know they were witnessing the first meeting of what was to become the most important court in the world, the Supreme Court of the United States. It began on February 2, 1790. Chief Justice John Jay from New York, Justice James Wilson from Pennsylvania, and Justice William Cushing from Massachusetts were the only three of the original six appointees who made it through the snowy roads to New York City. They met in the Royal Exchange Building, an open-air market for butchers, which was the seat of the new federal government. The term lasted ten days, there were no cases to hear, and there was no quorum. The time was devoted to the admission of lawyers to practice before the Court.[1]

Four years later, Chief Justice John Jay resigned, in part because the federal court system lacked "energy, weight, and dignity," and in part to become governor of New York. But by the end of Chief Justice John Marshall's service (1801–1835), the Supreme Court had taken its place as a coequal third branch of the federal government. In fact, foreigners are often amazed at the power Americans give their judges, especially their federal judges. In 1834, after his visit to the United States, French aristocrat Alexis de Tocqueville wrote: "If I were asked where I place the American aristocracy, I should reply without hesitation . . . that it occupies the judicial bench and bar.... Scarcely any political question arises in the United States that is not resolved, sooner or later, into a judicial question."[2] A century later the English writer Harold Laski observed, "The respect in which federal courts and, above all, the Supreme Court are held is hardly surpassed by the influence they exert on the life of the United States."[3]

Why do judges play such a central role in our political life? One reason, as we saw in Chapter 1, is that in *Marbury v Madison* (1803), Chief Justice John Marshall successfully claimed for judges the power of **judicial review,** that is, the power to interpret the Constitution authoritatively. Only a constitutional amendment or a later Supreme Court can modify the Court's doctrine. Justice Felix Frankfurter once put it tersely: "The Supreme Court is the Constitution."

Besides exercising the power of judicial review, judges—and not just those on the Supreme Court—resolve disputes involving millions of dollars, decide conflicts among interests, supervise the criminal justice system, and make rules that affect the lives of millions of people. They are not only resolvers of legal conflicts; through their equity powers they have, in effect, become managers of schools, prisons, mental hospitals, and complex businesses.[4] Sometimes, in fact, they decide the details of how these institutions should be run. Still, the role of our judges is limited by the scope and nature of judicial power.

THE SCOPE OF JUDICIAL POWER

The American judicial process rests on an *adversary system.* A court of law is a neutral arena in which two parties argue their differences and present their points of view before an impartial arbiter. The adversary system, or *fight theory,* may or may not be adequate to arrive at the truth, but it is the basis of our judicial system. The logic of the adversary system imposes formal restraints on the scope of judicial power, and its rhetoric leads us to conceive the role of the judge in a special way.

Judicial power is essentially *passive.* Judges cannot reach out and instigate a case. Further, not all disputes are within the scope of judicial power. Judges decide only **justiciable disputes**—those that grow out of actual cases and are capable of settlement by legal methods. Not all constitutional disputes are justiciable. Some raise **political questions,** which require knowledge of a nonlegal character, or the use of techniques not suitable for a court, or are explicitly assigned by the Constitution to Congress or the president. Which of two competing state governments is the proper one? What does the Constitution mean when it provides that the national government should guarantee to each state a republican form of state government? Which group of officials of a foreign nation should be recognized by the United States as the government of that nation?[5] These are all *political questions.*

Judges are not supposed to use their power unless there is a real *case or controversy.* "It was never thought that, by means of a friendly suit, a party beaten in the legislature could transfer to the courts an inquiry as to the constitutionality of a legislative act."[6] (This, of course, is exactly what is done in nonfriendly suits. In such cases, however, the two parties have an interest in getting the full facts before the court.) In addition, litigants must have *standing to sue;* that is, they must have sustained or be in immediate danger of sustaining a direct and substantial injury. It is not enough merely to have a general interest in a subject or to believe that a law is unconstitutional.[7]

Of increasing importance in recent years are **class action suits** in which a small number of persons are allowed to represent all other persons similarly situated—a suit on behalf of all students in a university, for example, or all patients in a hospital, or all persons who bought a particular model of an automobile. "Would-be class action litigants must show that they are proper representatives for the class of persons they seek to champion, that the types of issues they wish to raise are common to the class, and they must be able to demonstrate how a remedy can be formed that will meet the needs of the class."[8]

Do Judges Make Law?

"Do judges make law? Course they do. Made some myself," remarked Jeremiah Smith, judge of the New Hampshire Supreme Court.[9] Most judges, even today, are less candid. Judges obviously make law, but to admit it is somehow disturbing. Such statements do not conform to our notions of what a judge should do.

Why do we think judges should not make law? Many people equate a judge's role with that of a referee in a prizefight. We expect referees to be impartial and disinterested, to treat both parties as equals. We expect them to apply rules, not make them.

Laws are not made, however, in the same way as the rules of a sport, and herein lies the answer to our question. Not only *do* judges make law, but they *must.* Legislatures make law by enacting statutes, but judges apply statutes to concrete situations. In some cases, applicability is clear: "If anything is a vehicle, a motor-car is one."[10] But does the word "vehicle" in a statute include bicycles,

---

Types of Law

Statutory Law
Law that comes from authoritative and specific law-making sources, primarily legislatures but also including treaties and executive orders.

Common Law
Judge-made law that originated in England in the twelfth century, when royal judges traveled around the country settling disputes in each locality according to prevailing custom. The common law continues to develop according to the rule of *stare decisis,* which means "Let the decision stand." This is the rule of precedent, which implies that a rule established by a court is to be followed in all similar cases.

Equity Law
Law used whenever common law remedies are inadequate. For example, if an injury done to property may do irreparable harm for which money damages cannot provide compensation, under equity a person may ask the judge to issue an injunction ordering the offending person not to take the threatened action. If the wrongdoer persists, he or she may be punished for contempt of court.

Constitutional Law
Statements interpreting the United States Constitution that have been given Supreme Court approval.

Admiralty and Maritime Law
Law applicable to cases concerning shipping and waterway commerce on the high seas and on the navigable waters of the United States.

Administrative Law
Law relating to the authority and procedures of administrative agencies as well as to the rules and regulations issued by those agencies.

Criminal Law
Law that defines crimes against the public order and provides for punishment. Government is responsible for enforcing criminal law, the great body of which is enacted by states and enforced by state officials in state courts. However, the criminal caseload of federal judges is growing.

Civil Law
Law that governs the relations between individuals and defines their legal rights. However, the government can also be a party to a civil action. Under the Sherman Antitrust Act, for example, the federal government may initiate civil as well as criminal action to prevent violations of the law.

---

airplanes, and roller skates? A judge is constantly faced with situations that possess some features of similar cases but lack others. Statutes are drawn in broad terms: drivers shall act with "reasonable care"; no one may make "excessive noise" in the vicinity of a hospital; employers must maintain "safe working conditions." Such broad terms must be used because legislators cannot know exactly what will happen in the future.

These problems are intensified when judges are asked—as American judges are—to apply the Constitution, which was written more than two hundred years ago. The Constitution is full of generalizations: "due process of law," "equal protection of the laws," "unreasonable searches and seizures," "Commerce ... among the several States." Recourse to the intent of the framers or just to the words of the Constitution is not likely to help judges faced with cases involving electronic wiretaps, multinational corporations, or birth control pills.

Adherence to Precedent

Just because judges make policy, however, does not mean they are free to make it as they wish. They are subject to a variety of limits on what they decide—some imposed by the political system of which they are a part, some by their own professional obligations as lawyers. Among these constraints is the rule of *stare decisis,* the rule of precedent.

Stare decisis pervades our judicial system. Judges are expected to abide by all previous decisions of their own courts and all rulings of superior courts. Although adherence to precedent is normal, the doctrine of *stare decisis* is not nearly as restrictive as some people think.[11] Consider, for example, the father who, removing his hat as he enters a church, says to his son: "This is the way to behave on such occasions. Do as I do."[12] Like the judge trying to follow a precedent, the son has a wide range of possibilities open to him. How much of his father's behavior must be imitated? Does it matter if the hat is removed slowly or quickly? If the hat is put under the seat? If it is not replaced on the head inside the church? The judge can distinguish precedents by stating that a previous case does not control the immediate one because of differences in context. In addition, many areas of law have conflicting precedents, one of which can be chosen to support a decision for either party.

The doctrine of *stare decisis* is even less controlling in the field of constitutional law. Because the Constitution itself, rather than any one interpretation of it, is binding, the Court can reverse a previous decision it no longer wishes to follow, as it has done dozens of times. Supreme Court justices are, therefore, not seriously restricted by *stare decisis.* As Justice John Marshall Harlan told a group of law students, "I want to say to you young gentlemen that if we don't like an act of Congress, we don't have too much trouble to find grounds for declaring it unconstitutional."[13]

FEDERAL JUSTICE

"The judicial Power of the United States," says Article III of the Constitution, "shall be vested in one supreme Court, and in such inferior Courts as the Congress may from time to time ordain and establish." Courts created to carry out this judicial power are called *Article III* or *constitutional courts.* Congress may also establish *Article I* or *legislative courts* to carry out the legislative powers the Constitution has granted to it. The main difference between a legislative and a constitutional court is that the judges of the former need not be appointed to "hold their Offices during good Behavior" and may be assigned other than purely judicial duties.

The Constitution requires a Supreme Court. It is a necessity if the national government is to have the power to frame and enforce laws superior to those of the states. The lack of such an agency to maintain national supremacy, to ensure uniform interpretation of national legislation, and to resolve conflicts among the states was one of the glaring deficiencies of the central government under the Articles of Confederation.

Congress decides whether there will be national courts in addition to the one Supreme Court created by the Constitution. The Constitution also allows Congress to determine the size of the Supreme Court. The First Congress divided the nation into districts and created lower national courts for each district. That decision, though often supplemented, has never been seriously questioned.

Federal Courts of General Jurisdiction

Today the hierarchy of national courts of general jurisdiction consists of district courts, courts of appeals, and one Supreme Court (see Figure 12–1). Although the Supreme Court and its justices receive most of the attention, the workhorses of the federal judiciary are the district courts within the states, in the District of Columbia, and in the territories. Each state has at least one district court. Larger states have as many as the demands of judicial business and the pressure of politics require, although no state has more than four.

There are 623 permanent district judges organized into 94 district courts in the 50 states, in the District of Columbia, and the Commonwealth of Puerto Rico. There are also territorial district courts in Guam, the U.S. Virgin Islands, and the Northern Mariana Islands. Each has at least 2 judges, but may have as many as 28. District judges normally hold court by themselves. Except for the three territorial courts that are Article I courts, all district judges, like all Article III federal judges, hold office for life.

District courts are trial courts of **original jurisdiction.** They are the only federal courts that regularly employ **grand juries** (indicting) and **petit juries** (trial). Many cases tried before district judges involve citizens of different states, and the judges apply the appropriate state laws. Otherwise, district judges are concerned with federal laws. For example, they hear and decide cases involving crimes

"It's nothing personal, Prescott. It's just that a higher court gets a kick out of overturning a lower court."

Saturday Review, June 24, 1967.

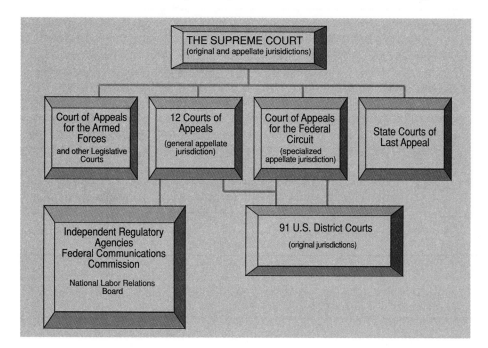

FIGURE 12-1   The Structure of the Federal Courts

Factors Constraining Federal Judges

- The Constitution
- Precedent (*stare decisis*)
- Statutory law
- Legal thought as found in books and law reviews
- Opinions of other courts
- Interest groups
- Public opinion
- Media opinion
- Views of colleagues
- Views of law clerks
- Contemporary events and general social environment
- Traditions of the law
- Actions of the legislature, past and future
- Actions of executives, past and future
- Limitations of time and staffing

These factors are not listed in any particular order. Some weigh more heavily at one time than at another, and on some judges more than on others.

against the United States—suits under the national revenue, postal, patent, copyright, trademark, bankruptcy, and civil rights laws.[14]

District judges are assisted by clerks, bailiffs, stenographers, law clerks, court reporters, probation officers, and United States magistrate judges. All these officials are appointed by the judges. The 406 full-time and 85 part-time *federal magistrate judges* are increasingly important.[15] After being screened by panels composed of residents of the judicial districts, full-time magistrates are appointed for eight-year renewable terms, part-time magistrates for four-year renewable terms.

Magistrates "look like a judge, act like a judge, and speak like a judge."[16] Magistrates, most of whom wear robes and since 1990 are called "Judge," issue warrants for arrest, hold hearings to determine whether arrested persons should be held for action by the grand jury, and, if so, set bail. They hear motions subject to varying kinds of review by their district judges. They preside over civil trials—jury and non-jury—with the consent of both parties, and over non-jury trials for petty offenses with the consent of the defendants.[17] Under the supervision of the district judge, and with the consent of the accused, they may preside over the selection of a jury for a felony trial.[18]

Except for the few cases that may be taken directly to the Supreme Court, a final decision of a district court is reviewable by a *court of appeals*. The United States is divided into 12 *judicial circuits*, one of which is the District of Columbia (see map). Each has a court of appeals consisting of 6 to 28 permanent judgeships (167 in all). The Court of Appeals for the Federal Circuit has national jurisdiction. Each court of appeals normally hears cases in panels of three, but for especially important and controversial cases all judges may be present, that is, they may sit *en banc*.

From Coast to Coast

The Thirteen Federal Judicial Courts

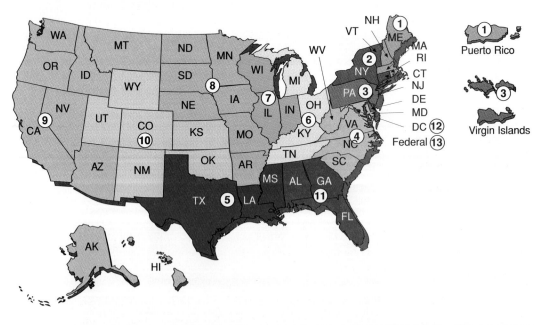

SOURCE: *The Federal Register.*

The Court of Appeals for the Ninth Circuit, the largest, has 28 circuit judges and 99 district judges who serve in California, Arizona, Nevada, Oregon, Washington, Idaho, Montana, Alaska, and Hawaii. The Ninth's liberalism often brings it into conflict with the more conservative United States and California supreme courts. Republicans are trying to split the Ninth, ostensibly because it is too large, but the battle is also over politics and public policy. The proposal currently before the U.S. Senate and House leaves only California, Hawaii, Guam, and the Northern Marinas in the Ninth. The northwestern states, along with Arizona and Nevada (Arizona and Nevada were added to the proposed new circuit in order to get the votes of the senators from those states) would become a new Twelfth circuit.[19] Senators from those states would have more influence over future nominations in their circuit. Proponents of the change hope it would also "isolate and diminish the power of progressive judges" from California left in the Ninth.[20] The mining and oil interests from the Northwest hope to remove judges from California who tend to be rigorous on environmental issues.

The last circuit to be divided was the old Fifth Circuit, which covered the Deep South. In 1981 it was split; Texas, Louisiana, and Mississippi remained in the Fifth, and Georgia, Florida, and Alabama became the Eleventh Circuit. This split was opposed by some of the more liberal judges who had presided over the abolition of public school segregation.

Courts of appeals have only **appellate jurisdiction**, the authority to review decisions of the district courts within their circuits and also some of the actions of the independent regulatory agencies, such as the Federal Trade Commission. These courts are powerful policy makers.[21] Less than 1 percent of the cases from these courts are looked at carefully by the Supreme Court. As the policy role of federal courts has become a prominent political issue, more attention is being focused on these courts and the judges who serve on them.[22]

State and Federal Courts

In addition to federal courts, each state maintains a judicial system of its own, and many large municipalities have judicial systems as complex as those of the states. State courts have sole jurisdiction to try all cases not within the judicial power the Constitution grants to the United States.

The federal and state court systems are related, but they do not exist in a superior-inferior relationship. Except for the limited **habeas corpus** jurisdiction of the district courts (the power to release persons from custody if the judge is not satisfied that the person is being constitutionally detained), the Supreme Court is the only federal court that may review state court decisions. And it may do so only under special conditions.

Other than the original jurisdiction the Constitution vests directly in the Supreme Court, no federal court has any jurisdiction except that granted to it by act of Congress. Congress also determines whether this judicial power of the United States will be exercised exclusively by federal courts or concurrently by both federal and state courts.

PROSECUTION AND DEFENSE

Federal Lawyers

Judges decide cases; they do not prosecute persons. That job, on the federal level, falls to the Department of Justice: the attorney general, the solicitor general, the 94 United States attorneys, and some 1,200 assistant attorneys. The president, with the consent of the Senate, appoints a United States attorney for each district court. United States attorneys serve a four-year term but may be dismissed by the president at any time. These appointments are of great interest to senators, who exercise significant influence over the selection process through **senatorial courtesy**—the presidential custom of submitting the names of prospective appointees for approval to senators from the states in which the appointees reside. Because U.S. attorneys are almost always members of the president's political party, it is customary for them to resign if the opposition party wins the White House.

The attorney general, in consultation with the U.S. attorney in each district, appoints assistant attorneys. Some districts have only one; the largest, the Southern District of New York, has more than 65. These attorneys, working with the U.S. attorney and assisted by the Federal Bureau of Investigation and other federal law-enforcement agencies, begin proceedings against those alleged to have broken federal laws. They also represent the United States in civil suits.

Prosecutors and the Solicitor General

Prosecutors decide whether to charge an offense and which offense to charge. They have largely unreviewable discretion. "So long as the prosecutor has probable cause to believe that the accused committed an offense defined by statute, the decision whether or not to prosecute, and what charge to file or bring before a grand jury, generally rests entirely in his [or her] discretion."[23]

Prosecutors negotiate with the lawyers for **defendants** (those accused of an offense) and often work out a **plea bargain** whereby defendants agree to plead guilty to one offense to avoid having to stand trial for a more serious offense. Prosecutors make recommendations to judges about what sentences to impose.

Attorneys from the Department of Justice and from other federal agencies participate in well over half the cases on the Supreme Court's docket. Of special importance is the *solicitor general* (SG), who represents the government before the Supreme Court. (When the SG appears before the Supreme Court, he wears a formal dark vest, tails, and striped pants.) When the solicitor general petitions the Supreme Court and asks it to review an opinion of a lower court, the Court is likely to do so. "Overall, the government is involved in about two-thirds of all cases heard during a term, and the solicitor general's record of wins has been fairly consistent in the past decade. About 75 percent of all rulings goes his way."[24] Moreover, no appeal may be taken by the United States to any appellate court without the approval of the solicitor general.[25]

Although the solicitor general reports to the attorney general and has always been responsive to the views of the president, the SG (sometimes called the "Tenth Justice") has traditionally been given some measure of independence from the White House. In recent decades that independence has been reduced. The Reagan administration used the SG to carry its social policy agenda to the Supreme Court—to try to persuade the justices, for example, to limit affirmative action and to restrict the right of women to have abortions.[26] The Clinton administration's first solicitor general, Drew S. Days, with his staff of 23 lawyers, continued in the activist manner of his immediate predecessors in the Reagan and Bush administrations, although on the opposite side on many issues.[27] His office became embroiled with the Republican-controlled Senate Judiciary Committee over whether it properly came to the aid of states in cases before the Supreme Court contending that they had invaded the constitutional rights of prisoners.[28]

A Department of Justice office that is becoming increasingly important is the *assistant attorney general*, who heads up the Office of Legal Counsel. The OLC is "the principal legal guardian in the executive branch of the constitutional prerogatives and powers of the presidency"[29] and works closely with the Office of the Counsel to the President located in the White House.

Federal Defense Lawyers

The federal government also provides lawyers for poor defendants in criminal trials. Each district court has some discretion as to how to provide this assistance. Most districts use the traditional system of assigning a private attorney. About half of the judicial districts, however, have opted to use the **public defender** system. These salaried public defenders operate under the general supervision of the Administrative Office of the United States Courts. The Judicial Conference of the United States has said that the most important problem confronting the federal defender program is lack of money.[30] Congress is now reviewing the effectiveness of these procedures.

The Legal Services Corporation (LSC) provides financial assistance to 323 organizations that furnish legal help to the poor in noncriminal legal matters.[31] The corporation is the center of controversy. There are those, primarily Republicans, who would like to abolish it and who have been able to slash its funding by 30 percent. They have barred it from filing class action suits and thus restricted its role to suing landlords, employers, husbands, or wives in traditional legal battles. On the other side are those, primarily Democrats, who would more adequately fund LSC and would allow it to use class action suits to challenge the status quo. It is governed by an 11-member board of directors appointed by the president with the advice and consent of the Senate. Hillary Rodham Clinton was chair of LSC when her husband was governor of Arkansas.

THE POLITICS OF JUDICIAL SELECTION

The selection of federal judges has always been part of the political process. It makes a difference who serves on the federal courts—a difference in how the Constitution is interpreted and how goods and services and values are distributed. It has always been so, but as the courts have come to play an even more important role in the political process, and as more and more interests—African Americans and women, for example—have become empowered to participate in that process, judicial selection politics have come front and center on the political stage.

The president selects federal judges with the advice and consent of the Senate. Political reality imposes constraints on the president's discretion, and the selection of a federal judge is actually a complex bargaining process. The principal figures involved are the candidates, the president, and the "subpresidency for judicial selection"[32] consisting of key members of the Department of Justice, United States senators, the Standing Committee on the Federal Judiciary of the American Bar Association, party leaders, and, increasingly, interest groups.

Recent presidents have inserted the White House much more directly into the process than did their predecessors. Department of Justice officials and key White House staff have met often to review proposed names. President Clinton, a former professor of constitutional law and a state attorney general, took a special interest in judicial appointments. He took an active role in finding and suggesting nominees to the Supreme Court and the courts of appeals, as did First Lady Hillary Rodham Clinton, also a lawyer.[33]

Before the White House submits names of nominees for the federal district courts to the Senate, the president observes the practice of *senatorial courtesy* by consulting with the senior senator from the president's party in the state. Even a senator from the opposition party is usually consulted. If negotiations are deadlocked between the senators or between the senators and the Department of Justice, a seat may stay vacant for years.[34]

The custom of senatorial courtesy no longer applies to Supreme Court appointments and is not often applied to the selection of judges for the courts of appeals

---

Jurisdiction of the Supreme Court

Original
   In all cases affecting ambassadors, other public ministers, and consuls.
   In cases in which a state is a party.

Appellate
   In all other cases arising under the judicial power of the United States. The Supreme Court has appellate jurisdiction—power to review decisions of other courts—except when Congress determines otherwise.

Jurisdiction of the Federal Courts

Federal Courts can hear and decide cases or controversies in law and equity if:

1. They arise under the Constitution, a federal law, or a treaty.
2. They arise under admiralty and maritime laws.
3. They arise because of a dispute involving land claimed under titles granted by two or more states.
4. The United States is a party to the case.
5. A state is a party to the case (but not if a suit was begun or prosecuted against a state by an individual or a foreign nation).
6. They are between citizens of different states.*
7. They affect the accredited representatives of a foreign nation.

*Congress has chosen to limit this *diversity jurisdiction* of federal courts, as it is called, to cases in which the amount in controversy exceeds $50,000.

The Liability Revolution: The Tort Law Explosion

In recent decades, there has been a huge increase in *tort law*, that part of civil law covering the liability of those whose conduct injures others and the compensation they must pay.

"Throughout most of American history, liability law has been an obscure legal byway . . . with little discernible effect on the wider society or economy."* Today liability has dramatically expanded, and the targets are mainly manufacturers, physicians, hospitals, towns, and counties, and their insurance carriers.

Judges have played a leading role in this liability revolution, to the praise of some who believe judges have provided protection for the weak against the powerful, to the criticism of others who believe judges have usurped legislative responsibilities and impaired the effectiveness of our economy.

This is yet another example of the important role judges play. They not only resolve disputes between individuals, but in so doing they are central policy makers.

*Walter Olson, "The Liability Revolution: New Directions in Liability Law," *Proceedings of the Academy of Political Science* 37, no. 1 (1988), p. 1.

because these judges do not serve in any one senator's domain. This difference in selection politics means that district court judges often reflect values different from those of persons appointed to the courts of appeal or the Supreme Court.[35]

President Clinton has given Democratic senators "clear guidelines about the kind of judges he wants."[36] These senators, however, have taken the initiative and sent names to the Department of Justice, rather than wait for names to be cleared with them. Most senators consult with screening panels they appoint. After the Republicans took control of the Senate in 1994, President Clinton, "using an approach that would have been unthinkable in recent administrations," instructed his "judge-pickers" to consult closely with Senator Orrin Hatch, chair of the Senate Judiciary Committee, and with "hostile senators to assuage their fears." Clinton dropped from consideration any candidates who were likely to "engender serious opposition," such as law professor Peter Edelman, husband of Marian Wright Edelman of the Children's Defense Fund.[37] As a result of Clinton's cooperative attitude, he moved quickly to fill the vacancies and was able to appoint 185 judges during his first three years.

The American Bar Association's Standing Committee on the Federal Judiciary plays a special role in the appointment process. Presidents are hesitant to submit for Senate confirmation a candidate rated "not qualified" by the ABA. During an earlier period, the American Bar Association was thought to introduce a bias favoring the conservative "corporation lawyer" into the selection process. In recent years, however, conservative groups have mounted an attack on the ABA's role, contending it reflects a liberal bias and gives low ratings to "sandbag conservative nominees." Bob Dole made the role of the ABA an issue in his campaign, saying, "It is time to remove the American Bar Association from its role in reviewing potential judicial appointees . . . In place of the narrowly partisan and ideologically liberal ABA, I will create a nonpartisan Judicial Integrity Panel, consisting of police, prosecutors, crime victims, legal scholars, and representatives of other legal and professional organizations."[38]

Liberal interest groups, such as People for the American Way and Alliance for Justice, as well as conservative groups, such as the Heritage Foundation and the Free Congress Foundation's Judicial Monitoring Project, have become active in the preliminaries, making known their views about nominees even before the names are released to the public or sent to the Senate Judiciary Committee for confirmation.[39]

The Senate: Advice and Consent

The normal presumption is that the president should be allowed considerable discretion in the selection of federal judges. Despite this presumption, the Senate takes seriously its responsibility to confirm presidential nominations, especially when the party controlling the Senate is different from that of the president.

Most nominations, especially those for the lower federal courts, are processed without much controversy, especially when a president whose party controls the Senate nominates a highly qualified candidate. This action usually results "in a lopsided, consensual vote." When the president nominates a less well-qualified candidate, especially when the president and a majority of the Senate are from different political parties, "then a conflictual vote is likely."[40]

The major battle over judicial confirmations, if there is one, ordinarily takes place before the Senate Judiciary Committee. The Senate usually goes along with the recommendations of its Judiciary Committee without much debate. Yet floor debates are not all that rare. Overall, the Senate has refused to confirm 29 of the 138 presidential nominations for Supreme Court justices, including 7 in this century.[41]

Prior to 1955, only two nominees for the Supreme Court made personal appearances before the Senate Judiciary Committee: Harlan Fiske Stone in 1925 and Felix Frankfurter in 1939. The common practice was for the Senate to look into candidates' qualifications and background yet not examine them in person. More recently, the committee has felt free to ask judicial candidates a full range of questions, since it is now crystal clear that a candidate's political orientation is the major factor in determining how he or she will vote on the cases that come before the Court. Except for Robert Bork, nominated by President Ronald Reagan in 1987, judicial nominees have steadfastly refused to answer questions when the answer might reveal how they would decide a case likely to come up to the Supreme Court. Judge Bork had written so many articles, made so many speeches, and decided so many cases that he thought he had to clarify his constitutional views. His candor may well have contributed to the Senate's rejection of him and is likely to scare off future nominees from responding to similar questions.

The Role of Party, Race, and Sex

Presidents so seldom nominate judges from the opposing party (around 90 percent of judicial appointments since the time of Franklin Roosevelt have gone to persons from the president's party) that partisan considerations are taken for granted and partisan affiliation is rarely mentioned (see Table 12-1). Today journalists pay more attention to other characteristics, such as race and sex.

President Jimmy Carter, who had no opportunity to appoint anyone to the Supreme Court, selected more African Americans, Hispanics, and women for the lower federal courts than all prior presidents combined—40 women, 38 African Americans, and 16 Hispanics. President Ronald Reagan, although the first to appoint a woman to the Supreme Court, appointed fewer minority members or women than did Carter, perhaps in part because fewer minorities and women could pass the Reagan administration's ideological screening. Twenty percent of

TABLE 12-1

Party Affiliation of District and Appeals Judges Appointed by Presidents from Franklin Roosevelt to Bill Clinton

President	Party	Appointees from Same Party
Roosevelt	Democrat	97%
Truman	Democrat	92
Eisenhower	Republican	95
Kennedy	Democrat	92
Johnson	Democrat	96
Nixon	Republican	93
Ford	Republican	81
Carter	Democrat	90
Reagan	Republican	94
Bush	Republican	89
Clinton	Democrat	89*

SOURCE: Sheldon Goldman, "Judicial Selection under Clinton: A Midterm Examination," *Judicature* 78 (May/June 1995), p. 280.

*Figures for President Clinton are for nominations through 1994. Figures for other presidents are for confirmed appointments.

The confirmation hearings of Clarence Thomas became a much-watched event because of the charges of sexual harassment raised by Anita Hill. Ms. Hill had worked for Thomas, and her comments before the all-male Senate Judiciary committee divided the nation. The Senate and the public were left with the choice of whom to believe, Ms. Hill or Mr. Thomas.

The Role of a Federal Judge

"What is it like to be a judge? Most of the time it is very satisfying. One enjoys the prestige. Courtrooms contain every symbol of authority that a set designer could imagine. Everyone stands up when you come in. You wear a costume identifying you as, if not quite divine, someone special. Attendants twitter all around. Most striking, at every sitting, at least two highly trained lawyers, whose job it is to talk, who love to talk, allow you to interrupt them whenever you want.

There are negatives, of course. We have been known to get frivolous cases, or splendidly prepared ones that are nevertheless boring almost beyond belief. Also, the system is designed to maximize the judge's anxiety—that he has just made a mistake, or is about to. It is not just that (as the egg sorter complained about his job) it is "decisions, decisions, decisions all day long"; it is that the system is designed to ensure that the questions presented to us are the hardest to resolve. Seeking a judicial solution to a problem is usually an act of last resort.

The judicial system is the most expensive machine ever invented for finding out what happened and what to do about it. When we judges get a question, it is almost always (a) very important, and (b) a tough case that is close enough to drive one mad. Hence the craft is hard. Much tension accompanies the job of deciding the questions that all the rest of the social matrix has found too hard to answer. But the effort is worth it. For the job of adjudication is to decide those questions according to particular rules and free of the influences that often affect decisions made outside the courtroom. We represent a third value that is not, and is trusted not to be, the prisoner of either wealth or popular prejudice.

Thus all the pleasing mummery in the courtroom, all our political insulation, indeed all our power, is designed to support a message: "Whichever side you're on, we are not on your side or your opponent's side; you must persuade us not that you've got money or that you've got votes, but that your cause is lawful and just." That is a role worth fulfilling."

SOURCE: From an address by Irving R. Kaufman, chief judge of the U.S. Court of Appeals for the Second Circuit, reprinted in *Time*, May 5, 1980, p. 70.

George Bush's appointees were women, 7 percent African Americans, and 4 percent Hispanics.[42]

Bill Clinton lived up to his pledge to appoint federal judges who would be more "representative" of the ethnic makeup of the United States. "There will not be an ideological blood test, like there was during the Reagan and Bush years, to see if the candidate is a moderate or liberal," said a prominent Democratic member of the Senate Judiciary Committee, "but there will be an insistence upon diversity."[43] President Clinton was slow in making his initial appointments, but by the end of 1996 he had appointed 187 federal judges, almost half of whom were women or minorities.[44]

The Role of Ideology

Finding a party member is not enough; presidents want to pick the "right" kind of Republican or "our" kind of Democrat to serve as judge. By and large they have been able to achieve this goal. Republican judges picked by Republican presidents tend to be judicial conservatives (with the notable exception of President Dwight Eisenhower's nomination of Chief Justice Earl Warren), and most Democratic judges picked by Democratic presidents are more likely to be liberals. Both of these orientations have been tempered by the fact that judges have had to go through a senatorial confirmation screen that during the administrations of Reagan, Bush, and Clinton was of the opposite persuasion from that of the White House.[45]

When the appointment is to the Supreme Court, the policy orientation of the nominee is likely to be foremost among presidential concerns. As President Abraham Lincoln told Congressman George S. Boutewell when he appointed Salmon P. Chase to the Supreme Court: "We wish for a Chief Justice who will sustain what has been done in regard to emancipation and legal tender."[46] Theodore Roosevelt voiced the same concern about appointing the "correct" person in a letter to Senator Henry Cabot Lodge about Judge Oliver Wendell Holmes, Jr., of the Massachusetts Supreme Judicial Court, whom he was considering for the Supreme Court: "Now I should like to know that Judge Holmes was in entire sympathy with our views, that is with your views and mine. I should hold myself guilty of an irreparable wrong to the nation if I should appoint any man who was not absolutely sane and sound on the great national policies for which we stand in public life."[47]

President Ronald Reagan's two terms made it possible for him to join Presidents Franklin D. Roosevelt and Dwight D. Eisenhower as the only presidents in modern times to appoint a majority of the federal bench. All told, Reagan appointed 346 lifetime judges. Like his predecessors, he was concerned about the ideologies of those he nominated, and his administration acted carefully to nominate only those whose views about the role of the courts and constitutional issues were consistent with Reagan's own.[48] Not only were a large number of judicial conservatives appointed, many of them—because they were comparatively young—will continue to have an effect on judicial policy making well into the next century. (Despite the care given in their selection, the Reagan judges may not be that much more conservative than judges appointed by other presidents.[49])

As President Bush's commitment to conservatism was somewhat less well established than Reagan's, conservatives and their organizations, such as the Heritage Foundation, the Pacific Legal Foundation, and the Federalist Society, focused their attention on Bush's judicial appointments, "turning on the heat . . . so that the Bush administration doesn't squander any opportunity to tip the U.S. Supreme Court further to the right or turn its back on President Reagan's legacy of appointing conservatives to the federal bench."[50] Bush, looking to lower federal and state courts for candidates, appointed 148 district judges, 37 appellate judges, and two Supreme Court justices—David Souter and Clarence Thomas. His appointees were among the most conservative in recent history.[51] Their conservative constitutional views helped consolidate the Court's "turn to the right," a turn President Bill Clinton is trying to reverse.[52]

The Role of Judicial Philosophy

What about a candidate's judicial philosophy? Does a candidate believe that judges should try to interpret the Constitution to reflect what the framers intended and what its words literally say; that is, does the candidate believe in **judicial restraint**? Or does the candidate believe the Constitution cannot and should not be interpreted literally, but rather be adapted to reflect current conditions and philosophies; that is, does the candidate believe in **judicial activism**?

Judicial philosophy is closely related to political ideology. Throughout most of our history, federal courts have been more conservative than Congress, the White House, or state legislatures. Prior to 1937, judicial self-restraint was the battle cry of liberals who objected to judges interpreting the due process clauses of the Fifth and Fourteenth Amendments to strike down many laws passed to protect labor and women and to keep the national and state governments from regulating the economy. These judges broadly construed the words of the Constitution to prevent what they thought to be unreasonable regulations of property.

By the time of Richard Nixon, Ronald Reagan, and George Bush, however, the judicial shoe was on the other foot, and it was conservatives who were advocates of judicial self-restraint. What is wanted, they argued, are judges who will let Congress, the president, and the state legislatures do what they want, unless it clearly contravenes the precise words of the Constitution: regulate or forbid abortions, for example, adopt prayers for public schools, impose capital punishment, or authorize police to engage in wiretapping.

It would be wrong to assume that judicial philosophy is nothing more than another way to argue about political ideology. Some conservatives, for example, favor judicial activism because they want current judges to reverse the last half century of precedents and actively seek to protect property rights from government regulation. Some liberals favor judicial restraint because they believe democracy will flourish when judges stay out of policy debates. Nonetheless, most of the country understands enough about the policy-making role of judges to recognize that the debates about the proper role of the courts and about how to interpret the Constitution are reflections of differing convictions about what policy outcomes are in the public interest. The debate over the Supreme Court's role today is less about activism and restraint than it is about competing conceptions of the proper balance between government authority and individual rights.

Judicial Longevity and Presidential Tenure

Ideology and judicial philosophy affect not only presidents' nominations for the federal courts but also *when* sitting judges choose to retire. Because federal judges serve for life, they may be able to schedule their retirement to allow a president whose views they approve to nominate their successors. Chief Justice Roger B. Taney stayed on the bench long after his health began to fail to prevent President Abraham Lincoln from nominating a Republican. In 1929 Chief Justice William Howard Taft wrote: "I am older and slower and less acute and more confused. However, as long as things continue as they are, and I am able to answer in my place, I must stay on the court in order to prevent the Bolsheviki [Herbert Hoover, a conservative Republican, was in the White House] from getting control."[53]

Although former Chief Justice Warren Burger denied that he retired in 1986 in order to permit President Ronald Reagan to replace him with a constitutional

CONFIRMATION POLITICS

Robert Bork.

David Souter.

Examination of recent nomination battles highlights the interplay of party, race, sex, ideology, and judicial philosophy in the process of selecting and confirming a Supreme Court justice.

The Bork Battle

When Justice Lewis F. Powell, Jr., who had had the swing vote on such critical issues as affirmative action and abortion, announced his retirement as he neared 80 years of age at the end of the term in July 1987, he made it possible for Ronald Reagan to select a justice who could have a decisive vote on many issues. President Reagan quickly nominated Judge Robert Bork, a member of the Court of Appeals for the District of Columbia and a noted jurist and legal scholar. Despite Bork's controversial writings on many current constitutional issues, his scholarly and legal qualifications made it appear initially that he would be confirmed. However, his nomination so offended women's and black organizations that they organized a campaign to block the Bork nomination. After almost four months of national debate, 12 days of acrimonious questioning by the members of the Senate Judiciary Committee, and 23 hours of debate on the Senate floor, the Senate voted 58 to 42 against Bork's confirmation.

The Souter Solution

The political bruises resulting from the Bork confirmation proceedings were traumatic. Political pundits speculated that in the future, presidents would seek noncontroversial candidates for the Supreme Court. This prediction came true in 1990 with George Bush's nominee to replace William J. Brennan, Jr., leader of the liberal bloc on the Supreme Court, who had been able to blunt the conservative impact of Rehnquist, Scalia, and Kennedy. President Bush chose David Souter, who had been on the Court of Appeals for three months and had been a member of the New Hampshire Supreme Court. Educated at Harvard and Oxford, he had written no law articles, made practically no speeches, and lived the secluded life of a sitting judge. When he appeared before the Judiciary Committee, Souter steadfastly refused to answer any questions that might reveal his orientation on abortion and privacy issues, to the frustration of the Senate Democrats. He was confirmed by an overwhelming vote.

The Thomas Tangle

Clarence Thomas.

When Justice Thurgood Marshall retired in 1991, President Bush sent to the Senate the name of a controversial jurist, Judge Clarence Thomas, then sitting on the Court of Appeals for the District of Columbia. Thomas is a conservative African American. Prior to his brief service on the Court of Appeals, he had served as chair of the Equal Employment Opportunity Commission (EEOC) and in the Office of Civil Rights. During five days of grueling questions about his constitutional views, Judge Thomas, as had his predecessor, refused to respond. The Senate Judiciary Committee narrowly recommended his confirmation.

Two days before the Senate was due to vote on his confirmation, documents leaked to the press revealed that a former associate of Judge Thomas, Anita Hill, had accused him of sexually harassing her when she worked for him in the Department of Education and the EEOC. Women's and liberal groups exploded in outrage. There followed three days of dramatic and emotion-charged hearings telecast to the nation in which Judge Thomas categorically denied the charges presented persuasively by his accuser. Panels of witnesses pro and con came forward to testify. Judge Thomas was confirmed by the Senate 52 to 48, the closest Supreme Court confirmation vote in modern times.

The Clinton Choices

Almost as soon as President Clinton took office, Justice Byron White announced he would leave the Court at the end of its 1992–1993 term. It was clear that with this appointment, Clinton could arrest the Court's conservative drift and fulfill his campaign pledge to appoint justices committed to protect the rights of privacy—that is, to preserve a woman's freedom to choose an abortion.

Ruth Bader Ginsburg.

After several months of deliberation, including the rather public consideration of other candidates, President Clinton nominated Ruth Bader Ginsburg. Judge Ginsburg was a 13-year veteran of the Court of Appeals for the District of Columbia, to which she had been appointed by President Carter. On the Court of Appeals she had earned a reputation for fairness and moderation. She was readily confirmed by the Senate and took her seat for the opening of the 1993-1994 term.

Clinton had a second opportunity when Harry A. Blackmun, at age 85, announced his intention to leave the Court during the spring of 1994. Blackmun, best known for writing the opinion in *Roe v Wade*, was thought at first to be a judicial conservative, but by the time of his retirement, he had become the most liberal member of the Court.

The leading candidates were all sitting judges except for Interior Secretary Bruce Babbitt and Senate Majority Leader George Mitchell. After Mitchell withdrew from consideration and Senate opposition developed against Babbitt, President Clinton nominated Stephen G. Breyer, Chief Judge of the First Circuit, a noncontroversial judicial moderate. Justice Breyer, a graduate of Stanford University, Oxford, and Harvard Law School, served as Supreme Court law clerk for Justice Arthur Goldberg and was a member of the faculty at Harvard Law School before being appointed by President Carter as a Federal Appeals Court judge. After a cordial hearing before the Senate Judiciary Committee in July 1994, Breyer was easily confirmed by the Senate.

Stephen G. Breyer.

conservative, his retirement did give Reagan an opportunity to rejuvenate the conservative wing of the Court by promoting the 61-year-old William H. Rehnquist, an articulate constitutional conservative, to replace the 78-year-old Burger. Reagan then picked another constitutional conservative, the 50-year-old Antonin Scalia, from the Court of Appeals for the District of Columbia, to take the seat vacated by Rehnquist.[54] Liberal Supreme Court justices William J. Brennan, Jr., and Thurgood Marshall held onto their seats well into their 80s, and many assumed that they were doing so in the hope that they might be able to stay on the Court until the time that a president more congenial to their views might be in the White House. They did not make it, and their successors were appointed by President Bush rather than by a Democrat.

Reforming the Selection Process

The televised Bork and Thomas confirmation hearings aroused considerable criticism from both liberals and conservatives and created widespread complaints that "something is wrong with the process." Everybody appeared to be dissatisfied with it. Democratic senators were frustrated by their inability to get nominees to explain their judicial philosophies or to reveal their constitutional values. They argued that unless candidates respond about their constitutional philosophy, the Senate should refuse to confirm. Republican senators and the Bush White House accused Senate Democrats of improperly trying to force candidates to commit how they would decide cases and thus jeopardize the independence of the courts and compromise their ability to be impartial judges. Senators, they argued, should content themselves with checking into candidates' integrity and legal background and not ask about political and constitutional orientation or badger candidates to reveal how they might vote on cases that will come before them for decision.[55]

A group of experts agreed that judicial appointments could not and should not be free of political considerations but recommended that an attempt be made to constrain the partisan politics surrounding the confirmation process for Supreme Court justices. They recommended, among other things, that "Supreme Court nominees should no longer be expected to appear as witnesses during the Senate Judiciary Committee's hearings on their confirmation" and that the Senate return to the practice of judging nominees on their written record and on the testimony of legal experts.[56] It is unlikely, however, that there will be any fundamental alteration in the selection process. Presidents of all persuasions are not likely to want to limit their discretion in selecting judges, and their political opponents are not likely to abandon their concern about the judicial views of presidential nominees. As one scholar pointed out:

> The cries to depoliticize the process are not only naive, but perhaps too hastily considered. The apparent decorum of the past was achieved at the expense of participation and accountability. Few who viewed the agony and personal tragedies of the Clarence Thomas proceedings can avoid the almost instinctive desire to return to less visible and contentious proceedings, but the stakes are too high and involve the vital interests of too many forces to seek refuge in the ways of the past.[57]

The politics of judicial selection may shock those who like to think judges are picked strictly in terms of legal merit and without regard for party, race, sex, or ideology. But as a former Justice Department official has said, "When courts cease being an instrument for political change, then maybe the judges will stop being politically selected."[58]

CHANGING THE NUMBERS   Partisan politics also affects decisions about the number of federal judges. One of the first actions of a political party after gaining control of the White House and Congress is to increase the number of federal

1. Courtyards
2. Solicitor General's Office
3. Lawyers' Lounge
4. Marshall's Office
5. Main Hall
6. Court Room
7. Conference and Reception Rooms

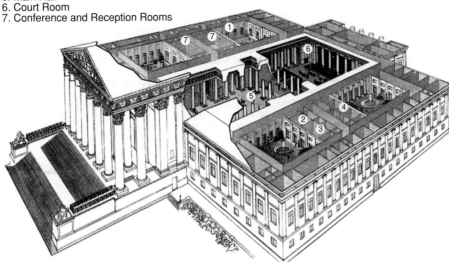

judgeships. With divided government, however, when one party controls Congress and the other holds the White House, a stalemate is likely to occur and relatively few new judicial positions will be created. During Andrew Johnson's administration, Congress went so far as to reduce the size of the Supreme Court to prevent the president from filling two vacancies. After Johnson left the White House, Congress returned the Court to its former size to permit Ulysses S. Grant to fill the vacancies. In 1937, President Franklin Roosevelt proposed an increase in the size of the Supreme Court by one additional justice for every member of the Court over the age of 70, up to a total of 15 members. Ostensibly, the proposal was aimed at making the Court more efficient. In fact, Roosevelt and his advisers were frustrated because the Court had declared much New Deal legislation unconstitutional. Despite Roosevelt's popularity, this "court-packing scheme" aroused intense opposition. Roosevelt's proposals to change the Court's size failed. He lost the battle, but he won the war, as the Court began to sustain some important New Deal legislation.

CHANGING THE JURISDICTION Congressional control over the structure and jurisdiction of federal courts has been used to influence the course of judicial policy making. Although unable to get rid of Federalist judges by impeachment, the Jeffersonians abolished the circuit courts created by the Federalist Congress just prior to their losing control. In 1869 radical Republicans in Congress altered the Supreme Court's appellate jurisdiction in order to snatch from the Court a case it was about to review involving the constitutionality of some Reconstruction legislation.[59]

During the Reagan administration, a number of bills were introduced in Congress either to eliminate the jurisdiction of all federal courts over cases relating to abortion, school prayer, and school busing, or to eliminate the appellate jurisdiction of the Supreme Court over such matters. These bills sparked debate about whether the Constitution gives Congress authority to take such actions. Congress has not yet decided to make what could amount to a fundamental shift in the nature of the relationship between Congress and the Supreme Court.

Thinking it Through

A national telephone survey of 603 adults found that 23 percent of all respondents said that justices' political views *should* influence their decisions, while 69 percent disagreed. When asked how much they think justices' political views influence their decisions, 44 percent responded "a lot," 44 percent answered "somewhat," and 8 percent said "not much."

How do you think responses to these questions vary among respondents with different political views of their own? Twenty-nine percent of liberals, 19 percent of moderates, and 24 percent of conservatives think justices should bring their political views to bear on their decisions. Conservatives are most likely (52 percent) to say justices' political views influence their decisions a lot, followed by moderates at 43 percent and liberals at 39 percent; 35 percent of conservatives, 47 percent of moderates and 50 percent of liberals say justices' decisions are influenced somewhat by their political views.

SOURCE: John M. Scheb, II, and William Lyons, "Public Holds U.S. Supreme Court in High Regard," *Judicature* 77 (March-April 1994), pp. 273–274.

Don't Call Me Judge

A member of the United States Supreme Court is called "Justice," not "Judge," and the chief justice is the "Chief Justice of the United States," not the "Chief Justice of the Supreme Court." Members of the Court call him "The Chief," but nobody else should. In the years before Justice Sandra Day O'Connor was appointed to the Court, justices were often called "Mr. Justice" and were collectively known as "The Brethren." Nowadays "Justice" will do, and so will "Your Honor."

A member of the lower federal court is "Judge," not "Justice." The practice among the states varies, but members of state supreme courts are coming to be called "Justices."

SOURCE: David Margolick, "Here Comes the Chief Justice (Please Don't Call Him Judge)," *The New York Times*, April 26, 1991, p. B1.

The Rise of the Law Clerks

Beginning in the 1930s, federal judges began the practice of hiring the best recent graduates of law schools to serve as clerks for a year or two. As the judicial work load increased, more law clerks have been appointed. Today each Supreme Court justice is entitled to four clerks (circuit judges have three, and each court of appeals has "staff attorneys"). Clerks draft opinions and screen writs of *certiorari*, which determine the cases the Court will review. Justices often talk through their cases with their law clerks.

Law clerks are young and energetic, and they know how to use computers to do research and prepare drafts of opinions. As the number of law clerks and computers has increased, so has the number of concurring and dissenting opinions. Further, today's opinions are longer and have more substantive footnotes and elaborate citations of cases and law review articles. As Justice Harry A. Blackmun said about his colleague, Justice John Paul Stevens, "He uses hundreds of footnotes. Sometimes I think what he does is to outline his opinion, give it to his clerks and say, 'You put the footnotes in,' and of course there's an ego trip for the clerks and they have all kinds of footnotes."*

*Harry A. Blackmun, quoted in Stuart Taylor, Jr., "When High Court's Away, Clerks' Work Begins," *The New York Times*, September 23, 1988, p. 22.

Supreme Court justices are in session from the first Monday in October through the end of June. They listen to oral arguments for two weeks and then adjourn for two weeks to consider the cases and write their opinions. By agreement, six justices must participate in each decision. Cases are decided by a majority. In the event of a tie vote, the decision of the lower court is sustained, although, on rare occasions, the case may be reargued.

At 10:00 A.M. on the days when the Supreme Court sits, the eight associate justices and the chief justice, dressed in their robes, file into the Court. (Chief Justice Rehnquist has four gold stripes on each sleeve of his robe.[60]) As they take their seats—arranged according to seniority, with the chief justice in the center—the clerk of the Court introduces them as the "Honorable Chief Justice and Associate Justices of the Supreme Court of the United States." Those present in the courtroom, asked to stand when the justices enter, are seated, and counsel take their places along tables in front of the bench. The attorneys for the Department of Justice, dressed in formal morning clothes, are at the right. The other attorneys are dressed conservatively; sport coats are not considered proper. Dress and ceremony are all part of the high ritual of the Court:

> The majesty of its courtroom; the black robes of the justices; the ritual of its proceedings at oral argument and on decision day; the secrecy and isolation of its decision-making conferences; the formal opinions invoking the symbols of Constitution, precedent, and framers' intent; and all the other elements of setting and conduct distinguish the Supreme Court, a body of constitutional guardians, from all other government officials.[61]

Which Cases Reach the Supreme Court?

When citizens vow they will take their cases to the highest court of the land even if it costs their last penny, they underestimate the difficulty of securing Supreme Court review, overestimate the cost (although it costs plenty), and reveal a basic misunderstanding of the Court's role. The rules for appealing a case to the Supreme Court are established by act of Congress. Today all appellate cases come before the Court by means of a discretionary **writ of *certiorari***, a formal writ used to bring a case up to the Court. (Until 1988 there were a few types of cases the Supreme Court was obliged by law to review.) In addition, the Constitution stipulates the Supreme Court has original jurisdiction in a few specified situations. But the fact is the Supreme Court has control of its agenda and decides which cases it wants to consider. In recent years the justices have closely reviewed and usually signed opinions in less than one hundred of the thousands of cases presented to them.[62]

It is not enough, for example, that Jones thinks he should have won his case against Smith. There probably has already been at least one appellate review of the trial, either in a federal court of appeals or in a state supreme court. The Supreme Court will review Jones's case only if his claim has broad public significance. For instance, the rulings among the courts of appeals may conflict; by deciding the Jones case, the Supreme Court can establish which rule is to be followed throughout the judicial system. Or Jones's case may raise a constitutional issue on which a state supreme court has presented an interpretation with which the Court disagrees. The crucial factor in determining whether the Supreme Court will hear a case is its importance not to Jones but to the operation of the governmental system as a whole.

The Court accepts cases under the *rule of four*. If four justices are sufficiently interested in a petition for a writ of *certiorari*, the petition will be granted and the case brought forward for review. Nowadays the law clerks (called the "cert pool") read the petitions and write a memorandum on each for circulation to all the justices in the pool. Only Justice John Paul Stevens stays out of the pool, and even he, it is rumored, divides up the cert petitions among his own clerks and reads only a few of them himself.[63]

Denial of a writ of *certiorari* does not mean that the justices agree with the decision of the lower court, nor does it establish precedents. Refusal to grant such a writ may indicate all kinds of possibilities: the justices may not wish to become involved in a political "hot potato," or the Court may be so divided on an issue that it is not yet prepared to take a stand.[64]

Briefs and Oral Arguments

Before a case is heard in open court, the justices receive printed briefs, perhaps hundreds of pages long, in which each side presents legal arguments, historical materials, and relevant precedents. In addition, the Supreme Court may receive briefs from **amici curiae** (literally, "friends of the court"), who may be individuals, organizations, or government agencies that have an interest in the case and claim they have information of value to the Court. This procedure guarantees that the Department of Justice is represented if a suit between two private parties calls the constitutionality of an act of Congress into question. The *amicus curiae* brief is also used by presidents, through the Department of Justice, to see that the views of the current administration are brought to the Court's attention.[65]

Often organizations file *amicus curiae* briefs before the Supreme Court grants a writ of *certiorari* in order to lobby the Supreme Court to review the case. Their doing so enhances the probability that the court will take the case for review,[66] but has almost no influence on how the case is decided.[67] A brief brought by a private party or interest group may help the justices by presenting an argument or point of law that the parties to the case have not raised. Often the briefs are filed as a means of pressuring the Court to reach a particular decision. In the *Bakke* case, in which the Supreme Court dealt substantively with affirmative action issues, 37 *amicus* briefs were filed for the University of California, 16 for Allan Bakke, and 5 that did not take sides. In *Webster v Reproductive Health Services,* argued in the spring of 1989 and dealing with a Missouri law regulating abortions and a request from both Missouri and the solicitor general for the Court to reverse *Roe v Wade,* 78 *amicus* briefs were filed.[68]

In *U.S. v. Lopez,* which challenged congressional authority to ban guns in and around schools, more than 40 parties filed a dozen amicus briefs. Ohio, New York, and the District of Columbia argued in favor of federal powers, as did associations of police chiefs and school officials. On the other side were some conservative public interest firms, the National Governors' Association, and the National League of Cities.[69]

Formal oratory before the Supreme Court, perhaps lasting for several days, is a thing of the past. As a rule, counsel for each side is limited to 30 minutes. Lawyers use a lectern to which two lights are attached. A white light flashes five minutes before time is up; when the red light goes on, the lawyer must stop, even in the middle of an "if."

The entire procedure is formally informal. Sometimes, to the annoyance of attorneys, justices talk among themselves or consult briefs or legal volumes during the oral presentation. Sometimes, if justices find a presentation particularly bad, they ostentatiously consult their watches. Justices freely interrupt the lawyers to ask questions and to request additional information. In recent years, especially with the addition of Justices Scalia and Ginsburg, "The justices seem

"We all make mistakes, as Your Honor knows, having been twice reprimanded by the New York State Commission on Judicial Conduct."

Drawing by Stevenson. © 1981 The New Yorker Magazine, Inc.

barely able to contain themselves, often interrupting the answer to one question with another query."[70] The 30-minute limit is becoming a problem, especially when the solicitor general participates, since his ten minutes comes out of the time of the two parties before the Court.[71]

If a lawyer seems to be having a difficult time, justices may try to help him or her present a better case. Occasionally, justices bounce arguments off a hapless attorney and at one another. Justice Antonin Scalia is a harsh questioner. "When Scalia prepares to ask a question, he doesn't just adjust himself in his chair to get closer to the microphone like the others; he looks like a vulture, zooming in for the kill. He strains way forward, pinches his eyebrows, and poses the question, like '… do you want us to believe….'"[72] Justice Sandra Day O'Connor commented about him, "Some of our members are former law professors and haven't lost their technique of asking questions."[73] Justice Thurgood Marshall did "a terrible job of keeping his mouth away from the mike" when whispering.[74] Justice Ruth Bader Ginsburg, in her early days on the Court, was a particularly persistent questioner, frequently rivaling Justice Scalia in asking the most questions. Justice Clarence Thomas almost never asks a question. Justice David Souter has a thick New England accent. He once asked an attorney during oral arguments in an affirmative action case, "What's the floor?" The attorney hemmed and hawed until, with a smile, Souter said he meant "flaw," not "floor."[75]

Behind the Curtains: The Conference

Wednesday afternoons and all day Friday the justices meet in conference. They have heard the oral arguments, read and studied the briefs, and examined the petitions. Before every conference, each justice receives a list of the cases to be discussed. Each brings to the meeting a red leather book in which the cases and the votes of the justices are recorded. These conferences are secret affairs, although in recent years the secrecy has been penetrated. They are marked by informality and by vigorous give and take; they are both "collegial and substantive."[76] The chief justice presides, usually opening the discussion by stating the facts, summarizing the questions of law, and making suggestions for disposing of the case. Each member of the Court is then asked, in order of seniority, to give his or her views and conclusions. Recently the justices have not

The Supreme Court.

bothered with formal votes because they express their views when they discuss the case.[77]

In a case challenging the constitutionality of a Texas law making it a crime to desecrate the American flag, Chief Justice Rehnquist called his colleagues' attention to an earlier dissent of his in which he had stated, "Flag-burning and fighting words may be punished constitutionally." Justice Brennan disagreed. This was, he argued, a classic case of speech being punished solely because of objection to the message. Justice White was next. He supported Chief Justice Rehnquist; to affirm the decision of the Texas Criminal Court of Appeals declaring the Texas statute to be an unconstitutional abridgment of the First Amendment rights would "run the First Amendment into the ground." Justice Marshall agreed with Brennan. Justice Stevens was "uncharacteristically tentative" and passed without giving his vote. Justice O'Connor appeared to support Justice Brennan: "This is core speech for political purposes." Nonetheless, she said that her decision to affirm the Texas Criminal Court of Appeals was still tentative and she would make a final decision after reading the circulated opinions. Justices Scalia and Kennedy agreed that this was a free-speech case and would affirm the Texas Court ruling declaring the statute unconstitutional. Justice Brennan, as the senior justice in the majority, had the responsibility to prepare the opinion for the Court.[78]

Opinions

As a general rule, Supreme Court opinions state the facts, present the issues, announce the decision, and, most important, explain the reasoning of the Court. These opinions are the Court's principal method of expressing its views to the world. Perhaps the most important function of opinions is to instruct the judges of all other state and federal courts in the United States on how to decide similar cases in the future.

Judicial opinions may be directed at Congress or at the president. If the Court regrets that "in the absence of action by Congress, we have no choice but to . . ." or insists that "relief of the sort that petitioner demands can only come from the political branches of government," it is clearly asking Congress to act.[79] The justices also use opinions to communicate with the public. A well-handled opinion may increase support among specialized groups—especially lawyers and judges—and among the general population for a policy the Court is stressing. For this reason, the Court delayed declaring school segregation unconstitutional until unanimity could be secured. The justices understood that any sign of dissension on the bench on this major social issue would be an invitation to evade the Court's ruling.

ASSIGNING OPINIONS   The justice to whom the writing of an opinion is assigned knows that he or she must influence the outcome, for no vote in conference is final. Justices are free to change their minds if persuaded by the draft opinion. When voting with the majority, the chief justice decides who drafts the opinion. When the chief justice is in the minority, the senior justice among the majority makes the assignment, often to himself or herself. Justices are free to write a **dissenting opinion** if they wish. Dissenting opinions are, in Chief Justice Charles Evans Hughes's words, "an appeal to the brooding spirit of the law, to the intelligence of a later day."[80] Dissenting opinions are common, as justices hope that someday these dissenting opinions will command a majority of the court. If a justice agrees with the majority on how the case should be decided but differs on the reasoning, that justice may write a **concurring opinion**.

CIRCULATING DRAFTS   Writing an opinion for the Court is an exacting task. The document must win the support of at least four—even more, if possible—

TABLE 12-2

Comparison of Dissent Rates

"The Great Dissenters"	Number of Dissenting Opinions
William Johnson, 1804–1834	30
John Catron, 1837–1865	26
Nathan Clifford, 1858–1881	60
John Marshall Harlan, 1877–1911	119
Oliver Wendell Holmes, Jr., 1902–1932	72
Louis D. Brandeis, 1916–1939	65
Harlan F. Stone, 1925–1946	93
Hugo Black, 1937–1971	310
Felix Frankfurter, 1939–1962	251
John Marshall Harlan, 1955–1971	242

The Burger and Rehnquist Courts	
William O. Douglas, 1969–1974	231
John Paul Stevens, 1975–1994	406
William Brennan, Jr., 1969–1990	402
Thurgood Marshall, 1969–1991	315
William H. Rehnquist, 1972–1994	272
Potter Stewart, 1969–1981	130
Byron R. White, 1969–1993	236
Harry A. Blackmun, 1970–1994	257
Antonin Scalia, 1986–1994	63
Lewis F. Powell, Jr., 1971–1987	159
Sandra Day O'Connor, 1981–1994	91
Warren Burger, 1969–1986	111
Anthony M. Kennedy, 1990–1994	45
David Souter, 1990–1994	67
Clarence Thomas, 1991–1994	77
Ruth Bader Ginsburg, 1993–1994	25

SOURCE: David M. O'Brien, *Storm Center: The Supreme Court in American Politics*, 3d ed. (W. W. Norton, 1993); "The Supreme Court, 1994 Term," *Harvard Law Review* 109 (November 1995), p. 352.

intelligent, strong-willed persons, all of whom may have voted the same way but for different reasons. Assisted by the law clerks, the assigned justice writes a draft and sends it to colleagues for comments. If the justice is lucky, the majority will accept the draft, perhaps with only minor changes. If the draft is not satisfactory to the other justices, it must be redrafted and recirculated until a majority can reach agreement.

If the initial version is not acceptable to a majority, an elaborate bargaining process occurs. The opinion ultimately published is not necessarily the opinion the author would have liked to write. Like a committee report, it represents the common denominator. Justice Oliver Wendell Holmes, Jr., bitterly complained to British political scientist Harold J. Laski that he had written an opinion in terms to suit the majority of the brethren, although it did not suit him.

> Years ago I did the same thing in the interest of getting a job done. I let the brethren put in a reason that I thought bad and cut out all that I thought good and I have squirmed ever since, and swore that never again—but again I yield and now comes a petition for rehearing pointing out all the horrors that will ensue from just what I didn't want to say.[81]

The two major weapons justices can use against their colleagues are their votes and their willingness to write separate opinions attacking a doctrine the majority wishes to see adopted. Especially if the Court is closely divided, one justice may be in a position to demand that a given argument be included in, or removed from, the opinion as the price of his or her vote. Sometimes this bargaining occurs even though the Court is not closely divided. An opinion writer who anticipates that a decision will bring critical public reaction may wish to have it presented as the view of a unanimous Court and may be prepared to compromise to achieve unanimity. See Table 12-2 for a comparison of dissent rates in various Courts.

In the Texas flag-salute case, Justice Brennan drafted a narrow opinion in an attempt to win the support of as many of his colleagues as possible. As James F. Simon wrote, "Justice Brennan approached his task of writing the majority opinion in *Texas v Johnson* cautiously. He could anticipate an unflinching opinion from the chief justice defending the government's right to protect the American flag. Justice White had made it clear that he would support the chief. Both O'Connor and Stevens had appeared to lean Brennan's way at conference, but none too confidently; Brennan could not depend on their votes."[82] And Justice Blackmun, "a usually reliable liberal justice," voiced uneasiness about the case in a note to Brennan, three months after the conference.[83] Ultimately, Brennan's draft was endorsed by Justices Kennedy, Blackmun, Marshall, and Scalia, but Justices O'Connor and Stevens, who in conference had kept their vote tentative, dissented. Thus the decision came down five to four against the law.

The Powers of the Chief Justice

The chief justice of the United States is appointed by the president and confirmed by the Senate and holds tenure for life. This method of selecting the chief justice gives him (so far they have all been men) greater visibility than if selected by rotation or by fellow justices, as is the case of the chief in the state supreme court, or by seniority, as is the practice in the federal courts of appeals. But as Chief Justice Rehnquist said when he was still an associate justice, the chief deals not with "eight subordinates whom he may direct or instruct, but eight associates who, like him, have tenure during good behavior, and who are as independent as hogs on ice."[84]

The ability of the chief justice to influence the Court has varied considerably.[85] Chief Justice Charles Evans Hughes ran the conferences like a stern schoolmaster, keeping the justices talking to the point, moving the discussion along, and doing his best to work out compromises. He tried to achieve unanimous votes in order to give decisions greater weight. Chief Justice Harlan F. Stone, on the other hand, encouraged justices to state their own points of view and let discussions wander. Chief Justice Warren Burger devoted much of his time to judicial reform, speaking to bar and lay groups and trying to build political support for modernizing the judicial process.

Chief Justice William H. Rehnquist had 15 years of Court experience prior to his elevation to the post of chief justice. He had demonstrated his personal warmth and charm. He "has not utilized his position as Chief Justice to shape the decisions of the Court,"[86] but as the Reagan-Bush justices are now a majority, his constitutional views, formerly expressed only in his dissenting opinions, are now the opinions of the Court.[87] "The chief justiceship does not guarantee leadership. It only offers its incumbent an opportunity to lead. Optimum leadership inheres in the combination of the office and an able, persuasive, personable judge."[88]

After the Lawsuit Is Over

Victory in the Supreme Court does not necessarily mean that winning parties get what they want. As a rule, the Court does not implement its own decision but "remands," that is, sends back, the case to the lower court with instructions to act in accordance with the Supreme Court's opinion. The lower court often has considerable leeway in interpreting the Court's mandate as it disposes of the case.

Although Congress or a president has occasionally "ignored" or "construed" a Supreme Court ruling to avoid its impact, decisions whose enforcement requires only the action of a central governmental agency usually become effective immediately. Thus, when the Supreme Court held that President Harry Truman lacked constitutional authority to seize steel companies temporarily to avoid a shutdown during the Korean War, the president promptly complied. Of course, subsequent presidents have great discretion in determining how that particular precedent should be applied to them.

The impact of a particular ruling announced by the Supreme Court on the behavior of those who are not immediate parties to a lawsuit is even more uncertain. Many of the more important decisions require further action by administrative and elected officials before they become the effective law of the land. Sometimes Supreme Court decisions are simply ignored. Despite the Supreme Court's holding that it is unconstitutional for school boards to require prayers within schools, for example, some school boards continue their previous practices.[89] And for years after the Supreme Court held public school segregation unconstitutional, many school districts remained segregated.[90]

The most difficult Supreme Court decisions to implement are those that require the cooperation of large numbers of officials. For example, a Supreme Court decision announcing a new standard for warrantless searches is not likely to have an impact on the way police make arrests for some time, since not many police officers subscribe to the *United States Supreme Court Reports*. The process is more complex. Local prosecutors, state attorneys general, chiefs of police, and state and federal trial court judges must all participate to give "meaning" to Supreme Court decisions.

The Constitution may be what the Supreme Court says it is, but a Supreme Court opinion, for the moment at least, is what a trial judge or police officer or a prosecutor or a school board or a city council says it is.

Chief Justice William Hubbs Rehnquist was formerly an assistant attorney general and was an associate justice of the Supreme Court from 1971 to 1986.

TABLE 12-3

U.S. Supreme Court Declarations of Unconstitutionality of Federal Statutes (in Whole or in Part)

Time Span	Chief Justice	Number of Declarations of Unconstitutionality
1798–1801	John Jay	0
	John Rutledge	0
	Oliver Ellsworth	0
1801–1835	John Marshall	1
1836–1864	Roger B. Taney	1
1864–1873	Salmon P. Chase	10
1874–1888	Morrison R. Waite	9
1888–1910	Melville W. Fuller	14
1910–1921	Edward D. White	12
1921–1930	William Howard Taft	12
1930–1936	Charles Evans Hughes	14
1936–1941	Charles Evans Hughes	0
1941–1946	Harlan F. Stone	2
1946–1953	Fred M. Vinson	1
1953–1969	Earl Warren	25
1969–1986	Warren Burger	34
1986–1996	William H. Rehnquist	16
Total		143

SOURCE: Adapted from Henry J. Abraham, *The Judicial Process*, 6th ed. (Oxford University Press, 1993), p. 273; also David M. O'Brien, "The Rehnquist Court and Federal Preemption," *Publius* 23 (1993), pp. 15–31. See also the Law Library of Cornell University on the Internet: http://www.law.cornell.edu/library/default.html.

JUDICIAL POWER IN A CONSTITUTIONAL DEMOCRACY

An independent judiciary is one of the hallmarks of a free society. As impartial dispensers of equal justice under the law, judges should not be dependent on the executive, the legislature, the parties to the case, the electorate, or a mob outside the courtroom. But this very independence, essential to protect judges in their roles as legal umpires, raises basic problems when a democratic society decides—as ours has—also to make these same judges policy makers. Perhaps in no other society do the people resort to litigation as a means of making public policy as much as they do in the United States.

The involvement of our courts in politics exposes the judiciary to political criticism. Throughout our history the Supreme Court has been attacked for engaging in "judicial legislation." This is nothing new. Yet the more active role of the federal courts since 1937 on behalf of liberal causes and the Reagan and Bush administrations' frontal attack on that role have returned these issues to the forefront of public debate.

Since the end of World War II, federal courts under the Supreme Court's leadership have removed most of the constitutional restraints on government regulation of business. At the same time, they have imposed many more restraints to protect civil liberties and civil rights, especially for the poor and minorities. Since 1943 the Supreme Court has declared unconstitutional more than 60 acts of Congress as well as more than 400 acts of state legislatures and city councils. Overall, the Supreme Court has struck down over 140 acts of Congress (see Table 12-3) and almost 1,100 pieces of state legislation and state constitutional provisions. In one 1983 decision, *INS v Chadha*, it called into question 200 provisions of various federal laws.[91]

Whereas in earlier times judges occasionally told public officials what they could not do, today they often tell them what they *must* do. For example, federal judges, responding to class action complaints, have told Congress, state legislatures, and local officials that they must provide attorneys for the poor, ensure adequate care for mental patients, modernize prisons, and even break up the telephone system (in this last case the Department of Justice initiated the action). Often judges retain jurisdiction for years as they preside over the implementation of the decrees they have issued.[92] Judges have always been policy makers; that role is not a matter of choice but flows from the roles they play in deciding cases. But today they also govern.[93]

The Great Debate over the Proper Role of the Courts

Some people contend that the courts have a duty to protect the long-range interests of the public as defined in the Constitution, even against the short-range wishes of the voters (but then what is and is not defined by the Constitution is the issue). Defenders of this activist judicial role argue that if Congress, the White House, and the state legislatures are unable to resolve pressing problems when people are being denied justice and their constitutional rights, then the courts should resolve those problems. The Supreme Court, they say, should be "a leader in a vital national seminar that leads to the formulation of values for the American people."[94]

Critics of judicial activism, on the other side, contend that for the last half a century the federal courts, in their zeal to protect the people, became unhinged from their political moorings in the political and constitutional system. These critics argue that even if courts make the "right" decisions, it is not right for courts to take over the legislative responsibilities of the people's elected representatives.

Others claim the debate between those who favor judicial restraint and those who favor judicial activism oversimplifies the choices. Judges, they argue, should take a leadership role in some areas but a restrained role in others. They stand with Justice Harlan F. Stone, who argued that courts have a special duty to intervene: (1) whenever legislation restricts the political process by which decisions are made, or (2) whenever legislation restricts the rights of "discrete and insular minorities." In all other areas, the political process should be allowed to work, and judges should not set aside legislation or interfere with administrative agencies merely because judges would prefer some other policy or even some other interpretation of the Constitution.[95]

For a brief time when the Reagan and Bush jurists dominated both the Supreme Court and lower federal courts, many conservatives supported an active judicial role, and some liberals were skeptical about conservative judges using judicial power.[96] When President Clinton was in a position to reverse the conservative makeup of the federal judiciary, liberals became less skeptical about an active judiciary, and conservatives were likely to prefer more restrained judges.

The People and the Court

Whether judges are liberal or conservative, defer to legislatures or not, try to apply the Constitution as they think the framers intended, or interpret it to conform to current values, there are linkages between what the judges do and what the people want done. The linkages are not direct, and the people never speak with one mind, but these linkages are the heart of the matter.[97] In the first place, the president and the Senate are likely to appoint justices whose decisions reflect contemporary values. When the people elected George Bush, they got judges who reflected his perspectives. When they elected Bill Clinton, they got judges who reflected his values and preferences.

Bush was able to pick two Supreme Court justices—David Souter and Clarence Thomas—who, as expected, joined the Reagan appointees to complete the Court's "turn to the right." Yet at the end of the 1991–1992 term, that Court, by a 5 to 4 vote in *Planned Parenthood v Casey*, nonetheless refused to overturn *Roe v Wade* and upheld its core holding that the Constitution protects the right of a woman to an abortion, although subjecting that right to state regulations that do not unduly burden it.[98] This close vote on abortion made it clear that the 1992 election would determine whether that right would continue to be protected by the Constitution. At stake was whether it would be George Bush or Bill Clinton who would nominate new members of the Supreme Court. Clinton pledged to nominate only persons committed to the view that the Constitution protects a woman's right to choose. Bush continued to disavow that he had any "litmus test" for his nominees and insisted that it would be improper to inquire how they would vote on specific issues, but he made it clear that he would continue to appoint conservative jurists who could be expected to vote to reverse *Roe v Wade*.

Influencing the course of constitutional interpretation by the federal judiciary has been an issue in all recent presidential elections. Voters have been given a choice. Most presidential candidates have been clear about what kind of judges they would nominate, and senatorial candidates have not been bashful in stating the advice and consent they would give to such presidential nominations.

Although voters in 1992 gave Democrats control over both the Congress and White House, in 1994 they put Republicans in charge of the Senate so that Clinton's judicial appointments had to be filtered through a conservatively dominated Senate Judiciary Committee with Republicans in control of the Senate. The Judiciary Committee began to slow down its processing of nominations,

Supreme Court Decisions Reversed by Constitutional Amendment

Chisholm v Georgia, 2 Dallas 419 (1793), allowed states to be sued in federal courts; reversed by the Eleventh Amendment, ratified 1795.

Dred Scott Case, 19 Howard 393 (1857), held that African Americans were ineligible for American citizenship; reversed by the Fourteenth Amendment, ratified 1868.

Pollock v Farmer's Land & Trust Co., 157 US 429 (1895), denied Congress authority to levy an income tax; reversed by the Sixteenth Amendment, ratified 1913.

ostensibly because some senators questioned whether there might be too many judges on the courts of appeals. In fact, the committee was following the historical pattern of slowing down the confirmation process "in the hopes that the election could give their party's candidate the possibility of filling those vacancies if elected."[99]

Clinton was able to increase substantially the number of African Americans and women on the federal bench. But some liberal critics accused him of working so closely with the Republicans that he was not able to reverse the conservative legacy of the Reagan/Bush years.[100] On the other side, conservative critics decried his appointments. They may be "no-name judges," they conceded, but they were nonetheless liberal judges. These conservatives expressed concern that, if reelected, Clinton could reverse the accomplishments of Presidents Reagan and Bush, who named roughly 70 percent of all federal judges. The courts were solidly in the hands of judicial conservatives when Bush left office.[101] "In a second term," they argued, "Mr. Clinton might come a bolder judge-picker, selecting name liberals from law faculties and displaying a willingness to duke it out with Senate Republicans."[102] Bob Dole described the 1996 election as a choice "between a candidate who will appoint conservative judges to the court and a candidate who appoints liberal judges who bend the laws to let drug dealers free."[103]

Also at stake was the tone and direction of Supreme Court constitutional interpretation. By the 1996 elections, the conservative hold on the Supreme Court was clear but tenuous. After decades of effort, the Nixon-Reagan-Bush attempts to alter the course of constitutional interpretation were having results. Chief Justice Rehnquist and Justices Thomas and Scalia were increasingly being joined by Justices Kennedy and O'Connor to provide a five-person majority on issues relating to the establishment clause, affirmative action, and criminal justice. The future direction of constitutional interpretation was once again a campaign issue in 1996.

When the voters returned Clinton for a second term but left Republicans in control of the Senate, they increased the probability that centrists would be selected to become federal judges, since only candidates who could please both President Clinton and the conservative Republicans who dominated the Senate judiciary committee were likely to be nominated and confirmed. But they also enhanced the likelihood that constitutional conservatives would not be able to consolidate their control over the Supreme Court.

Scholars debate how public opinion influences what judges decide, whether it is direct or indirect through presidential appointments and Senate confirmations, but there is little question that, sooner or later there is a correlation between public opinion and judicial decisions.[104] Judicial opinions that reflect what the people want have the greatest survival value. When a new political coalition takes over the White House or Congress, the old regime stays on in the federal courts, or as one unknown wit put it: "The good a president does is oft interred with his bones, but his choice of Supreme Court justices lives after him." New electoral coalitions eventually take over the federal courts, and before long, new interpretations of the Constitution reflect the dominant political ideology.[105]

Judges have neither armies nor police to execute their rulings. Although Congress cannot reverse Supreme Court decisions that relate to constitutional interpretations, and only three Supreme Court decisions have been reversed by formal constitutional amendment, the political system alters judicial policy in more subtle ways. Decisions are binding on the parties to a particular case, but the policies involved in judicial decisions are effective and durable only if they are supported by a considerable portion of the electorate. To win a favorable

Supreme Court decision is to win something of considerable political value, but the policies reflected by that decision may or may not alter the way people behave. "American courts are not all-powerful institutions."[106] If the Court's policies are too far out of step with the values of the country, the Court is likely to be "reversed." As Chief Justice William H. Rehnquist has written, "No judge worthy of his salt would ever cast his vote in a particular case simply because he thought the majority of the public wanted him to vote that way, but that is quite a different thing from saying that no judge is ever influenced by the great tides of public opinion that run a country such as ours."[107]

The American policy-making process is complex. What Congress and the White House and the state legislatures and police officers do has an effect on what the Supreme Court does, and what the Supreme Court does has an effect on what Congress and the White House and the state legislatures and the police do. Most important, what all these agencies do is related to what the various segments of "the people" want done. Consider, for example, the chain of developments that made the Constitution more reflective of the values of equal rights under the law. Changing economic and social conditions led to the growth of a black leadership, which in turn generated political power for blacks, which led presidents to care about what blacks wanted, which resulted in their appointing judges who reflected the values of civil rights advocates. And this action led to action and reaction in city councils, school boards, and state legislatures. The judges certainly played a leadership role in the development of a national civil rights consensus, and where they led the people followed. Today we are in the midst of a continuing debate about what the Constitution "means" about affirmative action. The answer is being decided only in part by what the judges say it means.

"The people" speak in many ways and with many voices. The Supreme Court—and the other courts—represent and reflect the values of some of these people. Although the Court is not the defenseless institution portrayed by some commentators, and its decisions are as much shapers of public opinion as reflections of it, ultimately the power of the Court in our constitutional democracy rests on retaining the support of most of the people most of the time. No better standard for determining the legitimacy of a governmental institution has been discovered.

SUMMARY

1. Judges in the United States play a more active role in the political process than they do in other democracies. Federal courts receive their jurisdiction directly from Congress, which must decide the constitutional division of responsibilities among federal and state courts.

2. Federal judges apply statutory law, common law, equity, admiralty, and maritime law, and administrative law. They apply federal, criminal, and civil law. Although bound by procedural requirements, including *stare decisis,* they have to exercise discretion.

3. Partisanship and ideology are important factors in the selection of federal judges, and these factors ensure a linkage between the courts and the rest of the political system so that the views of the people are reflected, even if indirectly, in the work of the courts.

4. The Supreme Court, which has almost complete control over the cases it reviews as they come up from the state courts, the courts of appeals, and district courts, is a revered but somewhat mysterious branch of our government. Annually its nine justices dispose of thousands of cases, but most of their time is concentrated on the 75 to 105 cases per year that establish guidelines for lower courts and the country.

5. A continuing concern of major importance is the reconciliation of the role of judges—especially those on the Supreme Court—as independent and fair dispensers of justice for the parties before them with their vital role as interpreters of the Constitution. This is an especially complex problem in our democracy because of the power of judicial review and the significant role courts play making public policy.

6. The debate about how judges should interpret the Constitution is almost as old as the Republic. More than two hundred years after the Constitution was adopted, the argument between those who contend judges should interpret the document literally and those who believe they cannot, and should not, has returned to the headlines.

FURTHER READING

HENRY J. ABRAHAM, *The Judiciary: The Supreme Court in the Governmental Process,* 9th ed. (Brown & Benchmark, 1994).

HENRY J. ABRAHAM, *Justices and Presidents: A Political History of Appointments to the Supreme Court,* 3d ed. (Oxford University Press, 1992).

ROBERT BORK, *The Tempting of America: The Political Seduction of the Law* (Macmillan, 1990).

ETHAN BRONNER, *Battle for Justice: How the Bork Nomination Shook America* (W. W. Norton, 1989).

BENJAMIN R. CARDOZO, *The Nature of the Judicial Process* (Yale University Press, 1921).

STEPHEN L. CARTER, *The Confirmation Mess: Cleaning Up the Federal Appointments Process* (Basic Books, 1994).

RICHARD DAVIS, *Decision and Images: The Supreme Court and the Press* (Prentice Hall, 1994).

JOHN HART ELY, *Democracy and Distrust: A Theory of Judicial Review* (Harvard University Press, 1980).

LEE EPSTEIN AND JOSEPH F. KOBYLKA, *The Supreme Court and Legal Change: Abortion and the Death Penalty* (University of North Carolina Press, 1993).

KERMIT L. HALL, ED., *The Oxford Companion to the Supreme Court of the United States* (Oxford University Press, 1992).

EUGENE W. HICKOK JR., ED., *The Bill of Rights: Original Meanings and Current Understanding* (University Press of Virginia, 1991).

PETER IRVING AND STEPHANIE GUITTON, EDS., *May It Please the Court: Transcripts of 23 Recordings of Landmark Cases as Argued Before the Supreme Court* (The New Press, 1993).

WILLIAM LASSER, *The Limits of Judicial Power: The Supreme Court in American Politics* (University of North Carolina Press, 1989).

LEONARD W. LEVY, *Original Intent and the Framers' Constitution* (Macmillian, 1988).

THOMAS R. MARSHALL, *Public Opinion and the Supreme Court* (Unwin Hyman, 1989).

JOHN MASSARO, *Supremely Political: The Role of Ideology and Presidential Management in Unsuccessful Supreme Court Nominations* (State University of New York Press, 1990).

DANIEL JOHN MEADOR AND JORDANA SIMONE BERNSTEIN, *Appellate Courts in the United States* (West Publishing, 1994).

WALTER F. MURPHY AND C. HERMAN PRITCHETT, *Courts, Judges and Politics: An Introduction to the Judicial Process,* 4th ed. (Random House, 1986).

DAVID M. O'BRIEN, *Storm Center: The Supreme Court in American Politics,* 3d ed. (W. W. Norton, 1993).

J. W. PELTASON, *Federal Courts in the Political Process* (Doubleday, 1955).

BARBARA A. PERRY, *A "Representative" Supreme Court? The Impact of Race, Religion, and Gender on Appointments* (Greenwood Press, 1991).

H. W. PERRY, JR., *Deciding To Decide* (Harvard University Press, 1991).

TIMOTHY H. PHELPS AND HELEN WINTERNITZ, *Capitol Games: Clarence Thomas, Anita Hill, and the Story of a Supreme Court Nomination* (Hyperion, 1992).

RICHARD A POSNER, *The Federal Courts* (Harvard University Press, 1985).

GERALD N. ROSENBERG, *The Hollow Hope: Can Courts Bring About Social Change?* (University of Chicago Press, 1991).

DAVID G. SAVAGE, *Turning Right: The Making of the Rehnquist Supreme Court* (John Wiley & Sons, 1992).

BERNARD SCHWARTZ, *A History of the Supreme Court* (Oxford University Press, 1993).

JAMES F. SIMON, *The Center Holds: The Power Struggle Inside the Rehnquist Court* (Simon & Schuster, 1995).

PAUL SIMON, *Advice and Consent: Clarence Thomas, Robert Bork, and the Intriguing History of the Supreme Court Battles* (National Press Books, 1992).

ELLIOT E. SLOTNICK, *Judicial Politics: Readings from "Judicature"* (Nelson-Hall, 1992).

LAURENCE H. TRIBE, *God Save This Honorable Court: How the Choice of Supreme Court Justices Shapes Our History* (Random House, 1985).

STEPHEN L. WASBY, *The Supreme Court in the Federal Judicial System,* 4th ed. (Nelson-Hall, 1993).

BARBARA M. YARNOLD, *Abortion Politics in the Federal Courts: Rights Versus Rights* (Praeger, 1995).

THE BUREAUCRACY: THE REAL POWER?

In the 1990s it seemed that everyone in this country had a gripe against the federal bureaucracy as arrogant, wasteful, lazy, overpaid, and underproductive. Even Democratic and Republican officials joined in the criticism. Republicans on the campaign trail and in Congress called for getting rid of the departments of Education, Energy, and Commerce. They also urged an end to funding for the Endowment for the Arts, the Public Broadcasting System (PBS), the U.S. Information Agency, and the Agency for International Development. Bill Clinton adroitly picked up on this theme in his State of the Union address in 1996, declaring that "the era of big government is over."

As candidates in 1992, Bill Clinton and Al Gore had attacked the federal bureaucracy and promised to cut its size and make it more responsive and efficient. With the help of Congress, they succeeded in cutting both the civilian and military bureaucracies by at least 10 percent.[1] But shrinking the bureaucracy remained a key issue again in 1996, as both parties claimed to have better ideas of how to make government leaner. Bob Dole stated: "I want to be president so we can rein in this big government of ours and eliminate some of the bureaucracy."[2] Other presidential candidates called for even more radical downsizing of the national government.

Bureaucrats aroused some sympathy when they were "furloughed" from their jobs in the pre-Christmas season of 1995 and the early weeks of 1996 during the unending tug of war between the president and Congress over balancing the budget. The nightly news on television showed their despair over having their salaries cut off as bills piled up for rent, food, and car payments. No Santa Claus for them.

But criticizing government bureaucracy is almost as traditional as kissing babies and marching in Fourth of July parades. Some members of Congress like to joke that there is a parlor game played in the nation's capital: "It's called Bureaucracy," they say. "And there is only one rule. The first one to move loses." There is another Washington saying: "When a bureaucrat makes a mistake and continues to make it, it usually becomes the new policy."

Public bureaucrats are an inviting target or scapegoat. There is hardly a citizen who has not been offended, irritated, or at least regulated at one time or another in dealing with the Internal Revenue Service (IRS), the FBI, the U.S. Army, the Environmental Protection Agency (EPA), or the Food and Drug Administration (FDA); and all of us have stood in lines at the post office or been kept waiting and gotten inept responses when we called government agencies. No matter that these agencies can also be a big help to us. We tend to remember the hassles and mistakes.

For most people, the government appears to have become increasingly distant and impersonal. Everything in life is regulated. Rules are numerous and inflexible. One critic writes that our government in the 1990s "acts like some extraterrestrial power, not an institution that exists to serve us. Its actions have an arbitrary quality. It almost never deals with real-life problems in a way that reflects our understanding of the situation."[3] We have, he adds, constructed a

Bureaucracies tend to create a lot of paperwork. Employees of a private company pose with the amount of paper they were required to file with the government in one year.

system of regulatory laws and rules "that basically outlaws common sense. Modern law, in an effort to be 'self-executing,' has shut out our humanity."[4]

Bureaucracy is a fact of modern life. Of course we have a lot of "red tape" and overlap in our public administration process—too much. It is important to ask, as we enter the twenty-first century, whether our bureaucracy and its methods are stifling innovation, productivity, and common sense.

In this chapter we explain who the bureaucrats are, examine the origins, functions, and realities of our national public bureaucracy, and explore how elected officials in both the Congress and the executive branch are trying to make the bureaucracy leaner, more responsive, and more accountable to the American people.

THE FEDERAL BUREAUCRACY

Bureaucrats, or career government employees, work in the executive branch, in the 14 cabinet-level departments, and in the more than 50 independent agencies embracing about 2,000 bureaus, divisions, branches, offices, services, and other subunits of government. Five big agencies—the Departments of Army, Navy, and Air Force, the Department of Veterans Affairs, and the U.S. Postal Service—tower over the others in size. Most agencies are directly responsible to the president, yet some, like the Postal Service, are partly independent. Agencies exist by act of Congress; legislators can abolish them either by passing a new law or by withholding funds.[5]

The terms "bureaucrat" and "bureaucracy" are of recent origin. Initially referring to a cloth covering the desks or flat writing tables of French government officials in the eighteenth century, the term "bureau" came to be linked with the suffix "ocracy" signifying rule of government (as in "democracy" or "aristocracy"). "Bureaucracy," as it came to be used 100 years ago, referred to a rational, efficient method of organization. "Bureaucracy" today can refer to a professional corps of officials organized in a pyramidal hierarchy and functioning under impersonal, uniform rules and procedures. The term "bureaucracy" typically refers to the whole body of nonelected and nonpresidentially appointed government officials in the executive branch who work for presidents and their political appointees. In this chapter we use the terms "bureaucracy" and "bureaucrat" in their neutral sense. Yet popular usage of these terms is typically negative.

Bureaucracies are public or private organizations that are large and hierarchical in structure, with each employee accountable to a superior through a chain of command. They provide each employee with a defined role or responsibility, base their decisions on impersonal rules, and hire and promote employees based on skills related to their jobs.[6] Bureaucracies in the modern sense came into being in government to provide predictability and efficiency and to minimize the arbitrary practices that so often characterized rule under dictatorial monarchs.

Critics believe the federal bureaucracy is an overzealous guardian of the status quo and is too lazy or unimaginative to innovate or experiment. Others fear that a powerful national bureaucracy is too liberal and encourages a wasteful welfare state. Many people also think the federal bureaucracy is too large, too powerful, too unaccountable. Indeed, 60 percent of a national survey by the Gallup organization in 1995 complained that the federal government had too much power. And nearly everyone was suspicious that there is waste and "fat" in government, especially those who had heard about Defense Department procurement cost overruns, welfare fraud, CIA tragedies, and general inefficiencies. Such stereotypes are widespread, for bureaucracies have never been popular, but the skepticism and hostility toward public bureaucracies seem greater today than before.

From Coast to Coast

Federal Employment Is Widely Dispersed

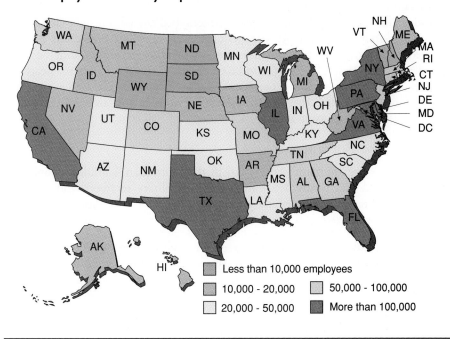

SOURCE: U.S. Census Bureau, Office of Personnel Management.

Bureaucracy in a large, complex society is virtually inevitable. Most of us will work in some public or private bureaucracy for part, if not most, of our careers. Public bureaucracies pose special challenges because they report to competing political institutions and must function within our constitutional democracy of shared powers and multiple checks and balances.

How Did the Bureaucracy Evolve?

From 1789 until about 1829, the federal service was drawn from an upper-class, white male elite. In 1829, President Andrew Jackson called for greater participation by the middle and lower classes. He employed a **spoils system** that was followed by his successors until well into the 1890s. This system, epitomized by the phrase "to the victor belong the spoils," operated on the theory that party loyalists should be rewarded and that government would be effective and responsive only if followers of the president held most key federal posts. Besides, it was thought that government should not be complicated; almost anybody should be able to do the job. With each new president came a full turnover in the federal service.

Later in the nineteenth century, however, a sharp reaction set in against this system. In response to the various abuses of the system and most immediately to the assassination of President James Garfield in 1881 by a disappointed office seeker, Congress passed the Pendleton Act. It set up a limited **merit system** based on a testing program to evaluate candidates. Federal employees were to be selected and retained according to their "merit," not their party loyalty. Federal service was placed under the control of a three-person bipartisan board called the Civil Service Commission, which functioned from 1883 to 1978.[7]

By the 1950s, coverage under the merit system had grown from 10 percent of all federal employees when it was first established to about 90 percent. In 1978

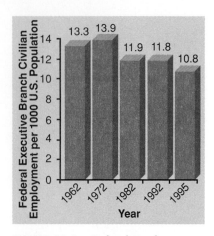

FIGURE 13-1 Federal Employment per 1,000 Americans

SOURCE: U.S. Census Bureau, Office of Personnel Management.

the Civil Service Reform Act abolished the Civil Service Commission and split its functions between two new agencies. This split was necessary to avoid a conflict of interest inherent in the agency that recruits, hires, and promotes employees also being the same agency that passes judgment on employee grievances about fairness and discrimination.

Today the Office of Personnel Management (OPM) administers civil service laws, rules, and regulations. An independent Merit Systems Protection Board is charged with protecting the integrity of the federal merit system and the rights of federal employees. The board conducts studies of the merit system, hears and decides charges of wrongdoing, considers employee appeals against adverse agency actions, and orders corrective and disciplinary actions against an agency executive or employee when appropriate.

Who Are the Bureaucrats?

In this chapter we are mainly interested in the more than 4 million people (2.7 million civilians and nearly 1.5 million in the military services) who make up the executive branch of the federal government. Certain facts about these people need to be emphasized:

1. Only about 10 percent of the career civilian employees work in the Washington area. The vast majority are scattered throughout the country and around the world. California alone has more federal employees than does the District of Columbia.

2. Nearly 30 percent of the civilian employees work for the army, the navy, the air force, or some other defense agency.

3. The welfare state may consume a sizable portion of our budget, yet the size of the federal bureaucracy that administers it is relatively small. Less than 15 percent of the bureaucrats work for welfare agencies such as the Social Security Administration or the Rural Electrification Administration. Almost half of those who do work for the Department of Veterans Affairs.

4. Federal employees are not all of one type. Indeed, in terms of social origin, education, religion, and other background factors, bureaucrats are more broadly representative of the nation than are legislators or politically appointed executives.

5. Federal employment per 1,000 people in the U.S. population has decreased steadily from over 14 percent in the early 1970s to little over 10 percent by the late 1990s (see Figure 13-1).

6. Bureaucrats work at an endless variety of jobs. More than 15,000 different personnel skills are represented in the federal government. Unlike Americans as a whole, however, most federal employees are white-collar workers: secretaries, clerks, lawyers, inspectors, engineers.

The vast number of senior bureaucrats are honest professionals and experts at their business. Presidents, Congress, and other elected officials ignore the bureaucracy's advice at their peril. A compelling example is provided by the Central Intelligence Agency's (CIA) perceptive memoranda (many of them later published in the celebrated *Pentagon Papers*) arguing that the Vietnam War as President Lyndon Johnson wanted to conduct it would be a failure. This was good advice from an expert bureaucracy, but Johnson disregarded it.

What Do Bureaucrats Do?

After the president has signed a bill into law or a regulatory agency has made its rules, they must be implemented. Legislation or administrative decisions are not self-implementing. Implementation of policy is the function of the executive branch, its bureaucracy, and in some instances, state, county, and local governments as well.

More is involved in policy implementation than the literal translation of goals into practice. Indeed, it is during this stage that many key decisions are made. The coalition that pushes a bill through Congress often does not stay together after the bill has been enacted. Congress often passes ambiguous legislation that conceals serious policy differences. Because of policy differences among the supporters of a bill, Congress sets general goals and passes the responsibility for interpretation on to the bureaucrats. Legislators are frequently more concerned with the symbolic potency of legislation than with its substantive content. As a result, the bureaucracy is given some latitude to translate general guidelines into specific directives. Bureaucrats are sometimes blamed for confusion, yet they are merely trying to carry out deliberately unclear policies in a political atmosphere characterized by conflict and competition.

Consider civil rights legislation. Often differences among women's groups, African American groups, Latino groups, employer groups, and trade unions are momentarily resolved and a bill becomes law. But after the bill has been enacted, the coalition that supported the bill falls apart, and the resulting conflicting pressures are felt by the agencies trying to implement the policies. Employers claim that the agencies' regulations are unrealistic and interfere with their rights; women's groups contend agencies are failing to enforce the law vigorously enough; black groups claim agencies favor the women's groups but ignore African Americans. The more controversial the issue, the greater the chance of delay, as powerful interest groups clash over a program and force bureaucrats to move cautiously.

The implementation process involves a long chain of decision points. At each decision point a public official or community leader often can advance or delay the program. The more decision points a program needs to clear, the greater the chance of failure or delay. Special problems result if the successful implementation of a national program depends on the cooperation of state and local officials. One state or community may be eager to help; another may be opposed to a program and try to stop it.

A number of federal programs have failed to accomplish their desired goals because of problems that occurred in administration. Sometimes these difficulties lead to the outright failure of a program, but more often they mean excessive delay, watered-down goals, or cost overruns. John Kennedy's economic reform programs in Latin America, Lyndon Johnson's Model Cities program, Richard Nixon's and Gerald Ford's crime control programs, George Bush's antidrug crusade, and Bill Clinton's national service program all faced problems of implementation. When such failures occur, it is easier to blame the original legislation rather than what happened after the bill became law. Of course, poorly written legislation and badly conceived policy yield poor results, but even the best legislation can fail because of problems encountered during implementation.

Like so much of politics, successful policy implementation cannot be guaranteed. It depends on the creation of stable routines for implementation, the ability to adjust to changing circumstances, the quality of the working relationship between implementers at various levels, the degree of conflict invoked by the policy, and the general level of public support for the program.

How Is the Bureaucracy Organized ?

FORMAL ORGANIZATION The executive branch departments are headed by cabinet members called *secretaries* (except Justice, which is headed by the attorney general). The secretaries are directly responsible to the president. Although

Executive Branch Departments

- Department of State (1789)
- Department of the Treasury (1789)
- Department of Defense (1947, originally War, 1789)
- Department of Justice (1789)
- Department of the Interior (1849)
- Department of Agriculture (1862)
- Department of Commerce (1913, originally Commerce and Labor, 1903)
- Department of Labor (1913, originally Commerce and Labor, 1903)
- Department of Health and Human Services (1979, originally Health, Education and Welfare, 1953)
- Department of Housing and Urban Development (1965)
- Department of Transportation (1966)
- Department of Energy (1977)
- Department of Education (1979)
- Department of Veterans Affairs (1989)

Dates indicate when the department was established.

The Federal Deposit Insurance Corporation, a government corporation, was set up to protect depositors' accounts in banks and savings and loans companies. Here an FDIC poster on a bank door announces the closing of the bank and informs depositors where to seek restitution of their money.

departments vary greatly in size, they have certain features in common. A deputy or an undersecretary takes part of the administrative load off the secretary's shoulders, and several assistant secretaries direct major programs. The secretaries have assistants who help them in planning, budget, personnel, legal services, public relations, and other staff functions.

Departments are subdivided into bureaus and smaller units, and the basis for their division may differ. The most common basis is *function*. For example, the Commerce Department is divided into the Bureau of the Census, the Patent and Trademark Office, and so on. The basis may also be *clientele* (for example, the Bureau of Indian Affairs of the Interior Department), or *work processes* (for example, the Economic Research Service of the Agriculture Department), or *geography* (for example, the Alaskan Air Command of the Department of the Air Force).

Government corporations, such as the Corporation for Public Broadcasting and the Federal Deposit Insurance Corporation, are a cross between business corporations and regular government agencies. Government corporations were designed to make possible a freedom of action and flexibility not always found in the regular agencies. These corporations have been freed from certain regulations of the Office of Management and Budget and the comptroller general. They also have more leeway in using their own earnings. Still, because these corporations are a part of the government, the government retains control over their activities.

Government entities that are not corporations and do not fall within cabinet departments are called **independent agencies**. They consist of many types of organizations with differing degrees of independence. Many, however, are no more independent of the president and Congress than the departments. The huge General Services Administration (GSA), for example, the function of which is to operate and maintain federal properties, is not represented in the cabinet, but its director is responsible to the White House and its actions are closely watched by Congress.[8]

Another type of agency is the **independent regulatory board or commission**. Examples are the Securities and Exchange Commission, the National Labor Relations Board, and the Federal Reserve Board. Congress deliberately set up these boards to keep them somewhat free from White House influence; the president nominates them and Congress confirms them, but the president can fire them. They exercise **quasi-legislative and quasi-judicial** functions. Congress has protected their independence in several ways: the boards are headed by three or more commissioners with overlapping terms; they often have to be bipartisan in membership (that is, they must have some Democrats as well as some Republicans); and members are appointed for fixed terms in office, some for only 3 years but others for up to 14 years.

Within each of the departments, corporations, and independent agencies are many subordinate units. The standard name for the largest subunit is the **bureau**, although it is sometimes called an office, administration, or service. Bureaus are the working units of the federal government. In contrast to the big departments, which often consist of a variety of agencies, bureaus usually have fairly definite and clear-cut duties, as their names show: the Bureau of the Census in the Commerce Department, the Forest Service in the Agriculture Department, the Social Security Administration in the Department of Health and Human Services, the Bureau of the Mint in the Treasury Department, the Bureau of Indian Affairs and the Park Service in the Interior Department, and the Bureau of Prisons, Federal Bureau of Investigation (FBI), and Drug Enforcement Administration in the Justice Department.

By assigning certain functions to each unit, placing an official at the head, and holding that official responsible for performance, formal bureaucracy allows for both specialization and coordination, permits ready communication, and in general makes a large and complex organization more manageable.

INFORMAL ORGANIZATION To look at a formal organization chart is only to *begin* to understand how an agency works, for we also need to understand the informal organization (see Figure 13-2). Bureaucrats differ in attitudes, motives, abilities, experiences, and political clout, and these differences matter. Leadership in an organization is exercised in a variety of places; some officials may have considerably more influence than others with the same formal status. Further, loyalties of officials cut across the formal aims of the agency.

Informal organization can have a significant effect on administration. A subordinate official in an agency might be especially close to the chief because they went to the same college, or they play racquetball together, or because the subordinate knows how to ingratiate himself with the chief. A staff official may have tremendous influence not because of formal authority but because of experience, fairness, common sense, and personality. In an agency headed by a chief who is weak or unimaginative, a vacuum may develop that encourages others to take over. Such informal organization and communication, cutting across regular channels, are inevitable in any organization—public or private, civilian or military.

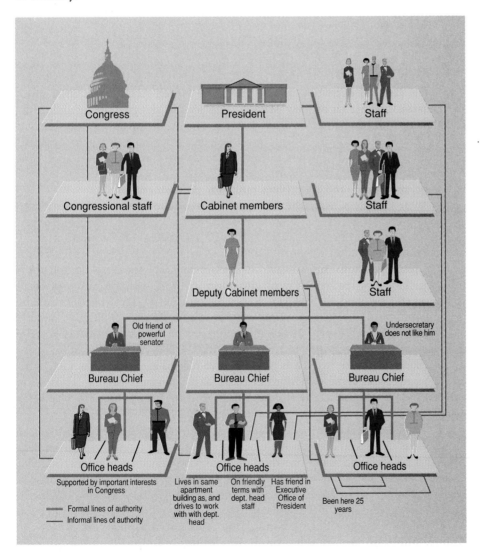

FIGURE 13-2 Hypothetical Relationships within the Executive Branch

Hatch Act Rules: What Federal Civilian Employees May and May Not Do

May register and vote as they choose

May assist in voter registration

May express opinions about candidates and issues

May participate in campaigns in their off-duty activities

May contribute money to political organizations or attend political fund-raising functions

May wear or display political badges, buttons, or stickers

May attend political rallies and meetings

May join political clubs or parties

May seek and hold positions in political parties

May campaign for or against referendum questions, constitutional amendments, municipal ordinances

May not be candidates for public office in partisan elections

May not use official authority to interfere with or affect the results of an election

May not collect contributions or sell tickets to political fund-raising functions from subordinate employees

May not solicit funds or discourage the political activity of any person who has business before the employee's office

May not solicit funds or discourage political activity by any person who is the subject of an ongoing audit, investigation, or enforcement action

These rules apply to nearly all federal civil servants. Rules are stricter for military personnel and certain agencies like the FBI, CIA, and Secret Service.

Hiring Practices in the Bureaucracy

Senior government administrators work with the Office of Personnel Management in staffing their agencies. OPM acts as a policy maker for recruiting, examining, and appointing government workers. It advertises for new employees, prepares and administers oral and written examinations throughout the country, and compiles a register of names of those who pass the tests. OPM delegates to individual agencies the responsibility for hiring new personnel, subject to its standards. Individual agencies may promote people from within or transfer a civil servant already in the government. If, however, they wish to consider an "outsider," they request OPM to certify possible candidates from its roster of applicants. OPM typically certifies the top three applicants who have applied for the departmental or agency opening, and the agency normally selects one of these. However, the agency can decide to make no appointment or to request other applicants if it thinks none of the three is qualified.

These procedures are intended to protect the merit principle and to meet agencies' needs for qualified personnel. In practice, the two objectives are not the same. Trade-offs have to be made, particularly between central control by OPM and delegation of discretionary authority to the agencies. Further, the pursuit of both objectives is enfeebled by the introduction of additional and often incompatible objectives—the veteran preference system, for example.

THE HATCH ACT, OLD AND NEW In 1939 Congress passed an Act to Prevent Pernicious Political Activities, usually called the **Hatch Act** after its chief sponsor, Senator Carl Hatch of New Mexico. The act was designed to neutralize the danger of a federal civil service being able to shape, if not dictate, the election of presidents and members of Congress. In essence, the Hatch Act permitted federal employees to vote, but not to take an active part in partisan politics. The Hatch Act also made it illegal to dismiss non-policy-making federal officials (those below cabinet and subcabinet rank) for partisan reasons.[9]

In 1993, Congress, with the encouragement of the Clinton administration, overhauled the old Hatch Act and made many forms of participation in partisan politics permissible. The revised Hatch Act still bars federal officials from running as candidates in partisan elections, but it does permit most federal civil servants to hold party positions and involve themselves in party fund raising and campaigning. This new law, which went into effect in 1994, was especially welcomed by those who believed the old Hatch Act discouraged political participation by over two million individuals who might otherwise be vigorous political activists.[10]

The new Hatch Act spells out many restrictions on federal bureaucrats to raise campaign funds in their agencies, and it specifically bars nearly all partisan activity for those who work in such highly sensitive federal agencies as the CIA, FBI, Secret Service, and certain divisions of the Internal Revenue Service. Those who work in the U.S. military have stricter rules regulating their political involvement.

EMPLOYEE UNIONS Since 1962, federal civilian employees have had the right to form unions or associations that represent them in seeking to improve government personnel policies, and about one-third of them have joined such unions. Some of the more important unions representing federal employees today are the American Federation of Government Employees, the National Treasury Employees Union, the National Association of Government Employees, and the National Federation of Federal Employees. Unlike unions in the private sector, these groups lack the right to strike and are not able to bargain over pay and benefits. What can they do? They attempt to negotiate better personnel policies and practices for federal workers, and they represent federal bureaucrats at grievance and disciplinary proceedings. They also lobby Congress on measures affecting personnel changes.

Principles of Bureaucratic Management

Early in this century, several scholars developed a formal model of administration from which they derived certain principles:

1. *Unity of command.* Every officer should have a superior to whom to report and from whom to take orders.
2. *Chain of command.* There should be a firm line of authority running from the top down and responsibility running from the bottom up.
3. *Line and staff.* The staff advises the executive but gives no commands, whereas the line has operating duties.
4. *Span of control.* A hierarchical structure should be established so that no individuals supervise more agencies directly than they can effectively handle.
5. *Decentralization.* When possible, administrators should delegate decisions and responsibilities to lower levels.

Woodrow Wilson, while still a Princeton University professor, adopted many of these views in his writings. Politics and public administration, he said, should be carefully separated. Leave politics to Congress and management to administrators who adhere to the laws passed by Congress. Followers of the noted German sociologist Max Weber contended that a properly run bureaucracy could be a model of efficiency based on rational and impartial management.[11]

According to the textbook model, bureaucrats should be closely controlled by established rules and regulations. Although this is not always true in practice, it is generally the case. Administrators are not free to make any rules they wish or to decide disputes any way they please. Several kinds of limitations exist:

1. The basic legislative power of Congress compels agencies to identify the will of Congress and to interpret and apply laws as Congress would wish. Congress can amend a law to make its intent clearer, conduct oversight hearings and investigations, or restrict appropriations.
2. Congress has closely regulated the procedures to be followed by regulatory agencies. Under the Administrative Procedures Act of 1946, agencies must publicize their procedures and organization, give advance information of proposed rules to interested persons, allow such persons to present written information and arguments, and allow parties appearing before the agency to be accompanied by counsel and to cross-examine witnesses.
3. Under certain conditions, final actions of agencies may be appealed to the courts.
4. Some federal agencies are created for the specific purpose of overseeing and limiting their fellow agencies. Examples are the Office of Management and Budget (OMB), which is supervised by the White House, and the General Accounting Office (GAO), which is supervised by Congress. In addition to reviewing an agency's budget requests annually in the name of the president, OMB reviews management, organization, and administrative practices on a more or less continuous basis. GAO conducts audits of agency spending and investigates the effectiveness of alternative programs designed for similar ends.

5. Administrators are constrained by informal political checks. They must keep in mind the demands of professional ethics, the advice and criticism of experts, and the attitudes of Congress, the president, interest groups, political parties, private persons, and so on. In the long run, these informal safeguards may be the most important of all.

This classical or textbook model remains influential because it reflects reality. Laws of Congress, although not the whole story, are an important part of the story. Federal agencies and career servants are creatures of the enabling laws under which they work.

Bureaucratic Realities

Suppose Congress passes a law setting federal standards for automobile safety and designates the Department of Transportation to carry out a law that all automobiles must have air bags by 1999. Conflicts over this requirement do not stop with the adoption of the law. Or suppose a president announces that we are about to wage war on drug abuse, and Congress appropriates funds and designates the agencies to carry out programs. Politics—conflicts over who is to get what and who is to do what—continue to be important as the policy is applied to changing conditions.

Career administrators are in a good position to know when a program is not operating properly and what action is needed. But one of the major complaints about bureaucrats is that they do not go out of their way to make things better. The problem is that many bureaucrats often learn by hard experience that they are more likely to get into trouble by attempting to improve or change programs than they are if they just do nothing. Hardening of administrative arteries is more likely, some critics say, than administrative aggressiveness.

Often the fiercest battles in Washington are not over principles or programs but over jurisdictional boundaries, personnel cuts, and fringe benefits. Career employees come to believe the expansion of their organization is vital to the public interest. They sometimes become more skillful at building political alliances to protect their own organization than at building alliances to ensure the effectiveness of the programs their organization administers.

Federal employees were caught in the middle of the battle between congressional Republicans and President Clinton over a balanced budget during the 1995 Christmas season. After Clinton vetoed continuing resolutions that imposed terms he could not accept, thousands of government workers were "furloughed" without pay. Nightly news broadcasts put a sympathetic face on the "faceless bureaucrats" who were deprived of money for gifts, rent, and food.

Organizations, both public and private, also tend to resist change and to resent "outside" direction, whether by a president or by other external supervisors or boards. A department head in the government, a large corporation, or a university is often likely to consider the president of the organization to be an outsider whose judgment in matters affecting his or her bureau is always suspect.

Career administrators often become involved in politics. Some of them have more bargaining and alliance-building skills than the elected and appointed officials to whom they report. In one sense, agency leaders are at the center of action in Washington. Over time, administrative agencies may come to resemble entrenched pressure groups in that they operate to advance *their own interests*. The FBI is a good example; it is always seeking more funds, new projects, and as much independence as possible from the Justice Department in which it is located.

Career bureaucrats develop a keen sensitivity to the political environment and get caught up in a network of issue experts and politicians who specialize in certain policy areas. The growth of federal programs from the 1930s through the 1970s brought an increase in the number of policy aides on Capitol Hill, of Washington law firms that specialize in assisting clients who are interested in policy developments, and of lobbyists (some say at least 40,000) who work with Congress and the federal bureaucracy to advance various economic and professional interests.

Groups that perceive real or potential harm to their interests cultivate the bureau chiefs and agency staffs of concern to their programs. They also work closely with the committees or subcommittees of Congress that authorize, appropriate, and oversee programs run by these key bureaucracies. One former cabinet member, testifying before a congressional committee, described the process this way:

> It is a fact, unknown to the general public, that some elements in Congress and some special interest lobbies have never really wanted the departmental Secretaries (cabinet members) to be strong. As everyone in this room knows but few people outside of Washington understand, questions of public policy nominally lodged with the Secretary are often decided far beyond the Secretary's reach by a trinity— not exactly a holy trinity—consisting of (1) representatives of an outside lobby, (2) middle-level bureaucrats, and (3) selected Members of Congress, particularly concerned with appropriations.
>
> In a given field these people may have collaborated for years. They may have formed deep personal and family friendships. They have traded innumerable favors. They have seen Secretaries come and go.... They have a durable alliance that cranks out legislation and appropriations in behalf of their special interest.[12]

Members of Congress cultivate bureau officials, just as special interests nurture close ties with both Congress and bureau heads. Congress controls agency budgets and has the power to approve or deny requests for relevant legislation. Bureau officials are especially careful to develop good relations with members of the congressional committees and subcommittees that handle their legislation and appropriations.

Some bureaucrats become more entangled than others with these external coalitions. Bureau chiefs are logical targets for the efforts of concerned interest groups. On the other hand, recognizing the power of interest groups, bureau chiefs frequently recruit them as allies in pursuing common goals. What these bureau officials have in common with interest groups and their allies in Congress is a shared view that more money should be spent on federal programs run by the bureau in question. These alliances—among bureaucrats, interest groups, and subcommittee members and their staffs on Capitol Hill—are sometimes described as **iron triangles**.

The executive branch is not the smooth operating hierarchy it is made to appear on an organization chart. The president, cabinet members, and their politically

Thinking it Through

Unannounced drug testing raises serious Fourth Amendment questions. The idea that a group of people should be subjected to random searches without reasonable individual cause has been resisted since the outset of our life as a nation. When Congress, or the president, or the head of a federal agency requires testing as a condition of employment, even if evidence of drug use would not be used to dismiss employees, skeptical judges must be persuaded that the testing is not an "unreasonable" search and seizure.

The Supreme Court ruled in two 1989 decisions involving railway workers and U.S. Customs Service employees that mandatory blood and urine tests may be required for certain workers without a showing of "individualized suspicion." Writing for the Court in the railway workers' case, Justice Anthony Kennedy said the government's interest in testing even without a showing of individual suspicion is compelling. Employees subject to the tests discharge duties fraught with such risks of injury to others that even a momentary lapse of attention can have disastrous results.

The two cases dealt with post-accident testing of railway personnel on duty at the time of a major accident and with customs officials who carry firearms, handle classified information, or intercept drugs.

Drug testing of all federal employees, or even only those in policy-making positions, presents difficult constitutional issues. Supporters of privacy rights and civil liberties are uncomfortable with carrying this policy too far. Drug testing, some concede, may be necessary for certain individuals where public safety is genuinely involved, but it is not needed and would be an unconstitutional deprivation of privacy rights under the Fourth Amendment as a general policy.

Admiral Hyman G. Rickover, Bureaucratic Rebel

The career of the late Admiral Hyman G. Rickover points up the limits on the authority of presidents and cabinet members over some bureaucrats. Rickover served as an officer for 63 years, longer than any other naval officer in American history. Hailed for supervising the production of the nuclear-powered submarine, he often bullied subordinates, intimidated superiors, and in general attacked the naval bureaucracy. For more than 30 years Admiral Rickover worked with powerful members of Congress to build a nuclear-powered navy, often in complete and open defiance of the chief of naval operations, the secretary of defense, and the president. He outlasted 14 secretaries of defense, 14 secretaries of the navy, and at least 10 chiefs of naval operations. Time and again Congress chose to listen to Rickover rather than to his superiors, even when they had vigorous backing from various presidents. Yet Rickover was an admiral in the U.S. Navy and as such was presumably subject to the authority of many of those whom he defied.

One reason for Rickover's success was that his ships worked better than promised. Another reason was that he had unwavering support from the members of the Armed Services Committees of both the House and the Senate and from members of the Joint Committee on Atomic Energy. "Rickover's skill at cultivating Congress—he works the hallways of congressional office buildings as assiduously as any lobbyist for a cause—has given his supporters on the Hill a sense that they also played a key role in creating the nuclear fleet."*

*Juan Cameron, "Admiral Rickover's Final Battle," *Fortune*, November 1976, p. 200.

appointed undersecretaries and assistant secretaries have their work cut out for them as they try to impose their will on the permanent civil service. Bureaucrats, with their strong allies in Congress and the interest groups, often resist change and direction from their appointed or elected political "superiors." Some view these external relations as "administrative guerrilla warfare" and a serious roadblock to holding elected leaders accountable. Others anticipate a clash over values as inevitable in a system that provides ample opportunities for such clashes. After all, the bureaus themselves are merely one more forum for registering the many demands that make up the people's will.

The Case of Bureau Chief George Brown

The following case is fictional, yet based on actual experiences of a typical bureaucrat. (Note that not only is our main character, George Brown, fictitious, but so are the Bureau of Erosion and the Department of Conservation. Other agencies mentioned do exist.) This case illustrates some of the painful choices bureaucrats have to make.

George Brown is chief of the Bureau of Erosion in the Department of Conservation. A graduate of North Dakota State University, Brown is a career official in the federal service and a member of the Senior Executive Service. He is 47; his appointment to the post was a result of both ability and luck. When his old bureau chief retired, the president wanted to bring in an erosion expert from Illinois, but influential members of Congress pressed for the selection of a recently "retired" (actually he was defeated in the last election!) member of the House of Representatives from a farm state. After deadlock and delay, Brown, then a division head in the Bureau of Erosion, was promoted to bureau chief as a compromise.

Early in March of Brown's second year in his new post, his boss, the secretary of conservation, summoned him and the other bureau heads to an important conference and informed them that he had just attended a cabinet meeting in which the president had called on each department to make at least a 10 percent cut in spending in the coming fiscal year. The president, the secretary reported, was responding to popular demands for federal fiscal restraint.

Brown quickly calculated what this cutback would mean for his agency. For several years the Bureau of Erosion had been spending about $800 million a year to help farmers protect their farmland. Could it get along on about $700 million, and where could savings be made? Returning to his office, Brown called a meeting of his personnel, budget, and management officials. After hours of discussion, it was agreed that savings could be effected only by decreasing the scope of the program, a step that would involve terminating about 1,500 of the bureau's employees. Brown asked his subordinates to prepare a list of employees who were the least useful to the bureau. He would decide which to drop after checking with the affected members of Congress.

A few weeks later Brown presented a $710 million budget to Secretary Jones, who approved it and passed it along to the White House. The president then went over the figures in a conference with the director of the Office of Management and Budget, and a few weeks later the White House submitted the budget for the whole executive department, incorporating the Erosion Bureau's $710 million, to Congress.

Meanwhile Brown was running into trouble. News of the proposed budget cut had leaked immediately to the bureau's personnel in the field. Nobody knew who would be dropped if the cut went through, and some officials were already looking around for other positions. Morale fell. Hearing of the cut, farmers' representatives in Washington notified local farm organizations throughout the country. Soon Brown began to receive letters demanding certain services be maintained. Members of the farm bloc in Congress were also becoming restless.

Shortly after the president's budget went to Congress, Representative Jim Smith of Kansas asked Brown to meet with him. Smith was chair of the Subcommittee on Agriculture of the influential House Appropriations Committee and thus a powerful factor in congressional treatment of the budget. Smith said he had consulted his fellow subcommittee members, both Democratic and Republican, and they all agreed the Erosion Bureau's cut must not go through. The farmers needed even more than the usual $800 million because of severe flood conditions in some sections of the country. He warned they would rise up in arms if the program were reduced. Members of Congress from agricultural areas, Smith went on, were under tremendous pressure. Leaders of farm groups in Washington were mobilizing farmers everywhere. Besides, Smith said, the president was unfair in cutting down on the farm program; he did not understand agricultural problems, and he failed to recognize that programs designed to increase agricultural output were the best way to reduce the trade imbalance. Let the cuts in federal programs be made elsewhere.

Smith then came to the point. Brown, he said, must vigorously oppose the budget cut. Hearings on appropriations would begin in a few days, and Brown as bureau chief would, of course, testify. At that time he must insist that the cuts would hurt the bureau and undermine its whole program. Brown would not have to volunteer this statement, Smith said. He could just respond to leading questions put by committee members. Brown's testimony, Smith thought, would help clinch the argument against the cut because the committee would respect the judgment of the administrator closest to the problem. Other bureaucrats were fighting to save their appropriations. Obviously, said Smith, they are counting on public reaction to get them exemptions from the 10 percent cutback, and Brown would be foolish not to do the same.

Brown was in an embarrassing position. He had submitted his estimates to the secretary of conservation and to the president, and it was his duty to back them up. The rules of the game demanded, moreover, that agency heads defend budget estimates submitted to Congress, whatever their personal feelings might be. The president had appointed Brown to his position and had a right to expect loyalty. On the other hand, Brown was on the spot with his own agency. The employees all expected their chief to look out for them. Brown had developed cordial relations with his staff, and he squirmed at the thought of having to let more than a thousand employees go. What would they think when they heard him defend the cut? More important, he wanted to maintain friendly relations with the farmers, the farm organizations, and the farm bloc in Congress. Finally, Brown was committed to his program. He grasped its true importance, whereas the president's budget advisers did not. And he knew that his pet project—aid to poverty-stricken areas in Appalachia—would probably be sacrificed because it was not supported by a powerful constituency.

Brown turned for advice to an old friend in the Office of Management and Budget. This friend urged him to defend the president's budget. He appealed to Brown's professional pride as an administrator and career public servant. He reminded him that the chief executive must have control of the budget and that agency heads must subordinate their interests to the executive program. He said the only way to balance the budget would be for all agencies to make program cuts. As for the employees to be dropped—well, that was part of the game. Some of them might be able to get jobs in other government agencies; civil service would protect their status. Anyway, they would understand Brown's position. In a parting shot he that mentioned the president had Brown in mind for bigger things.

The next day Brown had lunch with a North Dakota senator, wise and experienced in Washington ways, who had helped him get his start in government.

J. Edgar Hoover, Consummate Bureaucrat

J. Edgar Hoover (1895–1972), chief of the Federal Bureau of Investigation for almost half a century, was in theory subject to direction from the attorney general and the president of the United States. In fact, he was so popular with Congress and the public that he was practically immune to control. Part of this "popularity," we now know, came from his investigatory power, which was feared as well as abused. That immunity served the country poorly at times, such as when Hoover was able to wiretap Dr. Martin Luther King, Jr., or others he disliked, but it served the country well when Hoover was able to thwart President Richard Nixon and his aides in certain of their illegal efforts to undermine political opponents.* But how safe is a democracy when the administrative head of a major agency can defy even the elected president?

*See Anthony Summers, *Official and Confidential: The Secret Life of J. Edgar Hoover* (Putnam, 1993).

The senator was sympathetic. But there was no doubt about what Brown should do, the senator said. He should follow Representative Smith's plan, of course, being as diplomatic as possible about it. That way he would protect his position with those who would be most important in the long run.

"After all," the senator said, "presidents come and go, parties rise and fall, but Smith and the other members of Congress will be here a long time, and so will the farm organizations. They can do a lot for you in future years. And remember one other thing," the senator concluded. "These people are the elected representatives of the people. Constitutionally, Congress has the power to spend money as it sees fit. Why should you object if they want to spend an extra 70 or 80 million?"

Leaving the Dirksen Senate Office Building, Brown realized his dilemma was worse than ever. The arguments on both sides were persuasive. He felt hopelessly divided in his loyalties and responsibilities. The president expected one thing of him; Congress expected another. As a professional administrator, he felt obliged to side with the president. As head of a bureau, however, he wanted to protect his team and his programs. His future? Whatever decision he made, he was bound to antagonize important people and interests.

After much soul searching, Brown decided the issue involved more than loyalties, ambitions, and programs. Ultimately it boiled down to two questions: First, to whom was he, Brown, legally and administratively responsible? Formally, of course, he was responsible to the chief executive who appointed him, who was accountable to the people. Brown knew, too, that he was accountable to Congress, which after all has the power over all fiscal matters. Second, which course of action did he think was better for the welfare of all the people? Looking at the question this way, he believed the president was right in asking for fiscal restraint. As a taxpayer, Brown recognized the need to reduce the federal budget deficit. To be sure, Congress must make the final decision. Yet to make the decision, Congress had to act on the advice of the administration, and the administration should speak with one voice for the majority of the people, or it should not be speaking out at all.

With mixed feelings Brown decided to support the president. Being a seasoned alliance builder, however, he hedged his bets. He came out strongly for the president's budget, yet at the same time he sent friendly members of Congress some questions to be asked of him in future hearings so he could explain the impact of the cutbacks. He also circulated to some of these same members of Congress an analysis of the impact of personnel and funding cuts in their states and districts.

Our fictional account of George Brown and similar case studies leads to three important generalizations about bureaucrats:

1. Bureaucrats are people, not robots, and are subject to many influences—the president, OMB, the cabinet, the House, the Senate, the courts, competing interest groups, public opinion, as well as their own sense of what is right.

2. Bureaucrats do not respond merely to orders from the top but to a variety of motives stemming from their own personalities, political attitudes, educational and professional backgrounds, formal and informal organization and communication, and the political context in which they operate.

3. Bureaucrats are important in government. Some of them have considerable discretion and make decisions of great significance. The cumulative effect of all their policies and actions on our daily lives is enormous.

WHAT THE PUBLIC THINKS OF BUREAUCRATS AND THE BUREAUCRACY

Big bureaucracy in the abstract is unpopular, especially when it is out of sight and what it does is little understood. It engages in so many activities that most people find something it does offensive (like taxing them, inspecting them, or regulating them). Big bureaucracy is sometimes defined as that part of the government people dislike.

Civil servants, as individuals, are appreciated, but as a class they are not. Citizens who have dealings with federal employees on a face-to-face basis often say they are pleased by employees' performance. In contrast to scorn for bureaucrats and bureaucracy in the abstract, Americans seem to approve the conduct of individual federal employees—Postal Service delivery persons, forest rangers, Veterans Affairs Department officials, or the county field agents who help with the local 4-H programs. They also admire astronauts, marines, FBI agents, and Coast Guard officers, all of whom are also federal employees.

Still, bureaucrats as a group are a favorite punching bag—a convenient scapegoat—for reporters and politicians who want to place the blame on someone for things that go wrong in government. An irreverent journal in the nation's capital, *The Washington Monthly,* rails against clumsy bureaucracy in every issue. Most newspapers and magazines feature stories and cartoons critical of the federal bureaucracy.

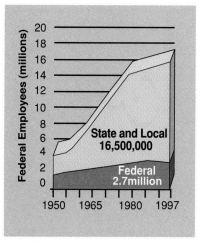

FIGURE 13-3   Civilian Government Employees

SOURCE: Bureau of Labor Statistics, U.S. Department of Labor.

Red Tape and Waste

We Americans are generally skeptical of, if not cynical about, big government. We equate bigness with remoteness, incompetence, and unresponsiveness. We also assume that the bigger government gets, the less efficient it is, and the more it wastes. Perhaps the most criticized aspect of the federal bureaucracy is that career public employees seem to enjoy the closest thing to job security; they are almost as secure in their jobs as if they were confirmed for life on the Supreme Court. For all practical purposes, federal workers can neither be fairly punished nor justly rewarded. Hence most of them, critics say, perform the bare minimum.

When Thomas Jefferson was president, the federal government employed 2,120 persons: Indian commissioners, postmasters, collectors of customs, tax collectors, marshals, lighthouse keepers, and clerks. Today the president heads an executive branch of, as noted earlier, more than 2.7 million civilians and slightly over 1.4 million military employees, who work in at least 2,000 units of federal administration (see Figure 13-3). Critics today say the federal bureaucracy is too large.

A central problem with the bureaucracy, critics say, is not that it exists, but that we have failed to subject it to the control and discipline alleged to operate in the private sector. Despite the great federal government shutdowns in late 1995 and early 1996, and the talk about numerous federal programs facing the guillotine, most federal agencies have survived. The tests of efficiency and cost effectiveness that are the basic standards of business are often absent or at least much less important in decisions about which federal programs survive. A number of outdated, ineffective, or wasteful programs endure because both Republicans and Democrats forge coalitions of convenience based on a desire to deliver favors and protect programs that help their particular districts.

One economics writer points to farm and maritime fleet subsidies, Amtrak, public-broadcasting subsidies, the Small Business Administration, and government-owned power plants as wasteful and no longer needed. "Some of these programs

THE BUREAUCRATS: PAPER SHUFFLERS OR EMPIRE BUILDERS?

One of the paradoxes of public attitudes toward bureaucrats is that some of the time we criticize federal employees for working too little, for being lazy, or for lacking initiative—for failing to abide by the so-called work ethic. Yet at the same time we view federal workers as too powerful and we accuse them of intervening in or regulating our lives far too much. Can bureaucrats in reality be both timid *and* empire builders? In fact, there are enough bureaucrats to fulfill all kinds of contrasting stereotypes, so despite the seeming contradiction, perhaps both views are valid.

Even federal employees gripe about the system. Although top federal employees say they like the challenge of their work, the opportunity to participate in forming and managing important policies, and the quality of people with whom they work, most workers dislike the rigidity, the red tape, and the frustrations of dealing with interest groups and politicians.

"Think of it. Presidents come and go, but WE go on forever!"

Berry's World. Reproduced by permission of Newspaper Enterprise Association, Inc.

CRITICISMS OF FEDERAL WORKERS

BUREAUCRATS AS PAPER-SHUFFLING CLERKS ARE:

Timid and indecisive

Flabby, overpaid, and lazy

Ruled by inertia

Unimaginative

Devoted to rigid procedures

Slow to accept new ideas

Slow to abandon unsuccessful policies

Impersonal and lacking individuality

Red tape artists

On "one long coffee break"

BUREAUCRATS AS THE REAL POWER IN WASHINGTON ARE:

A self-anointed elite in our nation's capital

An oppressive foreign power

The fourth branch of government

Intolerably meddlesome

A demanding giant

The permanent government

Superbureaucrats who wield vast power

Influential enough to do great injury

Intrusive, arrogant empire builders

WHAT TOP FEDERAL CAREER EMPLOYEES LIKE LEAST AND MOST ABOUT THEIR WORK

LIKE LEAST:

Inability to take personnel actions that should be a manager's prerogative (e.g., hiring and discipline)

Inadequate resources (e.g., personnel, budget)

Personal financial sacrifice

Red tape

Frustrations in dealing with interest groups and Congress

LIKE MOST:

Challenging assignments

Opportunity to have an impact on policy programs

Opportunity for public service

Opportunity to use and expand one's knowledge and skills

Caliber of colleagues

qualify as corporate welfare; all are unneeded. . . . Other programs should revert to the states."[13]

Defining what is truly in the national interest is hard. And deciding what is no longer in the national interest is also equally hard for presidents and members of Congress. Take, for example, the subsidies for public radio and public television. Many Republicans in the Newt Gingrich coalition in Congress would end support for public broadcasting, saying that "Sesame Street," "Car Talk," and "Wall Street Week" would all be picked up by the networks, and that today's diversity of cable television channels makes publicly subsidized broadcasting no longer necessary.[14]

Congress in the mid and late 1990s has taken several steps to downsize federal agencies: it has abolished the Interstate Commerce Commission; it has called for the gradual privatization of Amtrak; and it has scaled back the Environmental Protection Agency, the Bureau of Mines, the Bureau of Indian Affairs, and several scientific advisory boards and projects. Still, many Americans and many in Washington believe Congress has spared too many programs and agencies that do not serve us well.

Critics add, too, that the incentive system in the national bureaucracy seems to promote growth and inefficiency. Growth in a bureau improves employee chances for promotion and higher salaries, so a significant portion of time is devoted to its expansion. In short, one of the most common complaints is that our national civil servants seldom have any incentive to save taxpayers money. Systems that might encourage efficiency appear to be lacking; on the contrary, everything seems to tempt them in the opposite direction.

Another charge leveled against bureaucrats is that once a program is established, the people assigned to it become committed to the "cause." In the Office of Civil Rights in the Department of Education, for example, appointments generally go to those concerned about protecting the rights of women and minorities. The protection of rights is their assigned task, and in their zeal they strengthen their authority. Those assigned to the Drug Enforcement Administration are likely to be convinced that enforcement of the federal laws against narcotics is of supreme importance; in carrying out their duties, they sometimes go beyond their vested authority. Groups outside the government who want their programs carried forward pressure the agencies; women's groups and minority advocacy groups carefully watch the Office of Civil Rights, for instance.

A Positive Perspective

Bureaucracy is a function not only of governments but also of corporations, universities, and private associations. It is a reality of modern existence. The challenge in the 1990s is not to wish away big bureaucracies, but to learn how to improve their performance and make them more efficient and accountable. Recent efforts at some state and local government levels have made their bureaucracies more entrepreneurial. The cities of St. Paul, Minnesota, and Indianapolis, Indiana, and the states of Florida under Governor Lawton Chiles and Massachusetts under Governor William Weld have introduced various market incentives, rewards, and public/private partnerships that encourage efficiency and responsiveness. The strategies used in these places and elsewhere are detailed in David Osborne and Ted Gaebler's *Reinventing Government: How the Entrepreneurial Spirit Is Transforming the Public Sector*.[15] Competition and incentives can prudently be built into various government monopolies so that bureaucracies become more responsive to their customers.

A comparison of the performance of our bureaucracy with most bureaucracies in the world suggests we should be somewhat more grateful for the service we get from our public employees than we are. The U.S. Postal Service provides a

Do Government Agencies Ever Die?

Herbert Kaufman, a student of bureaucracies, set out a several years ago to study whether government agencies ever die. He began by looking at 175 agencies in selected areas of the national government that existed in 1923 and then traced them for the next 50 years. All but 27 were alive and well in 1973. In the meantime scores of new agencies had been created to work in these same areas. Death of a bureaucracy is the exception rather than the rule. The birth of new units continues, regardless of whether a Democrat or a Republican occupies the White House. Additional bureaucracies seem to be encouraged by sudden shifts in economic conditions or international tensions or by a "built-in thrust that...assists the even finer division of labor in organizations." Excessive workloads in existing agencies, pressure by groups who believe a new agency will be more sympathetic to their point of view, and a variety of societal change factors all work to create more units of government.

SOURCE: Herbert Kaufman, *Are Government Organizations Immortal?* (Brookings Institution, 1976), p. 67.

good example. Although it is criticized as being a dinosaur, it is more efficient and less costly than comparable services around the world. Another example is the United States tax system; it is the most effective such system in the world.

Compared to most other nations, U.S. government employment has not grown. Government employment grew by more than 20 percent in Sweden in the past generation and by over 11 percent in Italy and Germany during the same period. There has been a steady decline in U.S. government employment during the last ten years, especially in the mid-1990s. Moreover, government employment as a percentage of total employment in the United States is 30 to 50 percent lower than in these Western European democracies.

One recent study finds that American public bureaucracies respond well to effective political leadership. Under such conditions, federal bureaucracies are competitive, adaptable, and dynamic. "Agencies respond systematically to changes in political leadership, as manifested through appointments, changing budgets, reorganizations, and various other tools of administrative control."[16]

"Reinventing Government" in the 1990s

The Clinton administration worked hard to cut the size of the federal government's military and civilian employees. The end of the cold war made it easier to close military bases and to "downsize" the post-cold-war military ranks. Clinton pledged to cut the federal workforce by 273,000 positions and claimed he would eventually preside over a government that was the smallest since John Kennedy was in the White House. Clinton and Vice-President Gore insisted their efforts would create a federal bureaucracy that worked better and cost less. Major federal budget cuts, championed by the Republican-controlled Congress in the mid-1990s, often forced the White House to cut more and to cut faster than might otherwise have been the case.

By 1996, the executive branch claimed considerable progress on "putting customers first, empowering employees to get results, cutting red tape, and cutting back to basics." The departments and agencies "have established customer service standards and streamlined their operations," said Clinton. "They also are working with my Office of Management and Budget to focus more on 'performance'—what federal programs actually accomplish."[17]

Clinton and Gore were plainly responding to the popular perception that there was too much waste and inadequate responsiveness by federal bureaucrats. Thus they talked about introducing competition and a market orientation wherever possible. And they usually, though not always, went along with the Republican's call to shift responsibility to the states whenever possible.[18]

Gore's report on the bureaucracy's performance made hundreds of major recommendations for encouraging efficiency, productivity, and responsiveness in government operations. Some recommendations from the 1993 Gore report were:

- Close or consolidate 1,200 field offices of the Department of Agriculture.
- Allow the sale of the Alaska Power Administration.
- Reduce the number of Department of Education programs from 230 to 189.
- Eliminate federal support payments (subsidies) for mohair, wool, and honey.
- Remove people who are no longer disabled from disability insurance rolls.
- Allow all federal agencies funds for creative innovation.
- Encourage market-based approaches to reduce pollution.
- Eliminate the Government Printing Office's monopoly on publishing government documents and reports.

- Reduce the time required to fire incompetent federal employees by half.
- Insist that all agencies survey customers, measure customer satisfaction, and establish service standards equal to the best in business.

The Clinton-Gore reforms of the federal bureacracy have largely been ignored by the public and the media, yet they have had an impact on the way the national government operates. Several federal departments and agencies—though certainly not all—have begun to improve their procedures to encourage common sense and accountability. There is growing recognition, both in and out of government circles, that "A reinvented civil service will have to invest more in people than in process. People will have to be more mobile and faster to learn; agencies will have to acquire more flexibility to attract the people they need."[19]

People now realize that managers need greater freedom to hire, promote, and fire workers, based on merit performance and merit promotion, with systems in place to measure program effectiveness. Encrusted bureaucratic procedures of the past have so constrained executive discretion that managers could not apply common sense to making reasonable decisions.

The political climate of the 1990s is more favorable than ever to considering such reforms as the deregulation of the federal civil service, although vested interests and political and legal obstacles make the outcome dubious.

BUREAUCRATIC RESPONSIVENESS

One of the most complex questions concerning public bureaucracies is whether they are responsive enough to the citizens and the elected officials who represent them. Being *responsive* means being quick to react and treating those who need assistance sympathetically. Determining how responsive an agency is depends on the perceptions of the person involved. A person who has had to stand for hours in a long line, whether at the post office or at a welfare agency, will complain about unresponsive bureaucrats. Someone who feels that a federal bureaucrat treats her "by the book" rather than by common sense also develops a critical view.

Standard Operating Procedures

Bureaucracies develop routines and standard operating procedures to ensure efficiency and productivity. Unfortunately, reliance on routine reduces flexibility. Just about everyone has at one time or another been turned away from the local post office because a package to be mailed was too large, or too small, or in the wrong kind of container. It is hard on such occasions to hold back our anger: Why can't they be flexible? Why can't they be reasonable? Why can't they deal with me in a personal way?

Procedures that allow the post office, the army, or the Internal Revenue Service to perform efficiently sometimes also diminish their ability to respond to the personalized needs of individuals. Routines help to prevent chaos and allow government behavior to be consistent, uniform, and impartial. The inevitable and necessary result of big bureaucracy is often a trade-off; quick, personalized, and sympathetic service is sacrificed for order.

Privatization

Can certain problems be better handled by agencies other than government bureaucracies? For example, should the government run railways, prisons, and a public television channel, or should we encourage the private sector and free market mechanisms to handle these responsibilities?

To whom should bureaucrats be accountable?

One of the important challenges in American government is how to keep nonelected government workers (bureaucrats) accountable to the taxpayers. After all, whose bureaucracy is this, anyway? Part of the challenge is figuring out how accountability can be guaranteed. How should the day-to-day operations and behavior of the typical U.S. public bureaucrat be controlled? From this list of possibilities, select one or more as your preferences.

The Constitution

Laws and statutes

Congress

The president

Their administrative superiors, including bureau chiefs and cabinet officers

Their own view of "the public interest"

Court rulings

Public opinion

Interest groups

The media

Their profession

Public-employee unions

Political parties and their platforms

Intellectual opinion

Their co-workers and colleagues

Taxpayers

Privatization is the process of contracting public services to private organizations. Examples of privatization include the contracting out by San Francisco of its budget analysis to a private firm, contracting out by Massachusetts of much of its tax collecting, and contracting out by the city of Chelsea, Massachusetts, of the operation of its schools to Boston University. The National Aeronautics and Space Administration (NASA) contracts out most of the manufacturing of its space vehicles.

Private or nonprofit firms handle a vast array of services, from repairing ships to delivering "meals-on-wheels" to the home-bound elderly. Some people suggest that our state and federal prisons might be more effectively operated by private firms. Advocates of privatization claim it would reduce costs and provide better service than reliance on the federal bureaucracy.[20]

Critics of privatization point to the cost overruns and waste in the procurement of weapons systems as failures of privatization. Those who advocate privatization on the ideological grounds that business is always superior to government are, according to David Osborne and Ted Gaebler, "selling the American people snake oil." Privatization is one answer, they say, but not *the* answer:

> Services can be contracted out or turned over to the private sector. But *governance* cannot. We can privatize discrete [governmental programs], but not the overall process of governance. If we did, we would have no mechanism by which to make collective decisions, no way to set the rules of the marketplace, no means to enforce rules of behavior. We would lose all sense of equity and altruism: services that could not generate a profit, whether housing for the homeless or health care for the poor, would barely exist....
>
> Business does some things better than government, but government does some things better than business. The public sector tends to be better, for instance, at policy management, regulation, ensuring equity, preventing discrimination or exploitation, ensuring continuity and stability of services, and ensuring social cohesion....Business tends to do better at performing economic tasks, innovating, replicating successful experiments, adapting to rapid change, abandoning unsuccessful or obsolete activities, and performing complex or technical tasks.[21]

Would we be better off if the U.S. Postal Service were turned over to private firms? A business executive who recently served as postmaster general, Anthony Frank, says no. He praises the Postal Service for its high on-time delivery and points out that all Americans, no matter where they live, get essentially the same service at the same price. "If you privatize it," Frank pointed out, "the cost would go up for a lot of Americans. [Thirty-two] cents compared to anywhere else in the world is an incredible bargain," says Frank. "It's 67 cents in Germany, 47 cents in Japan, and 42 cents in Canada. And they don't have any overnight service."[22]

BUREAUCRATIC ACCOUNTABILITY

The question of *bureaucratic responsiveness* is extremely difficult to disentangle from the question of *bureaucratic accountability*. In determining the responsiveness of the U.S. Navy or the FBI or the Department of Transportation, we must also ask who should oversee and control them.

Should bureaucrats be accountable to the president's cabinet, the majority who elected the president, or the majority in Congress? Plainly, most Americans would like the bureaucracy to be responsive to the public interest. But defining the public interest is the crucial problem. The president and the House and the Senate and the committees of Congress all claim to speak on behalf of the public interest. Moreover, to whom bureaucrats should be accountable is an inherently *polit-*

ical question. Certain forms of accountability favor some groups and interests over others. Accountability to the White House, for example, depends in large measure on the supporters' partisanship toward the president. Republicans, not surprisingly, favor strong presidential control over the bureaucracy when Republicans occupy the White House, as do Democrats when their party wins the White House.

To the President

Modern presidents invariably contend the president should be in charge, for the chief executive is responsive to the broadest constituency. A president, it is argued, must see that popular needs and expectations are converted into administrative action. When the nation elects a conservative president who favors cutbacks in federal programs and less governmental intervention in the economy, his policies must be carried out by the bureaucracy. The voters' wishes can be translated into action only if the bureaucrats support presidential policies.

Yet, as we have seen, under the American system of checks and balances the party winning a presidential election does not acquire control of the national government or even of the executive branch itself. Under our Constitution, the president is not even the undisputed master of the executive structure. Congress sets up the agencies, broadly determines their organization, provides money, and establishes the ground rules under which they operate. Congress constantly reviews the activities of the bureaucrats in appropriation hearings, special investigations, or informal inquiries. And, as we have also seen, the Senate confirms important cabinet-level leaders.

Presidents come into an ongoing system over which they have little control and within which they have little leeway to make the bureaucracy responsive. Still, some presidential control over the bureaucracy may be exercised through the powers of *appointment, reorganization,* and *budgeting*. More specifically, a president can attempt to control the bureaucracy by appointing or promoting sympathetic personnel, mobilizing public opinion and congressional pressure, changing the administrative apparatus, influencing budget decisions, using extensive personal persuasion, and if all else fails, shifting a bureaucracy's assignment to another department or agency (although this requires tacit if not explicit congressional approval).

Presidents appoint about 4,000 people to top positions within the executive branch; however, many of these are confidential assistants or special aides to cabinet officers. Moreover, many require Senate confirmation and are not exclusively a president's choice. Some suggest that a president's hand could be strengthened if the chief executive were able to make two or three times as many political appointments.

ASSISTANT SECRETARIES: A WEAK LINK Although presidents can usually recruit to their cabinets people of prominence and influence, they find it much harder to hire outstanding people at the assistant secretary level. Assistant secretaries transmit the views and values of the White House into the federal bureaucracy. These citizen-leaders serve as links between the people who elect the presidents and the civil servants. Many people, however, are not willing to interrupt their professional or business careers to become assistant secretaries.

Over the last three decades the position has become one of relatively low pay, little prestige in Washington, short tenure (people stay, on average, barely two years in these posts), and high cost to one's family. As a result, presidents often fill these slots with relatively young people who, from the day they arrive in Washington, are looking for their next job. These assistant secretaries, or people in comparable appointed posts, are forced to wear "kid gloves" with those they are supposed to regulate because it is from them that their next job is often

Thinking it Through

Most bureaucrats, most of the time, follow guidelines provided either in the law or by their administrative superiors, but at times many factors come into play as bureaucrats have to exercise judgment and discretion. Many of the considerations listed in the You Decide box on the facing page shape bureaucratic behavior implicitly rather than explicitly. Much of this chapter has analyzed the question of bureaucratic accountability. Perhaps it will revise your thinking.

Why Presidents Like to Reorganize the Bureaucracy

- *Shake up* an organization to increase managerial control
- *Simplify or streamline* the bureaucracy or a specific agency
- *Reduce costs* by lessening overlap, duplication, inefficiencies
- *Symbolize priorities* by signaling new responsibilities in new agencies
- *Improve program effectiveness* by bringing separate but logically related programs to the same agency
- *Improve policy integration* by placing competitive or conflicting interests within a single organization
- *Downgrade* the importance of a program to weaken it
- *Increase power* over an unresponsive agency by installing their own people.

likely to come. Others have strong ideological convictions but little experience in administration and congressional politics. Still others use the position as a transition to retirement.

These presidential appointees have to deal with civil servants who know their "bosses" will not be there long. Most civil servants have virtually secure jobs, and sometimes all they have to do to ignore presidentially selected assistant secretaries is to wait them out for a year or two. Moreover, in and around Washington, government workers constitute a powerful political group. Assistant secretaries who try to significantly alter the policy directions of those who are supposedly under their supervision may do so at considerable political and legal peril.

THE SENIOR EXECUTIVE SERVICE   The Civil Service Reform Act of 1978 created a Senior Executive Service. This pool of about 8,000 career officials (which can include up to 10 percent political appointees by an administration) can be filled without senatorial confirmation, and its individual members are subject to transfer from one program to another within a department according to an administration's wishes. The service was created to make senior career bureaucrats—especially those enmeshed in issue networks—more responsive to the goals and policy preferences of the White House. This new service gave presidents greater flexibility in selecting, promoting, and rewarding with financial bonuses those in the top career service who are productive and responsive.

The Civil Service Reform Act of 1978 was viewed with skepticism. Some feared an executive service would be put to political use. Others worried that without strong White House support, the noble intentions of the act would not be achieved. The Senior Executive Service has not lived up to many of its creators' expectations. It has had little impact on the federal workers it was supposed to help. Because of federal budgetary problems, the bonuses and related incentives have been less than was expected. Morale in the senior ranks of the federal bureaucracy is pretty much the same as it was before the service was created. The White House, however, has enjoyed an increase in the flexibility of assignments, and recent presidents have shrewdly used this flexibility to their advantage to influence and discipline the upper reaches of the executive branch.

THE OFFICE OF MANAGEMENT AND BUDGET   Ever since Franklin Roosevelt strengthened the presidential staffs, the budget bureau (currently called the Office of Management and Budget) has been a key resource. OMB's primary task is to prepare the president's annual budget. The budget is a major vehicle for shaping a president's policy priorities. It is the place and the process that determines which programs will get more funds, which will be cut, and which will remain the same. Departments and agencies fight to win larger chunks of the president's budget projections. OMB supervises the preparation of the budget and hence assists very directly in the formulation of policy. It weighs and evaluates the merits of the countless proposals and pleas that constantly pour in upon the White House.

Ninety-six percent of OMB's staff are career officials trained to evaluate ongoing projects and new spending requests. OMB's top officials are presidential appointees, and they are often among a president's most important advisers. They help a president make critical decisions not only about the budget but also about management practices, collaborative efforts among government agencies, and legislative planning. OMB makes sure that both the departments and Congress are informed of the president's legislative preferences and plays an important role in expanding the policy and administrative options open to a president.[23]

To Congress

Congress has a number of ways to exercise control over the bureaucracy: by establishing agencies, formulating budgets, appropriating funds, confirming personnel, authorizing new programs or new shifts in direction, conducting investigations and hearings, reorganizing authority, and rebuking officials.

The foundation of this bureaucratic power is legal authority. A bureaucrat's information and expertise augment this legal authority. Ordinarily, bureaucrats know more than anyone else about their programs and the consequences of what they are doing. Recognizing this, Congress may request agency heads to make initial proposals and provide cost and price estimates. To reduce bureaucratic deception, Congress has imposed stiff penalties for providing misleading information.

Still, Congress is under fire, at least in some quarters, for encouraging the growth of federal spending and for deliberately allowing the bureaucracy to remain too independent. Members of Congress, so this reasoning goes, profit from the growth and complexity of the federal government. Most constituents, especially businesspeople, turn to their members of Congress for help as they battle federal red tape. Hence, as the federal bureaucracy and its funds grow, so does the influence of members of Congress. Members of Congress regularly earn political credit by interceding in federal agencies on behalf of their constituents.

> The brutal fact is that only a small minority of our 535 members of Congress would trade the present bureaucratic structure for one which was an efficient, effective agent of the general interest—the political payoffs of the latter are lower than those of the former. Congressional talk of inefficient, irresponsible, out-of-control bureaucracy is typically just that—talk—and when it is not, it usually refers to agencies under the jurisdiction of other legislators' committees. Why do reformers continually ignore the fact that Congress has all the power necessary to enforce the "people's will" on the bureaucracy? Congress can abolish or reorganize an agency. Congress can limit or expand an agency's jurisdiction, or allow its authority to lapse entirely. Congress can slash an agency's appropriations. Congress can investigate. Congress can do all these things, but individual congressmen generally find reasons not to do so.[24]

Congress, it is charged, anxious whenever possible to avoid conflict, adopts such sweeping legislation and delegates so much authority to the bureaucracy that bureaucrats, in effect, have become the nation's lawmakers. Congress could pass laws with precise wording, but it would get too bogged down in details to complete its work. Congress does not generally specify details. Instead, Congress declares its policy in general terms and empowers appropriate agencies to make appropriate decisions to meet varying circumstances throughout the nation.

It is not Congress as a whole that shares the direction over the bureaucracy with the president. More accurately, individual members and committees specialize in the appropriations and oversight processes. They oversee policies of a particular cluster of agencies—often the agencies serving constituents in their own districts. Some legislators stake out a claim over more general policies. Members of Congress, who see presidents come and go, come to think they know more about particular agencies than the president does (and often they do). Some congressional leaders prefer to seal off "their" agencies from presidential direction to maintain influence over public policy. Sometimes their power is institutionalized; the army chief of engineers, for example, is given authority by law to plan public works and report to Congress without going through the president.

Another factor works in favor of congressional control. Every day thousands of bureaucrats are involved in making millions of decisions. A president has limited time, limited resources, and limited political influence over many of these agencies. Presidents and their staffs can become involved only in matters of significant political interest. Members of Congress, with an institutional staff of well over 20,000, however, can operate in areas far from the presidential spotlight.

So, whose bureaucracy is this anyway? Presidents and members of Congress both strive to exercise control over the bureaucracy, each in their own way. Interest groups and court rulings also influence the way the bureaucracy operates. For their part, career bureaucrats say they are responsive to the laws and statutes they work under and to their own standards of professionalism and responsibility. No one answer exists to the question of who or what controls the bureaucracy. And because of this, there is a never-ending search for improved means of ensuring bureaucratic accountability. This search and the experiments with countless instruments—reorganization, deregulating the public service, sunset practices, selective privatization, budgetary planning, and oversight hearings—continue.

It is increasingly clear, moreover, that virtually all national bureaucracies are more responsive nowadays than once was the case. Even organizations such as the FBI or the Corps of Engineers are now reasonably accountable to Congress and the White House, and ultimately to the American people. "Thanks to Freedom of Information statutes and other 'sunshine' legislation, [the bureaucracy] has become less selective, and the weakening of iron triangles has made it much more responsive to broad constituencies and much less the creature of its own clients."[25] Also, new restrictions the Clinton administration is enforcing prohibit those who leave government from working for the agency they recently left on any contractual basis.

REFORM AND REORGANIZATION

Some writers call for a radical overhaul of the civil service system. One observer, for example, calls for appointments for only 6 to 12 years—term limits for civil servants. Job security creates deadwood, he argues, so periodic reexamination of employee qualifications would greatly increase employee productivity and responsiveness. Another suggestion is to rotate professionals from outside the government or from other agencies to loosen up stiffened joints, bring new blood, and encourage breadth. Such rotation might also break up the iron triangles—alliances that get fixed among senior civil servants, members of Congress, and outside client interest groups.

More realistic are the efforts to give more discretion to civil service executives and provide greater flexibility in the way government personnel systems operate. But members of Congress remain jealous of their prerogatives and are reluctant to delegate additional powers to the executive branch.

From 1949 to 1983, Congress delegated considerable discretion to presidents in reorganizing the executive departments. Each president made major reorganizing proposals, most of which Congress approved. Today presidential proposals for reorganization must be approved by a joint resolution of the two chambers, making reorganization more difficult.

Congress is always sensitive to the implications of any reorganization that may affect their committee structure. Congressional committee leaders are aware that if they restructure the executive branch, they may have to reorganize their own committee systems, and this might upset the balance of power in Congress. "A willingness to surrender turf is as rare among members of Congress as it is among cabinet secretaries."[26]

Presidents, however, still have reasonably broad powers to reorganize the bureaucracy within the various cabinet departments. Yet even here, congressional committees take an active interest in how and why these changes are implemented. Interest groups also watch proposed changes and try to calculate how they will affect pet programs. In short, changing the shape of an administration is more than a matter of efficiency and economy. It is also a matter of *policy outcomes:* who gets what, how, and why.

Although nearly everybody favors efficient government and responsive bureaucracy, difficulties arise when you get specific because the specifics often upset the already established distribution of power in the Washington power system. Still, thanks to the end of the cold war and to continuing efforts to eliminate budget deficits, the federal bureaucracy is shrinking and in many ways is also more efficient and responsive than in the past. But it has a long way to go before the public becomes a fan of its existence and performance.

SUMMARY

1. We often condemn bureaucracy and bureaucrats, yet we continue to turn to them to solve our toughest problems and to render more and better services. A survey of our bureaucratic agencies, then, is also a survey of how our political system has tried to identify our most important national goals and how policies are implemented.

2. The American bureaucracy does not adhere to the textbook model of management organization, as it is not fully subordinate to any branch of government. It has at least two immediate bosses: Congress and the president. It must pay considerable attention as well to the courts and their rulings and, of course, to well-organized interest groups and public opinion. In many ways the bureaucracy is a semi-independent force—a fourth branch of government—in American politics.

3. Debates and controversy over big government and big bureaucracy, and over how to reorganize and eliminate waste in them, continue. Compared with many other nations and their centralized bureaucracies, the hand of bureaucracy rests more gently and less oppressively on Americans than on citizens elsewhere.

4. Whom and how the government hires and what discretion or powers it grants its employees are controversial topics. To work in the career public service is to have the opportunity to serve people, solve problems, and try to bring about a better society. Efforts to make the bureaucracy more responsive are enduring struggles in a constitutional democracy. Such issues are rightly debated in every presidential election.

FURTHER READING

JOEL D. ABERBACH, *Keeping a Watchful Eye: The Politics of Congressional Oversight* (Brookings Institution, 1990).

JOHN J. DiIULIO, JR., ED. *Deregulating the Public Service: Can Government Be Improved?* (Brookings Institution, 1994).

JOHN J. DiIULIO JR., GERALD GARVEY, AND DONALD F. KETTL, *Improving Government Performances: An Owner's Manual* (Brookings Institution, 1993).

ANTHONY DOWNS, *Inside Bureaucracy* (Little, Brown, 1967).

JAMES W. FESLER AND DONALD F. KETTL, *The Politics of the Administrative Process* (Chatham House, 1991).

CHARLES T. GOODSELL, *The Case for Bureaucracy*, 3d ed. (Chatham House, 1994).

AL GORE, *Creating a Government That Works Better and Costs Less: The Report of the National Performance Review* (Plume-Penguin, 1993).

LARRY HILL, ED., *The State of Public Bureaucracy* (M. E. Sharpe, 1992).

PHILIP K. HOWARD, *The Death of Common Sense: How Law Is Suffocating America* (Random House, 1994).

PATRICIA INGRAHAM AND DAVID ROSENBLOOM, EDS., *The Promise and Paradox of Civil Service Reform* (University of Pittsburgh Press, 1992).

DONALD F. KETTL AND JOHN J. DiIULIO, JR. EDS., *Inside the Reinvention Machine: Appraising Governmental Reform* (Brookings Institution, 1995).

HERBERT KAUFMAN, *The Administrative Behavior of Federal Bureau Chiefs* (Brookings Institution, 1981).

PAUL C. LIGHT, *Thickening Government: Federal Hierarchy and the Diffusion of Accountability* (Brookings Institution, 1995).

PAUL C. LIGHT, *Monitoring Government: Inspectors General and the Search for Accountability* (Brookings Institution, 1993).

DAVID OSBORNE AND TED GAEBLER, *Reinventing Government: How the Entrepreneurial Spirit Is Transforming the Public Sector* (Addison-Wesley, 1992).

B. GUY PETERS, *The Politics of Bureaucracy*, 3d ed. (Longman, 1989).

DENNIS D. RILEY, *Controlling the Federal Bureaucracy* (Temple University Press, 1987).

JOHN T. TIERNEY, *The U.S. Postal Service* (Auburn House, 1988).

JAMES Q. WILSON, *Bureaucracy: What Government Agencies Do and Why They Do It* (Basic Books, 1989).

B. DAN WOOD AND RICHARD W. WATERMAN, *Bureaucratic Dynamics: The Role of Bureaucracy in a Democracy* (Westview Press, 1994).

Four useful journals are *Journal of Policy Analysis and Management, National Journal, Public Administration Review,* and *Government Executive.*

DOMESTIC POLICY

With the collapse of communism and the end of the cold war, the agenda of American politics shifted from foreign to domestic policy. For more than forty years we had been engaged in a world-wide effort to contain communism and defend our interests against a military super power with a global agenda. The cost of readiness for a possible war with the Soviet Union was tremendous, and the United States invested heavily in defense and a nuclear arsenal. In presidential elections, foreign policy leadership and national security experience were attributes Americans looked for when choosing a leader.

In the 1990s all this changed. Although we are still engaged in peacekeeping operations and occasional skirmishes around the world, the sense of a military threat to the United States is greatly reduced. George Bush, whose personal background and presidency emphasized foreign policy, lost the 1992 election to Bill Clinton, who understood that domestic policy had come to be the driving force in American politics. The presidential campaigns of 1992 and 1996 focused on the economy—jobs, growth, controlling the deficit, keeping inflation under control, as well as on health care reform, welfare reform, and crime. Downsizing government, a popular theme among Republicans in their 1994 election sweep and a centerpiece of Bob Dole's 1996 campaign, is also about domestic politics. This chapter is about domestic policy—how it is made, how it is implemented, and what the issues are in the current debate over domestic policy.

MAKING PUBLIC POLICY

Public policy is what government does. It is also what a government decides not to do. The policy-making process occurs within well-established boundaries or limits. Some policy ideas exist only in our dreams. The elimination of private property, for example, is outside the policy boundaries of the American political system.[1] Some of the boundaries of political acceptability stem from our political culture and ideology; others are the result of the structure of American government. Thousands of individuals are at work in the Washington policy-making process: White House staff and executive branch officials, congressional committee staff, lobbyists, professional political consultants, and unelected policy politicians in a variety of governmental and nongovernmental positions. They help clarify issues, resolve conflicts, and facilitate cooperation across institutions. Only by understanding their backgrounds, values, and responsibilities can we appreciate the complexities of national policy making.

Stages in the Policy-Making Process

There are numerous approaches to the study of public policy making. The choice of which approach is most appropriate depends on what policies are being considered, the particular stage of the process selected for analysis, and the analyst's assumptions and political values. Nevertheless, distinct stages in the policy-making process can be identified.

PROBLEM IDENTIFICATION What is the problem? How and by whom is the problem defined? Does the government need to intervene, regulate, or make some kind of decision? Should the problem be placed on the government's agenda? For example, if air pollution is making people sick, is this a matter for governmental attention? Which level of government—national, state, local, or all of them—should act? What forces determine whether a problem will reach the attention of government officials? A variety of factors and people are involved in the process of problem identification: events, crises, changes in expert opinion, changes in mass opinion, interest group agitation, and considerable involvement by elected officials and their staffs.

POLICY FORMULATION What should be done? How can we best assess the alternatives? Who should be involved in the planning and design of the policy? For example, if air pollution requires government action, what action is preferable? What alternatives should analysts consider?

POLICY ADOPTION Who needs to act? What branch of government should get involved? What constitutional, legal, or political requirements must be met? How specific or how general must the decision be? For example, should Congress pass a clean-air act, or should some regulatory body like the Environmental Protection Agency be asked to hold hearings and come up with recommendations? Or should the matter be turned over to the president, requiring an executive order and major addresses to the public?

POLICY IMPLEMENTATION Once the decisions are made, how should the policy be carried out? At what level of government will the policy be most effectively implemented? How much money should be spent, where, and how? How can the policy be effectively administered? During this stage policy is translated into practice. Congress often passes ambiguous legislation that conceals serious policy differences. As a result, the agencies responsible for implementing the policy are given considerable latitude to translate vague ideas into specific directives.[2]

POLICY EVALUATION Is the policy working? How is the impact of the policy measured? Who evaluates the policy? What are the consequences of policy evaluation and congressional oversight? For example, are antipollution laws really improving air quality? Are the administration's antidrug measures making any headway?

Program supporters and administrators tend to exaggerate the success of their favorite programs in order to justify the funds allocated to them. On the other hand, an agency may build in delays and deficiencies during evaluation to hide the real cost of its operations. Evaluation is never entirely nonpolitical; it is sometimes used by one party, branch of government, department, or agency against another.[3]

ECONOMIC POLICY

Our national government unquestionably has tremendous economic power. But soaring government spending and deficits have raised questions about how effectively the government is doing its job. Through two types of policy—**monetary policy** (control of the money supply) and **fiscal policy** (taxing and spending)—the government attempts to manage the economy's ups and downs, moderating both while encouraging steady economic growth. These powers emerged earlier this century through such developments as the Federal Reserve System, the income tax, and the growth of government spending.

Approaches to the Study of Public Policy

Despite their limitations, policy models help us understand some of the complexities of policy making. At least four approaches have been used to study policy making:

1. *Rational Person Model.* A policy is adopted if its benefits, broadly defined, outweigh its costs." The rationalist model requires an awareness of alternative courses of action, knowledge of the likely consequences of each alternative, substantial theoretical understanding of causal mechanisms, and choice among the alternatives on the basis of well-defined criteria."* This model is often called the *rational choice model.*
2. *Power Elite Model.* Businesses and wealthy individuals have a "privileged position" since politicians and the wealthy are mutually dependent for success. This approach advises that we should study government inaction as much as action.**
3. *Incremental Model.* Struggles for power among competing groups mean policy answers will be arrived at gradually. Our system of checks and balances promotes such a piecemeal approach to policy.†
4. *Policy Systems Model.* Policy "inputs," or the stages of the process, translate into "outputs," or laws. "The way policies are made affects the content of public policy."††

*Davis B. Bobrow and John S. Dryzek, *Policy Analysis by Design* (University of Pittsburgh Press, 1987), p.11. See also Frances Fox Piven and Richard Cloward, *Regulating the Poor: The Functions of Public Welfare* (Vintage Books, 1971).

**C. Wright Mills made the classic statement of this view in *The Power Elite* (Oxford University Press, 1956).

†Charles E. Lindblom, *The Intelligence of Democracy: Decision-Making through Mutual Adjustment* (Free Press, 1965).

††Thomas R. Dye, *Understanding Public Policy*, 8th ed. (Prentice Hall, 1995), p. 25.

The **Federal Reserve System,** or more simply "the Fed," is a private-public banking regulatory system established by Congress in 1913. The Fed consists of 12 regional banks and one central bank that have the job of controlling the monetary policy of the country as well as regulating and supervising the nation's banks and other financial institutions. While Congress and the President control *fiscal policy*—the taxing of citizens and spending of government revenues—the Fed controls *monetary policy*—policies that affect the growth rate of the nation's money supply, interest rates, and other economic activity.

The federal government has been involved from its start in setting policies that had economic consequences. The Constitution grants Congress power to regulate interstate and foreign commerce. This role was later broadened to include the power to provide internal improvements, which eventually led to the establishment of the Bank of the United States. With the Industrial Revolution came the need to deal with monopolies, child labor, and workplace safety. The government's involvement in the economy grew dramatically as a result of the Great Depression. The scale of social and economic dislocation prompted a governmental response well beyond anything seen before. In many ways it was those events more than a half century ago that today shape the way we approach the making of social and economic policy. Three approaches to the role of government in managing the economy deserve mention: Keynesian economics, supply-side economics, and monetarism.

KEYNESIAN ECONOMICS   Named after English economist John Maynard Keynes, this theory has influenced government policy makers since the 1930s. Keynes contended that government should take responsibility for increasing aggregate demand by spending during business slumps and curbing spending during booms. Politically, Keynesian economics present a problem. It is much easier to increase spending and government programs than it is to curb them. As a result, deficit spending has become the norm. To stimulate demand, the government spends more money than it takes in. For many years, this policy was thought to be beneficial to the economy; it was also convenient politically. However, the deficit has soared in recent years, and there have been no surpluses, even with economic growth.

SUPPLY-SIDE ECONOMICS   Ronald Reagan preached an alternative to Keynesian economics—despite the fact that he, more than any other president, relied on deficit spending to encourage economic growth. He pledged to balance the budget by cutting both taxes and government spending. In simple terms, supply-side economics holds that large cuts in taxes will inspire productive investment so that the initial loss of federal revenues will be offset by the taxes generated from expanded private economic activity.

MONETARISM   The core element of *monetarism* is the idea that prices, income, and economic stability are primarily the function of growth in the money supply. Monetarists contend the money supply is the key factor affecting the economy's performance. Further, they argue that there should be restrained yet steady growth in the money supply, enough to encourage solid economic growth but not inflation. Tightening the money supply can slow inflation, but that in turn can lead to a recession, as happened in the early 1980s.

Government Subsidies: How and Why?

All kinds of individuals and corporations benefit from government **subsidies,** which include tax reductions, government loans, special protections, outright cash, or credit assistance. Welfare programs for the needy may be the most publicized government assistance efforts, but "the preponderance of the benefits of many programs is garnered by profitable corporations and citizens in the top half of the nation's income distribution."[4] During the 1996 campaign, these subsidies were attacked by both Bob Dole and Bill Clinton as a form of "corporate welfare."

Computing how much is spent on subsidy programs is difficult because many federal subsidy programs are called something else: grants-in-aid, price supports, tax incentives, import quotas, stabilization programs, and loan guarantees. Government subsidy programs include:

1. *Cash benefits.* Cash payments help to support artists as well as researchers through federal agencies like the National Science Foundation and the National Endowment for the Humanities.

2. *Tax incentives.* Recipients of these subsidies receive no cash; they pay lower taxes than would normally be required. Tax deductions for mortgage interest on homes occupied by their owners are one example. The government makes no expenditure, but it still loses revenue.

3. *Credit subsidies.* Credit subsidies range from loans for financing students through college to the financing of a major public works project at a fraction of prevailing interest rates.

4. *Benefit-in-kind subsidies.* Recipients receive a product or service paid for by the government. Examples are food stamps and Medicare.

Other examples of federal subsidies are tariffs on imports that allow domestic producers to charge higher prices than free markets would bring. In fact, almost all economic groups at one time or another have benefited from government help. Many businesses have sought aid, and government has responded, for example, by bailing out savings and loan banks and the Chrysler Corporation, issuing government-backed loans to railroads, and building modern airports and interstate highways. Similarly, spokespersons for the poor seek a larger government role in providing health services, establishing a floor below which incomes are not allowed to fall, and subsidizing improved housing and employment opportunities. Governmental promotion can be used to help any group. But who shall be aided, in what way, and with what consequences? These are the important questions.

Promoting Commerce

Government's greatest help to commerce is probably maintaining peace and tranquility, providing the kind of environment in which people are free to pursue their economic interests. But the national government also supplies a number of specific services for the business community.

BUSINESS AND INDUSTRY   The Department of Commerce is sometimes known as the nation's "service center for business." Its National Institute of Standards and Technology (NIST) provides valuable technical assistance to corporations like General Electric, DuPont, and IBM.[5] The Department of Commerce also undertakes basic research in ocean science and engineering, meteorology, and weather forecasting. The Patent and Trademark Office (PTO) administers the patent system for new inventions and also issues trademarks to protect distinctive names for commercial purposes.

AGRICULTURE   The impressive success and competitiveness of American agriculture owes much to the federal government and its subsidies—almost as much as to fertile soil, hard work, and the technology revolution. Agriculture and food-related

American manufacturers urge customers to "buy American," but these same manufacturers often sell cars made abroad.

businesses are our largest industry, bigger than computers and automobiles or the movie and recording industries. Agriculture and food-related businesses generate nearly one out of every five jobs in our private sector; they account for almost 20 percent of the GDP and 15 percent of our exports and have a high rate of productivity.[6] The federal government has invested large sums of money in basic and applied agricultural research. Major federal initiatives in irrigation and rural electrification have also fostered significant strides in productivity. Loans and credit programs help farmers purchase needed equipment.

For decades Congress stabilized prices and output for a range of products, everything from tobacco to mohair, but two-thirds of the money went to grain. Then in 1996 Congress passed the Federal Agriculture Improvement and Reform Act (FAIR), which will remove subsidies on wheat, corn, feed grain, cotton, and rice, and reduce them on peanuts, sugar, and dairy products. For the next seven years farmers will receive Freedom to Farm payments that permit them to grow whatever they want. These payments are intended to ease the transition to a free market in agriculture.

Free Trade or Protectionism?

The United States used to be the leading exporting nation, but our competitive edge eroded in the 1970s and 1980s. Today the United States must strive to be an equal among peers. Our biggest challenge comes from Pacific Rim nations, such as Japan, Korea, Taiwan, and Singapore. Our international competitors have benefited from the spread of technology and capital, and many foreign governments have worked closely with industries in planning competitive products and maximizing export possibilities.

Our strong position in technology and our vast agricultural industry are both now threatened by other nations, which are quickly moving up and doing what we do, but at lower costs and with a fresh assertiveness. The implications for American industry are staggering. Thousands of plants have been closed; hundreds of thousands of workers at steel mills, machine-tool factories, textile and apparel manufacturing plants, and in the computer, electronics, and communications industries have been laid off. Industry and the unions blame the problem on imports.

But the problem is not that we are importing too much but that we are exporting too little. German cars, Japanese electronics, and Indonesian textiles are fine products, provided we are productive enough to pay for them. If other countries can produce better cars or shoes at a lower price, then free traders argue we should deploy our labor and capital to do what we can do better.

The question is also whether our products are given fair treatment by other nations. American agricultural products are denied entry into some countries, automobile manufacturers complain of unfair restrictions abroad, and some countries attempt to exploit the U.S. advantage in technology by copying our products and then selling them back to us or to other countries at a profit. Some countries practice *dumping,* selling products in another country below the cost of manufacturing, with the obvious intention of driving our producers out of the market and then raising prices to profitable levels. These products may be heavily subsidized by the country doing the dumping. The United States often reciprocates; in recent years, we have imposed "voluntary" limits on Japanese automobiles and European steel imports, and we have long subsidized our agricultural exports with price supports and inexpensive credit.

Protectionism—erecting tariff barriers to protect domestic industry—sounds like an easy and workable solution to the trade deficit, but the trade deficit itself is only symptomatic of more profound economic problems. Economists almost always favor free trade and strongly dislike protectionism. Protectionism, they

The vote on the North American Free Trade Agreement was preceded by battles between labor and management, between economists and environmentalists, and between free traders and protectionists.

say, prevents efficient use of resources, for consumers pay much more for protected products than they would otherwise. Tariffs also inevitably invite retaliation from foreign countries.[7]

Americans usually favor free trade, having learned that if we want people to buy our goods, we must be willing to buy theirs. Politicians and many chief executive officers of struggling companies often replace the concept of "free trade" with the nebulous term "fair trade." Elected officials from Bill Clinton down speak of the need to "level the playing field" against unfair competition. However, when politicians speak of unfair trade, they do not mean the trade transaction was somehow illegal or unfair to consumers, but that domestic industries are being hurt. They argue that "fair trade" and "protection" bestow benefits. Workers in unskilled or semi-skilled occupations, who may find a job change difficult, are allowed to keep their jobs. In addition, because industries like steel and textiles may be necessary for security reasons, the government must protect them, even though the cost may be high.

THE NORTH AMERICAN FREE TRADE AGREEMENT   On December 17, 1992, leaders of the United States, Canada, and Mexico signed the **North American Free Trade Agreement (NAFTA)**, which formed the largest free-trade zone in the world, even surpassing the European Union's 13-country conglomerate. Though trade between the United States, Canada, and Mexico will not be absolutely "free" or unimpeded, the agreement will have a tremendous impact on the economies of all three countries.

Critics of NAFTA are worried that Mexican environmental regulations are less stringent than those in the United States, and Mexican workers are willing to work for lower wages. Both of these factors may make relocation to Mexico attractive to many U.S. companies seeking to lower their labor and pollution costs.

Thinking it Through

What constitutes an "American" car? After finishing this short quiz you know (if you did not know already) that the company name has little relevance. Many foreign companies have plants in the United States that employ American workers and use a high percentage of American parts. General Motors, Ford, and Chrysler all have joint ventures with foreign-owned companies that place some of their models in the "import" category. Is a Toyota Camry an American car if it is built in Mexico in a plant partially owned by Ford? What defines an American product: ownership of company? nationality of employees? location of production? domestic content of components?

The "Buy American" movement reached its apex in 1992. In January of that year, the president of Monsanto (an American chemicals manufacturer) offered each of its 12,000 employees $1,000 to buy or lease a new American car. Other countries charged discrimination, arguing that our government should have no role in promoting homegrown products over imports; citizens, they maintained, should choose the best product available, not the one that says "Made in the U.S.A."

SOURCE: Jacqueline Mitchell, "Growing Movement To 'Buy American' Debates the Term," *The Wall Street Journal*, January 24, 1992, A1.

Advocates of NAFTA, including Gerald Ford, Jimmy Carter, George Bush, Bill Clinton, and Bob Dole, claim a free-trade zone will create jobs for Americans and increase profits for U.S.-owned companies. Proponents predict that our exports to Mexico will increase when tariff barriers are eliminated. In addition, they point out that Mexico has a responsibility to enforce health and environmental laws according to NAFTA's side agreements.

Some estimates indicate that 112,000 U.S. jobs will be eliminated as U.S. firms expand in Mexico, but as many as 130,000 new U.S. jobs will be created, many of them high-tech, high-wage jobs. Not all studies come to the same conclusion, however. Some studies estimate 1.5 million U.S. jobs will be created by the end of the decade due to NAFTA, while others conclude the United States will lose up to 900,000 jobs.[8]

THE BUDGET: POLICY BLUEPRINT

The implementation of public policies requires money. Nothing reflects the growth in public policy in the United States and the rise of big government more clearly than the increased spending by the federal government. As recently as 1933, the federal government spent only $4 billion, about $30 per capita. In 1997 the respective figures were $1,635 billion, about $6,100 per capita (see Table 14-1). Today federal, state, and local governments spend sums of money equal to about one third of the income of all Americans, and the national government is the biggest spender of all. In recent years, Washington has distributed more than all state and local governments combined. With revenues of $1.495 trillion and a national budget of about $1.635 trillion for 1997, our national government annually spends 22 percent of the gross domestic product (GDP), or nearly one dollar out of every four. The national debt reached about

"Remember, son, we are a government of loopholes, not of men."

Drawing by Dana Fradon. © 1976 The New Yorker Magazine, Inc.

TABLE 14-1

Presidents and Their Deficits in Billions of Dollars, 1934–1997

President	Fiscal Year Period*	Years in Office	Deficit at End of Period (billions)	Increase During Period (billions)
Franklin Roosevelt	1934–45	12	260.1	237.6
Harry Truman	1946–53	8	266.0	5.9
Dwight Eisenhower	1954–61	8	292.6	26.6
John Kennedy	1962–63	2	310.3	17.7
Lyndon Johnson	1964–69	6	365.8	55.5
Richard Nixon	1970–74	5	483.9	118.1
Gerald Ford	1975–77	3¼**	706.4	222.5
Jimmy Carter	1978–81	4	994.3	287.9
Ronald Reagan	1982–89	8	2,867.5	1,873.2
George Bush	1990–93	4	4,326.5	1,530.0
Bill Clinton	1994–97	4	5,566.2***	1,239.7***

SOURCE: *Budget of the United States Government, Fiscal Year 1992* (Government Printing Office, 1991); *Budget of the United States Government, Fiscal Year 1995* (Government Printing Office, 1994).

*Fiscal years shown approximate but do not exactly match presidential terms of office.

**Includes extra three months for change in fiscal year between 1976 and 1977.

***Projected.

$5.2 trillion in 1994, and we pay $232 billion each year in interest payments on that debt.[9]

The politics of budgeting and reducing the deficit resulted in a seven-month-long impasse between President Clinton and the Republican-controlled 104th Congress. Unable to pass a budget bill the president would sign, Congress had passed 14 partial spending bills to keep the government going for a few days or weeks. Twice the government was shut down in all but essential services. When a bill was finally agreed upon, both sides claimed victory—the Republicans in Congress because they forced the president to agree to large cutbacks in domestic spending and a balanced budget in seven years, and Bill Clinton because he had protected spending for education, job training, and the environment. Subsequent polls showed Clinton the winner in terms of public opinion, as more people blamed Congress for the government shutdown.

The battle over the budget and deficit reduction continued through the 1996 election campaign. Bob Dole's promised 15 percent tax reduction brought back the supply-side debate over whether the economic stimulus of a tax cut generated enough growth to cut the deficit. Clinton proposed a set of tax cuts targeted to college tuition, college savings accounts, and child-care. Ross Perot, who had made deficit reduction an issue in the 1992 election, stressed the issue again in 1996.

Where the Money Comes From

The federal government gets most of its funds from taxes (see Figure 14-1). Other monies come from borrowing, special fees and fines, grants and gifts, and from administrative and commercial revenues. Tax collecting is one of the oldest activities of government. Putting power over taxation into the hands of the people was a major achievement in the development of self-government. "No taxation without representation" has been a battle cry the world over.

Raising money is only one objective of taxation. Regulation and, more recently, promoting economic growth are others. In a broad sense all taxation regulates human behavior. For example, a **progressive income tax**—by which people with high incomes generally pay larger fractions of their incomes than people with lower incomes—has a leveling tendency on incomes.

In the federal budget for fiscal year 1997 federal receipts include the following:

1. *Individual income taxes.* Taxes on individuals' incomes account for about 43 percent of the federal government's tax revenue, or 39 percent of the government's *total revenue* when you include borrowing. Over the years, the income tax has grown increasingly complex as Congress has responded to claims for differing kinds of exemptions and rates. The great advantage of the income tax is its flexibility.

2. *Corporate income taxes.* These account for just over 11 percent of the national government's tax revenues. As late as 1942, revenue from corporate income taxes exceeded that from individual income taxes.

3. *Social insurance receipts.* This is the second largest and most rapidly rising source of federal revenue, accounting for 33 percent of all federal revenue, not including borrowing. These are highly regressive taxes; low-income people generally pay larger fractions of their income than do high-income people.

4. *Excise taxes.* These taxes account for roughly 4 percent of federal revenue. Federal taxes on liquor, tobacco, gasoline, telephones, air travel, and other so-called "luxury items" are projected to total about $60 billion in 1997.

5. *Customs duties and tariffs.* Although no longer the main source of federal income, in recent years these taxes provided an annual yield of almost $20 billion.

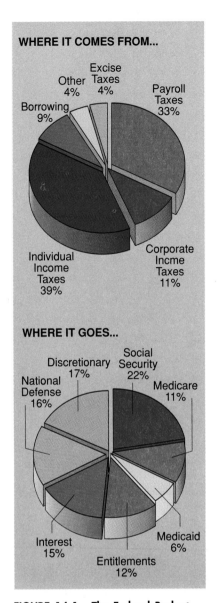

WHERE IT COMES FROM...

Excise Taxes 4%
Other 4%
Borrowing 9%
Payroll Taxes 33%
Individual Income Taxes 39%
Corporate Income Taxes 11%

WHERE IT GOES...

Discretionary 17%
National Defense 16%
Social Security 22%
Medicare 11%
Interest 15%
Entitlements 12%
Medicaid 6%

FIGURE 14-1   The Federal Budget.

SOURCE: "A Citizen's Guide to the Federal Budget," Executive Office of the President of the United States, February 1996.

A few years ago the idea of a flat tax was virtually unknown. But proposals of a flat tax system with just one tax rate instead of the several we now have, have recently gained momentum. Jerry Brown, former governor of California and 1992 Democratic presidential hopeful, made the flat tax an integral part of his campaign, but the idea did not gain much momentum. In 1996, several Republicans took up the same issue. Presidential candidate Steve Forbes made a flat tax the central theme of his campaign. He proposed a 17 percent rate, similar to the system introduced in Congress by Representative Dick Armey of Texas. House Speaker Newt Gingrich and Senator Bob Dole drafted former Housing and Urban Development Secretary Jack Kemp to chair the National Commission on Economic Growth and Tax Reform. This commission's report recommended a flat tax with a rate no higher than 19 percent.

The main appeal of the flat tax is its simplicity. One objection to Steve Forbes's proposal was that it did not allow deductions for mortgages or charitable donations. Critics speculate that flat tax rates as low as the 17 and 19 percent proposals would not raise enough tax revenue. Some studies indicate that a 21 to 23 percent rate would be needed to maintain current federal spending levels. Advocates counter that a simpler tax system and the reality of lowering taxes will spur economic growth enough to make up the difference.

GNP and GDP

National output is the total amount of goods and services produced by a country and is measured either by *gross national product* (GNP) or *gross domestic product* (GDP). GNP measures all output attributed to labor or property supplied by residents of the United States. A manufacturing plant in Singapore owned by the United States would increase GNP, but a Japanese-owned automobile plant located in the United States would not. On the other hand, GDP is the total amount of goods and services produced domestically—regardless of ownership. In this case, the automobile plant would count towards GDP; the manufacturing plant in Singapore would not. GDP is now the preferred measure of domestic economic activity.

6. *Borrowing*. Since World War II, the government has regularly resorted to borrowing money to finance itself. Since 1969, the government has never had a surplus, and it has resorted to borrowing in 38 of the last 42 years.

What is the best type of tax? Some say a progressive income tax because it is relatively easy to collect, hits hardest those who are most able to pay, and hardly touches those at the bottom of the income ladder. Others argue that excise taxes are the fairest because they are paid by people who spend money for luxury goods and thus obviously have money to spare. On the other hand, excise taxes are more expensive to collect than income taxes, and in some cases, such as the tax on tobacco, they may hit the poor the hardest. Excise taxes also face strong resistance from affected industries: tobacco, liquor, and airlines, for example. An excise tax on yachts passed by Congress in 1990 but later repealed in 1993, had the unintended consequence of putting several thousand yacht builders out of business.[10]

A type of tax often suggested is a *flat tax*, which requires wage-earners to pay one "flat" percentage for taxes, regardless of the size of their income. Several prominent Republicans, including House Majority Leader Dick Armey and Republican vice-presidential candidate Jack Kemp, advocated a flat tax. Steve Forbes, Republican presidential candidate in 1996, made a 17 percent flat tax the central theme of his campaign.

Where the Money Goes

Where does the money go? Much of it, of course, goes for benefit payments and national defense. In 1997, 16 percent went to national defense, 15 percent to interest on the national debt, 51 percent to direct benefit payments for individuals (such as Social Security and Medicare), and 17 percent for nondefense discretionary spending (programs such as education, training, science, technology, housing, transportation, and foreign aid).[11]

Another way of understanding how the money is spent is to consider federal outlays as a percentage of the nation's **gross domestic product** (GDP), an estimate of the total output of all U.S. economic activity. Gross National Product (GNP) was the standard measure of economic activity through the 1980s; GDP is now preferred by economists because it more accurately gauges the domestic economy. In fiscal year 1997, spending on **entitlement programs**—programs such as Social Security, Medicare, and unemployment insurance to which qualified persons are "entitled" by national legislation—was nearly 11 percent of the GDP; spending for defense went down from 5.3 percent in 1981 to 3.3 percent by 1997; payments on the deficit went up as a percentage of GDP from 2.3 percent in 1981 to 3.0 percent in 1997; and nondefense discretionary spending declined from 5.7 percent in 1981 to 3.6 percent by 1997.[12]

Years ago, federal revenues and outlays were so small that national taxing and spending had little impact on the overall economy. Today the federal government extracts billions of dollars from the economy and pumps them back, with profound effects on the U.S. and world economy. Much of the federal budget is "uncontrollable" in the sense that "mandatory growth" in many programs is built into the law. These are programs that do not come up for annual review or decision by either Congress or the president; they just keep on going and growing automatically. "Mandatory" programs now account for nearly 65 percent of the federal budget.[13]

The most important uncontrollable portions of the budget are the large entitlement programs for social welfare such as Social Security, Medicare, unemployment benefits, outstanding contracts, and other fiscal obligations. The most controllable part of the budget is defense spending. With the collapse of the Soviet Union, additional real cuts in defense spending were anticipated, but military expenses for peacekeeping and humanitarian aid may add to the outlay.

The Budget Process

Under our Constitution, Congress must authorize the spending of funds and appropriate the money, but in practice it is the president who first proposes the budget. The budget process involves a series of accommodations between the executive and legislative branches.

THE EXECUTIVE BRANCH   The budget process begins two years in advance, when the various departments and agencies estimate their needs and propose budgets to the president.[14] While Congress is debating the budget for the fiscal year immediately ahead, agencies are making estimates for the next year. (See Figure 14-2). Agency officials take into account not only their needs as they see them but also the overall presidential program and the probable reactions of Congress. Departmental budgets are detailed; they include estimates for personnel, supplies, office space, and the like.

Treasury Secretary Robert Rubin resorted to some creative financing to pay the government's bills when wrangling between Bill Clinton and Congress over continuing budget resolutions in 1996 cut off the money for government.

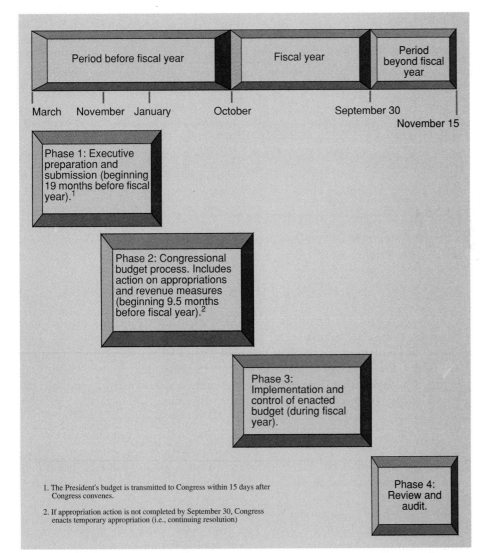

FIGURE 14-2   The Federal Budget-Making Process.

SOURCE: Based on data from *A Glossary of Terms Used in the Federal Budget* (General Accounting Office, 1981), p. 7.

The **Office of Management and Budget (OMB),** a staff agency of the president, handles the next phase. The OMB director and staff often prune the agencies' requests severely. Executive branch hearings are then held to give agency people a chance to clarify and defend their estimates.

Finally, the OMB director goes to the president with a single consolidated set of estimates of both revenue and expenditures, the product of perhaps a year's work. The president takes a few days to review these figures and make some adjustments. In January, soon after Congress convenes, the president submits his budget and an accompanying message.

THE LEGISLATIVE BRANCH Under the Constitution, only Congress can appropriate funds. Yet today, Congress essentially follows the lead of the president in making national budget decisions. In 1974 Congress adopted the Budget Reform Act, which was intended to give Congress a more effective role in the budget process. This act specifies that when submitting proposals, the president must include proposed changes in tax laws, estimates of amounts of revenue lost through existing preferential tax treatments, and five-year estimates of the costs of new and continuing federal programs. The act also calls on the president to seek authorizing legislation for a program a year before asking Congress to fund it.

After Congress appropriates money, it reserves the right to check how that money is being spent. The General Accounting Office (GAO) is headed by the comptroller general, who is appointed by the president with the approval of the Senate for a 15-year term. The GAO, which has more than 5,000 employees,[15] uses spot sampling methods to check up on the adequacy and effectiveness, as well as the honesty, of a program's performance.[16]

The Politics of Taxing and Spending

One function of tax policy is to decide who shall pay how much to finance government spending. Over the years tax legislation has also sought to promote economic growth of various kinds and to reward certain types of behavior, such as owning a home, contributing to charities, and investing in high-risk but desirable (from a national standpoint) energy or housing ventures. Cynics suggest, too, that from a member of Congress's point of view, tax legislation has the additional and important function of raising campaign funds. Whenever tax legislation is under consideration in Congress, swarms of lobbyists are eager to attend expensive campaign dinners and to contribute generously to campaign coffers.[17]

THE TAX BURDEN No one likes taxes. Most of us complain that our tax load is too heavy and that someone else is not paying a fair share. People with high incomes in the highest tax brackets grumble. People with low-incomes point out that even a low tax may deprive them of the necessities of life. People with middle-incomes consider their situation the worst of all. Their incomes are not high, but their taxes are.

THE DEFICIT The **deficit** is the difference between the revenues raised from the other sources of government income and the expenditures of government, including paying the interest on past borrowing. Today it reaches into the trillions of dollars. In the budget for fiscal year 1993, roughly one in four dollars was raised by borrowing.

When individuals are suddenly faced with emergency expenses greater than their incomes, they borrow money. The same used to be true of government. During military and economic crises, the federal government went heavily into debt; it engaged in *deficit spending*. But recently, we have also incurred great debt during a period of peace with a relatively healthy economy. We borrowed $23 billion during World War I, about $13 billion during the 1930s, and $200 billion during World War II. In 1995, the federal debt was estimated to be about $192 billion, increasing the gross federal deficit to about $5 trillion.[18] Borrowing costs money. Although the federal government can borrow at a relatively low rate, the interest on the federal debt is more than $230 billion a year.[19] The federal government borrows from investors who buy treasury notes, treasury bills, and U.S. savings bonds.

The size of the debt and the interest payments alarmed many Americans and became a central theme of recent presidential campaigns (see Table 14-2). How long can we allow the debt to grow at this rate? When dealing with this question, keep two considerations in mind. First, the government owes roughly 90 percent of the money to its own citizens rather than to foreign governments or investors, although the amount owed to foreigners is growing. Second, the economic strength and resources of the country are more significant than the size of the debt.

Why do we have huge annual deficits? These deficits are not the result of a weak economy, and they apparently cannot be cured simply by economic growth. The fact is that the United States is committed to spending more for defense and domestic programs than current tax revenues can provide, even though the economy is running at relatively full capacity. By tolerating unprecedented deficits in the 1980s, the Reagan administration was able to "create an austere political climate in which proposed cuts, not expected increases became the focus of discussions about federal domestic programs."[20] These budgetary

TABLE 14-2

Public Attitudes on Reducing the Deficit

Question: As you know, the president and Congress will be trying to cut federal programs in order to reduce the budget deficit. For each of the following programs, please tell me whether you think it is more important to reduce the federal budget deficit, or more important to prevent that program from being significantly cut.

	Reduce Deficit	No Serious Program Cuts	No Opinion
Medicare—the federal health program for the elderly	19	78	3
Medicaid—the federal health program for the poor	29	66	5
Social Security	20	77	3
Defense spending	52	43	5
Food stamps	60	35	5
School lunch programs	28	69	3
Grants to cities to put more police on the streets	28	68	4
Aid to farmers	43	52	5
Funding for the arts	66	29	5
Loans to college students	31	65	4
Welfare programs in general	65	30	5

Source: Gallup Poll, February 24–26, 1995.

The Republican party made reducing the deficit a major issue in the 1996 battle of the budget. Here Congressman John Kasich, Senator Bob Dole, and Congressman Newt Gingrich brief reporters on the impasse in budget negotiations.

limitations obviously carried over to the Bush and Clinton administrations (see Table 14-1). The massive deficit effectively stalled the development of social welfare policy in areas like health care and welfare reform.[21] Each individual's share of the deficit now exceeds $18,900.[22] House Speaker Newt Gingrich calls eliminating the budget deficit a matter of "fiscal honesty." Gingrich writes, "The American tradition used to be to pay off the mortgage and leave the kids the farm. New we are selling off the farm and leaving the kids the mortgage."[23]

The politics of balancing the budget were a major element in the 104th Congress. The protracted budget battles and government shutdowns hurt the Republicans more than they hurt the president. The Dole proposal for an across-the-board tax cut of 15 percent pushed deficit reduction to the forefront of the 1996 presidential election. Clinton's response was that the Dole tax "scheme" would "blow a hole in the deficit." Exit polls show that most voters agreed with Clinton on this issue.

THE BALANCED BUDGET AMENDMENT   The apparent inability of the federal government to balance its budget led many politicians and some economists to propose that a balanced budget be constitutionally mandated. A proposed Balanced Budget Amendment would require Congress to adopt a budget in which projected spending is no larger than projected tax receipts. In addition, the amendment would limit the increase in taxes (or spending or both) in any fiscal year to the percentage increase in the GDP during the previous calendar year. The amendment would have two escape clauses: Congress can waive the requirements of the amendment by a vote of three fifths of all members of both houses, and the provisions of the amendment would not apply in any year in which a war was declared.

Advocates of a Balanced Budget Amendment claim that such an amendment is necessary to correct what they call the "spending bias" in government decision making. Proponents claim that a structural deficiency in our political system causes higher levels of spending than the citizenry desires. They argue that well-organized, powerful, and heavily financed interest groups overwhelm relatively weak taxpayer lobbies and regularly win on spending measures in Congress.

Opponents of a Balanced Budget Amendment say that it would reduce the flexibility of economic policy makers and would virtually eliminate fiscal policy as a tool for managing the economy. In times of economic downturn, government spending in excess of revenues could increase employment, generate investment, stimulate demand, and prevent a recession from deepening into a depression, or respond to natural disasters. If a balanced budget were adopted, Congress might resort to subterfuges, "pretending" it balanced the books. Opponents also say it would be unwise to insert an economic theory into the Constitution, which should be, they contend, a broad charter of fundamental principles of governance, not a document with specific theories of economic management.

The Balanced Budget Amendment would clearly change the "rules of the game" and make it easier for social and economic conservatives to win more legislative battles. More votes would be required to adopt new programs, some requiring a three-fifths vote in order to appropriate money. During the 104th Congress, the House resoundingly passed a Balanced Budget Amendment 300 to 132. However, it failed by one vote to get the necessary two-thirds majority in the Senate.

THE ITEM VETO   In 1996, after years of debate, Congress passed and President Clinton signed into law the item veto, to take effect starting in 1997. The bill permits the president to strike specific items from the budget passed by Congress. Governors in 43 states have this power, sometimes called the line-item veto. Since the federal budget is not itemized by line like many state budgets, the new veto power given to the president is called the **item veto**.

The president may not lower appropriations for specific items to his preferred amount; he must either keep or reject the appropriation for the specific item. Existing entitlement programs like Medicare and Social Security are exempt from the item veto, but the president could apply the item veto to new entitlement programs. The item veto could be used to eliminate tax breaks enacted by Congress that affect 100 or fewer individual taxpayers or ten or fewer businesses. Congress granted the president the item veto power through a statute rather than a constitutional amendment, which means that Congress may at some future date decide it does not want the president to have this power and overturn the statute.

If the president strikes an item in the budget, such as a new entitlement program or a tax break for a small group, Congress can restore spending provisions or tax breaks by passing new legislation within 30 days. The president would be able to veto those measures, but his veto would be subject to the same override procedures as other vetoes—a two-thirds vote of both houses of Congress.[24]

Advocates of an item veto, including Bill Clinton and recent former presidents, contend that the reform will discourage "pork-barrel" spending since a president will not have to reject an entire appropriations bill because of a few objectionable sections.[25] The idea is not new; Ulysses S. Grant advocated an item veto in 1873. The item veto is available to most governors, and proponents assert that the process must be working at the state level because no state that has ever adopted it has abandoned it. Governors have also generally felt that it is an important bargaining tool with the legislature.[26]

Opponents of the change, like Senator Robert Byrd of West Virginia, term the law a "colossal mistake."[27] They argue that this measure muddies the waters of separation of powers too much, allowing a president excessive control over Congress. Congressional leadership has long combined multiple issues into single bills as a way of building a legislative majority and forcing the president to accept some things he does not want in order to get others he does want. The item veto enhances presidential power and diminishes Congress's constitutional grant of control over spending. Some argue that the item veto will inevitably lead to more presidential vetoes. Instead of presidents bargaining with Congress over the content of legislation, they may wait until the legislation has been passed and simply veto provisions they don't like. It may also mean that legislators will lobby the president to veto parts of bills they don't like but could not persuade Congress to change. Finally, opponents contend that there is little comparative or quantitative data for evaluation of the item veto across the states,[28] and that "the transferability of this experience to the federal sector is limited."[29]

As the president and Congress test this new procedure and apply it to actual legislation, the courts will be called upon to be the arbiter of this new separation of powers battle. At the state level, the item veto has proven to be a complex problem for the courts.[30] Courts may therefore become even more important in our political system, given the fact that they will ultimately decide the parameters of presidential and congressional power under the item veto.

REGULATORY POLICY

Regulation occurs when the government alters the natural workings of the open market. Governments regulate business activity in a variety of ways and for a variety of purposes. In all nations there is some regulation of business activity, for there are no totally unregulated market economies. In the United States we have less government regulation of business than most industrialized nations. We rely on private enterprise and market incentives to carry out most of our production and distribution.

The presumption in the United States is against regulation. People should be allowed to buy and sell their products and produce things with a minimum of government interference. However, regulation is necessary to protect people from undesirable side effects of the market, such as pollution or discrimination. Our government has to justify regulations, and does so only because people, through the representative process, come to demand certain protections from those who produce and sell various products and services.

Types of Regulation

It is customary to talk of two general categories of regulation: economic and social regulation. *Economic or traditional regulation* generally refers to government controls on the behavior of businesses in the marketplace: the entry of individual firms into particular lines of business, the prices that firms may charge, the standards of service they must offer. A host of **regulatory agencies, boards, or commissions** are responsible for enforcing statutes in particular industries.

Social regulation refers to government corrections of a variety of widely shared side effects, usually unintended, brought about by economic activity. Concerns for worker health and safety and for hazards to the environment have brought about social regulation. Whereas economic regulation is usually organized along industry lines, social regulation cuts across these lines. In economic terms, producers regulated by social regulation must now pay for external costs that once were free, such as using rivers, landfills, or the atmosphere for waste disposal. These costs are often passed along to the consumer, so the true cost of the product is more accurately reflected in its price. Some goods subsequently become too costly and demand drops; others become more popular (for instance, safe toys) and demand soars. The final goal of social regulation is a more socially beneficial allocation of resources.

The Politics of Regulation

A critical task of modern constitutional democracies is to make wise, balanced choices among courses of action and competing objectives, and regulation is no exception. Often the social benefits of regulation conflict with economic objectives. Critics say it contributes to higher inflation, lower productivity, and eco-

Cleaning up industrial pollution costs money, and ultimately it is the consumer who foots the bill.

nomic stagnation. Proponents point to improvements in environmental quality, worker safety, and consumer protection.

How desirable is it to have cleaner air or safer workplaces? Although it is relatively inexpensive to remove a large amount of air pollution, and therefore socially desirable, it becomes increasingly expensive to remove *all*, or even almost all, of it. To do so would require an allocation of resources that, from a taxpayer's point of view, might be better used for something else—perhaps new parks or public schools. Is there a socially optimal point of pollution control or worker safety beyond which it is too costly to go? The challenge for policy makers is to determine what this point is. In our political system, with its many competing interest groups, there is much difference of opinion on this matter.

Faced with this problem, Congress often legislates broad objectives for the regulatory agencies, which then set specific rules for meeting the goals. Agency regulations have been largely in the form of specific rules that a firm may not violate without being punished, which have been criticized as being arbitrary, costly, and inflexible. Recent presidents and their administrations have cut back some of these regulations, For example, the Occupational Safety and Health Administration (OSHA) trimmed more than 1,000 "nitpicking" regulations that governed such things as the shape of toilet seats.

Regulating Business

Business has never been free of regulation, but during most of the nineteenth century our national policy was to leave business pretty much alone. However, four major waves of regulatory legislation have occurred in our nation's history: at the turn of the century, in the 1910s, in the 1930s, and in the late 1960s through 1980. In each case, changing political circumstances and forces gave rise to the legislation. The primary reasons for regulation were controlling monopoly, compensating for market imperfections, and defending the economically weak.

ANTITRUST POLICY Social critics and populist reformers in the late nineteenth century believed consumers were being cheated, especially in the oil, sugar, whiskey, and steel industries, where monopolies controlled goods and services, often in combinations that worked to reduce competition, called **trusts**.

In 1890 Congress responded to this concern with monopolies by passing the **Sherman Antitrust Act.** Designed to foster competition and stop the growth of private monopolies, the act made clear its intention "to protect trade and commerce against unlawful restraints and monopolies." The Sherman Antitrust Act had little immediate impact. Presidents made little attempt to enforce it, and the Supreme Court's early interpretation of the act limited its scope.[31]

In 1914, during the administration of Woodrow Wilson, Congress added the **Clayton Act** to the antitrust arsenal. This act outlawed such specific abuses as charging different prices to different buyers in order to destroy a weaker competitor, granting rebates, making false statements about competitors and their products, buying up supplies to stifle competition, and bribing competitors' employees. In addition, *interlocking directorates* (by which an officer or director in one corporation serves on the board of a competitor) were banned, and corporations were prohibited from acquiring stock (amended in 1950 to include assets) in competing concerns if such acquisitions substantially lessened interstate competition. Also in 1914, Congress established the Federal Trade Commission (FTC), run by a five-person board, to enforce the Clayton Act and to prevent unfair competitive practices. The FTC was to be the "traffic cop" for competition.[32]

Antitrust laws may be missing their mark. While monopolies as such have virtually disappeared from the economic arena, in their place are two new threats to competition: the **oligopoly,** a situation in which a few firms dominate a market, such as in the automobile industry or the food-processing industry, and the **conglomerate,** a firm that owns businesses in many unrelated industries. About one third of our nation's manufacturing capacity is controlled by 50 companies, and about two thirds of all manufacturing assets are owned by only 500 corporations.

During recent years there has been a wave of corporate *mergers*, in which one company buys another out, or two companies pool assets to form a single larger company. Ten thousand such mergers took place in one five-year period, many of them among competing companies. General Motors bought Hughes Aircraft, R. J. Reynolds absorbed Nabisco, GE and RCA merged, ABC became part of Capital Cities Communications, Philip Morris merged with General Foods, and Warner Communications merged with Time. Several airlines have also merged. The effect of these mergers may have been to decrease competition, and many of them raised questions about whether consumers and stockholders suffered for the benefit of a few who made enormous short-term profits.

The Reagan and Bush administrations generally adopted a permissive policy toward mergers, and few were prevented. These Republican administrations assumed that most mergers were inherently good for the consumer and the economy, not—as the common wisdom had it in the 1960s—that such mergers were suspect.[33] The Clinton administration was somewhat more vigorous in enforcing antitrust laws, barring price fixing and other regulations that affect mergers.[34]

THE TELECOMMUNICATIONS ACT OF 1996 After years of debate, President Clinton signed into law the Telecommunications Act of 1996, the most sweeping regulatory reform of telecommunications since the Communications Act of 1934. The main objective of the new law is to increase competition among phone, cable, and other communications companies. Telephone companies that were once divided into seven local "mini-Bell companies" are now allowed to offer services outside their defined regions. Local telephone companies won the freedom to offer long distance service, manufacture communications equipment, and offer video service in competition with cable television. At the same time, local telephone companies must now open their network to competition for local telephone service from cable television and long distance companies. In short, a number of business restrictions were removed so that cable television and local and long distance telephone companies could effectively compete with one another. The bill thus opens up large areas of telecommunications to companies that once were regulated both in the services they could provide and the prices they could charge.

Advocates argue that this competition will not only lower prices but expand the range of service options. As in other deregulation efforts, there is some uncertainty about what will happen in areas where there is not much competition. Will prices soar? Will services even be available?

Two controversial aspects of the Telecommunications Act of 1996 are the regulation of the Internet content and the advent of the "v-chip" to allow parents to block out television shows with objectionable content. The act prohibits any person or company knowingly to make indecent material accessible to minors by a computer; selling or obtaining drugs are similarly prohibited. In reaction to President Clinton's signing of the bill, Internet activists organized a 48-hour blackout of World Wide Web pages. Congress has long been under pressure to regulate the increasingly violent content of television. The invention of the v-chip permits parents themselves to limit access. It works with ratings for television shows that allow parents to block out shows with ratings for excessive violence, offensive language, or nudity. The constitutionality of these restrictions has since been challenged and will be settled by the courts, and debate continues on who will decide what is deemed violent or offensive.

TRANSPORTATION No industry has undergone as extensive deregulation as has the transportation industry. Over the past generation airlines, trucking, and railroads have been granted more freedom in conducting their operations.

The Civil Aeronautics Board (CAB) was established by the federal government in 1938 to protect airlines from unreasonable competition by controlling rates and fares. Congress passed the Airline Deregulation Act in the fall of 1978.[35] The act phased out the CAB and relaxed restrictions on airline fares and routes. In effect, airlines were free to set whatever fares their markets would bear, and free entry and free exit were allowed in all markets. Critics say airlines have raised fares on routes over which they had monopolies in order to subsidize lower fares on more competitive routes, and that safety precautions and maintenance suffered as a result of cutthroat competition. A combination of tough economic conditions and competition forced about a dozen airline companies to

Deregulation of the airline industry altered service and caused confusion and delays at some airports, but it helped lower prices in other instances.

merge with others or go out of business since deregulation. Plainly, there have been many transitional problems as deregulation has been implemented. Overall, however, it has resulted in generally lower fares (after controlling for inflation), greater choice of routes and fares in most markets, and more efficient use of assets by the industry.[36]

Deregulation of the trucking and railroad industries soon followed airline deregulation. It is worth noting that in 1995 Congress abolished the Interstate Commerce Commission (ICC), the first major national independent regulatory commission established in 1887. The ICC dealt with all interstate surface transportation including trucks, buses, and trains. It was originally established to protect the public from unfair practices by railroad monopolies. Critics in Congress alleged that over time the ICC had become a defender of the interests of the transportation industry rather than protecting the public.

BANKING AND THE SAVINGS & LOANS The banking industry had long been regulated by the federal government. The trauma caused by the numerous bank failures during the Great Depression led to controls and regulations designed to ensure that such a shock would never recur. Because banks and other financial institutions control the flow of money, the lifeblood of the economy, some observers believe the federal government must supervise the industry to guarantee confidence.[37]

Regulation of the banking industry consisted mainly of protective devices. The federal government established the Federal Deposit Insurance Corporation (FDIC) to insure bank deposits up to a specified amount, and the Federal Savings and Loan Insurance Corporation (FSLIC), which performed a similar function for savings and loans institutions. The FSLIC has had enormous problems, and its lax regulations have been the biggest failure of government regulation in American history. During the 1980s, 525 insolvent savings and loan institutions were liquidated or sold at enormous loss to taxpayers.

What went wrong? Congress, the Reagan administration, and the regulatory agencies had created a flawed deposit insurance system and had allowed deregulation to go too far.[38] Under intense lobbying from the savings and loan industry, Washington policy makers had relaxed restrictions on how federally chartered S&Ls could invest money deposited by savers, many of which turned out to be high-risk ventures. Interest-rate ceilings were eliminated.

The federal government responded to the savings and loan mess with a massive bailout program and the imposition of new regulations to prevent this situation from happening again. Minimum capital requirements for federally insured savings institutions were raised to make capital requirements as stringent as those for national banks. Criminal and civil sanctions for illegal activities involving savings institutions were strengthened. The savings and loan debacle is a lesson in the perils of excessive deregulation. The net effect of the crisis has been to impose more regulations, not less—or what is now called *reregulation*.

Regulating Labor and Management

Government regulation of business is essentially restrictive. Most governmental laws and rules curb certain business practices and steer private enterprise into socially useful channels. But regulation cuts two ways. In the case of American workers, most laws passed in recent decades have tended not to restrict but rather to confer rights and opportunities. Actually, many labor laws do not touch labor directly; instead, they regulate its relations with employers.

Do unions need federal laws to protect their right to organize? The history of union efforts before 1933 suggests that organizing without federal protection was extremely difficult. Indeed, union membership and strength were waning fast until New Deal measures granted workers the right to organize and bargain collectively. The **National Labor Relations Act of 1935** (usually called the Wagner Act) made these guarantees permanent and gave them federal backing. Its preamble declared that workers in industries affecting interstate commerce (with certain exemptions) should have the right to organize and bargain collectively, and that inequality in bargaining power between employers and workers leads to industrial strife and economic instability. The act made five types of action unfair for employers: (1) interfering with workers in their attempt to organize unions or bargain collectively; (2) supporting company unions (unions set up and dominated by the employer); (3) discriminating against members of unions; (4) firing or otherwise victimizing an employee for having taken action under the act; and (5) refusing to bargain with union representatives. The act was intended to prevent employers from using violence, espionage, propaganda, and community pressure to resist unionization.

THE TAFT-HARTLEY ACT   A major modification to laws about unions was passed by Congress in 1947, the Labor-Management Relations Act, commonly called the **Taft-Hartley Act**. This act, which places various limitations on unions, applies (with certain exceptions) to industries dealing in interstate commerce. The act:

1. Outlaws the **closed shop** (a company that requires an employer to hire and retain only union members in good standing) and permits the **union shop** (a company in which new employees must join the union within a stated period of time) only under certain conditions.

2. Outlaws **jurisdictional strikes** (strikes arising from disputes between unions over whose members should perform a particular task); **secondary boycotts** (efforts by unions involved in disputes with employers to encourage other unions to boycott a third party—usually other employers—who, in response to such pressure, might put pressure on the original offending employers); excessive union dues or fees; and strikes by federal employees.

3. Makes it an unfair labor practice for unions to refuse to bargain with employers.

4. Permits employers and unions to sue each other in federal court for violation of contracts.

5. Allows limited use of the **labor injunction** (a court order forbidding specific individuals or groups to perform acts the court considers harmful to the rights or property of an employer or community).

6. Permits states to outlaw union shops. **Right-to-work laws,** which states could now adopt, typically make it illegal for **collective bargaining** agreements (terms and conditions of employment negotiated by representatives of the union and the employer) to contain closed shop, union shop, preferential hiring, or any other clauses calling for compulsory union membership.

The Taft-Hartley Act also set up machinery for handling disputes affecting an entire industry or a major part of it if a work stoppage would threaten national health or safety. The act has been invoked in the past against strikes in vital sectors of the economy such as atomic energy, coal, shipping, steel, and telephone service. Sometimes a president and the secretary of labor attempt to mediate strikes without resorting to the act.

Thinking it Through

Unemployment among young people is a serious problem. The youth unemployment rate is usually at least double that of the adult population; for black teenagers, it is several times that of all adults. A subminimum wage might encourage employers to put more young people to work. It would probably also create some jobs and provide training opportunities for unskilled workers.

But if there were a subminimum wage, young people would often displace older workers because they would be cheaper to hire. This debate over a subminimum wage for teenagers distracts attention from the more important issue of the substantial erosion in the minimum wage for all. Still a case can be made that a two-tier minimum wage should be tried for a period.

When a strike breaks out, the following steps are authorized:

1. The president appoints a special board to investigate and report the facts.
2. The president may then instruct the attorney general to seek an 80-day injunction against the strike in a federal court.
3. If the court agrees that national health or safety is endangered, it grants this injunction.
4. If the parties have not settled the strike within the 80 days, the board informs the president of the employer's last offer of settlement.
5. The National Labor Relations Board (NLRB) takes a secret vote among the employees to see if they will accept the employer's last offer.
6. If no settlement is reached, the injunction expires, and the president reports to Congress with such recommendations as he may wish to make.

The effectiveness of this act is difficult to assess because legislation is only one of the many factors that affect industrial peace. Labor unions are now so weak that the federal government seldom has to invoke Taft-Hartley to prevent strikes in vital services. Still, one basic issue remains unsolved. Strikes are part of the price we pay for the system of collective bargaining. But under what conditions does the price become so high that the federal government should intervene, stop the strike, and force a settlement?

Regulatory Outcomes and Issues

While the need for regulation, especially in areas affecting health and safety, is widely accepted, there are concerns about the negative consequences of regulation as well. A marked decrease in lead paint poisonings, childproof bottle tops, and the banning of many cancer-producing pesticides are all byproducts of federal regulatory activity. On the negative side, regulations have increased the cost of some products and may have hampered such industries as railroads.

The major criticisms of regulation can be summarized as follows:

• *Regulation Distorts and Disrupts the Operation of the Market* Sometimes governmental intervention upsets the normal adjustment processes of the market and thus encourages higher prices, misallocation of resources, and inefficiency.

• *Regulation Can Discourage Competition* Some forms of regulation (often the kind desired by industry) actually have the reverse of their desired effect. This is especially true when the government grants operating licenses and charters to maintain a certain level of quality or stability in the market. Regulatory red tape has also been charged with discouraging entry into industries and driving small businesses out.

• *Regulation May Discourage Technological Development* It is argued that the reward for innovation is a new set of rules and a struggle for permission to use a new product, business may not find it worth the effort to innovate.

• *Regulatory Agencies Are Often "Captured" by the Industries They Regulate* It is suggested, especially by those on the political left, that some regulatory bodies are controlled by the big businesses they are supposed to be regulating. For example, environmentalists concerned with western lands sometimes jokingly refer to the Bureau of Land Management (BLM) as the "Bureau of Logging and Mining." Some evidence of the capture thesis does exist in what has been described as the *revolving door*, in which federal regulators leave their jobs to take high-paying posts with the industries they

"I think we can agree, gentlemen, that one can respect Mother Nature without coddling her."

Drawing by Lorenz. © 1986 The New Yorker Magazine, Inc.

previously regulated. There is evidence, too, that some people consider jobs in regulatory agencies as stepping stones to lucrative careers in private industry, and the industries obviously benefit in several ways from hiring some of the more able regulators.

- *Regulation Increases Costs to Industry and to the Consumer* Federal regulations, as noted earlier, are costly. One conservative think tank estimates that government regulations cost more than $8,000 annually for every household in the United States.[39] Such figures are disputed by many labor and consumer advocates, who say health and safety standards are the best investment we can make. Every life and every limb we save, and every disease we prevent, represents not only a valuable achievement but also a reduction in the nation's enormous hospital and medical bills. Plainly, the side you take in the debate over the cost of federal regulations depends in part on where you sit—that is, on whether you favor labor or management, producer or consumer, energy developer or ecologist, and in part on how much you are willing to spend to move toward a risk-free society.

- *Regulation Has Often Been Introduced without Cost-Benefit Analysis* Critics say too little attention is given to whether the benefits of a particular piece of regulation are great enough to justify its cost. Is it worth it to restrict approval of new drugs if some who would benefit may die? Is it worth it to clean up 95 percent of automobile emissions if the cost is many times that of an 85-percent cleanup? One report claims we're spending $1.75 million per cancer case arising from exposure to hazardous waste.[40] Is that worth it?

- *Regulatory Agencies Lack Qualified Personnel* Critics of regulation, and some heads of regulatory agencies themselves, say regulators lack the expertise to do their jobs properly. Regulatory agencies complain they need larger budgets to do their job properly and attract more qualified staff. Critics argue, too, that government should not meddle in complex chemical or technological industries about which it knows little.

Evaluating Deregulation

For more than 30 years every president has proposed a program for regulatory reform. Economists from a variety of ideological perspectives are all but unanimous in their view that certain kinds of regulation are unnecessary and that some of it uses the wrong strategy. Even if various parties agree that reform is needed, heated debate arises over what specific actions to take.

The 104th Congress did not pass comprehensive regulatory reform but did pass a law giving Congress veto power over new small business regulations; the president can override the congressional veto. Although regulatory reform was not part of the Republican Contract with America, many Republicans wanted a moratorium on all new government agency regulations. Democrats contended that a moratorium would threaten the safety and health of the American people, because the Food and Drug Administration, Federal Aviation Administration, and other agencies need to be free to regulate as necessary. A proposed regulatory moratorium passed the House easily, but the Senate was slow to act. Democratic filibusters kept a less restrictive congressional veto of new regulations from coming to a vote. Republicans believe that their party's opposition to regulation is a popular position, while Democrats are just as sure that the public wants what they see as the benefits of regulation—safe airlines, clean water, and safe prescription drugs.

Deregulation appears to be working better in some areas than in others. In the area of drug deregulation, the results are mixed. The Food and Drug Administration, especially since 1981, relaxed the requirements for introducing

Living on Social Security Checks

The first Social Security check was paid in 1940 to Ida Fuller of Brattleboro, Vermont. She had contributed $22 in payroll taxes between 1937, when the system began, and the end of 1939, when she retired. Fuller's first monthly check was for $22.54. She continued to receive checks for 34 years, until her death in late 1974 (shortly after her 100th birthday). All told, Fuller collected almost $21,000.

For proponents and critics alike, Ida Fuller's story captures the essence of the Social Security system. Critics point out that Fuller joined late, paid almost nothing, and received benefits nearly a thousand times larger than the taxes she paid in. Proponents point with pride to a system that provides a reliable stream of benefits to someone lucky enough to live as long as Fuller did and to the comfort and peace of mind Social Security gave her. They also note that though she received a high return on her contributions, the system was only a small cushion for her. History does not record her other sources of support, but she could not have lived 34 years sustained only by her Social Security checks.

SOURCE: Herman B. Leonard, *Checks Unbalanced: The Quiet Side of Public Spending* (Basic Books, 1986), p. 51.

new medicines. People in the drug industry applaud these efforts. They argue that as a result of deregulation the public gets better medicines faster and cheaper. Opponents contend, and with some growing evidence, that the accelerated approval process is endangering public health by prematurely allowing potentially hazardous drugs on the market.[41]

Advocates of deregulation say consumers are capable of making intelligent choices and are profiting from the lower prices and expanded services brought about by deregulation. Opponents contend deregulation results in such confusion in the marketplace that consumers cannot make sensible choices. In the airline business, they say, even experienced travel agents often cannot figure out the cheapest way to go "from here to there."

One other point: In our federal system the mere fact that the national government stops regulating an industry does not mean the particular industry will be unregulated. On the contrary, sometimes 50 different state regulators take over, making it even more difficult for that industry to operate on a large scale.[42] California, for example, has much tougher automobile air-pollution rules than does the national government. This is why businesspeople themselves sometimes call for more, not less, national regulation; they would prefer one set of national regulations to 50 different state ones.

The overall effects of deregulation trends, especially as they affect traditional economic regulation, appear to be positive. A major exception, of course, was the deregulation of the savings and loan industry. Deregulation has forced some industries to become more efficient, and most consumers have had better services at less cost.

SOCIAL POLICY

What is the proper role of government in education, health care, housing, job security, care for the elderly, and public safety? These questions encompass a large part of the agenda of our national government today, yet such functions were once thought to be mostly private matters or were left to local government. As we noted in Chapter 2, debates over private versus public responsibilities and the role of different levels of government have shaped the partisan and ideological differences of this century, and they continue to be important as the nation considers major changes in social policy.

Public versus Private

Those who favor primarily private approaches to social policy do so for a host of reasons, including a belief that individuals need to take responsibility for their own lives rather than relying on the government to care for them. These people doubt the efficiency and effectiveness of public solutions to social problems and are confident the free market will provide opportunities for those with ambition and a willingness to work hard. Opponents of government solutions say public assistance robs people of their ambition and work ethic.

A preference for private solutions to social problems is closely linked with conservatism in American politics and has long been a central precept of the Republican party. Some conservatives today advocate a purely private form of health insurance, with employers getting out of the business of providing it as a benefit. Allowing parents to choose where to send their children to school by giving them vouchers that can be redeemed at any private or public school is another example of a conservative approach to a social policy issue.

Conservatives often point to the long-standing tradition in the United States that private charities, churches, and foundations should raise contributions from individuals and businesses to build hospitals and nursing homes, fund medical research, provide scholarships for students, feed and house the homeless, care for abandoned children, and perform many similar services. The private approach to social policy points to such activities as evidence that people can and will seek to remedy social problems on their own, without the higher taxes, bigger government, and wasteful bureaucracy they see connected to public remedies.

Advocates of public solutions to social problems believe it is the responsibility of government to provide some minimum standard of living—a job, an education, health care, housing, and basic nutrition—for all citizens. They argue that human dignity not only requires some minimum standard of living, but that such a policy is also pragmatic. Without it, our cities would have far more homeless and hungry people, desperate for survival. Advocates of public programs say that private solutions to social problems do not work because there is simply not enough charitable giving to address the social needs of poor people, the elderly, and those without health insurance. Moreover, they argue the United States is far behind other countries in social service programs and funding. Government support for public housing, welfare, health care, and education is simply a fact of life for the modern nation-state, they contend.

National versus State and Local

Social policy was long considered primarily a responsibility of state and local governments. Consequently, the ideological debate on social policy includes the question of federalism. Are social policy problems better addressed by the national government or by the state and local levels? Conservatives advocate leaving most social policy matters to states and localities, where programs can be adapted to local needs. Liberals counter that history has taught that state and local governments are unable or unwilling to address such problems on their own, so the national government needs to play a major role in funding programs and setting policy standards.

Governors of several states have become increasingly vocal about the tendency of the national government to mandate social policy programs that the states must administer but with little or no federal funding for implementation. Such *unfunded mandates* force state governments to raise taxes or reduce funding of various other state programs. With all the attention health care and welfare reform have received, the governors clearly want to make the point that whenever new programs are enacted, they need to be fully funded by the national government. The issue of federalism in social policy is this: Do Americans want a variety of social programs with some differences between the states, or should the poor, the young, and those with disabilities be treated the same, regardless of which state they live in?

A Brief History of Social Policy in the United States

Long after other Western democracies had expanded their social services, welfare in the United States was left to private charities and to local governments. Why? Part of the answer is that this nation has always been seen as the land of opportunity. Our millions of acres of free land, our enormous natural resources, and our technical advances all helped absorb people who otherwise might not have made a go of it. Closely linked with this growth and opportunity was the widely held philosophy of rugged individualism: If people did not get ahead, it was their own fault. For others, the idea of equality of opportunity meant that government played only a limited role in people's lives. Government's primary function was to secure traditional individual rights and provide public goods, such as roads, harbors, postal services, and public order. Rather grudgingly, state governments in the early twentieth century extended relief to needy groups, especially the old,

Thinking it Through

AFDC was designed to help single parents. If it is abolished, millions may be left homeless and destitute. But reforms that provide single parents with job training and child care are much more expensive than the current system, which makes talk of reform politically popular but economically difficult.

Most welfare reform packages propose that welfare recipients work or provide some community service in exchange for the benefits they receive. The rationale behind such ideas is popular with taxpayers whose stereotype of a welfare recipient is an able-bodied person who prefers the welfare check to working. In fact, there are many impediments to "workfare" welfare reform. They include the fact that employers often resist hiring people who have been stigmatized as being "on the dole." Proposals to create public sector jobs have been criticized by unions, who fear that the lower wages paid to such workers will undercut their own pay, and some see public sector employment as "dead-end jobs."

Head Start: A Great Society Success Story

Many Great Society programs have been politically controversial, but one program has enjoyed strong bipartisan support—Head Start. This preschool program prepares impoverished three- and four-year-olds for elementary school by teaching them basic academic and social skills. The program also teaches good nutrition and personal hygiene and provides immunizations and medical and dental screening. Parents of children in the program receive instruction on parenting. Since 1965 nearly 14 million children have participated in Head Start, but the 714,000 students enrolled in 1993 still represent only about half of all eligible children. Head Start makes extensive use of volunteers, with a ratio of volunteers to paid staff of nearly 10 to 1. Even with this large volunteer effort, the program costs taxpayers $3,758 per student per year, with an annual overall budget of more than $4 billion.

the blind, and the orphaned. But government aid was limited and much reliance was placed on private charity.[43]

Most Americans today expect government to play a greater role in the delivery of social services than did their predecessors. These expectations have changed as a result of wave after wave of reformers who pushed their agenda of social services. Two social policy reform efforts deserve special attention: The New Deal and the Great Society.

THE NEW DEAL The Great Depression of the 1930s drastically expanded the involvement of the national government in social programs. As the value of stocks and real estate fell after the 1929 stock market crash, and unemployment, homelessness, and poverty rose to unprecedented heights, the inadequacy of state and local government programs and private charities became apparent. In 1933 the federal government began making loans to states and localities for public relief. When state and local funds dried up, the federal government assumed more responsibility.

Franklin D. Roosevelt's administration established relief programs designed to stimulate the economy and put people back to work:

- The Works Progress Administration (WPA) spent billions of dollars on local projects such as public housing, courthouses, and parks.
- The Public Works Administration (PWA) built larger permanent projects, like dams and roads.
- The Agricultural Adjustment Act (AAA) raised farm prices.
- The Civilian Conservation Corps (CCC) put people to work protecting natural resources on federal land.
- The Tennessee Valley Authority (TVA) supervised the construction of dams and power plants on the Tennessee River to electrify and modernize the rural South.

SOCIAL SECURITY As a part of the New Deal, the United States inaugurated Social Security in 1935, perhaps the most significant social legislation in our his-

Breadlines like this provided handouts of food to thousands of unemployed and destitute people during the Great Depression.

tory. At the time it was controversial; today it is politically untouchable. Social Security is actually many programs, the most important being a retirement program supported by a combination of employee and employer taxes, now covering more than 90 percent of the American work force. Other Social Security programs include financial support for disabled workers and for children of deceased or disabled workers. Health insurance for retired and disabled persons is also part of Social Security.

Since Social Security began, the program has experienced steady growth and is now the world's largest insurance program for retirees, survivors, and people with disabilities. Combined with the cost of Medicare, its expenditures totaled about $493 billion by 1995.[44] Programs like Social Security are called entitlement programs because they provide a specified set of benefits as a matter of right to all who meet the criteria established by law.

Social Security pays over 43 million Americans every month, while 140 million working people contribute to it; the average retired person receives about $720 per month.[45] Full benefits are paid to those between the ages of 65 and 70 who are not currently earning wages of more than a certain amount; after age 70, people are entitled to retirement benefits regardless of wage earnings. The universal nature of Social Security is one reason it is politically so popular: everyone benefits, regardless of need.

Until the 1970s, growth in Social Security benefits was relatively noncontroversial, largely because "the costs were initially deceptively low," while benefits steadily increased, making the system politically painless.[46] The liberalization and expansion of benefits to include medical insurance for the elderly and poor were made possible by the steady economic growth of the 1950s and 1960s. But increased life expectancy and a steadily declining birthrate placed the burden of supporting the Social Security system for more and more senior citizens on fewer and fewer workers. Today the system provides monthly benefits to 26.6 million retired Americans, as well as benefits to 5.4 million widows and widowers, 4.2 million disabled workers, 3.8 million children of deceased or disabled persons, and 3.2 million entitled wives and husbands.[47]

Social Security, unlike many other welfare programs, is financed not from general taxes but from a trust fund into which taxes on employees and employers are placed—the Federal Insurance Contribution Act, commonly known as FICA. In some ways, this fund is like a private pension plan in which an investor puts money into a pension account. Over the years Congress has added benefits to the Social Security system without adding enough money to the trust fund to cover the added expense. In 1983, Congress was forced to put Social Security on a more sound financial foundation by passing reforms that raised the retirement age at which one qualifies for Social Security benefits, increased Social Security taxes, and taxed half of the Social Security payments of upper-income individuals, a figure that has more recently been raised to 85 percent.[48]

Social Security taxes have increased over time until they are now the largest tax paid by roughly two-thirds of all Americans, exceeding the amount they pay in income tax. Employees are required to pay 7.65 percent of their earnings to the Social Security fund, up to $4,085 per year, and employers match this amount for each employee. A single person with no dependents would have to earn $30,000 before paying more federal income tax than Social Security tax; families with two children would have to earn over $40,000 before the income tax would exceed the Social Security tax. Some experts believe that if Social Security expenditures are not controlled, more than half of every paycheck will be used to finance the program by 2040.[49]

Because people are living longer and demanding more benefits, concerns about the financial stability of Social Security over the long term have grown.

New Democrats

People who advocate government-sponsored solutions to social problems are considered liberals, and most often they are Democrats, but there are exceptions within both parties. Some Republicans favor universal health care, and some Democrats would vote to lower the minimum wage.

One prominent group of Democrats—calling themselves "New Democrats"—recently tried to establish an identity somewhere between the liberal and conservative positions. These New Democrats are usually affiliated with the Democratic Leadership Council (DLC), a group formed in 1985 to steer the Democratic party away from the more liberal elements and policy positions of the party. Bill Clinton served for a time as chair of the DLC, and seven members of his cabinet have been affiliated with it. Clinton has indicated that he is "proud to govern as a New Democrat."*

The DLC/New Democrat agenda includes support for the North American Free Trade Agreement, welfare and health care reform, deficit reduction, and the earned-income tax credit. New Democrats also advocate policies that encourage economic growth rather than redistribution, and they are willing to challenge popular government programs they believe are inefficient and ineffective. They emphasize the values of community and individual responsibility that conservatives long laid claim to. New Democrats emphasize reducing bureaucratic red tape, favor programs that are more decentralized, make use of market approaches, and place more reliance on individual responsibility.

*Quoted in David Corn, "Working with the New Democrats," *The Nation*, January 3–10, 1994, p. 16.

When the "baby boomers" retire, there will be a major increase in the number of people receiving benefits in proportion to those contributing to the system. This increase would not be a problem if the money being contributed to Social Security by today's workers was being saved for their eventual retirement. But much of the money taken from today's workers goes to pay for today's retirees. Social Security is thus a transfer program in which today's young workers finance the retirement of today's elderly. At some point, this reality is likely to foster intergenerational tension between workers and retirees.

Although the demographics of Social Security are a policy concern, the politics of Social Security are clear. Few politicians today would risk proposing changes that might be construed by the powerful constituency of elderly voters as cutting back on the program or its benefits. The 1993 budget, including an increase in taxes on Social Security earnings, passed on a party line vote in Congress. Democrats voted for the increase while Republicans voted against it. This action shows that retirement programs are not immune from change, but such votes are rare.

THE GREAT SOCIETY   Another significant expansion of social services came in the 1960s. At a commencement speech at the University of Michigan in May 1964, President Lyndon Johnson described a vision of a "great society," one that would end poverty and racial prejudice, in which education would be available to every child, and in which people residing in cities would live "the good life." In his State of the Union Address to Congress a few months earlier, Johnson had called for a "declaration of war on poverty in America." Johnson's agenda was as broad as his rhetoric, and as with the New Deal, Congress enacted much of it in a fairly short period of time. Great Society programs dramatically increased the role of the federal government in education, extended voting and civil rights, expanded Social Security to include medical benefits for retired Americans, provided health care to poor Americans, financed housing programs to provide decent housing to the poor, offered job training through the Job Corps, and provided preschool education to poor children in a program called Head Start.[50] Congress followed Johnson's lead, appropriating funds for most of what he had asked for in his first year of the War on Poverty.

The leadership and political skill of President Lyndon Johnson were critical. His motivation stemmed from his own values but also reflected a response to pressures within his party and the country and, some might argue, a desire to deflect attention away from the Vietnam War. Johnson combined a passion for the agenda with great skill in working with Congress. Within Johnson's five years as president, 1,902 proposals were submitted to Congress. Only 57 percent of them were approved, yet of Johnson's 115 Great Society proposals submitted to Congress, 78 percent were passed.[51] Johnson's effectiveness was enhanced by his party's large majority in Congress following his landslide victory in 1964, his ability to mobilize public opinion for his programs, and his skill in dealing with individual legislators, which came from his years of experience in Congress, including several years as leader of Senate Democrats.

The central article of faith in the Great Society agenda was that social and economic problems could be solved, or at least reduced, by government action. In the period since 1968, there has been considerable debate over whether the Great Society was a success or failure.[52] Some Great Society programs were later disbanded during the Reagan and Bush administrations, yet the belief remains that the federal government should play a major role in social policy. Many of the Great Society programs in housing, education, welfare, health care, crime control, and the environment have continued and even been expanded in recent years (see Table 14-3).

RONALD REAGAN AND THE CONTRACT WITH AMERICA   Republican administrations in the 1950s, 1960s, and 1970s did not expand the programs of the New Deal or the Great Society, but at the same time they did not directly challenge them. Ronald Reagan did. Reagan sought to change the agenda of politics in general and to close down increases in social spending in particular. Overall, Reagan called for cuts of $35 billion in social spending and succeeded in eliminating programs like the Comprehensive Employment and Training Act (CETA) and Community Services Administration (CSA). The size of many programs was reduced; for instance, the number of food stamp recipients dropped from 21.1 million in 1980 to 18.6 million in 1988. Proponents of a larger role for government in social policy shifted to a position of fighting to protect existing programs. The 1994 Republican Contract with America proposed further cuts in domestic social programs. The Republican-controlled 104th Congress passed, and Bill Clinton signed into law, welfare reform that replaces such federal welfare programs as Aid to Families with Dependent Children (AFDC) with an annual block grant to the states to implement their own welfare programs. The compromise legislation worked out between Clinton and Congress also imposes a five-year lifetime limit and a requirement that welfare recipients begin work within two years of the start of benefits. States may exempt up to 20 percent of welfare recipients like the blind or disabled from the time limit or work requirements. The reform may cut the federal budget but may result in higher state budgets.

Health Care

The federal government has three major approaches to health policy: research, cost control, and access. On research, the government has adopted a wide range of programs to promote research, target particular diseases, regulate drugs, monitor health care providers, gather and disseminate information, and in general deal with health issues with a public dimension. On cost control, government pays for approximately 44 percent of the nation's health care costs through veterans' hospitals and programs for the poor, elderly, and disabled (see Table 14-4). Developments in health care thus have a profound impact on the federal budget. Concerning access, most people feel that the United States provides the best medical care money can buy. But that is precisely the problem. Not everyone can afford our increasingly expensive medical care.

In 1965, as part of Lyndon Johnson's Great Society legislation, Congress passed Medicare and Medicaid. **Medicare** is the national health insurance program for the elderly and disabled; it provides hospital and medical insurance for people 65 years of age and older. Disabled people under age 65 are also entitled to Medicare. **Medicaid** provides medical benefits for low-income persons; it is funded largely by the federal government but also requires state funding and administration. Eligibility for Medicaid is limited to persons who receive welfare cash payments—the visually impaired, the elderly, the disabled, and families with dependent children where one parent is absent, incapacitated, or unemployed. Both programs took effect in 1966.[53]

The Medicare program covers most charges for most illnesses, but some catastrophic and long-term conditions result in major costs to patients for which there is no Medicare coverage. Responding to pressure to add catastrophic coverage and prescription drugs to the plan, Congress enacted the Medicare Catastrophic Coverage Act of 1988. To cover the costs of this expanded coverage, many senior citizens had to pay higher Medicare premiums—something they disliked—and a year later, Congress repealed the law. The lesson from this reversal has not been lost on members of Congress: The public wants expanded health care benefits but does not want to pay more for them.

TABLE 14-3

Entitlement Spending, 1940–1995
(in billions of 1995 dollars)

Year	Amount	Percent of Total Outlays
1940	$18.9	17.5%
1950	85.3	32.1
1960	118.8	26.2
1970	248.7	33.1
1980	534.4	47.1
1985	620.6	45.2
1987	637.8	46.9
1988	649.5	47.0
1989	663.6	46.9
1990	689.6	46.6
1991	732.5	49.1
1992	794.7	52.7
1993	831.9	55.6
1994	859.1	56.3
1995	887.4	56.8

Source: U.S. Bureau of the Census, *Statistical Abstract of the United States: 1993*, p. 331; and *Statistical Abstract of the United States: 1995*, p. 333.

TABLE 14-4

National Health Expenditures, 1970–1993
(billions of dollars)

Year	Total Amount Spent
1970	74.3
1975	132.6
1980	251.1
1981	291.4
1982	328.2
1983	360.8
1984	396.0
1985	434.5
1986	466.0
1987	506.2
1988	562.3
1989	623.9
1990	696.6
1991	755.6
1992	820.3
1993	884.2

Sources: U.S. Health Care Financing Administration, *Health Care Financing Review* (Winter 1994), adapted in U.S. Bureau of the Census, *Statistical Abstract of the United States, 1995* (Government Printing Office, 1996), p. 109.

Health Care Reform

President Clinton presented his health care reform plan during his first year in office, which faced more than twenty competing proposals. A partisan battle erupted as the 1994 election neared, and none of the reforms that had seemed inevitable just a short time before were enacted. In one summary of the failure to enact health care reform, Julie Rovner concludes that the debate "could be fairly summarized as the Democrats telling the public they could have health care nirvana, and the Republicans telling them they could not."[54] The stalemate resulted in failure to enact any meaningful reform. Despite many proposals and wide public support for reform in general, health care reform was not a priority of the Republican-controlled 104th Congress of 1995 and 1996.

SINGLE-PAYER   Many Americans advocate a single-payer system, like the system used in Canada. Under such a system the government, using broad-based taxes, covers the costs of health care and hospitalization and also sets the rates. The plan would provide universal coverage and benefits to all Americans. Proponents claim that the single-payer system would save billions of dollars in administrative expenses by reducing the number of insurers from about 1200 to 1. Opponents of the single-payer system claim it would lead to a bureaucratic mess, with little incentive for innovation, cost control, or diversity of coverage. They further

From Coast to Coast

The Uninsured, 1992

Percent Uninsured

- Highest: 19% or above
- Average: 13 -18.9%
- Below average: 10 -12.9%
- Lowest: below 10%

U.S. average: 15.3%

Growth in Uninsured

- Above average
- Average or below

U.S. average: 0.8 percentage points

SOURCE: Map by Deberah Bosanko, *American Demographics* (January 1994), p. 56.

These estimates do not include state-run programs other than Medicaid.

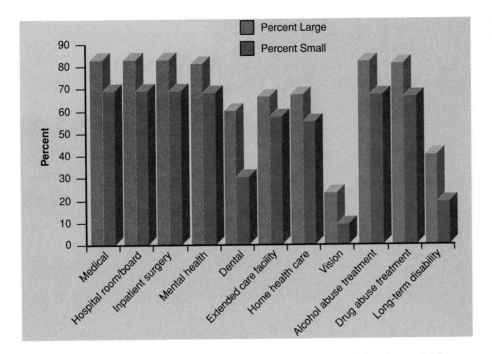

FIGURE 14-3 Percentage of Large and Small Businesses That Provide Employees with Certain Categories of Health Benefits

SOURCE: U.S. Bureau of the Census, *Statistical Abstract of the United States, 1993* (Government Printing Office, 1994), p. 431.

Thinking it Through

Although we all have our own ideas about health care reform, the American people are split over what approach is best. More than half do not want restrictions on their choice of doctors and hospitals, and almost half do not think that the country spends enough on health care. A 1993 Gallop poll found these results:

Do you think the nation spends too much, too little, or the right amount on health care?

	Too Much	Too Little	Right Amount
Total public	36%	49%	8%
Men	42	42	10
Women	31	56	7
With health insurance	38	47	9
Without health insurance	26	61	5
Practicing physicians	44	7	42
Influential physicians	32	4	35

Which approach to health care reform do you prefer?

Type	Percent
Tax incentive	37%
Managed competition	28
Leave it as it is	16
Single payer	13
None/other	6

SOURCES: *Gallup Poll Monthly*, October 1993, p. 39; "The Public, Their Doctors and Health Care Reform," *In Case You Missed Some of Them* ...(Times Mirror Center for the People and the Press, 1994), p. 9.

claim that the government would be put in the position of deciding which procedures to pay for and how to ration access to these procedures. As a result, they contend, Americans would lose not only quality in their health care but part of their freedom.

MANAGED COMPETITION   President Clinton has proposed managed care as part of the health care reform package developed by Hillary Clinton's task force. Its main features are greater use of health maintenance organizations (HMOs) and creation of large purchasing groups of employers (alliances) and other consumers powerful enough to bargain with the HMOs for lower costs. This plan would leave each person with some choices of the type of medical care he or she wants.

EMPLOYER-MANDATED COVERAGE   Most people get some form of medical insurance as a benefit that goes with their job (see Figure 14-3). President Clinton's plan recommended that all employers be required to provide their employees with health insurance, suggesting that employers pay 80 percent of the costs. But many small businesses assert they cannot afford to provide their employees with this benefit and stay in business. All employer-mandated plans raise questions about which procedures will be covered and at what cost, how access will be managed and regulated, and what will happen to people when they change jobs.

SPENDING CAPS   The cost of providing health care each year consumes a larger and larger share of our gross domestic product, and if we change the system, there is concern that the costs will go up even faster. Some have proposed an overall expenditure cap on health care that applies not only to public expenditures but to private ones as well. It is hard to know how such controls would really work, which evokes fear among health care providers. Opponents argue that spending caps would limit research and development in medicine and lower the quality of people entering the medical profession.

INDIVIDUAL RESPONSIBILITY FOR COVERAGE   Another proposal for health care reform seeks to apply a free-market approach to health care by abolishing all employer-provided benefits and encouraging individuals to buy health insurance

HEALTH CARE IN ADVANCED INDUSTRIAL DEMOCRACIES

Advanced industrial democracies like Canada, Germany, Japan, the Netherlands, and the United Kingdom provide health care for their entire population either through national health insurance or a national health service. Although one-seventh of all U.S. citizens do not have health insurance and do not regularly receive health care, the United States outspends all these countries in terms of health expenditures as a percent of the gross domestic product (GDP).

Our high spending on health care does not mean we are a more healthy population. Our infant mortality rates, for instance, are among the highest in all industrialized countries, and we rank below average in male and female life expectancy at birth.* However, the United States does rank first in the quality and access to first-rate medical technology, and for those Americans who can afford the best health care, our system is excellent.

The United States also differs from other countries in the extent to which health care costs are paid by public funds. Approximately three-quarters of the cost of health care in most advanced industrial democracies is funded by central or local governments. In 1990, for instance, the government paid 73 percent of the costs of health care in Canada and Germany, 72 percent in the Netherlands, and 84 percent in the United Kingdom. In 1990, the U.S. government paid 42 percent of the costs.†

Whether health care reform will actually lead to better or to poorer care is hotly debated, with those opposed to change heightening fears and those favoring reform seeking to reduce fears. Health care systems in other countries are often used by opponents of reform as examples of "socialized medicine." Proponents of reform point to high-quality health care in countries with greater government intervention.

*George Schieber, Jean-Pierre Poullier, and Leslie M. Greenwald, "U.S. Health Expenditure Performance: An International Comparison and Data Update," *Healthcare Financing Review* 13 (September 1992), pp. 64–65.
†Ibid., p. 4.

Per Capita Health Spending in the United States as Compared with Other Industrial Democracies, 1990

SOURCE: Based on data from George Schieber, Jean-Pierre Poullier, and Leslie M. Greenwald, "U.S. Health Expenditure Performance: An International Comparison and Update," *Health Care Financing Review* 13 (September 1992), pp. 1–15.

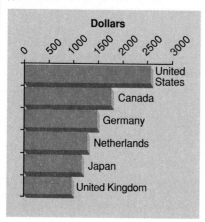

Total Health Care Expenditures as a Share of Gross Domestic Product, 1993

United States	12.2%
Canada	9.5
United Kingdom	6.0
France	8.8
Germany	8.8
Japan	6.7

SOURCE: "Spending," *Public Perspective* 5 (May/June 1994), p. 88.

Infant Mortality and Life Expectancy Rates in Ten Industrialized Nations, 1995

Country	Infant Mortality Rate*	Life Expectancy Rate
Japan	4.3	79.4
Sweden	5.6	78.4
Netherlands	6.0	78.0
Germany	6.6	76.1
France	6.3	76.6
Canada	6.8	78.3
Australia	7.1	77.8
United Kingdom	7.0	77.0
Italy	7.4	77.9
United States	7.9	76.0

SOURCE: U.S. Bureau of the Census, *Statistical Abstract of the United States, 1995* (Government Printing Office, 1995), pp. 489–50.

*Infant mortality rate is the number of deaths of children under one year of age per 1,000 live births in a calendar year.

on their own in much the same way that individuals are now responsible for purchasing their own automobile insurance. Those with low incomes, including people not now covered, would have tax credits or vouchers to assist in the purchase of insurance.

The complexity of financing health care means that it will be a recurrent issue in American politics. It is also central to the social policy agenda of the Clinton administration. Clinton's strong commitment to the issue helped move it to center stage in American politics. But interest groups, congressional committees, partisan politicians, the bureaucracy, and even the media all play a role in the development of this national issue and policy controversy. Most Americans agree that there is a crisis in health care but are satisfied with their own coverage. They want universal coverage without significant tax increases and lower costs without additional restrictions.

Welfare

Welfare programs in the United States are much more complex than merely handing out checks to poor people. They incorporate job training, transportation subsidies, housing subsidies, free school lunches, food stamps, food for pregnant mothers and babies, and tax credits for low-income people (see Table 14-5). The government also provides financial assistance to farmers and certain industries and underwrites the cost of such "middle-class welfare" as national parks (supported by taxpayers but rarely used by poor people) and loans to college students. But when we hear the term "welfare," we tend to think of public assistance for poor, handicapped, or disadvantaged people.

Public assistance can take many forms:

- Direct payments to single parents with young children, the unemployed, and the disabled
- Vouchers that can be exchanged for food
- Subsidies that reduce the cost of housing or the provision of public housing
- Reduced cost or free access to public transportation, higher education, or job training
- Subsidized medical care

These programs are targeted to the more than 37 million people living under the official poverty line of just under $14,000 for a family of four in 1993, or

Problems with Health Care

- *Cost* Health care costs in the United States have risen from $270 billion in 1970 to $884 billion in 1993 (in inflation-adjusted dollars), a 325 percent increase.

- *The Uninsured* At any one time, approximately 40 million people, over 15 percent of the U.S. population, are not covered by any private health insurance or state or federal Medicaid benefits.* A very large proportion of this number—84 percent—are full-time employees. Because these people often fall just above the poverty line, they do not qualify for Medicaid. And because they work near the minimum wage in jobs that are part-time, seasonal, or menial, their employer does not provide health insurance benefits.

- *Unnecessary Procedures* Doctors and insurance companies claim that they have to perform and pay for procedures that may be unnecessary medically but are needed to reduce the risk of being sued by patients. It is estimated that between 15 and 30 percent of all medical procedures in the United States are not necessary.**

- *Endless Paperwork* In medicine as in other activities, paperwork is necessary to document what services were provided and to prevent fraud. One avoidable expense that virtually all health care reformers agree on is the inefficient and uncoordinated system of paperwork in the present system.

- *Litigation Expenses* Physicians frequently complain about the high cost of malpractice insurance. Malpractice premiums in the United States are nine times higher than in Canada. Malpractice insurance for all physicians, on average, has climbed from an annual premium of $7,000 in 1983 to $15,000 in 1990, and is highest for doctors in specialties like anesthesia, obstetrics and gynecology, and heart and brain surgery.†

- *Prevention: Lifestyle and Environmental Causes of Illness* Part of the health care "crisis" in the United States is avoidable. Medicare alone will spend $16 billion in 1994 on treating cigarette-related diseases, and over the next 20 years the cost will be an estimated $800 billion.††

*U.S. Bureau of the Census, *Statistical Abstract of the United States: 1995* (Government Printing Office, 1995), p. 118.

**Arnold S. Relman, "Where Does all the Money Go?" *Health Management Quarterly* (Fall 1991), p. 324.

†Peter C. Coyte, Donald N. Dewees, and Michael Trebilock, "Medical Malpractice: The Canadian Experience," *New England Journal of Medicine* 324 (January 10, 1991), pp. 89–93; *Statistical Abstract, 1993*, p. 120.

††"Medicare Funds Going Up in Smoke," *Deseret News*, May 17, 1994, p. A1.

TABLE 14-5

Social Insurance and Benefit Program Payments, 1980–1995 (in billions of 1994 dollars)

Program	1980	1985	1990	1995
Social Security	$204.9	$242.8	$265.9	$286.0
Medicaid	44.0	53.8	77.8	118.1
Medicare	59.5	93.1	117.7	132.2
AFDC	22.1	21.9	22.7	24.9
Food Stamps	16.3	17.4	19.0	24.9

SOURCE: U.S. Bureau of the Census, *Statistical Abstract of the United States: 1993*, pp. 369, 371; and *Statistical Abstract of the United States: 1995*, pp. 369, 377.

Welfare Programs: Assisting the Poor

Welfare policy is made up of a combination of federal, state, and local programs. Most of the following programs are paid for by federal funds, but the administrative burden falls on state and local governments.

• *Food Stamps*—coupons that can be exchanged for food at most grocery stores. Originating in the New Deal as a way of helping feed the poor, this is the nation's largest single welfare program. It is administered by the U.S. Department of Agriculture with the assistance of state and local welfare offices. There are roughly twice as many people who use food stamps as receive AFDC benefits.

• *Job Training*—includes job-training programs administered by all levels of government ranging from student aid programs in public schools, to vocational rehabilitation programs for people who are disabled by physical or mental problems, to programs under the Job Training Partnership Act, which encourages private firms to hire and train poor people.

• *Aid to Families with Dependent Children (AFDC)*—provides federal funds administered by states to families with children who meet specified standards of need; originally part of the Social Security Act of 1935. The number of families receiving AFDC remained fairly constant throughout the 1970s and 1980s, at about 3.5 million families. By 1993, however, enrollment reached 14.2 million persons, including 5 million families and 9.6 million children, the highest levels in history.

• *Medicaid*—pays for medical care for eligible poor people, including the aged, the blind, the disabled, and AFDC families. The program is partially funded by the federal government but is administered by state agencies. Medicaid was created in 1965 as an amendment to the Social Security Act.

• *Public Housing*—the federal government assists local governments in building housing through a local housing authority that, with state permission, can sell bonds and spend federal funds provided for the program. Rents help to pay off the bonded indebtedness, but since rents are too low to provide enough money for this purpose, the government must make up the difference. The federal government also has a rent subsidy program to assist poor people with rent for private housing where public housing units are not available.

roughly 15 percent of the population. One study has estimated that there has been a 39 percent decline in poverty due to social welfare programs.[55]

The poor tend to be disproportionately African American, Hispanic, young, and female. More than half of all poor families are headed by females. The fact that more women and children are impoverished has been called the "feminization of poverty."[56] Examples of the range of problems encountered by women include the male-female wage gap for men and women doing the same work, the concentration of women in low-paying jobs, the differential economic impact of divorce on men and women, the disproportionate responsibility women assume for child care, the abandonment of family by men who fail to pay child support, and illegitimate births. Traditional welfare programs are aimed at these problems, but they have largely failed to solve them.

THE CURRENT WELFARE SYSTEM   As with much of social policy, the welfare system traces its roots to the New Deal. In the face of widespread unemployment and poverty during the Great Depression, the government enacted social policies intended to provide a system of "social security" for the nation's elderly and disabled as well as jobs programs for the unemployed. In 1950, the federal government contributed just 44 percent of all public assistance, but in 1990, the federal government paid over 72 percent of all benefits.[57] Federal funds flow to the states on certain conditions: each state sets requirements for eligibility and level of payments; the federal government sets overall standards.

During his 1992 presidential campaign, Bill Clinton promised to "end welfare as we know it" by providing education, training, day-care, and health coverage during the first two years on welfare, and then helping welfare recipients find work in private-sector or community service jobs as a way to eliminate the "permanent dependence on welfare."

Welfare reform was a major issue throughout the Republican-controlled 104th Congress. House and Senate reformers appeared to be reacting to a growing sentiment that welfare recipients are not victims; they just need some help to pull themselves up by their bootstraps. The "safety net" should be only a temporary aid, and more should be required of recipients. Republican proposals would reduce the role of the federal government and elevate the role of the state.

In early 1995, as part of the vigorous campaign to reduce the federal deficit, Congress proposed a slash in eligibility, a cap on federal spending, and state responsibility to run a revamped welfare program. House proposals attempted to combine dozens of welfare programs into large block grants to the states. Each state was to set eligibility requirements and administer child-care programs, school meals, nutrition programs for pregnant women and young children, and possibly cash welfare, child protection, and food stamps, through these block grants. With limited funds, the priority would be on American children; illegal immigrants would be excluded from 23 welfare programs and legal aliens from 19. These proposals required welfare recipients to find work after two years of benefits, and they set a lifetime cap for benefits at five years. House Republicans were criticized for these proposals because, in attempting to cut costs, they provided little help for getting and keeping jobs, and children were penalized if their parents did not move toward self-sufficiency.

President Clinton, who had advocated time limits for welfare, work requirements, tougher child support enforcement, and requiring minor mothers to live at home as a condition of assistance, vetoed the measure, saying the budget cuts were too deep. Congressional Republicans had attempted to implement welfare reform through the budget process, something Clinton also objected to. When they passed welfare reform legislation with essentially the same provisions, Clinton again vetoed it.

The National Governor's Association (NGA) then stepped in with some compromise welfare reform proposals of their own. The NGA plan is based on the defeated welfare bill in that it embraces the block-grant approach and state discretion and responsibility. With bipartisan support, the governors agreed that more money for child care was needed than Congress offered, that states must spend funds to match federal block grants, and that school lunch programs should stay intact and not become a block grant. Funds for most welfare programs would be sent to the states in a block grant with few strings attached. The states would be relatively free of interference from Washington, but they would have access to a federal "rainy-day fund" during times of recession or when demand for welfare services exceeded state capacity. Congress and the president reached a compromise in August 1996 on a welfare reform bill that incorporated the NGA block-grant idea. Proposals such as a lifetime limit on benefits and decreasing aid to legal immigrants were included, as was Clinton's proposal that welfare be linked to work and that welfare benefits have a time limit.

Everyone seems to agree that welfare does not work and should be changed so the cycle of dependency can be broken. But liberals fear that reform really means abandoning vulnerable people before they are ready. Conservatives criticize reforms as diluting similar but more meaningful reforms already in place at the state and local levels. The debate centers on several questions. Should there be a limit on how long welfare benefits can be received? To provide incentives to work, programs now place time limits on receiving benefits. Some states have proposed overall limits as well as phased-in reductions. Do we really have the resolve to punish children of parents who cannot or will not work by denying them food and shelter? President Clinton's task force on welfare reform proposed to make it easier for families to collect welfare if the father is present. Some oppose this idea; they think it will weaken the incentive for fathers to work.

Should a person have to work to earn welfare? About one-quarter of families who receive AFDC continue to do so for ten or more years.[58] A longstanding aspect of welfare policy was that public assistance was temporary, until people found jobs or received training for new jobs. But most people on welfare have little education, and they lack job skills. They are unemployable or they can only find jobs that pay less than their welfare payments. Some people on welfare may lack motivation to get off of public assistance or fear losing medical coverage. Putting the poor to work requires training and incentives to overcome weak motivation. Such a program would cost more than simply sending out welfare checks. Successful jobs programs may cost $10,000 to $15,000 to develop one job; training may cost an additional $5,000 to $10,000.[59]

EXPERIMENTS IN WELFARE REFORM   Welfare reform has become a major issue in most states as well as at the national level. Several governors have become outspoken critics of the federal bureaucracy, federal mandates for state spending, and the seeming inability to help people get off welfare, to reduce program costs, and to improve lives. But welfare reforms, especially reforms targeted to help people become self-sufficient, are expensive. The following proposals illustrate the range and nature of some of the reforms that have been proposed:

1. *Use tax credits.* The federal government's Earned Income Tax Credit (EITC) supplements the wages of the working person with tax credits and food stamps to lift recipients above the poverty level. EITC is available to families with working parents whose annual income is less than $23,050. In a sense, the EITC rewards those who are working but not making enough money to get them out of poverty. By encouraging those who are employed to maintain their jobs by supplementing their income with tax credits, the

We The People

People in Poverty

	Number (millions)	Percent
Race		
White	26.2	12.2%
Black	10.9	33.1
Hispanic	8.1	30.6
Age		
Under 18	15.7	22.7
18–24	4.9	19.1
25–34	5.8	13.8
35–44	4.4	10.6
45–54	2.5	8.5
55–59	1.1	9.9
60–64	1.1	11.3
65+	3.8	12.2
Education		
No High School Diploma	3.1	25.1
No College	2.5	11.7
Some College	1.3	8.0
BA	.4	2.3
All Persons	39.3	15.1

SOURCE: U.S. Bureau of the Census, *Statistical Abstract of the United States, 1995* (Government Printing Office, 1995), p. 481.

federal government hopes to reduce the number of eligible workers who are living solely on welfare checks and encourage people to find jobs, albeit low-paying ones.[60]

2. *Provide job training.* In 1988 Congress passed the Family Support Act, which established the Job Opportunities and Basic Skills (JOBS) program. It requires states to provide education and training opportunities and child-care assistance for recipients who do not have children under age three. Additional federal funds are made available to states to assist persons moving from welfare to work. JOBS has not been fully implemented, and no one knows how expensive it will end up being. According to its advocates, it gives people a way out of welfare by providing them the training they need as well as health and child care. Critics see a much-expanded federal welfare bureaucracy that will not deliver on its promises. The Congressional Budget Office has estimated that by the end of 1993, JOBS will have decreased the number of AFDC families by about 50,000, a 1.3 percent reduction in the number of families on the AFDC rolls.[61]

3. *Limit the time people can be on welfare.* Proposed limits on welfare are often conditioned on giving recipients a fixed period of time to find work. After that time expires, recipients in Massachusetts, for example, must accept a community service job or lose their benefits; in Colorado, they have the additional option to participate in a job-training program.

4. *Improve child-support enforcement.* To ensure that children are adequately cared for, the system of child support needs to reformed. One idea is to require states to enforce determinations of paternity so that children receive some support from fathers who are legally required to provide financial assistance. Another idea is to enforce child-support decrees by *garnishing* the wages (the state intervenes and takes part or all of the wages) of fathers who fail to provide the determined amount of financial assistance. One study has estimated that if "one-fourth of the $20 billion in unpaid child support could be collected on behalf of poor children, the poverty deficit could be reduced to $1.5 billion dollars."[62]

5. *Target teenage mothers.* Some argue that we should focus on working with teenagers to avoid pregnancies. If we can develop programs that reduce the number of "children having children," we could avoid major welfare costs. One expert suggests that reform is needed in how states reimburse child-care expenses for the poor. Paul Offner points out that states pay child-care costs only to licensed providers, and many poor women live in poor areas that have few licensed providers. As a result, many women stay home with their children when they could otherwise be working, going to school, or receiving job training.[63] Former Education Secretary Bill Bennett has argued that withdrawing welfare from unmarried mothers would give them an incentive to find employment.[64]

6. *Reduce fraud.* New York's former governor, Mario Cuomo, and California Governor Pete Wilson proposed that welfare recipients be fingerprinted as part of the enrollment process. Such a program could save states and the federal government money that is lost each year to abuse of the system by those who use illegal means and multiple applications to benefit from programs. By reducing fraud, the allocated funding could reach those it was intended to benefit and possibly cut the overall budget required to sustain the system.

7. *Consolidate programs.* Alabama, Washington, and Minnesota have combined various welfare programs into one package, and Oregon is about to do so. It is hoped that such consolidations can save dollars and help simplify the

procedures.[65] A draft report of the Department of Health and Human Services' inspector general found the federal government is spending from $6 to $8 billion a year to help states administer food stamps, AFDC, and Medicaid.[66] Between 1987 and 1991, administrative costs for these programs grew by 19 percent.[67] By reducing these administrative costs, it is hoped more funding will be available, and the overall costs of operating these programs will be reduced.

8. *Terminate welfare entirely.* Author Charles Murray has suggested abolishing AFDC health benefits, housing subsidies, and food stamps. Speaking of the problem of teenage mothers, he says, "If she wants to keep a child, she must enlist support from her parents, boyfriend, siblings, neighbors, church, or philanthropies. She must get support from somewhere, anywhere, other than the government."[68] Children would be supported by the state only if the child could not be adopted; then the child would be "adopted" by the state and kept in an orphanage.[69]

Welfare policies are often criticized because they fail to accomplish the purposes identified for them, but most have multiple goals that cannot all be achieved at the same time. Policies are bundles of compromises; they include contradictions that are responses to political demands, interests, and preferences. We try to help people who are poor as well as help prevent people from becoming poor. We try to eliminate the causes of poverty, so that welfare will eventually not be needed. But support payments may serve to reward the existing conditions and create disincentives for the changes necessary to become independent.

Crime

In recent years, crime control, once a state and local issue, has been forced onto the national political agenda. The 1995 bombing of a federal government office building in Oklahoma City gave rise to proposals in Congress to enact antiterrorist legislation that would give the federal government more authority to investigate and prosecute these types of actions.

More and more crimes are now defined as federal crimes—for instance, blocking entrance to abortion clinics—and federal laws are being interpreted more broadly by courts. Punishment for federal crimes has become more severe, and spending on federal prisons is increasing (see Table 14-6). As crime and violence in cities and small towns increases, the federal government is pressured to step in. But crime control is primarily a state and local matter (see Figure 14-4). The national government usually acts as a banker, providing grants to states and local governments to hire more police officers, improve the enforcement of drug laws, or deal with organized crime.

An exception to this decentralized criminal justice system is the Federal Bureau of Investigation (FBI), created in 1908 and charged with gathering and reporting evidence in matters relating to federal laws or to crimes that cross state boundaries. In addition, the FBI provides investigative services on a cooperative basis to local law enforcement in fingerprint identification and laboratory services. Other agencies of the federal government that take on law enforcement activities include the Drug Enforcement Agency (DEA), which is responsible for controlling the flow of illegal narcotics into the United States, patrolling U.S. borders, and conducting joint operations with countries where drugs are produced, and the Bureau of Alcohol, Tobacco, and Firearms (ATF), which monitors the sale of destructive weapons and guns inside the United States.

TABLE 14-6

The Cost of Crime in the United States, 1993 (in billions)

Criminal justice system	$78
Private protection	64
Loss of life and work	202
Crimes against business	120
Stolen goods and fraud	60
Drug abuse	40
Driving while intoxicated	110
Total	$674

SOURCE: "Cost of Crime," *U.S. News and World Report,* January 17, 1994, pp. 40–41.

Thinking it Through

Opponents of such limitations point to the Second Amendment, which protects the right to keep and bear arms as it relates to the militia—a right valued by more people than just gun owners. But as technology has created more powerful guns, we have had to define what types of arms are protected. Few would assert that individuals have the right to use their own bazookas; during Prohibition, Congress banned machine guns; and now we have added semiautomatic weapons to the list.

In 1994, Congress voted to ban 19 semiautomatic rifles while specifically exempting 670 guns used in hunting and target practice. In 1996 the House voted to overturn this ban, but the Senate took no action, so the ban remains in force. Though supporters of this measure say these guns have made killing humans much easier, opponents point out that less than 1 percent of all violent crime is committed by criminals using assault rifles.

Though banning only 19 out of nearly 700 assault rifles seems trivial, it could be regarded as a first step toward tight gun control. For two centuries, gun rights advocates have had the power and influence to stop any gun regulation in Congress; today, however, public demands for safe streets and a reduction in crime are pushing Congress to adopt controls.

The Underreporting of Crime

Data on crime are gathered either from police reports, which become part of the FBI's crime statistics, or in a Justice Department survey, which includes crimes never reported to the police. FBI statistics underestimate some crimes more than others. According to the Justice Department, in 1991, only 59 percent of rapes, 55 percent of robberies, 47 percent of assaults, 28 percent of personal larceny, 50 percent of household burglaries, and 74 percent of motor vehicle thefts were reported. Therefore, the number of crimes in the FBI reports is far fewer than the actual number of crimes committed.

SOURCE: U.S. Bureau of the Census, *Statistical Abstract of the United States, 1993* (Government Printing Office, 1994), pp. 189–90.

LYNDON JOHNSON'S WAR ON CRIME Just as Lyndon Johnson launched a "war on poverty" as part of his Great Society, he also launched a "war on crime." Johnson commissioned a blue-ribbon panel of experts to study the causes of crime and violence and propose remedies. These experts pointed out the relationship between poverty and crime and called attention to the understaffed and inefficient criminal justice system—police, prosecutors, judges, and prisons.[70]

Partly as a result of these studies, in 1965 Congress established the Law Enforcement Assistance Administration (LEAA), which over its 12 years of existence made grants exceeding $8 billion to state and local governments. These federal dollars were used to hire more police, purchase squad cars and radios, and provide for greater coordination within the criminal justice system. Part of the money was spent studying crime and identifying areas for future funding. Evaluations of the LEAA found that money was spent on what local governments could get grants for rather than on what the most pressing needs were. Other critics maintained that Washington gave up too much control over how the money was spent. Much of the LEAA money was wasted, and the program was abolished during the Carter administration.[71]

RECENT CRIME CONTROL LEGISLATION The growth of drug-related crime reignited the debate over how the federal government should assist in fighting crime. Since 1983, Congress has passed five anticrime grant programs:

1. In 1984 Congress overhauled the federal sentencing system, required mandatory minimum sentences for certain crimes, increased the maximum fines for serious drug offenses, and established a victim compensation program in the Department of Justice.

2. In 1986 Congress provided grants to state and local drug-enforcement programs.

3. In 1988 Congress again provided money for local and state drug enforcement, mandated tougher sentences, and coordinated federal antidrug efforts through the creation of a cabinet-level official to oversee these efforts—the "drug czar."

4. In 1990 additional federal grants were made available to establish more effective prison programs, including alternatives to traditional incarceration.

FIGURE 14-4 Federal and State Prisoners, 1960–1995

SOURCE: U.S. Bureau of the Census, *Statistical Abstract of the United States, 1993*, p. 210; and *Statistical Abstract of the United States, 1995*, p. 217; 1994 numbers from Bureau of Justice Statistics home page: http://www.ojb.usdoj.gov/pub/bjs/press/pi94.pr; 1995 numbers for June http://www.ojp.usdoj.gov/pub/bjs/press/pam95.pr.

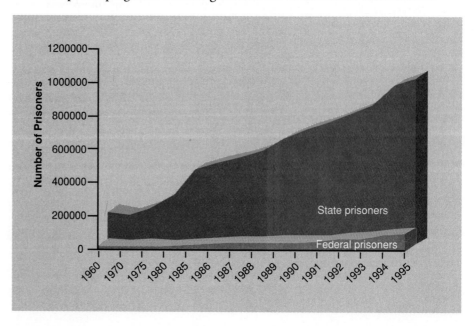

5. In 1994 Congress passed an omnibus anticrime bill that included federal funds to hire thousands of additional police officers, construct new prisons, and fund several crime prevention programs.

The crime rate early in Clinton's term was actually declining. There is good evidence that there is a systematic underreporting of some crimes, but that is not a new phenomenon. Statistics from the FBI indicate that the rate of crime as a whole declined 5 percent in the first six months of 1993 from that same period a year before, and the rate of violent crime dropped by 3 percent. But the widespread perception was that crime and violence were increasing and that the federal government needed to step in.

A recurring policy debate in Congress centers around gun control. The Brady Bill, which imposes a five-day waiting period on the purchase of handguns, permits law enforcement personnel to conduct background checks on prospective gun buyers. President Clinton also was successful in winning enough votes to ban the sale of some semiautomatic assault weapons, although the Republican-controlled House of Representatives voted in 1996 to repeal the ban. Both measures had a limited scope. The Brady Bill applies only to handguns, and the assault weapon ban was only for 19 types of guns. Despite these limitations, both laws are testing the strength of the National Rifle Association (NRA), long thought to be one of the most powerful lobbies in the country. President Clinton marshaled the support of police chiefs and victims of violent crime in a skillful campaign to pressure Congress to pass these two bills. The NRA, long an opponent of these bills, staged its own all-out campaign to defeat the legislation. The assault weapon ban passed by only two votes (216 to 214) in the House. After Republicans took control of the House in 1995, they voted to repeal this ban, but no action was taken in the Senate, so the ban remains in force.

Fighting crime may be the biggest social policy challenge of the 1990s. But the goal of reducing crime must compete with other expectations we have for government. Can we combat crime in ways that protect traditional civil liberties? Random drug tests, searches of private automobiles, curfews in urban areas, electronic eavesdropping, setting up sting operations to catch criminals, and other steps law enforcement officials believe are necessary often conflict with the individual liberty and freedom from government restraint that Americans cherish. Must we give up some of those individual freedoms in order to fight crime? Should we build more prisons and impose harsher sentences on convicted criminals? Or should we focus more on remedying the poverty and lack of opportunity that lead to criminal behavior? Like other social policies, those aimed at fighting crime must ultimately balance competing values, one of the most complex and difficult tasks we delegate to governments.

The Politics of Social Policy

Social policy issues now dominate the agenda of American politics. Crime, welfare, health care, and their costs are what people are concerned about. Both Republicans and Democrats are attempting to address these key domestic issues which win broad support. Recent elections demonstrate how unsettled public opinion is on these issues.

The nation long ago answered the questions about whether the government is responsible to provide decent housing, adequate health care, and a solid education to all of its citizens. The answer—to use Ronald Reagan's phrase—is that government provides a "safety net" for those who cannot provide for themselves. But how to provide that net, and what programs or approaches to try are very much debated. And what are we willing to pay for expanded social services? These questions will remain central to American politics as we enter the twenty-first century.

Guns and More Guns

The number of guns in the United States has increased dramatically since 1950, up from 54 million to more than 200 million today. Today, one of every four households in this country has a gun. Guns, particularly handguns, are used in violent crimes. Of all crime incidents by armed offenders, over 25 percent involved a handgun; almost 40 percent of all rapes and robberies involved a handgun; more than 11,000 murders were committed by handguns; and handguns accounted for almost 30,000 deaths in the United States in 1993 through murder, accident, or suicide. In 1993, there were an estimated 6 million incidents of violent crime; however, there were only about 130,000 convictions. As violent crime rises, conviction rates are falling.

SOURCES: Ted Gest, Gordon Witkin, Katia Hetter, and Andrea Wright, "Violence in America," *U.S. News and World Report,* January 17, 1994, p. 24; Shane Tritsch, "Will Handguns Keep You Safe?" *Safety and Health* 148 (August 1993), pp. 68–70; U.S. Bureau of the Census, *Statistical Abstract of the United States, 1993* (Government Printing Office, 1994), pp. 98, 195, 197.

SUMMARY

1. There are five stages in the policy-making process: problem identification, policy formulation, policy adoption, policy implementation, and policy evaluation. When the process turns to implementation and evaluation, new problems are identified, and the process begins again. Many problems exist, but do not result in policy or legislation. Similarly, many policies are proposed yet never adopted.

2. The role of government as promoter of economic growth and jobs is not new. Recent years have witnessed intense governmental concern with energy development, support of businesses such as Chrysler and the savings and loan banks, and human-resource assistance programs. The federal government uses fiscal policy (taxes and spending) and monetary policy (control of the money supply through interest rate adjustment) to promote economic change.

3. Many disagree with efforts by the national government to improve the quality of life, to focus resources and attention on the problems of the poor, and to improve the cities. They view with distaste the bureaucracy these programs require; allege that the programs cost far more than they might cost if administered at the local level; and claim that many of these programs create a dependency that undermines our traditional ethic of self-reliance. On the other hand, most of these problems developed because local, private, and voluntary sectors were overwhelmed by them and were unable to respond to social problems in a meaningful way.

4. The pressures are usually for more, not less, involvement by the national government. Once a subsidy or entitlement program is established, it is hard to eliminate it. In one way or another, the government subsidizes nearly every segment of our population. Which of these programs are justified and which are not is at the heart of American politics. One person's cherished subsidy is often seen by the next person as a wasteful boondoggle.

5. The commercial relations between our industries and those of other nations are a concern of the federal government. Decisions on free trade versus protectionism and alliances such as the North American Free Trade Agreement (NAFTA) affect our economic health. Internal policies on taxes and spending also affect the economy and are central to our politics.

6. Regulation in the United States is a set of government rules and laws issued to alter or control the operations of economic enterprises yet based on a widely held commitment to a free market economy. Although we often think of politics as the pursuit of private power and private interests, it is plainly also an effort to define the public interest. We set up regulatory agencies to enforce federal rules and regulations in an effort to interpret the public interest and to achieve various desired goals. Regulatory agencies can be very powerful.

7. Social issues like health care reform, welfare reform, and crime control are now the primary agenda of American politics. Conservatives advocate private solutions to most social problems, while liberals argue that it is the responsibility of government to provide a minimum standard of living—including a job, education, health care, housing, and nutrition—for all citizens. Since the New Deal, some government involvement in social programs has been widely accepted, although the extent of involvement has waxed and waned.

8. Social Security, inaugurated in 1935 as part of the New Deal, is perhaps the most significant social legislation in U.S. history. Through a system of employee and employer taxes, retired workers and disabled individuals receive monthly payments. With the country's changing demographic profile, tensions in the system are likely to increase.

9. The federal government supports medical research and has increased its role in health care cost control and access as the country's mostly private health care system is beset by rising costs, increasing numbers of uninsured Americans, unnecessary procedures, endless paperwork, high litigation costs, and limited access. A variety of proposals for reform are under consideration, including a single-payer system, managed competition, employer-mandated coverage, spending caps, and individual responsibility for coverage.

10. Welfare takes many forms, including direct payments to the poor, the unemployed, and the disabled; food stamps; job training; housing subsidies; free school lunches; tax credits; and subsidized medical care. Public assistance programs began with the New Deal and have grown ever since; the federal government pays about three-fourths of their costs. Welfare has long been criticized as creating disincentives to work, and many proposals have been put forward to make programs more effective and efficient. But because welfare problems embody competing political agendas and expectations, reform has seen little success.

11. Crime control has been forced onto the national agenda by publicly perceived increases in crime and violence and by politicians eager to accuse opponents of being "soft on crime." Pressures for federal action resulted in passage of the Brady Bill, which imposed a five-day waiting period on the sale of handguns, and in other proposals that would add to the number of police officers and further restrict gun sales. The Republican vote to overturn part of this legislation demonstrates the contentious nature of the crime and gun control issue.

FURTHER READING

Mary Jo Bane and David T. Ellwood, *Welfare Realities: From Rhetoric to Reform* (Harvard University Press, 1994).

James Barth, *The Great Savings and Loan Debacle* (American Enterprise Institute, 1991).

Gary C. Bryner, *Blue Skies, Green Politics: The Clean Air Act of 1990 and Its Implementation,* 2nd ed. (Congressional Quarterly Press, 1995).

Bryan Burrough and John Helyar, *Barbarians at the Gate: The Fall of RJR Nabisco* (Harper & Row, 1990).

David P. Calleo, *The Bankrupting of America: How the Federal Budget Is Impoverishing the Nation* (William Morrow, 1992).

Thomas E. Cronin, Tania Z. Cronin, and Michael E. Milakovich, *U.S. v. Crime in the Streets* (Indiana University Press, 1981).

Andrew W. Dobelstein, *Social Welfare: Policy and Analysis* (Nelson-Hall, 1990).

Frank Fischer, *Evaluating Public Policy* (Nelson-Hall, 1995).

James Grant, *Money of the Mind: Borrowing and Lending in America* (Farrar, Straus & Giroux, 1992).

Laurene A. Graig, *Health of Nations: An International Perspective on U.S. Health Care Reform* (Congressional Quarterly, Inc., 1993).

William Greider, *Secrets of the Temple: How the Federal Reserve Runs the Country* (Simon & Schuster, 1987).

Christopher Jencks, *The Homeless* (Harvard University Press, 1994).

Paul W. MacAvoy, *Industrial Regulation and Performance of the American Economy* (W.W. Norton, 1992).

Thomas E. Mann and Norman J. Ornstein, eds., *Intensive Care: How Congress Shapes Health Policy* (Brookings Institution, 1995).

Theodore R. Marmor, *Understanding Health Care Reform* (Yale University Press, 1994).

Theodore R. Marmor, Jerry L. Mashaw, and Phillip L. Harvey, *America's Misunderstood Welfare State: Persistent Myths, Enduring Realities* (Basic Books, 1990).

Daniel Patrick Moynihan, *Family and Nation* (Harvard University Press, 1986).

Charles Murray, *Losing Ground: American Social Policy, 1950–80* (Basic Books, 1984).

B. Guy Peters, *American Public Policy: Promise and Performance,* revised ed. (Chatham House, 1995).

Theda Skocpol, *Social Policy in the United States: Future Possibilities in Historical Perspective* (Princeton University Press, 1995).

Lawrence J. White, *The S&L Debacle: Public Policy Lessons for Bank and Thrift Regulation* (Oxford University Press, 1991).

Bob Woodward, *Agenda: Inside the Clinton White House* (Simon & Schuster, 1994).

FOREIGN AND DEFENSE POLICY

The United States finds itself today in a wholly new age of world affairs. "It is an age which, for all its confusions and dangers," observed distinguished diplomat George F. Kennan, "is marked by one major blessing: for the first time in centuries, there are no great-power rivalries that threaten immediately the peace of the world."[1] We have a vested interest in keeping it this way. Yet Kennan and nearly every U.S. citizen understand that even if the cold war is over and even if the United States is the world's dominant and unrivaled military power, the world is still full of violent conflicts between and within nations. In addition, the population explosion, drugs, poverty, environmental problems, and nuclear weapons create a highly unsettled and unstable world.

The debate among our parties and presidential candidates highlights a fundamental tension in how we shape foreign and defense policy. One of the main differences may simply be summarized as the persisting desire for America "to remain the premier global power and our ever deepening aversion to bear the costs of this position. Evidence of the contradiction is pervasive," writes Robert W. Tucker.[2]

Republican candidate Bob Dole tried to discredit President Clinton's foreign and defense policies in the 1996 election season, but most voters seemed indifferent if not apathetic about most world developments. Clinton and the Republican Congress now face critical international challenges and will have to provide global leadership.

How should we restructure our foreign policy to meet these new conditions? Should we pull back from the rest of the world, now that the cold war is over? How much have economic and trade competition replaced superpower military conflicts? What role do environmental and drug issues now play in foreign policy? How much should we try to link trade agreements with another nation's willingness to protect human rights? How much should we aid former enemies?

And is it possible—or desirable—to fashion a single grand strategy of foreign policy to replace our longtime goal of containing and defeating the Soviets? As the once-clear lines between foreign and domestic policy become irretrievably blurred, how will the increased participation by Congress and the increased influence of public opinion affect the traditional primacy of the American president in the politics of foreign policy decision making? In short, what should our new foreign policy be, and who should make it? In this chapter we explore possible answers to these difficult questions.

VITAL INTERESTS IN THE POST–COLD WAR WORLD

Defining and defending our vital national security interests was easier when we understood who the enemy was. In the cold war years, we concentrated on containing and undermining the Soviet threat, and that became the guiding plan of foreign policy. Now the cold war is over, and although the United States has emerged as the world's only military superpower, there are considerable limits on what we *can* do, as well as hard decisions about what we *should* do.

Over the past several generations, the United States has become involved in world affairs to a degree unprecedented in our history. Much of this activity was due to the cold war, 1945 to 1990. Yet there are other reasons as well. U.S. interests, security, and economy are so closely tied to what happens in the rest of the world that, whether we like it or not, events far from home affect our life, liberty, and pursuit of happiness.

Defining Our Vital Interests

America's political values are a factor in defining our vital interests. We want peace. We favor human rights. We generally support United Nations peacekeeping missions. The United States has a commitment to protect weaker nations against aggression. We want to encourage democracy and market-oriented economies. We want, where possible, to improve the standard of living in less-developed nations. We are also committed to improving the global environment. Our vital interests have long been defined by our commitment to free trade. As the world's principal trader, the United States needs markets for its products, imports of raw materials, and adequate supplies of energy.

Our foreign policy leaders see American power and purpose as a vital means of shaping not only a more secure world but also a more democratic world. According to the State Department, foreign policy priorities for the 1990s are:

1. *Promoting democratic values:* human rights, political choice, the rule of law, and self-determination. When barriers to these democratic values come down, prospects open wide for legitimate government, revitalized societies, and improved relations.

2. *Fostering global growth by promoting market principles.* The United States will pursue an active economic agenda bilaterally with our major trading partners and multilaterally through the International Monetary Fund, the World Bank, and the General Agreement on Tariffs and Trade (GATT).

3. *Promoting the secure global environment* that is vital if democratic and market values are to flourish.

Some Key Foreign Policy Terms

- *Internationalism:* A foreign policy that recognizes that concern for trade, human rights, and international peace requires not only a strong military but also the willingness to intervene where U.S. vital interests are at stake. The goal is to create an international order consistent with American values.

- *Isolationism:* A foreign policy that curtails U.S. military aid and intervention abroad as much as possible. It was the dominant policy in this country during the nineteenth century and to some degree in the 1920s and 1930s, and was put forward again by Pat Buchanan during the 1996 presidential primaries.

- *Realism or Realpolitik:* A foreign policy based on practical and self-interest factors rather than on moral, idealistic, or theoretical considerations. Realists say the United States should intervene in world affairs only if its vital interests are in jeopardy or if a dispute involves overt outside aggression, not simply internal rebellion.

- *Containment:* A foreign policy aimed at halting the spread of communism, especially the influence of the former Soviet Union. This was the underlying foreign and national security policy of the United States between 1947 and 1990.

- *New World Order:* A vague and often confusing label pinned on the post-cold war period—one in which the United States presumably plays a vital role as the only remaining superpower in preserving peace and encouraging economic and human rights throughout the world.

During a summit meeting in Russia in January 1994, Presidents Clinton, Yeltsin, and Kravchuk (*left to right*) agreed to stop aiming long-range nuclear missiles at each other's territory, and the Ukraine agreed to dismantle all of its nuclear warheads.

TABLE 15-1

Foreign Policy Goals: What Is Important?

	Percent Answering "Important" or "Very Important"	
	The Public	Leaders
Stopping flow of illegal drugs into U.S.	85%	57%
Protecting jobs of American workers	83	50
Preventing the spread of nuclear weapons	82	90
Controlling and reducing illegal immigration	72	28
Securing adequate supplies of energy	62	67
Reducing our trade deficits with foreign countries	59	49
Improving global environment	58	49
Combating world hunger	56	41
Protecting interests of America's business abroad	52	38
Strengthening United Nations	51	33
Maintaining superior military power worldwide	50	54
Defending our allies' security	41	60
Promoting and defending human rights in other countries	34	26
Helping to bring a democratic form of government to other nations	25	21
Protecting weaker nations against foreign aggression	24	21
Helping to improve standards of living in less-developed nations	22	28

Source: Adapted with permission from John E. Reilly, *American Public Opinion and U.S. Foreign Policy, 1995* (The Chicago Council on Foreign Relations, 1995), p. 15.

Public sample was N=1492. Leaders sample involved 383 elected officials, business leaders, educators, editors, and union officers.

4. *Working with all allies against new transnational threats,* such as environmental degradation, narcotics, and terrorism.

5. *Reshaping and renewing our alliances and other important ties.* We need to adjust our alliances to the largely favorable conditions that we and our Atlantic and Pacific partners created in the postwar period. [3]

New Foreign Policy Challenges

The end of the cold war did not mean that the United States no longer faced challenges to its security or economic well-being. The removal of communism as a constraint led to the reemergence of old national hatreds throughout Eastern Europe. Some nations, such as Yugoslavia and Czechoslovakia, broke apart. The Middle East remains unsettled, with a rising tide of Islamic fundamentalism challenging the West and threatening American energy supplies. In Latin America, democracies seem to be emerging, but there have been setbacks. In Asia, the countries of China, Burma, and Indonesia remain under military rule. The United States remains especially concerned with the proliferation of nuclear weapons, the invasion of drugs into our country, and the persistence of brutal civil wars in several countries around the globe.

The United States may be militarily strong, but it faces stiff competition for influence in the world as the power base shifts, at least in part, from military might to economic strength. The United States may be the world's most important military power, but in many regions of the world, it is not necessarily the most influential nation. Our foreign policy has to address vital issues that have been simmering for many years, plus some concerns that are very recent. The list of issues is long, and we can outline only a few, but Table 15-1 lists issues of major concern to both leaders and the general public.

POPULATION GROWTH Americans are alarmed at the world's population explosion in the face of widespread poverty. Most of the world's 5.5 billion people are already virtually excluded from economic opportunity. Moreover, there continues to be a significant transfer of wealth from poor countries to rich, and the information technology revolution will accelerate this disparity.

TRADE WITH JAPAN AND CHINA A serious trade imbalance exists between the United States and Japan. Some U.S. citizens believe we should force Japan to open its markets to imports of our products and impose restrictions on the manufacture of exported Japanese products, even if such restrictions would make those products cost more.

Trade with China poses different concerns. China has one of the fastest growing economies in the world. U.S. exports to China have tripled in the last several years. Human rights advocates believe we should link trade and tariff agreements to China's human rights record. It is well known that China does not regard human rights in the same way that constitutional democracies do. President Clinton threatened to withhold most favored nation status from China unless there was a marked improvement in their treatment of dissidents. **Most favored nation status** is an international trade policy whereby we grant to a country the same favorable trade concessions and tariffs that our best trading partners receive.

Loss of trade with China would deal a serious blow to the American economy, especially on the West Coast. This potential setback came into conflict with the desire to protect human rights. When push came to shove, Clinton "separated" the two issues and extended China's favored nation status. But today this issue is a persisting obstacle in U.S.–Chinese diplomatic and economic relations.

NUCLEAR, BIOLOGICAL, AND CHEMICAL ARMS CONTROL   Probably the single greatest threat to the security of the United States and the rest of the world is the proliferation of weapons of mass destruction. At present, only a handful of nations have usable nuclear weapons. What happens if such weapons fall into the hands of nations like Libya, Iraq, and North Korea who have no democratic controls on their government and whose leaders may have dreams of world conquest?

Twenty-seven nations, including the United States and Russia, have agreed to curb the sale of materials that could be used in the manufacture of nuclear weapons. This agreement was a direct result of a close call in early 1990 when Iraq was detected trying to build nuclear weapons. Although the agreement established limits on the sale of materials or machinery that can be used for peaceful purposes or for building nuclear bombs, experts still caution that "good intentions on export controls are often undermined by ignorance and greed."[4]

In the mid 1990s, America created an international coalition that seeks to end the threat of nuclear proliferation in North Korea. Former Secretary of Defense Caspar Weinberger calls it an "appeasement agreement" that gives North Korea two large plutonium reactors, years of free oil, and much else in return for that country's promise to stop making nuclear weapons.[5]

One expert thinks the United States may some day have to resort to an occasional "preemptive intervention" in nations like North Korea, Iran, Iraq, Syria, Libya, or Algeria to prevent a rogue nation-state from acquiring menacing nuclear weapons.[6] This is hardly a strategy most Americans would like, and no government official has espoused it.

The United States has entered into a variety of agreements that seek to restrict the use of biological or chemical materials. Restrictions on the use of land mines also won support.

THE FORMER SOVIET UNION AND EASTERN EUROPE   Several of the countries that emerged from the former Soviet Union and its satellites are now torn by economic chaos and shortages. Americans want to be of assistance but are weary of giving direct aid that will raise U.S. taxes and enlarge the U.S. national debt. Yet foreign policy experts contend such aid is essential to help with the transitions to a market economy and to encourage the gradual development of healthy constitutional democracies in that region.

THE EUROPEAN ECONOMIC UNION AND THE FUTURE OF NATO   The European Economic Union has adopted measures that bind European nations together for the purpose of economic growth. An economically powerful Europe poses challenges for U.S. companies and trade. With the end of the cold war, Europe, Canada, and the United States must redefine the mission and goals of the North Atlantic Treaty Organization (NATO). Some argue that NATO is no longer needed. There has been a significant downsizing of the U.S. military presence in Europe, but our policy toward this new Europe needs to be clarified. NATO forces were deployed in 1996 in an effort to maintain the Bosnia peace accord.

DRUG TRAFFIC   U.S. relations with Mexico, Colombia, and other Latin American nations are affected by drug traffic issues. The drug epidemic in the United States is fed by drugs smuggled into this country from Western hemisphere nations. Should the U.S. military be involved? Are drugs a domestic problem that needs to be solved at home, or should American addictions be perceived as a combined domestic, economic, and foreign policy problem?

THE GLOBAL ENVIRONMENT   The United States is at the same time one of the world's leading environmental forces and one of its major polluters. A 1992

"Dad, what was the Soviet Union?"
The Wall Street Journal.

George Marshall (Truman)

John Foster Dulles (Eisenhower)

Dean Rusk (Kennedy and Johnson)

Henry Kissinger (Nixon and Ford)

U.N. conference in Rio de Janeiro on conserving and improving the world's natural resources pointed the way toward many new policies, but most nations, including the United States, have moved slowly on implementing policies to achieve these goals.

KEY PLAYERS IN FOREIGN POLICY

Although presidents share with Congress the responsibility for making overall foreign policy decisions, the operations of foreign policy are directly under the president. In practice, a president has the primary responsibility to shape foreign policy. Presidents can bargain, negotiate, persuade, apply economic pressures, threaten, or even use armed force.

The Constitution put control of foreign policy in the hands of those who run the national government: the president, the Senate, and, in some cases, the Congress as a whole. In England, the king controlled foreign policy; our framers tried to redress the balance a bit. Many of the powers given to Congress by the Constitution reflect the decision to limit the powers of the executive branch. The framers wanted to make what had traditionally been a prerogative of the executive into a responsibility shared with the legislature. Thus Congress has the power to declare war, to appropriate funds, and to make rules for the armed forces. But the president is commander in chief of the armed forces and is expected to negotiate treaties and receive and send ambassadors—that is, to recognize or refuse to recognize other governments. The Senate confirms ambassadors and gives consent to treaty ratification. The courts have the power to interpret treaties, but by and large they have ruled that relations with other nations are matters for the executive to negotiate. The primacy of the executive in foreign policy is a fact of political life of all nations, including constitutional democracies. To appreciate this phenomenon, let us look at the people within the executive branch who make up much of the foreign policy establishment.

The President's Foreign Policy Advisers

The president's principal foreign policy adviser is the secretary of state. The secretary of state administers the State Department, receives visits from foreign diplomats, attends international conferences, and usually heads our delegation in the General Assembly of the United Nations. The secretary also serves as the administration's chief coordinator of all governmental actions that affect our relations with foreign nations. In practice, a secretary of state delegates the day-to-day responsibilities for running the State Department and spends most of his time negotiating with the leaders of other countries.[7]

At one time, only the secretary of state was called upon for advice in formulating and implementing foreign policies. Today, because of the interdependence of foreign, economic, and domestic policies, a president calls on an increasing number of civilian and economic advisers. The conduct of foreign affairs is now the business of several major departments and agencies: State, Defense, Treasury, Agriculture, Commerce, Labor, Energy, the Central Intelligence Agency (CIA), and others. The need for immediate reaction and preparedness has transferred more responsibilities directly to the president—and to a great extent, to the senior White House aides who assist in coordinating information and advice. Yet no matter what the system for advice and coordination, there is always overlap, redundancy, and competition to influence the president.

Secretaries, agency chiefs, and their senior subordinates are chosen by the president and are expected to support and carry out his decisions. Yet at the same time, they retain a measure of independence; they naturally tend to reflect and defend the views of the departments and agencies they head. As a result, our presidents have found a need to appoint White House advisers whose loyalties lie solely with the chief executive.

The National Security Council

The key coordinating agency for the president is the National Security Council (NSC). Created by Congress in 1947, it is intended to help presidents integrate foreign, military, and economic policies that affect national security. The National Security Council serves directly under the president. By law, it consists of the president, vice-president, secretary of state, and secretary of defense. Recent presidents have sometimes included the director of the CIA, the White House chief of staff, the attorney general, and the national security adviser as ex officio members of the NSC.

The national security adviser, appointed by the president, has gradually emerged as one of the most influential foreign policy makers, sometimes rivaling in influence the secretary of state. Presidents come to rely on these White House aides both because of their proximity (down the hall in the west wing of the White House) and because they owe their primary loyalties to the president, not to any department or program. Each president has shaped the NSC structure and adapted its staff procedures to suit his personal preferences, but over the years the NSC, as both a committee and a staff, has taken on a major role in making and implementing foreign policy.[8] President Clinton, for example, sees and talks with Anthony Lake, his NSC adviser, on a daily and sometimes hourly basis, while Clinton and his secretary of state may chat only twice a week.

The State Department

The primary duty of the State Department has always been the security of the nation. Although our armed forces remain the ultimate line of defense, the State Department is our first line. It is dedicated to an around-the-clock, worldwide effort to see that troops and weapons are not used except in genuine emergencies. It is also the central agency in the day-to-day management of foreign affairs. The State Department has six priorities:

1. To promote peace and human rights
2. To protect American citizens and interests abroad
3. To promote American commercial interests and enterprises
4. To collect and interpret intelligence
5. To represent an American "presence" abroad
6. To negotiate with other nations and international organizations

As the diplomatic arm of a superpower, the State Department has responded to American global concerns with continual reorganization. Among the cabinet departments, State's annual budget of about $5 billion in 1997 is the lowest—less than 2 percent of the Department of Defense's approximately $260 billion budget as of 1997. Considering the State Department's role and prestige, its staff of less than 24,000 worldwide is small, especially compared with the more than 2.2 million civilian and military personnel in the Department of Defense. Like most other federal agencies, State has had to eliminate nearly 10 percent of its staff in the 1990s. If Republican Senator Jesse Helms had his way, they would have cut at least twice that amount.

Cyrus Vance (Carter)

George Shultz (Reagan)

James Baker (Bush)

Warren Christopher (Clinton)

The Foreign Service

The American Foreign Service is the eyes and ears of the United States in other countries. Although part of the State Department, the service represents the entire government and performs jobs for many other agencies. Its main duties are to carry out foreign policy as expressed in the directives of the secretary of state, gather political, economic and intelligence data for American policy makers, protect Americans and American interests in foreign countries, and cultivate friendly relations with host governments and foreign peoples.

The Foreign Service is composed of Foreign Service officers, Foreign Service reserve officers, and Foreign Service staff officers. At the core of the service are the Foreign Service officers, comparable to army officers in the military. They are a select, specially trained group expected to take assignments any place in the world on short notice. There are approximately 4,300 such officers; in recent years fewer than 250 junior officers win appointment each year.

The Foreign Service is one of the most prestigious yet most criticized career services of the national government. Criticism sometimes comes as much from within as from outside. Critics claim the organizational culture of the Foreign Service: (1) stifles creativity; (2) attracts officers who are, or at least become, more concerned about their status than their responsibilities; and (3) requires new recruits to wait 15 to 20 years before being considered for positions of responsibility. The problems are recognized in Washington, and the task of improving the service continues. Outside critics point to a social homogeneity among the Foreign Service, but that is probably overstated. More women and minorities have been recruited in recent years.

The Foreign Service's problems of overstaffing, empty jobs, and tedious apprenticeships are common in many bureaucracies. Despite all these alleged problems, the Foreign Service attracts bright and able professionals, and, in general, members of the Foreign Service serve their country with distinction.

Intelligence and the CIA

What is the nuclear capability of the North Korean military? How strong are the rebel forces in rural Philippines? What are the internal political struggles in Bosnia and Haiti? How stable is the political situation in Colombia, Peru, or Venezuela? Before our foreign policy makers can act on important issues, they have to know as much as possible about other countries: their possible reactions to a particular policy, their strengths and weaknesses, the character of their leaders, and if possible, their strategic plans and intentions. Thus those who gather and analyze intelligence data are among the important aides to policy makers. They often become policy makers themselves.

The Central Intelligence Agency, an outgrowth of the World War II Office of Strategic Services, was created in 1947 to coordinate the gathering and analysis of information that flows into various parts of the U.S. government from all over the world. In recent years, the CIA has had nearly 20,000 employees and has helped direct and integrate the intelligence products of nearly a dozen other intelligence agencies, among them the State Department's Bureau of Intelligence and Research, the Defense Intelligence Agency (which combines the intelligence operations of the Army, Navy, Air Force, and Marine Corps), the National Security Agency (which specializes in electronic reconnaissance and code breaking), the supersecret National Reconnaissance Office (which runs the U.S. satellite surveillance programs), the Federal Bureau of Investigation (FBI), and a small intelligence operation run by the Departments of Energy and Treasury. In the late 1990s, these agencies were spending an estimated $30 billion a year on intelligence work.[9]

Although most of the information the CIA gathers comes from open sources, the term "intelligence" conjures up visions of spies and undercover agents. Secret intelligence occasionally does supply crucial data. But it is not all glamour; much is routine. Intelligence work involves three basic operations: reporting, research, and transmission. Reporting is based on the close and rigorous observation of developments around the world; research is the attempt to detect meaningful patterns out of what was observed in the past and to understand what appears to be going on now; and transmission means getting the right information to the right people at the right time.

CIA analysts detected the military buildup by Iraq's Saddam Hussein in 1990, but their warnings about an invasion of Kuwait were too cautious and too late, according to later analyses. Indeed, President Bush, himself a former CIA director, is reported to have been misinformed that Iraq really was not adequately recovered from its war with Iran to mount another military invasion.

For 40 years the CIA used its best personnel to understand and help undermine our primary enemy—the Soviet Union. Now that the Soviet Union is gone, the CIA has had to redefine its role, address new challenges, and reverse its long-term growth pattern. Among its new challenges are gathering intelligence on terrorism, on drug trafficking, and on the growing number of nations that have ballistic missiles with chemical, biological, and nuclear warheads. A recent addition has been preventing economic espionage by other nations.

What about the need for covert operations—operations that deliberately try to destabilize governments or insurgent groups in other nations? The CIA has been credited with both successful and failed covert operations abroad. The ill-fated Bay of Pigs invasion of Cuba in 1961 was directed by the CIA. Later the CIA organized and trained anticommunist forces in Laos and supported the anti-Allende forces in Chile. Because of its past record and because it must act when our government cannot intervene officially, there is a tendency to credit (or blame) the CIA for many coups, purges, and revolts whether the agency was involved or not.

In the Reagan years the CIA played an important role in several Central American nations. For example, we supported the government in El Salvador but aided the anti-government rebels in Nicaragua. Some observers believed these and related activities represented an integral part of U.S. diplomacy and preparedness and helped us achieve our goals in that region. Others denounced these activities as jeopardizing the values of freedom and liberty the United States is dedicated to defending.

The CIA's political leverage, its information, its secrecy, its speed in communication, its ability to act, and its enormous budget make it a potent force. These same characteristics also make the CIA controversial. Congress has tried to see that this power is used only by publicly accountable decision makers. Committees exist in both the Senate and the House of Representatives whose primary purpose is to hold the CIA accountable to Congress, although earlier efforts by similar committees sometimes failed to do an adequate job.

Congress became especially outraged at the CIA's leadership in 1994 when it was discovered that a senior CIA agent, Aldrich Ames, had spied for the Soviets and the KGB for much of the 1980s. Ames confessed to what is considered the worst betrayal of U.S. intelligence in the history of the CIA. It will take years for the CIA to recover the credibility it lost from this case.[10]

The CIA's role in the post-cold war era has been widely debated in the 1990s. Some politicians call for its abolition, saying its essential functions could just as easily and less expensively be carried out by the State and Defense departments. After an extensive review of the CIA in the mid-1990s, a bipartisan commission recommended strengthening the hand of the director of central

The Peace Corps

The Peace Corps, established by the Peace Corps Act of 1961 in the Kennedy administration, has a mission to encourage world peace and friendship, help other countries in meeting their social and development needs, and promote greater understanding between Americans and other peoples. Peace Corps volunteers are expected to serve in another nation for two years and become part of the community they are serving. Volunteers work on a variety of projects, such as teaching math and science, doing community development work, and improving water and sanitation systems.

What qualifications does one need to apply? Generally a college degree, experience, or a combination of both. There is no age limit. In fact, about 10 percent of the 6500 current volunteers are over 50 years old. The Peace Corps picks up the expenses and typically trains each volunteer in language and job skills for about three months prior to service abroad.

The Peace Corps in the 1990s operates in about 95 nations and has had funding of about $230 million a year. Nearly 150,000 Americans have been Peace Corps volunteers. Eight Peace Corps alumni serve in Congress, evenly divided between Republicans and Democrats. The Peace Corps is wholly separate from the State and Defense departments or the intelligence agencies. The Peace Corps motto to would-be volunteers says, "The Peace Corps—the toughest job you'll ever love."

For more information, write Peace Corps, Volunteer Service Office, 1990 K Street, NW, Washington, D.C. 20526, or call 1-800-424-8580. For a useful history of the origins and early years of the Peace Corps, see Gerald T. Rice, *The Bold Experiment: JFK's Peace Corps* (University of Notre Dame Press, 1985).

intelligence, reducing the workforce of intelligence agencies, and "refocusing its efforts or global crime such as terrorism, narcotics, trafficking, proliferation of weapons of mass destruction and international organized crime syndicates."[11] The commission's recommendation that the CIA continue yet with a new focus means that the CIA will survive into the Twenty-first century.

THE POLITICS OF MAKING FOREIGN AND DEFENSE POLICY

Foreign policy flows through the same institutional and constitutional structures as domestic policy. Public opinion, interest groups, members of Congress, elections, separation of powers, and federalism all affect the politics of making foreign policy. Yet these structures operate somewhat differently from the way they do in domestic affairs. Of course, international organizations and foreign governments and their embassies also play an important role.

Public Opinion

Different foreign and defense issues evoke different degrees of public interest and involvement. In crisis situations—such as the planning of Operation Desert Storm in Kuwait in 1991—decisions are made by a small group of persons. Yet even in these situations, presidents and their advisers know their decisions will ultimately require support from the public and from Congress.

In noncrisis situations, the public appears to consist of three subcategories. The largest, constituting perhaps as much as 75 percent of the adult population, is the *mass public*. This group knows little about the details of foreign affairs, despite the subject's importance. The mass public concerns itself with foreign affairs mainly in conflict situations, especially those involving the actual or possible use of American troops abroad. The second group is the *attentive public*, constituting perhaps 15 to 20 percent of the population. It maintains an active interest in foreign policy. The *opinion makers* are the third and smallest public; as editors, teachers, writers, political and business leaders, they transmit information and judgments on foreign affairs and mobilize the support of the other two publics.

Why are so many people in this country indifferent or uninformed? First, foreign affairs issues are usually more remote than domestic issues. People have more firsthand information about unemployment, inflation, crime, and hospital costs than about Ukrainian economic reform or Brazilian political problems. The worker in the factory and the boss in the front office know what labor-management relations are about, and they have strong opinions on the subject. They may also have strong opinions about gun control, capital punishment, and abortion. But most Americans have a poor sense of world geography and an even weaker grasp of geopolitics. Foreign policy seems to most people to be distant. Sometimes it seems that only when American soldiers or civilians overseas are killed does the mass public become directly concerned with foreign affairs.

Most Americans do recognize that their lives, jobs, and security are inevitably part of international developments. "Contrary to a widely held assumption, their concern does not stop at the water's edge," writes Steven Kull.[12] And a survey of American views on foreign and defense policy concludes that despite the absence of strong White House leadership on foreign affairs, most Americans accept that the United States has serious contributions to make in world affairs:

> Relief from the long competition with the Soviet Union and the lack of a clear external threat have made Americans more reluctant to use force abroad and become involved in

The American public concerns itself with foreign affairs mainly when it involves the use of our troops abroad.

the affairs of other countries. But they want to maintain current levels of defense in an uncertain world and are committed to diplomatic engagement through alliances and multilateral organizations.[13]

The State and Defense Departments make an effort to keep people informed about those areas of policy it thinks should be discussed publicly and to keep itself informed about public opinion. Yet despite occasional talk about open and democratic policy-making processes, most of the foreign policy negotiations in which our government has a major role are conducted in secret. Sometimes even Congress is kept at a distance.

Special Interests

The mass media can be powerful in shaping public opinion, a fact reflected in frequent disputes between the media and government. Certain reporters and newspapers have helped rally public opinion on behalf of human rights, for example, and press coverage of government treatment of dissidents in China and South Africa put pressure on the White House and Congress to reconsider our policies toward those countries.

It is difficult to generalize about the impact of interest groups on American foreign policies. At moments of international crisis, such as after Iraq invaded Kuwait, a president is usually able to mobilize so much public support that interest groups find it difficult to exert much influence. As a general rule, special interest groups other than major economic interests rarely have a decisive role in the formulation of foreign policy. Of course, what is more difficult to determine is the impact on policy caused by policy makers' anticipation of group reactions.

Ethnic interest groups can and do play an important role in foreign policy decisions in our country. As a nation of immigrants and the children and grandchildren of immigrants, our citizens often retain a special bond with their country of origin. Thus, Irish Americans, Jewish Americans, African Americans, Polish Americans, and Greek Americans are part of an attentive public that takes a keen interest in decisions affecting Ireland, Israel, South Africa, Poland, and Greece, for example. These interest groups sometimes exert powerful pressures on our policy makers to support the country to which they are emotionally linked. Congress, even more than the executive branch, is attuned to these pressures.

Foreign Countries and Foreign Companies

Most countries, large and small, have embassies lobbying for their interests in Washington, D.C. In addition, some countries like Japan have built up a powerful network of lawyers, lobbyists, and Washington-based publicists who are retained by Japanese companies and trade associations, as well as by the Japanese government, to defend their extensive economic interests in the United States.[14] Lobbyists representing newly industrialized countries like South Korea, Taiwan, Singapore, Brazil, and Mexico have also expanded their Washington lobbying efforts to fight U.S. protectionism and import quotas on textiles, shoes, and some of their other exports.

Political Parties

Political parties do not usually play a major role in shaping foreign and defense policy for two reasons: (1) many Americans still prefer to keep partisan politics out of foreign policy; (2) parties usually take less clear and candid stands on foreign policy than they do on domestic policy. Party platforms often obscure the issues instead of highlighting them, and many members of Congress fail to follow a general party line.

Lessons from the Iran-Contra Affair

In the mid 1980s the Reagan administration allowed the profits from the sale of weapons to Iran to be diverted to assist Contra rebels in Nicaragua. This was a deliberate violation of the law as well as a secret means to achieve the president's initiatives. Congress subsequently held lengthy televised hearings that condemned these deceptions. Some of the conclusions were:

"The U.S. Constitution specifies the process by which laws and policy are to be made and executed. Constitutional process is the essence of our democracy, and our democratic form of government is the basis of our strength. Time and again we have learned that a flawed process leads to bad results, and that a lawless process leads to worse."

"The theory of the Constitution is that policies formed through consultation and the democratic process are better, and wiser, than those formed without it.... Those who would take shortcuts in the constitutional process—mislead the Congress or withhold information—show their contempt for what the framers created. Shortcuts that bypass the checks and balances of the system, and excessive secrecy by those who serve the President, do not strengthen the President. They weaken the President and the constitutional system of government."

"Government officials must observe the law, even when they disagree with it."

"The Administration must not lie to Congress about what it is doing. Congress is the partner, not the adversary of the executive branch, in the formulation of policy."

"Excessive secrecy in the making of important policy decisions is profoundly antidemocratic and rarely promotes sound policy decisions."

SOURCE: Lee H. Hamilton and Daniel K. Inouye et al., *Iran-Contra Affair*, Report of the Congressional Committees Investigating the Iran-Contra Affair, H. Rpt 100–433 (Government Printing Office, 1987).

Should parties be concerned with foreign policy? At the end of World War II, sentiment grew stronger for a bipartisan approach to foreign policy. An ambiguous term, **bipartisanship** seems to mean: (1) collaboration between the executive and the congressional foreign policy leaders of both parties; (2) support of presidential foreign policies by both parties in Congress; and (3) downplaying foreign policy issues in national elections and especially in presidential debates. In general, bipartisanship is an attempt to remove the issues of foreign policy from partisan politics.

The Role of Congress

Despite the importance of foreign and defense policy, and even though Congress can block the president's policy and undermine the chief executive's decisions, Congress as an institution seldom directly makes foreign policy. Individual members of Congress, however, are sometimes included within the circle of those who make foreign and defense policy decisions. The power of Congress is mainly consultative, although the legislature has taken the initiative in some trade and foreign economic and military assistance questions. In addition, Congress has attempted to curb presidential war-making powers.[15] Congress is also a link between the policy makers and the public. Congress wants a voice—especially "meaningful consultation" with the president in matters of foreign relations. Congress, for example, played an important role in cutting off funds for bombing Cambodia in 1973 and in shaping U.S. foreign policy toward Haiti and Bosnia. But Congress is often divided on issues of foreign and defense policy.

For the most part, presidents and their advisers initiate most of our foreign policies, yet members of Congress, with predictable regularity, stimulate, prod, amend, and modify much of what the White House proposes.

The Potential for a Democratic Foreign Policy

A great paradox exists in conducting the foreign relations of a modern democracy. In the last century, Alexis de Tocqueville wrote that foreign relations "demand scarcely any of the qualities which are peculiar to a democracy; they require, on the contrary, the perfect use of all those in which it is deficient."[16] One leading scholar observed more directly that policy makers in our democracy "either . . . must sacrifice what they consider good policy upon the altar of public opinion, or they must by devious means gain support for policies whose true nature is concealed from the public."[17]

A democratic foreign policy is one in which policy makers are known and held accountable to the people. That is a tough test for any policy, but it is especially tough for foreign policy because of the need to act with speed, and sometimes with secrecy, the generally low level of information among the general public, the anonymity of most foreign policy leaders, and, of course, the complexity of issues and options. Still, the American public wants to be consulted and informed, and it wants its leaders accountable.

In Vietnam, American policy makers miscalculated the character of the war as well as the commitment of the Vietnamese who opposed the Saigon government. And because these policy makers knew to some extent that they had made mistakes and believed the American people and Congress might not support them in what they thought necessary, they sometimes concealed these difficulties.[18]

A constitutional democracy may not be able to keep leaders from making mistakes, especially when leaders work in secrecy and do not get advance approval for national security decisions. But in a policy area in which big mistakes can be made, the mistakes after a while become public. It is then that the safeguarding agencies of democracy—the opposition party, the press, and dissident opinion—go to work.

"Let me connect you with Edith, our specialist in ethnic conflict in the former Yugoslavia. My expertise happens to be in North Korean intransigence."

Drawing by Handelsman. © 1994 The New Yorker Magazine, Inc.

Changes are demanded, and policies are often changed. In the case of Vietnam, public resistance to the war eventually forced the United States to get out. The way in which these agencies of democracy worked in the United States doubtless encouraged the United States to exit from both the Vietnam and Somalia conflicts faster than the Soviets got out of their ill-fated engagement in Afghanistan.

FOREIGN AND DEFENSE POLICY STRATEGIES

How are foreign and defense policies actually implemented? As a major power, the United States can choose a variety of options, but it usually employs the following six, or some combination of them.

Conventional Diplomacy

Much of U.S. foreign policy is conducted by the foreign service and ambassadors in face-to-face discussions in Washington and other capitals, at the United Nations, in Geneva (at arms talks), and elsewhere around the world in regional or international organizations and world conferences. International summit meetings, with their high-profile pomp and drama, are another form of conventional diplomacy. Even though traditional diplomacy appears more subdued and somewhat less vital in this era of personal leader-to-leader communication by telephone, fax, and teleconferencing, it is still an important, if slow, process by which nations can gain information, talk about mutual interests, and try to resolve bilateral and multilateral disputes.

Much of the conventional diplomacy carried out by the State Department and its $5 billion budget may not produce important breakthroughs, yet it is difficult to measure the value of diplomatic representation. No price tag can be placed on close personal relations with foreign officials or on information gathered and arguments made to promote American interests around the world. Surely the closing of one embassy or the withdrawal from international organizations is unlikely to cause major setbacks for the Republic, yet a less active diplomacy could mean a less effective foreign policy.

Foreign Aid

The United States regularly grants economic and military assistance to foreign countries, in part for humanitarian reasons and in part to further good relations with other nations. The United States offers aid to more than 100 countries directly and to a number of other nations through our contributions to various United Nations development funds. Since 1945 we have provided about $250 billion in economic assistance to foreign countries—a figure that looks and sounds impressive. In 1997, U.S. foreign aid amounted to another $19 billion. Yet the United States devotes less of its gross national product to foreign aid and development than any other industrialized democracy. Most foreign aid goes to a few countries the United States deems to be of strategic importance—Israel, Egypt, Turkey, Pakistan, El Salvador, the Philippines, and now Russia. And much of what constitutes foreign aid is actually spent in the United States, where it pays for the purchase of American services and products being sent to those countries. It thus amounts to a hefty subsidy for American companies and their employees.

Ever since the United States began giving serious amounts of foreign aid after World War II, many Americans and members of Congress have opposed it. Few powerful interest groups or constituencies back foreign aid initiatives. State department officials are probably the biggest advocates of foreign aid. Presidents also recognize the vital role foreign aid plays in advancing U.S. interests, so presidents

Thinking it Through

Most American citizens say they would like to have their voice heard more often on major issues. But most political scientists, pollsters, and elected national officials oppose national polls that would in any way bind the national government. Franklin Roosevelt strongly opposed the idea of taking votes on whether we go to war, saying it would be impractical in its application and incompatible with our representative form of government. Political and public opinion analysts also point out that we would never have had a Marshall Plan in the 1940s if we had followed public opinion.

On most issues, the public does not have an opinion in any firm, definitive sense, and to try to discover one may be misguided. Most members of Congress say representatives owe their constituents their judgment, not just slavish deference to temporary passions of the moment. Indeed, critics go so far as to say one of the reasons we do not have a serious foreign policy is because we already pay too much attention to public opinion.

Still, the public would like to be heard, even if its voice is generally not clear on most issues and more likely to be reactive to headlines than the product of careful reflection.

SOURCE: Adapted from Adam Clymer, "Proposing to Eliminate a Polling Gap in Congress," *The New York Times,* May 15, 1994, p. 18.

keep asking Congress for funds for foreign aid. Successive presidents have all wanted to maintain the leverage with key countries that economic and military assistance aid provides. One of the major debates today is how much economic aid the United States should provide to Russia and the republics that once constituted the Soviet Union. Despite the assertion by presidents and their secretaries of state that foreign aid—scarcely more than one percent of the federal budget—is an investment to secure our vital national interests and a peaceful future, Congress invariably trims these requests by 15 to 20 percent, saying there is too much waste.

Economic Sanctions

The United States has frequently practiced the art of economic pressure in response to a nation's unwillingness to abide by what we perceive to be international law or proper relations. The U.S. and U.N. embargo against Haiti in 1994 is a classic example of economic sanctions. Economic sanctions imposed on South Africa helped in encouraging democracy in that nation. But sanctions imposed on Iraq and Cuba did not have much effect on dislodging Saddam Hussein or Fidel Castro.

The popularity of economic sanctions has waxed and waned over the years, yet it is still a potentially important weapon in the arsenal of diplomatic and foreign policy strategies. "Economic sanctions often emerge as the centerpiece when a balance is needed between actions that seem too soft or too strident. In these situations, sanctions are seldom regarded as the 'ideal' weapon; rather they are seen as the 'least bad' alternative."[19] One study of economic sanctions since World War I found that economic sanctions helped achieve foreign policy goals only about one-third of the time.[20] Such sanctions are obviously not popular among the farmers or corporations that have to sacrifice part of their overseas markets to comply with government sanctions or controls. Nevertheless, the United States has employed this strategy more than 70 times since World War I.

Political Coercion

When relations between nations become especially strained, diplomatic relations are sometimes broken as a means of political coercion. When the United States breaks diplomatic ties, it greatly restricts tourist and business travel to a country

United States troops sent to Haiti to restore order quickly overcame pockets of resistance and were warmly received by most of the Haitian people.

and, in effect, curbs political as well as certain economic relations with a nation. The consequences are thus more than merely symbolic.

Breaking off diplomatic relations, however, is a next-to-last resort (force is the last resort), for such action undermines the ability to reason with a nation's leaders or to use other diplomatic strategies to resolve conflicts. It also undermines our ability to get valuable information about what is going on in a nation and to have a presence in that nation.

Covert Operations

President Dwight Eisenhower used the Central Intelligence Agency to engage in covert or quasi-military ventures, both to avoid deploying the military and to advance U.S. foreign policy interests. U.S. support for the Shah of Iran and the overthrow of the government in Guatemala in the 1950s are examples. During the cold war years, several presidents authorized covert operations in Vietnam and neighboring nations. Covert activities are planned and executed to conceal the identity of the sponsor. But covert activities in Cuba, Chile, and elsewhere have backfired, and support for this strategy has cooled in the post–cold war era.[21] Clinton's CIA director, John M. Deutch, insists, however, that "espionage is the core of the CIA . . . Despite the setbacks, we must continue to take risks."[22]

Military Intervention

War, it is said, is not merely an extension of diplomacy; it is also a total breakdown of diplomacy. The United States has intervened militarily in other nations on the average of almost once a year since 1789, although usually in relatively minor or short-term episodes, such as Ronald Reagan's use of troops in Grenada, George Bush's invasion of Panama in 1989 and Clinton's peaceful invasion of Haiti in 1994. Of course, these may not be considered minor events by the target nations.

Intervention with force is plainly the ultimate strategy—the last resort—in trying to resolve a conflict. Military action by the United States is often successful when it involves small and even medium-sized countries (Grenada, Panama, and Kuwait). But military intervention "often proves ineffective in the context of national civil wars (the United States in Vietnam; Israel in Lebanon)."[23] This is why Americans have been reluctant about U.S. intervention in Haiti and Bosnia.

THE UNITED NATIONS

The United States belongs to the 185-nation United Nations and is a member of at least 200 other international organizations. The United Nations was set up in 1945 by the victors of World War II. Its main goal was to promote peace. But when the two superpowers—the United States and the former Soviet Union—became major military rivals, the United Nations was less able to achieve its central objectives.

For most of its first 45 years, the United Nations earned a reputation for ineffectiveness. Critics contend it either ducked or was politically unable to tackle crucial global issues. During much of that time, the U.N. General Assembly, dominated by a combination of Third World and communist nations, was hostile to many U.S. interests. The General Assembly often became a talk shop, passing vague resolutions.

But when the cold war ended, the five permanent members of the U.N. Security Council—the United States, China, Russia (which replaced the Soviet Union), Britain, and France—usually worked in harmony. Moreover, the U.N.'s assumption

Thinking it Through

A 1996 CNN-Time survey found that 25 percent of an American adult sample favored getting out of the United Nations; 69 percent opposed our leaving, and the rest were undecided. A 1995 poll sponsored by the Americans Talk Issues Foundation found 66 percent of their respondents believed American troops should take part in UN military operations only if they are under U.S. command.

There have always been Americans who wanted to "go it alone." And there are quite a number, perhaps a majority in the U.S. Congress, who want to emasculate UN peacekeeping missions and to end UN-sponsored conferences on major social and scientific issues. Republican presidential candidate Pat Buchanan struck a responsive chord with his supporters through his criticism of the UN.

Defenders of the UN claim that the United States has a complete veto over anything the UN does, so it is complete nonsense to say anyone in this country puts the UN's interests ahead of our own. Defenders also point out that the UN is neither more wise nor more farsighted than the governments that compose it, and thus is subject to the same kind of waste, inefficiency, and abuse. "Without the United Nations," writes Ted Sorensen, "the instrument of peace preferred by our allies despite its many limitations—the United States would be required to put out threatening brushfires on its own or not at all." Sorensen adds, "Must we learn all over again that we save neither American money nor American lives by rendering the world's only global fire department too weak to contain those conflagrations that ultimately engulf our interests?"*

*Theodore Sorensen, "Is America the Dutiful in Trouble? We Abandon Our Role As World Leader at Our Own Peril," *The Washington Post National Weekly Edition*, July 10–16, 1995, Commentary page.

TABLE 15-2

How Is the United Nations Doing?

Question: In general, do you feel that the United Nations is doing a good job or a poor job in trying to resolve the problems it has had to face?

	1975	1985	1993	1995
Good job	33%	38%	52%	35%
Poor job	51	44	44	56
Don't know or no answer	16	18	4	9

SOURCE: Gallup Organization, 1996.

of responsibilities in the Persian Gulf War and its extensive peacekeeping missions in places such as Cyprus and Lebanon won it respect in recent years (see Table 15-2). U.N. efforts in Cambodia, Somalia, and in Bosnia were less successful.

Blue-helmeted U.N. peacekeeping forces are now monitoring cease-fires, elections, and human rights in a dozen places, yet these efforts are costly. The United Nations constantly finds itself pleading with leading nations, such as the United States, to help underwrite the costs of these peace initiatives. Many of the U.N.'s peacekeeping missions are popular, yet as these efforts increase in number and in cost, the negotiations to raise funds for this new international peace army get harder.

Some conservatives have long been skeptical of U.S. involvement in the United Nations, fearing that the United States risks being trapped or outvoted. Critics across the ideological spectrum question whether it makes sense to give every U.N. member an equal vote in the General Assembly, regardless of its size, population, and contribution to the U.N. budget. Critics worry also about creating a standing U.N. army with a large contingent of U.S. troops under foreign command. Some U.S. officials call this current system "taxation without representation." Critics also continue to question the efficiency of the U.N.'s bureaucracy.

Republican Bob Dole says Congress needs to have a greater say in how the United Nations uses U.S. taxpayers' dollars and puts U.S. soldiers' lives at risk. Dole says that the examples of Somalia and Bosnia show it is not in the best interests of the United States to let the United Nations define U.S. foreign policy. "When the U.N. Security Council votes," writes Dole, "American taxpayers should grab their wallets. Once the council approves a peacekeeping operation, the United States is obligated to pay nearly one-third of the cost."[24] Several members of Congress have introduced legislation that would bar U.S. forces from any standing U.N. army and prohibit U.S. troops from serving under foreign command in U.N. operations.

Many critics, both on the left and right, suggest that the United Nations be allowed to wither away into irrelevance.[25] The UN has certainly disappointed many of the grander hopes of its ardent founders. The United States, which is assessed 25 percent of the UN's annual budget, is almost always delinquent in its payment. Both the U.S. Congress and recent presidents have urged the UN to trim its peacekeeping operations and end its bureaucratic inefficiencies. "The UN," said President Clinton, "must be able to show that the money it receives supports saving and enriching people's lives, not unneeded overhead."[26] Clinton worked, with mixed success, with Congress to get the United States to pay its regular UN dues assessment. Meanwhile, the UN has significantly reduced its budgets and cut staff. Secretary-general Boutrous Boutrous Ghali claimed it was in deep financial trouble.[27]

Still, the United Nations is an important international instrument for the promotion of peace and the prevention of war. If the United Nations did not exist, something else much like it would have to be invented to settle quarrels and lessen violence among sovereign nations.

U.S. SECURITY AND DEFENSE OBJECTIVES

The overriding mission of the U.S. defense program is to provide for the physical protection of the country and to protect American interests at home and abroad. We want to deter a nuclear attack against the United States, and we seek to restrain the proliferation of armaments, especially weapons of mass destruction. We are committed to defend our allies and friends from armed aggression. We are also eager to forestall regional conflicts that might threaten the vital interests of the United States or its allies. Further, the United States seeks multilateral alliances or mechanisms such as the United Nations or NATO to provide for the collective security and rule of law among all nations.

The United States has a long history of involvement in world affairs, often by means of military interventions. We have formally declared war by an act of Congress on only five occasions. Although the Persian Gulf War was not declared formally, Congress, in effect, declared war when it authorized the use of troops to repel Iraq. But we have intervened with military forces on about 190 occasions, and military intervention is likely to continue. In this new post–cold war era, "We are the ones who can deter," says General Colin Powell, former chair of the Joint Chiefs of Staff. "We have the overwhelming power, and we have demonstrated the willingness to use it."[28]

Some Americans are concerned the United States will use its military clout unwisely or irresponsibly. Some believe we should resist the temptation to send our military into regional conflicts around the world when other means are available to achieve our objectives.[29] And there is probably widespread agreement that we should not intervene in conflicts unless the action is backed by broad public consensus and a well-heeled international alliance of nations, similar to the U.N. coalition in the Persian Gulf War. Still, virtually all Americans want to maintain our ability to advance the United States' interests around the globe. They say it would be a grave mistake to forsake our leadership position and abandon our friends and allies at this time of global change.

U.S. Formal Military Alliances

- The North Atlantic Treaty Organization (NATO)
- The Australian–New Zealand–United States (ANZUS) Alliance (although U.S. obligations to New Zealand are suspended)
- The Treaty of Mutual Cooperation and Security between the United States and Japan
- The Mutual Defense Treaty between the United States and the Republic of Korea
- The Mutual Defense Treaty between the United States and the Republic of the Philippines
- The Southeast Asia Collective Defense Treaty (which remains in effect on a bilateral basis with Thailand)
- The InterAmerican Treaty of Reciprocal Assistance between the United States and most Latin and Central American countries (Rio Treaty)

THE DEFENSE DEPARTMENT STRUCTURE

Civilian Control over the Military

One of the bedrock principles of our constitutional democracy is that the president of the United States, the people's elected representative, is the commander in chief. Those in the military have freedom of speech, yet to ensure civilian supremacy, commissioned officers who use "contemptuous words" against a president are subject to punishment. When a two-star general made rude and critical remarks about President Bill Clinton in a speech, he was fined $7,000 and retired from the service. And when a popular World War II hero, General Douglas MacArthur, challenged President Harry Truman's decisions, MacArthur was forced to resign. Constitutional democracy is a remarkable achievement because it is the consent of the governed, not the force of arms, that determines who wields the power of our government.

Defense Organization

The president, Congress, the National Security Council, and the State Department make overall defense policy and attempt to integrate U.S. national security programs. But the day-to-day work of organizing for defense is the job of the Defense Department. Its headquarters, the Pentagon, houses within its miles of corridors 25,000 top military and civilian personnel. The offices of several hundred generals and admirals are there, as is the office of the secretary of defense, which provides civilian control of the armed services.

A major issue in recent decades has been how to organize the Department of Defense to ensure that it can provide both strategic vision and practical coordination among the military services. Prior to 1947 there were two separate military departments, War and Navy. The difficulty of coordinating them during World War II led to demands for unification. In 1947 the Air Force, already an autonomous unit within the War Department, was made an independent unit, and all three military departments—Army, Navy, and Air Force—were placed under the general

General John M. Shalikashvili heads the Joint Chiefs of Staff.

supervision of the secretary of defense. The Unification Act of 1947 was a bundle of compromises between the Army, which favored a tightly integrated department, and the Navy, which wanted a loosely federated structure. The act at least brought the military services under a common organizational chart.

The Joint Chiefs of Staff (JCS) serves as the principal military adviser to the president, the National Security Council, and the secretary of defense. It includes the military heads of the three armed services, the commandant of the Marine Corps, a chair, and a vice chair. All the service chiefs are appointed by the president with the consent of the Senate for four-year, nonrenewable terms. The chair of the JCS, a top-ranking military officer from one of the three services or the Marine Corps, is appointed by the president with the consent of the Senate for a two-year term that may be renewed once. The current chair of the Joint Chiefs is Army General John Shalikashvili. Air Force General Joseph Ralston serves as vice chair. Note that their short two-year term is part of the process of ensuring civilian control over the military.

Before 1986 the members of the Joint Chiefs of Staff were, collectively, all powerful. They advised the president and the secretary of defense. Because they functioned as a committee and could not act until unanimous agreement was reached, they often produced overly broad decisions. Critics, therefore, viewed much of the work of the Joint Chiefs as wasteful and even dangerous.

The Department of Defense Reorganization Act of 1986 changed that. This legislation shifted considerable power to the chair. Reporting through the secretary of defense, the chair advises the president on military matters, exercises authority over the forces in the field, and is responsible for overall military planning. In theory, the chair of the Joint Chiefs can even make a military decision that the chiefs of the other services oppose. On paper at least, these other chiefs now serve the chair merely as advisers, and even the chair's deputy, the vice chair, outranks the other service chiefs. It gave the chair a mandate to encourage "jointness in military education and in other spheres to integrate the services for maximum effectiveness." Disputes still continue, but the chair is now much stronger than was previously the case. All of this makes the chair of the Joint Chiefs in the 1990s the most powerful peacetime military officer in U.S. history. The Reorganization Act also strengthened the powers of the theater commanders who actually command forces in various parts of the world.

It is critical to appreciate, however, that the chair of the Joint Chiefs is not the head of the military. The chair and the JCS are the principal advisers to the secretary of defense and the president. The president can and has on occasion disregarded their advice; a president must weigh military action or inaction against the larger foreign and security interests of the nation.

The Confederational Nature of the Defense Bureaucracy

It is common to hear criticisms of the "Pentagon machine" or the "national military establishment." The defense bureaucracy is, however, best understood—as is any bureaucracy—as something less than a monolith. In practice, the Defense

The Pentagon—headquarters for the Department of Defense and the Joint Chiefs of Staff. It is the world's largest building and has 20 miles of corridors. It houses nearly 25,000 workers, who tell time by 4,200 clocks, drink water from 685 fountains, consume 30,000 cups of coffee daily, and place 200,000 phone calls a day on 87,000 phones connected by 100,000 miles of cable.

Department is comprised of four major components: (1) the Office of the Secretary of Defense and the civilians in the Department of Defense; (2) the organization of the Joint Chiefs of Staff; (3) the individual armed services (Army, Navy, Air Force, Marines); and (4) the intelligence community (Defense Intelligence Agency and National Security Agency).

Reflecting the fragmented nature of the larger American political system, defense policy is thrashed out in a day-to-day process of give-and-take among these constituent units in the Defense Department along with officials in the State Department, Central Intelligence Agency, and the National Security Council at the White House. Insiders often stress that this policy-making structure is best thought of as a *confederation*, or bargaining arena, as opposed to a tight chain-of-command hierarchy. In fact, in recent years, strong sentiment has emerged for more centralized control and direction of the nation's defense bureaucracy.

Disputes among military services involve more than professional jealousies. The technological revolution in warfare has rendered obsolete many concepts about military missions, thereby threatening certain roles of some of the services. In the past it made sense to divide command among land, sea, and air forces. Defense research and development are constantly altering these formerly established roles and missions. Yet the individual services are reluctant to give up their traditional function or to serve each other's crucial needs. The Navy, for example, is interested in waging sea warfare, not in running a freight service for the Army. Each branch supports weapons that bring it prestige. This often leads to such interservice rivalries as the Army and Air Force quarrel over who should provide air support for ground troops, and the Air Force and Navy dispute over land versus sea-based missiles.

Whether strategic policies are worked out within the Defense Department, the White House, or Congress, the decisions result from a political process in which some measure of consensus is essential. The Joint Chiefs engage in the same type of vote trading used in Congress. On budget issues the chiefs often endorse all the programs desired by each service. When forced to choose on an issue of policy, the chiefs have traditionally compromised among the different service positions rather than attempt to develop a position based on a unified military point of view.

Women in the Military and in Combat

Women constitute 11 percent of the total enlistment in the armed forces; 6 percent of our forces in the Persian Gulf War were female; about 25 percent of R.O.T.C. cadets are women. The women in Operation Desert Storm routinely piloted troop transport and supply aircraft, helped to operate Patriot antimissile systems, and worked as tank mechanics and military police guarding Iraqi prisoners of war.

Women now attend the military academies and war colleges once reserved exclusively for males. And as the military has become more technically sophisticated, the role of women has increased. As one member of Congress put it: "It does not take much muscle to launch an ICBM." And, if brains rather than brawn are needed, women in the military usually have more formal education and higher intelligence scores than their male counterparts.

Women in the armed forces have faced many problems. There have been problems of sexual harassment, and women officers have complained of men refusing to take orders from them and giving them inappropriate assignments. Yet, by and large, women have been accepted and are playing an increasingly significant role in virtually all aspects of the armed forces.

Congress has lifted legal restrictions on air force and navy women becoming combat pilots. And the Pentagon, after prodding by the Clinton administration, has now opened thousands of combat-related positions in the military services

The National Guard: How It Works

At one time the National Guard was called the state militia. Today the National Guard is a volunteer armed forces unit within each state. As of the mid-1990s, about 500,000 serve in these units around the country, either in the Army or Air Force National Guard. The governor of each state is the commander in chief of the state National Guard and may call it out in times of emergency, such as floods, inner-city riots, and similar civil disorders.

They are called "National" because these guard units are funded and organized by Congress and may be called to serve in U.S. wars, as had been the case in World Wars I and II. The president, as national commander in chief, presides over guard units that are mobilized for national service. Guard units were cut back in size and funding as part of the general demobilization taking place in the 1990s.

THE DRAFT OR AN ALL-VOLUNTEER FORCE?

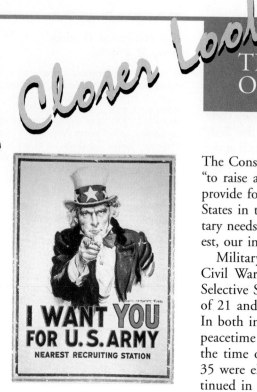

The Constitution authorizes Congress to do what is "necessary and proper" "to raise and support Armies," "to provide and maintain a Navy," and "to provide for calling the Militia." The problem is that the role of the United States in the world has changed dramatically since 1789, as have our military needs. Although our boundaries once defined our major national interest, our interests now reach around the globe.

Military conscription (the *draft*) was first instituted in 1862 during the Civil War. It was used during World War I, when Congress passed the Selective Service Act. This act called for a draft of males between the ages of 21 and 30, with exemptions for certain public officials and for clergy. In both instances, conscription ended when the conflicts ended. The first peacetime draft began in 1940, with the Selective Service Training Act. By the time of Pearl Harbor in late 1941, men between the ages of 18 and 35 were eligible for the draft. When World War II ended, the draft continued in various forms for almost three decades. Soon after the Vietnam War, the all-volunteer force (AVF) was established by Congress. This force was charged with providing for our peacetime military personnel needs; in time of war, a draft could be reinstituted.

Full-time, active military personnel in all services is now about 1.7 million. Minorities are overrepresented in the armed services, notably in the army, where African Americans constitute about 30 percent of the enlisted ranks. Women are underrepresented, although the proportion of women to men in the armed forces has grown. About 80 percent of all new enlisted troops have graduated from high school, a higher level than the eligible pool.

Since its beginning, the all-volunteer force has been much debated. Some experts contend the AVF has worked, that the quality and quantity of recruits are better than under the draft, and that the social costs are much lower. Other experts say quality has dropped and that the AVF is inadequate to defend our vital interests abroad. Most analysts say the all-volunteer force performed in a highly professional manner in the Persian Gulf War. There remain questions, as there always will, as to whether such a force would be adequately prepared to fight a longer war against stronger enemies.

for women. The military is redesigning its assignments to ensure equal opportunity exists within its ranks.

A majority of Americans think women should be assigned to ground combat units, but others are still concerned about women in combat situations. According to reports from the Persian Gulf front, few women who served in combat support units recommended the experience. Similarly, many women in the military have said that while they would like to have the right to serve in combat positions, most of them would not opt for these roles.

The difficulty in deciding whether women should participate in combat often comes in defining what is combat. Women working in support units in the Panama conflict of 1989 engaged in fighting. "I find it very difficult to separate this from other jobs where women are at risk, on police and fire departments, as truck drivers," says retired Air Force General Wilma Vaught.[30]

Women now make up 11 percent of the total enlistment in the armed forces. During the Persian Gulf War, 6 percent of our forces were women.

The Gay Ban Controversy

Another persisting controversy in the 1990s is whether the military has the right to expel homosexuals from the military services. Even as recently as 1993, the U.S. military expelled about 1,000 men and women every year because of sexual preference. The Pentagon defended the ban on homosexuals by saying that homosexuals in a military setting create difficulty because there is no privacy, no choice of association or living quarters, and no provision for those who prefer gay and lesbian lifestyles.

Many leaders in and out of Congress criticized the ban, calling it the final bastion of discrimination in the military and saying it reminded them of the army's former official opposition to African Americans in uniform. Bill Clinton called for a complete end to the ban when he ran for the presidency. Once in office, however, he had to settle for a compromise that merely modified the ban. Under a "don't ask, don't tell" policy, military officials are not permitted now to question recruits about their sexual orientation, and gays and lesbians are required to refrain from sexual practices while on duty or assignments. Thus those who commit homosexual acts are still subject to discharge.

Americans are deeply divided over this new policy. Many conservatives are upset that the president and Congress modified the old policy. However, former Republican presidential candidate Barry Goldwater said that "you don't need to be 'straight' to fight and die for your country. You just need to shoot straight."[31]

Even after the Clinton compromise was implemented, there was evidence that harassment of gays was still common. "The evidence suggests that some military commanders continue to ask. And under duress, some soldiers continue to tell."[32] The percent of homosexuals discharged from the military went up, and many critics believe the new policy in practice was as bad, if not worse, than its predecessors.

As predicted, gay and homosexual groups have gone to the courts to try to get the ban and the new Clinton-era regulations overruled as unconstitutional. Some U.S. district courts have ruled that the military may not discharge a person simply because of declared sexual orientation. Yet a 1996 ruling by the full U.S. Court of Appeals for the Fourth Circuit upheld the regulations as set by the Clinton White House, saying they were properly based on a law enacted by Congress and that courts are traditionally obligated to defer to the other branches of government, especially when the matter involved military policy.[33]

This constitutional issue is destined for Supreme Court review. The Court will have to balance the seldom-questioned authority of Congress and the president to set the rules for the conduct of the armed forces against constitutional protections of freedom from government interference in our individual choices, actions, and speech.

THE POLITICS OF DEFENSE SPENDING

The U.S. defense budget is about $265 billion a year. Over half the people employed by the national government work in the Defense Department. About three-quarters of federal purchases of goods and services originate in the defense budget; moreover, a few thousand defense installations are scattered across the country. Contracts in excess of $100 billion result in defense-related

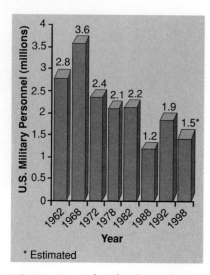

FIGURE 15-1 The Shrinking of the Military: U.S. Personnel in Military Service

SOURCE: *Fiscal Year 1997 Budget of the United States*, Historical Tables (Government Printing Office, 1996), p. 267.

*Estimated.

Newt Gingrich on Defense Spending

"I am a hawk but a cheap hawk. I don't think we ought to salute waste just because it is in uniform. I also don't think the Pentagon should be any more exempt from reengineering, downsizing, and rethinking than any other part of the federal government. . . .

While I am a cheap hawk, I remain a hawk. I believe the world is a dangerous place. I believe there are active enemies who would love to destroy the United States. I believe our opponents are clever and determined and deserve our respect. I believe we need to have a much bigger investment in intelligence and make a bigger effort to stop terrorism. . . .

The Romans had a simple rule: If you want peace, prepare for war. George Washington echoed the same theme as the result of his lifetime struggle for the cause of freedom. Peace through strength will work. Peace through weakness is impossible."

Newt Gingrich, *To Renew America* (HarperCollins, 1995), p. 184.

civilian employment of nearly 2 million workers. More than 1.5 million retired Defense Department personnel draw pensions and other fringe benefits. Thus, the Defense Department's size and impact on our society raise questions about how it can be controlled.

In the 1990s defense spending decreased, weapons systems were canceled or postponed, bases were closed, navy ships were retired, and large numbers of troops have been brought home from Germany, the Philippines, and elsewhere (see Figure 15-1). This downsizing reflects the end of the cold war, the demise of the Soviet Union, and the lack of popular support for maintaining defense spending at the 1980s level.

Most Americans believed that once the cold war was won, there would be a huge "peace dividend," and that much of the spending needed to defeat the Soviet Union could be shifted to domestic priorities or tax cuts. Defense spending has declined steadily, and in 1997 it is about 33 percent lower, adjusted for inflation, than it was in 1985. Still, the United States is "now spending more on defense than all of its NATO allies, Japan, Israel and South Korea combined. The U.S. defense budget is more than triple Russia's. And it is higher, in real terms, than it was in 1980."[34]

The United States now accounts for nearly 40 percent of the world's annual military spending. But many Republican leaders—including Bob Dole, Newt Gingrich, and Strom Thurmond—say the Clinton administration cut too fast and failed to appreciate the urgent need for an effective ballistic missile defense system.

In the 104th Congress, Republicans aggressively pushed for the cutting of most domestic programs and went along with many of the base closings and reductions in force for military personnel. But congressional Republicans and some congressional Democrats are worried about new threats to U.S. security.

Clinton and Defense Secretary William Perry insist they have cut but not gutted the nation's defense preparedness. If we are ever going to even come close to balancing the budget, the military will have to accept its share of cuts, they insist. Clinton vetoed the initial 1996 defense budget authorization bill because it called for too much of an increase in defense technologies and weapons systems.

Clinton maintains we are strong militarily. He admits that "We can't be the world's policeman. We can't be everywhere. We can't do everything. But we can make a difference, and when it is consistent with out values and our interests, we have to try. That's what the effort in Bosnia is all about."[35]

It is no secret in Washington that the Pentagon's top military brass would like to see Congress appropriate significantly more funds for new weapons systems, new ships, and new technologies.[36] The 1990s have seen constant U.S. involvement in international peacekeeping and humanitarian relief operations that have strained the military's resources and energy. Yet, it is difficult for anyone—defense expert or average citizen, Republican or Democrat—to estimate with any accuracy how much is enough to spend on military preparedness.

Pressures to Promote Military Spending

One of the problems of cutting defense spending is that it immediately costs jobs in congressional districts. Weapons systems such as the Seawolf submarine and the B-2 bomber continue to be protected even though they were designed to combat the Soviet threat.[37]

The B-2 is a notable case in point. After 15 years of design and manufacturing, the Stealth bomber apparently can't distinguish a rainstorm from a mountain. The Pentagon has not asked for more of these billion-dollar planes, yet Congress keeps approving funds to build more of them. This congressional decision has more to do with jobs and reelection hopes than strategic needs.

Cuts and plant closings mean not only that people in the Defense Department and on bases lose their jobs, but also that shopkeepers, bankers, lawyers, doctors, contractors, housekeepers, baby sitters—the list goes on and on—also lose their jobs.

Weapons are a major American industry, and the industry and members of Congress work hard to promote its products. The agreement that operates in other **pork-barrel** areas works here as well: "You help me in my district, and I'll help you in yours." Even the most anti-deficit, balance-the-budget conservatives alter their tune when a contract termination hits close to their district. Similarly, the most vigorous anti-war doves in Congress shout the loudest when a base closing is proposed for their home region.

This is not to say that members of Congress cast their vote on military spending solely on whether the legislator's district would profit from the decision. An analysis of the relationships between campaign contributors and votes on weapons systems concludes that issues of defense strategy, cost, and a legislator's political philosophy are equally important.[38]

The Politics of Base Closings

The Defense Department was repeatedly frustrated in the 1960s and 1970s by the efforts of Congress to overturn proposed closings of no longer needed or uneconomical military bases in the United States. Influential members of Congress went to great lengths lobbying their colleagues that the base in their district was too important to shut down. Eventually military spokesmen and members of Congress realized that new procedures were needed to handle congressional approval of base closings.

Congress enacted legislation in 1988 setting up a blue-ribbon panel that would identify military bases that should be closed for budget savings. Congress invented this new procedure to thwart efforts by legislators to block closings of individual bases. This bypass strategy has succeeded. Dozens of bases have now been closed or are in the process of being shut down—and the savings will run into billions of dollars.

This is how the procedure works. The blue-ribbon panel is appointed by Congress and the president, but it works independently of both branches. It reviews the base-closing suggestions made by the Pentagon and makes its recommendations, which have to be accepted in toto or else be rejected by the president. If the president accepts the closings, the package then goes to Congress, where each chamber is allowed 45 days to consider the entire package. Congress has to accept the entire package or else no closings take place.

Initial experience with the Defense Base Closure and Realignment Commission process has been positive—although not without some predictable grumbling from the big losers and some lawsuits. But the federal courts have upheld these procedures, and dozens of additional bases will be closed in the late 1990s.

Weapons Systems and Defense

A number of major weapons systems whose primary justification was to fight the former Soviet Union have been canceled or their production greatly curtailed in the past few years. All the services have lost personnel and may continue to do so for the next few years. The National Guard and the military reserve have also been cut back about 25 percent.

The nation's primary defense against nuclear attack has been a strategy of *deterrence*, or maintaining the ability to threaten massive retaliation on any nation that attacked us. Effective deterrence is commonly measured by the strength of survivable second-strike force. Thus, the United States has maintained a large,

A "Military-Industrial Complex"?

By its nature, the defense industry is different from most other large industries in the United States. National defense is what economists call a "public good." There is no way to exclude citizens from "consuming" national defense, whether they wish to pay for it or not. Thus, the government must provide for defense by taxing citizens.

Critics sometimes charge that the military conspires with defense contractors and other strategic elites to maintain a vast network of bases and fleets around the world. They contend that the "military-industrial complex"—the alleged alliance between top military and industrial leaders who have a common interest in arms production—has a life of its own, is too big to be managed or controlled, spends too large a share of our national wealth, and is dedicated to exaggerating what was once "the Soviet menace," or "the Iranian or Iraqi menace," or whatever new enemy might emerge in the post–cold war era.

Military leaders deny the existence of a military-industrial complex. They point to the reduced size of the military and note that since its wartime peak in 1968, the number of military personnel will have dropped from 3.5 million in the late 1960s to about 1.4 million in 1997. Fewer people are in uniform now than at any time since 1950, and fewer U.S. troops are abroad than at any time since 1940. Further, our active fleet has been reduced and will be greatly reduced by the late 1990s.

Although defense contractors and pro-defense legislators in Congress still press for major military weapons developments, they are usually outnumbered by those who emphasize domestic and economic policy needs as we shift to a post–cold war economy.

TABLE 15-3

Public Opinion
and Defense Spending

*Question: Is the U.S. spending too
much, about right, or too little on
defense?*

Year	Too Much	About Right	Too Little	No Opinion
1995	42%	40%	15%	3%
1993	42	38	17	3
1991	50	36	10	4
1989	49	37	11	3
1987	44	36	14	6
1986	47	36	13	4
1980	14	24	49	13
1976	36	32	22	10
1974	44	32	12	12
1971	49	31	11	9
1969	52	31	8	9

SOURCE: Gallup poll index and 1995 data from
Greenberg and Stephen, Polls from Americas
Talk Issues Foundation, cited in *National Journal*,
September 2, 1995, p. 2185.

diversified, and well-protected defense system so that a first strike by another nation would not cripple our ability to retaliate decisively.

The United States has sought to prevent a major war by maintaining military forces and demonstrating the determination to use them, if needed, in ways that would persuade opponents that the cost of any attack on our interests would exceed any benefit they could possibly hope to gain. This strategy of *mutual assured destruction* is still the core of American defense policy in the 1990s. Pentagon officials claim it has worked (although at a very high cost). At least, they point out, it has succeeded in winning for the United States and our allies more than five decades of peace—a period twice as long as the period between World Wars I and II.

SECURITY AND LIBERTY: NOT BY FORCE ALONE

What should be the role of the military in a constitutional democracy? Although Americans have reasonably high confidence in the military, fear of the abuse of military force is also deeply rooted in the American tradition. And the unpopularity of the Vietnam War, together with the belief that vast military expenditures are giving undue influence to the military and their allies in the industrial community, has aroused concern about how to ensure civilian control over the so-called military-industrial complex (see Table 15-3).

The framers in 1787, recognizing that military domination is incompatible with free government, wove into the Constitution several precautions. The military is under civilian control. The president, an elected official, is the commander in chief of the armed forces; with the Senate's consent, the chief executive commissions all officers. Constitutional provisions grant Congress the power to raise and support armies, to make military law, to declare war, and to appropriate funds for the military for no more than two-year periods. Congress has also, by law, enacted requirements that the secretary of defense and the secretaries of the army, navy, and air force must be civilians. Yet sometimes the separation between military and civilian spheres of activity is less clear. On occasion, for example, the military decides what information must remain top secret. Members of Congress and the general public are thus sometimes at a disadvantage. With a large standing army and complicated intelligence and weapons systems invariably also come increased centralization of power and responsibility in the president. A nation preoccupied with defense is sometimes tempted to suppress dissent and to label critics as unpatriotic or subversive.

National debates about foreign policy, foreign aid, the military budget, deterrence strategies, missile defense systems, weapons systems, arms control, procurement processes, and force levels are commonplace in American politics, as they should be. The objectives of an ever-more-effective, yet ever-more-efficient, military preparedness effort will guide these debates. Although we recognize that true security for our constitutional democracy lies in more than troops and weapons, providing for the nation's common defense is a requirement that must be satisfied before a nation can go about its other business.

SUMMARY

1. American foreign policy from 1945 through 1990 was shaped and at times completely dominated by relations with the superpower rival, the Soviet Union. The competition between these two military giants dominated our foreign policy and world politics. With the passing of the cold war has come a major debate over foreign policy goals. The rise of Japan and Europe as economic powers and the increasing importance of economic and trading interests have transformed foreign policy debates in the 1990s.

2. Presidents, Congress, and the American people all become involved in defining our vital national security interests. Today there is an increased emphasis on trade and jobs, the well-being of the global environment, and the role of the United Nations and NATO as peacekeeping forces in the world.

3. Presidents must sometimes act swiftly and decisively. Plainly, the role of the president in foreign affairs was strengthened during the cold war years as the United States developed an enormous standing military capability and an extensive intelligence network. Presidents are often in a good position to see the nation's long-run interests above the tugging of bureaucratic and special interests. But in our constitutional democracy, presidents and their advisers must consult with Congress and inform the American people.

4. U.S. foreign policy interests are advanced by one or a combination of the following strategies or means: diplomacy, foreign aid, economic sanctions, political coercion (including the breaking off of diplomatic relations), covert action, and military intervention.

5. The United States is an active participant in numerous international organizations, especially the United Nations. The United Nations is likely to play an even greater role in the post–cold war world. The future of the nation-state is not in question, yet more and more of our global policy problems will be solved through international organizations of one type or another.

6. Our system is designed to provide civilian control over the military. Although the military in any society has enormous potential for direct political involvement, this has not occurred in the United States. The president, Congress, the secretary of defense, and other cabinet officers continually weigh national security against competing claims.

7. Although the 1990s witnessed major reductions in the size of the military and a large cut in military spending, many critics say the defense budget can be cut much further. Critics on the right, however, claim we have seriously weakened our defense preparedness. Nuclear missile blackmail and other instabilities around the globe are as great a threat today as the Soviet Union once was.

FURTHER READING

C. Kenneth Allard, *Command Control and the Common Defense* (Yale University Press, 1991).

Stephen E. Ambrose, *Rise to Globalism: American Foreign Policy Since 1938*, 6th ed. (Penguin, 1991).

James Baker with Thomas M. DeFrank, *The Politics of Diplomacy* (Putnam's Sons, 1995).

Angelo Codevilla, *Informing Statecraft: Intelligence for a New Century* (Free Press, 1992).

Louis Fisher, *Presidential War Power* (University Press of Kansas, 1995).

John Lewis Gaddis, *The United States and the End of the Cold War* (Oxford University Press, 1992).

Loch K. Johnson, *America's Secret Power: The CIA in a Democratic Society* (Oxford University Press, 1989).

Henry Kissinger, *Diplomacy* (Simon & Schuster, 1994).

Harold Hongju Koh, *The National Security Constitution: Sharing Power after the Iran-Contra Affair* (Yale University Press, 1990).

Kenneth R. Mayer, *The Political Economy of Defense Contracting* (Yale University Press, 1991).

Robert S. McNamara, *In Retrospect: The Tragedy and Lessons of Vietnam* (Times Books, 1995).

Ralph Nader et al., *The Case Against Free Trade: GATT, NAFTA, and the Globalization of Corporate Power* (Earth Island Press, 1993).

John Prados, *Keepers of the Keys: A History of the National Security Council from Truman to Bush* (William Morrow, 1991).

Rosemary Righter, *Utopia Lost: The United Nations and World Order* (Twentieth Century Fund, 1995).

Joseph Romm, *Defining National Security: The Nonmilitary Aspect* (Council on Foreign Relations, 1993).

James N. Rosenau, *The United Nations in a Turbulent World* (Lynne Rienner, 1992).

George Shultz, *Turmoil and Triumph: My Years as Secretary of State* (Scribner's, 1993).

Ronald Steel, *Temptations of a Superpower* (Harvard University Press, 1995).

Robert W. Tucker and David C. Hendrickson, *The Imperial Temptation: The New World Order and American Purpose* (Council on Foreign Relations, 1992).

Stephen R. Weissman, *A Culture of Deference: Congress's Failure of Leadership in Foreign Affairs* (Basic Books, 1995).

Bob Woodward, *The Commanders* (Simon & Schuster, 1991).

APPENDIX

THE DECLARATION OF INDEPENDENCE

Drafted mainly by Thomas Jefferson, this document adopted by the Second Continental Congress, and signed by John Hancock and fifty-five others, outlined the rights of man and the rights to rebellion and self-government. It declared the independence of the colonies from Great Britain, justified rebellion, and listed the grievances against George the III and his government. What is memorable about this famous document is not only that it declared the birth of a new nation, but that it set forth, with eloquence, our basic philosophy of liberty and representative democracy.

IN CONGRESS, JULY 4, 1776
(The unanimous Declaration of the Thirteen United States of America)

Preamble
When, in the course of human events, it becomes necessary for one people to dissolve the political bands which have connected them with another, and to assume, among the powers of the earth, the separate and equal station to which the laws of nature and of nature's God entitle them, a decent respect to the opinions of mankind requires that they should declare the causes which impel them to the separation.

New Principles of Government

We hold these truths to be self-evident; that all men are created equal, that they are endowed by their Creator with certain unalienable rights, that among these are life, liberty, and the pursuit of happiness.

That, to secure these rights, governments are instituted among men, deriving their just powers from the consent of the governed.

That whenever any form of government becomes destructive of these ends, it is the right of the people to alter or to abolish it, and to institute new government, laying its foundation on such principles, and organizing its powers in such form, as to them shall seem most likely to effect their safety and happiness. Prudence, indeed will dictate that governments long established should not be changed for light and transient causes; and accordingly all experience hath shown that mankind are more disposed to suffer while evils are sufferable, than to right themselves by abolishing the forms to which they are accustomed. But when a long train of abuses and usurpations, pursuing invariably the same object, evinces a design to reduce them under absolute despotism, it is their right, it is their duty, to throw off such government, and to provide new guards for their future security.

Reasons for Separation

Such has been the patient sufferance of these colonies; and such is now the necessity which constrains them to alter their former systems of government. The history of the present king of Great Britain is a history of repeated injuries and usurpations, all having in direct object the establishment of an absolute tyranny over these states. To prove this, let facts be submitted to a candid world.

He has refused his assent to laws, the most wholesome and necessary for the public good.

He has forbidden his governors to pass laws of immediate and pressing importance unless suspended in their operation till his assent should be obtained; and when so suspended, he has utterly neglected to attend to them.

He has refused to pass other laws for the accommodation of large districts of people, unless those people would relinquish the right of representation in the legislature, a right inestimable to them, and formidable to tyrants only.

He has called together legislative bodies at places unusual, uncomfortable, and distant for the depository of their public records, for the sole purpose of fatiguing them into compliance with his measures.

He has dissolved representative houses repeatedly, for opposing, with manly firmness, his invasions on the rights of people.

He has refused, for a long time after such dissolutions, to cause others to be elected; whereby the legislative powers incapable of annihilation, have returned to the people at large for their exercise; the state remaining, in the meantime, exposed to all the dangers of invasion from without and convulsions within.

He has endeavored to prevent the population of these states; for that purpose obstructing the laws of naturalization of foreigners, refusing to pass others to encourage their migration hither, and raising the conditions of new appropriations of lands.

He has obstructed the administration of justice, by refusing his assent to laws for establishing judiciary powers.

He has made judges dependent on his will alone for the tenure of their offices, and the amount and payment of their salaries.

He has erected a multitude of new offices, and sent hither swarms of officers to harass our people and eat out their substance.

He has kept among us, in times of peace, standing armies, without the consent of our legislature.

He has affected to render the military independent of, and superior to, the civil power.

He has combined with others to subject us to jurisdiction foreign to our constitution and unacknowledged by our laws, giving his assent to their acts of pretended legislation:

For quartering large bodies of armed troops among us;

For protecting them, by a mock trial, from punishment for any murders which they should commit on the inhabitants of these states;

For cutting off our trade with all parts of the world;

For imposing taxes on us without our consent;

For depriving us, in many cases, of the benefits of trial by jury;

For transporting us beyond seas, to be tried for pretended offenses;

For abolishing the free system of English laws in a neighboring province, establishing therein an arbitrary government, and enlarging its boundaries, so as to render it at once an example and fit instrument for introducing the same absolute rule into these colonies;

For taking away our charters, abolishing our most valuable laws, and altering, fundamentally, the forms of our governments;

For suspending our own legislatures, and declaring themselves invented with power to legislate for us in all cases whatsoever.

He has abdicated government here, by declaring us out of his protection and waging war against us.

He has plundered our seas, ravaged our coasts, burned our towns, and destroyed the lives of our people.

He is at this time transporting large armies of foreign mercenaries to complete the works of death, desolation, and tyranny already begun with circumstances of cruelty and perfidy scarcely paralleled in the most barbarous ages and totally unworthy of the head of a civilized nation.

He has constrained our fellow-citizens, taken captive on the high seas, to bear arms against their country, to become the executioners of their friends and brethren, or to fall themselves by their hands.

He has excited domestic insurrections among us, and has endeavored to bring on the inhabitants of our frontiers the merciless Indian savages, whose known rule of warfare is an undistinguished destruction of all ages, sexes, and conditions.

In every stage of these oppressions we have petitioned for redress in the most humble terms; our repeated petitions have been answered only by repeated injury. A prince whose character is thus marked by every act which may define a tyrant is unfit to be the ruler of a free people.

Nor have we been wanting in attention to our British brethren. We have warned them, from time to time, of attempts by their legislature to extend an unwarrantable jurisdiction over us. We have reminded them of the circumstances of our emigration and settlement here. We have appealed to their native justice and magnanimity; and we have conjured them, by the ties of our common kindred, to disavow these usurpations, which would inevitably interrupt our connections and correspondence. They, too, have been deaf to the voice of justice and of consanguinity. We must, therefore, acquiesce in the necessity which denounces our separation, and hold them, as we hold the rest of mankind, enemies in war, in peace, friends.

We, therefore, the representatives of the United States of America, in General Congress assembled, appealing to the Supreme Judge of the world for the rectitude of our intentions, do, in the name and by authority of the good people of these colonies, solemnly publish and declare, that these united colonies are, and of right ought to be, free and independent states; that they are absolved from all allegiance to the British crown, and that all political connection between them and the state of Great Britain is, and ought to be, totally dissolved; and that, as free and independent states, they have full power to levy war, conclude peace, contract alliances, establish commerce, and do all other acts and things which independent states may of a right do. And, for the support of this declaration, with a firm reliance on the protection of Divine Providence, we mutually pledge to each other our lives, our fortunes, and our sacred honor.

THE FEDERALIST, NO. 10, JAMES MADISON

The Federalist, No. 10, written by James Madison soon after the Constitutional Convention, was prepared as one of several dozen newspaper essays aimed at persuading New Yorkers to ratify the proposed constitution. One of the most important basic documents in American political history, it outlines the need for and the general principles of a democratic republic. It also provides a political and economic analysis of the realities of interest group or faction politics.

To the People of the State of New York: Among the numerous advantages promised by a well-constructed union, none deserves to be more accurately developed than its tendency to break and control the violence of faction. The friend of popular governments, never finds himself so much alarmed for their character and fate, as when he contemplates their propensity of this dangerous vice. He will not fail, therefore, to set a due value on any plan which, without violating the principles to which he is attached, provides a proper cure for it. The instability, injustice, and confusion introduced into the public councils, have, in truth, been the mortal diseases under which popular governments have everywhere perished; as they continue to be the favorite and fruitful topics from which the adversaries to liberty derive their most specious declamations. The valuable improvements made by the American constitutions on the popular models, both ancient and modern, cannot certainly be too much admired; but it would be an unwarrantable partiality, to contend that they have as effectually obviated the danger on this side, as was wished and expected. Complaints are everywhere heard from our most considerate and virtuous citizens, equally the friends of public and private faith, and of public and personal liberty, that our governments are too unstable; that the public good is disregarded in the conflicts of rival parties; and that measures are too often decided, not according to the rules of justice, and the rights of the minor party, but by the superior force of an interested and overbearing majority. However anxiously we may wish that these complaints had no foundation, the evidence of known facts will not permit us to deny that they are in some degree true. It will be found, indeed, on a candid review of our situation, that some of the distresses under which we labor have been erroneously charged on the operations of our governments; but it will be found, at the same time, that other causes will not alone account for many of our heaviest misfortunes; and, particularly, for that prevailing and increasing distrust of public engagements, and alarm for private rights, which are echoed from one end of the continent to the other. These must be chiefly, if not wholly, effects of the unsteadiness and injustice, with which a factious spirit has tainted our public administrations.

By a faction, I understand a number of citizens, whether amounting to a majority of the whole, who are united and actuated by some common impulse of passion, or of interest, adverse to the rights of other citizens, or to the permanent and aggregate interests of the community.

There are two methods of curing the mischiefs of faction: the one, by removing its causes; the other, by controlling its effects.

There are again two methods of removing the causes of faction: the one, by destroying the liberty which is essential to its existence; the other, by giving to every citizen the same opinions, the same passions, and the same interests.

It could never be more truly said, than of the first remedy, that it was worse than the disease. Liberty is to faction what air is to fire, an aliment without which it instantly expires. But it could not be a less folly to abolish liberty, which is essential to political life, because it nourishes faction, than it would be to wish the annihilation of air, which is essential to animal life, because it imparts to fire its destructive agency.

The second expedient is as impracticable, as the first would be unwise. As long as the reason of man continues fallible, and he is at liberty to exercise it, different opinions will be formed. As long as the connection subsists between his reason and his self-love, his opinions and his passions will have a reciprocal influence on each other; and the former will be objects to which the latter will attach themselves. The diversity in the faculties of men, from which the rights of property originate, is not less an insuperable obstacle to an uniformity of interests. The protection of these faculties is the first object of government. From the protection of different and unequal faculties of acquiring property, the possession of different degrees and kinds of property immediately results; and from the influence of these

on the sentiments and views of the respective proprietors, ensues a division of the society into different interests and parties.

The latent causes of faction are thus sown in the nature of man; and we see them everywhere brought into different degrees of activity, according to the different circumstances of civil society. A zeal for different opinions concerning religion, concerning government, and many other points, as well of speculation as of practice; an attachment to different leaders ambitiously contending for preeminence and power; or to persons of other descriptions whose fortunes have been interesting to the human passions, have, in turn, divided mankind into parties, inflamed them with mutual animosity, and rendered them much more disposed to vex and oppress each other, than to cooperate for their common good. So strong is this propensity of mankind, to fall into mutual animosities, that where no substantial occasion presents itself, the most frivolous and fanciful distinctions have been sufficient to kindle their unfriendly passions and excite their most violent conflicts. But the most common and durable source of factions, has been the various and unequal distribution of property. Those who hold, and those who are without property, have ever formed distinct interests in society. Those who are creditors, and those who are debtors, fall under a like discrimination. A landed interest, a manufacturing interest, a mercantile interest, a moneyed interest, with many lesser interests, grow up of necessity in civilized nations, and divide them into different classes, actuated by different sentiments and views. The regulation of these various and interfering interests forms the principal task of modern legislation, and involves the spirit of the party and faction in the necessary and ordinary operations of the government.

No man is allowed to be a judge in his own cause; because his interest will certainly bias his judgment, and, not improbably, corrupt his integrity. With equal, nay, with greater reason, a body of men are unfit to be both judges and parties at the same time; yet what are many of the most important acts of legislation, but so many judicial determinations, not indeed concerning the right of single persons, but concerning the rights of large bodies of citizens? And what are the different classes of legislators, but advocates and parties to the causes which they determine? Is a law proposed concerning private debts? It is a questions to which the creditors are parties on one side, and the debtors on the other. Justice ought to hold the balance between them. Yet the parties are, and must be, themselves the judges; and the most numerous party, or, in other words, the most powerful faction, must be expected

to prevail. Shall domestic manufacturers be encouraged, and in what degree, by restrictions on foreign manufacturers? Are questions which would be differently decided by the landed and the manufacturing classes; and probably by neither with a sole regard to justice and the public good. The apportionment of taxes, on the various descriptions of property, is an act which seems to require the most exact impartiality; yet there is, perhaps, no legislative act, in which greater opportunity and temptation are given to a predominant party to trample on the rules of justice. Every shilling, with which they overburden the inferior number, is a shilling saved to their own pockets.

It is in vain to say, that enlightened statesmen will be able to adjust these clashing interests, and render them all subservient to the public good. Enlightened statesmen will not always be at the helm, nor, in many cases, can such an adjustment be made at all, without taking into view indirect and remote considerations, which will rarely prevail over the immediate interest which one party may find in disregarding the rights of another, or the good of the whole.

The inference to which we are brought is, that the causes of faction cannot be removed; and that relief is only to be sought in the means of controlling its *effects*.

If a faction consists of less than a majority, relief is supplied by the republican principle, which enables the majority to defeat its sinister views, by regular vote. It may clog the administration, it may convulse the society; but it will be unable to execute and mask its violence under the forms of the Constitution. When a majority is included in a faction, the form of popular government, on the other hand, enables it to sacrifice to its ruling passion or interest, both the public good and the rights of other citizens. To secure the public good, and private rights, against the danger of such a faction, and at the same time to preserve the spirit and the form of popular government, is then the great object to which our inquiries are directed. Let me add, that it is the great desideratum, by which alone this form of government can be rescued from the opprobrium under which it has so long laboured, and be recommended to the esteem and adoption of mankind.

By what means is this object attainable? Evidently by one of two only. Either the existence of the same passion or interest in a majority, at the same time, must be prevented; or the majority, having such coexistent passion or interest, must be rendered, by their number and local situation, unable to concert and carry into effect schemes of oppression. If the impulse and the opportunity be suffered to coincide, we well know that neither moral nor religious motives can be relied on as an adequate control. They are not found to be such on the injustice and violence of individuals, and lose their efficacy in proportion to the number combined together; that is, in proportion as their efficacy becomes needful.

From this view of the subject, it may be concluded, that a pure democracy, by which I mean a society consisting of a small number of citizens, who assemble and administer the government in person, can admit of no cure for the mischiefs of faction. A common passion or interest will, in almost every case, be felt by a majority of the whole; a communication and concert, results from the form of government itself; and there is nothing to check the inducements to sacrifice the weaker party, or an obnoxious individual. Hence, it is, that such democracies have ever been spectacles of turbulence and contention; have ever been found incompatible with personal security, or the rights of property; and have in general been as short in their lives, as they have been violent in their deaths. Theoretic politicians, who have patronized this species of government, have erroneously supposed, that by reducing mankind to a perfect equality in their political rights, they would, at the same time be perfectly equalized and assimilated in their possessions, their opinions, and their passions.

A republic, by which I mean a government in which the scheme of representation takes place, opens a different prospect, and promises the cure for which we are seeking. Let us examine the points in which it varies from pure democracy, and we shall comprehend both the nature of the cure and the efficacy which it must derive from the union.

The two great points of difference, between a democracy and a republic, are, first, the delegation of the government, in the latter, to a small number of citizens, elected by the rest; secondly, the greater number of citizens, and greater sphere of country, over which the latter may be extended.

The effect of the first difference is, on the one hand, to refine and enlarge the public views, by passing them through the medium of a chosen body of citizens, whose wisdom may best discern the true interest of their country, and whose patriotism and love of justice, will be least likely to sacrifice it to temporary or partial considerations. Under such a regulation, it may well happen, that the public voice, pronounced by the representatives of the people, will be more consonant to the public good, than if pronounced by the people themselves, convened for the purpose. On the other hand the effect may be inverted. Men of factious tempers, of local prejudices, or of sin-

ister designs, may by intrigue, by corruption, or by other means, first obtain the suffrages, and then betray the interest of the people. The question resulting is, whether small or extensive republics are most favourable to the election of proper guardians of the public weal; and it is clearly decided in favour of the latter by two obvious considerations.

In the first place, it is to be remarked that, however small the republic may be, the representatives must be raised to a certain number, in order to guard against the cabals of a few; and that however large it may be, they must be limited to a certain number, in order to guard against the confusion of a multitude. Hence, the number of representatives in the two cases not being in proportion to that of the constituents, and being proportionally greatest in the small republic, it follows, that if the proportion of fit characters be not less in the large than in the small republic, the former will present a greater option, and consequently a greater probability of a fit choice.

In the next place, as each representative will be chosen by a greater number of citizens in the large than in the small republic, it will be more difficult for unworthy candidates to practice with success the vicious arts, by which elections are too often carried; and the suffrages of the people being more free, will be more likely to centre in men who possess the most attractive merit, and the most diffusive and established characters.

It must be confessed, that in this, as in most other cases, there is a mean, on both sides of which inconveniences will be found to lie. By enlarging too much the number of electors, you render the representatives too little acquainted with all their local circumstances and lesser interests; as by reducing it too much, you render him unduly attached to these, and too little fit to comprehend and pursue great and national objects. The federal constitution forms a happy combination in this respect; the great and aggregate interests being referred to the national, the local and particular to the state legislatures.

The other point of difference is, the greater number of citizens, and extent of territory, which may be brought within the compass of republican, than of democratic government; and it is this circumstance principally which renders factious combinations less to be dreaded in the former, than in the latter. The smaller the society, the fewer probably will be the distinct parties and interests composing it; the fewer the distinct parties and interests, the more frequently will a majority be found of the same party; and the smaller the number of individuals composing a majority, and the smaller the compass within which they are placed, the more easily will

they concert and execute their plans of oppression. Extend the sphere, and you take in a greater variety of parties and interests; you make it less probable that a majority of the whole will have a common motive to invade the rights of other citizens; or if such a common motive exists, it will be more difficult for all who feel it to discover their own strength, and to act in unison with each other. Besides other impediments, it may be remarked, that where there is a consciousness of unjust or dishonourable purposes, communication is always checked by distrust, in proportion to the number whose concurrence is necessary.

Hence, it clearly appears, that the same advantage, which a republic has over a democracy, in controlling the effects of faction, is enjoyed by a large over a small republic—is enjoyed by the union over the states composing it. Does this advantage consist in the substitution of representatives, whose enlightened views and virtuous sentiments render them superior to local prejudices, and to schemes of injustice? It will not be denied that the representation of the union will be most likely to possess these requisite endowments. Does it consist in the greater security afforded by a greater variety of parties, against the event of any one party being able to outnumber and oppress the rest? In an equal degree does the increased variety of parties, comprised within the union, increase the security? Does it, in fine, consist in the greater obstacles opposed to the concert and accomplishment of the secret wishes of an unjust and interested majority? Here, again, the extent of the union gives it the most palpable advantage.

The influence of factious leaders may kindle a flame within their particular states, but will be unable to spread a general conflagration through the other states; a religious sect may degenerate into a political faction in a part of the confederacy; but the variety of sects dispersed over the entire face of it, must secure the national councils against any danger from that source: a rage for paper money, for an abolition of debts, for an equal division of property, or for any other improper or wicked project, will be less apt to pervade the whole body of the union than a particular member of it; in the same proportion as such a malady is more likely to taint a particular county or district, than an entire state.

In the extent and proper structure of the union, therefore, we behold a republican remedy for the diseases most incident to republican government. And according to the degree of pleasure and pride we feel in being republicans, ought to be our zeal in cherishing the spirit, and supporting the character of federalists.

THE FEDERALIST, NO. 51, JAMES MADISON

The Federalist, No. 51, also written by Madison, is a classic statement in defense
of separation of powers and republican processes. Its fourth paragraph is especially
famous and is frequently quoted by students of government.

To what expedient, then, shall we finally resort, for maintaining in practice the necessary partition of power among the several departments as laid down in the Constitution? The only answer that can be given is that as all these exterior provisions are found to be inadequate the defect must be supplied, by so contriving the interior structure of the government as that its several constituent parts may, by their mutual relations, be the means of keeping each other in their proper places. Without presuming to undertake a full development of this important idea I will hazard a few general observations which may perhaps place it in a clearer light, and enable us to form a more correct judgment of the principles and structure of the government planned by the convention.

In order to lay a due foundation for that separate and distinct exercise of the different powers of government, which to a certain extent is admitted on all hands to be essential to the preservation of liberty, it is evident that each department should have a will of its own; and consequently should be so constituted that the members of each should have as little agency as possible in the appointment of the members of the others. Were this principle rigorously adhered to, it would require that all the appointments for the supreme executive, legislative, and judiciary magistracies should be drawn from the same fountain of authority, the people, through channels having no communication whatever with one another. Perhaps such a plan of constructing the several departments would be less difficult in practice than it may in contemplation appear. Some difficulties, however, and some additional expense would attend the execution of it. Some deviations, therefore, from the principle must be admitted. In the constitution of the judiciary department in particular, it might be inexpedient to insist rigorously on the principle: first, because peculiar qualifications being essential in the members, the primary consideration ought to be to select that mode of choice which best secures these qualifications; second, because the permanent tenure by which the appointments are held in that department must soon destroy all sense of dependence on the authority conferring them.

It is equally evident that the members of each department should be as little dependent as possible on those of the others for the emoluments annexed to their offices. Were the executive magistrate, or the judges, not independent of the legislature in this particular, their independence in every other would be merely nominal.

But the great security against a gradual concentration of the several powers in the same department consists in giving to those who administer each department the necessary constitutional means and personal motives to resist encroachments of the others. The provision for defense must in this, as in all other cases, be made commensurate to the danger of attack. Ambition must be made to counteract ambition. The interest of the man must be connected with the constitutional rights of the place. It may be a reflection on human nature that such devices should be necessary to control the abuses of government. But what is government itself but the greatest of all reflections on human nature? If men were angels, no government would be necessary. If angels were to govern men, neither external nor internal controls on government would be necessary. In framing a government which is to be administered by men over men, the great difficulty lies in this: you must first enable the government to control the governed; and in the next place oblige it to control itself. A dependence on the people is, no doubt, the primary control on the government; but experience has taught mankind the necessity of auxiliary precautions.

This policy of supplying, by opposite and rival interests, the defect of better motives, might be traced through the whole system of human affairs, private as well as public. We see it particularly displayed in all the subordinate distributions of power, where the constant aim is to divide and arrange the several offices in such a manner as that each may be a check on the other—that the private interest of every individual may be a sentinel over the public rights. These inventions of prudence cannot be less requisite in the distribution of the supreme powers of the State.

But it is not possible to give to each department an equal power of self-defense. In republican government, the legislative authority necessarily predominates. The remedy for this inconveniency is to divide the legislature into different branches; and to render them, by modes of election and different principles of action, as little connected with each other as the nature of their common functions and their common dependence on the society will admit. It may even be necessary to guard against dangerous encroachments by still further precautions. As the weight of the legislative authority requires that it should be thus divided, the weakness of the executive may require, on the other hand, that it should be fortified. An absolute negative on the legislature appears, at first view, to be the natural defense with which the executive magistrate should be armed. But perhaps it would be neither altogether safe nor alone sufficient. On ordinary occasions it might not be exerted with the requisite firmness, and on extraordinary occasions it might be perfidiously abused. May not this defect of an absolute negative be supplied by some qualified connection between this weaker department and the weaker branch of the stronger department, by which the latter may be led to support the constitutional rights of the former, without being too much detached from the rights of its own department?

If the principles on which these observations are founded be just, as I persuade myself they are, and they be applied as a criterion to the several State constitutions, and to the federal Constitution, it will be found that if the latter does not perfectly correspond with them, the former are infinitely less able to bear such a test.

There are, moreover, two considerations particularly applicable to the federal system of America, which place that system in a very interesting point of view.

First. In a single republic, all the power surrendered by the people is submitted to the administration of a single government; and the usurpations are guarded against by a division of the government into distinct and separate departments. In the compound republic of America, the power surrendered by the people is first divided between two distinct governments, and then the portion allotted to each subdivided among distinct and separate departments. Hence a double security arises to the rights of the people. The different governments will control each other, at the same time that each will be controlled by itself.

Second. It is of great importance in a republic not only to guard the society against the oppression of its rulers, but to guard one part of the society against the injustice of the other part. Different interests necessarily exist in different classes of citizens. If a majority be united by a common interest, the rights of the minority will be insecure. There are but two methods of providing against this evil: the one by creating a will in the community independent of the majority—that is, of the society itself; the other, by comprehending in the society so many separate descriptions of citizens as will render an unjust combination of a majority of the whole very improbable, if not impracticable. The first method prevails in all governments possessing an hereditary or self-appointed authority. This, at best, is but a precarious security; because a power independent of the society may as well espouse the unjust views of the major as the rightful interests of the minor party, and may possibly be turned against both parties. The second method will be exemplified in the federal republic of the United States. Whilst all authority in it will be derived from and dependent on the society, the society itself will be broken into so many parts, interests and classes of citizens, that the rights of individuals, or of the minority, will be in little danger from interested combinations of the majority. In a free government the security for civil rights must be the same as that for religious rights. It consists in the one case in the multiplicity of interests, and in the other in the multiplicity of sects. The degree of security in both cases

will depend on the number of interests and sects; and this may be presumed to depend on the extent of country and number of people comprehended under the same government. This view of the subject must particularly recommend a proper federal system to all the sincere and considerate friends of republican government, since it shows that in exact proportion as the territory of the Union may be formed into more circumscribed Confederacies, or States, oppressive combinations of a majority will be facilitated; the best security, under the republican forms, for the rights of every class of citizen, will be diminished; and consequently the stability and independence of some member of the government, the only other security, must be proportionally increased. Justice is the end of government. It is the end of civil society. It ever has been and ever will be pursued until it be obtained, or until liberty be lost in the pursuit. In a society under the forms of which the stronger faction can readily unite and oppress the weaker, anarchy may as truly be said to reign as in a state of nature, where the weaker individual is not secured against the violence of the stronger; and as, in the latter state, even the stronger individuals are prompted, by the uncertainty of their condition, to submit to a government which may protect the weak as well as themselves; so, in the former state, will the more powerful factions or parties be gradually induced, by a

like motive, to wish for a government which will protect all parties, the weaker as well as the more powerful. It can be little doubted that if the State of Rhode Island was separated from the Confederacy and left to itself, the insecurity of rights under the popular form of government within such narrow limits would be displayed by such reiterated oppressions of factious majorities that some power altogether independent of the people would soon be called for by the voice of the very factions whose misrule had proved the necessity to it. In the extended republic of the United States, and among the great variety of interests, parties, and sects which it embraces, a coalition of a majority of the whole society could seldom take place on any other principles than those of justice and the general good; whilst there being thus less danger to a minor from the will of a major party, there must be less pretext, also, to provide for the security of the former, by introducing into the government a will not dependent on the latter, or, in other words, a will independent of the society itself. It is no less certain that it is important, notwithstanding the contrary opinions which have been entertained that the larger the society, provided it lie within a practicable sphere, the more duly capable it will be of self-government. And happily for the *republican cause,* the practicable sphere may be carried to a very great extent by a judicious modification and mixture of the *federal principle.*

THE FEDERALIST, NO. 78, ALEXANDER HAMILTON

The Federalist, No. 78, written by Alexander Hamilton, explains and praises the provisions for the judiciary in the newly drafted Constitution. Notice especially how Hamilton asserts that the courts have a key responsibility in determining the meaning of the Constitution as fundamental law. Hamilton is outlining here the doctrine of *judicial review* as we now know it.

We proceed now to an examination of the judiciary department of the proposed government.

In unfolding the defects of the existing Confederation, the utility and necessity of a federal judicature have been clearly pointed out. It is the less necessary to recapitulate the considerations there urged as the propriety of the institution in the abstract is not disputed; the only questions which have been raised being relative to the manner of constituting it, and to its extent. To these points, therefore, our observations shall be confined.

The manner of constituting it seems to embrace these several objects: 1st. The mode of appointing the judges. 2nd. The tenure by

which they are to hold their places. 3rd. The partition of the judiciary authority between different courts and their relations to each other.

First. As to the mode of appointing the judges: this is the same with that of appointing the officers of the Union in general and has been so fully discussed in the two last numbers that nothing can be said here which would not be useless repetition.

Second. As to the tenure by which the judges are to hold their places: this chiefly concerns their duration in office, the provisions for their support, the precautions for their responsibility.

According to the plan of the convention, all judges who may be appointed by the Unit-

ed States are to hold their offices *during good behavior;* which is conformable to the most approved of the State constitutions, and among the rest, to that of this State. Its propriety having been drawn into question by the adversaries of that plan is no light symptom of the rage for objection which disorders their imaginations and judgments. The standard of good behavior for the continuance in office of the judicial magistracy is certainly one of the most valuable of the modern improvements in the practice of government. In a monarchy it is an excellent barrier to the despotism of the prince; in a republic it is a no less excellent barrier to the encroachments and oppressions of the representative body. And it is the best expedient which can be devised in any government to secure a steady, upright, and impartial administration of the laws.

Whoever attentively considers the different departments of power must perceive that, in a government in which they are separated from each other, the judiciary, from the nature of its functions, will always be the least dangerous to the political rights of the Constitution; because it will be least in a capacity to annoy or injure them. The executive not only dispenses the honors but holds the sword of the community. The legislature not only commands the purse but prescribes the rules by which the duties and rights of every citizen are to be regulated. The judiciary, on the contrary, has no influence over either the sword or the purse; no direction either of the strength or of the wealth of the society, and can take no active resolution whatever. It may truly be said to have neither FORCE NOR WILL but merely judgment; and must ultimately depend upon the aid of the executive arm even for the efficacy of its judgments.

This simple view of the matter suggests several important consequences. It proves incontestably that the judiciary is beyond comparison the weakest of the three departments of power; that it can never attack with success either of the other two; and that all possible care is requisite to enable it to defend itself against their attacks. It equally proves that though individual oppression may now and then proceed from the courts of justice, the general liberty of the people can never be endangered from that quarter; I mean so long as the judiciary remains truly distinct from both the legislature and the executive. For I agree that "there is no liberty if the power of judging be not separated from the legislative and executive powers." And it proves, in the last place, that as liberty can have nothing to fear from the judiciary alone, but would have everything to fear from its union with either of the other departments, that as all the effects of such a union must ensue from a dependence of the former on the latter, notwithstanding a nominal and apparent separation; that as, from the natural feebleness of the judiciary, it is in continual jeopardy of being overpowered, awed, or influenced by its co-ordinate branches; and that as nothing can contribute so much to its firmness and independence as permanency in office, this quality may therefore be justly regarded as an indispensable ingredient in its constitution, and, in a great measure, as the citadel for the public justice and the public security.

The complete independence of the courts of justice is peculiarly essential in a limited Constitution. By a limited Constitution, I understand one which contains certain specified exceptions to the legislative authority; such, for instance, as that it shall pass no bills of attainder, no *ex post facto* laws, and the like. Limitations of this kind can be preserved in practice no other way than through the medium of courts of justice, whose duty it must be to declare all acts contrary to the manifest tenor of the Constitution void. Without this, all the reservations of particular rights or privileges would amount to nothing.

Some perplexity respecting the rights of the courts to pronounce legislative acts void, because contrary to the Constitution, has arisen from an imagination that the doctrine would imply a superiority to the judiciary to the legislative power. It is urged that the authority which can declare the acts of another void must necessarily be superior to the one whose acts may be declared void. As this doctrine is of great importance in all the American constitutions, a brief discussion of the grounds on which it rests cannot be unacceptable.

There is no position which depends on clearer principles than that every act of a delegated authority, contrary to the tenor of the commission under which it is exercised, is void. No legislative act, therefore, contrary to the Constitution, can be valid. To deny this would be to affirm that the deputy is greater than his principal; that the servant is above his master; that the representatives of the people are superior to the people themselves; that men acting by virtue of powers do not authorize, but what they forbid.

If it be said that the legislative body are themselves the constitutional judges of their own powers and that the construction they put upon them is conclusive upon the other departments it may be answered that this cannot be the natural presumption where it is not to be collected from any particular provisions in the Constitution. It is not otherwise to be supposed that the Constitution could intend to enable the representatives of the people to substitute their *will* to that of their constituents. It is far more rational to suppose that the courts were designed to be an intermediate body between the people and the legislature in order, among other things, to keep the latter within the limits assigned to their authority. The interpretation of the laws is the proper and peculiar province of the courts. A constitution is, in fact, and must be regarded by the judges as, a fundamental law. It therefore belongs to them to ascertain its meaning as well as the meaning of any particular act proceeding from the legislative body. If there should happen to be an irreconcilable variance between the two, that which has the superior obligation and validity ought, of course, to be preferred; or, in other words, the Constitution ought to be preferred to the statute, the intention of the people to the intention of their agents.

Nor does this conclusion by any means suppose a superiority of the judicial to the legislative power. It only supposes that the power of the people is superior to both, and that where the will of the legislature, declared in its statutes, stands in opposition to that of the people, declared in the Constitution, the judges ought to be governed by the latter rather than the former. They ought to regulate their decisions by the fundamental laws rather than by those which are not fundamental.

This exercise of judicial discretion in determining between two contradictory laws is exemplified in a familiar instance. It not uncommonly happens that there are two statutes existing at one time, clashing in whole or in part with each other and neither of them containing any repealing clause or expression. In such a case, it is the province of the courts to liquidate and fix their meaning and operation. So far as they can, by any fair construction, be reconciled to each other, reason and law conspire to dictate that this should be done; where this is impracticable, it becomes a matter of necessity to give effect to one in exclusion of the other. The rule which has obtained in the courts for determining their relative validity is that the last in order of time shall be preferred to the first. But this is a mere rule of construction, not derived from any positive law but from the nature and reason of the thing. It is a rule not enjoined upon the courts by legislative provision but adopted by themselves, as consonant to truth and propriety, for the direction of their conduct as interpreters of the law. They thought it reasonable that between the interfering acts of an *equal* authority that which was the last indication of its will should have the preference.

But in regard to the interfering acts of a superior and subordinate authority of an original and derivative power, the nature and reason of the thing indicates the converse of that rule as proper to be followed. They teach us that the prior act of a superior ought to be preferred to the subsequent act of an inferior and subordinate authority; and that accordingly, whenever a particular statute contravenes the Constitution, it will be the duty of the judicial tribunals to adhere to the latter and disregard the former.

It can be of no weight to say that the courts, on the pretense of a repugnancy, may substitute their own pleasure to the constitutional intentions of the legislature. This might as well happen in the case of two contradictory statutes; or it might as well happen in every adjudication upon any single statute. The courts must declare the sense of the law; and if they should be disposed to exercise WILL instead of JUDGMENT, the consequence would equally be the substitution of their pleasure to that of the legislative body. The observation, if it prove anything, would prove that there ought to be no judges distinct from that body.

If, then, the courts of justice are to be considered as the bulwarks of a limited Constitution against legislative encroachments, this consideration will afford a strong argument for the permanent tenure of judicial offices, since nothing will contribute so much as this to that independent spirit in the judges which must be essential to the faithful performance of so arduous a duty.

This independence of the judges is equally requisite to guard the Constitution and the rights of individuals from the effects of those ill humors which the arts of designing men, or the influence of particular conjunctures, sometimes disseminate among the people themselves, and which, though they speedily give place to better information, and more deliberate reflection, have a tendency, in the meantime, to occasion dangerous innovations in the government, and serious oppressions of the minor party in the community. Though I trust the friends of the proposed Constitution will never concur with its enemies in questioning that fundamental principal of Republican government which admits the right of the people to alter or abolish the established Constitution whenever they find it inconsistent with their happiness; yet it is not to be inferred from this principle that the representatives of the people, whenever a momentary inclination happens to lay hold of a majority of their constituents incompatible with the provisions in the existing Constitution would, on that account, be justifiable in a violation of those provisions; or that the courts would be under a greater obligation to connive at infractions in this shape than when they had proceeded wholly from the cabals of the representative body. Until the people have, by some solemn and authoritative act, annulled or changed the established form, it is binding upon themselves collectively, as well as individually; and no presumption, or even knowledge of their sentiments, can warrant their representatives in a departure from it prior to such an act. But it is easy to see that it would require an uncommon portion of fortitude in the judges to do their duty as faithful guardians of the Constitution, where legislative invasions of it had been instigated by the major voice of the community.

But it is not with a view to infractions of the Constitution only that the independence of the judges may be an essential safeguard against the effects of occasional ill humors in the society. These sometimes extend no farther than to the injury of the private rights of particular classes of citizens, by unjust and partial laws. Here also the firmness of the judicial magistracy is of vast importance in mitigating the severity and confining the operation of such laws. It not only serves to moderate the immediate mischiefs of those which may have been passed but it operates as a check upon the legislative body in passing them; who, perceiving that obstacles to the success of iniquitous intention are to be expected from the scruples of the courts, are in a manner compelled, by the very motives of the injustice they mediate, to qualify their attempts. This is a circumstance calculated to have more influence upon the character of our governments than but a few may be aware of. The benefits of the integrity and moderation of the judiciary have already been felt in more States than one; and though they may have displeased those whose sinister expectations they may have disappointed, they must have commanded the esteem and applause of all the virtuous and disinterested. Considerate men of every description ought to prize whatever will tend to beget or fortify that temper in the courts; as no man can be sure that he may not be tomorrow the victim of a spirit of injustice, by which he may be a gainer today. And every man must now feel that the inevitable tendency of such a spirit is to sap the foundations of public and private confidence and to introduce in its stead universal distrust and distress.

That inflexible and uniform adherence to the rights of the Constitution, and of individuals, which we perceive to be indispensable in the courts of justice, can certainly not be expected from judges who hold their offices by a temporary commission. Periodical appointments, however regulated, or by whomsoever made, would, in some way or other, be fatal to their necessary independence. If the power of making them was committed either to the executive or legislature there would be danger of an improper complaisance to the branch which possessed it; if to both, there would be an unwillingness to hazard the displeasure of either; if to the people, or to persons chosen by them for the special purpose, there would be too great a disposition to consult popularity to justify a reliance that nothing would be consulted by the Constitution and the laws.

There is yet a further and a weighty reason for the permanency of the judicial offices which is deducible from the nature of the qualifications they require. It has been frequently remarked with great propriety that a voluminous code of laws is one of the inconveniences necessarily connected with the advantages of a free government. To avoid an arbitrary discretion in the courts, it is indispensable that they should be bound down by strict rules and precedents which serve to define and point out their duty in every particular case that comes before them; and it will readily be conceived from the variety of controversies which grow out of the folly and wickedness of mankind that the records of those precedents must unavoidably swell to a very considerable bulk and must demand long and laborious study to acquire a competent knowledge of them. Hence it is that there can be but few men in the society who will have sufficient skill in the laws to qualify them for the stations of judges. And making the proper deductions for the ordinary depravity of human nature, the number must be still smaller of those who unite the requisite integrity with the requisite knowledge. These considerations apprise us that the government can have no great option between fit characters; and that a temporary duration in office which would naturally discourage such characters from quitting a lucrative line of practice to accept a seat on the bench would have a tendency to throw the administration of justice into hands less able and less well qualified to conduct it with utility and dignity. In the present circumstances of this country and in those in which it is likely to be for a long time to come, the disadvantages on this score would be greater than they may at first sight appear; but it must be confessed that they are far inferior to those which present themselves under the other aspects of the subject.

Upon the whole, there can be no room to doubt that the convention acted wisely in copying from the models of those constitutions which have established *good behavior* as the tenure of their judicial offices in point of duration, and that so far from being blamable on this account, their plan would have been inexcusably defective if it had wanted this important feature of good government. The experience of Great Britain affords an illustrious comment on the excellence of the institution.

Presidential Election Results 1789–1996

Year	Candidates	Party	Popular Vote	Electoral Vote
1789	George Washington			69
	John Adams			34
	Others			35
1793	George Washington			132
	John Adams			77
	George Clinton			50
	Others			5
1796	John Adams	Federalist		71
	Thomas Jefferson	Democratic-Republican		68
	Thomas Pinckney	Federalist		59
	Aaron Burr	Democratic-Republican		30
	Others			48
1800	Thomas Jefferson	Democratic-Republican		73
	Aaron Burr	Democratic-Republican		73
	John Adams	Federalist		65
	Charles C. Pinckney	Federalist		64
1804	Thomas Jefferson	Democratic-Republican		162
	Charles C. Pinckney	Federalist		14
1808	James Madison	Democratic-Republican		122
	Charles C. Pinckney	Federalist		47
	George Clinton	Independent-Republican		6
1812	James Madison	Democratic-Republican		128
	DeWitt Clinton	Federalist		89
1816	James Monroe	Democratic-Republican		183
	Rufus King	Federalist		34
1820	James Monroe	Democratic-Republican		231
	John Quincy Adams	Independent-Republican		1
1824	John Quincy Adams	Democratic-Republican	108,740(30.5%)	84
	Andrew Jackson	Democratic-Republican	153,544(43.1%)	99
	Henry Clay	Democratic-Republican	47,136(13.2%)	37
	William H. Crawford	Democratic-Republican	46,618(13.1%)	41
1828	Andrew Jackson	Democratic	647,231(56.0%)	178
	John Quincy Adams	National Republican	509,097(44.0%)	83
1832	Andrew Jackson	Democratic	687,502(55.0%)	219
	Henry Clay	National Republican	530,189(42.4%)	49
	William Wirt	Anti-Masonic		7
	John Floyd	National Republican	33,108(2.6%)	11
1836	Martin Van Buren	Democratic	761,549(50.9%)	170
	William H. Harrison	Whig	549,567(36.7%)	73
	Hugh L. White	Whig	145,396(9.7%)	26
	Daniel Webster	Whig	41,287(2.7%)	14
1840	William H. Harrison	Whig	1,275,017(53.1%)	234
	Martin Van Buren	Democratic	1,128,702(46.9%)	60
1844	James K. Polk	Democratic	1,337,243(49.6%)	170
	Henry Clay	Whig	1,299,068(48.1%)	105
	James G. Birney	Liberty	63,300(2.3%)	
1848	Zachary Taylor	Whig	1,360,101(47.4%)	163
	Lewis Cass	Democratic	1,220,544(42.5%)	127
	Martin Van Buren	Free Soil	291,163(10.1%)	
1852	Franklin Pierce	Democratic	1,601,474(50.9%)	254
	Winfield Scott	Whig	1,386,578(44.1%)	42
1856	James Buchanan	Democratic	1,838,169(45.4%)	174
	John C. Fremont	Republican	1,335,264(33.0%)	114
	Millard Fillmore	American	874,534(21.6%)	8
1860	Abraham Lincoln	Republican	1,865,593(39.8%)	180
	Stephen A. Douglas	Democratic	1,381,713(29.5%)	12
	John C. Breckinridge	Democratic	848,356(18.1%)	72
	John Bell	Constitutional Union	592,906(12.6%)	79
1864	Abraham Lincoln	Republican	2,206,938(55.0%)	212
	George B. McClellan	Democratic	1,803,787(45.0%)	21
1868	Ulysses S. Grant	Republican	3,013,421(52.7%)	214
	Horatio Seymour	Democratic	2,706,829(47.3%)	80
1872	Ulysses S. Grant	Republican	3,596,745(55.6%)	286
	Horace Greeley	Democratic	2,843,446(43.9%)	66
1876	Rutherford B. Hayes	Republican	4,036,571(48.0%)	185
	Samuel J. Tilden	Democratic	4,284,020(51.0%)	184
1880	James A. Garfield	Republican	4,449,053(48.3%)	214
	Winfield S. Hancock	Democratic	4,442,035(48.2%)	155
	James B. Weaver	Greenback-Labor	308,578(3.4%)	
1884	Grover Cleveland	Democratic	4,874,986(48.5%)	219
	James G. Blaine	Republican	4,851,931(48.2%)	182
	Benjamin F. Butler	Greenback-Labor	175,370(1.8%)	

Presidential Election Results 1789–1996

Year	Candidates	Party	Popular Vote	Electoral Vote
1888	Benjamin Harrison	Republican	5,444,337(47.8%)	233
	Grover Cleveland	Democratic	5,540,050(48.6%)	168
1892	Grover Cleveland	Democratic	5,554,414(46.0%)	277
	Benjamin Harrison	Republican	5,190,802(43.0%)	145
	James B. Weaver	Peoples	1,027,329(8.5%)	22
1896	William McKinley	Republican	7,035,638(50.8%)	271
	William J. Bryan	Democratic; Populist	6,467,946(46.7%)	176
1900	William McKinley	Republican	7,219,530(51.7%)	292
	William J. Bryan	Democratic; Populist	6,356,734(45.5%)	155
1904	Theodore Roosevelt	Republican	7,628,834(56.4%)	336
	Alton B. Parker	Democrat	5,084,401(37.6%)	140
	Eugene V. Debs	Socialist	402,460(3.0%)	0
1908	William H. Taft	Republican	7,679,006(51.6%)	321
	William J. Bryan	Democratic	6,409,106(43.1%)	162
	Eugene V. Debs	Socialist	420,820(2.8%)	0
1912	Woodrow Wilson	Democratic	6,286,820(41.8%)	435
	Theodore Roosevelt	Progressive	4,126,020(27.4%)	88
	William H. Taft	Republican	3,483,922(23.2%)	8
	Eugene V. Debs	Socialist	897,011(6.0%)	0
1916	Woodrow Wilson	Democratic	9,129,606(49.3%)	277
	Charles E. Hughes	Republican	8,538,211(46.1%)	254
1920	Warren G. Harding	Republican	16,152,200(61.0%)	404
	James M. Cox	Democratic	9,147,353(34.6%)	127
	Eugene V. Debs	Socialist	919,799(3.5%)	0
1924	Calvin Coolidge	Republican	15,725,016(54.1%)	382
	John W. Davis	Democratic	8,385,586(28.8%)	136
	Robert M. La Follette	Progressive	4,822,856(16.6%)	13
1928	Herbert C. Hoover	Republican	21,392,190(58.2%)	444
	Alfred E. Smith	Democratic	15,016,443(40.8%)	87
1932	Franklin D. Roosevelt	Democratic	22,809,638(57.3%)	472
	Herbert C. Hoover	Republican	15,758,901(39.6%)	59
	Norman Thomas	Socialist	881,951(2.2%)	0
1936	Franklin D. Roosevelt	Democratic	27,751,612(60.7%)	523
	Alfred M. Landon	Republican	16,681,913(36.4%)	8
	William Lemke	Union	891,858(1.9%)	0
1940	Franklin D. Roosevelt	Democratic	27,243,466(54.7%)	449
	Wendell L. Wilkie	Republican	22,304,755(44.8%)	82
1944	Franklin D. Roosevelt	Democratic	25,602,505(52.8%)	432
	Thomas E. Dewey	Republican	22,006,278(44.5%)	99
1948	Harry S. Truman	Democratic	24,105,812(49.5%)	303
	Thomas E. Dewey	Republican	21,970,065(45.1%)	189
	J. Strom Thurmond	States' Rights	1,169,063(2.4%)	39
	Henry A. Wallace	Progressive	1,157,172(2.4%)	0
1952	Dwight D. Eisenhower	Republican	33,936,234(55.2%)	442
	Adlai E. Stevenson	Democratic	27,314,992(44.5%)	89
1956	Dwight D. Eisenhower	Republican	35,590,472(57.4%)	457
	Adlai E. Stevenson	Democratic	26,022,752(42.0%)	73
1960	John F. Kennedy	Democratic	34,227,096(49.9%)	303
	Richard M. Nixon	Republican	34,108,546(49.6%)	219
1964	Lyndon B Johnson	Democratic	43,126,233(61.1%)	486
	Barry Goldwater	Republican	27,174,989(38.5%)	52
1968	Richard M. Nixon	Republican	31,783,783(43.4%)	301
	Hubert H. Humphrey	Democratic	31,271,839(42.7%)	191
	George C. Wallace	American Independent	9,899,557(13.5%)	46
1972	Richard M. Nixon	Republican	46,632,189(61.3%)	520
	George McGovern	Democratic	28,422,015(37.3%)	17
1976	Jimmy Carter	Democratic	40,828,587(50.1%)	297
	Gerald R. Ford	Republican	39,147,613(48.0%)	240
1980	Ronald Reagan	Republican	42,941,145(51.0%)	489
	Jimmy Carter	Democratic	34,663,037(41.0%)	49
	John B. Anderson	Independent	5,551,551(6.6%)	0
1984	Ronald Reagan	Republican	53,428,357(59%)	525
	Walter F. Mondale	Democratic	36,930,923(41%)	13
1988	George Bush	Republican	48,881,011(53%)	426
	Michael Dukakis	Democratic	41,828,350(46%)	111
1992	Bill Clinton	Democratic	38,394,210(43%)	370
	George Bush	Republican	33,974,386(38%)	168
	H. Ross Perot	Independent	16,573,465(19%)	0
1996	Bill Clinton	Democratic	45,628,667(49%)	379
	Bob Dole	Republican	37,869,435(41%)	159
	H. Ross Perot	Reform	7,874,283(8%)	0

GLOSSARY

We have tried to write a readable book about American politics and government. We realize, however, that certain legal terms and political science phrases may not be familiar to some readers. To make such words or phrases (which appear in the text in boldface type) more understandable, we have compiled this glossary.

Affirmative action   Remedial actions—originally relating to employment but now also covering college and university admissions, contracting, and other areas—designed to overcome effects of past societal and individual discrimination against minorities and women.

American Dream   The widespread belief that individual initiative and hard work can result in economic success, that the next generation can have a better standard of living than the former, and that the United States is a land of opportunity.

Amicus curia ("friend of the court") brief   A brief filed by an individual or organization with the permission of the court. It provides arguments in addition to those presented by the immediate parties to the case.

Annapolis Convention   A convention held in August 1786 that issued the call to Congress and the states for what became the Constitutional Convention. Attended by delegates from five states, it was called to consider problems of trade and navigation.

Antifederalists   Persons opposed to more nationally centralized government in general, and to the ratification of the 1787 Philadelphia Constitution in particular.

Antitrust policy   Federal laws (of which the Sherman Act of 1890 is most prominent), supplemented by state laws, that try to prevent one or a few business firms from dominating a particular market through monopoly or restraint of trade.

Appellate jurisdiction   Authority to review decisions of lower courts, administrative tribunals, and some independent regulatory agencies.

Articles of Confederation   The first constitution of the newly independent American states. It was drafted in 1777, ratified in 1781, and replaced by the present Constitution in 1789.

Attentive public   Those who follow public affairs fairly carefully, reading newspapers and magazines and watching television news broadcasts to keep informed about politics and world affairs.

Australian ballot   A ballot printed by the state, which the voter marks and then places in a ballot box. Also called a **secret ballot.**

Bad tendency doctrine   Interpretation of the First Amendment that would permit legislatures to make illegal speech that can reasonably be said to have a tendency to cause people to engage in illegal action.

Bicameralism   Two-house legislature; form for 49 of the states as well as for the U.S. Congress.

Bill of attainder   Legislative act that inflicts punishment, including deprivation of property without judicial trial, on named individuals or members of a specified group.

Bipartisanship   A policy that emphasizes cooperation and a united front between the major political parties, especially on sensitive foreign policy issues.

Block grant   Broad grant of funds made by one level of government to another for prescribed activities—for example, health programs or crime prevention—with few strings attached.

Bureau   Generally, the largest subunit of a government department or agency.

Bureaucracy   Large private or public organizations that are hierarchical in structure, provide each employee with clearly defined responsibility, base actions and decisions on impersonal rules, and hire and promote employees based on skills and training.

Bureaucrat   Career government employee, normally one who gains office by appointment rather than election.

Capitalism   An economic system characterized by private property, competitive markets, economic incentives, and limited government involvement.

Caucus (legislative) or conference   Meeting of the members of a party in a chamber of legislature to select the party leadership in that chamber and to take party positions on pending legislative issues.

Caucus (local party)   Meeting of party members in a ward or town to choose party officials and/or candidates for public office and to decide platforms.

Centralists   Those who favor national rather than state or local action.

Charter   A city "constitution" that outlines the structure of city government, defines the authority of various officials, and provides for their selection.

Checks and balances   Constitutional grant of powers that enables each of the three branches of government—legislative, executive, and judicial—to stop some of the acts of the other branches. Ensures each branch a sufficient role in the actions of the others so that no one branch may dominate. The branches must work together if governmental business is to be performed.

Class action suit   Lawsuit brought by a person or group of persons on behalf of all persons similarly situated. The class may consist of a few persons or of thousands of persons. An example of a class action would be a suit by one person against an airline, alleging overcharges on behalf of that person and all others charged the same price for the same kind of flight.

Classical liberalism   A political philosophy that stresses the importance of the individual and of freedom, equality, private property, limited government, and popular consent.

Clayton Act   Act passed by Congress in 1914 that expanded governmental antitrust policy by outlawing specific abuses, such as charging different prices to different buyers in order to destroy a weaker competitor, granting rebates, making false statements about competitors and their products, buying up supplies to stifle competition, and bribing competitors' employees.

Clear and present danger doctrine   Interpretation of the First Amendment first announced by Justice Oliver Wendell Holmes. This doctrine would not let laws that directly or indirectly restrict freedom of speech be applied unless the particular speech, article, or book in question presents a clear and present danger that it will lead to acts that the government may make illegal.

Closed primary   A primary in which only persons registered in the party holding the primary may vote.

Closed rule   A procedural rule in the House of Representatives that prohibits any amendments to bills or provides that only members of the committee reporting the bill may offer amendments.

Closed shop   A company in which new employees and retained employees must be union members in good standing.

Cloture   Procedure for terminating debate (especially filibusters) in the U.S. Senate.

Collective bargaining   Method whereby representatives of the union and the employer determine wages, hours, and other conditions of employment through direct negotiation.

Commerce clause   The clause of the Constitution giving Congress the power to regulate all business activities that cross state lines or affect more than one state, and also prohibiting states from unduly burdening or discriminating against the business activities of other nations or states.

Common law   Body of judge-made law developed as judges decided cases; part of the English and American systems of justice.

Comparable worth   The idea that jobs should be paid at the same rate if they require comparable skills and contributions. Advocated by those who believe jobs traditionally dominated by women—nurses, secretaries, and elementary school teachers, for example—are held down in wage rates compared to equivalent type jobs traditionally dominated by men—plumbers and janitors, for example—because of discrimination and role stereotyping.

Concurrent powers   Powers the Constitution gives to both the national and state governments, such as the power to levy taxes.

Concurring opinion   An opinion in which a judge explains why he or she agrees with the majority opinion but differs on the reasoning.

Confederation   Government created when nation-states, by compact, create a new central government and limit its powers, especially the power to regulate the conduct of individuals directly.

Conference committee   Committee appointed by the presiding officers of each house of the legislature to adjust differences on a particular bill. The report of the conference committee back to each chamber cannot be amended but must be accepted or rejected as it stands.

Conglomerate   Firm that owns businesses in many unrelated industries.

Connecticut Compromise   Agreement by delegates to the Constitutional Convention to give each state two senators, regardless of population. This would offset the decision to allocate representatives in the House of Representatives according to population.

Conservatism   Philosophical approach to the role of government that generally favors local or state governmental action over federal governmental action. Both Barry Goldwater in 1964 and Ronald Reagan in the 1980s were major proponents of this approach.

Conservative coalition   A coalition in Congress of Republicans and southern Democrats who often vote together, at least in recent years, especially on social policy and welfare legislation.

Constitutional Convention   The convention in Philadelphia in 1787 (May 25–September 17) that framed the Constitution of the United States. It invented the presidency, electoral college, federalism, and separation of powers—features that are still the central elements of American government. This draft had to be approved by nine states before it was ratified in 1788.

Constitutional democracy   A government that enforces recognized limits on those who govern and allows the voice of the people to be heard through free and fair elections.

Constitutionalism   The set of arrangements and processes—checks and balances, federalism, separation of powers, rule of law, due process, and a bill of rights—that disperses and limits the power of government officials. Constitutionalism provides for the granting as well as restraining of powers and seeks to ensure that a government's leaders and representatives are accountable to the citizens.

Continuing resolution   A bill passed by Congress and the president that allows the federal government to continue paying its bills until a new budget is passed.

Convention   See Party convention.

Cross-cutting cleavages   Divisions within society that make groups more heterogeneous or different.

Crossover voting   A member of one party voting for a candidate of another party. Open primaries encourage crossover voting and may result in a situation in which nonparty members determine the party's nominee for a particular office.

Cross-pressure   A pressure that pulls an individual in different directions, often related to conflicting racial, religious, ethnic, union, or other group values.

Custom   Practices of nongovernmental institutions, such as political parties or the electorate, not specified in the Constitution.

De facto segregation   Racial segregation that results not from governmental practices or pressures but from social customs or personal choice, including residential housing patterns.

De jure segregation   Racial segregation that results from governmental actions. See also **Jim Crow laws**.

Dealignment   Dramatic change in the composition of the electorate or its partisan preferences that points to a rejection of both major parties and a move to Independent status.

Decentralists   Those who favor state or local action rather than national action.

Defendant   In a civil action, the party defending himself or herself against charges brought by the plaintiff; in a criminal action, the person charged with the offense.

Deficit   The difference between the revenues raised from sources of income other than borrowing and the expenditure of government, including paying the interest on past borrowing.

Deficit spending   Spending by increasing the debt.

Delegate   A view of the role of a member of a legislature which holds that, as delegates, legislators should represent the views of constituents even when personally holding different views.

Demagogue   Leader who gains power by means of impassioned appeals to the prejudices and emotions of the masses.

Democracy   Government by the people, either directly or indirectly, with free and frequent elections.

Demographics   The study of the characteristics of populations.

Deregulation   Efforts to reduce or eliminate governmental controls, rules, or regulation of economic activity.

Direct democracy   A government in which citizens come together to discuss and pass laws and select rulers. May also refer to the initiative, referendum, and recall.

Direct primary   Election open to all members of the party in which voters choose the persons who will be the party's nominees in the general election.

Discharge petition   Petition that, if signed by a majority of the members of the House of Representatives, will pry a bill from committee and bring it to the floor for consideration.

Dissenting opinion   An opinion in which a judge explains why he or she disagrees with the decision of the majority.

Distribution   Proportion of the population that holds a particular opinion.

Divided government   Governance divided between the parties, as when one controls the White House and the other Congress.

Double jeopardy   Trial or punishment for the *same* crime by the *same* government. Such a practice is forbidden by the Constitution.

Due process clauses   Clauses in the Fifth and Fourteenth Amendments that state that the national (Fifth) and the state (Fourteenth) governments shall not deprive any person of life, liberty, or property without due process of law.

Electoral college   The gathering in each state of electors from that state who formally cast their ballots for their parties' candidates for president and vice-president. The electoral college is largely a formality.

Eminent domain   Power of governments to take private property for public use. The Constitution requires governments to provide just compensation for property so taken.

Entitlements or Entitlement programs   Programs such as Social Security, Aid to Families with Dependent Children, Medicare, and unemployment insurance to which qualified citizens are "entitled" by definitions in national legislation.

Equal protection clause   Clause in the Fourteenth Amendment that forbids any state to deny to any person within its jurisdiction the equal protection of the laws. By interpretation, the Fifth Amendment imposes the same limitation on the national government. This is the major constitutional restraint on the power of governments to discriminate against persons because of race, national origin, or sex.

Equal-time requirement   Requirement of Congress and Federal Communications Commission that radio and television licensees must give opposing candidates for public office equal air time.

Establishment clause   Clause in the First Amendment that states that Congress shall make no law respecting an establishment of religion. By interpretation, the Fourteenth Amendment imposes the same limitation on state legislatures. It has been interpreted by the

Supreme Court to forbid governmental support to any or all religions.

Ethnicity Identification with a group based upon national origin, religion, language, and often race.

Ethnocentrism A selective perception based on individual background, attitudes, and biases that leads one to believe in the superiority of one's nation or ethnic group.

Excise tax Consumer tax on a specific kind of merchandise, such as tobacco.

Exclusionary rule Rule that evidence unconstitutionally obtained cannot be used in a criminal trial as part of the government's main case against persons from whom it was seized.

Executive Office of the President Cluster of staff agencies created by the Reorganization Act of 1939 to help the president. Currently the Executive Office includes an Office of Management and Budget, the Council of Economic Advisers, the National Security Council, and a number of specialized offices.

Executive privilege The claim by presidents that they have the discretion to decide that the national interest will be better served if certain information is withheld from the public, including the courts and Congress. In *United States v Nixon* the Supreme Court ruled that even though presidents are entitled to the privilege, the privilege is not unlimited, and its extent is subject to judicial determination.

Ex post facto law Retroactive criminal law that works to the disadvantage of an individual.

Express powers Powers specifically granted to one of the branches of the national government by the Constitution.

Extradition Legal process whereby an alleged criminal offender is surrendered by the officials of one state to officials of the state in which the crime is alleged to have been committed.

Faction What we call "interest groups" today, James Madison called factions. He also thought of political parties as factions.

Fairness doctrine Doctrine interpreted by the Federal Communications Commission that imposed on radio and television licensees an obligation to ensure that differing viewpoints were presented about controversial issues or persons. Repealed by the FCC in 1987.

Federal mandate A requirement imposed by the federal government as a condition of receipt of federal funds.

Federal Reserve System The private-public banking regulatory system created by Congress in 1913 to establish banking practices and regulate currency in circulation and the amount of credit available. It is comprised of 12 regional banks, and its major responsibilities are supervised by a seven-member presidentially appointed Federal Reserve Board of Governors in Washington, D.C.

Federalism Constitutional arrangement whereby power is divided by a constitution between a national government and constituent governments, called states in the United States. The national and the constituent governments both exercise direct authority over individuals.

The Federalist Series of essays favoring the new Constitution, written by Alexander Hamilton, John Jay, and James Madison in 1787 and 1788, during the debate over ratification.

Federalists Persons who supported the Constitution before its ratification in 1787 to 1788. After ratification, a Federalist party developed under the leadership of Alexander Hamilton, George Washington's first secretary of the treasury. Federalists like John Adams and John Marshall generally favored a strong central government and a fiscal policy of assuming state debts and establishing a national bank.

Fighting words Words that by their very nature inflict injury upon those to whom they are addressed or cause acts of violence by them.

Filibuster Holding the floor of the U.S. Senate to delay proceedings and thereby prevent a vote on a controversial issue.

Fiscal policy Government policy that attempts to manage the economy by controlling taxing and spending.

Franchise The right to vote.

Free exercise clause Clause in the First Amendment that states that Congress shall make no law prohibiting the free exercise of religion; extended by the Fourteenth Amendment as a limit on the states.

Free rider An individual who does not join an interest group representing his or her interests, yet receives the benefit of the influence the group achieves.

Full faith and credit clause Clause in the Constitution requiring each state to recognize the civil judgments rendered by the courts of the other states and to accept their public records and acts as valid documents.

Gender gap The difference between the political opinions or political behavior of men and women.

Gerrymandering Drawing an election district in such a way that one party or group has a distinct advantage. The strategy is to provide a close but safe margin in numerous districts while concentrating (and hence wasting) the opposition's vote in a few districts.

Government corporation Cross between a business corporation and a government agency, created to secure greater freedom of action and flexibility for a particular program.

Grand jury A jury comprising 12 to 23 persons who, in private, hear evidence presented by the government to determine whether persons shall be required to stand trial. If the jury believes there is sufficient evidence that a crime was committed, it issues an indictment.

Gross domestic product (GDP) An estimate of the total output of all economic activity in the nation, including goods and services.

Gross national product (GNP) The monetary values of all goods and services in the nation in a given year.

Habeas corpus See Writ of habeas corpus.

Hatch Act Federal statute barring federal employees from active participation in certain kinds of politics and protecting them from being fired on partisan grounds.

Honeymoon A period at the beginning of a new president's term in which the president enjoys generally positive relations with the press and Congress, usually lasting about six months.

Ideology One's basic beliefs about power, political values, and the role of government—beliefs that arise out of educational, economic, and social conditions and experiences.

Impeachment Formal accusation against a public official and the first step in removal from office.

Implied powers Powers given to Congress by the Constitution that allow Congress to do whatever is necessary and proper in order to carry out one of the express powers or any combination of them.

Impoundment Presidential refusal to allow an agency to spend funds authorized and appropriated by Congress.

Independent agency A government agency that is not part of the legislative, executive, or judicial branch, such as the Interstate Commerce Commission. The term also describes a nonregulatory agency that is not part of a cabinet department, such as the National Aeronautics and Space Administration. Members of independent agencies are appointed by the president, confirmed by the Senate, and removable only for some specific "cause." Also called an **independent regulatory agency.**

Inherent powers Those powers of the national government in the field of foreign affairs that the Supreme Court has declared do not depend upon constitutional grants but rather grow out of the very existence of the national government.

Initiative Procedure whereby a certain number of voters may, by petition, propose a law or constitutional amendment and get it submitted to the people for a vote. Initiatives may be direct (if the proposed law is voted on directly by the people) or indirect (if the proposal is submitted first to the legislature and then to the people, if the legislature rejects it).

Intensity How strongly people feel about an issue or candidate.

Interest group A collection of people who share some common interest or attitude and seek to influence government for specific ends. Interest groups usually work within the framework of government and employ tactics such as lobbying to achieve their goals.

Interested money Financial contributions made by persons or groups in the hopes of influencing the outcome of an election and subsequently influencing policy.

Interstate compacts Agreements among the states. The Constitution requires that most such agreements be approved by Congress.

Iron triangle A mutually supporting relationship among interest groups, congressional committees or subcommittees, and government agencies that share a common policy concern. Also called **Issue network**.

Item veto Authority given to the president and most governors to veto parts of a legislative spending bill without having to veto the entire bill.

Jim Crow laws Laws that required public facilities and places of public accommodation, including those privately owned and operated, to be segregated by race.

Joint committee Committee composed of members of both houses of a legislature. Such committees are intended to speed up legislative action. Some oversee institutions such as the Library of Congress or conduct congressional investigations.

Judicial activism Philosophy proposing that judges cannot decide cases strictly by applying the literal words of the Constitution or by discerning the intention of the framers, but that they could and should openly recognize that judicial decision making is choosing among conflicting values. Judges should so interpret the Constitution as to keep it reflecting the current values of the American people.

Judicial restraint Philosophy proposing that, in deciding cases, judges should declare unconstitutional only those legislative acions and executive actions that clearly violate the words of the Constitution or the intent of the framers and that constitutional changes should be left to the formal amendatory process.

Judicial review The power of a court to refuse to enforce a law or government regulation that in the opinion of the judges conflicts with the Constitution. This authority was spelled out by Chief Justice John Marshall in *Marbury v Madison* (1803).

Jurisdictional strike Strike arising from disputes between unions over whose members should perform a particular task.

Justiciable dispute A dispute that grows out of an actual case and is capable of settlement by legal methods. Those constitutional disputes that are political are not justiciable.

Keynesian economics Economic theories based on the principles advocated by John Maynard Keynes: increasing government spending during business slumps and curbing spending during booms.

Labor injunction Court order forbidding specific individuals or groups from performing certain acts, such as striking, that the court considers harmful to the rights and property of an employer or community.

Laissez faire Doctrine opposing governmental interference in economic affairs beyond what is necessary to protect life and property.

Lame duck A politician in office who cannot, or has announced that he or she will not, run again.

Latency Political opinions that exist only as a potential.

Libel Written defamation of another person. Especially in the case of public officials and public figures, the constitutional tests designed to restrict libel actions are very rigid.

Liberalism Philosophical approach to the role of government that generally favors the positive uses of government to bring about justice and equality of opportunity.

Libertarianism Philosophical approach to the role of government that cherishes individual liberty and favors as limited a government as

possible. Libertarians believe in free-market economics and a noninterventionist foreign policy.

Literacy test Requirement imposed by some states that prospective voters must prove they understand national and state laws. Now illegal, such tests were used too disqualify blacks from voting in the South.

Lobby/lobbying Activities aimed at influencing public officials, especially legislators, and the policies they enact. This is, of course, part of the citizen's right to petition the government.

Lobbyist Person who is employed by and acts for an organized interest group or corporation to try to influence policy decisions and positions in the executive and legislative branches.

Log rolling Mutual aid and vote trading among legislators.

Majority leader Legislative position held by an important party member selected by the majority party in caucus or conference. The majority leader helps frame party strategy and tries to keep the membership in line. In the U.S. Senate the majority leader (in consultation with the minority leader) determines the agenda and has strong influence in committee selection.

Manifest destiny A notion held by many nineteenth-century Americans that the United States was destined to rule the continent, from the Atlantic to the Pacific oceans.

Mass media Means of communication that reach the mass public. The mass media include newspapers and magazines, radio and television (cable and satellite), and films, recordings, and books.

Medicaid Federal program that provides medical benefits for low-income persons.

Medicare National health insurance program for the elderly and disabled.

Merit system A system of public employment in which selection and promotion depend on demonstrated performance rather than on political patronage.

Military-industrial complex Alleged alliance between top military and industrial leaders who have a common interest in arms production.

Minor party Small political party, more persistent than a third party, and generally composed of ideologues on the right or left.

Minority leader Party leader in each house of a legislature, elected by the minority party as spokesperson for the opposition.

Monetary policy Government policy that attempts to manage the economy by controlling the money supply.

Monopoly Domination of an industry by one company.

Most-favored nation Trade policy whereby countries give each other the same favorable treatment given to other trade partners.

Movement A large body of people united around a central idea whose goal is to change attitudes or institutions, not only policies. Movements tend to feel "left out" of government and may sometimes resort to extreme measures to advance their cause.

National Labor Relations Act (1935) Guarantees workers the right to organize and bargain collectively with management. Also known as the **Wagner Act**.

National party convention The national meeting of delegates elected in primaries, caucuses, or state conventions who assemble once every four years for the purpose of nominating candidates for president and vice-president, ratifying the party platform, electing officers, and adopting rules.

National Security Council Planning and advisory board that confers with the president on matters relating to national security. Permanent members include the president, vice-president, secretary of state, secretary of defense, and the chair of the joint chiefs of staff.

National supremacy Constitutional doctrine that whenever conflict occurs between the constitutionally authorized actions of the national government and those of a state or local government, the actions of the national government take priority.

Nationalism A consciousness of the nation-state and of belonging to that entity.

Natural law God or nature's law that defines right from wrong and is higher than human law.

Natural rights Rights of all citizens to dignity and worth; also called **human rights**.

Naturalization Process by which persons acquire citizenship in a country other than the nation of their birth.

Necessary and proper clause Clause of the Constitution setting forth the implied powers of Congress. It states that Congress, in addition to its express powers, has the power to make all laws necessary and proper for carrying out all powers vested by the Constitution in the national government.

Neoconservativism A pragmatic form of traditional liberalism that accepts some of the welfare state but believes affirmative action has gone too far. Neoconservatives also support military spending to ensure that the United States can defend its global interests.

Neoliberalism A political ideology that is left-of-center yet distrustful or skeptical of large bureaucracies and traditional welfare strategies. Neoliberals believe in relying on the marketplace and favor middle-of-the-road tax and defense policies.

New Jersey Plan Plan presented by William Paterson of New Jersey at the Constitutional Convention as a counterproposal to the Virginia Plan. The New Jersey Plan proposed only modifications in the Articles of Confederation and provided for a confederation built around powerful state governments.

New judicial federalism The practice of some state courts of using the bill of rights in their state constitutions to provide more protection for some rights than is provided by Supreme Court interpretation of the Bill of Rights in the Constitution.

North American Free Trade Agreement (NAFTA) Agreement signed by the United States, Canada, and Mexico in 1992 to form the largest free-trade zone in the world.

Obscenity Quality or state of a work that taken as a whole appeals to a prurient interest in sex by depicting sexual conduct as specifically defined by legislation or judicial interpretation in a patently offensive way and that lacks serious literary, artistic, political, or scientific value.

Office block ballot Method of voting in which all candidates are listed under the office for which they are running. Sometimes called the **Massachusetts ballot**.

Office of Management and Budget (OMB) Presidential staff agency that serves as a clearinghouse for budgetary requests and management improvements. It advises the president in detail about hundreds of government agencies—how much money they should be allotted in the budget and what kind of job they are doing—and it seeks to improve the planning, management, and statistical work of the agencies.

Oligopoly Situation in which a few firms dominate an industry.

Open primary A primary in which any voter, regardless of party, can vote.

Open rule A procedural rule in the House of Representatives that permits floor amendments within the overall time allocated to the bill.

Open shop Labor arrangement in which union membership cannot be required as a condition of employment.

Original jurisdiction The authority of a trial court to hear a case "in the first instance."

Override An action by Congress to try to reverse a presidential veto of legislation by a two-thirds vote in both chambers.

Partisan identification Sense of identification with a political party; a longstanding preference for one party.

Party column ballot Method of voting in which all candidates are listed under their party designations, making it easy for the voters to cast votes for all the candidates of one party. Sometimes called the **Indiana ballot**.

Party convention A meeting of party delegates to pass on matters of policy and in some cases to select party candidates for public office. Conventions are held on county, state, and national levels.

Party identification Subjective affiliation with a political party, usually acquired in childhood.

Party platform The official statement of party policy.

Party registration The act of declaring party affiliation, in some states required when one registers to vote.

Patronage Dispensing government jobs to persons who belong to the winning political party. Also called **spoils system.**

Petit jury The jury for the trial of a civil or criminal action.

Plea bargaining Negotiations between prosecutor and defendant aimed at getting the defendant to plead guilty in return for the prosecutor's agreeing to reduce the seriousness of the crime for which the defendant will be convicted.

Pocket veto Special veto power exercised by a chief executive after a legislative body has adjourned. Bills that a chief executive does not sign within ten days of adjournment do not become law and are not returned to the chamber of origin for a possible override. In effect, by such an action, a governor or president "puts the bill in his or her pocket," and the bill thus dies.

Police powers Powers of a government to regulate persons and property in order to promote the public health, welfare, safety, and morals. In the United States, the states, but not the national government, have such general police power.

Political action committee (PAC) The political arm of a business, labor, trade association, or other interest group that is legally entitled to raise money on a voluntary basis from members, stockholders, or employees in order to contribute to favored candidates or political parties.

Political culture Political beliefs, values, and norms most citizens share concerning the relationship of citizens to government and to one another.

Political question A dispute that requires knowledge of a nonlegal character or the use of techniques not suitable for a court or that are explicitly addressed by the Constitution to Congress or the president. Judges refuse to answer constitutional questions that they declare are political.

Political party An organization that seeks political power by electing people to office so that its positions and philosophy become public policy.

Political socialization The process by which we develop our political attitudes, values, and beliefs.

Poll tax Payment by a person, formerly required in some states, as a condition for voting.

Popular consent The idea that a just government must derive its powers from the consent of the people.

Populists Adherents of a movement and political party of the 1880s and 1890s. Their geographical base was rural—in the Midwest, South, and Southwest especially. Waging "reformist" efforts against the banks, railroads, and other establishments, populists raised issues that influenced the Progressive movement and the Democratic party after 1892.

Pork-barrel Government benefits or programs that help the economy of a member's district—as in "bringing home the bacon."

Preemption The right of a federal law or regulation to preclude enforcement of a state or local law or regulation.

Preferred position doctrine Interpretation of the First Amendment that holds that no law restricting expression is constitutional unless the government can demonstrate convincingly to a court that the law is absolutely necessary to prevent serious injury to the public well-being.

President pro tempore Officer of the U.S. Senate chosen from the ranks—often a junior member of the majority party—who serves as president of the Senate in the absence of the vice-president.

Prior restraint Restraint imposed prior to a speech's being made, a newspaper's being published, or a motion picture's being shown. The restraint may be of various kinds—for example, a requirement that a license be granted or that the approval of a censorship board be given.

Privatization The contracting out to the "for profit" private sector of services that are typically provided by public organizations. Trash collection, ambulance, and fire protection services have been the most common privatizations of public services. The objectives are to obtain the public services at lower costs, and sometimes to shrink the public bureaucracy to encourage additional efficiencies.

Procedural due process Constitutional requirement that governments proceed by proper methods.

Progressive income tax A tax whereby upper-income citizens pay a larger fraction of their income in taxes than do lower-income citizens.

Progressives Adherents of a "good government" movement in the first two decades of this century, who advocated measures that would open up the system and weaken party bosses. They favored nonpartisan elections, participatory primaries, and direct elections of senators.

Property rights The rights of an individual to own, use, rent, invest in, buy, and sell property.

Proportional representation An election system in which each party running receives the proportion of legislative seats corresponding to its proportion of the vote.

Protectionism The erecting of tariff barriers to protect domestic industry.

Public defender Public official whose job is to provide legal assistance to those persons accused of crimes who are unable to hire their own attorneys.

Public goods Services or commodities that individuals benefit from but that cannot be separately sold or given to individuals. Examples are clean air, national defense, and public safety.

Public opinion The distribution within a population of individual views about a given issue, candidate, or institution.

Public policy The substance of what government does. More generally, public policy reflects the intentions of a government and the subsequent actions to implement laws and other decisions of governmental bodies.

Quasi-legislative and quasi-judicial Phrase coined by the Supreme Court to permit noncourt and nonlegislative bodies to decide disputes and make rules. Decisions must, however, be subject to court review, and rules must be within the general guidelines established by the legislature.

Race A grouping of human beings with common characteristics presumed to be transmitted genetically. In the United States, race issues focus on African Americans, Asian Americans, and sometimes Hispanics, although, technically, Hispanics can be of any race.

Racial gerrymandering The drawing of election districts so as to ensure that members of a certain race are a minority in all districts.

Random sampling In public opinion polls creating a representative sample through random selection—for example, by shuffling housing tracts and interviewing individuals in every fifth, tenth, or fifteenth house.

Reaganomics Ronald Reagan's version of supply-side economics, which held that by cutting taxes and government spending in nondefense areas the economy would be stimulated enough to fund Reagan's other priority, national defense.

Realignment A dramatic change in the composition of the electorate or its partisan preferences, or both.

Recall Election in certain states or communities to determine whether an official should be removed from office before the end of his or her term. A certain number of voters, typically 25 percent of those who voted in the last election, must petition to hold a recall election.

Recidivist One who habitually relapses into crime.

Redistricting The redrawing of congressional and other legislative district lines following the census. Also called **reapportionment**.

Referendum Practice of submitting to popular vote measures passed by the legislature or proposed by initiative. Use of the referendum may be required or optional.

Regulation Governmental order having the force of law and designed to control or govern the behavior of a business, union, or similar organizations and individuals. Governmental regulation seeks to alter the natural workings of the open market to achieve some desired goal.

Regulatory agency, board, or commission Government agency responsible for enforcing particular statutes. Generally such an agency has quasi-legislative and quasi-judicial functions as well as executive powers.

Regulatory taking Government regulation of property so extensive that government is deemed to have taken the property and thus exercised the power of eminent domain, for which it must compensate the property owners.

Reinforcing cleavages Divisions within society that reinforce one another, making groups more homogeneous or similar.

Republic Form of government that derives its powers directly or indirectly from the people. Those chosen to govern are accountable, directly or indirectly, to those whom they govern. In contrast to a direct democracy, in which the people make rules directly, in a republic the people select representatives who make the rules. Also called **representative democracy**.

Restrictive covenant A restriction in a deed limiting to whom property may be sold and how it may be used.

Revenue sharing Program whereby federal funds are provided to state and local governments to be spent largely at the discretion of the receiving governments, subject to few and very general conditions.

Revolving door The employment cycle in which individuals work, in turn, for governmental agencies regulating interests and then for businesses representing those interests.

Rider A provision that might not have much chance to pass on its own merits but is attached to another bill, often unrelated, to secure its legislative passage. Often bills that have little to do with spending money are attached as riders to appropriations bills, because appropriations bills are rarely defeated or vetoed.

Right-to-work law Provision in state laws that prohibits arrangements between a union and an employer requiring membership in a union as a condition for getting or keeping a job.

Safe seat Electoral office, usually in legislature, for which the party or the incumbent is so strong that reelection is almost taken for granted.

Salience Extent to which people believe issues are relevant.

Search warrant A warrant that authorizes the police to search a particular place or person. A search warrant must specify the place to be searched and the objects to be seized in order to protect people from unreasonable government intrusion.

Secondary boycott Efforts by a union involved in a dispute with an employer to place pressure on a third party, who—in response to such pressure—might put pressure on the original offending employer. Such boycotts are forbidden by the 1947 Taft-Hartley Act.

Sedition Attempting to overthrow the government by force or to interrupt its activities by violence.

Select or special committee A congressional committee created for a specific purpose, sometimes to conduct an investigation.

Selective exposure Screening out messages that do not conform to one's own biases.

Selective incorporation The doctrine that some, but not all, provisions of the Bill of Rights should be included within the Fourteenth Amendment as a limitation on state and local governments.

Selective perception Individuals perceiving what they want to in media messages and disregarding the rest.

Senatorial courtesy Presidential custom of submitting the names of prospective appointees for approval to senators from the states in which the appointees reside.

Seniority rule A practice in legislatures that assigns the chair of a committee or subcommittee to the member of the majority party who has had the longest continuous service on the committee.

Separation of powers Constitutional division of power among legislative, executive, and judicial branches. The legislative branch is assigned the power to make laws; the executive is charged with the power to apply the laws; and the judiciary receives the power to interpret laws.

Shays's Rebellion Rural rebellion in 1786–87 protesting mortgage foreclosures in western Massachusetts. Led by Daniel Shays, it promoted conservative support for a stronger national government.

Sherman Antitrust Act Act passed by Congress in 1890 that attempted to foster competition and stop the growth of private monopolies by making it unlawful to form a combination that acted to restrain trade.

Socialism Philosophical approach to the role of government that favors national planning and public ownership of the means of production and exchange.

Social Security A combination of entitlement programs paid for by employer and employee taxes. Includes retirement benefits, health insurance, and support for disabled workers and children of deceased or disabled workers.

Socioeconomic status (SES) A measure of one's standing that combines in one index such factors as education, income, and occupation.

Soft money Money contributed to a state or local political party for nonfederal uses, such as voter registration drives and party mailings, that does not have to be reported under the Federal Election Campaign Act and is often not reported because of tax disclosure laws at that level.

Speaker The presiding officer in the House of Representatives, formally elected by the House but actually selected by the majority party. The Speaker's powers include referring legislation to committees, making appointments to the House Rules Committee, recognizing members who wish to speak, ruling on questions of parliamentary procedure, and appointing special conference committees. There is a similar office in state legislatures.

Split ticket Voting for some of one party's candidates and some candidates from other political parties.

Spoils system Rewarding those who support victorious candidates with profitable contracts or jobs in government; in the nineteenth century often an important incentive for political participation.

Stare decisis The rule of precedent, whereby a rule or law contained in a judicial decision is commonly viewed as binding on judges whenever the same question is presented.

State delegation The senators and representatives from the same state, who often help each other secure choice committee assignments, work to promote each other in leadership positions, and watch out for state interests.

Statism Belief in the rights of the state over those of the individual—the opposite of the American tradition that the individual is exalted above the state.

Straight ticket Voting for all of one party's candidates.

Substantive due process Constitutional requirement that governments act reasonably and that the substance of the laws themselves be fair and reasonable.

Sunset process Process that calls for the termination of a program after a certain number of years, often six or seven, unless it is certified to be doing what it was intended to do. The word comes from the expression that "the sun should set" on programs that have outlived their usefulness.

Suspect class Racial or national origin classifications created by law and subject to careful judicial scrutiny. Suspect classifications are likely to be declared unconstitutional unless they can be justified by overwhelmingly desirable state purposes that can be achieved in no other way.

Taft-Hartley Act Act passed by Congress in 1947 that elaborates the terms of labor-management bargaining, the conditions under which strikes can occur, and related aspects of union organization. It worked to restrict some union activities.

Tariff Tax levied on imports to help protect a nation's industries, labor, or farmers from foreign competition. It can also be used merely to raise additional revenue.

Three-fifths compromise North-South agreement at the Constitutional Convention of 1787 to count only three-fifths of the slave population in determining direct taxation and apportionment in the House of Representatives.

Tort law Law, primarily judge made, dealing with damages to compensate people through a civil trial, for legal wrongs done to them, including injuries to person, reputation, or property.

Treason Carefully defined by the Constitution to consist only of levying war against the United States, adhering to its enemies, or giving the latter aid and comfort. No person can be convicted of treason unless the accused confesses in open court or unless two witnesses testify in court that they saw the acts of treason being committed.

Trustee A view of the function of a member of a legislature which holds that legislators may believe that they were sent to Washington or the state capitals to think and vote independently for the general welfare, and not as their constituents determine.

Trusts Monopolies that control goods and services, often in combinations that reduce competition.

Turnout The proportion of the voting-age public that votes.

Two-party system Electoral system in which two major political parties dominate.

Unicameralism, unicameral legislature One-house legislature. Nebraska and almost all cities use this form.

Union shop A company in which new employees must join the union within a stated period of time.

Unitary system or unitary government Government with power concentrated by the constitution in a central government; also an election system in which voters elect legislators who, in turn, elect the prime minister or head of state.

Usage Long-standing practices of Congress, the president, and the courts not specified in the Constitution.

Veto Rejection of proposed legislation by a president or governor.

Virginia Plan Proposal made at the Constitutional Convention by the Virginia delegation that provided for a strong legislature with representation in each house determined by wealth or population. It thus favored the large states.

Voter registration A system designed to reduce voter fraud such as multiple voting and to limit voting to those who have established eligibility by submitting the appropriate form.

Whip Party leader who is the liaison between the leadership and the rank-and-file in the legislature.

White primary Under the pretense that it was not governmental action, officials of the Democratic party in the South used to admit only white persons to its primaries. Candidates of the Democratic party were the only ones with any chance of winning in the following general election; blacks were thus excluded from the only election that counted. The white primary in all its various forms was declared unconstitutional by the Supreme Court in *Smith v Allwright* (1944).

Winner-take-all An electoral practice in which the candidate with the most votes wins. In American presidential elections, the winner of the popular vote in nearly all states receives all the electoral votes of the state.

Women's suffrage The right of women to vote; denied in federal elections in the United States before passage of the Nineteenth Amendment in 1920.

Writ of certiorari Writ used by the Supreme Court to review decisions of lower courts, federal and state, that are within the discretionary appellate jurisdiction of the Supreme Court. It is a formal device regularly used to bring a case up to the Court.

Writ of habeas corpus Court order requiring explanation to a judge why a prisoner is held in custody.

Writ of mandamus Court order directing an official to perform a nondiscretionary act as required by law.

NOTES

CHAPTER 1

1. For a major theoretical work on the principle of majority rule, see Robert A. Dahl, *Democracy and Its Critics* (Yale University Press, 1989).

2. James Madison, *The Federalist*, No. 51.

3. For a discussion of the importance for democracy of such overlapping group memberships, see David Truman's seminal work, *The Governmental Process*, 2d ed. (Knopf, 1971).

4. Robert A. Dahl, *A Preface to Democratic Theory* (University of Chicago Press, 1956), p. 132.

5. See the essays in Thomas E. Cronin, ed., *Inventing the American Presidency* (University Press of Kansas, 1989).

6. Charles A. Beard and Mary R. Beard, *A Basic History of the United States* (New Home Library, 1944), p. 136.

7. Herbert J. Storing, ed., abridgment by Murray Day, *The Anti-Federalist: Writings by the Opponents of the Constitution* (University of Chicago Press, 1985).

8. Mercy Warren, quoted in Pauline Maier, *The Old Revolutionaries* (Knopf, 1980), p. 284.

9. On the role of the promised bill of rights amendments in the ratifications of the Constitution, see Leonard W. Levy, *Constitutional Opinions* (Oxford University Press, 1986), chap. 6.

10. Herbert Storing, "The Constitution and the Bill of Rights," in *Essays on the Constitution of the United States*, ed. M. Judd Harmon (Kennikat Press, 1978), pp.36–37, points out that many Antifederalists remained unsatisfied with the Bill of Rights.

11. Max Lerner, *Ideas for the Ice Age* (Viking, 1991), pp. 241–42. See also "The American Public's Knowledge of the U.S. Constitution" (Hearst Corporation, 1987).

12. Sanford Levinson, *Constitutional Faith* (Princeton University Press, 1988), pp. 9–52.

13. Thomas Jefferson, quoted in Alpheus T. Mason, *The Supreme Court: Palladium of Freedom* (University of Michigan Press, 1962), p. 10.

14. Richard E. Neustadt, *Presidential Power* (Free Press, 1990), p. 29.

15. Edward S. Corwin, "The Constitution as Instrument and as Symbol," *American Political Science Review* (December 1936), p. 1078. J. M. Sosin argues that these earlier precedents do not support the view that judicial review was "in the air," in *The Aristocracy of the Long Robe: The Origins of Judicial Review in America* (Greenwood Press, 1989).

16. 1 Cranch 137 (1803).

17. Dumas Malone, *Jefferson the President: First Term, 1801–1805* (Little, Brown, 1970), p. 145.

18. *Dred Scott v Sandford*, 19 Howard 393 (1857).

19. Robert Lowry Clinton, *Marbury v. Madison and Judicial Review* (University Press of Kansas, 1989), pp. 4–42.

20. J. W. Peltason, *Federal Courts in the Political Process* (Random House, 1955).

21. James L. Sundquist, "Needed: A Political Theory for the New Era of Coalition Government in the United States," *Political Science Quarterly* (Winter 1988–89), pp. 613–35; Robert A. Godwin and Art Kaufman, eds., *Separation of Powers: Does It Still Work?* (AEI Press, 1986).

22. Charles O. Jones, "The Separate Presidency," in *The New American Political System*, ed. Anthony King, 2d ed. (AEI Press, 1990), p. 3.

23. Morris P. Fiorina, "An Era of Divided Government," *Political Science Quarterly* 107, no. 3 (1992), p. 407.

24. David R. Mayhew, *Divided We Govern: Party Control, Lawmaking, and Investigations, 1946–1990* (Yale University Press, 1991), p. 4. See also James A. Thurber, ed., *Divided Democracy: Presidents and Congress in Cooperation and Conflict* (Congressional Quarterly, 1991).

25. Charles O. Jones, *Separate But Equal Branches: Congress and the Presidency* (Chatham House, 1995).

26. See Eleanore Bushnell, *Crimes, Follies, and Misfortunes: The Federal Impeachment Trials* (University of Illinois Press, 1992).

27. *Nixon v United States*, 506 US 224 (1993).

28. John R. Labovitz, *Presidential Impeachment* (Yale University Press, 1978).

29. Neustadt, *Presidential Power*, pp. 180–81.

30. Jones, *Separate But Equal Branches*, p. viii.

31. Sanford Levinson, ed., *The Theory and Practice of Constitutional Amendment* (Princeton University Press, 1995).

32. For a debate among scholars about whether or not Article V is the only way to amend formally the Constitution, see Sanford Levinson ed., *Responding to Imperfection: The Theory and Practice of Constitutional Amendment* (Princeton University Press, 1995).

33. See Committee on the Constitutional System, *A Bicentennial Analysis of the American Political Structure: Report and Recommendations of the Committee on the Constitutional System* (1987), for recommendations of a committee co-chaired by Senators Nancy L. Kassebaum, C. Douglas Dillon, and Lloyd Cutler. For critical comments, see Mark P. Petracca, "To Right What the Constitution Has Wrought or to Wrong What Is Right," presented at the annual meeting of the American Political Science Association, Washington, D.C., 1988.

34. Ann Stuart Diamond, "A Convention for Proposing Amendments: The Constitution's Other Method," *Publius* (Summer 1981), pp. 113–46; Wilbur Edel, "Amending the Constitution by Convention: Myths and Realities," *State Government* 55 (1982), pp. 51–56.

35. Russell L. Caplan, *Constitutional Brinkmanship: Amending the Constitution by National Convention* (Oxford University Press, 1988) p. x.

36. Ibid.

37. For an analysis of more than 40 proposals for structural change, see John R. Vile, *Rewriting the United States Constitution: An Examination of Proposals from Reconstruction to the Present* (Praeger, 1991), chap. 8.

38. Samuel S. Freedman and Pamela J. Naughton, *ERA: May a State Change Its Vote?* (Wayne State University Press, 1979).

39. Alan P. Grimes, *Democracy and Amendments to the Constitution* (Lexington Books, 1978), p. 95. See also Clement E. Vose, *Constitutional Change* (Lexington Books, 1972), pp. 342–44, which focuses on amendment politics in the case of women's suffrage, child labor, and prohibition.

40. *Dillon v Gloss*, 256 US 368 (1921).

41. William Van Alstyne, "What Do You Think About the Twenty-seventh Amendment?" *Constitutional Commentary* 10, no. 1 (University of Minnesota Law School, 1993), p. 15. Sanford Levinson, "Authorizing Constitutional Text: On the Purported Twenty-seventh Amendment," *Constitutional Commentary* 11 (1994), p. 101.

42. Gregory A. Caldeira, "Constitutional Change in America: Dynamics of Ratification under Article V," *Publius* (Fall 1985), p. 29.

CHAPTER 2

1. For background, see Samuel H. Beer, *To Make a Nation* (Harvard University Press, 1993).

2. Ronald L. Watts, "Canadian Federalism in the 1990's: Once More in Question," *Publius* 21 (Summer 1991), pp. 169–90; Robert C. Vipond, "The Canadian Constitutional Crisis: Who's Right on Rights?" *Intergovernmental Perspective* (Fall 1991), pp. 49–52; Robert C. Vipond, *Liberty and Community: Canadian Federalism and the Failure of the Constitution* (State University of New York Press, 1991).

3. John Darnton, "Nationalist Winds Pick Up Again in Scotland," *The New York Times*, October 17, 1995, p. A1.

4. James M. Perry, "After Years of Trying, GOP Is on the Threshold of Making History by Scaling Back Federalism," *The Wall Street Journal*, October 27, 1995, p. A 16.

5. *U.S. Terms Limits, Inc. v Thorton*, 131 L Ed 2d 881 (1995).

6. *United States v Lopez*, 131 L Ed 2d 626 (1995).

7. William H. Stewart, *Concepts of Federalism* (Center for the Study of Federalism and University Press of America, 1984). See also Edward L. Rubin and Malcolm Feeley, "Federalism: Some Notes on a National Neurosis," *UCLA Law Review* 41 (April 1994), pp. 903–952.

8. Daniel J. Elazar, *Exploring Federalism* (University of Alabama Press, 1987), p. 6.

9. See Beer, *To Make a Nation*.

10. William H. Riker, *The Development of American Federalism* (Academic Publishers, 1987), pp. 14–15. Riker contends that not only does federalism not guarantee freedom but that the framers of our federal system, as well as those of other nations, were not animated by considerations of safeguarding freedom but by practical considerations of preserving unity.

11. "Local Government's Deceptive Charms," *Business Week*, May 1, 1995, p. 166.

12. *Gibbons v Ogden*, 9 Wheaton 1 (1824).

13. *Heart of Atlanta Motel v United States*, 379 US 241 (1964).

14. *United States v. Lopez*, 131 L Ed 2d 626 (1995).

15. Nina Totenberg, quoted by Joseph Calve, "Anatomy of a Landmark," *The Recorder*, August 3, 1995, p. 10.

16. *US Steel Corporation v Multistate Tax Commission*, 434 US 452 (1978).

17. *Luther v Borden*, 7 How. 1 (1849).

18. *California v Superior Court of California*, 482 US 400 (1987).

19. *Puerto Rico v Brandstadt*, 483 US 219 (1987); Kenyon Bunch and Richard J. Hardy, "Continuity or Change in Interstate Extradition? Assessing *Puerto Rico v Brandstadt*," *Publius* (Winter 1991), pp.51–67. David C. Nice, "State Participation in Interstate Compacts," *Publius* 17 (Spring 1987), p. 70.

20. Advisory Commission on Intergovernmental Relations, *Restoring Confidence and Competence* (ACIR, 1981), p. 30.

21. Cynthia Cates Colella, "The Creation, Care and Feeding of the Leviathan: Who and What Makes Government Grow," *Intergovernmental Perspective* (Fall 1979), p. 9.

22. Aaron Wildavsky, "Bare Bones: Putting Flesh on the Skeleton of American Federalism," in Advisory Commission on Intergovernmental Relations, *The Future of Federalism in the 1980s* (ACIR, 1981), p. 79.

23. Paul E.Peterson, *The Price of Federalism* (Brookings Institution, 1995), p. 182.

24. Coined by Richard P. Nathan in testimony before the Senate Finance Committee, as quoted by Daniel Patrick Moynihan, "The Devolution Revolution," *The New York Times*, August 6, 1995, p. B15.

25. David Wessel, "Federal Deficit Shrank in Fiscal 1993 to Below Predictions of Two Agencies," *The Wall Street Journal*, October 29, 1993, p. A2.

26. Quoted by James M. Perry, "After Years of Trying, GOP Is on the Threshold of Making History by Scaling Back Federalism," *The Wall Street Journal*, October 27, 1995, p. A 16.

27. *U.S. Terms Limits, Inc. v Thorton*, 131 L Ed 2d 881 (1995).

28. *United States v Darby*, 312 US 100 (1941).

29. 4 Wheaton 316 (1819).

30. *Missouri v Jenkins*, 495 US 33 (1990). *Missouri v Jenkins*, 132 L Ed 263 (1995).

31. *Oklahoma City v Tuttle*, 471 US 808 (1985); *Mainer v Thiboutot*, 488 US (1980); *Monell v New York City Dept. of Social Welfare*, 436 US 658 (1978).

32. David Rapp, "The FEDS: Washington and the States: The Politics of Distrust," *Governing*, September 1, 1992, p. 67.

33. Joseph F. Zimmerman, "Federal Preemption under Reagan's New Federalism," *Publius* 21 (Winter 1991), pp. 7–28.

34. *Webster v Reproductive Health Services*, 492 US 490 (1989).

35. Oliver Wendell Holmes, Jr., *Collected Legal Papers* (Harcourt, 1920), pp. 295–96.

36. Robert Pear, "Shifting Where the Buck Stops," *The New York Times*, October 29, 1995, p. E2.

37. Peterson, *The Price of Federalism*, p. 127.

38. William Weld, "The States Won't Be Cruel," *The New York Times*, February 9, 1996, p. A15; *Congressional Quarterly* 54, August 3, 1996, pp. 2190–96.

39. Deil S. Wright, *Understanding Intergovernmental Relations*, 3d ed. (Brooks-Cole, 1982).

40. Harold Seidman and Robert Gilmour, *Politics, Position and Power*, rev. ed. (Oxford University Press, 1985).

41. John E. Chubb, "The Political Economy of Federalism," *American Political Science Review* 79 (December 1985), p. 1005.

42. Donald F. Kettl, *The Regulation of American Federalism* (Johns Hopkins University Press, 1987), pp. 154–55.

43. Norman Beckman, "Developments in Federal-State Relations," *The Book of the States: 1990–91* (Council of State Governments, 1990), p. 528.

44. Joseph F. Zimmerman, "Congressional Regulation of Subnational Governments," *PS: Political Science and Politics* 26 (June 1993), p. 180.

45. Ron Suskind, "Health-Care Reform May Seem Like a Bitter Pill to Localities Sick of Unfunded Federal Mandates," *The Wall Street Journal*, December 21, 1993.

46. *Congressional Quarterly*, April 15, 1995, p. 1087.

47. Zimmerman, "Congressional Regulation of Subnational Governments," p. 179.

48. Mel Dubnick and Alan Gitelson, "Nationalizing State Policies," in *The Nationalization of State Government*, ed. Jerome J. Hanus (D.C. Heath, 1981), pp. 56–57.

49. Timothy J. Conlan, "And the Beat Goes On: Intergovernmental Mandates and Preemption in an Era of Deregulation," *Publius* 21 (Summer 1991), p. 46.

50. John Kincaid, "American Federalism: The Third Century," *Annals of the American Academy of Political and Social Sciences* 509 (May 1990), p. 9. See also Zimmerman, "Federal Preemption under Reagan's New Federalism," pp. 7–28.

51. Thomas R. Dye, *American Federalism: Competition Among Governments* (Lexington Books, 1990), p. 199.

52. Ibid., p. 26.

53. Daniel J. Elazar, *American Federalism: A View from the States*, 3d ed. (Harper and Row, 1984), p. 241.

54. Debra A. Stewart, "State Initiatives in the Federal System: The Politics and Policy of Comparable Worth in 1984," *Publius* (Summer 1985), p. 83.

55. Martha M. Hamilton, "If You Want Something Done Right, Do It Yourself," *Washington Post National Weekly Edition*, September 5–11, 1988, p. 31.

56. Edward Felsenthal, "Firms Ask Congress to Pass Uniform Rules," *The Wall Street Journal*, May 10, 1993, p. B4.

57. John Herbers, "The New Federalism: Unplanned, Innovative, and Here to Stay," *Governing* 1 (October 1987), pp. 28–34.

58. Virginia I. Pastrel, "States' Rights, or Dereliction of Duty?" *Washington Post National Weekly Edition*, July 22–28, 1991, p. 23.

59. Beverly A. Cigler, "Challenges Facing Fiscal Federalism in the 1990s," *PS: Political Science and Politics* 26 (June 1993), p. 183; Bowman and Pagano, "State of American Federalism, 1989–1990," p. 7; U.S. General Accounting Office, *Federal-State-Local Relations: Trends of the Past Decade and Emerging Issues* (GAO, March 1990).

60. Pear, "Shifting Where the Buck Stops," p. E1.

61. Richard P. Nathan, "Federalism: The Great Composition," in *The New American Political System*, 2d ed., ed. Anthony King, (AEI Press, 1990), pp. 234–35.

62. Steven D. Gold, ed., *The Fiscal Crisis of the States* (Georgetown University Press, 1995), p. 29.

63. Brad C. Johnson, "Washington Should Look at the Damage It's Doing," *Washington Post National Weekly Edition*, July 22–28, 1991, p. 24; Susan A. MacManus, "Mad about Mandates: The Issue of Who Should Pay for What Resurfaces in the 1990s," *Publius* 21 (Summer 1991), pp. 59–75.

64. Cigler, "Challenges Facing Fiscal Federalism," p. 183.

65. Sam Howe Verhovek, "With Power Shift, State Lawmakers See New Demands," *The New York Times*, September 24, 1995, p. 12.
66. Steven D. Gold, director of the Center for the Study of the States at the State University of New York at Albany, quoted by Verhovek, "With Power Shift."
67. Luther Gulick, "Reorganization of the States," *Civil Engineering* (August 1933), pp. 420–21.

68. David E. Osborne, *Laboratories of Democracy* (Harvard Business School Press, 1988), p. 363.
69. Peterson, *The Price of Federalism*, p. 195.
70. John J. DiIulio, Jr., and Donald F. Kettl, *Fine Print: The Contract With America, Devolution, and the Administrative Realities of American Federalism* (Brookings Institution, 1995), p. 60.

CHAPTER 3

1. Craig Smith, *To Form a More Perfect Union: The Ratification of the Constitution and the Bill of Rights, 1788–1791* (University Press of America, 1993).
2. *Barron v Baltimore*, 7 Peters 243 (1833).
3. *Gitlow v New York*, 268 US 652 (1925).
4. Ibid.
5. *Richmond Newspapers Inc. v Virginia*, 448 US 555 (1980).
6. "Project Report: Toward an Activist Role for State Bills of Rights," *Harvard Civil Rights-Civil Liberties Law Review* 8 (March 1973), p. 274.
7. Stanley H. Friedelbaum, ed., *Human Rights in the States: New Directions in Constitutional Policy Making* (Greenwood, 1988); Shirley S. Abrahamson and Diane S. Gutmann, "The New Federalism: State Constitutions and State Courts," *Judicature* (August/September 1987), pp. 88–99; Stanley H. Friedelbaum, "Independent State Grounds: Contemporary Invitations to Judicial Activism," in *State Supreme Courts: Policy Makers in the Federal System*, eds. Mary Cornelia Porter and G. Alan Tarr (Greendwood, 1982), p. 46.
8. Peter J. Galie, "State Supreme Courts, Judicial Federalism and the Other Constitutions," *Judicature* (August/September 1987), pp. 100–110. See also Jeff Rosen, "Altered States: Liberals and Forgotten Constitutions," *The New Republican*, July 1, 1991, p. 19; Steven Pressman, "Protecting Rights in State Courts," Editorial Research Reports, *Congressional Quarterly* 1, no. 20 (1988), p. 277; Dorothy Beasley, "State Bills of Rights: Dead or Alive?" *Intergovernmental Perspective* (June 1989), pp. 13–17.
9. Rosen, "Altered States," p. 20.
10. Miranda S. Spivack, "How States' Rights Can Rectify the Wrongs of the Supreme Court," *The Los Angeles Times*, June 16, 1991, p. M2.
11. Barry Latzer, "The Hidden Conservatism of the State Court 'Revolution,' " *Judicature* (December 1990/January 1991), p. 193.
12. Ibid.
13. *Lemon v Kurtzman*, 403 US 602 (1971).
14. Dissenting in *Rosenberger v University of Virginia*, 132 L Ed 2d 700 (1995).
15. *Everson v Board of Education*, 333 U.S. 203 (1947); Leonard W. Levy, *The Establishment Clause: Religion and the First Amendment* (Macmillan, 1986).
16. *Walz v Tax Commission*, 397 U.S. 664 (1970); *Lemon v Kurtzman*, 403 U.S. 602 (1971). For a review of these and other cases, see John Swomley, *Religious Liberty and the Secular State: The Constitutional Context* (Prometheus Books, 1987).
17. See their dissenting opinions in *Rosenberger v University of Virginia*, 132 L Ed 2d 700 (1995).
18. *Capital Square Review Board v Pinette*, 132 L Ed 2d 650 (1995).
19. *Lynch v Donnelly* 465 U.S. 669 (1984). *Allegheny County v Greater Pittsburgh ACLU*, 492 US 573 (1989).
20. *Allegheny County v. Greater Pittsburgh ACLU*, 492 US 573 (1989).
21. *Lee v Weisman*, 505 US 577 (1992).
22. *Board of Education of Kiryas Joel Village School District v Grumet*, 129 L Ed 2d 546 (1994).
23. *Harvard Law Review*, "Leading Cases," (November 1995), p 219.
24. *Capital Square Review Board v Pinette*, 132 L Ed 2d 650 (1995).
25. *Bowen v Kendrick*, 487 US 589 (1988); *Texas Monthly, Inc. v Bullock*, 489 U.S. 1 (1989); *Lee v Weisman*, 505 US 577 (1992). *Board of Education of Kiryas Joel Village School District v Grumet*, 129 L Ed 2d 546 (1994).
26. *Engel v Vitale*, 370 US 421 (1962).
27. *Lee v Weisman*, 505 US 577 (1992).
28. *Edwards v Aguillard*, 482 US 578 (1987).
29. *Marsh v Chambers*, 463 US 783 (1983).
30. *Witters v. Washington Department of Service for Blind*, 474 US 481 (1986).
31. Donald L. Brakeman, *Church-State Constitutional Issues: Marking Sense of the Establishment Clause* (Greenwood, 1991), p. 125.
32. *Mueller v Allen*, 463 US 388 (1983).
33. *Wolman v Walter*, 433 US 229 (1977).

34. *Zobrest v Catalina Foothills School District*, 509 US 1 (1993).
35. *Walz v Tax Commission*, 397 US 644 (1970).
36. *Board of Education of Westside Community Schools (Dist. 66) v Mergens*, 496 US 226 (1990).
37. *Rosenberger v University of Virginia*, 132 L Ed 2d 700 (1995).
38. *Frazee v Illinois Department of Employment Security*, 489 US 829 (1989).
39. *Wisconsin v Yoder*, 406 US 205 (1972).
40. *Employment Division, Department of Human Resources of Oregon v Smith*, 494 US 872 (1990).
41. *Lukumi Babalu Aye, Inc. v City of Hialeah*, 125 L Ed 2d 472 (1993).
42. *Lamb's Chapel v Center Moriches Union Free School District*, 124 L Ed 2d 352 (1993).
43. *Bob Jones University v United States*, 461 US 574 (1983).
44. *Hernandez v Commissioner*, 489 US 1027 (1989).
45. Jesse H. Choper, *Securing Religious Liberty: Principles for Judicial Interpretation of the Religion Clauses* (University of Chicago Press, 1995), p. 55.
46. *Congressional Record*, 139, no. 65, May 11, 1993.
47. *Weekly Compendium of Presidential Documents* 2377, November 16, 1993.
48. John Stuart Mill, Essay on Liberty (1859), in *The English Philosophers from Bacon to Mill*, ed. Arthur Burtt (Modern Library, 1939), p. 961.
49. *West Virginia State Board of Education v Barnette*, 319 US 624 (1943).
50. *Hustler Magazine v Falwell*, 485 US 46 (1988); *United States v Schriummer*, 279 US 644 (1928).
51. For a thoughtful statement of a somewhat contrary point of view, see Walter Berns, *First Amendment and the Future of American Democracy* (Basic Books, 1976). For a review of the classics and a call for a review of the civil liberties traditional to deal with issues such as the regulation of campaign finance and other matters designed to equalize the competition in the marketplace of ideas, see Mark A. Graber, *Transforming Free Speech: The Ambiguous Legacy of Civil Libertarianism* (University of California Press, 1991).
52. *R.A.V. v St. Paul*, 505 US 377 (1992).
53. *Gitlow v New York*, 268 US 652 (1925).
54. *Brown v Hartlage*, 456 US 45 (1982), in which the Supreme Court reversed a decision of the Kentucky Court of Appeals based on the bad tendency doctrine.
55. *Schenck v United States*, 249 US 47 (1919).
56. *Whitney v California*, 274 US 357 (1927).
57. *Nebraska Press Association v Stuart*, 427 US 539 (1976). See also Fred W. Friendly, *Minnesota Rag: The Dramatic Story of the Landmark Supreme Court Case That Gave New Meaning to Freedom of the Press* (Random House, 1981).
58. *Hazelwood School District v Kuhlmeier*, 484 US 260 (1988).
59. *Lanzetta v New Jersey*, 306 US 451 (1939).
60. *Winters v New York*, 333 US 507 (1948); *Burstyn v Wilson*, 343 US 495 (1952).
61. *Regan v Time, Inc.*, 468 US 641 (1984).
62. *R.A.V. v St. Paul* 505 US 377 (1992). See also Edward J. Cleary, *Beyond the Burning Cross: The First Amendment and the Landmark R.A.V. Case* (Random House, 1995) by the attorney for the cross burner.
63. *Dun & Bradstreet v Greenmoss Builders*, 472 US 749 (1985), citing *First National Bank of Boston v Bellotti*, 435 US 765, 766 (1978). See also Edward V. Heck and Albert C. Ringelstein, "The Burger Court and the Primacy of Political Expression," *Western Political Quarterly* 40 (September 1987), pp. 411–23.
64. *Board of Trustees, State University of New York v Fox*, 492 US 469 (1989).
65. Lee C. Bollinger, *Images of a Free Press* (University of Chicago Press, 1991), p. 63.
66. *Lovell v Griffin*, 303 US 444 (1938).
67. *Richmond Newspapers, Inc. v Virginia*, 448 US 555 (1980). For a comprehensive history, see David A. Anderson, "The Origins of the Press Clause," *UCLA Law Review* (February 1983), pp. 455–537.

68. *Philadelphia Newspapers v Hepps*, 475 US 767 (1986); Richard Labunski, *Libel and the First Amendment: Legal History and Practice in Print and Broadcasting* (Transaction Books, 1987).

69. *Cohen v Cowles Media Co., 501 US 663 (1991).*

70. *Dun & Bradstreet v Greenmoss Builders*, 472 US 749 (1985). See also William W. Van Alstyne, *Interpretations of the First Amendment* (Duke University Press, 1984), pp. 50–67.

71. *Hazelwood School District v Kuhlmeier*, 484 US 260 (1988).

72. *Richmond Newspapers, Inc. v Virginia*, 448 US 555 (1980); David M. O'Brien, *The Public's Right to Know: The Supreme Court and the First Amendment* (Praeger, 1981).

73. *United States v Nixon*, 418 US 683 (1974). See also Daniel N. Hoffman, *Governmental Secrecy and the Founding Fathers: A Study in Constitutional Controls* (Greenwood, 1981).

74. Stephen Labaton, "President Agrees to Release Notes on Whitewater," *New York Times*, December 22, 1995, P.A1.

75. *Gentile v State Bar of Nevada*, 501 US 1030 (1991).

76. Susanna Barber, *News Cameras in the Courtroom: A Free Press–Fair Trial Debate* (Ablex, 1987), p. 9.

77. *Milwaukee Pub. Co. v Burleson*, 255 US 407 (1921).

78. *Lamont v Postmaster General*, 381 US 301 (1965).

79. *Rowan v Post Office Department*, 397 US 728 (1970).

80. *Southeastern Promotions, Ltd. v Conrad*, 420 US 546 (1975).

81. *California v LaRue*, 409 US 109 (1972); see also *Barnes v Glen Theatre, Inc.*, 501 US 560 (1991).

82. *McIntyre v Ohio Election Commission*, 131 L Ed 2d 426 (1995).

83. Ibid.

84. *Burson v Freeman*, 504 US 191 (1992).

85. Lucas A. Powe, Jr., *American Broadcasting and the First Amendment* (University of California Press, 1987).

86. *Federal Communications Commission v League of Women Voters of California*, 468 US 364 (1984).

87. Bruce Fein, "Cable Discretion and the First Amendment," *Washington Times*, December 2, 1992, p. G1.

88. *Denver Area Consortium v Federal Communications Commission*, 134 L Ed 2d 888 (1996).

89. Edmund L. Andres, "Robotic Telephone Sales Calls Come Under Fire in Congress," *New York Times*, October 30, 1991, p. A1.

90. James Barron, "Watch What You Say on the Cordless Phone," *New York Times*, November 9, 1991, p. 9.

91. *Sable Communications v Federal Communications Commission*, 492 US 115 (1989).

92. *Federal Communications Commission v Pacifica Foundation et al.*, 438 US 726 (1978). The Court, however, has refused to review a decision of the Court of Appeals for the District of Columbia, which declared unconstitutional a complete 24-hour ban on the televising of indecent materials.

93. Linda Greenhouse, "Supreme Court Roundup," *The New York Times*, March 3, 1992, p. A2.

94. Barnaby J. Feder, "Toward Defining Free Speech in the Computer Age," *The New York Times*, November 3, 1991, p. E5; Don Oldenburg, "Computers: Rights on the Line," and "The Law: Lost in Cyberspace," *The Washington Post*, October 1, 1991, p. E5. Dan Carney, "TeleCommunications: Conferees Favor 'Indency' Standard," *Congressional Quarterly Weekly Report*, December 9, 1995, p. 3734.

95. Benjamin Wittes, "Taming Cyberspace," *The Recorder*, December 29, 1995, p. 5. See also Peter H. Lewis, "Judges Turn Back Law to Regulate Internet Decency," *The New York Times*, June 13, 1996, p. A1.

96. *Amalgamated Food Employees v Logan Plaza*, 391 US 308 (1968).

97. *Frisby v Schultz*, 487 US 474 (1988).

98. *Madsen v. Women's Health Center, 129 L Ed 2d 593 (1994).*

99. *Boos v Barry*, 485 US 312 (1988).

100. *United States v O'Brien*, 391 US 367 (1968).

101. *Paris Adult Theatre v Slaton*, 413 US 49 (1973).

102. *United States v O'Brien*, 391 US 367 (1968).

103. *Clark v Community for Creative Non-Violence*, 468 US 288 (1984).

104. *R.A.V. v St. Paul*, 505 US 377 (1992).

105. *Clark v Community for Creative Non-Violence*, 468 US 288 (1984).

106. *Barnes v Glen Theatre, Inc.*, 501 US 560 (1991).\

107. *The New York Times v Sullivan*, 376 US 254 (1964). See also Anthony Lewis, *Make No Law: The Sullivan Case and the First Amendment* (Random House, 1991), p. 140.

108. *Harte-Hanks, Inc. v Connaughton*, 491 US 657 (1989).

109. *Hustler Magazine v Falwell*, 485 US 46 (1988).

110. *Masson v New Yorker Magazine, Inc.*, 501 US 496 (1991).

111. Robert Scheer, "Pornography Commissioners Founder on the Limits of Sex," *The Los Angeles Times*, May 1, 1986, p. 19.

112. *Brockett v Spokane Arcades, Inc.*, 472 US 491 (1985).

113. *Miller v California*, 413 US 15 (1973).

114. *Memoirs v Massachusetts*, 383 US 413 (1966).

115. *Jenkins v Georgia*, 418 US 153 (1974).

116. *Young v American Mini Theatres*, 427 US 51 (1976). See also *Renton v Playtime Theatres, Inc.*, 475 US 41 (1986).

117. "From Preamble to Indianapolis City-County Ordinance," cited by Joel B. Grossman, "The First Amendment and the New Anti-Pornography Statutes," *News for Teachers of Political Science* (American Political Science Association, 1985), p. 18. See also Catharine A. MacKinnon, *Only Words* (Harvard University Press, 1993). For a rebuttal to MacKinnon by another femenist, see Nadine Strossen, *Defending Pornography: Free Speech, Sex, and the Fight for Women's Rights* (Scribner's, 1995).

118. Cass R. Sunstein, *The Partial Constitution* (Harvard University Press, 1993), p. 268.

119. Suzanne Stefanac, "Sex and the New Media," *The Recorder*, September 8, 1993, p. 14.

120. Barry Sussman, "With Pornography, It All Depends on Who's Doing the Looking," *Washington Post*–ABC News Poll, *The Washington Post*, National Weekly Edition, March 24, 1986, p. 37.

121. "Anti-Pornography Laws and First Amendment Values," Harvard Law Review 98 (1984), p. 460. See also Donald Alexander Downs, *The New Politics of Pornography* (University of Chicago Press, 1990); Sunstein, *Partial Constitution*, pp. 261–70.

122. *Butler v Her Majesty the Queen* 1 S.C.R. 452 (1992). See also "Pornography, Equality, and a Discrimination-Free Workplace: A Comparative Perspective," *Harvard Law Review* 106 (March 1993), pp. 1075–92; Kent Greenawalt, *Fighting Words* (Princeton University Press, 1995), pp. 113–23.

123. *Hudnut v American Booksellers*, 475 US 1001 (1986); *Sable Communications v Federal Communications Commission*, 492 US 115 (1989).

124. *Chaplinsky v New Hampshire*, 315 US 568 (1942)

125. *Cohen v California*, 403 US 115 (1971). See also *NAACP v Claiborne Hardware Co.*, 458 US 886 (1982); *R.A.V. v St. Paul*, 505 US 377 (1992).

126. *Cohen v California*, 403 US 115 (1971).

127. *United States v Eichman*, 496 US 310 (1990), repeated and reemphasized in *Simon & Schuster v New York State Crime Victims Board*, 502 US 105 (1991).

128. *R.A.V. v St. Paul*, 505 US 377 (1992).

129. David M. Hamlin, "Swastikas and Survivors: Inside the Skokie-Nazi Free Speech Case," *Civil Liberties Review* (March/April 1978).

130. Lee C. Bollinger, *The Tolerant Society: Freedom of Speech and Extremist Speech in America* (Oxford University Press, 1986), pp. 24–32. See also Donald A. Downs, *Nazis in Skokie: Freedom, Community, and the First Amendment* (University of Notre Dame Press, 1985).

131. Bollinger, *Images of a Free Press*.

132. *Walker v Birmingham*, 388 US 307 (1967).

133. "Senate Passes Bill Making Blockades of Abortion Clinics a Federal Crime," *The New York Times*, May 13, 1994, pp. A1, A12.

134. *Madsen v Women's Health Center*, 129 L Ed 2d 593 (1994).

135. *Pruneyard Shopping Center v Robins*, 447 US 74 (1980).

136. *National Association for the Advancement of Colored People v Alabama*, 357 US 449 (1958).

137. *Roberts v United States Jaycees*, 465 US 609 (1984).

138. J. Skelly Wright, "Politics and the Constitution: Is Money Speech?" *Yale Law Journal* 85 (1976), pp. 1001–21.

139. *Buckley v Valeo*, 424 US 1 (1976).

140. *Federal Election Commission v National Political Action Committee*, 470 US 480 (1985).

141. *West Virginia State Board of Education v Barnette*, 319 US 624 (1943).

142. See two works by Leonard W. Levy: *Legacy of Suppression* (Harvard University Press, 1960), and *Freedom of the Press from Zenger to Jefferson* (Bobbs-Merrill, 1966).

143. The Sedition Act of 1798, quoted in James Morton Smith, *Freedom's Fetters: The Alien and Sedition Laws and American Civil Liberties* (Cornell University Press, 1956), p. 442.

144. *Dennis v United States*, 341 US 494 (1950).

145. *Yates v United States*, 354 US 298 (1957).

146. *Brandenburg v Ohio*, 395 US 444 (1969).

CHAPTER 4

1. Martin Edelman, *Democratic Theories and the Constitution* (State University of New York Press, 1984), p. 304; Judith N. Shklar, *American Citizenship: The Quest for Inclusion* (Harvard University Press, 1991), p. 3.
2. *Vance v Terrazas*, 444 US 252 (1980).
3. *San Antonio School District v Rodriguez*, 411 US 1 (1973).
4. *Washington v Davis*, 426 US 229 (1976). See also *Hunter v Underwood*, 471 US 522 (1985).
5. Justice Sandra Day O'Connor, concurring in *Hernandez v New York*, 500 US 352 (1991).
6. *Personnel Administrator of Massachusetts v Feeney*, 442 US 256 (1979).
7. C. Vann Woodward, *The Strange Career of Jim Crow* (Oxford University Press, 1968).
8. *Plessy v Ferguson*, 163 US 537 (1896).
9. *Brown v Board of Education of Topeka*, 347 US 483 (1954). See also J. W. Peltason, *Fifty-eight Lonely Men: Southern Federal Judges and School Desegregation* (University of Illinois Press, 1971), p. 248.
10. *Brown v Board of Education*, 349 US 294 (1955). For a comprehensive history of the events leading up to Brown, see Richard Kluger, *Simple Justice* (Knopf, 1976). Earl Black, *Southern Governors and Civil Rights: Racial Segregation as a Campaign Issue in the Second Reconstruction* (Harvard University Press, 1977), shows response, reaction, and eventually neutralization of race as a political issue following the *Brown* decision.
11. *Alexander v Board of Education*, 396 US 802 (1969).
12. *Missouri v. Jenkins*, 132 L Ed 2d 63 (1995).
13. Alex M. Johnson, Jr., "Bid Whist, Tonk, and *United States v. Fordice*: Why Integrationism Fails African-Americans Again," *California Law Review*, 81 (December 1993,) pp. 401-ff.
14. Gary Orfield, *Must We Bus? Segregated Schools and National Policy* (Brookings, 1979); Jennifer L. Hochschild, *The New American Dilemma: Liberal Democracy and School Desegregation* (Yale University Press, 1984).
15. *Swann v Charlotte-Mecklenburg Board of Education*, 402 US 1 (1971).
16. *Milliken v Bradley*, 418 US 717 (1974); Bernard Schwartz, *The School Busing Case and the Supreme Court* (Oxford University Press, 1986).
17. Gary Orfield, "Separate Societies: Have the Kerner Warnings Come True?" in *Quiet Riots: Race and Poverty in the United States–The Kerner Report Twenty Years Later*, eds. Fred Harris and Roger Welkins (Pantheon, 1988), p. 116. See also "Segregation's Threat to the Economy," *The New York Times*, December 19, 1993, p. A12.
18. *Missouri v. Jenkins*, 495 US 33 (1990).
19. *Missouri v. Jenkins*, 132 L Ed 2d 63 (1995).
20. *Freeman v. Pitts*, 503 US 467 (1992). See also Julie Johnson, "Deciding What to Do Next about Civil Rights," *The New York Times*, March 12, 1989, p. E5; Norman C. Amaker, ed., *Civil Rights and the Reagan Administration* (Urban Institute, 1988).
21. Peter Applebome, "Opponents' Moves Refueling Debate on School Busing," *The New York Times*, September 26, 1995, p. A1.
22. William Celis, III, "Study Finds Rising Concentration of Black and Hispanic Students," *The New York Times*, December 14, 1993, p. A1.
23. Raymond Hernandez, "N.A.A.C.P. Suspends Yonkers Leader After Criticism of Usefulness of School Busing," *The New York Times*, November 1, 1995, p. A13.
24. Quoted by Applebome, *The New York Times*, p. A1.
25. Quoted in Celis, "Study Finds Rising Concentration," p. A11.
26. V. O. Key, Jr., *Southern Politics* (Knopf, 1949), p. 555. For a history of the rise and fall of black disenfranchisement, see Steven F. Lawson, *Black Ballots: Voting Rights in the South, 1944-1969* (Columbia University Press, 1976).
27. *Smith v Allwright*, 321 US 649 (1944).
28. *Gomillion v Lightfoot*, 364 US 339 (1960).
29. *Harper v Virginia Board of Elections*, 383 US 663 (1966).
30. *Morse v Republican Party of Virginia*, 134 L Ed 2d 347 (1996).
31. *Report of the United States Commission on Civil Rights* (Government Printing Office, 1959), pp. 103–104.
32. David J. Garrow, *Protest at Selma: Martin Luther King and the Voting Rights Act of 1965* (Yale University Press, 1978).
33. Abigail M. Thernstrom, *Whose Votes Count? Affirmative Action and Minority Voting Rights* (Harvard University Press, 1987), p. 15. For a contrary view, see Bernard Grofman, Lisa Handley, and Richard Niemi, *Minority Representation and the Quest for Voting Equality* (Cambridge University Press, 1992).
34. *Morse v Republican Party of Virginia*, 134 L Ed 2d 347 (1996).
35. *Presley v Etowah County Commission*, 502 US 491 (1992).
36. *Holder v Hall*, 129 L Ed 2d 687 (1994).
37. Ellen Perlman, "Feds on Remaps: No Go," *City and State*, July 29–August 11, 1991.
38. *Shaw v. Reno*, 125 L Ed 511 (1993).
39. Ibid.
40. Ibid.
41. Ibid; *Johson v De Grandy*, 129 L Ed 2d 775 (1994).
42. *Miller v. Johnson*, 132 L Ed 2d 762 (1995).
43. *Bush v Vera; Shaw v Hunt*, as reported in *The New York Times*, June 13, 1996.
44. Justice William O. Douglas, dissenting in *Moose Lodge No. 107 v Irvis*, 407 US 163 (1972).
45. *New York State Club Association v New York City*, 487 US 1 (1988).
46. *Civil Rights Cases*, 109 US 3 (1883).
47. *Heart of Atlanta Motel v United States*, 379 US 421 (1964).
48. Paul Burstein, *Discrimination, Jobs, and Politics: The Struggle for Equal Employment Opportunity in the United States since the New Deal* (University of Chicago Press, 1985); Kathanne W. Greene, *Affirmative Action and Principles of Justice* (Greenwood Press, 1989).
49. *Meritor Savings Bank v Vinson*, 477 US 57 (1986); *Harris v Forklift Systems, Inc.* 126 L Ed 2d 295 (1993).
50. Hanes Walton, Jr., *When the Marching Stopped: The Politics of Civil Rights Regulatory Agencies* (State University of New York Press, 1988). See also David E. Rovella, "EEOC Chairman Casellas: 'We Are Being Selective'," *The National Law Journal*, November 20, 1995, p. 1.
51. Rovella, op. cit.
52. *Shelley v Kraemer*, 334 US 1 (1948).
53. Timothy Noah, "Housing Report Says Racial Bias Remains Prevalent," *The Wall Street Journal*, August 30, 1991; findings of report prepared by the Urban Institute commissioned by the Department of Housing and Urban Development.
54. Daniel Mitchell, quoted in *CQ Researcher, Housing Discrimination*, 5 (February 24, 1995), p. 174.
55. "The Racism Next Door: Segregated Housing Is Still a Blight in Most Neighborhoods," *Time*, June 30, 1986, p. 40. See also Alan Finder, "Housing Bias Still Pervades the New York Region," *The New York Times*, March 13, 1989, p. A16.
56. Justice John Marshall Harlan, dissenting in *Plessy v Ferguson*, 163 US 537 (1896).
57. *University of California Regents v Bakke*, 438 US 265 (1978).
58. Justice Byron White, concurring in *Wygant v Jackson Board of Education*, 476 US 267 (1986).
59. Justice Sandra Day O'Connor, majority opinion, and Justice Thurgood Marshall, dissenting in *Richmond v Croson*, 488 US 469 (1989).
60. Justice William J. Brennan, majority opinion, and Justice Sandra Day O'Connor, dissenting in *Metro Broadcasting v Federal Communications Commission*, 497 US 547 (1990).
61. *Adarand Constructors, Inc. v. Pena*, 132 L Ed 2d 158 (1995).
62. Justice Sandra Day O'Connor, majority opinion in *Richmond v Croson*, 488 US 469 (1989).
63. *Home Building & Loan Assn. v Blaisdell*, 290 US 398 (1934).
64. Richard A. Epstein, *Taking: Private Property and the Power of Eminent Domain* (Harvard University Press, 1985).
65. *First English Evangelical v Los Angeles County*, 482 US 304 (1987).
66. *United States v 564.54 Acres of Land*, 441 US 506 (1979).
67. Ibid.
68. *Nollan v California Coastal Commission*, 483 US 825 (1987). See also *Dolan v City of Tigard*, discussed in *The New York Times*, June 25, 1994.
69. *Mathews v Eldridge*, 424 US 319 (1976), restated in *Connecticut v Doeher*, 115 L Ed 2d 1 (1991).
70. *Leary v United States*, 395 US 6 (1969); *Turner v United States*, 369 US 398 (1970).
71. *Meyer v Nebraska*, 262 US 390 (1923).
72. *Meachum v Fano*, 427 US 215 (1976).
73. *Cleveland Board of Education v Loudermill*, 470 US 532 (1985).
74. *Morrissey v Brewer*, 408 US 471 (1972).
75. Philip B. Kurland, *Some Reflections on Privacy and the Constitution* (University of Chicago Center for Policy Study, 1976), p. 9. A classic and influential

article about privacy is S. D. Warren and L. D. Brandeis, "The Right to Privacy," *Harvard Law Review*, December 15, 1980, pp. 193–220.

76. *Roe v Wade*, 410 US 113 (1973).

77. *Planned Parenthood of Southeastern Pennsylvania v Casey*, 505 US 833 (1992).

78. *Ohio v Akron Center for Reproductive Health*, 497 US 502 (1990); *Hodgson v Minnesota*, 497 US 417 (1990); *Planned Parenthood of Southeastern Pennsylvania v Casey*, 505 US 833 (1992).

79. *Bowers v Hardwick*, 478 US 186 (1986); *Romer v Evans*, *The New York Times*, May 21, 1996, p. C18. See also Linda Greenhouse, "Gay Rights Laws Can't Be Banned, High Court Rules," *The New York Times*, May 21, 1996, p. 1.

80. The most comprehensive analysis of these complicated issues is Wayne R. LaFave, *Search and Seizure: A Treatise on the Fourth Amendment*, 2d ed. (West Publishing, 1987).

81. *County of Riverside v McLaughlin*, 500 US 44 (1991).

82. *Wilson v Arkansas*, 131 L Ed 2d 976 (1995).

83. *California v Hodari D.*, 499 US 621 (1991).

84. *Mincey v Arizona*, 437 US 385 (1978), reaffirmed in *California v Acevedo*, 500 US 565 (1991).

85. *United States v Ross*, 456 US 798 (1982).

86. *Terry v Ohio*, 392 US 1 (1968); *United States v Sharpe*, 470 US 675 (1985); *Hayes v Florida*, 470 US 811 (1985).

87. *Minnesota v Dickerson*, 508 US 366 (1993).

88. *Adams v Williams*, 407 US 143 (1972).

89. *Chimel v California*, 395 US 752 (1969); *United States v Edward*, 415 US 800 (1974); *Illinois v Lafayette*, 462 US 640 (1983).

90. *Cupp v Murphy*, 412 US 291 (1973).

91. *Florida v Wells*, 495 US 1 (1990).

92. *Schneckloth v Bustamonte*, 412 US 218 (1973); *United States v Matlock*, 415 US 164 (1974).

93. *Almeida-Sanchez v United States*, 413 US 266 (1973); *United States v Ortiz*, 422 US 891 (1975).

94. *United States v Ramsey*, 431 US 606 (1977).

95. *Torres v Puerto Rico*, 442 US 465 (1979).

96. *Coolidge v New Hampshire*, 403 US 443 (1971); *Texas v Brown*, 460 US 730 (1983); *Arizona v Hicks*, 480 US 321 (1987).

97. *Michigan v Tyler*, 436 US 499 (1978); *Mincey v Arizona*, 437 US 385 (1978).

98. Benjamin Wittes, "Ames Case Leads to More Powerful Spy Court," *The Recorder*, November 8, 1994, p. 16.

99. *Tennessee v Garner*, 471 US 1 (1985).

100. *Olmstead v United States*, 227 US 438 (1928).

101. *Florida v Riley*, 488 US 445 (1989).

102. *Katz v United States*, 389 US 347 (1967).

103. *Mapp v Ohio*, 367 US 643 (1961).

104. *United States v Leon*, 468 US 897 (1984).

105. *United States v Payner*, 447 US 727 (1980).

106. *Blau v United States*, 340 US 332 (1951).

107. *Mincey v Arizona*, 437 US 385 (1978).

108. *Miranda v Arizona*, 384 US 436 (1966). Liva Baker, *Miranda: Crime, Law and Politics* (Atheneum, 1983), explores every aspect of the decision, including subsequent controversy about its effects.

109. *Presier v Rodriguez*, 411 US 475 (1973).

110. 28 *United States Code* 2454.

111. *Stone v Powell*, 428 US 465 (1976); *McCleskey v Zant*, 499 US 467 (1991); *Withrow v Williams*, 123 L. Ed. 2d 407 (1993). For a review of these decisions, see Jordan Steiker, "Innocence and Federal Habeas," *UCLA Law Review* 41 (December 1993), pp. 303–89.

112. *Felker v Turpin*, 134 L Ed 2d 827 (1996).

113. Felix Frankfurter, dissenting in *United States v Rabinowitz*, 339 US 56 (1950).

114. *Johnson v Zerbst*, 304 US 458 (1938); *Gideon v Wainwright*, 372 US 335 (1963). Anthony Lewis, *Gideon's Trumpet* (Random House, 1964), has become a classic on this issue.

115. *United States v Salerno*, 481 US 739 (1987).

116. *United States v R.Enterprises, Inc.*, 498 US 292 (1991).

117. *Blanton et al. v North Las Vegas*, 489 US 538 (1989).

118. *The New York Times*, September 1, 1995, p. A14.

119. *J. E. B. v Alabama ex rel T. B.*, 128 L Ed 2d 89 (1994). *Batson v Kentucky*, 476 US 79 (1986); *Powers v Ohio*, 499 US 400 (1991); *Hernandez v New York*, 500 US 352 (1991); *Georgia v McCollum*, 505 US 42 (1992).

120. *Rhodes v Chapman*, 452 US 337 (1981); *Wilson v Seiiter*, 501 US 294 (1991).

121. *Hutto v Davis*, 454 US 370 (1982).

122. *Solem v Helm*, 463 US 277 (1983).

123. From Scott Graham: "The Death Penalty Backlog," in *The California Supreme Court At Mid-Decade*, *The Recorder* (Winter 1994–1995), p. 36.

124. *Benton v Maryland*, 395 US 784 (1969).

125. Jerome Frank, *Courts on Trial* (Princeton University Press, 1949), p. 122. See also Rita James Simon, ed., *The Jury System in America: A Critical Overview* (Sage Publications, 1975); John Guinther, *The Jury in America* (Facts-on-File Publications, 1988); Steven Brill, *Trial by Jury* (American Lawyer Books/Touchstone, 1989).

126. "Race Seems to Play an Increasing Role in Many Jury Verdicts," *The Wall Street Journal*, October 4, 1995, p. A1.

127. Laura Mansnerus, "Rewriting the Rules of the Jury System," *The New York Times*, November 4, 1995, p. A7.

128. See comments of Jeffrey Abramson, *The New York Times*, November 4, 1995, p. A7.

129. Harry Kalven, Jr., and Hans Zeisel, *The American Jury* (University of Chicago Press, 1971), p. 57. See also Jeffrey Abramson, *We, The Jury: The Jury System and the Ideal of Democracy* (Basic Books, 1994).

130. William O. Douglas, dissenting in *United States v Mara*, 410 US 19 (1973).

131. Bryan Abas, "The Ruckus out of Rocky Flats–Empowering the People Through Grand Juries," *The Recorder*, February 1, 1994, p. 16.

132. "Race and the Criminal Process," *Harvard Law Review* 101 (May 1988), p. 1493.

133. Ibid., p. 1476.

134. Dean Alfred Blumstein and Joan Petersilia, quoted in Norval Morris, "Race and Crime: What Evidence Is There That Race Influences Results in the Criminal Justice System?" *Judicature* (August/September 1988), p. 112.

135. Norval Morris, "Race and Crime," p. 112.

136. Gunnar Myrdal, *An American Dilemma* (Harper and Brothers, 1944).

137. Cassia C. Spohn, "Courts, Sentences, and Prisons," *Daedalus, Journal of the American Academy of Arts and Sciences* (Winter, 1995), p. 136.

138. Jonathan Kaufman, Wade Lambert, Benjaim A. Holden, "Fuhrman's Comments Bolster Black Concerns About Police Conduct," *The Wall Street Journal*, August 31, 1995, p. A1.

139. George Edwards, *The Police on the Urban Frontier* (Institute of Human Relations Press and the American Jewish Committee, 1968), p. 28.

140. Norval Morris, "Race and Crime," p. 113.

141. *West Virginia State Board of Education v Barnette*, 319 US 624 (1943).

142. Robert H. Jackson, *The Supreme Court in the American System of Government* (Harvard University Press, 1955), pp. 81–82.

CHAPTER 5

1. Dexter Waugh, "'Mistake' to End UC Racial Policy: Peltason Writes to Regents, Asks Them to Resist Dumping Admission Practices," *San Francisco Standard Examiner*, July 11, 1995, p. A8.

2. Clinton Rossiter, *Conservatism in America* (Vintage, 1962), p. 72.

3. *Marbury v Madison*, 1 Cranch 137 (1803).

4. See, generally, Bernard Bailyn, *The Ideological Origins of the American Revolution* (Harvard University Press, 1967).

5. Robert A. Dahl, "Liberal Democracy in the United States," in *A Prospect of Liberal Democracy*, ed. William Livingston (University of Texas Press, 1979), p. 64.

6. Franklin D. Roosevelt, State of the Union Address, January 11, 1944, *The Public Papers of the President of the United States, 1944* (Government Printing Office, 1962), pp. 371–94.

7. Bill Clinton, Address to Congress on Health Care, *The New York Times*, September 23, 1993, pp. A24–25.

8. Newt Gingrich, *To Renew America* (HarperCollins, 1995), p. 71.
9. Bill Bradley, *Time Present, Time Past: A Memoir* (Knopf, 1996), p. 406.
10. Dick Armey, *The Freedom Revolution* (Regnery Publishing, 1995), p. 150.
11. When adjusted using the Consumer Price Index, the percentage of households earning over $75,000 a year has risen from 6.4 percent in 1970 to 12.5 percent in 1993, while the percentage earning less than $10,000 a year remained relatively constant at 15.0 percent in 1970 and 14.2 percent in 1993. *Statistical Abstract of the United States, 1995* (Government Printing Office, 1995), p. 469.
12. Harry S Truman, State of the Union Address, 1949, *The Public Papers of the President of the United States, 1949* (Government Printing Office, 1964), pp. 1–7.
13. David Spitz, "A Liberal Perspective on Liberalism and Conservatism," in *Left, Right and Center*, ed. Robert Goldwin (Rand McNally, 1965), p. 31.
14. See also Charles Peters and Philip Keisling, eds., *A New Road for America: The Neoliberal Movement* (University Press of America, 1984); Randall Rothenberg, *The Neoliberals: Creating the New American Politics* (Simon & Schuster, 1984).
15. Armey, *The Freedom Revolution*, pp. 291–93.
16. Kevin Phillips, *The Politics of Rich and Poor: Wealth and the American Electorate in the Reagan Aftermath* (Random House, 1990), pp. 220–21.
17. Michael Barone, *Our Country: The Shaping of America from Roosevelt to Reagan* (Free Press, 1990), p. xii.
18. Kenneth R. Hoover, *Ideology and Political Life* (Brooks/Cole, 1987), p. 34.
19. See the writings of Milton Friedman, *Capitalism and Freedom* (University of Chicago, 1962). See also Friedrich A. Hayek, *The Road to Serfdom*, (University of Chicago Press, 1944).
20. Gingrich, *To Renew America*, p. 102.
21. Paula Poundstone, "He Didn't Even Like Girls," *Mother Jones* (May 1993), p. 37.
22. Dan Balz and Ronald Brownstein, "God's Fixer: Christian Coalition Leader Ralph Reed Has a Strategy: Instead of Chasing Republican Politicians, He Wants the Party to Come to Him," *The Washington Post*, January 28, 1996, p. W8.
23. "Mostly Protestant Christian Coalition Gains Catholic Alliance," *The New York Times*, December 9, 1995, p. A48.
24. Barry Goldwater with Jack Casserly, *Goldwater* (Doubleday, 1988), p. 387.
25. Ronald Reagan, Inaugural Address, 1981, *The Public Papers of the President of the United States: Ronald Reagan, 1981* (Government Printing Office, 1982), p. 1.
26. Kathleen Day, *S & L Hell: The People and the Politics Behind the $1 Trillion Savings and Loan Scandal* (W.W. Norton & Co., 1993).
27. See Edward A. Snyder, "The Effects of Higher Criminal Penalties on Antitrust Enforcement," *Journal of Law and Economics* 33 (October 1990), pp. 439–62; also Brian Burrough and John Helyar, *Barbarians at the Gate: The Fall of RJR Nabisco* (Harper, 1990).
28. Dan Goodman, "Bleeding-Heart Conservatives," *Time*, May 18, 1992, p. 37.
29. Ronald Reagan, Address to the Nation on the Economy, February 5, 1981, *Public Papers of the Presidents: Ronald Reagan, 1981* (Government Printing Office, 1982), p. 81.
30. Sylvia Nasar, "Even among the Well-Off, the Rich Get Richer," *The New York Times*, March 5, 1992, p. A1.
31. Karl Marx, "Critique of the Gotha Program," in *Marx Selections*, ed. Allen W. Wood (Macmillan Publishing, 1988), p. 190.
32. Irving Howe, *Socialism and America* (Harcourt, 1985); Michael Harrington, *Socialism: Past and Future* (Arcade, 1989).
33. Eric R. A. N. Smith, *The Unchanging American Voter* (University of California Press, 1989), pp. 171–72.
34. Center for Political Studies, University of Michigan, *American National Election Study, 1994*.
35. Herbert McClosky and Alida Brill, *Dimensions of Tolerance: What Americans Believe about Civil Liberties* (Russell Sage Foundation, 1983), pp. 274–75.
36. Dinesh D'Souza, *Illiberal Education: The Politics of Race and Sex on Campus* (Free Press, 1991), p. 3.

CHAPTER 6

1. Clay Robison, "Judge Defends His Order That Mom Speak English," *The Houston Chronicle*, August 30, 1995, p. A1; Scott Parks, "Judge Defends Telling Mom to Speak English to Girl; AG, Others Question Ruling in Custody Case," *The Dallas Morning News*, August 30, 1995, p. A1; and Patty Reinert, "Speak English Only, Judge Orders Mother," *The Houston Chronicle*, August 29, 1995, p. A1.
2. Albert Einstein, quoted in Laurence J. Peter, *Peter's Quotations* (William Morrow, 1977), p. 358.
3. Alexis de Tocqueville, *Democracy in America*, ed. J. P. Mayer, trans. George Lawrence (Doubleday and Company, 1969), p. 278.
4. Ibid., p. 280.
5. U.S. Bureau of the Census, *Statistical Abstract of the United States, 1982–83* (Government Printing Office, 1983), p. 488.
6. U.S. Bureau of the Census, *Statistical Abstract of the United States, 1995* (Government Printing Office 1995), p.289
7. V. O. Key, Jr., *Politics, Parties, and Pressure Groups*, 5th ed. (Thomas Y. Crowell, 1964), p. 232.
8. Tocqueville, *Democracy in America*, p. 68.
9. Robert S. Erickson, Gerold C. Wright, and John P. McIver, *Statehouse Democracy: Public Opinion and Policy in the American States* (Cambridge University Press, 1993).
10. U.S. Bureau of the Census, *Statistical Abstract, 1995*, p. 28.
11. Holly Idelson, "Count Adds Seats in Eight States," *Congressional Quarterly Weekly Report* 48 (December 29, 1990), p. 4240.
12. U.S. Bureau of the Census, Release CB 91–24, January 25, 1991.
13. U.S. Bureau of the Census, *Population Profile of the United States, 1993* (Government Printing Office, 1993), p. 34.
14. U.S. Bureau of the Census. *Statistical Abstract of the United States, 1995*, pp. 44–46.
15. Ibid., pp. 40–42.
16. U.S. Bureau of the Census Home Page, http://www.census.gov/ftp/pub/population/www/metropop.html.
17. U.S. Bureau of the Census, *Statistical Abstract, 1995*, p. 14.
18. U.S. Bureau of the Census, *Population Profile of the United States, 1993*, p. 3.
19. Dale Rogers Marshall, "The Continuing Significance of Race: The Transformation of American Politics," *American Political Science Review* 84 (June 1990), pp. 611–16.
20. Robert D. Ballard, "Introduction: Lure of the New South," in *Search of the New South: The Black Urban Experience in the 1970s and 1980s*, ed. Robert D. Ballard (University of Alabama Press, 1989), p. 5.
21. U.S. Bureau of the Census, *Statistical Abstract, 1995*, p. 36. Based on projections for 1995.
22. U.S. Bureau of the Census, *Population Profile of the United States: 1993*, p. 5.
23. Ibid., p. 48.
24. U.S. Bureau of the Census, *Household Wealth and Asset Ownership, 1991* (Government Printing Office, 1991), table H.
25. U.S. Bureau of the Census, *Statistical Abstract of the United States, 1995*, p. 469.
26. Ibid., p. 157.
27. Ibid., p. 174.
28. Ibid., pp. 22-23.
29. Mark R. Levy and Michael S. Kramer, *The Ethnic Factor: How America's Minorities Decide Elections* (Simon & Schuster, 1973).
30. Mark Stern, "Democratic Presidency and Voting Rights," in *Blacks in Southern Politics*, eds. Lawrence W. Mooreland, Robert P. Steed, and Todd A. Baker (Praeger, 1987), pp. 50–51.
31. David Bositis, *Blacks and the 1993 Republican National Convention* (Joint Center for Political and Economic Studies, 1992), p. 5.
32. U.S. Bureau of the Census, *Statistical Abstract, 1995*, pp. 34–36. Based on projections for 1995.
33. See Frank R. Parker, *Black Votes Count: Political Empowerment in Mississippi After 1965* (University of North Carolina Press, 1990).
34. National Black Caucus of State Legislatures, Washington, D.C.
35. U.S. Bureau of the Census, *Statistical Abstract, 1995*, p. 14.
36. Bureau of the Census Home Page, http://www.census.gov/ftp/pub/population/socdem/race/api/tab3.txt, March 1994.

37. U.S. Bureau of the Census, *Statistical Abstract, 1995*, p. 14.

38. Gary D. Sandefur and Arthur Sakamoto, "American Indian Household Structure and Income," *Demography* 25 (February 1988), p. 74.

39. U.S. Bureau of the Census, *We, The First Americans* (Government Printing Office, 1989), pp. 5–7.

40. Richard Santillan and Carlos Munoz, Jr., "Latinos and the Democratic Party," in *The Democrats Must Lead*, eds. James MacGregor Burns, William Crotty, Lois Lovelace Duke, and Lawrence D. Longley (Westview Press, 1992), pp. 182–83.

41. Rodolfo O. de la Garza, Louis DeSipio, F. Chris Garcia, John Garcia, and Angelo Falcon, *Latino Voices: Mexican, Puerto Rican, and Cuban Perspectives on American Politics* (Westview Press, 1992), p. 13.

42. Ibid., p. 14.

43. U.S. Bureau of the Census, Current Population Reports, *The Hispanic Population in the United States* (Government Printing Office, 1992), p. 302.

44. de la Garza, *Latino Voices*, p. 14.

45. U.S. Bureau of the Census, *Statistical Abstract, 1995*, p. 37.

46. Ibid., p. 10.

47. James West Davidson, William E. Gienapp, Christine Leigh Heyrman, Mark H. Lytle, and Michael B. Stoff, *Nation of Nations* (McGraw-Hill, 1990), pp. 833–34.

48. G. Thomas Edwards, *Sowing Good Seeds: The Northwest Suffrage Campaigns of Susan B. Anthony* (Oregon Historical Society Press, 1990), p. 136.

49. Paul Kleppner, *Continuity and Change in Electoral Politics, 1893–1928* (Greenwood Press, 1987), p. 172.

50. Carol Mueller, "The Gender Gap and Women's Political Influence," *Annals of the American Academy of Political and Social Sciences* 515 (May 1991), p. 25.

51. Self-reported turnout in the *American National Election Studies, 1978–88*, shows women voting at 2.2 percent less than men on average.

52. United Press International, "Is Year of the Woman for Real? Voters Will Settle the Matter," *Deseret News*, November 2, 1992, p. A4.

53. Barbara C. Burrell, *A Woman's Place Is in the House: Campaigning for Congress in the Feminist Era* (University of Michigan Press, 1994).

54. Diane L. Fowlkes, "Feminist Theory: Reconstructing Research and Teaching About American Politics and Government," *News for Teachers of Political Science* (Winter 1987), pp. 6–9. See also Andrea Dworkin, *Right-Wing Women* (Putnam's, 1983); Zillah R. Eisenstein, ed., *Feminism and Sexual Equality: Crisis in Liberal America* (Monthly Review Press ,1984); Ethel Klein, *Gender Politics* (Harvard University Press, 1984); Rebecca E. Klatch, *Women of the New Right* (Temple University Press, 1987).

55. U.S. Bureau of the Census, *Statistical Abstract, 1995*, p. 436.

56. Ibid., p. 478.

57. U.S. Bureau of the Census, *Population Profile of the United States, 1993*, p. 27

58. U.S. Bureau of the Census, *Statistical Abstract, 1995*, p. 479.

59. E. J. Dionne, Jr., "Struggle for Work and Family Fueling Women's Movement," *The New York Times*, August 22, 1989, p. A1.

60. Jeffrey Schmalz, "Clinton Carves a Wide Path Deep into Reagan Country," *The New York Times*, November 4, 1992, p. B1.

61. Times Mirror Center for the People and the Press, *Jury Still Out on Clinton's Success* (August 5, 1993), p. 27.

62. For a discussion of the holocaust, see Leni Yahil, *The Holocaust: The Fate of European Jewery* (Oxford University Press, 1990).

63. Stephen C. LeSuer, *The 1838 Mormon War in Missouri* (University of Missouri Press, 1987), pp. 151–53.

64. John Conway, "An Adapted Organic Tradition," *Daedalus* 117 (Fall 1988), p. 382. For an extended comparison of the impact of religion on politics in the United States and Canada, see Seymour Martin Lipset, *Continental Divide: The Values and Institutions of the United States and Canada* (Routledge, 1990), pp. 74–89.

65. Robert N. Bellah, *Beyond Belief: Essays on Religion in a Post-Traditional World* (University of California Press, 1991), pp. 168–90.

66. *1994 American National Election Study*, Center for Political Studies, University of Michigan.

67. William H. Flanigan and Nancy H. Zingale, *Political Behavior of the American Electorate*, 8th ed. (CQ Press, 1994), p. 122.

68. Karl Cordell, "The Role of the Evangelical Church in the GDR," *Government and Opposition* 25 (Winter 1990), pp. 48–59.

69. Taylor Branch, *Parting the Waters: America in the King Years, 1954–63* (Simon & Schuster, 1988), p. 3.

70. Kevin Lange, "An Energized Religious Right? Strategies for the Clinton Era," *Christian Century* 110 (February 17, 1993), pp. 177–79.

71. *1992 American National Election Study*, Center for Political Studies, University of Michigan.

72. Ibid.

73. Telephone survey of 113,000 households in the 48 contiguous states, April 1989-April 1990, Graduate School of the City University of New York.

74. Raymond E. Wolfinger, Fred I. Greenstein, and Martin Shapiro, *Dynamics of American Politics*, 2d ed. (Prentice Hall, 1980), p. 19.

75. U.S., Bureau of the Census, *Historical Statistics of the United States, Colonial Times to 1970* (Government Printing Office, 1976), p. 297; U.S. Bureau of the Census, *Statistical Abstract of the United States, 1993* (Government Printing Office, 1994), p. 457.

76. Stanley Fischer, "Symposium on the Slowdown in Productivity Growth," *Journal of Economic Perspectives* 2 (Fall 1988), pp. 3–7.

77. Organization for Economic Cooperation and Development (OECD), *National Accounts*, vol. 1, *Main Aggregates, 1960–89* (OECD, 1991), p. 145.

78. U.S. Department of Education, *Digest of Education Statistics, 1991* (Government Printing Office, 1991), p. 294.

79. U.S. Bureau of the Census Home Page, http://www.os.dhhs.gov/progorg/ aspe/poverty/poverty.html.

80. U.S. Bureau of the Census, *Statistical Abstract, 1995*, p. 483.

81. Ibid.

82. Many of those classified as poor at the beginning of the 1980s climbed out of poverty over the course of the decade, but others fell into poverty during the same time. Overall, the proportion of the population classified as in poverty increased during the 1980s. See David Wessel, "Low-Income Mobility Was High in the 1980s," *Wall Street Journal*, June 2, 1992, p. A.2.

83. In 1993, there were 32.8 million Americans over the age of 65 and 39.3 million people who fell below the poverty line. U.S. Bureau of the Census, *Statistical Abstract of the United States, 1995*, pp. 15 and 480.

84. Thomas Jefferson, "Autobiography," in *The Life and Selected Writings of Thomas Jefferson*, eds. Adrienne Koch and William Peden (Modern Library, 1944), p. 38.

85. Stanley Lebergott, *The Americans: An Economic Record* (W.W. Norton, 1984), p. 66.

86. U.S. Bureau of the Census, *Statistical Abstract, 1995*, p. 451.

87. Daniel Bell, *The Coming of Post-Industrial Society: A Venture in Social Forecasting* (Basic Books, 1973), p. xviii.

88. U.S. Bureau of the Census, *Statistical Abstract, 1995*, p. 451.

89. U.S. Department of Education, *Digest of Education Statistics, 1991* (Government Printing Office, 1991), p. 11.

90. U.S., Bureau of the Census, *Statistical Abstract, 1990*, p. 339.

91. *Griggs v Duke Power Company*, 401 US 424 (1971). See also *Wards Cove v Antonio*, 490 US 642 (1989).

92. Joan Biskupic, "Bush Signs Anti-Job Bias Bill amid Furor over Preferences," *Congressional Quarterly Weekly Report* 49 (November 23, 1991), p. 3463.

93. Stephen J. Rose, *American Profile Poster* (Pantheon Books, 1986), p. 9.

94. U.S. Bureau of the Census, *Money, Income and Poverty Status in the United States, 1990* (Government Printing Office, 1991), p. 49.

95. Mattei Dogan and Dominique Pelassy, *How to Compare Nations: Strategies in Comparative Politics*, 2d ed. (Chatham House, 1990), p. 47.

96. Responses for subjective social class vary somewhat with wording of the question. The data on Great Britain are from the *Index to International Public Opinion, 1991–92* (Greenwood Press, 1992), p. 462.

97. Seymour Martin Lipset, *Continental Divide: The Values and Institutions of the United States and Canada* (Routledge, 1990), p. 170.

98. U.S. Bureau of the Census, *Statistical Abstract of the United States, 1995*, pp. 15 and 117.

99. U.S. Bureau of the Census, Current Population Reports P 20, no. 446, *Voting and Registration in the Election of November 1992* (Government Printing Office, 1993).

100. U.S. Bureau of the Census, *Statistical Abstract, 1995*, p. 481.

101. *The New York Times*, September 23, 1993, pp. A24–25.

102. Seymour Martin Lipset, *Political Man* (Doubleday, 1963), pp. 283–86.

103. Thomas Jefferson to P. S. du Pont de Nemours, April 24, 1816, *The Writings of Thomas Jefferson*, ed. Paul L. Ford (G. P. Putnam's Sons, 1899), 10:25.

104. U.S. Bureau of the Census, *Statistical Abstract, 1995*, p. 151.

105. Ibid., p. 158.

106. U.S. Bureau of the Census Home Page, http://gopher.census.gov:70/0/ bureau/pr/subject/income/cb95-185.txt.

107. World Development Report, *The Challenge of Development* (Oxford University Press, 1991), p. 261.
108. U.S. Bureau of the Census, *Statistical Abstract, 1992*, p. 144.
109. Herbert McClosky and John Zaller, *The American Ethos: Public Attitudes Toward Capitalism and Democracy* (Harvard University Press, 1984), p. 261.

110. John Gunther, *Inside U.S.A.* (Harper and Brothers, 1947), p. 911.
111. Alan Ehrenhalt, *The United States of Ambition: Politicians, Power, and the Pursuit of Office* (Times Books, 1991), p. 275.
112. Carl N. Degler, *Out of Our Past: The Forces That Shaped Modern America*, 3rd ed. (Harper & Row, 1984), p. 322.

CHAPTER 7

1. John E. Mueller, "Choosing among 133 Candidates," *Public Opinion Quarterly* 34 (Fall 1970), pp. 395–402.
2. E. E. Schattschneider, *Party Government* (Holt, Rinehart & Winston, 1942), p. 1.
3. L. Sandy Maisel, *Parties and Elections in America: The Electoral Process* (Random House, 1987), chap. 5.
4. Charles O. Jones, *The Trusteeship Presidency: Jimmy Carter and the United States Congress* (Louisiana University Press, 1988). See also Charles O. Jones, "Ronald Reagan and the U.S. Congress: Visible Hand Politics," and Paul E. Peterson and Mark Rom, "Lower Taxes, More Spending and Budget Deficits," in *The Reagan Legacy*, ed. Charles O. Jones (Chatham House, 1988), pp. 30–59, 213–40, for discussions of the role of party in Congress during the last two administrations.
5. William H. Riker, "The Two-Party System and Duverger's Law: An Essay on the History of Political Science," *American Political Science Review* (December 1982), pp. 753–66. For a classic analysis, see Schattschneider, *Party Government*.
6. Federal Election Commission, "Summary of 1989–90 Political Party Finances," March 15, 1991, August 6, 1991, and October 31, 1991.
7. See John E. Chubb and Paul E. Peterson, eds., *The New Direction in American Politics* (Brookings, 1985).
8. John F. Bibby, *Politics, Parties, and Elections in America* (Nelson-Hall, 1992). For further data on these roles, see Cornelius P. Cotter, James L. Gibson, John F. Bibby, and Robert J. Huckshorn, *Party Organizations in American Politics* (Praeger, 1984).
9. See James L. Gibson, Cornelius P. Cotter, John F. Bibby, and Robert J. Huckshorn, "Assessing Party Organizational Strength," *American Journal of Political Science* 27 (May 1983), pp. 193–222; Cotter et al., *Party Organizations in American Politics*.
10. Paul S. Herrnson, *Party Campaigning in the 1980s: Have the National Parties Made a Comeback as Key Players in Congressional Elections?* (Harvard University Press, 1988), p. 122.
11. See Bruce E. Keith, David B. Magleby, Candice J. Nelson, Elizabeth Orr, Mark C. Westlye, and Raymond E. Wolfinger, *The Myth of the Independent Voter* (University of California Press, 1992), p. 148.
12. Thomas J. Weko, *The Politicizing Presidency: The White House Personnel Office, 1948–1994* (University of Kansas Press, 1995).
13. John Massaro, *Supremely Political: The Role of Ideology and Presidential Management in Unsuccessful Supreme Court Nominations* (State University of New York Press, 1990).
14. See Angus Campbell, Philip E. Converse, Warren E. Miller, and Donald E. Stokes, *The American Voter* (Wiley, 1960); Norman A. Nie, Sidney Verba, and John R. Petrocik, *The Changing American Voter*, enlarged ed. (Harvard University Press, 1979).
15. Campbell et al., *American Voter*, pp. 121–28.
16. Keith et al., *Myth of the Independent Voter*.
17. Hedrick Smith, *The Power Game: How Washington Works* (Random House, 1988), p. 671.
18. Keith et al., *Myth of the Independent Voter*, p. 51.
19. Eleanor Flexner, *Century of Struggle* (Harvard University Press, 1975), pp. 7–8, 63–65.
20. Abigail Adams to John Adams, March 31, 1776, in Miriam Schneir, ed., *Feminism: The Essential Historical Writings* (Vintage Books, 1972), p. 3.
21. Milton Cantor and Bruce Laurie, eds., *Class, Sex and the Woman Worker* (Greenwood, 1977).
22. *Roe v Wade*, 410 U.S. 113 (1973).
23. For a discussion of the response of established groups and interests to two recent movements, see L. Marvin Querby and Sarah J. Ritichie, "Mobilized Masses and Strategic Opponents: A Resource Mobilization Analysis of the Clean Air and Nuclear Freeze Movements," *Western Political Quarterly* 44 (June 1991), pp. 329–51.

24. Robert D. Putnam, *Making Democracy Work: Civic Traditions in Modern Italy* (Princeton University Press, 1993) p. 167. For more discussion of social capital, see James S. Coleman, *Foundations of Social Theory* (Harvard University Press, 1990), pp. 300–21 and Glenn Loury, "A Dynamic Theory of Racial Income Differences," in *Women, Minorities, and Employment Discrimination*, eds. P. A. Wallace and A. Le Mund (Lexington Books, 1977). See also Michael J. Sandel, *Democracy's Discontent: America in Search of a Public Philosophy* (Harvard University Press, 1996).
25. Robert D. Putnam, "Bowling Alone: America's Declining Social Capital," *Journal of Democracy* 6 (January 1995), pp. 65–78.
26. "Union Membership Drops to 16.4 Percent of Employees," *Wall Street Journal*, February 9, 1990, p. B6; Frank Swoboda, "AFL-CIO Membership Is Shifting: Survey Shows Growing Strength among Government, Service Unions," *Washington Post*, October 31, 1991, p. A17.
27. James MacGregor Burns and Stewart Burns, *A People's Charter: The Pursuit of Rights in America* (Knopf, 1991).
28. American Civil Liberties Union home page at http://www.aclu.org/about/aclumem.html., May 1996.
29. Michael Lienesch, "Right-Wing Religion: Christian Conservatism as a Political Movement," *Political Science Quarterly* 97 (Fall 1982), pp. 403–25.
30. Frank Swoboda, "AFL-CIO Membership Is Shifting: Survey Shows Growing Strength among Government Service Unions," *The Washington Post*, October 31, 1991, p. A17.
31. There is a debate in the literature about whether group membership has grown. For the view that it has, see Frank R. Baumgartner and Jack L. Walker, "Survey Research and Membership in Voluntary Associations," *American Journal of Political Science* 32 (November 1988), pp. 908–27. For a different perspective, see Tom W. Smith, "Trends in Voluntary Group Membership: Comments on Baumgartner and Walker," *American Journal of Political Science* 34 (August 1990), pp. 646–61, which in turn led to Frank R. Baumgartner and Jack L. Walker, "Measurement Validity and the Continuity of Results in Survey Research," *American Journal of Political Science* 34 (August 1990), pp. 662–70.
32. William P. Browne, "Organized Interests and Their Issue Niches: A Search for Pluralism in a Policy Domain," *Journal of Politics* 52 (May 1990), pp. 477–509.
33. V. O. Key, Jr., *Public Opinion and American Democracy* (Knopf, 1961), pp. 504–507.
34. R. Kenneth Godwin, *One Billion Dollars of Influence: The Direct Marketing of Politics* (Chatham House, 1988).
35. Joan Biskupie, "NRA, Gun-Control Supporters Take Aim at Swing Votes," *Congressional Quarterly Weekly Report*, March 9, 1991, p. 604.
36. Lucius J. Barker, "Third Parties in Litigation: A Systemic View of the Judicial Function," *Journal of Politics* (February 1967), pp. 41–69; Jethro K. Lieberman, *Litigious Society*, rev. ed. (Basic Books, 1983).
37. Gregory A. Calderia and John R. Wright, "Organized Interests and Agenda Setting in the U.S. Supreme Court," *American Political Science Review* 82 (December 1988), pp. 1109–27. See also Gregory A. Calderia and John R. Wright, "Amici Curiae before the Supreme Court: Who Participates, When, and How Much?" *Journal of Politics* 52 (August 1990), pp. 782–806.
38. One indication of the importance of transmitting information may be the frequency of contact by lobbyists. See John R. Wright, "Contributions, Lobbying, and Committee Voting in the U.S. House of Representatives," *American Political Science Review* 84 (June 1990), pp. 418–38.
39. Ruth Marcus, "Lobby Law Puts New Spin on Revolving Door," *The Washington Post*, March 26, 1996, p. 1.
40. Herbert E. Alexander, *PACs: What They Are, How They Are Changing Political Campaign Financing Patterns* (Grass Roots Guides, 1979), p. 3.

41. For evidence of the impact of PAC expenditures on legislative committee behavior and legislative involvement generally, see Richard L. Hall and Frank W. Wayman, "Buying Time: Moneyed Interests and the Mobilization of Bias in Congressional Committees," *American Political Science Review* 84 (September 1990), pp. 797–820.

42. Factors that predict the formation of PACs include company size and the degree of regulation for corporations. See Craig Humphries, "Corporations, PACs and the Strategic Link between Contributions and Lobbying Activities," *Western Political* Quarterly 44 (June 1991), pp. 353–72.

43. Harold W. Stanley and Richard G. Niemi, *Vital Statistics on American Politics* (Congressional Quarterly Inc., 1995), p. 164.

44. Charles Keating, quoted in David J. Jefferson, "Keating of American Continental Corporation Comes Out Fighting," *Wall Street Journal*, April 18, 1989, p. B2.

45. Senator Charles C. Mathias, statement in *New York Times*, February 27, 1986, p. A31.

46. Philip D. Duncan and Christine C. Lawrence, *Politics in America 1996* (Congressional Quarterly, Inc., 1995), pp. 1508–31.

47. Douglas Jehl and Sara Fritz, "Clinton Team Issues Ethics Rules for Top Appointees," *Los Angeles Times*, 10 December 1992, p. A26.

48. Alexander, *PACs*, p. 5.

49. Adam Clymer, "Congress Sends Lobbying Overhaul to Clinton," *New York Times*, December 16, 1995, sect. 1, p. 36.

50. David B. Magleby and Candice J. Nelson, *The Money Chase: Congressional Campaign Finance Reform* (Brookings, 1990), p. 20. See also Brooks Jackson, *Honest Graft: Big Money and the American Political Process* (Knopf, 1988), pp. 72–97.

51. Michael J. Malbin, "Campaign Financing and the 'Special Interest,' " *Public Interest* (Summer 1979), pp. 21–42. But for a somewhat different view, see David Cohen and Wendy Wolff, "Freeing Congress from the Special Interest State: A Public Interest Agenda for the 1980s," *Harvard Journal of Legislation* 17, 2 (1980), pp. 253–93.

52. Gary Jacobson, *The Politics of Congressional Elections*, 3d ed. (HarperCollins, 1992), p. 53. For a different assessment, see Donald P. Green and Jonathan S. Krasno, "Salvation for the Spendthrift Incumbent: Reestimating the Effects of Campaign Spending in House Elections," *American Journal of Political Science* 32 (1988), pp. 884–907.

53. See David Jessup, "Can Political Influence Be Democratized? A Labor Perspective," in *Parties, Interest Groups, and Campaign Finance Laws*, Michael J. Malbin, ed. (American Enterprise Institute for Public Policy, 1980), pp. 26–55.

CHAPTER 8

1. Norman Ornstein, "A Vote Cheapened," *The Washington Post*, February 8, 1996, p. A25.

2. Robert Coles, *The Political Life of Children* (Atlantic Monthly Press, 1986), pp. 59–60.

3. Pamela Johnston Conover, "The Influence of Group Identifications on Political Perception and Evaluation," *Journal of Politics* (August 1984), pp. 760–85; Henry E. Brady and Paul M. Sniderman, "Attitude Attribution: A Group Basis for Political Reasoning," *American Political Science Review* (December 1985), pp. 1061–78.

4. Russell J. Dalton, "Reassessing Parental Socialization: Indicator Unreliability versus Generational Transfer," *American Political Science Review* (June 1980), pp. 421–31.

5. Suzanne Koprince Sebert, M. Kent Jennings, and Richard G. Niemi, "The Political Texture of Peer Groups," in Jennings and Niemi, *The Political Character of Adolescence* (Princeton University Press, 1974), p. 246.

6. Kenneth Feldman and Theodore M. Newcomb, *The Impact of College on Students*, Vol. 2 (Jossey Bass, 1969), pp. 16–24, 49–56.

7. Alexander N. Astin and Eric L. Dey, *The American Freshman: Twenty-five Year Trends, 1966–1990* (Higher Education Research Institute, 1991), and *The American Freshman: National Norms for Fall 1995* (Higher Education Research Institute, 1996).

8. Benjamin Page and Robert Shapiro, *The Rational Public* (University of Chicago Press, 1992) p. 237.

9. John Zaller, "The Converse-McGuire Model of Attitude Change and the Gulf War Opinion Rally." *Political Communication* (1993) 10:369–88.

10. George J. Church, "What in the World Are We Doing?" *Time*, October 18, 1993, p. 42.

11. Thomas E. Mann and Raymond E. Wolfinger, "Candidates and Parties in Congressional Election," *American Political Science Review* 74, 3 (September 1980), pp. 617–40.

12. Robert S. Erikson and Kent L. Tedin, *American Public Opinion*, 5th ed. (Allyn and Bacon, 1995), p. 304.

13. Neil S. Newhouse and Christine L. Matthews, "NAFTA Revisited: Most Americans Just Weren't Deeply Engaged," *Public Perspective* 5 (January/February 1994), pp. 31–32.

14. *American National Election Studies 1960–92*, Center for Political Studies, University of Michigan, Ann Arbor.

15. For a discussion of the differences in the turnout between presidential and midterm elections, see James E. Campbell, "The Presidential Surge and Its Midterm Decline in Congressional Elections, 1868–1988," *Journal of Politics* 53 (May 1991), pp. 477–87.

16. G. Bingham Powell, Jr., "American Voter Turnout in Comparative Perspective," *American Political Science Review* 80 (March 1986) p. 38.

17. Raymond E. Wolfinger and Steven J. Rosenstone, "The Effect of Registration Laws on Voter Turnout," *American Political Science Review* (March 1978), p. 24.

18. "The National Voter Registration Act of 1993, 1995: The First Year" (New York, March 1996). Prepared by HumanSERVE for the National Motor Voter Coalition. See also http://www.essential.org/human_serve/human.html.

19. *The New York Times*, November 9, 1988, p. A24.

20. Powell, "American Voter Turnout in Comparative Perspective," pp. 17–43.

21. B. Grofman and L. Handley, "The Impact of the Voting Rights Act on Black Representation in Southern State Legislatures," *Legislative Studies Quarterly* (February 1991), pp. 118–22.

22. Ruy A. Teixeira, "Will the Real Nonvoter Please Stand Up?," *Public Opinion* (July/August 1988), pp. 41–59.

23. Raymond E. Wolfinger, David P. Glass, and Peverill Squire, "Predictors of Electoral Turnout: An International Comparison," *Policy Studies Review* 9 (Spring 1990), pp. 567–68. The impact of registration requirements is not greater for poorly educated persons as was once thought. See Jonathan Nagler, "The Effect of Registration Laws and Education on U.S. Voter Turnout," *American Political Science Review* 85 (December 1991), p. 1402.

24. U.S. Bureau of the Census, *Statistical Abstract of the United States: 1995*, 115th ed. (Washington, D.C., 1995), pp. 290–1.

25. Wolfinger and Rosenstone, Who Votes?, p. 102. See also Sandra Baxter and Marjorie Lansing, *Women and Politics: The Visible Majority* (University of Michigan Press, 1983), pp. 35–37.

26. Wolfinger and Rosenstone, *Who Votes?* pp. 90–91.

27. See Angus Campbell, Philip E. Converse, Warren E. Miller, and Donald E. Stokes, *The American Voter* (Wiley, 1960). This volume is a foundation of modern voting analysis despite much new evidence and reinterpretation. See also Norman H. Nie, Sidney Verba, and John R. Petrocik, *The Changing American Voter* (Harvard University Press, 1976); Ruy A. Teixeira, *Why Americans Don't Vote: Turnout Decline in the United States, 1960–1984* (Greenwood, 1987).

28. Wolfinger and Rosenstone, *Who Votes*, p. 38.

29. Baxter and Lansing, *Women and Politics: The Visible Majority*, Chapter 5. See also Claire Knoche Fulenwider, *Feminism in American Politics: A Study of Ideological Influence*, revised ed. (Praeger, 1983). On age as a key correlation with high turnout, see Lee Sigelman, Philip W. Roeder, Malcolm E. Jewell, and Michael A. Baer, "Voting and Nonvoting: A Multi-Election Perspective," *American Journal of Political Science* (November 1985), pp. 749–65.

30. 1990 American National Election Studies, Center for Political Studies, University of Michigan.

31. Michael B. MacKuen, Robert S. Erikson, and James A. Stimson, "Macropartisanship," *American Political Science Review* 83 (December 1989), pp. 1125–42.

32. *American National Election Studies, 1960–94*, Center for Political Studies, University of Michigan, Ann Arbor. A pure Independent does not lean toward the Democratic or Republican parties in response to survey questions. For a discussion of this issue see Bruce E. Keith, David B. Magleby, Candice J. Nelson, Elizabeth Orr, Mark C. Westlye, and Raymond E.

Wolfinger, *The Myth of the Independent Voter* (University of California Press, 1992), pp. 60–75.

33. Martin P. Wattenberg, *The Rise of Candidate Centered Politics: Presidential Elections of the 1980s* (Harvard University Press, 1991), p. 1.

34. William H. Flanigan and Nancy H. Zingale, *Political Behavior of the American Electorate*, 8th ed. (Congressional Quarterly Press, 1994), pp. 172–73.

35. See Flanigan and Zingale, *Political Behavior of the American Electorate*, Chapter 6.

36. Amihai Glazer, "The Strategy of Candidate Ambiguity," *American Political Science Review* 84 (March 1990), pp. 237–41.

37. Robert S. Erikson and David W. Romero, "Candidate Equilibrium and the Behavioral Model of the Vote," *American Political Science Review* 84 (December 1990), p. 1122.

38. Morris P. Fiorina, *Retrospective Voting in American National Elections* (Yale University Press, 1981).

39. See, for example, Gerald H. Kramer, "Short-Term Fluctuations in U.S. Voting Behavior, 1896–1964," *American Political Science Review* (March 1971), pp. 131–43. See also Edward R. Tufte, "Determinants of the Outcomes of Midterm Congressional Elections," *American Political Science Review* (September 1975), pp. 812–26.

40. John R. Hibbing and John R. Alford, "The Educational Impact of Economic Conditions: Who Is Held Responsible?" *American Journal of Political Science* (August 1982), pp. 423–39; Morris P. Fiorina, "Who Is Held Responsible? Further Evidence on the Hibbing-Alford Thesis," *American Journal of Political Science* (February 1983), pp. 158–64.

41. Robert M. Stein, "Economic Voting for Governor and U.S. Senator: The Electoral Consequences of Federalism," *Journal of Politics* 52 (February 1990), pp. 29–53.

42. M. Stephen Weatherford, "Economic Voting and the 'Symbolic Politics' Argument: A Reinterpretation and Synthesis," *American Political Science Review* (March 1983), pp. 158–74.

43. This same rule permitted Lloyd Bentsen to run for both offices in 1988.

44. Washington voters enacted term limits in 1992 after defeating them in 1991.

45. *U.S. Term Limits Inc. v. Thornton*, 114 S.Ct. 2703.

46. For an insightful examination of electoral rules, see Bernard Grofman and Arend Lijphart, eds., *Electoral Laws and Their Political Consequences* (Agathon Press, 1986).

47. Arend Lijphart, "The Political Consequences of Electoral Laws, 1945–85," *American Political Science Review* 84 (June 1990), pp. 481–95.

48. George Rabinowitz and Stuart Elaine MacDonald, "The Power of the States in U.S. Presidential Elections," *American Political Science Review* (March 1986), pp. 65–87.

49. Alan Ehrenhalt, *The United States of Ambition: Politicians, Power, and the Pursuit of Office* (Times Books, 1991).

50. David R. Mayhew, *Congress: The Electoral Connection* (Yale University Press, 1974).

51. Linda L. Fowler and Robert C. McClure, *Political Ambition: Who Decides to Run for Congress* (Yale University Press, 1989); David T. Canon, "Political Conditions and Experienced Challengers in Congressional Elections, 1972–1984," paper presented to the American Political Science Association Annual Meeting, New Orleans, Louisiana, September 1985.

52. Keith Drehbiel and John R. Wright, "The Incumbency Effect in Congressional Elections: A Test of Two Explanations," *American Journal of Political Science* (February 1983), p. 140.

53. See, for example, Alan I. Abramowitz, "Party and Individual Accountability in the 1978 Congressional Election," in *Congressional Elections*, L. Sandy Maisel and Joseph Cooper, eds. (Russell Sage Foundation, 1981); Thomas E. Mann and Raymond E. Wolfinger, "Candidates and Parties in Congressional Elections," *American Political Science Review* 74, 3 (September 1980), pp. 617–32.

54. Gary C. Jacobson and Samuel Kernell, *Strategy and Choice in Congressional Elections* (Yale University Press, 1981).

55. David B. Magleby and Candice J. Nelson, *The Money Chase: Congressional Campaign Finance Reform* (Brookings Institution, 1990), p. 37.

56. Albert D. Cover, "One Good Term Deserves Another: The Advantages of Incumbency in Congressional Elections," *American Journal of Political Science* 21 (August 1977) pp. 523–42; Morris P. Fiorina, *Congress: Keystone of the Washington Establishment* (Yale University Press, 1978).

57. Mayhew, *Congress*; Richard F. Fenno, Jr., *Congressmen in Committees* (Little, Brown, 1973); Steven S. Smith and Christopher J. Deering, *Committees in Congress* (Congressional Quarterly Press, 1984).

58. Candice J. Nelson, "Campaign Finance in Presidential and Congressional Elections," *The Political Science Teacher* (Summer 1988), p. 6.

59. Alan I. Abramowitz, "Explaining Senate Election Outcomes," *American Political Science Review* (June 1988), pp. 385–403.

60. Jonathan S. Krasno, *Challengers, Competition, and Reelection: Comparing Senate and House Elections* (Yale University Press, 1994).

61. *Congressional Quarterly* January 13, 1996, pp. 98–99.

62. Paul T. David and James W. Caesar, *Proportional Representation in Presidential Nominating Politics* (University Press of Virginia, 1980).

63. For a discussion of the 1996 primary rules see, Rhodes Cook, "GOP's Rules Favor Dole, If He Doesn't Stumble." *Congressional Quarterly Weekly Report*, Vol. 54, No. 4, (January 27, 1996): pp. 228–31.

64. Jeff Fishel, *Presidents and Promises* (Congressional Quarterly Press, 1984).

65. Jules Witcover uses the image of a marathon to describe the 1976 presidential campaign in *Marathon: The Pursuit of the Presidency, 1972–1976* (Viking, 1977).

66. Robert S. Erikson, "Economic Conditions and the Presidential Vote," *American Political Science Review* 83 (June 1989), pp. 567–75. Class based voting has also become more important. See Robert S. Erikson, Thomas O. Lancaster, and David W. Romers, "Group Components of the Presidential Vote, 1952–1984," *Journal of Politics* 51 (May 1989), pp. 337–46.

67. On the key factor of personal attributes in presidential campaigning, see David P. Glass," Evaluating Presidential Candidates: Who Focuses on Their Personal Attributes?" *Public Opinion Quarterly* (Winter 1985), pp. 517–34. See also Herbert B. Asher, *Presidential Elections and American Politics*, 4th ed. (Dorsey Press, 1988).

68. Sidney Kraus, *The Great Debates: Kennedy vs. Nixon*, 1960 (Indiana University Press, 1962). See also Myles Martel, *Political Campaign Debates* (Longman, 1983).

69. See Robert Hunter, ed., *Electing the President: A Program for Reform, Final Report of the Commission on National Election* (Center for Strategic and International Studies, 1986); James L. Sundquist, *Constitutional Reform* (Brookings Institution, 1986); Edward N. Kearny, "Presidential Nominations and Representative Democracy: Proposals for Change," *Presidential Studies Quarterly* (Summer 1984), pp. 348–56.

70. "A National Agenda for the Eighties," Report of the *President's Commission for a National Agenda for the Eighties* (Government Printing Office, 1980), p. 97, proposes holding only four presidential primaries, scheduled about one month apart.

71. Nelson Polsby, *Consequences of Party Reform* (Oxford University Press, 1983), p. 118.

72. Thomas E. Cronin and Robert Loevy, "The Case for a National Primary Convention Plan," *Public Opinion* (December/January 1983), pp. 50–53.

73. For a broader discussion of the plan and the problem, see Thomas E. Cronin, "Choosing a President," *The Center Magazine* (September/October 1978), pp. 5-15; William R. Keech, *Winner Take All: Report of the Twentieth Century Fund Task Force on Reform of the Presidential Election Process* (Holmes & Meier, 1978).

74. Jeffrey Schmalz, "Clinton Carves a Wide Path into Reagan Country," *The New York Times*, November 4, 1992, p. B1.

CHAPTER 9

1. John Kifner, "66 Die as Shell Wrecks Sarajevo Market," *New York Times*, February 6, 1994, p. 1.

2. *USA Today/CNN* Gallup Survey, January 8, 1994.

3. Elaine Sciolino, "Clinton Rules Out a Quick Response to Bosnia Attack," *New York Times*, February 7, 1994, p. A1.

4. Elaine Sciolino, "Conflict in the Balkans: Clinton Aides Seek Approval by NATO on Bosnia Air Raids," *New York Times*, February 8, 1994, p. A1.

5. Gallup Survey, February 13, 1994.

6. William Rivers, *The Other Government* (Universe Books, 1982); Douglas Cater, *The Fourth Branch of Government* (Houghton Mifflin, 1959); Dom

Bonafede, "The Washington Press: An Interpreter or a Participant in Policy Making?" *National Journal*, April 24, 1982, pp. 716–21; Michael Ledeen, "Learning to Say 'No' to the Press," *Public Interest* (Fall 1983), p. 113.

7. Leslie G. Moeller, "The Big Four: Mass Media Actualities and Expectations," in *Beyond Media: New Approaches to Mass Communication*, eds. Richard W. Budd and Brent D. Ruben (Transaction Books, 1988), p. 15.

8. Times Mirror Center for the People and the Press, "Campaign '92: The Politics of the Economy," press release, January 16, 1992.

9. Ibid.

10. See Ray Hiebert, Donald Ungarait, and Thomas Bohn, *Mass Media VI* (Longman, 1991), chap. 11.

11. See Robert A. Rutland, *Newsmongers: Journalism in the Life of the Nation, 1690–1972* (Dial Press, 1973).

12. Frank Luther Mott, *American Journalism*, 3d ed. (Macmillan, 1962), p. 123.

13. See Culver Smith, *The Press, Politics, and Patronage* (University of Georgia Press, 1977).

14. James Pollard, *Presidents and the Press* (Macmillan, 1947), pp. 351–59.

15. Thomas C. Leonard, *The Power of the Press* (Oxford University Press, 1986), p. 93.

16. Whitelaw Reid, quoted in Mott, *American Journalism*, p. 412.

17. Frances Perkins, quoted in James MacGregor Burns, *Roosevelt: The Lion and the Fox* (Harcourt Brace, 1956), p. 205.

18. Edward W. Chester, *Radio, Television and American Politics* (Sheed and Ward, 1969), p. 62.

19. Ben H. Bagdikian, *The Media Monopoly* (Becon Press, 1983).

20. See Doris A. Graber, *Mass Media and American Politics* (Congressional Quarterly Press, 1989); Gina M. Garramone and Charles K. Atkin, "Mass Communication and Political Socialization: Specifying the Effects," *Public Opinion Quarterly* 50 (Spring 1986), pp. 76–86.

21. Stephanie Strom, "Mergers for Year Approach Record," *New York Times*, October 31, 1995, p. A1.

22. Shanto Iyengar and Donald R. Kinder, *News That Matters* (University of Chicago Press, 1987).

23. Richard Davis, *The Press and American Politics: The New Mediator* (Longman, 1992), p. 100.

24. For a discussion of advocacy journalism, see Morris Janowitz, "Professional Models in Journalism: The Gatekeeper and the Advocate," *Journalism Quarterly* (Winter 1975), pp. 618–25.

25. Peter Stoler, *The War Against the Press: Politics, Pressure, and Intimidation in the 80s* (Dodd, Mead, 1986).

26. William Safire, "Blizzard of Lies," *New York Times*, January 8, 1996, p. A13.

27. Neil A. Lewis, "White House Says President Would Like to Punch Safire," *New York Times*, January 10, 1996, p. A11.

28. Harvey G. Zeidenstein, "News Media Perceptions of White House News Management," *Presidential Studies Quarterly* 24 (Summer 1984), pp. 391–98.

29. See, for example, Jack Dennis, "Preadult Learning of Political Independence: Media and Family Communications Effects," *Communication Research* 13 (July 1987, pp. 401–33; Olive Stevens, *Children Talking Politics* (Martin Robertson, 1982).

30. Elihu Katz and Paul Lazarsfeld, *Personal Influence The Part Played by People in the Flow of Mass Communications* (Free Press, 1955).

31. See another classic, Angus Campbell, Philip E. Converse, Warren E. Miller, and Donald E. Stokes, *The American Voter* (Wiley, 1960).

32. See the classic works, Paul Lazarsfeld, Bernard Berelson, and Hazel Gaudet, *The People's Choice: How the Voter Makes Up His Mind in a Presidential Campaign*, 3d ed. (Columbia University Press, 1968); Bernard Berelson, Paul Lazarsfeld, and William McPhee, *Voting: A Study of Opinion Formation in a Presidential Campaign* (University of Chicago Press, 1954).

33. Stuart Oskamp, ed., *Television as a Social Issue* (Sage Publications, 1988); James W. Carey, ed., *Media, Myths, and Narratives: Television and the Press* (Sage Publications, 1988).

34. Doris A. Graber, *Processing the News: How People Tame the Information Tide*, 2d ed. (Longman, 1988), pp. 107–13.

35. Times Mirror Center for the People and the Press, "Times Mirror News Interest Index," press releases, January 16, 1992, and February 28, 1992.

36. John K. Robinson and Mark R. Levy, eds., *The Main Source: Learning from Television News* (Sage Publications, 1986).

37. Graber, *Processing the News*, p. 115.

38. Times Mirror Center for the People and the Press, "Times Mirror News Interest Index," press release, January 16, 1992.

39. Fred Smoller, "The Six O'Clock Presidency: Patterns of Network News Coverage of the President," *Presidential Studies Quarterly 26* (Winter 1986), p. 34.

40. See Nelson Polsby, *Consequences of Party Reform* (Oxford University Press, 1983), pp. 142–46. See also Stanley Rothman and S. Robert Lichter, "Media and Business Elites: Two Classes in Conflict!" *The Public Interest* (Fall 1982), pp. 119–25.

41. David Broder, "Beware of the 'Insider' Syndrome: Why Newmakers and News Reporters Shouldn't Get Too Cozy," *Washington Post*, December 4, 1988, Outlook Section; see also Broder, "Thin-Skinned Journalists," *Washington Post*, January 11, 1989, p. A21.

42. See, for example, William A. Rusher, *The Coming Battle for the Media* (William Morrow, 1988).

43. Rush Limbaugh, *See, I Told You So* (Pocket Books, 1993), p. 326.

44. *Public Opinion* (August/September 1985), p. 7.

45. See, for example, Michael Parenti, *Inventing Reality* (St. Martin's Press, 1986); Todd Gitlin, *The Whole World Is Watching: Mass Media in the Making and Unmaking of the New Left* (University of California Press, 1980).

46. Daniel P. Moynihan, "The Presidency and the Press," *Commentary* (March 1971), p. 43.

47. S. Robert Lichter, Stanley Rothman, and Linda S. Lichter, *The Media Elite* (Adler and Adler, 1986).

48. See, for example, Michael J. Robinson and Margaret A. Sheehan, *Over the Wire and on TV: CBS and UPI in Campaign '80* (Russell Sage Foundation, 1983); Lichter, Rothman, and Lichter, *Media Elite*.

49. Among others researching this topic, see Doris A. Graber, "Say It with Pictures: The Impact of Audio–Visual News on Public Opinion Formation," paper presented to the Midwest Political Science Association Annual Meeting, Chicago, April 1987; Benjamin I. Page, Robert Y. Shapiro, and Glenn R. Dempsey, "What Moves Public Opinion?" *American Political Science Review* 76 (March 1987), pp. 23–43.

50. Shanto Iyengar, Mark D. Peters, and Donald R. Kinder, "Experimental Demonstrations of the 'Not–So–Minimal' Consequences of Television News Programs," *American Political Science Review* (December 1982), pp. 848–58.

51. Maxwell E. McCombs and Donald L. Shaw, "The Agenda-Setting Function of the Mass Media," *Public Opinion Quarterly* 36 (1972), pp. 176–87; Iyengar, Peters, and Kinder, "Experimental Demonstrations," pp. 848–58; Maxwell E. McCombs and Sheldon Gilbert, "News Influence on Our Pictures of the World," in *Perspectives on Media Effects*, eds. Jennings Bryant and Dolf Gillman (Lawrence Erlbaum, 1986); Iyengar and Kinder, *News That Matters*.

52. Walter Mondale, quoted in Robinson and Sheehan, *Over the Wire and on TV*, p. xiii.

53. Iyengar and Kinder, *News That Matters*.

54. Robert M. Entman, "How the Media Affect What People Think: An Information Processing Approach," *Journal of Politics* 51 (May 1989), pp. 346–70.

55. Shanto Iyengar, "Television News and Citizens Explanations of National Affairs," *American Political Science Review* 81 (September 1987), pp. 815–32; Iyengar and Kinder, *News That Matters*, pp. 82–89.

56. David B. Magleby, *Direct Legislation: Voting on Ballot Propositions in the United States* (Johns Hopkins University Press, 1984).

57. Steven J. Simmons, *The Fairness Doctrine and the Media* (University of California Press, 1978).

58. Norman E. Issacs, *Untended Gates: The Mismanaged Press* (Columbia University Press, 1985), p. 143.

59. Ibid.

60. S. Robert Lichter and Linda S. Lichter, "Covering the Convention Coverage," *Public Opinion* (September/October 1988), p. 41.

61. Davis, *Press and American Politics*, p. 279.

62. Frank I. Luntz, *Candidates, Consultants, and Campaigns* (Basil Blackwell, 1988), chap. 7.

63. Michael J. Robinson, "Where's the Beef? Media and Media Elites in 1984," in *The American Elections of 1984*, ed. Austin Ranney (Duke University Press, for the American Enterprise Institute, 1985), pp. 172–77.

64. Richard Armstrong, *The Next Hurrah: The Changing Face of the American Political Process* (Beech Tree Books, 1988), pp. 19–21.

65. See, for example, Kathleen Hall Jamieson, *Packaging the Presidency*, 2d ed. (Oxford University Press, 1992).

66. Frank Rich, "Journal: The Log Cabin Lesson," *New York Times*, October 21, 1995, p. A21.

67. John B. Judis, "The Porn Broker," *The New Republic*, June 5, 1995, pp. 14–16; Sam Howe Verhovek, "The Contenders: Phil Gramm's Offbeat Charm as a Persistent Conservative," *New York Times*, December 17, 1995, p. A1.

68. Larry J. Sabato, *The Rise of Political Consultants* (Basic Books, 1981).

69. Mimi Hall and Judy Keen, "Hillary Clinton's Image Undergoes a Change," *USA Today*, July 16, 1992, p. A4.

70. See in general, Sabato, *Rise of Political Consultants*, James David Barber, *The Pulse of Politics: Electing Presidents in the Media Age* (Norton, 1980). See also Fred Barnes, "The Myth of Political Consultants," *The New Republic*, June 16, 1986, p. 16.

71. Quoted in Sabato, *Rise of Political Consultants*, p. 144.

72. Thomas E. Patterson, *The Mass Media Election: How Americans Choose Their President* (Praeger, 1980), chap. 12.

73. See John H. Aldrich, *Before the Convention* (University of Chicago Press, 1980), p. 65, a study of candidates' choices and strategies. See also Patterson, *Mass Media Election*.

74. John Foley et al., *Nominating a President: The Process and the Press* (Praeger, 1980), p. 39. For the press's treatment of incumbents, see James Glen Stovall, "Incumbency and News Coverage of the 1980 Presidential Election Campaign," *Western Political Quarterly* (December 1984), p. 621.

75. Thomas E. Patterson and Robert McClure, *The Unseeing Eye: The Myth of Television Power in National Elections* (Putnam, 1976); Patterson, *Mass Media Election*, chap. 13.

76. Edwin Diamond and Stephen Bates, *The Spot: The Rise of Political Advertising on TV* (MIT Press, 1984). For a historical look at political advertising see Jamieson, *Packaging the Presidency*.

77. Priscilla Southwell, "Voter Turnout in the 1986 Congressional Elections: The Media as Demobilizer?" *American Politics Quarterly* 19 (January 1991), pp. 96–108.

78. David B. Magleby, "Direct Legislation in the American States," in *Referendums Around the World: The Growing Use of Direct Democracy*, eds. David Butler and Austin Ranney (AEI Press, 1994), pp. 218–257.

79. Patterson, *Mass Media Election*, pp. 115–17.

80. Raymond Wolfinger and Peter Linguiti, "Tuning In and Tuning Out," *Pubic Opinion* 4 (February/March 1981), pp. 56–60.

81. Walter Lippmann, *Public Opinion* (Macmillan, 1938), p. 364.

82. Davis, *Press and American Politics*, p. 205.

83. Bernard Cohen, *The Press and Foreign Policy* (Princeton University Press, 1963); Gary Orren, "Thinking About the Press and Government," in *Impact: How the Press Affects Federal Policymaking*, ed. Martin Linsky (Norton, 1986), pp. 1–20.

84. Lewis Wolfson, *The Untapped Power of the Press* (Praeger, 1985), p. 79.

85. Stephen Hess, *The Government/Press Connection* (Brookings Institution, 1984), p. 106.

86. Lloyd Cutler, "Foreign Policy on Deadline," *Foreign Policy* (Fall 1984), p. 114.

87. Michael B. Grossman and Martha Joynt Kumar, *Portraying the President* (Johns Hopkins University Press, 1981), pp. 255–63; Smoller, "Six O'Clock Presidency," pp. 31–49.

88. Michael J. Robinson and Kevin R. Appel, "Network News Coverage of Congress," *Political Science Quarterly* (Fall 1979), pp. 407–18; Charles Tidmarch and John C. Pitney, Jr., "Covering Congress," *Polity* (Spring 1985), pp. 463–83.

89. Susan Heilmann Miller, "News Coverage of Congress: The Search for the Ultimate Spokesperson," *Journalism Quarterly* (Autumn 1977), pp. 459–65.

90. See Stephen Hess, *Live from Capitol Hill: Studies of Congress and the Media* (Brookings Institution, 1991), pp. 102–10.

91. Richard Davis, "Whither the Congress and the Supreme Court? The Television News Portrayal of American National Government," *Television Quarterly* (1987), pp. 55–63.

92. For a discussion of the Supreme Court and public opinion, see Thomas R. Marshall, *Public Opinion and the Supreme Court* (Unwin Hyman, 1989); Gregory Caldiera, "Neither the Purse nor the Sword: Dynamics of Public Confidence in the Supreme Court," *American Political Science Review* (December 1986), pp. 1209–28.

93. For a discussion of the relationship between the Supreme Court and the press, see Richard Davis, "Lifting the Shroud: News Media Portrayal of the U.S. Supreme Court," *Communications and the Law* (October 1987), pp. 43–58; Elliot E. Slotnick, "Media Coverage of Supreme Court Decision Making: Problems and Prospects," *Judicature* (October/November 1991), pp. 128–42.

94. Thomas E. Patterson, "The Press and Its Missed Assignment," in *The Elections of 1988*, ed. Michael Nelson (Congressional Quarterly Press, 1989), pp. 107–8.

95. Times Mirror Center for the People and the Press, "Campaign '92: The Politics of the Economy," press release, January 16, 1992.

96. Theodore White, quoted in Herbert Schmertz, "The Making of the Presidency," *Presidential Studies Quarterly* (Winter 1986), p. 25.

CHAPTER 10

1. David Broder, "Mandate Missing for Anyone," *The Oregonian*, November 7, 1996, p. D15. See also "Clinton II," *Newsweek Special Edition*, November 18, 1996.

2. See Paul S. Herrnson, *Congressional Elections* (Congressional Quarterly Books, 1994).

3. For an examination of this practice, see Michael Lyons and Peter F. Galderisi, "Incumbency, Reapportionment, and U.S. House Redistricting," *Political Research Quarterly* (December, 1995), pp. 857–71.

4. See *Wesberry v Sanders*, 376 US 1 (1964).

5. *Davis v Bandemer*, 478 US 109 (1986).

6. *Shaw v Reno*, 125 L ED 2d 511 (1993).

7. Norman I. Ornstein, Thomas E. Mann, and Michael J. Malbin, eds., *Vital Statistics on Congress, 1995–1996* (Congressional Quarterly Books, 1995). See also Robert Goehlert, Fenton Martin, and John Sayre, eds., *Member of Congress: A Bibliography* (Congressional Quarterly Books, 1995).

8. For a brief discussion of the speakership in the 1990s, see Barbara Sinclair, "House Majority Party Leadership in an Era of Legislative Constraint," in *The Postreform Congress*, ed. Roger H. Davidson (St. Martin's Press, 1992), pp. 91–111. See also Ronald M. Peters, Jr., ed., *The Speaker: Leadership in the U.S. House of Representatives* (Congressional Quarterly Books, 1995).

9. Quoted in Adam Clymer, "Firebrand Who Got Singed Says Being Speaker Suffices," *New York Times*, January 22, 1996, p. 1.

10. Newt Gingrich, *To Renew America* (HarperCollins, 1995).

11. Steven S. Smith, "The Senate in the Postreform Era," in *Postreform Congress*, ed. Roger H. Davidson (St. Martin's Press, 1992), pp. 169–92.

12. For an insightful set of essays on Senate leadership, see Richard A. Baker and Roger H. Davidson, eds., *First Among Equals: Outstanding Senate Leaders of the Twentieth Century* (Congressional Quarterly Books, 1991).

13. Stephen Hess, *The Ultimate Insiders: U.S. Senators and the Media* (Brookings Institution, 1986).

14. For a criticism of recent confirmation hearings and various reform proposals, see Stephen L. Carter, *The Confirmation Mess: Cleaning Up the Federal Appointments Process* (Basic Books, 1994).

15. See Gingrich, *To Review America*, p. 121. See also Timothy Penny and Major Garrett, *Common Cents* (Little, Brown, 1995), p. 209.

16. Robert C. Byrd, quoted in David J. Vogler, *The Politics of Congress* (Allyn and Bacon, 1983), p. 77.

17. Melissa Weinstein Kaye, "Most Votes Ever Were Taken, With Fewer Votes Missed," *Congressional Quarterly*, January 27, 1996, p. 205.

18. Harold W. Stanley and Richard G. Niemi, *Vital Statistics on American Politics*, 4th ed. (Congressional Quarterly Press, 1994), p. 216.

19. R. Douglas Arnold, *The Logic of Congressional Action* (Yale University Press, 1990).

20. See Richard Morrin, "Tuned Out, Turned Off: Millions of Americans Know Little About How Their Government Works," *The Washington Post National Weekly Edition*, February 5–11, 1996, pp. 6–7.

21. Bill Bradley, *Time Past, Time Present: A Memoir* (Knopf, 1996), Chap. 4.

22. Dan Carney, "As Hostilities Rage on the Hill, Partisan Vote Rate Soars," *Congressional Quarterly*, January 27, 1996, p. 199.

23. Mark A. Peterson, *Legislating Together: The White House and Capital Hill from Eisenhower to Reagan* (Harvard University Press, 1990).

24. For two case studies on the way bills get treated in Congress, see Janet M. Martin, *Lessons From the Hill: The Legislative Journey, of an Education Program* (St. Martin's Press, 1993); and Steven Waldman, *The Bill: How Legislation Really Becomes Law: A Case Study of the National Service Bill* (Penguin, 1996).

25. Woodrow Wilson, *Congressional Government* (Houghton, Mifflin & Co., 1885; reprint Johns Hopkins University Press, 1981), p. 69.

26. Steven S. Smith and Christopher J. Deering, *Committees in Congress* (Congressional Quarterly Press, 1984).

27. Bradley, *Time Present*, p. 84.

28. Richard F. Fenno, Jr., *Congressman in Committees* (Little, Brown, 1972). See also Glen R. Parker and Suzanne L. Parker, *Factions in House Committees* (University of Tennessee Press, 1985).

29. Gingrich, *To Renew America*, p. 121.

30. Joel D. Aberbach, *Keeping a Watchful Eye: The Politics of Congressional Oversight* (Brookings Institution, 1990).

31. For studies of the role of congressional investigations, see James Hamilton, *The Power To Probe: A Study of Congressional Investigations* (Vintage, 1976); Morris S. Ogul, *Congress Oversees the Bureaucracy* (University of Pittsburg Press, 1976); Loch Johnson, *A Season of Inquiry: The Senate Intelligence Investigation* (University of Kentucky Press, 1985).

32. David J. Vogler, *The Politics of Congress*, 5th ed. (Allyn and Bacon, 1988), p. 213.

33. William S. Cohen, "Why I Am Leaving," *The Washington Post National Weekly Edition*, January 28–February 4, 1996, p. 29.

34. John Rhodes, *The Futile System* (EPM Publications, 1976), p. 15. See also Gregg Easterbrook, "What's Wrong with Congress?" *The Atlantic Monthly*, December 1984, pp. 57–84.

35. James L. Sundquist, *Constitutional Reform and Effective Government*, rev. ed. (Brookings Institution, 1992); James MacGregor Burns, *The Power To Lead* (Simon & Schuster, 1984). The vast majority of political scientists disagree with these ideas. See, for example, Charles O. Jones, *The Presidency in a Separated System* (Brookings Institution, 1994).

36. James Madison, *The Federalist*, No. 57, in Jacob E. Cooke, ed., *The Federalist* (Meridian Books, 1961), p. 385.

CHAPTER 11

1. Glenn A. Phelps, *George Washington and American Constitutionalism* (University Press of Kansas, 1993).

2. John Steinbeck, *American and Americans* (Bonanza Books, 1966), p. 46.

3. Charles O. Jones, *The Presidency in a Separated System* (Brookings Institution, 1994), p. 295. See also Jean Reith Schroedl, *Congress, The President and Policymaking* (M.E. Sharpe, 1994).

4. See, for example, Terry Eastland, *Energy in the Executive* (Free Press, 1992), and Harvey Mansfield, Jr., *Taming the Prince: The Ambivalence of Modern Executive Power* (Free Press, 1989).

5. See Louis Fisher, *Presidential War Power* (University Press of Kansas, 1995) and David Gray Adler and Larry N. George, eds., *The Constitution and the Conduct of American Foreign Policy: Essays on Law and History* (University Press of Kansas, 1996).

6. Louis Fisher, *Constitutional Conflicts Between Congress and the President*, 3d ed. (University Press of Kansas, 1991), p. 285.

7. Gerald Ford, informal talk at the Hinckley Institute of Politics, University of Utah, Salt Lake City, Utah, February 1982.

8. Our analysis here borrows and benefits from ideas in James A. Thurber, "The Roots of Divided Democracy," in *Divided Democracy*, ed. James A. Thurber (Congressional Quarterly Press, 1991).

9. Paul Brace and Barbara Hinckley, *Follow the Leader: Opinion Polls and the Modern Presidents* (Basic Books, 1992), p. 87.

10. Roger H. Davidson and Walter J. Oleszek, *Congress and Its Members*, 4th ed. (Congressional Quarterly Press, 1994), p. 239. See also Mark A. Peterson, *Legislating Together* (Harvard University Press, 1990); David R. Mayhew, *Divided We Govern: Party Control, and Investigations, 1946–1990* (Yale University Press, 1991).

11. G. Calvin Mackenzie, *The Politics of Presidential Appointments* (Free Press, 1981).

12. See Thomas J. Weko, *The Politicizing Presidency: The White House Personnel Office, 1948–1994* (University Press of Kansas, 1995).

13. "Leadership in Jeopardy: The Fraying of the Presidential Appointments System," *National Academy of Public Administration Report* (November 1985), p. 3.

14. *United States v Curtiss-Wright Export Corp.*, 299 US 304 (1936).

15. For those who believe the *Curtiss Wright* ruling was too sweeping, see Harold H. Koh, *The National Security Constitution* (Yale University Press, 1990); Louis Fisher, *Presidential War Power* (University Press of Kansas, 1995); and David Gray Adler and Larry N. George, eds., *The Constitution and the Conduct of American Foreign Policy: Essays on Law and History* (University Press of Kansas, 1996).

16. See, in general, Bob Woodward, *The Agenda: Inside the Clinton White House* (Simon & Shuster, 1994).

17. See Robert J. Spitzer, *The President and Congress: Executive Hegemony at the Crossroads of American Government* (McGraw-Hill, 1993); Lester G. Seligman and Cary R. Covington, *The Coalition Presidency* (Dorsey Press, 1989).

18. Jon Healey, "Clinton Success Rate Declined to a Record Low in 1995," *Congressional Quarterly*, January 27, 1996, pp. 193–96.

19. William J. Keefe, *Congress and the American People*, 3d ed. (Prentice Hall, 1988), p. 151.

20. Robert J. Spitzer, "Regular Veto" in *Encyclopedia of the American Presidency*, eds. Leonard W. Levy and Louis Fisher (Simon & Shuster, 1994), p. 1555.

21. Alison Mitchell, "With Ceremony, Clinton Signs a Line-Item Veto Measure," *The New York Times*, April 10, 1996, p. C20.

22. Senator Robert Byrd, quoted in Andrew Taylor, "Congress Hands President a Budgetary Scalpell," *Congressional Quarterly*, March 30, 1996, p. 866.

23. For a detailed review of the arguments for and against the item veto, see Thomas E. Cronin and Jeffrey Weill, "An Item Veto for Presidents?" *Congress and the Presidency*, 1985), pp. 127–51.

24. See Kenneth T. Walsh, *Feeding the Beast: The White House versus the Press* (Random House, 1996).

25. For an overview of how presidents try to organize their White House and their key advisers, see James P. Pfiffner, *The Strategic Presidency*, 2d ed, revised (University Press of Kansas, 1996).

26. Howard E. Shuman, *Politics and the Budget*, 2d ed. (Prentice Hall, 1988).

27. See Thomas E. Cronin, *The State of the Presidency* (Little, Brown, 1980).

28. For an analysis of the role of the vice-president as a potential adviser to the president, see Thomas E. Cronin, "Rethinking the Vice Presidency," in *Rethinking the Presidency*, ed. Thomas E. Cronin (Little, Brown, and Co., 1982), pp. 324–48; Report of the Twentieth Century Fund Task Force on the Vice-Presidency, *A Heartbeat Away* (Priority Press, 1988). See also Dan Quayle, *Standing Firm* (Harper Paperbacks, 1995).

29. Useful books on the vice-presidency are Jules Witcover, *Crapshoot: Rolling the Dice on the Vice Presidency* (Crown, 1992); Paul Light, *Vice Presidential Power* (Johns Hopkins University Press, 1984); Joel Goldstein, *The Modern Vice Presidency* (Princeton University Press, 1982).

30. See Stephen Skowronek, *The Politics Presidents Make: Leadership from John Adams to George Bush* (Harvard University Press, 1993), chaps. 1–3.

31. Mark Hertsgaard, *On Bended Knee: The Press and the Reagan Presidency* (Farrar, Straus, Giroux, 1988). See also John A. Maltese, *Spin Control* (University of North Carolina Press, 1992).

32. Thomas Griffith, "Goodbye to All That," *Time*, April 18, 1988, p. 47.

33. Richard Ellis and Aaron Wildavsky, "'Greatness' Revisited: Evaluating the Performance of Early American Presidents in Terms of Cultural Dilemmas," *Presidential Studies Quarterly* (Winter 1991), p. 17. See also the book by the same authors, *Dilemmas of Presidential Leadership from Washington through Lincoln* (Transaction Press, 1990).

34. Ellis and Wildavsky, "'Greatness' Revisited," p. 17.

35. Ibid., p. 18.

36. Paul Kennedy, *The Rise and Fall of the Great Powers* (Random House, 1987), p. 534.

37. Richard Rose, *The Postmodern President: George Bush Meets the World*, 2d ed. (Chatham House, 1991); Barbara Kellerman and Ryan J. Barilleaux, *The President as World Leader* (St. Martin's Press, 1991); Richard Rose and Robert Thompson, "The President in a Changing International System," *Presidential Studies Quarterly* (Fall 1991), pp. 751–70.